GEOGRAPHY
THE WORLD AND ITS PEOPLE
VOLUME 2

GEOGRAPHY
THE WORLD AND ITS PEOPLE

VOLUME 2

NATIONAL
GEOGRAPHIC
SOCIETY

Richard G. Boehm, Ph.D.
David G. Armstrong, Ph.D.
Francis P. Hunkins, Ph.D.

GLENCOE

McGraw-Hill

New York, New York
Columbus, Ohio
Woodland Hills, California
Peoria, Illinois

About the Authors

National Geographic Society

The National Geographic Society, founded in 1888 for the increase and diffusion of geographic knowledge, is the world's largest nonprofit scientific and educational organization. Since its earliest days, the Society has used sophisticated communication technologies, from color photography to holography, to convey geographic knowledge to a worldwide membership. The Educational Media Division supports the Society's mission by developing innovative educational programs—ranging from traditional print materials to multimedia programs including CD-ROMS, videodiscs, and software.

Richard G. Boehm

Richard G. Boehm, Ph.D., was one of seven authors of *Geography for Life,* national standards in geography, prepared under Goals 2000: Educate America Act. He was an author of the *Guidelines for Geographic Education,* in which the five themes of geography were first articulated. In 1990 Dr. Boehm was designated "Distinguished Geography Educator" by the National Geographic Society. In 1991 he received the George J. Miller award from the National Council for Geographic Education (NCGE) for distinguished service to geographic education. He was President of the NCGE and has twice won the *Journal of Geography* award for best article. He has received the NCGE's "Distinguished Teaching Achievement" award and currently occupies the Jesse H. Jones Distinguished Chair in Geographic Education at Southwest Texas State University in San Marcos, Texas.

David G. Armstrong

David G. Armstrong, Ph.D., is Dean of the School of Education at the University of North Carolina at Greensboro. A social studies education specialist with additional advanced training in geography, Dr. Armstrong was educated at Stanford University, University of Montana, and University of Washington. He taught at the secondary level in the state of Washington before beginning a career in higher education. Dr. Armstrong has written books for students at the secondary and university levels, as well as for teachers and university professors. He maintains an active interest in travel, teaching, and social studies education.

Francis P. Hunkins

Francis P. Hunkins, Ph.D., is Professor of Education at the University of Washington. He began his professional career as a teacher in Massachusetts. He received his masters degree in education from Boston University and his doctorate from Kent State University with a major in general curriculum and a minor in geography. Dr. Hunkins has written numerous books and articles dealing with general curriculum, social studies, and questioning and thinking for students and educators at elementary, middle school, high school, and university levels. As a student of geography, he has traveled extensively to all of the continents, with the exception of Antarctica.

Glencoe/McGraw-Hill

A Division of The **McGraw-Hill** Companies

Printed in the United States of America.

Send all inquiries to:
Glencoe/McGraw-Hill, 8787 Orion Place, Columbus, Ohio 43240

ISBN 0-02-821492-7 (Student Edition) 0-02-821486-2 (Teacher's Wraparound Edition)

3 4 5 6 7 8 9 027/043 04 03 02 01

Consultants

General Content Consultant
NATIONAL GEOGRAPHIC SOCIETY

Multicultural Consultants
Ricardo L. García, Ed.D.
Professor
University of Wisconsin
Stevens Point, Wisconsin

Sayyid M. Syeed, Ph.D.
Secretary General, Islamic Society of
    North America
Plainfield, Indiana

Introduction to Geography
Theodore H. Schmudde, Ph.D.
Professor of Geography
University of Tennessee
Knoxville, Tennessee

United States and Canada
Frederick Isele, Ph.D.
Former Assistant Professor
School of Education
Indiana State University
Terre Haute, Indiana

Latin America
Frank de Varona
Region Superintendent
Dade County Public Schools
Hialeah, Florida

Europe
Sarah W. Bednarz, Ph.D.
Assistant Professor
Department of Geography
Texas A&M University
College Station, Texas

Russia and the Independent Republics
A. Naklowycz
President, Ukrainian-American
    Academic Association of California
Carmichael, California

Alfred Bell, Ed.S.
Social Studies Supervisor
Knox County Schools
Knoxville, Tennessee

North Africa and Southwest Asia
Mounir Farah, Ph.D.
Associate Director,
Middle East Studies Program
University of Arkansas
Fayetteville, Arkansas

Africa South of the Sahara
Mary Jane Fraser, Ph.D.
Teacher and Social Studies Curriculum
    Project Leader
Seattle High School
Seattle, Washington

Asia
Kenji K. Oshiro, Ph.D.
Professor of Geography
Wright State University
Dayton, Ohio

Australia, Oceania, and Antarctica
Marianne Kenney
Social Studies Specialist
Colorado Department of Education
Denver, Colorado

Teacher Reviewers

Charles M. Bateman
Social Studies Teacher and
    Department Chair
Halls Middle School
Knox County District
Knoxville, Tennessee

Rebecca A. Corley
Social Studies Teacher
Evans Junior High School
Lubbock Independent School District
Lubbock, Texas

Carole Mayrose
Social Studies Teacher
Northview High School
Clay Community School District
Brazil, Indiana

Don Mendenhall
Social Studies Teacher and
    Department Chair
Coleman Junior High School
Van Buren, Arkansas

Rebecca M. Revis
Social Studies Teacher
Sylvan Hills Junior High School
Pulaski County Special School District
Sherwood, Arkansas

Marita E. Sesler
Social Studies Specialist
Knoxville County School District
Knoxville, Tennessee

Cathy Walter
World Geography Teacher
Colony Middle School
Palmer, Alaska

v

Contents

VOLUME 2

GEOGRAPHY & MAP SKILLS HANDBOOK

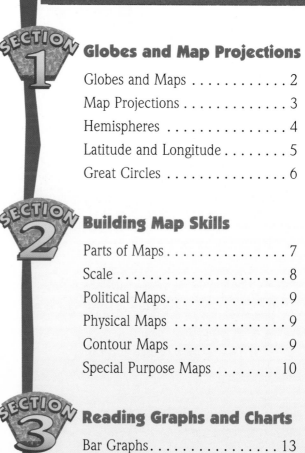

SECTION 1

Globes and Map Projections

SECTION 2

Building Map Skills

SECTION 3

Reading Graphs and Charts

REGIONAL REVIEW HANDBOOK

CONTENTS

Features

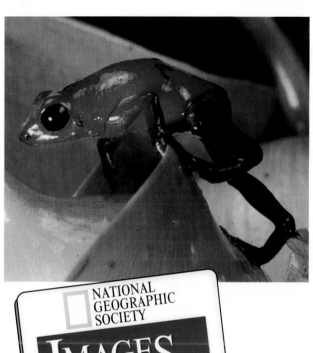

VOLUME 1

VOLUME 2

VOLUME 1

VOLUME 2

BUILDING GEOGRAPHY SKILLS

VOLUME 1

Using Technology

VOLUME 2

Using Technology

MAKING CONNECTIONS

| MATH | SCIENCE | HISTORY | LITERATURE | TECHNOLOGY |

VOLUME 1

Koala Mom and Joey

VOLUME 2

Teen Scene

What in the World?

GeoLab ACTIVITY

Cultural HERITAGE:

Multimedia Activities

NATIONAL GEOGRAPHIC SOCIETY **Picture Atlas of the World**

Surfing the "Net"

Maps

VOLUME 1

Unit 1 Geography of the World

Unit 2 The United States and Canada

CONTENTS

VOLUME 2

Unit 5 Russia and the Independent Republics

Graphs, Tables, and Diagrams

VOLUME 1

Unit 1 Geography of the World

Unit 2 The United States and Canada

Unit 3 Latin America

Unit 4 Europe

VOLUME 2

Unit 5 Russia and the Independent Republics

Unit 6 Southwest Asia and North Africa

Unit 7 Africa South of the Sahara

Unit 8 Asia

Unit 9 Australia, Oceania, and Antarctica

REFERENCE

ATLAS

Contents

ATLAS KEY

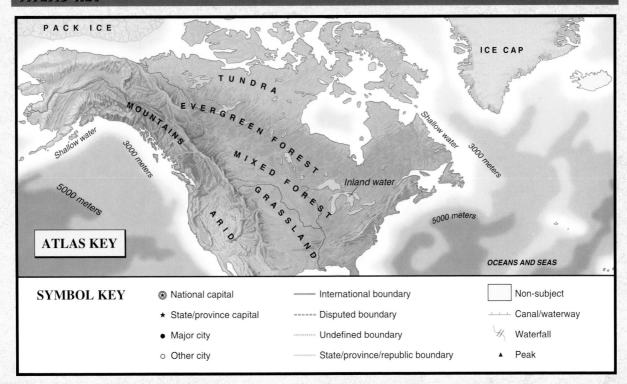

PACK ICE

ICE CAP

TUNDRA

EVERGREEN FOREST

MOUNTAINS

Shallow water

3000 meters

5000 meters

MIXED FOREST

Inland water

GRASSLAND

ARID

Shallow water

3000 meters

5000 meters

OCEANS AND SEAS

ATLAS KEY

SYMBOL KEY

⊛ National capital	—— International boundary	▢ Non-subject
★ State/province capital	----- Disputed boundary	⊢⊢⊣ Canal/waterway
● Major city	.... Undefined boundary	⚡ Waterfall
○ Other city	— State/province/republic boundary	▲ Peak

THE WORLD PHYSICAL/POLITICAL

- ● World's most populous cities
- —— International boundary
- – – – Disputed boundary
- ········ Undefined boundary

0   1000   2000 Miles
0   1000   2000 Kilometers

Projection: Robinson

CENTRAL AMERICA AND WEST INDIES

Projection: Bipolar Oblique Conic Conformal

0   250   500 Miles
0   250   500 Kilometers

A2

REFERENCE ATLAS

ARCTIC OCEAN

COMMONWEALTH OF INDEPENDENT STATES

1	ARMENIA	6	KYRGYZSTAN
2	AZERBAIJAN	7	MOLDOVA
3	BELARUS	8	RUSSIA
4	GEORGIA	9	TAJIKISTAN
5	KAZAKHSTAN	10	TURKMENISTAN
		11	UKRAINE
		12	UZBEKISTAN

EUROPE

Projection: Azimuthal Equal Area

0   250   500 Miles

0   250   500 Kilometers

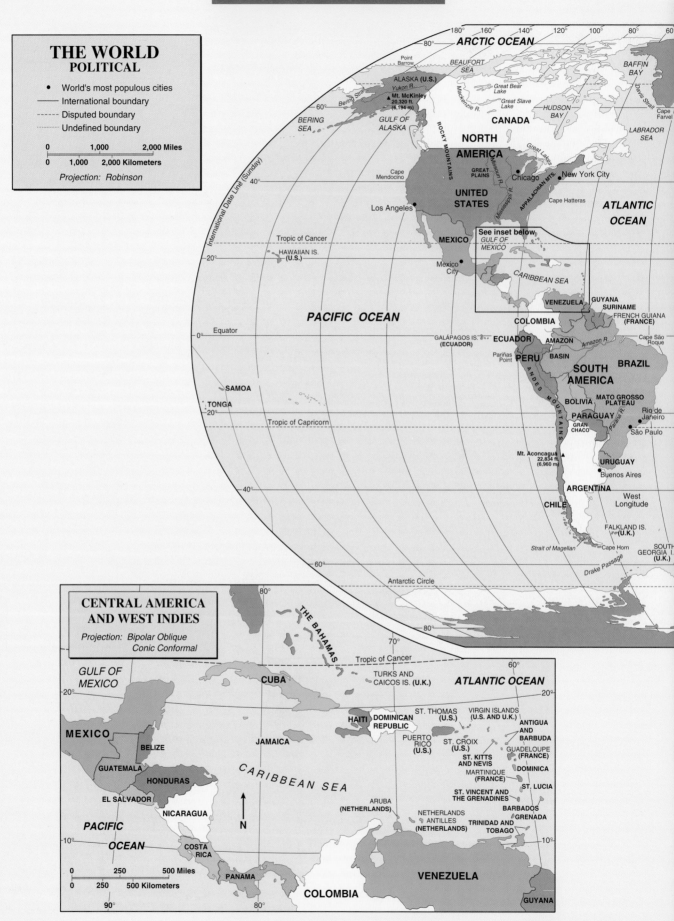

THE WORLD
POLITICAL

- World's most populous cities
— International boundary
‑‑‑ Disputed boundary
····· Undefined boundary

| 0 | 1,000 | 2,000 Miles |
| 0 | 1,000 | 2,000 Kilometers |

Projection: Robinson

CENTRAL AMERICA AND WEST INDIES

Projection: Bipolar Oblique Conic Conformal

| 0 | 250 | 500 Miles |
| 0 | 250 | 500 Kilometers |

ARCTIC OCEAN
BEAUFORT SEA
BAFFIN BAY
Point Barrow
ALASKA (U.S.)
Yukon R.
Mt. McKinley 20,320 ft. (6,194 m)
Great Bear Lake
Mackenzie R.
Great Slave Lake
HUDSON BAY
Davis Strait
Cape Farvel
BERING SEA
Bering Strait
GULF OF ALASKA
ROCKY MOUNTAINS
CANADA
NORTH AMERICA
LABRADOR SEA
Cape Mendocino
GREAT PLAINS
Missouri R.
Great Lakes
Chicago
New York City
APPALACHIAN MTS.
UNITED STATES
Mississippi R.
Cape Hatteras
ATLANTIC OCEAN
Los Angeles
MEXICO
Tropic of Cancer
See inset below
GULF OF MEXICO
HAWAIIAN IS. (U.S.)
Mexico City
CARIBBEAN SEA
GUYANA
SURINAME
VENEZUELA
FRENCH GUIANA (FRANCE)
COLOMBIA
PACIFIC OCEAN
Equator
GALÁPAGOS IS. (ECUADOR)
ECUADOR
AMAZON
Amazon R.
Cape São Roque
Pariñas Point
PERU
BASIN
BRAZIL
SOUTH AMERICA
SAMOA
ANDES MOUNTAINS
BOLIVIA
MATO GROSSO PLATEAU
TONGA
PARAGUAY
Rio de Janeiro
Tropic of Capricorn
GRAN CHACO
Paraná R.
São Paulo
Mt. Aconcagua 22,834 ft. (6,960 m)
URUGUAY
Buenos Aires
ARGENTINA
West Longitude
CHILE
FALKLAND IS. (U.K.)
Strait of Magellan
Cape Horn
SOUTH GEORGIA I. (U.K.)
Drake Passage
Antarctic Circle
International Date Line (Sunday)

THE BAHAMAS
Tropic of Cancer
GULF OF MEXICO
CUBA
TURKS AND CAICOS IS. (U.K.)
ATLANTIC OCEAN
ST. THOMAS (U.S.)
VIRGIN ISLANDS (U.S. AND U.K.)
HAITI
DOMINICAN REPUBLIC
ANTIGUA AND BARBUDA
MEXICO
JAMAICA
PUERTO RICO (U.S.)
ST. CROIX (U.S.)
GUADELOUPE (FRANCE)
BELIZE
ST. KITTS AND NEVIS
DOMINICA
GUATEMALA
MARTINIQUE (FRANCE)
ST. LUCIA
HONDURAS
CARIBBEAN SEA
ST. VINCENT AND THE GRENADINES
EL SALVADOR
BARBADOS
NICARAGUA
ARUBA (NETHERLANDS)
GRENADA
NETHERLANDS ANTILLES (NETHERLANDS)
TRINIDAD AND TOBAGO
PACIFIC OCEAN
COSTA RICA
PANAMA
VENEZUELA
COLOMBIA
GUYANA
N

REFERENCE ATLAS

UNITED STATES

Symbol	Description
◉	National capital
★	State capital
●	Major city
○	Other city
⣿⣿⣿	International boundary
──	State boundary

0	150	300 Miles
0	150	300 Kilometers

Projection: Albers Equal Area

PACIFIC OCEAN

WASHINGTON
- Seattle
- ★ Olympia

OREGON
- Portland
- ★ Salem

IDAHO
- ★ Boise

MONTANA
- Helena ★

WYOMING

NEVADA
- Carson City
- Sacramento

CALIFORNIA
- San Francisco
- Oakland
- San Jose
- Los Angeles
- San Bernardino
- Long Beach
- San Diego
- Las Vegas

UTAH
- Salt Lake City

COLORADO
- Denver

ARIZONA
- Phoenix
- Tucson

NEW MEXICO
- Santa Fe

NORTH DAKOTA
- Bismarck

SOUTH DAKOTA
- Pierre

NEBRASKA
- Cheyenne

KANSAS

OKLAHOMA
- Oklahoma City

TEXAS
- Fort Worth
- Austin
- San Antonio

MEXICO

Columbia River
Missouri River
Snake River
Great Salt Lake
Sacramento River
Colorado River
Gila River
Rio Grande
Pecos River
North Platte River
South Platte River
Platte River
Arkansas River
Red River
Brazos River
Colorado River
Rio Grande

GULF OF CALIFORNIA

HAWAII
PACIFIC OCEAN
- Honolulu ★

0   100 Miles
0   100 Kilometers

Arctic Circle
Bering Strait
Yukon River
ALASKA
CANADA
- Juneau ★
GULF OF ALASKA
BERING SEA

0   250   500 Miles
0   250   500 Kilometers

CANADA

MAINE
★ Augusta

MINNESOTA

Lake Superior

MICHIGAN

Lake Huron

St. Lawrence River

Montpelier ★   N.H.
VT. ★ Concord
Lake Ontario
Albany ★   Boston ★
Rochester   Syracuse   MASS.
Minneapolis ● St. Paul ★   WISCONSIN
Hudson River   Providence ●
Buffalo   Hartford ★   R.I.
Mississippi River   CONN.
NEW YORK   ★ Bridgeport

Lake Michigan   Grand Rapids
Madison ★   Milwaukee ●   Lansing ★   Detroit
IOWA   Lake Erie

Newark ●   New York
Chicago ●   Gary   Toledo   Cleveland   Youngstown   Harrisburg ★   N.J.
Omaha ●   Des Moines ★   Hammond   Akron   Canton   Pittsburgh ●   Trenton ★
Lincoln   Philadelphia   Camden
                OHIO   Dayton   Columbus   Dover
ILLINOIS   Springfield ★   Indianapolis ★   Cincinnati   MD.   DEL.
                INDIANA   River   Ohio River   Frankfort ★   Baltimore   Annapolis ★
Topeka ●   Kansas City   St. Louis   East St. Louis   Louisville ●   Charleston ●   D.C.   Washington
       Kansas City ●   Jefferson City ★   WEST   Richmond ●   ATLANTIC
Kansas City   VIRGINIA   Newport News
       MISSOURI   KENTUCKY   VIRGINIA   Norfolk   OCEAN

Tulsa ●   Nashville ★   Raleigh ●

ARKANSAS   Memphis ●   TENNESSEE   NORTH CAROLINA
       Little Rock ★   Mississippi River   Tennessee R.

Dallas ●   Columbia ★   SOUTH
       Birmingham ●   Atlanta ●   CAROLINA
       LOUISIANA   Jackson ●   ALABAMA   GEORGIA
                   Montgomery ★
       MISSISSIPPI
Baton Rouge ★   Jacksonville ●
Houston ●   New Orleans ●   Tallahassee ★
                                     FLORIDA

GULF   OF   MEXICO   Orlando ●

                                     Tampa ●
                          St. Petersburg ●

N

                                     Miami ●

THE
BAHAMAS

CUBA

ATLANTIC OCEAN

UNITED STATES

⊚ National capital
★ State capital
● Major city
━━ International boundary
── State boundary

|0   150   300 Miles|
|0   150   300 Kilometers|

Projection: Albers Equal Area

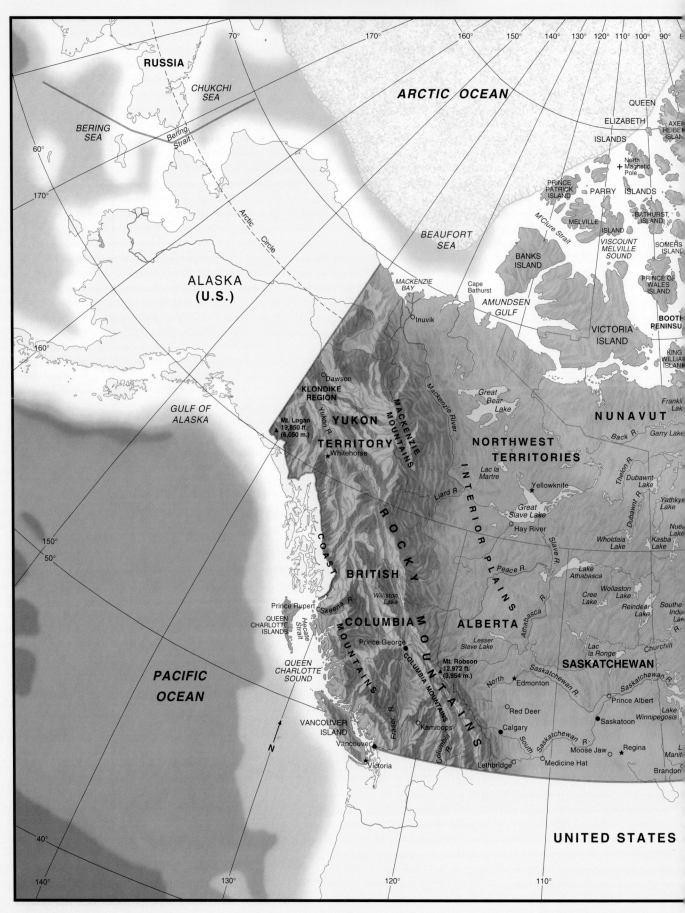

RUSSIA

CHUKCHI
SEA

BERING
SEA

*Bering
Strait*

ARCTIC OCEAN

QUEEN
ELIZABETH
ISLANDS

AXEL
HEIBE
ISLAN

North
Magnetic
Pole

PRINCE
PATRICK
ISLAND

PARRY   ISLANDS

M'Clure Strait

MELVILLE
ISLAND

VISCOUNT
MELVILLE
SOUND

BATHURST
ISLAND

SOMERS
ISLAND

PRINCE OF
WALES
ISLAND

BOOTH
PENINSU

60°

170°

Arctic   Circle

ALASKA
(U.S.)

BEAUFORT
SEA

*MACKENZIE
BAY*

Cape
Bathurst

AMUNDSEN
GULF

BANKS
ISLAND

VICTORIA
ISLAND

KING
WILLIAM
ISLAND

Inuvik

160°

GULF OF
ALASKA

Dawson

KLONDIKE
REGION

Mt. Logan
19,850 ft.
(6,050 m.)

Yukon R.

YUKON
TERRITORY

Whitehorse

MACKENZIE
MOUNTAINS

Mackenzie River

Great
Bear
Lake

NUNAVUT

Franklin
Lake

NORTHWEST
TERRITORIES

*Lac la
Martre*

Yellowknife

Back R.

Garry Lake

Thelon R.

Dubawnt
Lake

Yathkye
Lake

150°
50°

Liard R.

INTERIOR   PLAINS

Great
Slave Lake

Hay River

Slave R.

Wholdaia
Lake

Dubawnt R.

Kasba
Lake

Nue
Lake

ROCKY

BRITISH

COAST

Williston
Lake

Prince Rupert

QUEEN
CHARLOTTE
ISLANDS

Skeena R.

Hecate
Strait

COLUMBIA
MOUNTAINS

Prince George

Peace R.

ALBERTA

Athabasca R.

Lake
Athabasca

Cree
Lake

Wollaston
Lake

Reindeer
Lake

Lake
la Ronge

Southe
India
Lake

Churchill

QUEEN
CHARLOTTE
SOUND

PACIFIC

OCEAN

MOUNTAINS

COLUMBIA MOUNTAINS

Mt. Robson
12,972 ft.
(3,954 m.)

Lesser
Slave Lake

North

Saskatchewan R.

Edmonton

SASKATCHEWAN

Saskatchewan R.

Prince Albert

Lake
Winnipegosis

VANCOUVER
ISLAND

Fraser R.

Kamloops

Columbia R.

Red Deer

Calgary

Saskatoon

Vancouver

Victoria

South

Saskatchewan R.

Lethbridge

Medicine Hat

Moose Jaw

Regina

L
Manit

Brandon

40°

UNITED STATES

N

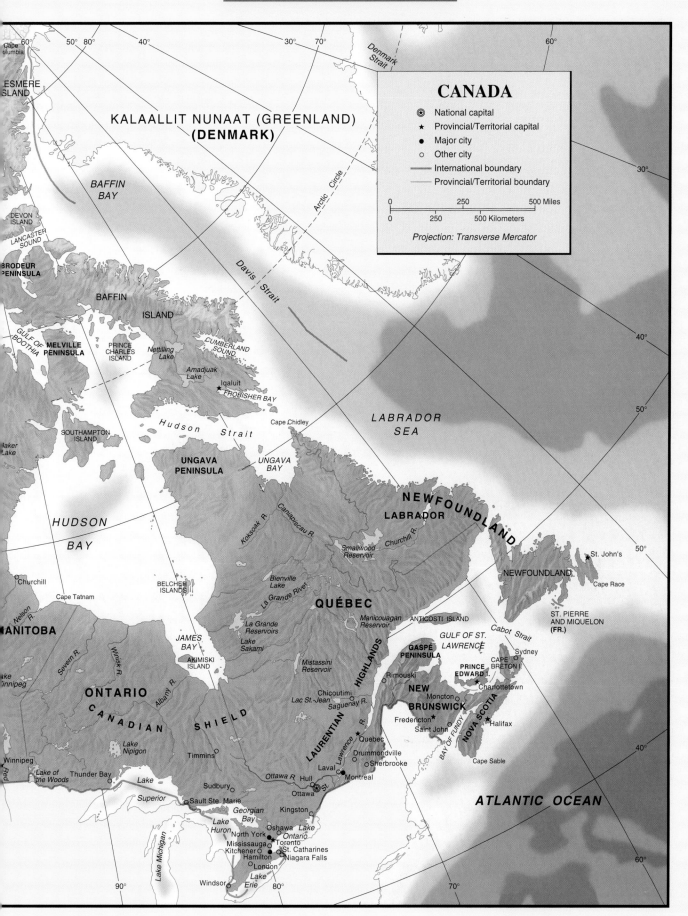

CANADA

- ◎ National capital
- ★ Provincial/Territorial capital
- ● Major city
- ○ Other city
- ━━ International boundary
- ─── Provincial/Territorial boundary

0   250   500 Miles
0   250   500 Kilometers

Projection: Transverse Mercator

KALAALLIT NUNAAT (GREENLAND)
(DENMARK)

BAFFIN BAY

BAFFIN ISLAND

Denmark Strait

Davis Strait

LABRADOR SEA

ESMERE ISLAND
Cape Columbia
DEVON ISLAND
LANCASTER SOUND
BRODEUR PENINSULA
GULF OF BOOTHIA
MELVILLE PENINSULA
PRINCE CHARLES ISLAND
Nettilling Lake
Amadjuak Lake
★ Iqaluit
FROBISHER BAY
Hudson Strait
Cape Chidley
SOUTHAMPTON ISLAND
Baker Lake
UNGAVA PENINSULA
UNGAVA BAY
CUMBERLAND SOUND

NEWFOUNDLAND
LABRADOR

HUDSON BAY

Churchill
Cape Tatnam
BELCHER ISLANDS
Bienville Lake
La Grande River
Koksoak R.
Caniapiscau R.
Smallwood Reservoir
Churchill R.

★ St. John's
Cape Race

NEWFOUNDLAND

ST. PIERRE AND MIQUELON (FR.)

QUÉBEC
La Grande Reservoirs
Lake Sakami
Manicouagan Reservoir
ANTICOSTI ISLAND
Mistassini Reservoir

MANITOBA
Nelson R.
JAMES BAY
AKIMISKI ISLAND
GULF OF ST. LAWRENCE
GASPÉ PENINSULA
Sydney
CAPE BRETON I.
Rimouski
PRINCE EDWARD I.
★ Charlottetown
NEW BRUNSWICK
Moncton

Cabot Strait

ONTARIO
CANADIAN SHIELD
Severn R.
Winisk R.
Albany R.
Lake Winnipeg
Lake Nipigon
Chicoutimi
Lac St.-Jean
Saguenay R.
LAURENTIAN HIGHLANDS
Fredericton ★
Saint John
BAY OF FUNDY
NOVA SCOTIA
★ Halifax
Cape Sable

Winnipeg
Red R.
Lake of the Woods
Thunder Bay
Timmins
Lake Superior
Sudbury
Sault Ste. Marie
Georgian Bay
Lake Huron
Kingston
★ Quebec
St. Lawrence R.
Drummondville
Laval
Hull
● Montreal
Ottawa R.
◎ Ottawa St.
Sherbrooke

ATLANTIC OCEAN

Lake Michigan
North York
Mississauga
Kitchener
Hamilton
London
Windsor
Lake Erie
Oshawa
Toronto
St. Catharines
Niagara Falls
Lake Ontario

MEXICO, the CARIBBEAN, and CENTRAL AMERICA

⊛ National capital
• Major city
── International boundary

| 0 | 250 | 500 Miles |
| 0 | 250 | 500 Kilometers |

Projection: Azimuthal Equal Area

BAJA CALIFORNIA PENINSULA

GULF OF CALIFORNIA

SIERRA MADRE OCCIDENTAL

SIERRA MADRE ORIENTAL

MEXICAN PLATEAU

MEXICO

SIERRA MADRE DEL SUR

San Pedro River

Balsas River

Rio Grande

Ciudad Juárez

Chihuahua

Monterrey

León

Guadalajara

Mexico City

Puebla

Tampico

Veracruz

Tropic of Cancer

CAMPECHE BAY

GULF OF MEXICO

YUCATÁN PENINSULA

Mérida

Belize

Belmopan

BELIZE

Dolores

GULF OF HONDURAS

El Progreso

GUATEMALA

Guatemala

Tegucigal

Quezaltenango

Santa Ana

San Salvador

EL SALVADOR

PACIFIC OCEAN

N

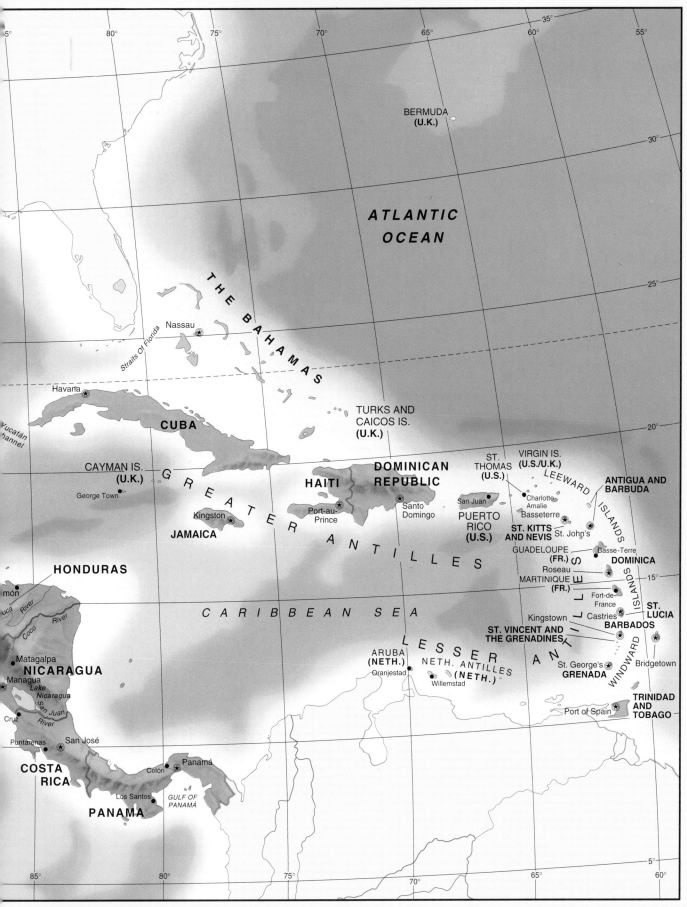

ATLANTIC OCEAN

BERMUDA (U.K.)

THE BAHAMAS

Nassau

Straits Of Florida

Havana

Yucatán Channel

CUBA

TURKS AND CAICOS IS. (U.K.)

CAYMAN IS. (U.K.)

George Town

G R E A T E R   A N T I L L E S

DOMINICAN REPUBLIC

HAITI

Port-au-Prince

Santo Domingo

Kingston

JAMAICA

ST. THOMAS (U.S.)

San Juan

PUERTO RICO (U.S.)

VIRGIN IS. (U.S./U.K.)

L E E W A R D

Charlotte Amalie

Basseterre

ST. KITTS AND NEVIS

St. John's

ANTIGUA AND BARBUDA

I S L A N D S

GUADELOUPE (FR.)

Basse-Terre

DOMINICA

Roseau

MARTINIQUE (FR.)

Fort-de-France

ST. LUCIA

Castries

Kingstown

ST. VINCENT AND THE GRENADINES

BARBADOS

Bridgetown

W I N D W A R D   I S L A N D S

St. George's

GRENADA

TRINIDAD AND TOBAGO

Port of Spain

HONDURAS

món

uca

River

Coco

River

River

Matagalpa

NICARAGUA

Managua

Lake Nicaragua

San Juan

River

Cruz

Puntarenas

San José

COSTA RICA

PANAMA

Colón

Panamá

Los Santos

GULF OF PANAMÁ

C A R I B B E A N   S E A

L E S S E R   A N T I L L E S

ARUBA (NETH.)

Oranjestad

NETH. ANTILLES (NETH.)

Willemstad

NORTH AMERICA

- ⊛ National capital
- ● Major city
- ○ Other city
- —— International boundary

0 250 500 750 Miles
0 250 500 750 Kilometers

Projection: Azimuthal Equal Area

SOUTH AMERICA

- ⊚ National capital
- ● Major city
- ○ Other city
- ‒‒‒‒ International boundary

0   250   500 Miles
0   250   500 Kilometers

Projection: Azimuthal Equal Area

EUROPE

⊛ National capital
● Major city
○ Other city
▥▥▥ International boundary
——— Republic boundary
⊥⊥ Canal

| 0 | 100 | 200 | 300 Miles |
| 0 | 100 | 200 | 300 Kilometers |

Projection: Azimuthal Equal Area

ICELAND
Reykjavik
Arctic Circle

FAROE IS. (DEN.)

NORWEGIAN SEA

SCANDINAVIAN HIGHLANDS

Trondheim

GULF OF BOTH

NORWAY
▲ Galdhöpiggen 8,097 ft. (2,468 m.)
Bergen
Oslo
SWEDEN
Lake Vänern
Uppsala
Stockholm

ÅLAND

HIIUMAA
SAAREMAA
GOTLAND I.

SHETLAND IS. (U.K.)

OUTER HEBRIDES IS.
Cape Wrath
ORKNEY ISLANDS
SCOTLAND

NORTH SEA

Skagerrak
Kattegat
Göteborg

ÖLAND I.

JUTLAND
Copenhagen
DENMARK
Odense
Malmö
BORNHOLM I.
BALTIC SEA

NORTHERN IRELAND (U.K.)
Glasgow
Edinburgh
Belfast
IRISH
ISLE OF MAN SEA
PENNINE RANGE
UNITED KINGDOM
Manchester
Liverpool
Leeds
Sheffield
ENGLAND
Birmingham

Kiel Canal
Hamburg
Elbe R.
Bremen
Rostock
Szczecin
Gdańsk
RUSS
NORT

Dublin
IRELAND
Cork
Cape Clear
St. George's Channel
WALES
Cardiff
Bristol
London

NETHERLANDS
Amsterdam
The Hague
Rotterdam
Antwerp
BELGIUM
Brussels
Liège
Bonn
LUXEMBOURG
Luxembourg
Berlin
Hannover
Magdeburg
Leipzig
Dresden
Chemnitz
GERMANY
Cologne
Essen
Dortmund
Mittelland Canal

POLAND
Poznań
Warsaw
Wrocław
Katow
Kra
Prague
CZECH REPUBLIC
Brno
Ostrava
Vista
Oder R.

ATLANTIC OCEAN

GUERNSEY I. (U.K.)
JERSEY I. (U.K.)
English Channel
Strait of Dover

BRETON PEN.
Le Havre
Seine River
Paris
Marne R.
Marne-Rhine Canal
Frankfurt
Stuttgart
Danube
Munich
Bodensee
Rhine River
Strasbourg

Nantes
Loire
FRANCE

CENTRAL MASSIF

Bordeaux
Garonne R.
Toulouse
Midi Canal

LIECHTENSTEIN
Zürich
Bern
SWITZERLAND
Lausanne
Geneva
L. Geneva
Vaduz
Innsbruck
AUSTRIA
Salzburg
Linz
Vienna
Bratislava
SLOVAK
Budapest
HUNGARY
Graz
Miskc
L. Balaton
Pécs

Cape Finisterre
BAY OF BISCAY

Lyon
Mt. Blanc 15,774 ft. (4,807 m.)
▲ Mt. Rosa 12,203 ft. (4,634 m.)
Milan
Turin
PO VALLEY
Po R.
Genoa
Venice
ALPS
Ljubljana
SLOVENIA
Zagreb
CROATIA
Novi Sa
DINARIC ALPS
Sava R.
Belgrade
BOSNIA-HERZEGOVINA
Saraje
Split

Cape St. Vincent
Strait of Gibraltar

CANTABRIAN MTNS.
Bilbao
Porto
PYRENEES
Valladolid
Ebro River
Duero River
PORTUGAL
IBERIAN
Zaragoza
Aneto Peak 11,168 ft. (3,404 m.)
ANDORRA
Andorra la Vella
Marseille
GULF OF LION
Montpellier
Nice
Monaco
MONACO
Florence
Bologna
SAN MARINO
San Marino
APENNINES
ADRIATIC SEA
FORMER YUGOSLAV REPUBLIC MACEDO
MONTENE

Lisbon
Setúbal
Tagus River
Madrid
PENINSULA
Guadiana River
Murcia
Valencia
Barcelona

CORSICA (FR.)
VATICAN CITY
Rome
ITALY
Bari
Tirane
ALBAN

SIERRA MORENA
SPAIN
Seville
Granada
Málaga
GIBRALTAR (U.K.)

Palma
BALEARIC IS. (SP.)

SARDINIA (IT.)
Cagliari
TYRRHENIAN SEA
Naples

G. OF TARANTO
IONIAN SEA
KEFALLINIA

Strait of Gibraltar

AFRICA

MEDITERRANEAN
Strait of Sicily
Palermo
SICILY
Catania
PANTELLERIA (IT.)
MALTA
Valletta

SEA

BARENTS SEA

Murmansk

KOLA PENINSULA

TIMAN RIDGE

Pechora R.

URAL MOUNTAINS

ASIA

WHITE SEA

Arkhangel'sk

N. Dvina River

Vychegda River

Mt. Konzhakovskiy ▲ 5,147 ft. (1,569 m.)

FINLAND

White Sea-Baltic Waterway

Lake Onega

Sukhona River

Kama R.

Perm

70°

Tampere

Lake Saimaa

Lake Ladoga

Volga-Baltic Waterway

Rybinsk Reservoir

Kazan

Kama River

Ufa

50°

Helsinki
rku
poo

St. Petersburg

Yaroslavl

Kuybyshev Reservoir

GULF OF FINLAND

Tallinn

Chudskoye Lake

Nizhniy Novgorod

Samara

Orenburg

ESTONIA

GULF OF RIGA

LATVIA

Riga
W.

PLAIN

Volga River

Volga-Baltic Waterway

Moscow

Dvina River

Oka

River

Tula

RUSSIA

Saratov

VOLGA UPLAND

Volga River

Volgograd Reservoir

Ural River

BALTIC PLAIN

LITHUANIA
aunas

Vilnius

EUROPEAN

Minsk

CENTRAL RUSSIAN UPLAND

Smolensk

Don R.

Voronezh

Volga River

KAZAKHSTAN

ARAL SEA

BELARUS

Pripet River

Desna R.

Kursk

River

Volgograd

Volga River

DEPRESSION

Kiev

Kremenchug Reservoir

Kharkov

Lugansk

Tsimlyansk Reservoir

Astrakhan

CASPIAN

Delta of the Volga

Lvov

UKRAINE

DNIEPER UPLAND

Dnieper R.

Dnester

Dnepropetrovsk

Krivoy Rog

Donetsk

Zaporozhye

Don River

Rostov

Volga River

CASPIAN SEA

CARPATHIAN MTNS.

MOLDOVA

Chisinau

DNIEPER LOWLAND

Dniep River

Kakhovka Res.

SEA OF AZOV

Debrecen

Prut River

Odessa

CRIMEA

Krasnodar

Grozny

Cluj-Napoca

ROMANIA

Brasov

CAUCASUS MTNS.

Timişoara

Bucharest

Mt. Elbrus 18,510 ft. (5,642 m.)

WALLACHIA PLAIN

River

Constanta

BLACK SEA

Danube

SERBIA

Ruse

Varna

Nis

BULGARIA

kopje

Sofia

Burgas

Plovdiv

Musala Peak 9,536 ft. (2,926 m.)

Bosporus

PENINSULA

TURKEY

Salonika

Dardanelles

SEA OF MARMARA

LKAN

Làrissa

AEGEAN SEA

ASIA

GREECE
Patras

Athens

Piraeus
PELOPONNESE
EN.

RHODES

CRETE (GR.)
Iraklion

30°

40°

70°

50°

60°

60°

70°

50°

40°

60°

30°

50°

ARCTIC OCEAN

FRANZ JOSEF ISLANDS

Cape Zelaniya

EUROPE

BARENTS SEA

Murmansk

KOLA PENINSULA

NOVAYA ZEMLYA

KARA SEA

BALTIC SEA

WHITE SEA

Kara Strait

GULF OF FINLAND

Baltic-White Sea Canal

Arkhangel'sk

YAMAL PEN.

(RUSSIA)

Lake Ladoga

St. Petersburg

Lake Onega

Volga-Baltic Waterway

N. Dvina River

TIMAN RIDGE

Yenisey River

GYDAN PENINSULA

Minsk

BELARUS

VALDAI HILLS

Vologda

Sukhona R.

Vychegda

Pechora River

URAL MOUNTAINS

Ob River

WEST SIBERIAN PLAIN

Lvov

DNIEPER UPLAND

Dnieper R.

Rybinsk Res.

Yaroslovl

NORTHERN HILLS

Urengoy

Kiev

DNIEPER LOWLAND

Moscow

Ivanovo

Volga

UKRAINE

Tula

Nizhniy Novgorod

Kamsk Res.

Izhevsk

Perm

Mt. Konzhakovskiy 5,147 ft. (1,569 m.)

Ob

MOLDOVA

Chisinau

Ryazan'

Kazan

R.

Kama

Ob

Vakh R.

Odessa

Nikolayev

Kharkov

Krivoy Rog

Voronezh

Kuybyshev Res.

Ul'yanovsk

Yekaterinburg

Irtysh River

Dnepropetrovsk

Don River

Penza

VOLGA UPLAND

Saratov

Tol'yatti

Ufa

Chelyabinsk

Tobol R.

Zaporozh'ye

Samara

Tom

Donetsk

Lugansk

Mariupol

SEA OF AZOV

Rostov

Volgograd Reservoir

Volgograd

Ural R.

Orenburg

Ishim R.

Omsk

L. Chany

Novosibirsk

Kemerovo

BLACK SEA

Krasnodar

Tsimlyansk Res.

Volga

CASPIAN DEPRESSION

Astrakhan

KYRGYZ STEPPE

TURGAY PLATEAU

Astana

Novosibirsk

Novokuznetsk

Barnaul

CAUCASUS MTNS.

Mt. Elbrus 18,510 ft. (5,642 m.)

KAZAKHSTAN

KAZAKH UPLAND

Mt. Belukha 14,783 ft. (4,506 m.)

GEORGIA

Tbilisi

ARMENIA

Yerevan

AZERBAIJAN

AZERBAIJAN

Baku

CASPIAN SEA

USTYURT PLATEAU

ARAL SEA

Syr

Karaganda

Semipalatinsk

L. Zaysan

BETPAK-DALA DESERT

Kzyl-Orda

Lake Balkhash

L. Alakol

PLAINS OF TURAN

Darya

ASIA

KARA BOGAZ GOL GULF

TURKMENISTAN

UZBEKISTAN

Ili R.

Almaty

KARAKUM DESERT

Amu

Darya

Samarkand

Tashkent

Bishkek

KYRGYZSTAN

L. Issyk-Kul

Ashkhabad

ALAY MOUNTAINS

Dushanbe

TAJIKISTAN

Communism Pk. 24,590 ft. (7,495 m.)

North Pole

ARCTIC OCEAN

Cape Arkticheski

SEVERNAYA ZEMLYA

Vil'kitskiy Strait

BYRRANGA MTNS.

TAYMYR PENINSULA

L. Taymyr

Noril'sk

Kotuy R.

CENTRAL SIBERIAN

Tura · Tunguska

Lower

PLATEAU

RUSSIA

Yenisey River

Angara R.

Bratsk

Krasnoyarsk

Krasnoyarsk Reservoir

Bratsk Reservoir

SAYAN MOUNTAINS

ALTAI MTNS.

80°

70°

CHUKCHI SEA

Bering Strait

WRANGEL ISLAND

Long Strait

CHUKOTSK PENINSULA

60°

170°

BERING SEA

180°

170°

Cape Navarin

EAST SIBERIAN SEA

KOLYMA PLAIN

Cherskiy

Kolyma

KOLYMA RANGE

Anadyr R.

KORYAK MTNS.

NEW SIBERIAN ISLANDS

Sannikov Strait

Laptev Strait

LAPTEV SEA

CHERSKIY RANGE

Indigirka

River

Evensk

KARAGIN ISLAND

KOMANDORSKIY ISLANDS

160°

SHELIKHOV GULF

SREDINNY RA.

▲ Mt. Kiyuchevsk 15,584 ft. (4,750 m.)

VERKHOYANSK RANGE

Verkhoyansk

River

KAMCHATKA PENINSULA

160°

Petropavlovsk-Kamchatskiy

S I B E R I A

Olenёk

Lena

R.

Markha

Vilyuy R.

River

Yakutsk

Magadan

Cape Lopatka

50°

SEA OF OKHOTSK

S

LENA PLATEAU

Vilyuysk Reservoir

R.

River

Aldan

ALDAN MTNS.

River

DZHUGDZHUR RA.

Cape Yelizavety

KURIL ISLANDS

150°

Vitim R.

STANOVOY UPLAND

Lena R.

YABLONOVY RANGE

STANOVOY RANGE

Uda R.

SAKHALIN ISLAND

Tatar

Strait

Terpeniya Point

R.

Komsomol'sk

Amur

River

Lake Baikal

Bratsk Reservoir

Chita

Shilka

Ulan-Ude

Irkutsk

R.

Khabarovsk

Ussuri River

SIKHOTE-ALIN RA.

La Pérouse Strait

140°

40°

L. Khanka

Vladivostok

ASIA

SEA OF JAPAN

30°

100°

110°

120°

130°

RUSSIA AND THE EURASIAN REPUBLICS

⊛ National capital

● Major city

○ Other city

— International boundary

| 0 | 250 | 500 Miles |

| 0 | 250 | 500 Kilometers |

Projection: Two-Point Equidistant

REFERENCE ATLAS

EUROPE

BLACK SEA

10°

20°

30°

40°

Istanbul • Bosporus
SEA OF MARMARA
Dardanelles

PONTUS MTNS. Samsun

ANATOLIAN

ASIA MINOR

AEGEAN SEA

Bursa   Eskisehir   ⊛ Ankara

Izmir

TURKEY

PLATEAU

Kayseri

Erciyes Dagi
12,369 ft.
(3,770 m.)

Denizli   Konya

Bizerte
⊛ Tunis

Cape Bon

TAURUS MTNS.

Antalya

Adana

Sfax

TUNISIA

GULF OF GABÈS

MEDITERRANEAN SEA

Nicosia ⊛
CYPRUS

Lataki

Trip

Beirut

LEBAN

Tripoli ⊛

Misrátah

Cape Hilâl

GOLAN HEIGHTS
Haifa

ISRAE

Nâbulus
Tel Aviv-Yafo

Jerusalem
GAZA STRIP

Banghâzî

GULF OF SIDRA

CYRENAICA

Matrûh

LIBYAN
PLATEAU

QATTARA
DEPRESSION

Delta of the Nile

Alexandria

Damanhûr Tanta Ismailia

Port
Said

Suez
Canal

DEAD SEA
DEPRESSION

SINAI

30°

El Giza ● Cairo

Suez

Al 'Aqabah

PENINSULA

El Faiyûm

LIBYA

Beni Suéf

El Minya

GULF OF SUEZ

Sardalas

Asyût

ARABIAN DESERT

GULF AQA

LIBYAN DESERT

EGYPT

Qena

Luxor

Tropic of Cancer

10°

Al Jawf

Aswân

Lake
Nasser

Nile

Inset map

Antalya

TAURUS MTNS.

Adana

Gaziantep

20°

Nicosia ⊛
CYPRUS

Latakia

● Aleppo

Euphrates River

Hamâh

Deir-ez-
Zor

MEDITERRANEAN
SEA

Tripoli

Beirut

Hims

SYRIA

Damascus ⊛

River

LEBANON

GOLAN HEIGHTS

SYRIAN

AFRICA

Haifa

Nâbulus
Tel Aviv-Yafo

ISRAEL

ISRAELI-OCCUPIED

WEST

Zarqa

Jerusalem ⊛
GAZA
STRIP

BANK

DESERT

Delta of the Nile
Damanhûr

Port
Said

Amman ⊛

Nile

Tanta
Ismailia

Suez
Canal

DEAD
SEA
DEPRESSION

JORDAN

El Giza ● Cairo

Suez

SINAI

El Faiyûm

Nile River

PENINSULA

Al 'Aqabah

AN NAFUD
DESERT

Beni Suéf

ARABIAN DESERT

Tabûk

Blue

Nile

R.

El Minya

EGYPT

GULF OF SUEZ

GULF OF AQABA

White Nile R.

0   50   100 Miles
0   50   100 Kilometers

MIDDLE EAST

⊛ National capital
● Major city
○ Other city
——— International boundary
- - - - Disputed boundary
······· Undefined boundary

0   100   200   300 Miles
0   100   200   300 Kilometers

Projection: Azimuthal Equal Area

N

20°

30°

ASIA

Trabzon

Erzurum Mt. Ararat ▲
16,945 ft.
(5,165 m.)
*Lake
Van*

Malatya   Diyarbakir   Urmia   Tabrîz
*Lake
Urmia*

Gaziantep   ELBURZ   Rasht   Mashhad
Aleppo   Qazvin   MTNS.
                         Mosul   Irbîl   ▲ Mt. Demavend
Hamâh Deir-ez-   Kirkuk   18,386 ft.
SYRIA   Zor   Z   Hamadân   Tehran   (5,604 m.)
Hims   M E S   IRAQ A   Bâkhtarân   GREAT SALT DESERT
Damascus   O P   G   Arâk
            SYRIAN O T   R   Baghdad   Bîrjand
ISRAELI-OCCUPIED   A   O   Karbalâ   Esfahân   PLATEAU
JORDAN   M   S   Al Hillah   M   OF
Zarqa   DESERT I   An Najaf   O   Ahvâz   IRAN
Amman   A   An   U   Kermân   30°
                              Nâsirîyah N   Shîrâz   Zâhedân
Tabûk   AN NAFUD   Al Başrah T Abadan
              DESERT   KUWAIT A
                               Hawalli Kuwait   Bûshehr
See inset below   Ha'il   Al Ahmadî   Bandar 'Abbâs

                NAJD PLATEAU   Buraydah   Ad Dammâm   Manama   Strait of Hormuz   GULF OF OMAN
                                            BAHRAIN   PERSIAN   Dubai
            Madinah   Al Hufûf QATAR GULF
RED   Doha Abu   Tropic of Cancer
        Yanbu al Bahr   Riyadh   Dhabi   Muscat
                    SAUDI   ARABIA   Cape Al Hadd
        Jiddah Makkah   UNITED ARAB
SEA   At Ta'if ARABIAN PENINSULA EMIRATES   OMAN
                                                                        20°
                    TUWAYQ MTNS. RUB AL   Duqm
        ASIR MOUNTAINS   KHALI

                                                      Salâlah

                San'a
        Mt. Nabî Shu'ayb ▲   ARABIAN SEA
        12,336 ft.   Al Ghaydah
Al Hudaydah (3,760 m.) YEMEN   Al Mukallâ
*Lake   Ta'izz
Tana*   Bab el   SOCOTRA
              Mandeb Aden   (YEMEN)
              GULF OF ADEN   Cape Asir
        40°   50°   60°

AFRICA

- ⊛ National capital
- ● Major city
- ○ Other city
- — International boundary
- ┄ Disputed boundary

0   500   1000 Miles
0   500   1000 Kilometers

Projection: Azimuthal Equal Area

A22

SOUTH ASIA

- ⊛ National capital
- ● Major city
- ○ Other city
- —— International boundary
- ----- Disputed boundary

| 0 | 250 | 500 Miles |
| 0 | 250 | 500 Kilometers |

Projection: Mercator

Mazār-i-Sharīf

HINDU KUSH

KARAKORAM RANGE

Godwin Austen Pk. (K2)
28,251 ft.
▲ (8,611 m.)

Kabul

AFGHANISTAN

Peshāwar
Srīnagar
Islāmābād
Rāwalpindi
Herāt
Siālkot
Gujrānwāla
Sargodha
Lahore
Amritsar
Faisalabad
Jhelum R.
Ravi
Multan
R.
Quetta
Sutlej
River
Indus

PAKISTAN

BALUCHISTAN

SULAIMĀN RANGE

CENTRAL MAKRĀN RANGE

Sukkur

THAR
DESERT

Delhi
New Delhi
Jaipur
Āgra
Yamuna River

GANGES

Mt. Dhaulagiri
26,971 ft.
(8,221 m.)
NEPAL
Kathmandu
Mt. Everest
29,028 ft.
(8,848 m.)
Mt. Kanchenjunga
28,208 ft.
(8,598 m.)
Thimphu
BHUTAN

Ghāghara River

Lucknow
Kānpur
Ganges
Patna
River
Vārānasi
PLAIN
Brahmaputra
Gauhāti
Imphāl
Sylhet
River
PĀTKAI RANGE

Hyderābād

Sonmiāni
Bay
Karāchi
RANN OF
KUTCH

Tropic of Cancer

Gāndhi
Reservoir

INDIA

VINDHYA RANGE
Ahmadābād
Indore
Narmada

BANGLADESH
Dhaka
Govind Ballaldh
Pant Res.
River
Khulna
Howrah
Calcutta
Barisāl
Karnaphuli
Reservoir
Chittagong
Delta of The Ganges
(Sundarbans)
Palmyras
Point

GULF OF KUTCH
KĀTHIĀWAR
PENINSULA
Vadodara
SĀTPURA RANGE
Tāpti River
Surat
GULF
OF
KHAMBHĀT
Mahānadi
River
DECCAN

Mumbai
(Bombay)
Poona
Godavari
River
PLATEAU
Sholapur
Bhima
Hyderābād
River
Vishākhapatnam

BAY OF
BENGAL

Krishna River
Vijayawāda

ARABIAN
SEA

HINDUSTAN

WESTERN

GHATS

EASTERN

GHATS
Coast

NORTH ANDAMAN
MIDDLE ANDAMAN
ANDAMAN IS.
(INDIA)
SOUTH ANDAMAN

Bangalore
Chennai (Madras)

LACCÁDIVE IS.
(INDIA)

Coimbatore

Coromandel

ANDAMAN

SEA

Malabar
Calicut
Madurai
Cochin
Coast
Point Calimere
Point Pedro
Jaffna
Park
Strait
Trincomalee

NICOBAR IS.
(INDIA)

LACCADIVE

SEA

Cape
Comorin
GULF
OF
MANNAR
SRI
LANKA
Colombo
Dehiwala
Moratuwa

GREAT
NICOBAR I.

Cape Dondra

⊛ Male

MALDIVES

Equator

INDIAN OCEAN

80°　　　　　　90°　　　　　　100°　　　　110°

50°

L. Uvs
Ulaangom
ALTAI
SHAN
L. Hyargas
L. Har Us
Dund-Us
L. Har
Ertix He
(Irtysh R.)
Ulungur
L. Ulungur

L. Hövsgöl
Sühbaatar
Orhon R.
Ulaanbaatar
(Ulan Bator)

Uliastay

MONGOLIA

Bayanhongor

MONGOLIAN
PLATEAU

DZUNGARIAN BASIN
Karamay
L. Ebinur

Ürümqi

Dalandzadgad

TURFAN
DEPRESSION

G O B I

TIAN SHAN
Pobedy Pk.
24,406 ft.
(7,439 m.)

L.
Bosten

Kongi He

Lop Nur

He
Tarim

40°

Kashi
Kongur Pk.
25,324 ft.
▲ (7,719 m.)

Yarkant He

Holan He

TAKLIMAKAN

ALTUN SHAN

Yumen

Mt. Qilian
18,198 ft.
(5,547 m.)

QILIAN ▲

SHAN

Yinchuan

HUANGTU

QAIDAM

BASIN

L. Har

CHINA

PLATEAU

Godwin Austen Pk. (K2)
28,251 ft.
▲ (8,611 m.)

KUNLUN SHAN

HOH XIL SHAN

PLATEAU OF XIZANG

L.
Ulan Ul

A'NYÊMAQÊN SHAN

L.
Qinghai

Golmud

Xining

Huang

He

Lanzhou

Jing He

Wei He

QIN LING

Xi'

TIBET

TANGGULA SHAN

Siling L.

Jinsha

BAYAN HAR SHAN

Jiang

Yalong

Min Jiang

Jiang

Chengdu

SICHUAN
BASIN

Chongqing

H
I
M
A
L
A
Y
A
S

Mapam
Yarung
L. Zhari

L. Tangra

Nam L.

Lhasa

Zangbo

Jiang

(Brahmaputra R.)

Yamzho
L.

Nu Jiang

HENGDUAN SHAN

Mt. Everest
29,028 ft.
(8,848 m.) ▲

Mt. Kanchenjunga
28,208 ft.
▲ (8,598 m.)

30°

Mt. Gongga
24,790 ft.
(7,556 m.) ▲

YUNGUI

Guiyang

PLATEAU

Kunming

Hongshui Jiang

Yuan Jiang (Red R.)

Nanpan Jiang

You Jiang

Nanning

(Salween R.)

BAY OF
BENGAL

20°

GULF
OF
TONK

80°　　　　　　90°　　　　　　100°

120°   130°   140°   150°

Amur R.
Heilong Jiang
XIAO HINGGAN LING
Choybalsan
Kerulen R.
L. Hulun
L. Buyr
Hailar He
Nen Jiang
Qiqihar
NORTHEAST (MANCHURIAN) PLAIN
Buyant-Uhaa
INNER MONGOLIA
DA HINGGAN LING
Songhua Jiang
Harbin
NORTHEAST (MANCHURIA)
Amur R.
(Sungari R.)
Jiang
Ussuri R.
L. Khanka
50°
WIN SHAN
Xar Moron He
Liao He
Changchun
Jilin
Songhua Res.
Baotou
Datong
Sanggan He
Beijing
Tangshan
Fushun
Shenyang
Anshan
Fengcheng
Dandong
Sinuiju
Yalu Jiang
NORTH KOREA
Tumen Jiang
Ch'ongjin
Kimch'aek
Asahikawa
HOKKAIDŌ
Sapporo
Kushiro
Cape Erimo
Hakodate
LÜLIANG SHAN
TAIHANG SHAN
Taiyuan
Shijiazhuang
Tianjin
LIAODONG PENINSULA
Dalian
KOREA BAY
Hamhung
Wonsan
SEA OF JAPAN
Akita
HONSHŪ
40°
Fen He
Quzhou
Jinan
Zibo
BO HAI
YELLOW SEA
Namp'o
Pyongyang
Kaesong
Sendai
NORTH CHINA PLAIN
Tai'an
Qingdao
SHANDONG PENINSULA
Cape Chengshan
Inchon
Seoul
Ansong
SOUTH KOREA
Niigata
Toyama
Kanazawa
Utsunomiya
Mt. Fuji 12,388 ft. (3,776 m.)
Tokyo
Cape Inubō
Kawasaki
Luoyang
Zhengzhou
Wei Res.
Huang He
Kuai He
Hongze Res.
Grand Canal
Gaoyou Res.
Zaozhuang
Huaian
Kunsan
Kwangju
Mokp'o
Taegu
Pusan
Korea Strait
Kyōto
Kōbe
Osaka
Nagoya
Yokohama
JAPAN
Han Shui
Huai He
Nanjing
L. Chao
CHEJU IS. (S. KOR.)
Kitakyūshū
Fukuoka
Hiroshima
SHIKOKU
Kōchi
DABA SHAN
Chang Jiang
Wuhan
Huzhou
Hangzhou
Shanghai
Nanchang
L. Tai
EAST CHINA SEA
Nagasaki
KYŪSHŪ
Kagoshima
Cape Sata
PACIFIC OCEAN
Dongting L.
Yueyang
Changsha
Nanchang
L. Poyang
Gan Jiang
30°
Yuan Jiang
Xiang Jiang
WUYI SHAN
Fuzhou
Taipei
Chilung
RYUKYU IS. (JAP.)
OKINAWA
N
Xi Jiang
Guangzhou
Kowloon
Victoria
HONG KONG
MACAO
Macao
Dongshan
Formosa Strait
Hsinchu
T'aichung
TAIWAN
Yü Shan 13,113 ft. (3,997 m.)
Chiai
Fengshan
Kaohsiung
Tropic of Cancer
Binyang
LEIZHOU PENINSULA
Cape Tungku
Bashi Channel
HAINAN
SOUTH CHINA SEA
Luzon Strait
PHILIPPINE SEA
20°

110°   120°   130°   140°

EAST ASIA

⊛ National capital
● Major city
○ Other city
— International boundary
--- Disputed boundary

0   150   300 Miles
0   150   300 Kilometers

Projection: Robinson

SOUTHEAST ASIA

◉ National capital
● Major city
○ Other city
—— International boundary

| 0 | 200 | 400 Miles |

| 0 | 200 | 400 Kilometers |

Projection: Mercator

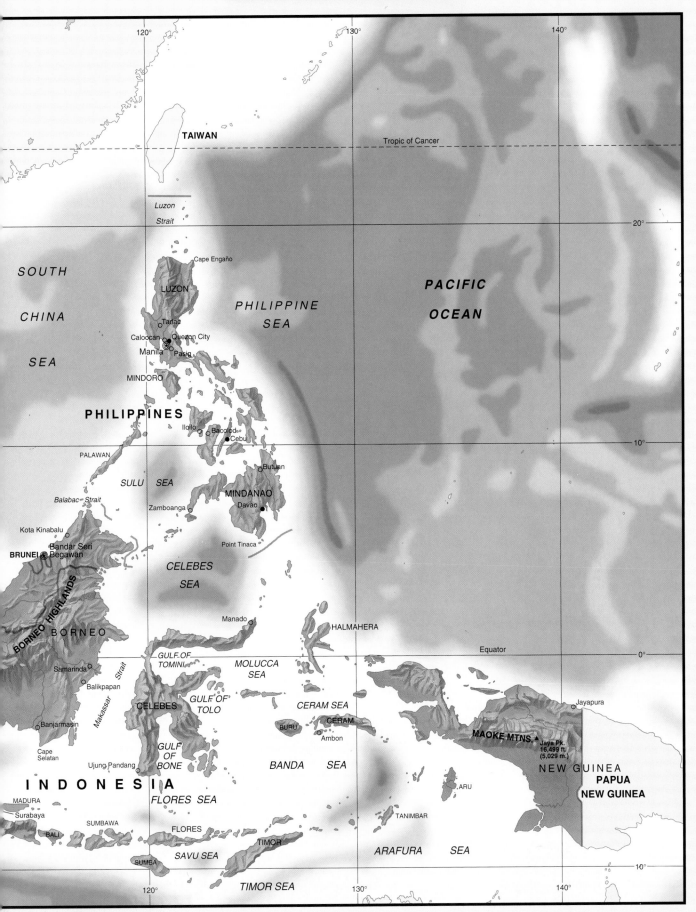

TAIWAN

Tropic of Cancer

Luzon Strait

SOUTH

CHINA

SEA

Cape Engaño

LUZON

PHILIPPINE
SEA

PACIFIC
OCEAN

Tarlac

Caloocan   Quezon City
Manila   Pasig

MINDORO

PHILIPPINES

Iloilo   Bacolod
Cebu

PALAWAN

SULU   SEA

Butuan

Balabac Strait

MINDANAO
Zamboanga   Davao

Kota Kinabalu

Bandar Seri
Begawan
BRUNEI

Point Tinaca

CELEBES

SEA

BORNEO HIGHLANDS

B O R N E O

Manado

HALMAHERA

Equator

Samarinda

GULF OF
TOMINI

MOLUCCA
SEA

Balikpapan

CELEBES

GULF OF
TOLO

CERAM SEA

CERAM

Jayapura

Banjarmasin

BURU
Ambon

MAOKE MTNS.

Jaya Pk.
16,499 ft.
(5,029 m.)

Cape
Selatan

GULF
OF
BONE

BANDA   SEA

Ujung Pandang

NEW GUINEA

PAPUA
NEW GUINEA

MADURA

I N D O N E S I A

ARU

Surabaya

FLORES SEA

SUMBAWA

BALI

FLORES

TANIMBAR

TIMOR

SAVU SEA

ARAFURA   SEA

SUMBA

TIMOR SEA

Makassar Strait

SOUTH
CHINA
SEA

PHILIPPINE
SEA

NORTHERN
MARIANA IS.
(U.S.)
• Saipan

GUAM
(U.S.)

M I C R O N E S I A

CELEBES
SEA

CAROLINE ISLANDS

Koror ⊛
PALAU

• Palikir

ASIA

FEDERATED STATES
OF MICRONESIA

JAVA SEA

BANDA SEA

M E L A N E S I A

ADMIRALTY IS.

BISMARCK
SEA

NEW IRELAND

Yaren
NAURU

NEW
GUINEA

Wewak

PAPUA NEW GUINEA
CENTRAL
RANGE
Mt. Wilhelm
15,400 ft.
(4,694 m.)

• Madang

Rabaul

BOUGAINVILLE
I.   Bougainville Strait
SOLOMON
SANTA ISABEL I.
ISLANDS   MALAITA I.

TIMOR SEA

ARAFURA SEA

Lae

NEW BRITAIN

SOLOMON
SEA

• Honiara ⊛

MELVILLE
BATHURST I.

GULF OF
PAPUA

Port Moresby
Torres Strait
Cape York

GUADALCANAL I.

LOUISIADE
ARCH.

INDIAN
OCEAN

ASHMORE AND
CARTIER IS.
(AUSTRAL.)

JOSEPH
BONAPARTE
GULF

★ Darwin
ARNHEM LAND

GOVE
PENINSULA
GULF OF
GROOTE I.
CARPENTARIA
WELLESLEY
IS.

CAPE
YORK
PENINSULA

CORAL

SEA

KING SOUND

L. Argyle

BARKLY
TABLELAND

CORAL SEA
IS. TERR.
(AUSTRAL.)

KIMBERLEY
PLATEAU

Fitzroy R.

NORTHERN

TERRITORY

Flinders

• Cairns

HALIFAX BAY
Townsville

BARROW I.

GREAT

SANDY

DESERT

GREAT
DIVIDING RANGE

Reef

NEW CALEDONIA
(FR.)

• Nouméa

HAMERSLEY
RANGE

AUSTRALIA

Mt. Ziel
4,955 ft.
(1,510 m.)

MACDONNELL
RANGES

GREAT

ARTESIAN

Sandy Cape
FRASER I.

SHARK BAY

WESTERN

GIBSON

DESERT

BASIN

QUEENSLAND

WESTERN

PLATEAU

MUSGRAVE
RANGE

EYRE
DEPRESSION

Warrego R.

• Brisbane

AUSTRALIA

GREAT
VICTORIA DESERT

SOUTH

Lake Eyre

LORD HOWE I.
(AUSTRAL.)

Perth ★

NULLARBOR   PLAIN

AUSTRALIA

FLINDERS
RANGE

Darling R.

NEW SOUTH WALES

• Newcastle

GEOGRAPHE
BAY

Whyalla
EYRE
PEN.

Murray

Lachlan R.

★ Sydney

GREAT AUSTRALIAN

BIGHT

SPENCER
GULF

Adelaide
Stirling ★

Murrumbidgee R.

Canberra ⊛
RIVERINA   AUST. CAP. TERR.

KANGAROO I.
ENCOUNTER
BAY

VICTORIA

Murray R.

AUSTRALIAN
ALPS

Mt. Kosciusko
7,310 ft.
(2,228 m.)

TASMAN

Geelong ★
Melbourne

SEA

KING I.

Bass Strait

FLINDERS I.

INDIAN OCEAN

TASMANIA

• Launceston
Hobart

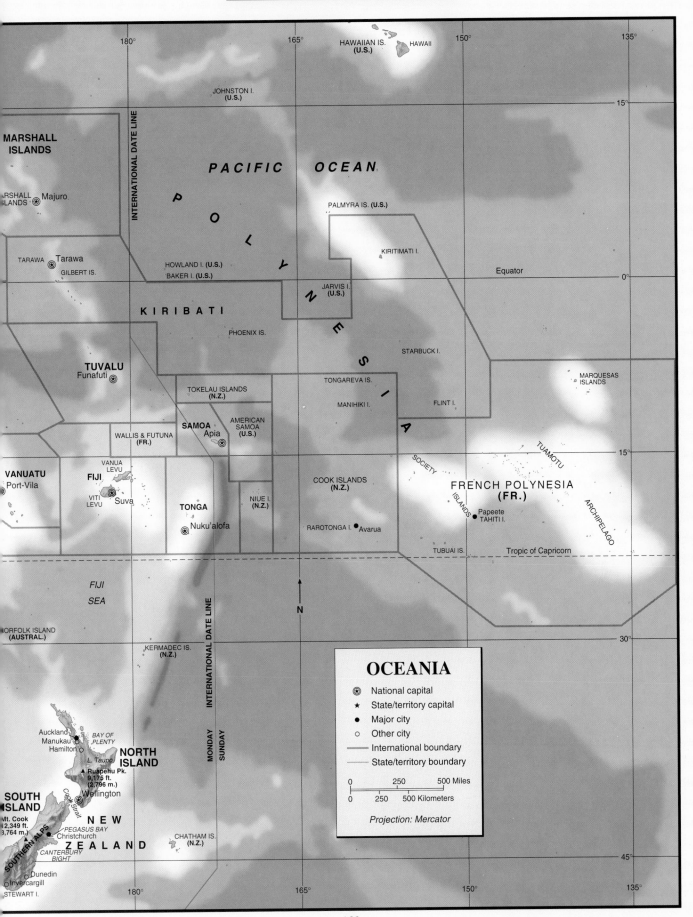

180°   165°   HAWAIIAN IS.   150°   135°
                (U.S.)   HAWAII

15°

JOHNSTON I.
(U.S.)

**MARSHALL
ISLANDS**

PACIFIC   OCEAN

RSHALL
LANDS   Majuro   P   PALMYRA IS. (U.S.)

                        O   KIRITIMATI I.

TARAWA   Tarawa   L   HOWLAND I. (U.S.)   Equator   0°
         GILBERT IS. Y   BAKER I. (U.S.)

                        N   JARVIS I.
K I R I B A T I   (U.S.)

                        E   PHOENIX IS.

                        S   STARBUCK I.
TUVALU
Funafuti   I   TONGAREVA IS.   MARQUESAS
                                                            ISLANDS
            TOKELAU ISLANDS A
            (N.Z.)   MANIHIKI I.   FLINT I.

                    SAMOA AMERICAN
SAMOA SAMOA   TUAMOTU
VANUATU WALLIS & FUTUNA Apia (U.S.)   15°
Port-Vila   (FR.)   SOCIETY
         VANUA   **FRENCH POLYNESIA**
         LEVU   **(FR.)**
FIJI   COOK ISLANDS ISLANDS   ARCHIPELAGO
                              (N.Z.)   Papeete
  VITI   Suva   NIUE I.   TAHITI I.
  LEVU   **TONGA** (N.Z.)
                    Nuku'alofa   RAROTONGA I. Avarua
                                                    TUBUAI IS.   Tropic of Capricorn

*FIJI
SEA*

NORFOLK ISLAND
(AUSTRAL.)   30°
                KERMADEC IS.
                (N.Z.)

                                    ┌─────────────────────────────────┐
                                    │   **OCEANIA**   │
Auckland   │ ⊛ National capital   │
Manukau   BAY OF   │ ★ State/territory capital   │
Hamilton PLENTY   │ ● Major city   │
         L. Taupo **NORTH**   │ ○ Other city   │
         Ruapehu Pk. **ISLAND**   │ ──── International boundary   │
         9,175 ft.   │ ──── State/territory boundary │
         (2,796 m.)   │   │
         Wellington   │ 0   250   500 Miles   │
SOUTH   │ ├───┬───┬───┬───┤   │
ISLAND **N E W**   │ 0   250   500 Kilometers   │
Mt. Cook   │   │
12,349 ft. PEGASUS BAY   │ *Projection: Mercator*   │
3,764 m.) Christchurch   └─────────────────────────────────┘
SOUTHERN ALPS **Z E A L A N D** CHATHAM IS.
CANTERBURY   (N.Z.)
BIGHT

Dunedin   45°
Invercargill
STEWART I.

180°   165°   150°   135°

165° Yukon River 150° Mt. McKinley 20,320 ft. (6,194 m.) ALASKA (U.S.) GULF OF ALASKA 135° Mackenzie R. 120° Great Bear Lake ROCKY MOUNTAINS Great Slave Lake 105° CANADA 90° Arctic Circle 75° 60° HUDSON BAY 60°

NORTH AMERICA

Lake Winnipeg Missouri River Lake Superior Lake Michigan Chicago Lake Huron 45° Lake Ontario Lake Erie New York APPALACHIAN MTNS.

UNITED STATES Great Salt Lake Mississippi R. Los Angeles

BERMUDA (U.K.) 30°

MEXICO GULF OF MEXICO THE BAHAMAS

Tropic of Cancer Mexico City CUBA DOMINICAN REPUBLIC

HAWAIIAN ISLANDS (U.S.) BELIZE JAMAICA HAITI CARIBBEAN SEA 15° HONDURAS GUATEMALA EL SALVADOR NICARAGUA

PACIFIC OCEAN COSTA RICA PANAMA VENEZUELA Bogotá COLOMBIA

Equator GALÁPAGOS ISLANDS (ECUADOR) ECUADOR 0° Amazon R. Marañón R. BRAZIL PERU SOUTH AMERICA

KIRIBATI

AMERICAN SAMOA (U.S.) Lima 15° BOLIVIA

COOK ISLANDS (N.Z.) FRENCH POLYNESIA (FR.) ANDES MOUNTAINS PARAGUAY

NIUE (N.Z.) PITCAIRN (U.K.) Tropic of Capricorn CHILE

30° Mt. Aconcagua 22,834 ft. (6,960 m.) Santiago

THE PACIFIC RIM

- Most populous cities
— International boundary
--- Disputed boundary

0   750   1500 Miles
0   750   1500 Kilometers

Scale at Equator

Projection: Miller Cylindrical

ARGENTINA

45°

165° 150° 135° 120° 105° 90° 75° 60°

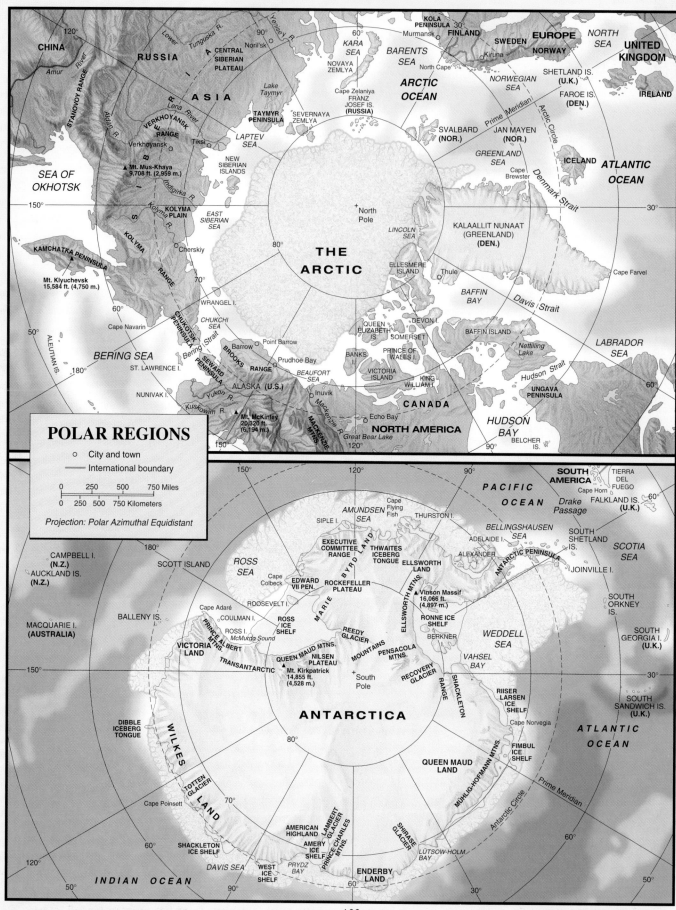

POLAR REGIONS

○ City and town

— International boundary

0   250   500   750 Miles

0   250   500   750 Kilometers

Projection: Polar Azimuthal Equidistant

THE ARCTIC

CHINA — RUSSIA — ASIA — CENTRAL SIBERIAN PLATEAU — STANOVOV RANGE — VERKHOYANSK RANGE — Amur River — Lower Tunguska R. — Noril'sk — Yenisey R. — Lena River — Aldan R. — Verkhoyansk — Tiksi — Mt. Mus-Khaya 9,708 ft. (2,959 m.) — SEA OF OKHOTSK — Indigirka R. — Kolyma R. — KOLYMA PLAIN — KOLYMA RANGE — Cherskiy — KAMCHATKA PENINSULA — Mt. Klyuchevsk 15,584 ft. (4,750 m.) — CHUKOTSK PENINSULA — CHUKCHI SEA — WRANGEL I. — Cape Navarin — BERING SEA — ST. LAWRENCE I. — ALEUTIAN IS. — NUNIVAK I. — Bering Strait — SEWARD PENINSULA — BROOKS RANGE — Barrow — Point Barrow — Prudhoe Bay — BEAUFORT SEA — Yukon R. — Kuskowim R. — ALASKA (U.S.) — Mt. McKinley 20,320 ft. (6,194 m.) — MACKENZIE MTNS. — Inuvik — Echo Bay — Great Bear Lake — NORTH AMERICA — CANADA

KOLA PENINSULA — Murmansk — FINLAND — SWEDEN — NORWAY — EUROPE — NORTH SEA — UNITED KINGDOM — KARA SEA — BARENTS SEA — Kiruna — SHETLAND IS. (U.K.) — IRELAND — NOVAYA ZEMLYA — Cape Zelaniya — FRANZ JOSEF IS. (RUSSIA) — ARCTIC OCEAN — North Cape — NORWEGIAN SEA — FAROE IS. (DEN.) — SEVERNAYA ZEMLYA — SVALBARD (NOR.) — JAN MAYEN (NOR.) — ICELAND — ATLANTIC OCEAN — GREENLAND SEA — Cape Brewster — Denmark Strait — North Pole — LINCOLN SEA — KALAALLIT NUNAAT (GREENLAND) (DEN.) — Cape Farvel — ELLESMERE ISLAND — Thule — BAFFIN BAY — Davis Strait — LABRADOR SEA — QUEEN ELIZABETH IS. — DEVON I. — SOMERSET — BAFFIN ISLAND — Nettling Lake — BANKS I. — PRINCE OF WALES I. — VICTORIA ISLAND — KING WILLIAM I. — Hudson Strait — UNGAVA PENINSULA — HUDSON BAY — BELCHER IS. — NEW SIBERIAN ISLANDS — TAYMYR PENINSULA — LAPTEV SEA — EAST SIBERIAN SEA — Prime Meridian — Arctic Circle

ANTARCTICA

PACIFIC OCEAN — SOUTH AMERICA — TIERRA DEL FUEGO — Cape Horn — FALKLAND IS. (U.K.) — Drake Passage — BELLINGSHAUSEN SEA — SOUTH SHETLAND IS. — SCOTIA SEA — ANTARCTIC PENINSULA — Adelaide I. — Alexander I. — JOINVILLE I. — SOUTH ORKNEY IS. — SOUTH GEORGIA I. (U.K.) — WEDDELL SEA — Vinson Massif 16,066 ft. (4,897 m.) — ELLSWORTH MTNS. — RONNE ICE SHELF — BERKNER I. — VAHSEL BAY — SOUTH SANDWICH IS. (U.K.) — ATLANTIC OCEAN — RIISER LARSEN ICE SHELF — Cape Norvegia — FIMBUL ICE SHELF — MÜHLIG-HOFMANN MTNS. — QUEEN MAUD LAND — Prime Meridian — SHIRASE GLACIER — LÜTSOW-HOLM BAY — Antarctic Circle — ENDERBY LAND — PRINCE CHARLES MTNS. — AMERY ICE SHELF — LAMBERT GLACIER — AMERICAN HIGHLAND — PRYDZ BAY — WEST ICE SHELF — DAVIS SEA — INDIAN OCEAN — SHACKLETON ICE SHELF — Cape Poinsett — TOTTEN GLACIER — WILKES LAND — DIBBLE ICEBERG TONGUE — MACQUARIE I. (AUSTRALIA) — BALLENY IS. — CAMPBELL I. (N.Z.) — AUCKLAND IS. (N.Z.) — SCOTT ISLAND — ROSS SEA — Cape Colbeck — EDWARD VII PEN. — ROCKEFELLER PLATEAU — ROOSEVELT I. — Cape Adaré — COULMAN I. — PRINCE ALBERT MTNS. — ROSS I. — McMurdo Sound — ROSS ICE SHELF — VICTORIA LAND — TRANSANTARCTIC — QUEEN MAUD MTNS. — NILSEN PLATEAU — Mt. Kirkpatrick 14,855 ft. (4,528 m.) — REEDY GLACIER — MARIE BYRD LAND — MOUNTAINS — PENSACOLA MTNS. — RECOVERY GLACIER — South Pole — SHACKLETON RANGE — SIPLE I. — EXECUTIVE COMMITTEE RANGE — THWAITES ICEBERG TONGUE — ELLSWORTH LAND — Cape Flying Fish — AMUNDSEN SEA — THURSTON I. — ANTARCTICA

A32

Geography and Map Skills Handbook

CONTENTS

SECTION 1 — Globes and Map Projections

SECTION 2 — Building Map Skills

SECTION 3 — Reading Graphs and Charts

Globes and Map Projections

PREVIEW

Words to Know

- projection
- hemisphere
- latitude
- longitude
- grid system
- absolute location
- great circle route

Read to Learn . . .

1. how mapmakers represent a round globe on a flat map.
2. what projections are useful for different purposes.
3. how to find an exact location.

Globes and the Earth

Although a globe is the most accurate way to represent the earth, using one presents some serious disadvantages. First, it is hard to carry a globe around in your pocket. Then try to imagine a globe large enough to show your community in detail. For these reasons, geographers use maps.

A globe—like the earth—is a sphere. A map, however, is a flat piece of paper. These facts explain why a flat map always distorts the surface of the earth it is showing.

Drawing Maps

Imagine taking the whole peel from an orange and trying to flatten it on a table. You would either have to cut it or stretch parts of it. Mapmakers face a similar problem in showing the surface of the round earth on a flat map. The different ways they have found to do this are called **projections**. Mapmakers call these different ways projections because a source of light, such as a flashlight, is placed inside of a globe and the light projects, or throws, the image onto a flat piece of paper.

Goode's Interrupted Projection

Goode's projection is called an equal-area projection. This means the projection quite accurately presents the size and shape of the continents. Distances—especially in the oceans—are less accurate. Researchers might use this type of projection to compare continent statistics according to area.

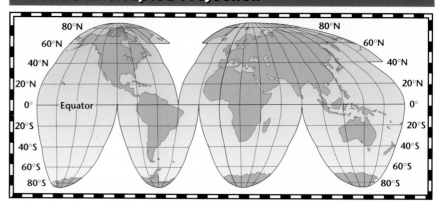

Goode's Interrupted Projection

Mercator Projection

A Mercator projection was one of the earliest types of maps drawn. Mapmaker Gerardus Mercator first created this projection in 1569. This kind of projection shows land shapes fairly accurately, but not size or distance. Areas that are distant from the Equator are quite distorted on this projection. Alaska, for example, appears much larger on a Mercator map than it does on a globe. This map projection does show true directions, however, making it very useful for sea travel.

Mercator Projection

Robinson Projection

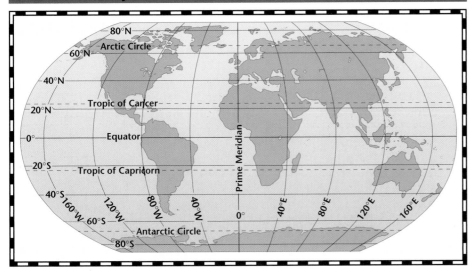

Robinson Projection

The Robinson projection shows both the size and shape of oceans and continents quite accurately. The shapes of the continents also appear much as they do on a globe. The areas most distorted on this projection are near the North and South poles. Textbook and atlas maps are often Robinson projections.

Hemispheres

Remember that a globe is the most accurate way to represent the earth. To locate places on the earth, geographers set up a system of imaginary lines that crisscross the globe. One of these lines, the Equator, circles the middle of the earth like a belt. It divides the earth into "half spheres," or **hemispheres**. Everything north of the Equator is in the Northern Hemisphere. Everything south of the Equator is in the Southern Hemisphere.

Another imaginary line running from north to south divides the earth into half spheres in the other direction. Find this line—the Prime Meridian—on a globe. It is located at 0° longitude. Everything east of the Prime Meridian is in the Eastern Hemisphere. Everything west of the Prime Meridian is in the Western Hemisphere. North America lies in the Northern Hemisphere and the Western Hemisphere.

Hemispheres

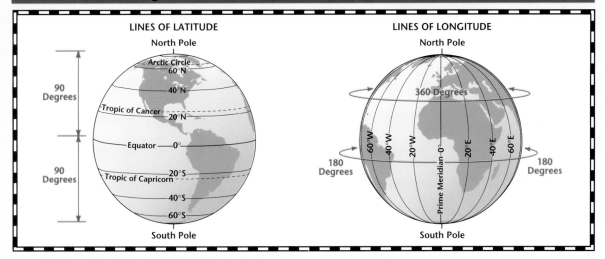

LINES OF LATITUDE

North Pole
Arctic Circle
60°N
40°N
Tropic of Cancer
20°N
Equator — 0°
20°S
Tropic of Capricorn
40°S
60°S
South Pole

90 Degrees
90 Degrees

LINES OF LONGITUDE

North Pole
360 Degrees
60°W 40°W 20°W Prime Meridian–0° 20°E 40°E 60°E
180 Degrees
180 Degrees
South Pole

Latitude and Longitude

Parallels The Equator and the Prime Meridian are the starting points for two sets of lines used to find any location. Parallels circle the earth and show **latitude**, which is distance measured in degrees north and south of the Equator at 0° latitude. The letter *N* or *S* following the degree symbol tells you if the location is north or south of the Equator. The North Pole is at 90° North *(N)* latitude, and the South Pole is at 90° South *(S)* latitude.

Two important parallels in between the poles are the Tropic of Cancer at 23½°N latitude and the Tropic of Capricorn at 23½°S latitude. You can also find the Arctic Circle at 66½°N latitude and the Antarctic Circle at 66½°S latitude.

Meridians Meridians run north to south from pole to pole. These lines signify **longitude**, which is distance measured in degrees east *(E)* or west *(W)* of the Prime Meridian at 0° longitude. On the opposite side of the earth is the International Date Line, or the 180° meridian.

Lines of latitude and longitude cross each other in the form of a **grid system**. Knowing a place's latitude and longitude allows you to locate it exactly on a map or globe. You can name an **absolute location** by naming the latitude and longitude lines that cross nearest to that location. For example, Tokyo is located at about 36°N latitude and 140°E longitude. Where those two lines cross is the absolute location of the city.

Japan

128°E 132°E 136°E 140°E 144°E 46°N

RUSSIA
CHINA
Sapporo
42°N
Bonne projection
NORTH KOREA
Sea of Japan
Sendai
38°N
SOUTH KOREA
JAPAN Tokyo
Kyoto
Kobe Yokohama
Osaka
34°N
Hiroshima
Kitakyushu

0   150   300 mi.
0   150   300 km

N
W E
S

30°N

Great Circles

The idea of a great circle illustrates one important difference between using a map and using a globe. Because both the earth and a globe are round, they accurately show great circles.

A great circle is the shortest distance between two points on earth. A great circle is any circle you can draw on the earth that divides it into two equal parts. A line drawn along the Equator around the entire earth is an example of a great circle. Traveling along a great circle is called following a **great circle route**. Airplane pilots and ship captains often use great circle routes to shorten their trips and cut down on the amount of fuel needed. These routes often take pilots over the North Pole. A trip between Moscow, Russia, and New York, New York, over the North Pole is an example of a great circle route. Other great circles lie along the routes between Hong Kong, China, and Washington, D.C., and between Cape Town, South Africa, and Washington, D.C. Find these routes on a globe.

The great circle route between two points may not appear to be the shortest distance on a flat map. On this map, the great circle route between Tokyo, Japan, and Los Angeles,

Great Circle Routes

California, appears to be far longer than the straight line route. Actually, the great circle is more than 345 miles (550 km) shorter!

SECTION 1 ASSESSMENT

REVIEWING GLOBES AND MAP PROJECTIONS

1. **Define the following:** projection, hemisphere, latitude, longitude, grid system, absolute location, great circle route.
2. Why does every map projection distort some parts of the earth?
3. What imaginary line divides the earth into the Northern Hemisphere and Southern Hemisphere? Where is it located?
4. **ACTIVITY** Look at a globe or world map to discover more of earth's great circles. Make a list of airplane flights that could follow great circle routes between New York City and other major world cities.

SECTION 2

Building Map Skills

PREVIEW

Words to Know

- key
- cardinal direction
- compass rose
- intermediate direction
- scale bar
- scale
- relief
- elevation
- contour line
- elevation profile
- population density
- climate region

Read to Learn . . .

1. how you can find a place's exact location on a map.
2. how to recognize the special parts of a map.
3. how to identify different kinds of maps.

Parts of Maps

Maps can direct you down the street, across the country, or around the world. There are as many different kinds of maps as there are uses for them. Being able to read a map begins with learning about its parts.

Map Key The map **key** unlocks the information presented on the map. The key explains the symbols used on the map. On this map of Germany, for example, dots mark cities and towns.

On a road map, the key tells what map lines stand for paved roads, dirt roads, and interstate highways. A pine tree symbol may represent a park, while an airplane is often the symbol for an airport.

Compass Rose An important first step in reading any map is to find the direction marker. A map has a symbol that tells you where the **cardinal directions**—north, south, east, and west—are positioned. Sometimes all of these directions are shown with a **compass rose**. An intermediate direction, such as southeast, may also be on the compass rose. **Intermediate directions** fall between the cardinal directions.

GERMANY: Political

- — National boundary
- ✪ National capital
- ● Other city

Lambert Conformal Conic projection

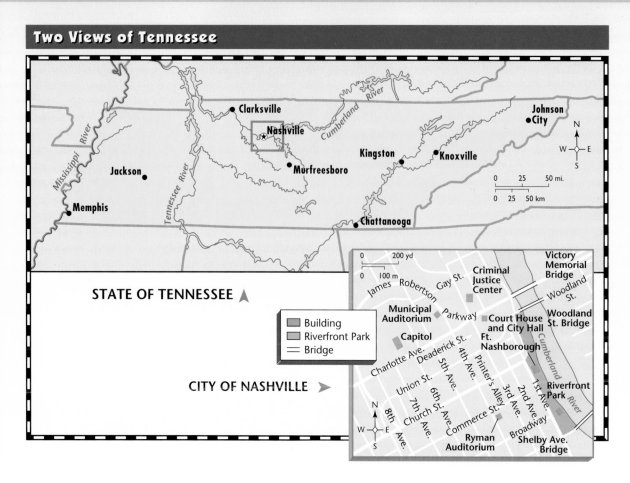

STATE OF TENNESSEE ▲

CITY OF NASHVILLE ➤

Building
Riverfront Park
Bridge

Scale A measuring line, often called a **scale bar**, helps you find distance on the map. The map's **scale** tells you what distance on the earth is represented by the measurement on the scale bar. For example, 1 inch on the map may represent 100 miles on the earth. Map scale is usually given in both miles and kilometers, a metric measurement of distance.

Each map you use might have a different scale. What scale a mapmaker uses depends on the size of the area the map shows. If you were drawing a map of a house, you might use a scale of 1 inch equals 5 feet. In contrast, the scale bar on the map of the city of Nashville shows that ⅜-inch represents 200 yards.

Scale is important when you are trying to compare the size of one area with another. You can't make a true comparison of the continental United States and Africa unless you are using maps drawn to the same scale. You will find similar maps comparing different countries to the continental United States (not including Alaska and Hawaii) throughout your book.

AFRICA AND THE UNITED STATES: Land Comparison

Different Kinds of Maps

Maps that show a wide range of general information about an area are called general purpose maps. Two of the most common general purpose maps are political and physical maps.

Political Maps Political maps generally show political, or human-made, divisions of countries or regions. The political map of Germany on page 7, for example, shows boundaries between Germany and other countries. It also shows cities within Germany and bodies of water surrounding Germany.

Physical Maps A physical map shows the physical features of an area, such as its mountains and rivers. The colors used for some features on physical maps are standard—brown or green for land, blue for water. Physical maps use colors and shadings to show **relief**—how flat or rugged the land surface is. Colors also may be used to show **elevation**—the height of an area above sea level.

Mapmakers also use color to show rainfall, types of soil, or plant life. Physical maps, like political maps, have a key that explains what each color and symbol stands for.

Contour Maps One kind of physical map scientists use may not look like a map at all to some people. This map—called a contour map—shows elevation. A contour map has **contour lines**—one for each major level of elevation. All the land at the same elevation is connected by a line. These lines usually form circles or ovals—one inside the other. If contour lines come very close together, the surface is steep. If the lines are spread far apart, the land is flat or rises very gradually.

Another way to show relief is to look at the landscape from the side, or profile. This **elevation profile** is a cutaway diagram. It clearly shows level land, hills, and steeper mountains.

PUERTO RICO

Contour Map

ATLANTIC OCEAN

150 m
300 m
500 ft.
1000 ft.
500 ft.
1000 ft.
600 m
1000 ft.
2000 ft.
600 m
300 m
2000 ft.
150 m

N
W—E
S

Caribbean Sea

0   125   250 mi.
0   125   250 km

Elevation Map

San Juan ★

ATLANTIC OCEAN

ELEVATIONS

Feet	Meters
10,000	3,000
5,000	1,500
2,000	600
1,000	300
0	0

★ Capital

Polyconic projection

Mayagüez

Ponce

Caribbean Sea

N
W—E
S

0   125   250 mi.
0   125   250 km

Special Purpose Maps

Besides showing political or physical features, some maps have a special purpose. They may show cultural features, historical changes, unique physical features, population, or climates. The map's title tells what kind of specialized information it shows. Colors and symbols in the map key are especially important on this type of map.

When looking at a special purpose map, it is important to remember that you are seeing only the information that relates to the map's special purpose. For example, on a population map you will see indications of where and how many people live in a country. The map will probably not show you anything about what crops the people there raise.

Land Use and Resources Maps Look at this map of land use and resources in South Africa. Colors identify parts of the area where people follow certain ways of life, such as farming or herding. Places where manufacturing takes place are also marked with color. The symbols stand for the different kinds of natural resources found in or on the land. The number and type of symbols can vary from map to map depending upon the area shown. Diamonds, for example, are not found in all parts of the world as they are in South Africa. So diamonds might not always be in a resource map key. Resources can include minerals, timber, and important crops.

SOUTH AFRICA: Land Use and Resources

Resources

Coal	Fish & other seafood	Tin
Copper	Gold	Magnesium
Diamonds	Iron ore	Uranium

Azimuthal Equal-Area projection

Agriculture
- Nomadic Herding
- Little or no farming
- Ranching
- Plantation farming
- Subsistence farming
- Manufacturing area

Plate boundary
Earthquake
Volcano

Miller projection

Some special purpose maps have a very limited use. You may have seen a map in your school, for example, that shows the boundaries of your school district. A map such as that would probably only be useful to people in your community and state. Other special purpose maps that show a wide area, such as the entire world, hold information that affects many more people.

Geological Maps Special purpose maps can show information about something that you cannot readily see, such as geological information. Geological maps explain the structure of the earth and how it is believed to have been formed. In addition to giving you new information, such maps might also help you make connections between events and their causes. It is often helpful to compare a special purpose map to another map to receive a complete picture of how the earth's elements work together.

Look at the Earthquake and Volcano Zones map above. It gives you a view of three things: the location of major plates that make up the earth's crust, where volcanoes have erupted, and where earthquakes have occurred most frequently. You will read in Chapter 2 about the plates that make up the earth's crust and how they move. On this map you can see—and make the connection—that earthquakes and volcanoes seem to occur where these plates meet. Geologists call the area of earthquake and volcano activity near the Pacific Ocean the Ring of Fire.

Population Density Maps Another special purpose map uses colors to show **population density**, or the average number of people living in a square mile or square kilometer. As with other specialized maps, it is important to first read the title and the key. The population density map of Brazil gives a striking picture of its differences in population density. You can see large coastal cities where the population is very crowded, as well as inland spaces where fewer people live.

Climate Maps What do climate maps show? They summarize information about an area's rain, snow, and temperatures throughout the year. A climate map can help you see similarities and differences in climates between different places. A **climate region**, broad areas that have the same climate, is readily seen on a climate map. Geographers often divide the earth into four major climate regions—tropical, dry, mid-latitude, and high latitude. In which climate region do you live?

BRAZIL: Population Density

Persons per

sq. mi.	sq. km
Uninhabited	Uninhabited
Under 2	Under 1
2-60	1-25
60-125	25-50
125-250	50-100
Over 250	Over 100

Goode's Interrupted Homolosine projection

CITIES

■ City with more than 5,000,000 people

● City with 1,000,000 to 5,000,000 people

○ City with 500,000 to 1,000,000 people

SECTION 2 ASSESSMENT

Reviewing Map Skills

1. **Define the following:** key, cardinal direction, compass rose, intermediate direction, scale bar, scale, relief, elevation, contour line, elevation profile, population density, climate region.

2. What kinds of features does a physical map include?

3. What special purpose do geological maps serve?

4. To draw a map showing your route to school, would you use a large scale or a small scale? Why?

5. **ACTIVITY** Use the following grid system "addresses" to find the three cities located at these coordinates: 55°N, 35°E; 23°S, 43°W; 1°N, 103°E.

SECTION 3 Reading Graphs and Charts

PREVIEW

Words to Know

- axis
- bar graph
- line graph
- circle graph
- pictograph
- climograph
- climate
- diagram
- flow chart
- chart
- table

Read to Learn . . .

1. how different types of graphs present information.
2. how charts, tables, and diagrams make data easier to understand.
3. how to read a flow chart.

Graphs

Think of the different places you see graphs and diagrams. They appear in newspapers, magazines, and even on television.

Graphs summarize and present information visually. Each part of a graph gives useful information. First read the graph's title to find out its subject. Then read the labels along the graph's **axes**—the vertical and horizontal lines along the bottom and sides of the graph. One axis will tell you what is being measured. The other axis tells what units of measurement are being used.

Bar Graphs Look carefully at this **bar graph** of the world's five most heavily populated countries. The vertical axis lists the countries. The horizontal axis gives the units of population measurement. By comparing the lengths of the bars you can quickly tell which country has the largest population. Bar graphs are especially useful for comparing quantities, and they may show the bars running across the graph or rising up from the bottom.

Comparing Population

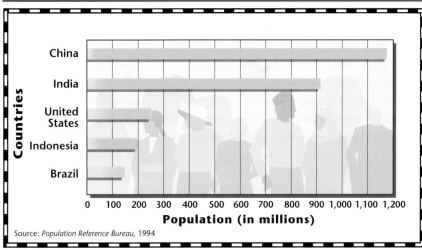

Source: *Population Reference Bureau, 1994*

Line Graphs A tool that is especially good for plotting changes in something over a period of time is a **line graph**. The amounts being plotted on this graph are shown by dots. These dots are connected by a line. Line graphs sometimes have two or more lines plotted on them.

This line graph shows how the population density of India has changed since 1978. The vertical axis lists people per square mile. The horizontal axis shows the passage of time in four-year periods from 1978 to 1994.

INDIA: Population Density

Source: *World Almanac*, 1980-1992; *Population Reference Bureau*, 1994

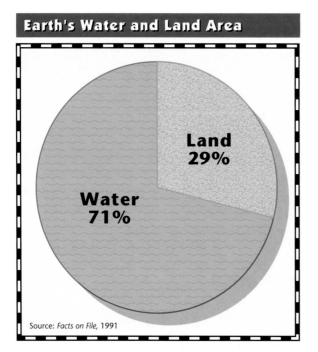

Earth's Water and Land Area

Land 29%

Water 71%

Source: *Facts on File*, 1991

Circle Graphs When you want to show how the *whole* of something is divided into its *parts*, you should use a **circle graph**. Because of their shape, circle graphs are often called pie graphs. Each "slice" represents a part or percentage of the whole "pie." Circle graphs are also good for making comparisons between two or more whole things that are broken into parts.

On this graph, the circle represents the whole surface area of the earth. Land and water each occupy a certain percentage of that whole, as shown by the way the circle is divided. You could easily compare this to another circle graph showing the total surface of another planet with land and water indicated.

Pictographs Like bar graphs, pictographs are good for making comparisons. **Pictographs** use rows of small symbols or pictures, each standing for an amount. This pictograph shows oil production in Venezuela. The key tells you that each oil rig stands for 20 million metric tons of oil. Pictographs are read like a bar graph. The total number of oil rigs in a row adds up to the production for that year.

Oil Production in Venezuela

1970
1975
1980
1985
1990

= 20 million metric tons

Source: *Statistical Abstract*, 1994

Climographs A **climograph**, or climate graph, combines a line graph and a bar graph. It gives an overall picture of the **climate**—the long-term weather patterns—in a specific place. Because climographs include several kinds of information, you need to read them carefully.

Note that the vertical bars on the climograph represent average amounts of precipitation in each month of the year. To measure these bars, use the scale on the right-hand axis of the graphs.

The line above the bars, like those on other line graphs, represents changes in the average temperature based on the scale on the left. The months are abbreviated on the bottom axis of the graph.

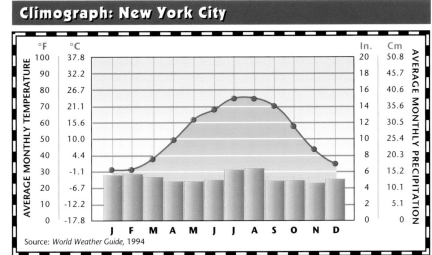

Climograph: New York City

Source: *World Weather Guide*, 1994

Diagrams

If you enjoy science, mechanics, or working with your hands, you have probably come across diagrams. **Diagrams** are drawings that either show steps in a process, point out the parts of an object, or explain how something works. You can follow a diagram to connect parts of a stereo system or to repair a bicycle. If you have ever tried to use a diagram, you know that the simpler it is, the easier it is to follow.

Another kind of diagram can show you a cross section—or profile—of something such as landforms. Profiles can be helpful when comparing the elevations of an area. You will find elevation profile diagrams in each unit of this book.

Flow Chart A **flow chart** combines elements of a diagram and a chart. It can show the cause-and-effect process of how things happen. Or a flow chart can present the steps in a process. This type of chart often uses arrows to help you see how one step leads to another. For example, you might draw a flow chart to describe the steps needed to film a video. Arrows would link each step, from first to last. A flow chart could also show how things are interconnected. A chart of a governmental body would show how an idea flows from one part to another.

The flow chart on this page illustrates the impact of computers on different areas of life. Notice how the chart uses the arrows to show the direction in which the effects move. You might be able to think of other areas of computer use that could have been added to the chart. What are they?

The Impact of the Computer

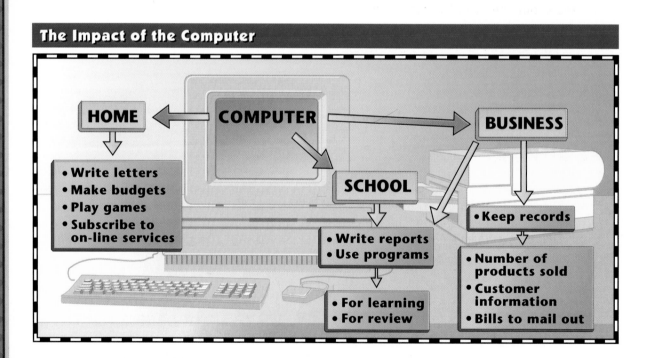

HOME
- Write letters
- Make budgets
- Play games
- Subscribe to on-line services

COMPUTER

SCHOOL
- Write reports
- Use programs
- For learning
- For review

BUSINESS
- Keep records
- Number of products sold
- Customer information
- Bills to mail out

Charts and Tables

Charts and tables present organized facts and statistics so they are easier to read. These graphics can also show how things are organized or how things are related. To understand a chart or table, first read the title. It tells you what information the chart or table contains. Next, read the labels at the top of each column and the left-hand side of the table or chart. They will tell you what data you are working with.

Tables are especially useful in organizing statistics in an easy-to-read way. This table shows data about the world's leading wheat-producing countries. Others might show many more columns and rows of numbers that would be difficult to understand if they were not organized in a table.

World's Leading Wheat Producers

COUNTRY	METRIC TONS PRODUCED
China	101,003,000
United States	66,920,000
India	55,087,000
Russia	46,000,000
France	32,600,000
Canada	29,871,000
Ukraine	19,473,000
Turkey	19,318,000
Kazakhstan	18,500,000
Pakistan	15,684,000

Source: *The Statesman's Yearbook, 1994-1995*

SECTION 3 ASSESSMENT

Reviewing Graphs and Charts

1. **Define the following:** axis, bar graph, line graph, circle graph, pictograph, climograph, climate, diagram, flow chart, chart, table.
2. If you wanted to show how the population of Mexico City changed from 1850 to 1990, what kind of graph would you draw?
3. What two features of climate does a climograph show?
4. **ACTIVITY** Draw a flow chart showing and labeling the steps in some simple process—for example, making a sandwich or using a pay telephone. Give your flow chart to a classmate to follow it and complete the task described. Write a sentence or two about how easy your chart was to follow. See if your classmate agrees or has suggestions for improvement.

Introduction

Geographers often think about the world in regions, or areas that share some common characteristics. An area can be called a region because of its physical features, such as landscape or climate. A region also can be determined by human traits, such as language, political boundaries, religion, or the kinds of work the people there do.

Before you begin your study of *Geography: The World And Its People, Volume Two* take time to read this special Regional Review Handbook. It will help you remember what you learned about the physical and cultural geography of the United States and Canada, Latin America and Europe.

Jasper National Park, Canada

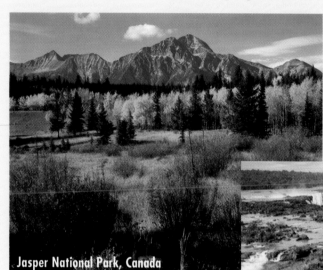

Iguaçú Falls, Brazil

GeoJournal Activity

You are about to journey to remote rain forests, bleak deserts, bustling marketplaces, and mountainous villages. You are entering the world of geography—the study of the earth and its people. Imagine that you could visit any place in the world. Where would you go? What would you want to see? Jot down your thoughts in your journal.

Loch Ness, Scotland

WHAT IS THE . . .	ANSWER	LOCATION	SIZE
largest continent?	Asia	Eastern Hemisphere	17,400,000 sq. miles
smallest continent?	Australia	South Pacific	2,941,290 sq. miles
largest nation?	Russia	Europe-Asia	6,592,800 sq. miles
smallest nation?	Vatican City	Europe	0.2 sq. miles
largest ocean?	Pacific		64,186,300 sq. miles
longest river?	Nile	East Africa	4,160 miles long
largest lake?	Caspian Sea	Eurasia	143,244 sq. miles
deepest lake?	Baikal	Asia	5,315 feet deep
highest mountain?	Mt. Everest	Nepal-Tibet	29,028 feet high
highest waterfall?	Angel Falls	Venezuela	3,212 feet high
largest desert?	Sahara	North Africa	3,500,000 sq. miles
highest continental point?	Mt. Everest	Nepal-Tibet	29,028 feet high
lowest continental point?	Dead Sea	Israel-Jordan	1,312 feet below sea level

19

Regional Focus

The United States and Canada are huge countries. Together they reach from the Arctic Ocean in the north to the country of Mexico in the south. West to east, they stretch from the Pacific Ocean to the Atlantic Ocean. The United States and Canada—with Mexico—form the continent of North America.

Region

The Land

The United States and Canada cover more than 7 million square miles (18 million sq. km). They share many of the same landscapes. Mountain ranges, basins, and plateaus run through the western part of both countries. The largest range is the massive Rocky Mountains, stretching more than 3,000 miles (4,800 km) from Alaska to New Mexico.

East of the Rockies spread the broad, rolling Great Plains. This flat area runs through the central part of the United States and Canada. The plains reach to the Canadian Shield—a huge, mineral-rich area of ancient rock—in Canada's far north. Find the Rockies and the Great Plains on the map on page 82.

Low mountains and coastal plains cover the eastern part of the United States and Canada. Here you will discover North America's second-longest mountain range, the Appalachians. East and south of these low mountains lie coastal lowlands that fan out westward to Texas.

Waterways The Mississippi River is the largest river system in North America. It flows from near the United States-Canadian border in the north to the Gulf of Mexico in the south. The Missouri River, the Ohio River, and their tributaries merge into the Mississippi River system. The largest lake system is the Great Lakes—Superior, Huron, Michigan, Erie, and Ontario. The waters of these five lakes are interconnected and eventually meet with the St. Lawrence River, which flows into the Atlantic Ocean.

Place

Climate and Vegetation

The vast size of landforms affects climate, soils, and vegetation in the United States and Canada. The forests and flatlands in far northern Canada and Alaska have short, cool summers and long, cold winters. The Pacific coast from southern Alaska to northern California has a mild, humid climate. Mist-covered forests and lush

Southwest Vegetation

The huge saguaro cactus grows only in the desert climates of the southwestern United States and Mexico.
PLACE: Where do you find the only deserts in the United States and Canada?

green plants cover this area. Pacific mountain ranges keep ocean rain clouds from reaching inland areas. Just east of the mountains lie the only deserts in the region.

The Great Plains The Great Plains has a humid continental climate of cold winters and hot summers. This region receives rain from the Gulf of Mexico and the far north. Before settlers arrived in the 1800s, grasses covered much of the Great Plains. Now the land is covered with farms and cities.

Other Areas The Northeast region of the United States and Canada has the same climate as the Great Plains. Most of the southern states, however, are in a humid subtropical region that experiences mild winters. Only the tip of Florida is far enough south to have a tropical climate. The Hawaiian Islands—the only other area of the United States with a tropical climate—lie 2,400 miles (3,862 km) from the United States mainland in the Pacific Ocean.

Region
Economy

The United States and Canada base their economies on the free enterprise system. This means that individuals and groups—rather than the government—run businesses. Skilled workers, many natural resources, and the use of advanced technology have brought prosperity to the United States and Canada.

Agriculture United States and Canadian farmers raise many meats, grains, vegetables, and fruits. Up-to-date farming methods have increased the size of farms and the amount of food produced. At the same time, they have decreased the number of farms and farm workers. Fertile soil and many waterways make the Great Plains, the Pacific coast, and the Northeast major agricultural areas.

The Pacific Coast

The city of Vancouver on Canada's Pacific coast is the country's busiest port.
PLACE: On what does Canada base its economy?

UNIT 2 ATLAS

Industry The United States and Canada are rich in such mineral resources as copper, iron ore, nickel, silver, oil, natural gas, and coal. Both countries are world leaders in manufactured goods. Their service industries—stores, banking, insurance, and entertainment—provide jobs for the largest number of people.

Movement
People

Throughout their histories, the United States and Canada have become home to settlers from almost every part of the world. Some of these people came to find a better way of life. Still others were forced to come as enslaved laborers.

Ethnic Groups Today the people of this region come from many different backgrounds. Most Americans and Canadians are European in origin. Others are African Americans, Hispanics, Asian Americans, and Native Americans. English is the major language of the United States and Canada, but French is the dominant language of Canada's Quebec Province. Other languages are also spoken in both countries.

Population About 300 million people live in the United States and Canada. In land area, Canada is the second-largest country in the world. Yet most of its 31 million people live in urban areas close to its border with the United States. The United States is the world's third-largest country in population. Most of its 270 million people live in urban areas along the coasts or in the Great Lakes region. Among the largest cities are New York City, Los Angeles, Chicago, and Dallas. The area from Washington, D.C., to Boston is almost continuously urban and is called a megalopolis.

Place
Culture

At least 12,500 years ago, the ancestors of Native Americans settled North America. Europeans arrived between the 1500s and 1700s. During the late 1700s, colonists along the Atlantic coast successfully fought the British for their freedom. They founded the United States of America. In the 1800s the new Americans moved into new lands, fought a great Civil War, and then reunited. Immigrants arriving by the thousands transformed the economy from an agricultural one to an industrial one. During the 1900s, the United States fought two world wars and became a major world power.

Canada, on the other hand, stayed apart from the United States. It gradually won its independence from the British during the 1800s and early 1900s. As in the United States, many immigrants made their homes in Canada. People moved westward and developed the economy, although differences between English-speaking and French-speaking Canadians threatened national unity. In the 1900s, Canada began to play an active role in world affairs.

Nature's Light Show

The colorful glow of the northern lights flickers in Alaska and northern Canada.
REGION: What do you think causes the northern lights?

Multimedia Unit 2 Activities

NATIONAL GEOGRAPHIC SOCIETY

Picture Atlas of the World

Economic Geography

Using the CD-ROM The physical features of a region influence its type of economic activity. As a result, the economies of the United States and Canada differ from region to region. Assemble a file of economic activity information. (See the User's Guide for information on how to use the Collector button.) Include essays on the United States and Canada and these photographs: New York City, the Hawaiian pineapple industry, Newfoundland fishermen, and Saskatchewan wheat fields. Then use the file to answer the following questions:

1. Many of the largest cities in the United States are located east of the Mississippi River. Why were cities able to grow and prosper on the eastern coast of the United States?
2. What makes Hawaii one of the world's top producers of pineapples?
3. How has economic activity in Newfoundland contributed to the decline of the physical environment?
4. Which region of Canada is known as the country's granary?

Surfing the "Net"

Regional Trade

In the early 1990s the United States and Canada, along with Mexico, established an agreement called the North American Free Trade Agreement, or NAFTA. These countries wanted to create an economic trading bloc. However, there were some groups in the United States and Canada that were opposed to NAFTA. To find out more about the reasons why NAFTA was opposed, look on the Internet.

Getting There

Follow these steps to gather information on why certain groups were opposed to NAFTA.

1. Use a search engine. Type in the name *North American Free Trade Agreement.*
2. After typing *North American Free Trade Agreement*, enter words like the following to focus your search: *NAFTA, economics, government, United States,* and *Canada.*
3. The search engine will provide you with a number of links to follow.

What To Do When You Are There

Organize the class into two groups. One group will represent the people who were opposed to NAFTA, and one group will represent the people who supported NAFTA. Click on the links to navigate through the pages of information and gather your findings. Each group should use a word processor to create a report about why they oppose or support NAFTA. Share the reports with the class.

Regional Focus

Latin America is the name given to the vast region that lies south of the United States. The map on page 144 shows you that Latin America begins at the Rio Grande, a river dividing the United States and Mexico. It ends at the southern tip of the continent of South America.

Region
The Land

Latin America covers some 7,900,000 square miles (20,400,000 sq. km)—about 16 percent of the earth's surface. This region includes Mexico and the countries of Central America and South America. It also takes in the West Indies island countries in the Caribbean Sea.

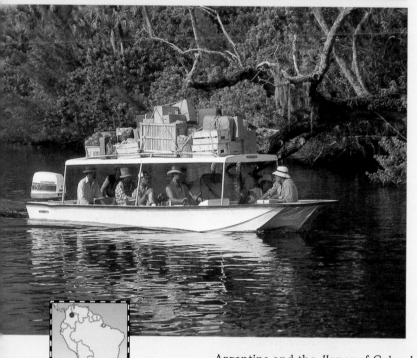

Cruising the Magdalena River in Colombia

Mountains High mountains can be found in much of Latin America. In Mexico, three mountain ranges meet to form what looks like the letter *Y.* Mountains also run south through much of Central America. Most of the West Indies islands are the tops of volcanic mountains rising up from the Caribbean Sea. Along the west coast of South America, you will find the Andes—the world's longest mountain chain. Volcanic activity and earthquakes are common in these mountainous areas of Latin America.

Plains Vast plains cover other areas of Latin America. You will find plains along the coasts of Mexico and Central America. Broad inland plains also can be found in parts of South America. The two major South American plains are the *pampas* of Argentina and the *llanos* of Colombia and Venezuela. These plains areas are made up of rolling grassland with few trees.

A river ferry carries passengers and their luggage down the Magdalena River.
LOCATION: What other major rivers are found in South America?

Rivers The map on page 144 shows you that South America has five major rivers: the Magdalena, the Orinoco, the Río de la Plata, the São Francisco, and the Amazon. The Amazon is the longest river in the Western Hemisphere. It stretches for about 4,000 miles (6,436 km) across South America from the Andes eastward to the Atlantic Ocean. It carries 20 percent of the world's unfrozen freshwater and drains a basin of more than 3 million square miles (7.8 million sq. km).

Natural Resources The countries of Mexico and Venezuela are among the world's leading producers of oil and natural gas. Latin America in general is rich in natural resources such as copper, iron ore, silver, tin, lead, oil, and natural gas. Rivers and waterfalls provide electric power to many countries. Farmers use the rich soil in many areas of Latin America to grow grains, fruits, and coffee.

Region
Climate and Vegetation

Latin America has a variety of climates and different types of vegetation. Traveling through the region, you can journey through deserts and rain forests and from grassy plains to empty plateaus.

Elevation Most of Latin America lies in the tropics and has some form of tropical climate. Elevation, however, affects climate throughout the region. Land at low elevations is hot and humid with green tropical vegetation. Crops such as sugarcane, bananas, and cacao beans grow well here. At higher elevations, you will notice that the climate becomes milder and temperatures cooler. Crops such as coffee, corn, and wheat grow in this area. In the highest areas, you will see very little plant life and may even spot frost and snow.

Rain Forests Rain forests cover lowland areas of Latin America. They are rainy and hot all the time. Rain forests have more kinds of plants and animals than anywhere else on the earth. The world's largest tropical rain forest is in Brazil in the Amazon basin. Other rain forests grow along the eastern coast of Central America and in some of the Caribbean islands.

Amazon Rain Forest

Plants in the Amazon basin provide sources for one-fourth of the world's medicines.
LOCATION: Where are other rain forests in Latin America?

Goods to Market

Workers load cases of bananas onto a waiting ship in the port of Guayaquil *(top)*. A woman from Ecuador weaves hats that she will sell in the city's market *(bottom)*.
PLACE: What percentage of Latin Americans live in cities?

Region
Economy

Latin America's economies are based partly on agriculture. Fertile soil and a warm, wet climate allow farmers to grow tropical crops—coffee, bananas, and sugarcane—in parts of the region. In addition, Latin Americans also make use of grasslands to raise livestock. Argentina, Mexico, and Brazil are among the world's leaders in cattle raising and meat production.

Service industries and manufacturing have grown rapidly in Latin America. In countries such as Venezuela, Mexico, and Brazil, workers produce cars, textiles, cement, chemicals, and electrical goods. Some countries, however, lack the money, skilled labor, and transportation systems needed to build industries. Rugged mountains and thick tropical vegetation provide physical barriers to movement.

Movement
The People

Latin America has about 500 million people, about 12 percent of the world's population. Most Latin Americans live either along the coasts of South America or in a broad strip of land reaching from Mexico into Central America. In recent years, many Latin Americans have moved from the countryside to the cities. About 70 percent of the region's people are now city dwellers. Four Latin American cities rank among the 15 largest urban areas in the world. They are Mexico City, Mexico; São Paulo and Rio de Janeiro, Brazil; and Buenos Aires, Argentina.

Latin Americans include Native Americans, Europeans, Africans, and Asians. All of these groups have left their mark on the culture of the region. Ancient Native American peoples, such as the Maya, Aztec, and Inca, had advanced civilizations long before Europeans arrived in the Americas. During the 1500s, Europeans enslaved and destroyed the Native American civilizations. They later enslaved Africans and brought them to work their plantations.

Spain and Portugal ruled most of Latin America from the 1500s to the early 1800s. The Spanish and Portuguese brought the Roman Catholic faith and their languages to the region. Because these languages are based on Latin, the region became known as Latin America. Most Latin Americans today are Roman Catholics.

Many Latin American countries won their freedom in the early 1800s. Wealthy landowners and military officials, however, controlled governments and often ignored the needs of poor farmers and workers. By the mid-1900s, the rise of cities and industries challenged these leaders. With wide public support, new democratic governments emerged.

Picture Atlas of the World

A Regional Study

Using the CD-ROM Create a file about Latin America. (See the User's Guide on how to use the Collector button.) Read the essays and vital statistics, look at the photos, map, and videos; and listen to the musical selections for each country. Make sure your file includes the following information:

1. most heavily and sparsely populated countries
2. major cities in the region
3. major physical features of the region
4. examples of colonial influences in architecture, religions, music, and languages
5. examples of Native American culture and traditions

Use your file to write an essay describing the regional characteristics of Latin America.

Surfing the "Net"

Latin American Culture

Latin American culture has been influenced by its history of colonial rule. Over time groups from Spain and Portugal, as well as Britain, France, and the Netherlands, settled in the region. These groups introduced elements of their cultures to the region. Some of these European influences can still be seen in Latin American culture today. To find out more about the influence of colonial rule on Latin American culture, search the Internet.

Getting There

Follow these steps to gather information on Latin American culture.

1. Use a search engine. Type in the words *Latin America.*
2. Enter words like the following to focus your search: *culture, history, colonization,* and *Europe.*
3. The search engine will provide you with a number of links to follow.

What To Do When You Are There

Click on the links to navigate through the pages of information and gather your findings. Use your findings to create an illustrated time line that identifies when and where each group of Europeans settled. Be sure to describe what each group contributed to Latin American culture. Display your time line for your classmates. Discuss the similarities and differences you found about colonial influences on Latin American culture.

Regional Focus

Europe is both a continent and a region. It is a huge peninsula that runs westward from the landmass of Asia. More than 30 countries make up Europe. Their peoples speak about 50 different languages.

Region

The Land

Europe covers about 1.9 million square miles (5.1 million sq. km). The map on page 246 shows you that several bodies of water touch Europe. The largest of these are the Arctic Ocean, the Mediterranean Sea, the Baltic Sea, and the Atlantic Ocean.

The Canals of Amsterdam in the Netherlands

Houseboats and tall, narrow apartment buildings line the banks of Amsterdam's many canals.
PLACE: What is western Europe's major river?

Seas and Coasts Europe's long, jagged coastline has many peninsulas and offshore islands. Deep bays, narrow seas, and well-protected inlets shelter fine harbors. Closeness to the sea has enabled Europeans to trade with other lands. Many Europeans also depend on the sea for food.

Mountains Europe is a continent almost completely covered by mountains. You will find low mountains in the British Isles, Scandinavia, and parts of France, Germany, and eastern Europe. Mountains elsewhere on the continent are higher and more rugged. They include the Pyrenees, which form the border between France and Spain, and the Alps. Europe's highest mountain range, the Alps sweep across southern and central parts of the continent. Joined to the Alps are the Carpathians, a chain of mountains that towers over the landscape of eastern Europe.

Plains Broad, fertile plains curve around Europe's mountains. The North European Plain stretches from the British Isles to Russia. Farms, towns, and cities dot its rolling land. You will find other plains in the peninsulas of southern and eastern Europe.

Rivers Europe's rivers provide trade links between inland areas and coastal ports. The Rhine—western Europe's major river—begins in the Alps, flows through northwestern Europe, and empties into the North Sea. Europe's other important waterway—the Danube River—flows eastward from central Europe to the Black Sea.

Region
Climate and Vegetation

Europe's small land area offers many contrasts in its climate. Europe's northern location and closeness to the sea are key to this variety of climates.

A Mild Climate Europe lies far north, but many areas of the continent enjoy mild temperatures year-round. This happens because of an ocean current known as the North Atlantic Current. It brings warm Atlantic Ocean waters and winds, which provide rainfall, to Europe's western coast.

Europe's northern location also influences the climate of the region. Northern Europe has longer, colder winters and shorter, cooler summers than southern Europe. Eastern Europe lies farther inland from the Atlantic and its mild current. Therefore, its winters are longer and colder—and its summers shorter and hotter—than those in western Europe.

Vegetation In the far north of Europe, mosses and small shrubs blanket the land. Mixed forests and grasslands are found in the milder climate regions of northwestern and eastern Europe. Air pollution from Europe's factories and cars, however, has harmed many woodlands throughout the continent. In the south the hot, dry summers of the Mediterranean area produce shrubs and short trees.

Region
The Economy

Agriculture, manufacturing, and service industries are Europe's leading economic activities. Skilled workers, a few key natural resources, and closeness to waterways have made Europe one of the economic giants of the world.

Agriculture Europe has some of the world's most productive farmland. European farmers use modern equipment to produce huge yields of grains, fruits, and vegetables on small areas of land. They also raise some of the world's finest breeds of cattle and sheep.

Industry Iron ore, coal, and other minerals are found throughout the North European Plain. Vast reserves of oil and natural gas lie beneath the North Sea and in southeastern Europe. Most of Europe's industrial centers have developed near major mineral deposits.

Many European countries are among the world's leading manufacturing centers. They produce steel, machinery, cars, textiles, electronic equipment, food products, and household goods. Service industries such as banking, insurance, and tourism are also important to Europe's economy.

Moving Products Along the Danube

Barges line the banks of the Danube River in Bratislava, Slovakia.
REGION: What factors have made Europe an economic giant?

243

UNIT 4 ATLAS

Region
The People

Some European countries have one main ethnic group; others are made up of two or more ethnic groups. Differences among Europe's many peoples have often led to conflicts such as civil war in the former Yugoslav republics.

Population The region of Europe has about 520 million people—a large number for a small space. It is one of the world's most densely populated areas. Most Europeans live in urban areas, while large stretches of countryside have few people. Many of the world's leading cities are in Europe. They include London, Paris, Rome, Berlin, and Warsaw. Europe's cities have historical palaces and churches as well as modern skyscrapers and shopping malls. In rural areas life still centers on villages and small towns.

History The ancient Greeks and Romans laid the foundation of European government, law, and thought. They left behind graceful works of art and architecture, such as the Parthenon in Athens. From A.D. 500 to 1500, Christianity shaped a new European civilization. The Gothic style of many cathedrals built during this time reflects Europe's Christian heritage.

Beginning in the 1400s and 1500s, Europeans advanced learning and the arts. The Renaissance—or "rebirth" of art and scholarly activities—advanced learning and the value of the individual person. After the 1700s, political changes increased freedom for the common people. An interest in science and the invention of machines during the Industrial Revolution changed the economy and, in the long run, raised standards of living. In eastern Europe once-powerful empires faced growing challenges from ethnic groups that wanted independence.

Europeans also explored, settled, and conquered other lands. They brought their ways of life to every part of the globe. Competition for land and trade among Europe's nations, however, eventually led to two world wars that put an end to Europe's global power. After World War II, Europe was split into noncommunist and communist areas. The fall of communism in the late 1980s brought about a new era. Many European countries joined the European Union to bring their governments and economies closer together.

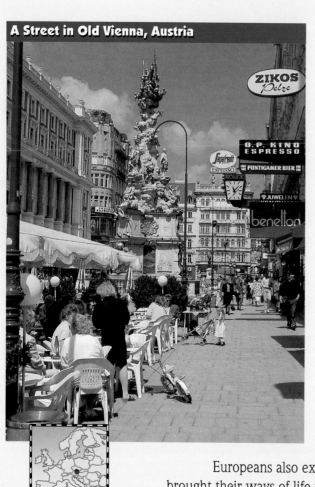

A Street in Old Vienna, Austria

People gather at sidewalk cafes in Vienna's historic Inner City to socialize and enjoy pastries and coffee.
REGION: What is the population of Europe?

Multimedia Unit 4 Activities

NATIONAL GEOGRAPHIC SOCIETY

Picture Atlas of the World

Culture and Tourism

Using the CD-ROM Each European country contributes its own history, language, and culture to the continent. Some of the most fascinating countries of Europe are also the smallest ones. Monaco, Andorra, San Marino, Liechtenstein, and Vatican City claim small populations and cover relatively small areas. Find out more about the allure of these tiny European countries. Assemble a file of information that a tourist might find interesting and helpful. (See the User's Guide for information on how to use the Collector button.) Use your findings to create a travel brochure titled "Europe: Little Places with Colossal Lure." Remember to include the following:

1. population and economic statistics
2. location of the country within Europe
3. information about the climate
4. charming photos of the people and countries
5. fascinating facts about the countries

Surfing the "Net"

Economic Unity

The goal of the European Union (EU) is to unify and strengthen the economies of member nations by removing all economic restrictions across their borders. To find out more about the reasons why the EU was created and how it benefits its member nations, search the Internet.

Getting There

Follow these steps to gather information on the EU:

1. Use a search engine. Type in the name *European Union, European Community,* or *European Common Market.*
2. Select two members of the EU on which to focus. Type in those countries' names to focus your search.
3. The search engine will provide you with a number of links to follow.

What To Do When You Are There

Click on the links to navigate through the pages of information and gather your findings. Use the information to create a chart of population and economic statistics. Note what the country produces and to whom it sells its products. Include this information in your chart. Prepare answers to the following questions: How does being a member of the EU benefit the country you selected? How do relationships among countries in the European Union compare with those among states in the United States? As a class, compare charts and discuss the questions above.

Unit 5
Russia and the Independent Republics

What Makes Russia and the Independent Republics a Region?

The people share . . .

• a vast land—8.5 million square miles!

• very diverse cultures within republics.

• geographic features.

• the change to a capitalist economy.

To find out more about Russia and the independent republics, see the Unit Atlas on pages 346–357.

St. Petersburg, Russia

EXPLORING THE INTERNET

To learn more about Russia and the independent republics, visit the Glencoe Social Studies Web site at **www.glencoe.com** for information, activities, and links to other sites.

GeoJournal Activity

As you read Unit 5, imagine you are living in a city in Russia or the independent republics. In your journal, write a story that describes one day in your life. Include a sketch map of the countryside surrounding the city.

UNIT 5 ATLAS

1

NATIONAL
GEOGRAPHIC
SOCIETY

IMAGES
of the
WORLD

7

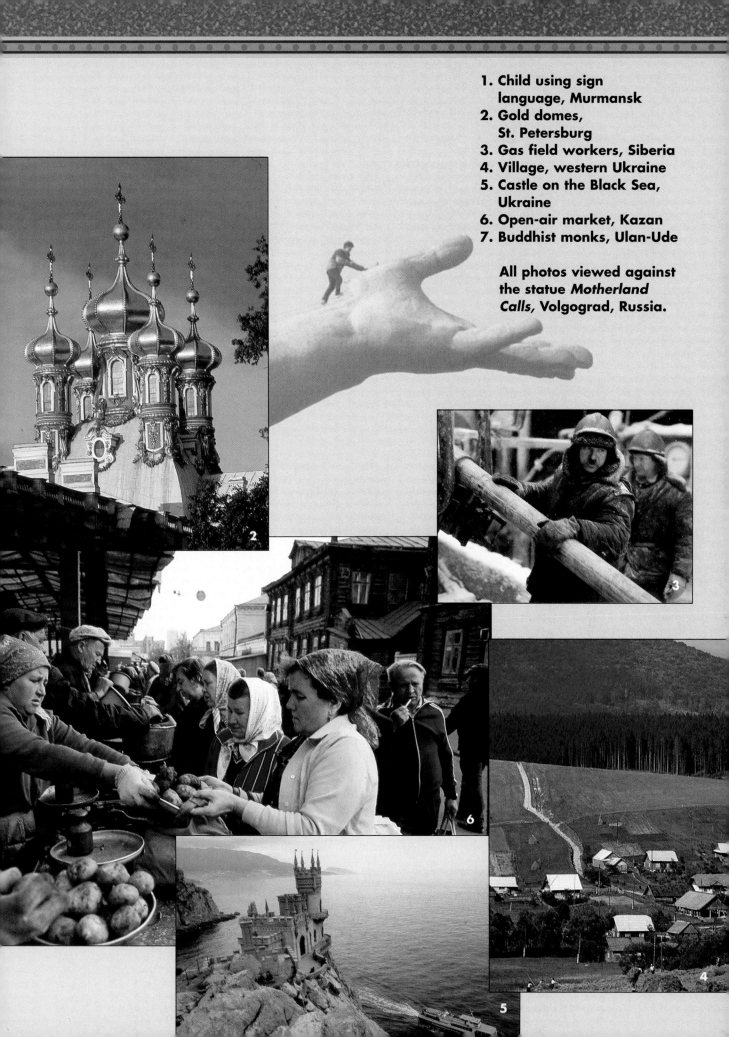

1. Child using sign language, Murmansk
2. Gold domes, St. Petersburg
3. Gas field workers, Siberia
4. Village, western Ukraine
5. Castle on the Black Sea, Ukraine
6. Open-air market, Kazan
7. Buddhist monks, Ulan-Ude

All photos viewed against the statue *Motherland Calls*, Volgograd, Russia.

Regional Focus

Russia and the other independent republics span the continents of Europe and Asia. Russia is the largest republic in area and population. The other republics in the region are Ukraine, Belarus, Moldova, Armenia, Georgia, Azerbaijan, Kazakhstan, Uzbekistan, Turkmenistan, Kyrgyzstan, and Tajikistan.

Region
The Land

The region of Russia and the independent republics covers about 8 million square miles (20.7 million sq. km). This land area is greater than the size of Canada, the United States, and Mexico combined.

Overlooking the Ural Mountains

The Ural Mountains separate European Russia from the Asian part of Russia known as Siberia. **HUMAN/ENVIRONMENT INTERACTION: Why do you think most Russians live west of the Urals?**

The North The far north of Russia is made up of low hills. Snow and ice cover the land for most of the year. The few people who live in the far north either fish, hunt, or herd reindeer. Farther south you will find deep, thick forests. In some areas farmers have cleared the woods to grow crops.

South of the forests is a vast open plain. It stretches more than 3,000 miles (4,800 km) from eastern Europe to Asia. For centuries routes across this plain brought invading armies. Today it is an important agricultural and industrial area for Russia, Ukraine, Moldova, and Belarus. The plain's fertile soil is among the best in the world for farming.

Mountains Mountains cover many areas in Russia and the independent republics. You will find two mountain ranges in areas where the continents of Europe and Asia meet. The Ural Mountains divide Russia into European and Asian parts. To the south, the Caucasus range rises along the borders of Russia, Georgia, and Azerbaijan. Find these mountains on the map on page 352.

Mountains also cross through several republics in central Asia. The Pamirs in Tajikistan have some of the region's highest peaks. The Tian Shan range in Kyrgyzstan holds some of the world's largest glaciers.

Bodies of Water Russia and the independent republics contain many bodies of water. You will find two of the world's largest lakes here. One is the Caspian Sea, which is really a salt lake. The other is Lake Baikal, the deepest lake in the world. The region also has long rivers. Some of the rivers flow eastward, like the Amur, which forms Russia's border with China. Others, like the Volga and the Dnieper, flow south through plains. Many that flow north, such as the Lena, Ob, and Yenisey, are frozen much of the year.

Region
Climate and Vegetation

The far northern location of Russia and the independent republics affects their climates. Most of the republics lie far from great bodies of water that keep land temperatures mild. Also, the region's flat lands do not provide shelter from hot summer winds and freezing winter storms.

Far northern areas have tundra and subarctic climates with cold temperatures most of the year. Most of the deep soil is always frozen. Farther south, forests stretch to a grass-covered plains area, which has a humid continental climate of short, hot summers and long, cold winters. Desert regions of central Asia have long, hot summers and short, cold winters. Plant life is very sparse there. The Black Sea coast, with its humid subtropical and Mediterranean climates, is known for subtropical plants and citrus fruits.

Vineyards in Moldova

Enough wine is produced from Moldova's vineyards to export to Russia and other independent republics.
PLACE: What crops grow well along the Black Sea?

Region
The Economy

For many years, Russia and the independent republics formed one country called the Soviet Union. It had an economy planned and run by the communist leaders. In 1991 each republic became independent and responsible for its own economy. The republics now allow people to run their own businesses and farms. This change to free enterprise has been a challenge for the people in the region.

Russia and the independent republics grow mainly wheat, rye, oats, barley, sugar beets, and cotton. The region is rich in minerals such as coal, oil, natural gas, copper, silver, manganese, and gold. Dams on rivers in Russia and Ukraine supply electric power to factories and cities. Rivers, roads, and railroads link industrial areas. Industrial growth under Soviet rule, however, led to widespread pollution of the air and water.

Place
The People

About 283 million people live in Russia and the independent republics. Russia has the region's largest population with 147 million people.

Population Climate and landscape affect where people live in Russia and the independent republics. Most people in the region live west of the Urals, where the climates are mild and the land is fertile. In the past most people lived in the countryside. Today most are urban dwellers. The three largest cities are Moscow, St. Petersburg, and Kiev.

Ethnic Groups Each of the republics has a major ethnic group, language, and culture. There are also many smaller groups in each republic. More than 100 different ethnic groups live throughout the entire region. Slavs (Russians, Ukrainians, and Belarusians) make up the region's largest ethnic group. They speak Slavic languages and practice Eastern Orthodox Christianity. Turkic ethnic groups (Uzbeks, Kazakhs, and Turkmenis) predominate in central Asia. They have their own languages and practice the religion of Islam. Various ethnic groups known as Caucasian inhabit Armenia and Georgia. They practice their own forms of Orthodox Christianity.

History Russia and the independent republics have a rich history. Centuries ago Slavs set up city-states along rivers in present-day Ukraine and Russia. By the 1400s powerful rulers called czars ruled Russia. Over several centuries, the Russians took over all of the region that is today Russia and the independent republics. Their territory was called the Russian Empire.

In 1917 the rule of the czars ended. A communist dictatorship emerged, and the Russian Empire became the Union of Soviet Socialist Republics. The Communists made the Soviet Union an industrial power but denied the people basic freedoms. In 1991 the Communists fell from power, and the separate parts of the Soviet Union became independent republics. Under Russian president Boris Yeltsin, Russia allied with the other former Soviet republics to form a loose union called the Commonwealth of Independent States, or CIS.

The Arts The arts of Russia and the independent republics include architecture, painting, music, and dance. Each republic has its own rich heritage. You probably have seen pictures of Russia's onion-domed churches and heard the classical music of Peter Tchaikovsky and other Russian composers. Ukraine is known for its lively folk music and colorfully decorated Easter eggs. Ancient churches with drumlike tops and bells dot the rugged countryside of Armenia and Georgia. In the central Asian republics, you will see beautiful tiles in swirling patterns decorate Islamic mosques.

Shopping in Moscow

The GUM department store—Russia's largest shopping mall—sells everything from coats to caviar *(above).*
REGION: How have the economies of Russia and the independent republics changed since 1991?

Multimedia Unit 5 Activities

NATIONAL GEOGRAPHIC SOCIETY

Picture Atlas of the World

Economic Restructuring

Using the CD-ROM Today Russia and the independent republics are struggling to come to terms with the changes brought about by independence. Use the CD-ROM and other reference works to analyze the economies of these countries. Record your findings in a chart. Use the following criteria to help you assess the economic status of each country:

- number of schools
- annual per capita income
- amount of food and housing per resident
- extent of communication and transportation networks
- literacy rate
- life expectancy
- infant mortality rate
- population growth rate

Compare your chart with your classmates' charts to see how your assessments of each country differ.

Surfing the "Net"

Security, Expansion, and Geography

Throughout history countries wishing to expand their borders have targeted neighboring nations. The former Soviet Union targeted Estonia, Latvia, and Lithuania. In 1990 Estonia, Latvia, and Lithuania became the first republics to declare their independence from the Soviet Union. To find out more about the struggle for self-rule in these countries, search the Internet.

Getting There

Follow these steps to gather information on the Baltic countries:

1. Use a search engine. Type in the names of the countries.
2. Enter words like the following to focus your search: *history*, *politics*, and *independence*.

3. The search engine will provide you with a number of links to follow.

What To Do When You Are There

Complete the following activity individually or in groups. Build a presentation that explores the history and results of political revolution in Estonia, Latvia, or Lithuania. Your presentation should depict one or more of the following events: the periods of independence and control of the country, the reactions of the country's citizens to control or independence, the buildup to revolution, how and when the revolution occurred, or the results of revolution. Share your presentation with the class.

Physical Geography

RUSSIA AND THE INDEPENDENT REPUBLICS: Physical

ARCTIC OCEAN

EUROPE

Baltic Sea

BELARUS

North European Plain

UKRAINE

MOLDOVA

GEORGIA

CAUCASUS MTS.

Mt. Elbrus
18,510 ft.
(5,642 m)

AZERBAIJAN

ARMENIA

Caspian Sea

TURKMENISTAN

Dnieper R.

Don R.

Volga R.

Black Sea

Kama R.

Ural R.

Kyrgyz Steppe

KAZAKHSTAN

Aral Sea

Kara Kum

UZBEKISTAN

TIAN SHAN
Communism Peak
▲ 24,590 ft. (7,495 m)

TAJIKISTAN

Lake Balkhash

KYRGYZSTAN

ASIA

URAL MOUNTAINS

R U S S I A

West Siberian Plain

Ob R.

Irtysh R.

SAYAN MOUNTAINS

Yenisey River

Barents Sea

Novaya Zemlya

Arctic Circle

Central Siberian Plateau

Lake Baikal

YABLONOVY MOUNTAINS

New Siberian Islands

VERKHOYANSKIY RANGE

CHERSKOGO RANGE

Kolyma R.

Lena R.

Kamchatka Peninsula

Klyuchevskaya
15,584 ft.
(4,750 m)

Bering Sea

Sea of Okhotsk

Sakhalin Island

N
W E
S

0   250   500 mi.
0 250 500 km

60°E   80°E   100°E   120°E

20°E   40°N   40°E   60°N   80°N   60°N

160°E   140°E

180°

ELEVATIONS

Feet	Meters
10,000	3,000
5,000	1,500
2,000	600
1,000	300
0	0

— National boundary
⬚ Desert
▲ Mountain peak

Lambert Equal-Area projection

Map Study

1. **LOCATION** What two mountain ranges border the Central Siberian Plateau on the south?
2. **LOCATION** What large desert is found in Turkmenistan?

ELEVATION PROFILE: Russia

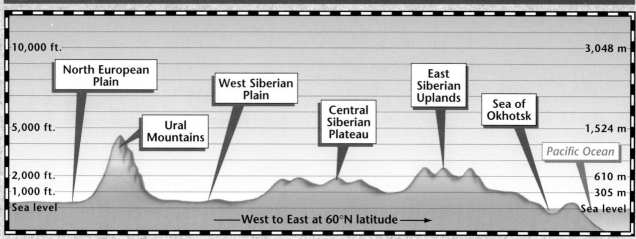

10,000 ft. — 3,048 m

North European Plain

Ural Mountains

West Siberian Plain

Central Siberian Plateau

East Siberian Uplands

Sea of Okhotsk

5,000 ft. — 1,524 m

Pacific Ocean

2,000 ft. — 610 m
1,000 ft. — 305 m
Sea level — Sea level

← West to East at 60°N latitude →

Source: *Goode's World Atlas*, 19th edition

GeoFacts

Highest point: Communism Peak (Tajikistan) 24,590 ft. (7,495 m) high

Lowest point: Caspian Sea (Russia, Azerbaijan) 92 ft. (28 m) below sea level

Longest river: Ob-Irtysh 3,362 mi. (5,409 km) long

Largest lake: Caspian Sea (Eurasia) 143,244 sq. mi. (371,002 sq. km)

Deepest lake: Lake Baikal (Russia) 5,315 ft. (1,620 m) deep

Largest desert: Kara Kum (Turkmenistan) 120,000 sq. mi. (310,800 sq. km)

RUSSIA/INDEPENDENT REPUBLICS AND THE UNITED STATES: Land Comparison

Graphic Study

1. LOCATION Where are the highest elevations found in Russia?

2. REGION About how much larger in area are Russia and the independent republics than the continental United States?

Cultural Geography

RUSSIA AND THE INDEPENDENT REPUBLICS: Political

ARCTIC OCEAN

Barents
Sea

Bering
Sea

EUROPE

Baltic Sea

Arctic Circle

Sea
of
Okhotsk

BELARUS
⊛ Minsk
Chisinau
⊛ Kiev
⊛ Moscow

RUSSIA

UKRAINE
MOLDOVA

Black Sea

GEORGIA
Tbilisi ⊛
Yerevan

⊛ Astana

KAZAKHSTAN

Lake
Baikal

Lake
Balkhash

ASIA

Sea
of
Japan

AZERBAIJAN
⊛ Baku

Aral
Sea

UZBEKISTAN

ARMENIA

Caspian
Sea

Bishkek

Ashkhabad ⊛
TURKMENISTAN

Tashkent ⊛
Dushanbe ⊛
TAJIKISTAN

KYRGYZSTAN

N
W   E
S

PACIFIC
OCEAN

— National boundary
⊛ National capital

Lambert Equal-Area
projection

0   250   500 mi.
0   250 500 km

60°E
80°E
100°E
120°E

Map Study

1. **PLACE** What is the largest independent republic after Russia?
2. **PLACE** What is the capital of Belarus?

Population: Russia and the Independent Republics

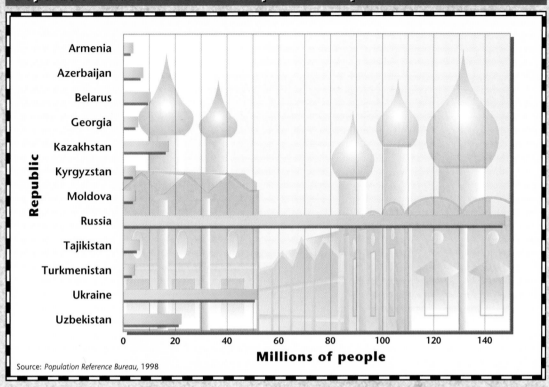

Republic

Armenia
Azerbaijan
Belarus
Georgia
Kazakhstan
Kyrgyzstan
Moldova
Russia
Tajikistan
Turkmenistan
Ukraine
Uzbekistan

0   20   40   60   80   100   120   140

Millions of people

Source: *Population Reference Bureau, 1998*

GeoFacts

Biggest country (land area):
Russia 6,520,656 sq. mi.
(16,888,499 sq. km)

Smallest country (land area):
Armenia 10,888 sq. mi.
(28,200 sq. km)

Largest city (population):
Moscow (1998) 9,269,000
(2015 projected) 11,000,000

Highest population density:
Armenia 349 people per sq. mi.
(134 per sq. km)

Lowest population density:
Kazakhstan 15 people per sq. mi.
(6 people per sq. km)

COMPARING POPULATION: Russia/Independent Republics and the U.S.

Russia/
Independent
Republics

United
States

= 50,000,000

Source: *Population Reference Bureau, 1998*

Graphic Study

1. PLACE What is the combined population of Russia and the independent republics?

2. PLACE Which country in the chart above has the second-highest population?

Countries at a Glance

Armenia

Yerevan

CAPITAL:
Yerevan
MAJOR LANGUAGE(S):
Armenian
POPULATION:
3,800,000

LANDMASS:
10,888 sq. mi./
28,200 sq. km
MONEY:
Dram
MAJOR EXPORT:
Machinery
MAJOR IMPORT:
Machinery

Azerbaijan

Baku

CAPITAL:
Baku
MAJOR LANGUAGE(S):
Azeri, Turkish, Russian
POPULATION:
7,700,000

LANDMASS:
33,436 sq. mi./
86,599 sq. km
MONEY:
Manat
MAJOR EXPORT:
Food Products
MAJOR IMPORT:
Food Products

Belarus

Minsk

CAPITAL:
Minsk
MAJOR LANGUAGE(S):
Belorussian, Russian
POPULATION:
10,200,000

LANDMASS:
80,108 sq. mi./
207,480 sq. km
MONEY:
Belarus Ruble
MAJOR EXPORT:
Machinery
MAJOR IMPORT:
Machinery

Georgia

Tbilisi

CAPITAL:
Tbilisi
MAJOR LANGUAGE(S):
Georgian, Russian
POPULATION:
5,400,000

LANDMASS:
26,911 sq. mi./
69,699 sq. km
MONEY:
Lari
MAJOR EXPORT:
Food
MAJOR IMPORT:
Machinery

Kazakhstan

Astana

CAPITAL:
Astana
MAJOR LANGUAGE(S):
Kazakh, Russian, German
POPULATION:
15,600,000

LANDMASS:
1,031,170 sq. mi./
2,670,730 sq. km
MONEY:
Tenge
MAJOR EXPORT:
Raw Materials
MAJOR IMPORT:
Raw Materials

Kyrgyzstan

Bishkek

CAPITAL:
Bishkek
MAJOR LANGUAGE(S):
Kyrgyz
POPULATION:
4,700,000

LANDMASS:
74,054 sq. mi./
191,800 sq. km
MONEY:
Som
MAJOR EXPORT:
Machinery
MAJOR IMPORT:
Light-industrial Products

Moldova

Chisinau

CAPITAL:
Chisinau
MAJOR LANGUAGE(S):
Romanian, Ukrainian
POPULATION:
4,200,000

LANDMASS:
12,730 sq. mi./
32,971 sq. km
MONEY:
Leu
MAJOR EXPORT:
Food Products
MAJOR IMPORT:
Machinery

Russia

Moscow

CAPITAL:
Moscow
MAJOR LANGUAGE(S):
Russian, Ukrainian,
Belorussian, Uzbek
POPULATION:
147,000,000

LANDMASS:
6,520,656 sq. mi./
16,888,499 sq. km
MONEY:
Ruble
MAJOR EXPORT:
Fuels
MAJOR IMPORT:
Machinery

Tajikistan

Dushanbe

CAPITAL:
Dushanbe
MAJOR LANGUAGE(S):
Tadzhik, Russian
POPULATION:
6,100,000

LANDMASS:
54,286 sq. mi./
140,601 sq. km
MONEY:
Ruble
MAJOR EXPORT:
Aluminum
MAJOR IMPORT:
Chemicals

Turkmenistan

Ashkhabad

CAPITAL:
Ashkhabad
MAJOR LANGUAGE(S):
Turkmen, Russian
POPULATION:
4,700,000

LANDMASS:
181,440 sq. mi./
470,000 sq. km
MONEY:
Manat
MAJOR EXPORT:
Natural gas
MAJOR IMPORT:
Machinery

Countries not drawn to scale.

Lunch in Moscow

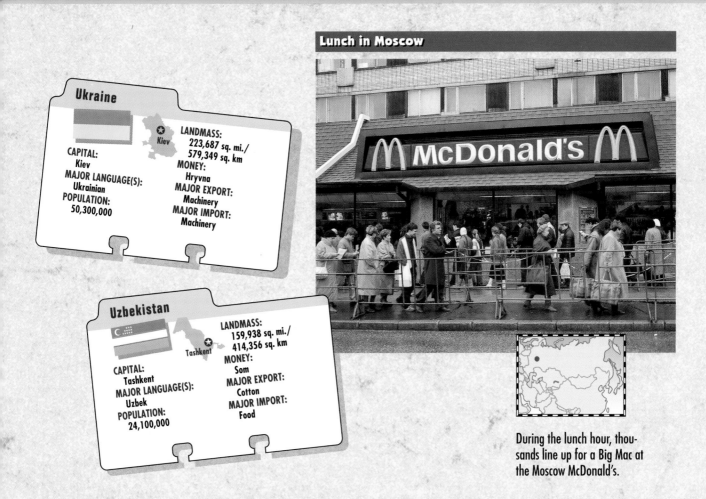

Ukraine

CAPITAL:
Kiev
MAJOR LANGUAGE(S):
Ukrainian
POPULATION:
50,300,000

LANDMASS:
223,687 sq. mi./
579,349 sq. km
MONEY:
Hryvna
MAJOR EXPORT:
Machinery
MAJOR IMPORT:
Machinery

Uzbekistan

CAPITAL:
Tashkent
MAJOR LANGUAGE(S):
Uzbek
POPULATION:
24,100,000

LANDMASS:
159,938 sq. mi./
414,356 sq. km
MONEY:
Som
MAJOR EXPORT:
Cotton
MAJOR IMPORT:
Food

During the lunch hour, thousands line up for a Big Mac at the Moscow McDonald's.

Street Scene in Lvov, Ukraine

The city of Lvov has large squares and narrow streets much like the cities of Europe.

В универмаге Гостиный Двор

Map of Russia (Lambert Equal-Area projection)

Cities and features labeled on the map:

ARCTIC OCEAN

Barents Sea

Baltic Sea

EUROPE

Murmansk

St. Petersburg

Moscow

Nizhniy Novgorod

Voronezh

Kazan

Perm

Saratov

Samara

Ufa

Yekaterinburg

Chelyabinsk

Volgograd

Astrakhan

Black Sea

Caspian Sea

Aral Sea

Omsk

Novosibirsk

R U S S I A

Krasnoyarsk

Irkutsk

Lake Baikal

Yakutsk

Khabarovsk

Vladivostok

Petropavlovsk-Kamchatski

Sea of Okhotsk

Bering Sea

Sea of Japan

ASIA

Arctic Circle

Legend:
— National boundary
⊛ National capital
• Other city

Lambert Equal-Area projection

Scale: 0 250 500 mi.
0 250 500 km

Compass: N, S, E, W

MAP STUDY ACTIVITY

As you read Chapter 14, you will learn about the land, people, and history of Russia.

1. In what part of Russia is its capital located?

2. What sea borders Vladivostok?

3. About how many miles (km) separate Moscow and St. Petersburg?

The Land

PREVIEW

Words to Know
- tundra
- taiga
- permafrost

Places to Locate
- North European Plain
- West Siberian Plain
- Central Siberian Plateau
- East Siberian Uplands
- Ural Mountains
- Volga River
- Caspian Sea
- Lake Baikal
- Kamchatka Peninsula

Read to Learn . . .
1. where Russia is located.
2. what landforms are found in Russia.
3. what two major climates Russia has.

Brown bear, elk, and fox roam this "green ocean"—a vast forest area that stretches across the northern part of Russia. Few people visit or live here, however. Why? Although summers are warm, snow covers the ground for as long as eight months a year!

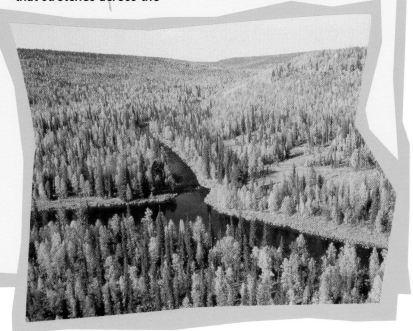

If you had to describe Russia in one word, that word would be "BIG!" Russia is the largest country in the world in area. Its almost 6.6 million square miles (17,075,400 sq. km) are spread across two continents—Europe and Asia. If you crossed Russia by train, it would take about one full week of travel and you would pass through 11 time zones!

Location
A Northern Country

The map on page 358 shows you two important facts about Russia—its far northern location and its isolation. Russia's longest coastline faces the Arctic Ocean. Along the Arctic coast, ice makes shipping difficult or impossible most of the year. Although Russia does have ports on the Baltic Sea, the Black Sea, and the Pacific Ocean, many of these are frozen for several weeks each winter.

ARCTIC OCEAN

New Siberian Islands

Bering Sea

EUROPE

Barents Sea

Kola Peninsula

Novaya Zemlya

Baltic Sea

Kamchatka Peninsula

Klyuchevskaya 15,584 ft. (4,750 m)

North

European

Plain

Moscow

R U S S I A

West

Siberian

Plain

Central

Siberian

Plateau

Arctic Circle

Yakutsk

East

Siberian

Uplands

Sea of Okhotsk

Sakhalin Island

URAL MOUNTAINS

Yenisey River

Lena R.

Kolyma R.

CHERSKOGO RANGE

VERKHOYANSKIY RANGE

Don R.

Volga R.

Ural R.

Irtysh R.

Lake Baikal

SAYAN MOUNTAINS

YABLONOVY MOUNTAINS

Black Sea

CAUCASUS MTS.

Caspian Sea

Aral Sea

Mt. Elbrus 18,510 ft. (5,642 m)

A S I A

0   250   500 mi.
0   250 500 km

ASIA

ELEVATIONS

Feet	Meters
10,000	3,000
5,000	1,500
2,000	600
1,000	300
0	0

⊛ National capital
▲ Mountain peak

Lambert Equal-Area projection

MAP STUDY

Most of Russia's people live on the North European Plain.

LOCATION: On what rivers do these people depend for water and transportation?

Ural Mountains Find the Ural Mountains on the map above. Can you see why geographers use them to mark the boundary between the continents of Europe and Asia? The Ural Mountains extend for 1,500 miles (2,414 km) from the Arctic Ocean in the north to near the Aral Sea in the south. The Urals—worn by erosion—are old mountains, rising only a few thousand feet.

Plains and Highlands West of the Urals lies a vast area known as the North European Plain. About 75 percent of the Russian people live on this plain. Russia's largest cities are located here, including its capital, Moscow, and St. Petersburg, a leading industrial and cultural center. Most of Russia's industries and farms dot this region, too.

Now look east of the Urals. This is the Asian part of Russia known as Siberia. Another plain lies on this side of the mountains—the West Siberian Plain. It is the world's largest area of flat land.

As you move farther east of the West Siberian Plain, you come to the Central Siberian Plateau. It rises in elevation from the Arctic Ocean in the north to the Sayan Mountains in the south. Another highland area—the East Siberian Uplands—forms the largest region of Siberia. This wilderness of forests, mountains, and plateaus runs from the Central Siberian Plateau to Russia's eastern coast. The endangered Siberian tiger, among other animals, makes its home here.

In Siberia's far north, large areas of **tundra,** or cold treeless plains, stretch along the Arctic shore. South of the tundra is a vast area of evergreen forests known as the **taiga.** It has so many trees that it is called a "green ocean." On its far eastern edges, a finger of land called the Kamchatka Peninsula stretches south between the Bering Sea and Sea of Okhotsk.

Caucasus Mountains In southwest Russia you can see the mighty Caucasus (KAW•kuh•suhs) Mountains. An extension of the Alps, the Caucasus are thickly covered with pines and other trees. Mount Elbrus in the Caucasus rises 18,510 feet (5,642 m). It is the tallest mountain on the continent of Europe.

Inland Water Areas Russia's landscape also includes many inland bodies of water. In the south Russia borders on the Caspian Sea—a saltwater lake. About the size of the state of California, it is the largest inland body of water in the world. The Caspian Sea lies 92 feet (28 m) *below* sea level.

RUSSIA: Climate

CLIMATE
High latitude
- Subarctic
- Tundra

Mid-latitude
- Humid continental

Dry
- Steppe (partly dry)

Lambert Equal-Area projection

MAP STUDY
The Arctic Circle passes through northern Russia.
PLACE: What two types of climates are found between the Arctic Circle and 80°N?

In Yakutsk, a city in north-eastern Siberia, temperatures have plunged as low as −108°F (−77°C).
REGION: What kind of climate prevails in northern Siberia?

Farther east is Siberia's Lake Baikal (by•KAHL). It is the deepest lake in the world—about 5,315 feet (1,620 m) deep. It also holds more water than any other freshwater lake—about 20 percent of the world's unfrozen freshwater.

Many rivers fan across Russia's landscape. Rivers in Siberia, such as the Lena (LEE•nuh), the Ob (AHB), and the Yenisey (YEH•nuh•SAY), are among the longest in the world. Most of them flow south to north into the Arctic Ocean.

Rivers in European Russia, on the western side of the Urals, are connected to one another and to the Caspian Sea by canals. This flow of river traffic has helped unify the country. European Russia's longest river—the Volga—flows 2,193 miles (3,528 km) southward from the Moscow area to the Caspian Sea.

Region
Climate

Russia's northern location near the cold Arctic Ocean results in short, warm summers and long, cold winters for most of the country. Imagine traveling west across the forested southern parts of Siberia. These areas have a subarctic climate. Summers are cool, and snow is on the ground eight to nine months each year. Average temperatures in January plunge to -45°F (-42.8°C).

The region north of the Arctic Circle has a tundra climate with perhaps the coldest winters in the world. Across much of Siberia, a permanently frozen layer of soil called **permafrost** lies beneath the ground's surface.

Temperatures warm on the North European Plain. This area has a humid continental climate. Winters are cold, but not so brutally cold as farther north and east. Summers are rainy and warm. In the city of Moscow, snow falls only five months each year, and rainfall averages 20 inches (50 cm) in the summer.

Farmers in some areas of southern Russia are not as fortunate regarding rainfall. Here rainfall is scarce. These areas have a steppe, or partly dry, climate. The natural vegetation in this area is largely grasses.

SECTION 1 ASSESSMENT

REVIEWING TERMS AND FACTS
1. Define the following: tundra, taiga, permafrost.
2. LOCATION How does Russia's location affect its climate?
3. REGION In what area do most of Russia's people live?

MAP STUDY ACTIVITIES
4. Look at the physical map on page 360. What oceans and seas border Russia?
5. Turn to the climate map on page 361. How would you describe the climate in the far north of Siberia?

BUILDING GEOGRAPHY SKILLS

Reading a Transportation Map

Transportation maps show how people and goods move from place to place. Lines and colors represent different types of transportation. Areas with many transportation routes through them are *accessible*, or easy to reach. These areas usually have more trade, industry, and population. When reading a transportation map, apply these steps:

Glencoe's **Skillbuilder Interactive Workbook, Level 1** provides instruction and practice in key social studies skills.

- Read the title and the map key to find the region and the kinds of transportation shown on the map.
- Find the areas that are most and least accessible.
- Determine what kinds of transportation are most important to this region.
- Use the map to conclude how transportation affects the region.

RUSSIA: Transportation Routes

Map key:
- National boundary
- Sea route (dashed)
- Railroad
- Trans-Siberian Railroad
- ★ National capital
- ● Other city
- ⚓ Seaport

Lambert Equal-Area projection

Geography Skills Practice

1. What region and kinds of transportation are shown on this map?

2. Which major railroad extends to the far eastern part of Russia?

3. Which parts of Russia are most accessible? Least accessible?

The Economy

Words to Know
- communism
- command economy
- heavy industry
- light industry
- free enterprise system
- consumer goods

Places to Locate
- Moscow
- St. Petersburg
- Siberia

Read to Learn . . .
1. what Russia's economy was like under communism.
2. how Russia's economy has changed in recent years.
3. what economic regions make up Russia.

You may not be able to tell by looking at it, but there is something special about this electronics factory in Russia. What is it? In the past, this same factory made weapons for the military. For years the communist Russian government told workers what to produce. Today Russians are making their own decisions about what to make and sell. They are entering the growing world economy.

If you travel across Russia, you will see people farming the land and working in factories. Others take resources from the earth, forests, and rivers. Russia is rich in natural and human resources, but its economy has gone through many ups and downs in this century.

Place
Today's Challenges

From 1922 to 1991, Russia was part of an even larger empire called the Soviet Union. The Soviet Union practiced **communism,** an authoritarian political system in which the government controls the economy. Private ownership of property is not allowed.

Government Controls The Soviet Union's Communist leaders created the world's largest command economy. In a **command economy,** the national government owns all land, resources, industries, farms, and railroads. The government also makes all economic decisions.

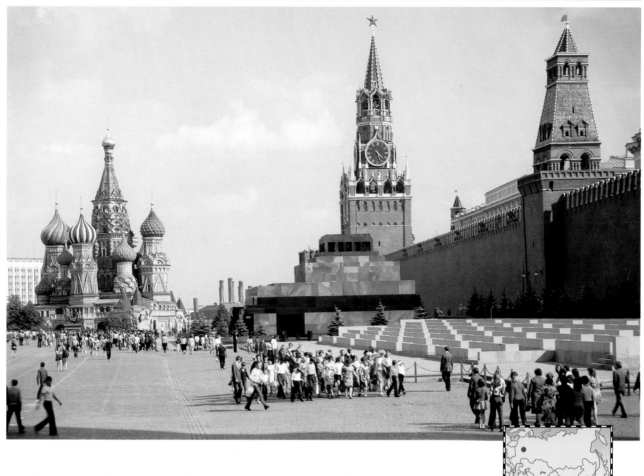

Communist leaders used five-year plans to run the Soviet economy. These plans set production goals, prices of goods, and workers' wages. Plans emphasized **heavy industry,** or the making of goods such as machinery, mining equipment, and military weapons. They gave less attention to **light industry,** or the making of such goods as clothing, shoes, furniture, and household products.

The colorful domes of St. Basil's Cathedral stand just outside the Kremlin in Moscow's Red Square.
PLACE: Why do you think the Kremlin was surrounded by a wall?

Collapse of Communism Many workers in the Soviet Union made the change from farmers to factory workers under communism. In the 1970s, however, inefficiencies in the centrally controlled communist system gradually weakened the economy. In 1985 the Soviet leader Mikhail Gorbachev (GOR•buh•CHAWF) pushed to rebuild the economy. He reduced some of the national government's rigid controls and allowed more decisions to be made at the local level. Before his plans could bring about change, however, the Soviet Union collapsed. In 1991 Russia and the other parts of the Soviet Union became independent countries.

A New Beginning Independence turned Russia's economy upside down. The Russians are making the painfully slow change to a **free enterprise system** like that of the United States. Under free enterprise, businesses are privately owned, operating for profit with little government control. Today Russia's economy is still struggling. Goods are often scarce, and prices have steadily risen. Some Russians even favor a return to government controls.

ARCTIC OCEAN

Bering Sea

Barents Sea

Baltic Sea

R U S S I A

Arctic Circle

Sea of Okhotsk

St. Petersburg

Flax

Yaroslavl

Corn

Moscow

EUROPE

Barley

Oats

Kazan

Samara

Saratov

Wheat

Magnitogorsk

Yekaterinburg

Chelyabinsk

Omsk

Wheat

Novosibirsk

Lake Baikal

ASIA

Vladivostok

Black Sea

Aral Sea

ASIA

Caspian Sea

| 0 | 250 | 500 mi. |
| 0 | 250 500 km | 60°E |

Agriculture

Ranching	Commercial farming
Nomadic herding	Subsistence farming
Hunting and gathering	Little or no activity
Forestry	Manufacturing area

Resources

Bauxite	Gold	Nickel
Coal	Iron ore	Petroleum
Copper	Lead	Tin
Fishing	Natural gas	Zinc

Lambert Equal-Area projection

MAP STUDY

Much of Russia is unsuitable for farming because of its cold climate. **REGION:** What type of agriculture is practiced in the area around Moscow?

Region
Economic Regions

Look at the map above. You see that most of Russia's industries are located west of 60°E in the European part of the country. Most farms are in this area of Russia, too. Although the country has a short growing season, its farmland is extremely productive. A dark, fertile soil spreads across part of the North European Plain into southwestern Siberia. Farmers in this area grow wheat, barley, rye, and sugar beets.

MOSCOW Russia's rich history shines in the city of Moscow located in the western part of Russia. About 800 years old, Moscow is the political, economic, and cultural center of Russia. This major industrial city produces textiles, electrical equipment, and automobiles. Moscow's factories recently have started to make more **consumer goods,** or household and electronics products.

Ivan Borisov, a Moscow teenager, enjoys greater freedom of choice than his parents or grandparents did. Ivan and his family—among Moscow's 9.3 million people—live in one of the city's many tall apartment houses. Ivan likes to take foreign visitors on a trip through the Metro, the Moscow subway that links every part of the city. His favorite stop is near Red Square in the center of Moscow.

"Chizburger," Anyone?

The familiar hamburger chain, McDonald's, has introduced the people of Moscow to the "chizburger." Russians, like Americans, are enthusiastic burger fans. Daily, more than 50,000 people pack into the Moscow McDonald's to get lunch.

St. Petersburg Northwest of Moscow lies St. Petersburg, Russia's second-largest city. Located on the Neva River near the Gulf of Finland, St. Petersburg is noted for shipbuilding. Its factories produce light machinery, textiles, and scientific and medical equipment.

St. Petersburg's 5.1 million residents take pride in their beautiful city. Built in the early 1700s, St. Petersburg spreads over about 100 islands. A network of graceful bridges and streets joins the islands.

The Volga and Urals Tucked between European Russia and Siberia lies the industrial region of the Volga River and the Ural Mountains. The Volga carries almost one-half of Russia's river traffic. It also provides water for hydroelectric power and irrigation. Both the Volga and the Urals contain large deposits of oil and natural gas. The Ural Mountains are rich in other minerals, too, such as tungsten, zinc, iron ore, and nickel.

Siberia East of the Volga and the Urals spreads Siberia, a promising economic region. Siberia has the largest supply of mineral resources in the country, including iron ore, uranium, gold, diamonds, and coal. In the Arctic region, huge deposits of oil and natural gas lie below the permafrost. About two-thirds of Siberia is covered by forests that provide lumber. In spite of this wealth in natural resources, Siberia is mostly undeveloped because of its climate and isolation. Since the late 1800s, the governments ruling Russia have built roads and railroads there to encourage development.

SECTION 2 ASSESSMENT

REVIEWING TERMS AND FACTS
1. **Define the following:** communism, command economy, heavy industry, light industry, free enterprise system, consumer goods.
2. **PLACE** Before 1991, how was the Soviet Union's economy run?
3. **REGION** What are Russia's four major economic regions?
4. **HUMAN/ENVIRONMENT INTERACTION** What region has the most promising future? Why?

MAP STUDY ACTIVITIES
5. Look at the land use map on page 366. What resources are found in Siberia? What kind of industry might locate there?

MAKING CONNECTIONS

MATH **SCIENCE** **HISTORY** **LITERATURE** **TECHNOLOGY**

A road that is 2,000 years old? It sounds unbelievable. Yet stretching 7,000 miles (11,263 km) across central Asia and Russia lies the ancient Silk Road. For about 14 centuries, this road was a vital trade route between Asia and Europe. Armies, merchants, missionaries, and adventurers from both eastern and western worlds traveled this road.

THE ROUTE Beginning in northern China about 100 B.C., the Silk Road wound its way from oasis to oasis across Asia's great deserts. To the south, always in plain view, were majestic snowcapped mountains. Beyond the deserts, travelers began the terrifying climb through the Himalayas. On the other side of these mountains, the road split. One branch continued westward toward Europe, winding through what is today Russia and the independent republics. Another branch turned south into India.

THE REASON Again and again, travelers on the Silk Road braved fierce desert sandstorms, howling Himalaya blizzards, and murderous thieves. Why? The only land route between

Asia and Europe, the Silk Road made it possible for costly Chinese goods to reach Europe. The most valuable of these goods was silk—the soft, shiny fabric that gave the road its name. Wealthy Europeans were willing to pay handsomely for this luxurious cloth.

The Silk Road

THE RESULT Heavily laden camels formed caravans that transported the silk. They also carried gemstones, perfumes, tea, fine china, and gunpowder. More importantly, travelers on the Silk Road traded ideas and customs. This cultural exchange greatly enriched the peoples of central Asia, China, India, Southwest Asia, and eventually, western Europe.

Making the Connection

1. What and where was the Silk Road?
2. What products did Silk Road travelers carry from China?

SECTION 3

The People

PREVIEW

Words to Know
- czar
- serf
- cold war
- *glasnost*
- ethnic group

Places to Locate
- Muscovy
- Union of Soviet Socialist Republics (Soviet Union)
- Commonwealth of Independent States (CIS)

Read to Learn . . .
1. what groups influenced Russia's culture.
2. how city life differs from country life in Russia.
3. what makes up Russia's culture today.

These Russian teenagers are enjoying a weekend outing in Moscow. After eating a "chizburger" at a fast-food restaurant, they will explore the city. In recent years, they and other Russians have seen two amazing changes in their country—the fall of communism and the first stirrings of democracy. Like teenagers around the world, these young people hope for a better future.

Russia and the other countries that were once part of the Soviet Union have a dramatic history. Today these countries are independent republics, trying to build democracies and a better way of life for their people.

Movement
A Dramatic Past

To understand the challenges facing Russia today, let's look back through Russia's history. As an early Russian you would have belonged to a loose union of people called Eastern Slavs who dominated the area from the 900s to the 1200s. Then Mongols swept in from central Asia in the 1200s and ruled the Slavic territories in eastern Europe for 200 years. During this time, what is now Moscow became the center of a territory called Muscovy (MUHS•kuh•vee). As a citizen in the late 1400s, you would have rejoiced when Ivan III, a prince of Muscovy, drove out the Mongols and made the territory independent.

Out With the Old

Nadia Abramov often visits the park near her family's apartment in Moscow. Sometimes she climbs on the toppled statues of former Communist leaders. The fallen statues remind her of the many changes that Russians have experienced since the breakup of the Soviet Union in 1991. Nadia is happy with most of the changes, especially those at school. She still goes to school six days a week, but she doesn't have to wear uniforms anymore. The classes on communism have been dropped, and her new history books are filled with information that was once forbidden by the former government. For the first time, she can also take religion courses if she wants to.

Strong Rulers Muscovy slowly developed into the country we know today as Russia. The Muscovite rulers extended their power and began calling themselves **czars,** or emperors. As a Muscovite, you would have feared Czar Ivan IV, who used a secret police force to keep his people under control. He also expanded Russia's territory by conquest eastward into the Volga region and Siberia.

Over the centuries the country grew as czars conquered other lands. Many non-Russian peoples came into the Russian Empire. Czars such as Peter I and Catherine II pushed the empire's borders westward and southward. They also tried to make Russia more like Europe. A new capital—St. Petersburg—was built in the early 1700s to look like a European city. If you had been a Russian noble at this time, you would have worn European clothes and spoken French instead of Russian.

The actions of the czars, however, had little effect on ordinary citizens. Most Russians were **serfs,** or laborers who were bound to the land. They were too poor to be interested in European ways and kept their Russian culture.

Toward Revolution In 1861 Czar Alexander II freed the serfs. At about the same time, Russia began to set up industries like those of other European countries. Railroads, including the famous Trans-Siberian Railroad, spread across the country. It linked Moscow in the west with Vladivostok on Russia's Pacific coast.

Russia, however, did not progress politically. The czars clung to their power and rejected democracy. Revolution brewed. In 1917 the political leaders and workers forced Czar Nicholas II to give up the throne. At the end of the year, a group of Communists led by Vladimir Ilyich Lenin came to power. They set up a Communist government and soon moved its capital to Moscow.

The Soviet Union In 1922 the Communists formed the Union of Soviet Socialist Republics, or the Soviet Union. The new country included Russia and most of the conquered territories of the old Russian Empire. During the late 1920s, Joseph Stalin became the ruler of the Soviet Union and set out to make it a great industrial power. To reach this goal, the government took control of all industry and farming. Stalin, a cruel dictator, put down any opposition to his rule. Millions of people were either killed or sent to prison labor camps.

After World War II the Soviet Union further expanded its territory and extended communism to eastern Europe. From the late 1940s to the late 1980s, the Soviet Union and the United States waged a **cold war.** They competed for world influence without actually waging war on one another.

A New Beginning In 1985 Mikhail Gorbachev came to power in the Soviet Union. In addition to economic changes, He supported a policy of **glasnost,** or openness. He wanted people to speak freely about the Soviet Union's problems. Gorbachev's efforts, however, failed to stop the collapse of the Soviet Union. Many of the non-Russian nations had long resented Russian rule and wanted independence. By late 1991 the Soviet Union had broken apart, and Russia had a new leader, Boris Yeltsin. Russia and the newly independent countries formed a loose union called the Commonwealth of Independent States (CIS).

Place
City and Country Life

The teens you read about earlier are part of Russia's 147 million people. Look at the graph below to see how Russia's population compares with that of the United States. Russian Slavs make up about 80 percent of the population, and Russian is the official language. The country, however, has hundreds of smaller **ethnic groups,** or people who have a common language, culture, and history.

City Life Nearly three-fourths of Russia's people live in cities and towns. The map on page 372 shows that a large part of Russia's population lives around Moscow. Many cities are crowded, and residents face severe housing shortages. Whole families often live in one- or two-room apartments. City residents in Russia also have to deal with other problems such as food shortages, high prices, crime, and pollution from factories. The government is trying to correct such concerns and is also working to improve medical care. When people in cities relax, they spend time with family and friends, taking walks through parks, or attending concerts, movies, and the circus.

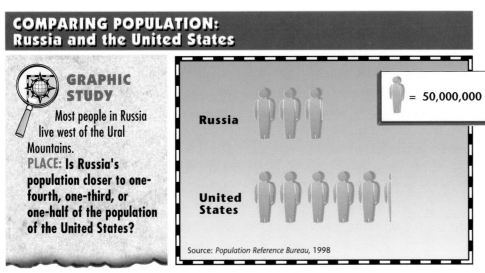

**COMPARING POPULATION:
Russia and the United States**

GRAPHIC STUDY
Most people in Russia live west of the Ural Mountains.
PLACE: Is Russia's population closer to one-fourth, one-third, or one-half of the population of the United States?

Russia

United States

= 50,000,000

Source: *Population Reference Bureau, 1998*

Country Life If you visit a village in Russia today, you will find that most people live in houses built of wood. In some rural areas, people live without heat, electricity, or plumbing. Consumer goods are scarce in the countryside, but food is more plentiful than in some cities. The quality of health care, education, and cultural activities is lower in rural areas than in urban areas. Over the years, many people have left the villages to find work in the cities.

Place
The Arts and Recreation

Russia has a rich tradition of art, music, and literature. The Russian people view their country's cultural achievements with pride. Some of their finest works of art depict religious and historical themes. Others reflect the daily lives of ordinary people.

Religion Communist rulers of the Soviet Union banned religion. They often closed houses of worship and persecuted religious people. Since the fall of communism, many Russians have returned to their religious traditions. Russians are Jews, Protestants, and Roman Catholics. Most Russians, however, follow Eastern Orthodox Christianity. Orthodox churches in Russia that have survived are excellent examples of Russian architecture. Many contain religious works of art that are hundreds of years old.

Arts and Music If you want to see Russian culture at its best, where do you go? If you enjoy dance, you might attend a ballet performed at Moscow's Bolshoi Theater. Russia has long been a world leader in ballet.

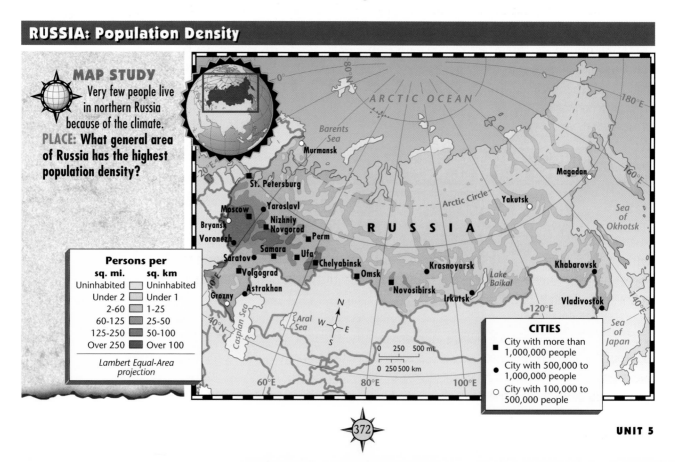

RUSSIA: Population Density

MAP STUDY
Very few people live in northern Russia because of the climate.
PLACE: What general area of Russia has the highest population density?

Persons per	
sq. mi.	**sq. km**
Uninhabited ☐	Uninhabited
Under 2 ☐	Under 1
2-60 ☐	1-25
60-125 ☐	25-50
125-250 ☐	50-100
Over 250 ☐	Over 100

Lambert Equal-Area projection

CITIES
■ City with more than 1,000,000 people
● City with 500,000 to 1,000,000 people
○ City with 100,000 to 500,000 people

If you enjoy painting, you might stroll through the Hermitage, St. Petersburg's most famous museum. Works of noted Russian as well as western European painters hang in the Hermitage. In the early 1900s, Russia led the modern art movement. Two of the most famous Russian-born painters of this movement are Kazimir Malevich and Wassily Kandinsky.

Perhaps you prefer music. Classical music fills concert halls throughout Russia. Many of the world's greatest composers were Russian. They include Peter Tchaikovsky and Nikolay Rimsky-Korsakov. You may be familiar with Tchaikovsky's *Nutcracker Suite* and his *1812 Overture.*

The 1800s and 1900s saw a great flowering of Russian literature. Among the best Russian writers of the nineteenth century were Alexander Pushkin, Leo Tolstoy, and Fyodor Dostoyevsky. Their works vividly describe the lives of nobles, merchants, serfs, and city workers. In this century, the leading Russian writers include Maxim Gorky and Alexander Solzhenitsyn. They and other modern writers have discussed the lack of individual freedom in Russia and the hopes for a better society.

Celebrations Russians enjoy small family get-togethers as well as national celebrations. New Year's Eve is the most festive nonreligious holiday for the Russian people. On this day children decorate a fir tree and exchange presents with their families. Another important holiday is May Day. In parades and speeches, May Day celebrates Russian workers and their contributions to their country.

Food If you have dinner with a Russian family, you might begin with a big bowl of *borsch,* a soup made from beets, or *shchi,* a soup made from cabbage. Next you might be served meat turnovers called *pirozhki.* For the main course, you would have meat, poultry, or fish with boiled potatoes. If you were having a

The wooden houses in rural Russia *(left)* have much more room than the cramped apartment buildings in Russia's cities *(right).*
PLACE: About how many of Russia's people live in cities?

Ballet Practice

Dedicated young dancers practice at a ballet school in St. Petersburg.
LOCATION: What famous ballet theater is located in Moscow?

special holiday dinner, you might have caviar, or fish eggs, fresh from the Caspian Sea.

Sports Russians love soccer, tennis, and ice hockey. On the lakes and in the mountains, you will find Russians skiing, hiking, camping, mountain climbing, and hunting. Reindeer races and dog-team competitions are popular sports in the cold lands of Siberia. And if you watch the Olympics, you know that Russians are major competitors in the games.

SECTION 3 ASSESSMENT

REVIEWING TERMS AND FACTS
1. Define the following: czar, serf, cold war, *glasnost,* ethnic group.
2. PLACE What was life like for most Russians under the czars?
3. PLACE How does city life differ from country life in Russia?
4. HUMAN/ENVIRONMENT INTERACTION How would you compare the practice of religion in Russia before and after 1991?

MAP STUDY ACTIVITIES
5. Turn to the population density map on page 372. Which region of Russia is sparsely populated? Why is this so?
6. Look again at the same map. About how many people live in Murmansk?

Important Things to Know About Russia

SECTION 1 THE LAND

- Russia is the largest country in the world in area.
- Russia extends across both Europe and Asia.
- Russia is a vast lowland divided or surrounded by mountains.
- Inland waterways help connect Russia's widespread regions.
- Much of Russia's climate is subarctic or humid continental.

SECTION 2 THE ECONOMY

- Russia's economy is moving from government control to a free enterprise system.
- Russia's leading industrial centers are located in Moscow, St. Petersburg, the Volga and the Urals, and Siberia.
- Oil and gas are important resources in Russia.
- Siberia, the Asian part of Russia, has vast timber resources.

SECTION 3 THE PEOPLE

- Russia was the center of a powerful empire under rulers known as czars.
- A revolution in 1917 overthrew the czars; later a communist empire called the Union of Soviet Socialist Republics, or Soviet Union, was established.
- Russia and other parts of the Soviet Union have become independent republics since the fall of communism in the early 1990s.
- Most Russians live in urban areas in the European part of Russia.
- Russia has a rich tradition of art, music, literature, and dance.

St. Petersburg, Russia ▶

Chapter 14 Assessment and Activities

REVIEWING KEY TERMS

Match the numbered terms in Set A with their lettered definitions in Set B.

A

1. taiga
2. command economy
3. czar
4. heavy industry
5. tundra
6. serf
7. permafrost
8. light industry
9. free enterprise system

B

A. permanent layer of frozen soil
B. Russian ruler
C. economy planned and directed by the communist government
D. production of household products
E. privately owned businesses with little government control
F. cold, treeless plain
G. farmers bound to the land
H. production of machinery, mining equipment, and military weapons
I. vast forest area of Siberia

REVIEWING THE MAIN IDEAS

Mental Mapping Activity

Draw a freehand map of Russia. Label the following:
- Black Sea
- Volga River
- Moscow
- Caspian Sea
- Central Siberian Plateau
- St. Petersburg

Section 1

1. REGION What is the world's largest region of flat land?
2. REGION What Russian lake is the deepest in the world?

Section 2

3. HUMAN/ENVIRONMENT INTERACTION What changes have come to Russia's economy since the fall of communism?
4. HUMAN/ENVIRONMENT INTERACTION Why is the Volga River important to Russia?

Section 3

5. MOVEMENT What railroad links Moscow with Russia's eastern coast?
6. PLACE What effect did Mikhail Gorbachev's changes have on the Soviet Union?

CRITICAL THINKING ACTIVITIES

1. **Determining Cause and Effect** How do you think climate affects the way Russians make a living?
2. **Evaluating Information** What problems did Russia face after becoming independent in the early 1990s?

CONNECTIONS TO WORLD HISTORY

Cooperative Learning Activity Work in groups to plan a trip to one of the following areas to learn more about the history and people of the area: (1) the Volga River; (2) the Ural Mountains; (3) Lake Baikal; or (4) an area of your choice. Each member of the group will do one of the following: (a) locate historic places to visit; (b) learn about the different people who live in the region; or (c) make a list of important historical events that have happened in the area. Combine your findings in a travel information packet.

GeoJournal Writing Activity

Imagine you are a friend of Ivan Borisov. He has asked you to join his family on a trip to Siberia. Write about your visit to this region of Russia. You may use the maps in your text or a reference book to help you.

TECHNOLOGY ACTIVITY

Using a Computerized Card Catalog Use a computerized card catalog to locate sources about the history of Russian czars. Create a genealogy chart of the Romanov dynasty. Include a short report explaining why the empire of the czars ended and how it affected Russian culture. Share your genealogy chart and summary with the class.

PLACE LOCATION ACTIVITY: RUSSIA

Match the letters on the map with the places and physical features of Russia. Write your answers on a separate sheet of paper.

1. Vladivostok
2. West Siberian Plain
3. Ural Mountains
4. Caspian Sea
5. Lena River
6. Kamchatka Peninsula
7. Lake Baikal
8. Caucasus Mountains
9. Moscow
10. Sea of Okhotsk

ACTIVITY

From the classroom of
Dana Moseley,
Carl Stuart Middle School,
Conway, Arkansas

MAPMAKING: Dough It!

Background

Russia can be divided into five major geographic regions: the North European Plain, the West Siberian Plain, the Central Siberian Plateau, the East Siberian Uplands, and the lowland region east of the Caspian Sea. In this activity, you will make a salt-dough relief map of these regions.

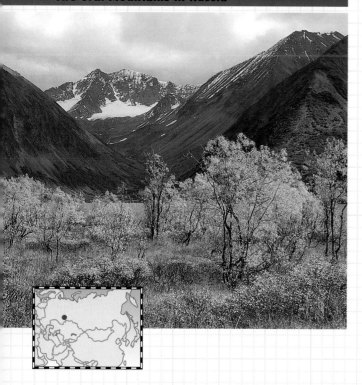

The Ural Mountains in Russia

Verkhoyansk is a small Russian town in northeast Siberia. It has one of the world's most extreme climates. In January, the coldest month, the average temperature plunges to -58.2°F.

This is one group's salt-dough map.

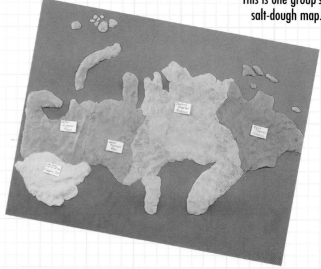

Materials

- 1 poster board
- outline map of Russia
- physical map of Russia
- salt dough (see recipe on page 379)
- glue
- food coloring

378

What To Do

A. Draw an outline map of Russia onto the poster board.

B. Mix the salt dough using this recipe:
- *1 cup flour*
- *1/2 cup salt*
- *1 cup water*
- *1 tablespoon vegetable oil*
- *2 teaspoons cream of tartar*

Heat all ingredients in a saucepan over medium heat, stirring about 4 minutes or until mixture forms a ball. Remove from saucepan and let dough cool on counter for 5 minutes. Knead dough about 1 minute or until it is smooth and blended. Let cool completely before using on map.

C. Separate the dough into five sections and use the food coloring to make each region a different color—brown, green, red, yellow, and blue.

D. Press the colored salt dough into the appropriate places on your outline map of Russia. Make sure you recreate the correct geographic landforms and regions.

E. Label each region.

Lab Activity Report

1. Which region covers the greatest area?

2. Which region has the highest relief overall?

3. Describe the relief of each region.

4. **Drawing Conclusions**
What adjustments in your life would you have to make if you lived in each region?

Go A Step Further!

Activity
Research and create a time line depicting Russia's history. Include important people, places, and events. Illustrate your time line with small, colorful pictures that focus on important events in Russia's history.

Cultural HERITAGE:

RUSSIA AND THE INDEPENDENT REPUBLICS

RELIGIOUS ART ▶ ▶ ▶ ▶

Icons hang on the walls of many homes and churches in Russia and the independent republics. Icons are paintings of Christian religious figures on wood panels. Many are hundreds of years old.

◀ ◀ ◀ ◀ MUSIC

Folk music is very popular in all the independent republics, especially Ukraine. This Ukrainian student plays the *bandura,* a multistringed instrument that is plucked like a guitar. Her brightly embroidered blouse and skirt are traditional Ukrainian clothing.

PAINTING ▶ ▶ ▶ ▶

Kazimir Malevich was one of the first painters to introduce modern art to Russia. This painting from the early 1900s does not show real objects. Instead Malevich used shapes and pure colors on plain backgrounds to represent objects.

◄ ◄ ◄ ◄ WEAVING

The people of Uzbekistan take great pride in their beautiful wool carpets and rugs. Each year, factories in the area weave more than 3 million square miles (7.9 million sq. km) of carpet. The bright colors and bold patterns of the rugs reflect the influence of Islamic ancestors.

ARCHITECTURE ▶ ▶ ▶ ▶

Churches, mosques, and synagogues reflect the many types of architecture found in Russia and the independent republics. This old church with a round tower in Msteka, Georgia, is made of stone. Others have elaborate onion-shaped domes and colorful mosaics.

FABERGÉ EGG ▲ ▲ ▲ ▲

Russia's most famous jeweler, Carl Fabergé, designed this beautiful egg for a Russian czar. He crafted a series of these elaborate eggs from gold, silver, enamel, and precious stones.

APPRECIATING CULTURE

1. Russia and the independent republics have a rich and varied history. How has some of that history been recorded in artwork from this area?

2. Which type of art shown here most appeals to you? Why?

The Independent Republics

EUROPE

BELARUS
Minsk

Gomel
Lvov • Kiev

UKRAINE
Kharkov

MOLDOVA
Chisinau
Dnepropetrovsk

Odessa
Donetsk

Sevastopol

Black Sea

GEORGIA

Tbilisi

Yerevan
Baku

ARMENIA

Mediterranean
Sea

AZERBAIJAN

Ashkhabad

TURKMENISTAN

RUSSIA

Astana

Karaganda

KAZAKHSTAN

Aral
Sea

Lake
Balkhash

Almaty

Bishkek
KYRGYZSTAN

UZBEKISTAN
Tashkent

Samarkand

Dushanbe

TAJIKISTAN

Caspian Sea

ASIA

	National boundary
⊛	National capital
•	Other city

Lambert Equal-Area projection

0   250   500 mi.
0   250 500 km

MAP STUDY ACTIVITY

As you read Chapter 15, you will learn about the independent republics that, like Russia, were once part of the former Soviet Union.

1. How many independent republics are there?

2. What republics share a border with Russia?

PREVIEW

Words to Know
- steppe

Places to Locate
- Ukraine
- Black Sea
- Dnieper River
- Dniester River
- Crimean Peninsula
- Kiev
- Odessa
- Donets Basin

Read to Learn . . .
1. what landforms are found in Ukraine.
2. why Ukraine is known as the breadbasket of Europe.
3. what challenges Ukraine faces as an independent country.

The sputtering of this tractor and the "whoosh" of harvested wheat echo across the broad plains of Ukraine. Farmers grow a variety of grains in Ukraine's rich soil and ship them abroad to foreign markets. Because of the abundance of its grain harvests, Ukraine has been called the breadbasket of Europe.

Ukraine and many of its neighbors were once part of the Soviet Union. Since the breakup of the Soviet Union in 1991, they have been independent republics. To help their economies grow, these new countries and Russia have formed the Commonwealth of Independent States (CIS).

Human/Environment Interaction

Land, Climate, Economy

Ukraine—a word meaning "frontier" in a Slavic language—was named for its location. It once marked the far western edge of the Russian empire. With 223,687 square miles (579,349 sq. km), Ukraine is about the size of Texas.

Landforms Find Ukraine on the map on page 384. Lowlands dotted with farms and forests spread across the north. Eastern highlands stretch toward the Black Sea. A coastal plain curves along the Black Sea. From the plain, a landmass juts into the water. This landmass, the Crimean Peninsula, is one of the Black Sea's most scenic areas.

MAP STUDY
All of the independent republics are located in the western half of what once was the Soviet Union.

LOCATION: On what sea is Ukraine located?

ELEVATIONS

Feet	Meters
10,000	3,000
5,000	1,500
2,000	600
1,000	300
0	0

— National boundary
⬚ Desert
▲ Mountain peak

Lambert Equal-Area projection

Vast treeless plains called **steppes** sweep through the center of Ukraine. Rich, fertile soil and plentiful rainfall make these steppes the most productive farmland in the region. Through the steppes to the Black Sea flows Ukraine's important river—the Dnieper (NEE•puhr). The Dniester (NEES•tuhr) also flows through the area. These rivers and other waterways link Ukraine's industrial areas with the Black Sea and world markets. The city of Odessa is Ukraine's major port.

The Climate Most of Ukraine has a humid continental climate of cold winters and warm summers. Rainfall is more plentiful in the northern and central parts of the country than in the south. On the Crimean Peninsula, mountains shield the Black Sea coast from the cold northern winds.

The Economy Under Soviet rule, what Ukraine produced was controlled by the government. Today Ukraine is changing its economy to one based on free enterprise. Farming and industry are the mainstays of Ukraine's economy. Farmers harvest grains, potatoes, sugar beets, and dairy products.

Ukraine is more than a breadbasket, however. The country is rich in coal, iron ore, manganese, potash, and natural gas. The Donets Basin in eastern Ukraine contains one of the largest coal deposits in the world. It also is the country's major industrial area. A gigantic dam on the Dnieper River supplies electricity to the region's factories.

Place
People

Ukraine has a population of about 50 million. About 75 percent of the people—including Anna Lyashenko, a 13-year-old citizen of Ukraine's capital—are ethnic Ukrainians. They have their own language and culture. The rest of Ukraine's population are mostly Russian. Eastern Orthodox Christianity is the country's main religion.

From Past to Present About two-thirds of Ukraine's people live in urban areas. Kiev (KEE•EHF), the capital and largest city, has about 2.8 million people. Located on the Dnieper River, Kiev is a transportation, industrial, and cultural center. In history class, Anna has learned that, from A.D. 900 to the 1200s, Kiev was the center of a group of powerful Slavic city-states. In past centuries, outsiders such as the Poles and the Russians ruled Anna's country, and Ukrainians suffered. Independence, Anna admits, has not solved all problems. Ukraine's economy is shaky. Many people have lost their jobs as factories change ways of producing goods. Prices are high in the stores, and some goods are scarce. In addition, the growth of heavy industry during the years of Soviet rule has seriously harmed Ukraine's environment. Factory smoke and other wastes have polluted the air and water.

Ukrainian and Russian Proverbs

- Where the road is straight, don't look for a short cut.

- A bad peace is better than a good war.

- There is plenty of sound in an empty barrel.

- A near neighbor is better than a distant relative.

- When the Czar has a cold, all Russia coughs.

Source: *The Prentice-Hall Encyclopedia of World Proverbs*

 GRAPHIC STUDY
A proverb is a saying that describes a truth.
HUMAN/ENVIRONMENT INTERACTION: On this chart, which proverb might be rewritten as "don't take the easy way out"?

Culture and Celebrations The people of Ukraine take pride in a rich cultural heritage. Ukrainians are famous for their folktales and proverbs. The chart above lists several favorite proverbs of Ukraine and Russia.

During the Easter season, Ukrainian families observe the ancient tradition of decorating eggs with colorful designs. Folk music is popular, and many Ukrainian musicians perform on a stringed instrument called the *bandura*. In a popular dance—the *hopak*—male dancers make astounding acrobatic leaps!

SECTION 1 ASSESSMENT

REVIEWING TERMS AND FACTS
1. Define the following: steppe.
2. PLACE How does the climate of Ukraine differ from north to south?
3. HUMAN/ENVIRONMENT INTERACTION How is the Donets Basin important to Ukraine's industrial growth?

 MAP STUDY ACTIVITIES
4. Turn to the physical map on page 384. What major body of water lies south of Ukraine?

BUILDING GEOGRAPHY SKILLS

Reading a Historical Map

Suppose you tried to draw a map of your town as it looked 100 years ago. You would not include roads or bridges as they are today. You certainly wouldn't find any airports. Perhaps there was no town at all!

A historical map shows the cultural and political features of an area in an earlier period. Physical features of a landscape may stay much the same. Cultural features, however, change dramatically over time. To read a historical map, apply these steps:

- Read the title to identify the region and time period.
- Use the key to locate political units.
- Compare the map with a recent physical map to observe changes.
- Compare the map with a recent political map to observe changes.

Glencoe's **Skillbuilder Interactive Workbook, Level 1** provides instruction and practice in key social studies skills.

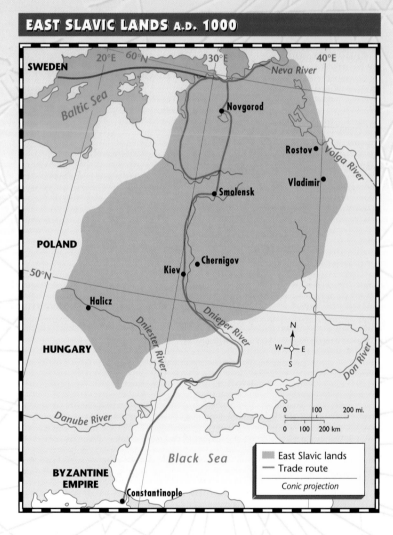

EAST SLAVIC LANDS A.D. 1000

SWEDEN
20°E · 60°N · 30°E · 40°E
Neva River
Baltic Sea
Novgorod
Rostov · Volga River
Vladimir
Smolensk
POLAND
50°N
Chernigov
Kiev
Halicz
Dniester River · Dnieper River
HUNGARY
Don River
Danube River
Black Sea
BYZANTINE EMPIRE
Constantinople

0   100   200 mi.
0   100   200 km

■ East Slavic lands
— Trade route
Conic projection

Geography Skills Practice

1. What region and time period are shown in this map?

2. Near what rivers did city-states develop?

3. What present-day independent republics were once part of the East Slavic lands?

Belarus and Moldova

Words to Know
- nature preserve

Places to Locate
- Belarus
- Minsk
- Moldova
- Chisinau

Read to Learn . . .
1. where Belarus and Moldova are located.
2. what Belarus and Moldova produce.
3. what groups of people live in Belarus and Moldova.

What makes this farmer in Belarus so happy? Is it a good crop of potatoes, flax, or wheat? Or is he feeling successful because he tends his own land? While most rural families in Belarus work on government-owned farms, many have been encouraged to run their own farms and businesses.

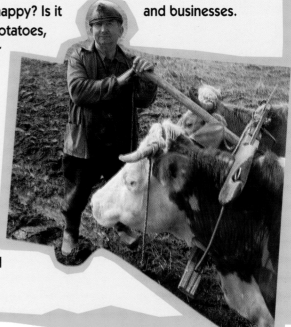

Belarus (BEE•luh•ROOS) lies north of Ukraine, and the country of Moldova (mahl•DOH•vuh) lies south. Like Ukraine, Belarus and Moldova—both land-locked countries—were once part of the Soviet Union. Today they are independent but have joined other former Soviet republics in the CIS.

Place
Belarus

Belarus covers 80,108 square miles (207,480 sq. km)—roughly the area of the state of Kansas. The people of Belarus, or Belarusians, are Slavs who are closely related to the Ukrainians and Russians. They also have close cultural ties to Poland, another neighboring Slavic country.

The Land and Climate Dense green undergrowth, towering trees, and wide marshes mark an area Belarus and Poland also share—Belovezha (BEHL•oh•VYEH•zah) Forest. This unique stretch of land is a famous **nature preserve,** or land set aside by the government to protect plants and wildlife. Rare European bison, similar to the American buffalo, graze in the woods and meadows of the forest. Low flatlands cover the rest of Belarus in the north. Marshes, swamps, and forests are found in the south.

The map below shows that Belarus has a humid continental climate with cold winters and warm summers. The temperature averages about 22°F (-6°C) in January, the coldest month. In July—the hottest month—the temperature averages about 65°F (18°C).

The Economy Most Belarusians earn their livings as factory workers and farmers. They also work in service industries. Factory workers in Belarus make trucks, tractors, engineering equipment, and consumer goods such as television sets and refrigerators. The country's farmers produce barley, flax, potatoes, rye, sugar beets, dairy products, and livestock. Forests supply wood products that include furniture, matches, and paper goods.

The People Belarus's 10.2 million people are mostly Slavs who are proud of their separate language and culture. Smaller ethnic groups in the country include Russians, Ukrainians, and Poles. Two-thirds of the population live in cities. Minsk, the capital and largest city, has a population of 1.8 million. Belarus became independent in 1991. Minsk was chosen as the headquarters of the CIS.

Nina Muzychenko lives in Neglyubka—a village known for its textiles woven in elaborate patterns. Like most Belarusians, Nina follows the Eastern Orthodox Christian religion. Her family lives in a wooden home decorated with roof carvings.

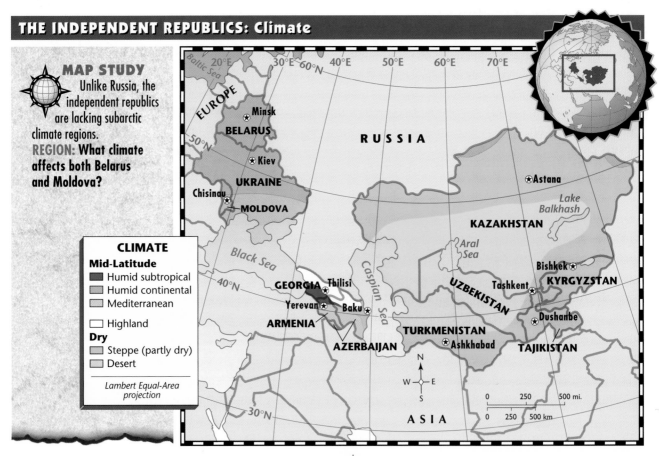

THE INDEPENDENT REPUBLICS: Climate

MAP STUDY
Unlike Russia, the independent republics are lacking subarctic climate regions.
REGION: What climate affects both Belarus and Moldova?

CLIMATE
Mid-Latitude
- Humid subtropical
- Humid continental
- Mediterranean
- Highland

Dry
- Steppe (partly dry)
- Desert

Lambert Equal-Area projection

Place
Moldova

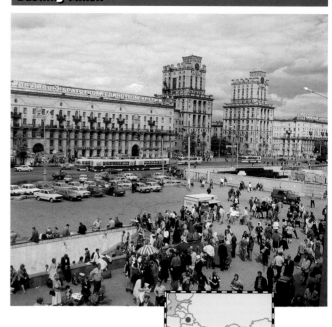

A small country of 12,730 square miles (32,971 sq. km), landlocked Moldova broke away from the Soviet Union and became independent in 1991. Most of northern and central Moldova is hilly. Many rivers and streams flow through the rolling countryside. The river valleys of Moldova boast dark, fertile soil. Grassy plains sweep across much of the country's southern area. The map on page 388 shows you that northern Moldova has a humid continental climate of long, cold winters and short, hot summers. The southern part of the country has a steppe climate of cold, snowy winters and hot, dry summers.

Human/Environment Interaction Moldova relies on farming as its major economic activity. Farmers pluck grapes to make the country's popular wines. On the plains of the south, farmers harvest corn and wheat. In addition to farming, Moldova's light industries produce a variety of consumer and household goods. Like the other countries of the former Soviet Union, however, Moldova is struggling to move from a government-run economy to a privately owned economy with an expanded service sector.

Minsk, the capital of Belarus, is an important center of science, industry, and culture.
PLACE: In what year did Moldova and Belarus gain their independence from the Soviet Union?

The population of Moldova totals about 4.2 million people. It is one of the most densely populated countries in this region. Most of Moldova's people trace their language and culture to neighboring Romania. The rest of Moldova's population are Ukrainians, Russians, and Turks. Such diverse ethnic and national backgrounds often lead to conflict.

Moldova's capital and largest city is Chisinau (KEE•shih•NOW). More than half of Moldova's people, however, live in the countryside. Much of Moldova's culture is based on rural ways of life. Villagers celebrate special occasions with folk music and good food. Moldovan feasts include lamb, cornmeal pudding, and cheese made from goat's milk.

SECTION 2 ASSESSMENT

REVIEWING TERMS AND FACTS
1. Define the following: nature preserve.
2. PLACE Why is the Belovezha Forest unique?
3. PLACE How do the economies of Belarus and Moldova differ?

MAP STUDY ACTIVITIES
4. Turn to the map on page 388. What republics share a border with Moldova?
5. Look at the map on page 388. In what climate region is the city of Minsk?

MAKING CONNECTIONS

In this excerpt from *The First Song,* a Russian boy tells about moving to a new home. He and his family are leaving Mariopol on the Azov Sea to live in the port city of Odessa on the Black Sea.

I had spent most of my life here in Mariopol. In the summer, I would almost live on the beach, baking myself on the hot light-yellow sand, and when I was overcome with the heat, I would throw myself into the green transparent water of the Azov Sea, swim and dive. Here, also, [about two-thirds of a mile] from the city, on the Kalka—a river associated with many legends about the fighting between the Russians and the invading Mongols, centuries ago—we boys would often make our way across in an old flat-bottomed rowboat. Tall reeds grew thickly on the opposite shore—this was almost the beginning of the Don Cossack Region. On this spot we had made a momentous decision: to explore this land of the Cossacks for buried Tartar [Mongol] treasure, hoping to find a cauldron of gold, a trunkful of daggers, and a chestful of ornamented saddles and harness. Yes, I was leaving behind me a great deal, and my spirit was heavy.

. . . We soon came to the end of the Azov Sea and entered the Kerchinsky Strait, and after passing one more floating beacon, we were on the Black Sea. But I experienced a

Port of Odessa

real disappointment now—this sea was not at all black. And no one was able to explain why it was called black. I thought even the Azov was darker. However, when I found out that the Black Sea was bigger and deeper, and that its water was bitter and salty and never froze over, while the water of the Azov Sea was sweet and fresh and froze over for several months in the year, I unwillingly felt respect for its vastness and depth.

From *The First Song* by Semyon E. Rosenfeld, in *A Harvest of Russian Children's Literature,* University of California Press, 1967. Reprinted by permission of the Estate of Miriam Morton.

Making the Connection   ▼ ▲

1. What activities with friends was this boy leaving behind?
2. How is the Black Sea different from the Azov Sea?

The Caucasus Republics

Words to Know
- fault
- food processing
- ethnic group

Places to Locate
- Caucasus Mountains
- Armenia
- Yerevan
- Georgia
- Tbilisi
- Azerbaijan

Read to Learn . . .
1. what major landform is found in the Caucasus republics.
2. what farm products are grown in this region.
3. how people live in the republics of the Caucasus.

Imagine living alongside a mountain range that seems to touch the sky! You can enjoy such a view in the country of Armenia. There snow-topped peaks form part of an enormous chain of mountains called the Caucasus, which stretches about 750 miles (1,210 km) between the Black and Caspian seas.

Armenia shares the Caucasus Mountains with two neighboring countries: Georgia and Azerbaijan (A•zuhr•BY•JAHN). Together these three lands are known as the Caucasus republics. All of them lie south of Russia. Once part of the Soviet Union, they are now independent countries.

Place
Armenia

Tiny landlocked Armenia takes pride in a history that reaches back to the ancient world. The map on page 382 shows that today Armenia is without a coastline. Centuries ago—as early as 800 B.C.—Armenia ruled a large empire that reached from the Caspian Sea to the Mediterranean Sea.

Rugged Land Most of Armenia is a rugged plateau of ridges, narrow valleys, and lakes. Formed millions of years ago by volcanic eruptions, this plateau today sits across many **faults,** or openings in the earth's crust. What occurs near faults? If you guessed earthquakes, you are correct. Earthquakes occur quite frequently in Armenia. In 1988 a severe quake shook the country, killing thousands of people and destroying many villages and towns.

The Economy How do people in Armenia earn a living? In years past, many Armenians left their own country to work in the oil fields of neighboring Azerbaijan. Today they work in their own factories, making chemicals, electronic goods, machinery, and textiles. Armenia's miners take copper, gold, lead, and zinc out of the earth. Farmers—although few in number—grow wheat, barley, grapes, and other fruits in the hot, dry climate of the valleys.

Overlooking Tbilisi, Georgia

The ruins of an ancient castle and fort stand guard over the Georgian capital of Tbilisi. PLACE: Why is Georgia popular with tourists?

The People Armenia's 3.8 million people are mostly ethnic Armenians who share a unique language, culture, and the Christian religion. In recent centuries Turkey and Russia ruled Armenia. The Armenians suffered under foreign rule, and many settled in other countries.

During the years of foreign rule, the Armenians protected their culture. They now value their newly won independence. Today about 70 percent of Armenia's people live in urban areas. Yerevan (YEHR•uh•VAHN), the capital, has broad streets, attractive fountains, and colorful buildings made of volcanic stone. Founded in 782 B.C., Yerevan is one of the ancient cities of the world.

Victor Basmajian is a teenager who lives in Yerevan. Like most Armenians, Victor and his family share close ties and like to entertain friends at home. Victor enjoys foods such as shish kebab, or meat and vegetables cooked on an iron skewer, and cabbage leaves stuffed with rice and meat. He also likes to play chess and a board game called backgammon.

Place
Georgia

A Georgian poet once said, "Three divine gifts have been bestowed on us by our ancestors: language, homeland, faith." The homeland of Georgia, as you can see on the map on page 384, lies north of Armenia. Georgia's west coast touches the Black Sea.

Mountains and Highlands Sandwiched between two mountain ranges, Georgia is a rugged land said to have been named for St. George, a Christian saint. Fertile mountain valleys and lowlands along the Black Sea coast are home to most of Georgia's people.

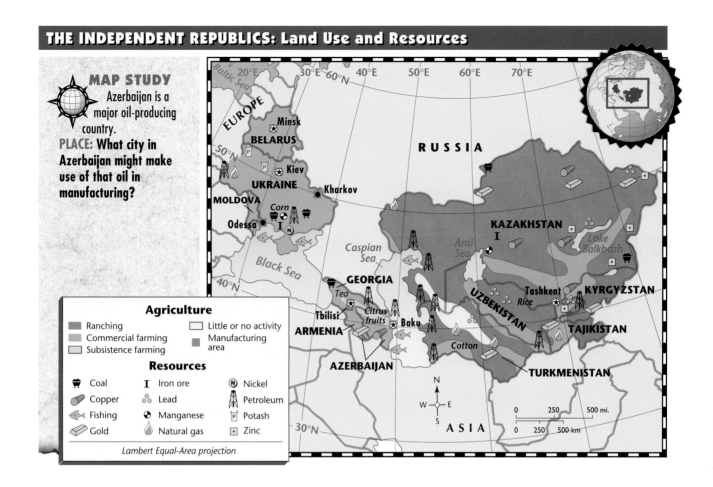

MAP STUDY
Azerbaijan is a major oil-producing country.
PLACE: What city in Azerbaijan might make use of that oil in manufacturing?

Agriculture
- Ranching
- Commercial farming
- Subsistence farming
- Little or no activity
- Manufacturing area

Resources
- Coal
- Copper
- Fishing
- Gold
- I Iron ore
- Lead
- Manganese
- Natural gas
- N Nickel
- Petroleum
- Potash
- Zinc

Lambert Equal-Area projection

Farms and Industries The map above shows you that farming ranks as Georgia's major economic activity. What would you grow if you were a Georgian farmer? You would probably harvest citrus fruits, tea, grapes, or wheat.

Georgia's major industries are wine making and **food processing,** or the preparing of foods as products for sale. Another leading industry is tourism. Resorts along the mild, scenic Black Sea coast draw thousands of visitors each year.

The People About 70 percent of Georgia's 5.4 million people are ethnic Georgians who are proud of their language, unique alphabet, and Christian heritage. The rest of Georgia's people belong to a number of other **ethnic groups**, or people having a common language, culture, and history. Since independence in 1991, conflict has broken out between Georgians and other ethnic groups. These groups want to separate from Georgia and create their own countries. Georgia first rejected membership in the Commonwealth of Independent States, but later joined in 1993.

More than half of Georgia's people live in cities and towns. Tbilisi (tuh•BEE•luh•see), the capital and largest city, prizes its warm mineral springs and scenic location. Georgians are known for their business skills, love of festivals, and friendliness to foreign visitors. They also maintain close family ties. Popular Georgian foods at family gatherings include shish kebab, pressed fried chicken, cheese, olives, and fruit.

An Azerbaijani family prepares vegetables for an outdoor lunch.
PLACE: What is Azerbaijan's most important natural resource?

Place
Azerbaijan

Also bordering Armenia is Azerbaijan, a country about the size of the state of Maine. It lies on the Caspian Sea. A narrow piece of Azerbaijan is separated from the rest of the country by Armenia. Since winning independence in 1991, Azerbaijan and Armenia have battled for control of territory and people.

The Land and Climate Like Armenia and Georgia, Azerbaijan is a mountainous country. The Caucasus ranges, having a highland climate, spread through the northern and western parts of Azerbaijan. A Mediterranean climate runs along the Caspian Sea. A dry coastal plain stretches to the north. Most of Azerbaijan is partly dry, with hot summers and mild winters.

The Economy Azerbaijan is largely agricultural. The country's farmers grow cotton, wheat, rice, fruits, and tobacco. Yet, along the shore of the Caspian Sea, countless oil-drilling rigs rise above the water. As you can see on the map on page 393, petroleum, lumber, and gold are Azerbaijan's main natural resources.

The People The 7.7 million people of Azerbaijan are mostly Azeris, a people distantly related to the people of Turkey in Southwest Asia. Armenians and Russians make up a small part of the population. The major faith of Azerbaijan is the religion of Islam.

About 55 percent of Azerbaijan's people live in cities. Baku (bah•KOO), the capital and largest city, has a population of 1.8 million. Founded more than 1,000 years ago, Baku got its name from Persian words meaning "windy town." Baku lies in one of the world's major oil-producing areas.

SECTION 3 ASSESSMENT

REVIEWING TERMS AND FACTS
1. Define the following: fault, food processing, ethnic group.
2. REGION What two bodies of water lie on either side of Armenia, Georgia, and Azerbaijan?
3. PLACE What kind of landscape is found in Armenia?
4. PLACE What is Azerbaijan's major religion?

MAP STUDY ACTIVITIES
5. Look at the land use map on page 393. What is Georgia's major economic activity?

SECTION 4

The Central Asian Republics

PREVIEW

Words to Know
- nomad
- oasis

Places to Locate
- Kazakhstan
- Astana
- Kyrgyzstan
- Bishkek
- Uzbekistan
- Tashkent
- Tajikistan
- Dushanbe
- Turkmenistan
- Ashkhabad
- Aral Sea
- Kara Kum

Read to Learn . . .
1. what landforms and climates are found in the Central Asian republics.
2. how people earn a living in these republics.
3. how cultures here blend traditions with modern ways.

Have you ever bargained for goods at a market? This seller displays tomatoes and dill at a market in Almaty, a city in Kazakhstan. Taking its first steps toward capitalism, the country is building a free market economy. Many people in Kazakhstan's cities and towns now own small businesses.

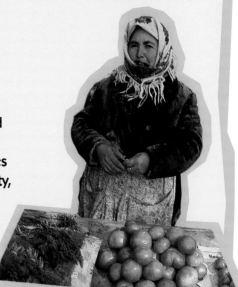

The Central Asian republics include Kazakhstan (KA•zak•STAN), Kyrgyzstan (KIHR•gih•STAN), Tajikistan (tah•JIH•kih•STAN), Turkmenistan (turk•MEH•nuh•STAN), and Uzbekistan (uz•BEH•kih•STAN). Reaching from east of the Caspian Sea to the borders of China, these republics cover an immense area. Once part of the Soviet Union, these countries became independent in 1991.

Place

Kazakhstan

Kazakhstan is a large country covering 1,031,170 square miles (2,670,730 sq. km). About one-third the size of the United States, this country lies south of Russia in central Asia.

A Variety of Landscapes Kazakhstan has lowlands, steppes, deserts, and mountains. The map on page 384 shows you that the Tian Shan (tee•AHN SHAHN) mountain range extends through the eastern part of Kazakhstan. Major rivers, such as the Irtysh (ihr•TISH), provide water to farms in dry areas.

Kazakhstan as a whole receives very little rainfall. Its people endure very cold winters and long, hot summers. Wheat farming and sheep raising are the country's major economic activities. Kazakhstan is also rich in minerals such as coal and oil. Some 9 billion barrels of oil may lie beneath its soil. The map on page 393 shows natural resources of Kazakhstan. The government recently opened its border with China, hoping to increase trade with Asia.

The People Many Kazakhs and other people of the region trace their ancestry to the Mongols. Kazakhs make up about 40 percent of Kazakhstan's population. Most follow Islam and live in rural areas. Russians, who form the second-largest group, live in the major cities. In 1998 the Kazakh government moved the country's capital from Almaty in the south to Astana in the north.

Kazakh culture is rich in folk songs and legends. At one time Kazakhs were **nomads,** or people who moved with their flocks in search of pasture. Today Kazakhs live in rural houses or city apartments.

Place

Kyrgyzstan

The country of Kyrgyzstan—one of the most southern republics—lies southeast of Kazakhstan. Kyrgyzstan's 74,054 square miles (191,800 sq. km) make it about the size of the state of Minnesota.

THE INDEPENDENT REPUBLICS: Population Density

MAP STUDY About two-thirds of the people in Ukraine live in cities.

PLACE: What is the population density of central Kazakhstan?

Persons per

sq. mi.	sq. km
Uninhabited	Uninhabited
Under 2	Under 1
2-60	1-25
60-125	25-50
125-250	50-100
Over 250	Over 100

Lambert Equal-Area projection

CITIES
- City with more than 1,000,000 people
- City with 500,000 to 1,000,000 people
- City with 100,000 to 500,000 people

A Land of Mountains The Tian Shan mountain range covers a large area of Kyrgyzstan. Nestled between the mountains lie high grassy plains and low river valleys. As in other highland areas, the climate of Kyrgyzstan differs with elevation. Lower valleys and plains have warm, dry summers and chilly winters. Highland areas have cool summers and bitterly cold winters. Most of Kyrgyzstan's people raise livestock or grow cotton, vegetables, and fruits.

The People More than half of Kyrgyzstan's 4.7 million people belong to the Kyrgyz (kihr•GEEZ) ethnic group. Russians make up the rest of the country's population. The Kyrgyz tend to live in rural areas, and the Russians live in the cities. Bishkek, with a population of about 616,000, is the capital and largest city.

Place
Tajikistan

Southwest of Kyrgyzstan lies the mountainous country of Tajikistan. Covering an area of 54,286 square miles (140,601 sq. km), Tajikistan is about the size of the state of Iowa.

Mountains and Valleys "Roof of the World" is what some people call Tajikistan's mountains. In one spot there, four major Asian mountain ranges come together. The map on page 384 shows that the Pamir Mountains rise in southeastern Tajikistan. Here Communism Peak reaches 24,590 feet (7,495 m).

Tajikistan is a farming country that depends on irrigation. In the river valleys, Tajik farmers grow cotton, rice, and fruits. In highland areas, coal, lead, and zinc are mined.

The People Most Tajiks are Muslims who speak a language similar to that spoken in Iran. About two-thirds of Tajikistan's people live in villages along the rivers. The largest city is Dushanbe (doo•SHAM•buh), the capital.

Place
Turkmenistan

Turkmenistan has some of the most isolated areas in the Central Asian republics. Covering 181,440 square miles (470,000 sq. km), it is slightly larger than the state of California.

Desert Country More than 85 percent of Turkmenistan is a vast desert known as the Kara Kum (KAHR•uh•KOOM), which means "black sand." For their water supply, the people of Turkmenistan rely on a few rivers and **oases**, or fertile desert areas watered by underground springs.

Teen Scene
Making His Mark

Kasim Ben Amir has found a way to be creative and earn money at the same time. Fifteen-year-old Kasim lives near Khodzent, Tajikistan. Much of the cotton and silk produced on Tajikistan farms is made into textiles here. Kasim buys plain shirts for a few rubles and then stamps them with designs that he creates. He sells his creations at a nearby market. Kasim gives some of the money he earns to his family. He's saving the rest to pay for a trip to Iran to visit his cousins.

Cotton, Turkmenistan's major crop, covers acres of irrigated land. Other farm products include grains, grapes, and potatoes. Turkmenistan's natural resources include natural gas, petroleum, copper, gold, and lead.

The People Most of Turkmenistan's 4.7 million people belong to the Turkmen ethnic group. Islam is Turkmenistan's major religion. The population is fairly evenly divided between rural and urban dwellers. Ashkhabad (ASH•kuh•BAD), with about 518,000 people, is the capital and largest city.

Place

Uzbekistan

Like Turkmenistan, Uzbekistan is slightly larger than California—about 159,938 square miles (414,356 sq. km). But Uzbekistan has about 8 times as many people as Turkmenistan.

Stranded ships lie aground on the shoreline of the shrinking Aral Sea.
HUMAN/ENVIRONMENT INTERACTION: What two countries share the Aral Sea?

Cotton Country Deserts and high plains cover much of Uzbekistan. In the west are dry lowlands around the Aral Sea, a large inland salt lake. In the east are fertile valleys that receive plenty of water from the Tian Shan mountain range. Uzbekistan's economy relies on cotton, grains, fruits, and vegetables that are grown in irrigated areas.

Cotton growing in Uzbekistan has taken its toll on the environment. Under the Soviets, farmers were ordered to irrigate crops with water drained from the rivers flowing into the Aral Sea. Since the 1960s the Aral Sea has shrunk drastically in size, and its salt content has increased. Fish and other wildlife have disappeared. Salt particles carried by wind from the lake pollute the air and soil.

The People Most of Uzbekistan's 24.1 million people are Uzbeks. More than 2.2 million people live in the capital city of Tashkent—the largest city in all of central Asia. Most Uzbeks practice Islam and live in rural areas.

SECTION 4 ASSESSMENT

REVIEWING TERMS AND FACTS

1. Define the following: nomad, oasis.

2. REGION What type of landscape covers most of Turkmenistan?

3. PLACE What is the capital of Uzbekistan?

4. HUMAN/ENVIRONMENT INTERACTION What caused the Aral Sea to shrink?

MAP STUDY ACTIVITIES

5. Look at the population density map on page 396. What Central Asian republic is the most densely populated?

Chapter 15 Highlights

Important Things to Know About the Independent Republics

SECTION 1 UKRAINE

- Ukraine's landscape consists of lowlands, highlands, a coastal plain, and a central plains area.
- Ukraine is called the breadbasket of Europe because of its fertile farmland.
- Ukraine's capital, Kiev, was the center of an early Slavic civilization.

SECTION 2 BELARUS AND MOLDOVA

- The major economic activities of Belarus are farming, manufacturing, and service industries.
- Moldovans have strong ties to Romanians in language and culture.

SECTION 3 THE CAUCASUS REPUBLICS

- The Caucasus Mountains cover most of Armenia, Georgia, and Azerbaijan.
- The people of Armenia and Georgia have separate cultures, languages, and heritages.
- Located on the Caspian Sea, Azerbaijan is a major oil-producing country.

SECTION 4 THE CENTRAL ASIAN REPUBLICS

- Mountains, deserts, and plains form the landscapes of the Central Asian republics.
- Most of the peoples of the Central Asian republics practice the Islamic religion.
- Farmers in these republics depend on irrigation to grow cotton, grains, fruits, and vegetables.

Ukrainian folk dancers ▶

REVIEWING KEY TERMS

Match the numbered terms in Set A with their lettered definitions in Set B.

A

1. nomad
2. steppe
3. landlocked
4. oasis
5. food processing
6. fault

B

A. having no coastline
B. break in the earth's crust
C. fertile place in a desert area supplied by underground water
D. vast treeless plain
E. person who travels in search of pasture for grazing animals
F. the preparing of food for sale as products

Mental Mapping Activity

Draw a freehand map of the independent republics. Label the following:

• Kiev
• Black Sea
• Tian Shan Mountains
• Dnieper River
• Aral Sea
• Georgia

REVIEWING THE MAIN IDEAS

Section 1

1. LOCATION   Describe the location of Ukraine.
2. REGION   Why is Ukraine called a breadbasket?

Section 2

3. REGION   What landforms are found in Belarus?
4. HUMAN/ENVIRONMENT INTERACTION   What agricultural products come from Moldova?

Section 3

5. MOVEMENT   Why did many Armenians migrate to other countries?
6. REGION   What are the two major religions of the Caucasus republics?

Section 4

7. REGION   What countries make up the Central Asian republics?
8. HUMAN/ENVIRONMENT INTERACTION   What is the role of rivers in the Central Asian republics?

CRITICAL THINKING ACTIVITIES

1. **Drawing Conclusions**   Why do you think Moldova is a densely populated country?
2. **Evaluating Information**   Did years of Soviet rule help or harm the development of the independent republics? Explain.

CONNECTIONS TO ECONOMICS

Cooperative Learning Activity Organize into 11 groups, and then choose one of the republics discussed in this chapter. Each group will research the economy of its republic. Consider the following: What industries are strongest? What economic problems does the republic face? Groups should combine their information to present to another class.

GeoJournal Writing Activity

Imagine you are vacationing in Ukraine and the other independent republics. Write a letter home describing what you are seeing and where you are staying. Use travel books and your text to describe in detail each of your stops. In your letter, describe the scenery, climate, and the activities of the people you see.

TECHNOLOGY ACTIVITY

Developing Multimedia Presentations
Conduct research to find information about the Chernobyl power station. Then imagine that you are a news reporter covering the nuclear disaster. Create a short multimedia presentation about the disaster and its effects on Ukraine and surrounding areas. Incorporate images, mock interviews, and maps in your presentation.

PLACE LOCATION ACTIVITY: THE INDEPENDENT REPUBLICS

Match the letters on the map with the places of the independent republics. Write your answers on a separate sheet of paper.

1. Black Sea
2. Caucasus Mountains
3. Ukraine
4. Crimean Peninsula
5. Aral Sea
6. Dnieper River
7. Kazakhstan
8. Kara Kum
9. Baku
10. Minsk

CHERNOBYL

NUCLEAR DISASTER

PROBLEM

On April 26, 1986, Reactor Number 4 of the Chernobyl Nuclear Power Plant exploded. Radioactive material flew more than 3 miles into the air. Blown by the wind, radioactive clouds contaminated thousands of square miles. Nearly 5 million people in Ukraine, Belarus, and Russia were affected.

Authorities quickly encased the reactor in a steel-and-concrete shell. They evacuated 116,000 people from the area and scraped away tons of contaminated topsoil. The cleanup continues to this day.

SOLUTIONS

- Ukraine authorities have agreed to shut down the 3 nuclear reactors remaining in Chernobyl and to work with the United States to replace electricity generated by the plants.
- Russia has agreed to encourage the use of natural gas instead of nuclear energy.
- Better worker-training programs, improved operating procedures, and fire safety measures have been started at nuclear plants.

Reindeer move up a ridge in Lapland. Radiation from the Chernobyl explosion contaminated reindeer herds, making the meat and milk unsafe for human consumption.

CHERNOBYL FACT BANK

- The Chernobyl accident was the worst nuclear-power-plant disaster of all time. An estimated 5,000 people died and 30,000 were disabled.

- More than 30,000 square miles of farmland were contaminated. Nothing can be grown there again for 100 years.

- About 23 percent of the land in Belarus was contaminated.

- Cases of thyroid cancer in children and birth defects have increased in the area near the reactor and in the path of the radioactive cloud.

- Penguins in Antarctica, reindeer in Lapland, and countless other animals have suffered the effects of the radioactive clouds that encircled the planet.

USE ALTERNATIVE ENERGY

402

At 1:23 A.M. on April 26, 1986, a test on emergency systems in the Chernobyl Nuclear Power Plant went wrong—and led to the explosion of Reactor Number 4. As pictured in this illustration, the explosion ripped apart the reactor and sent radioactive material high into the atmosphere on a plume of intense heat.

environmental activities

TEEN TRIBUTE

In April 1986, a group from Ramapo High School in Spring Valley, New York, was visiting Leningrad (now St. Petersburg) when the Chernobyl reactor blew up. The visitors returned home—their trip cut short by the disaster. Since then, Ramapo students and their teacher, working with community leaders and drug companies, have provided more than $11 million worth of medicine, vitamins, and toys to hospitals in Belarus and Russia.

WHAT CAN YOU DO?

TAKE A CLOSER LOOK

1 What disaster occurred in Ukraine at the Chernobyl Nuclear Power Plant?

2 What were the lasting effects of the Chernobyl disaster?

 SAVE ENERGY–ride a bike!

 Support a group working for safe disposal of toxic and nuclear wastes.

 Don't add to toxic waste–use fewer batteries and buy only rechargeable ones.

 SAVE ENERGY– encourage your parents to lower the thermostat 6 degrees in winter. If all Americans did, we'd save more than 500,000 barrels of oil a day!

This Ukrainian couple had to resettle after the accident, with only their colorful wall hangings to remind them of their lost home.

Unit 6

Southwest Asia and North Africa

What Makes Southwest Asia and North Africa a Region?

The people share . . .

- a constant quest for water.

- Mediterranean, steppe, and desert climates.

- an abundance of oil and natural gas reserves.

- the historical beginnings of the Islamic, Jewish, and Christian religions.

To find out more about Southwest Asia and North Africa, see the Unit Atlas on pages 406–417.

The Great Sphinx near Giza, Egypt

EXPLORING THE INTERNET

To learn more about Southwest Asia and North Africa, visit the Glencoe Social Studies Web site at **www.glencoe.com** for information, activities, and links to other sites.

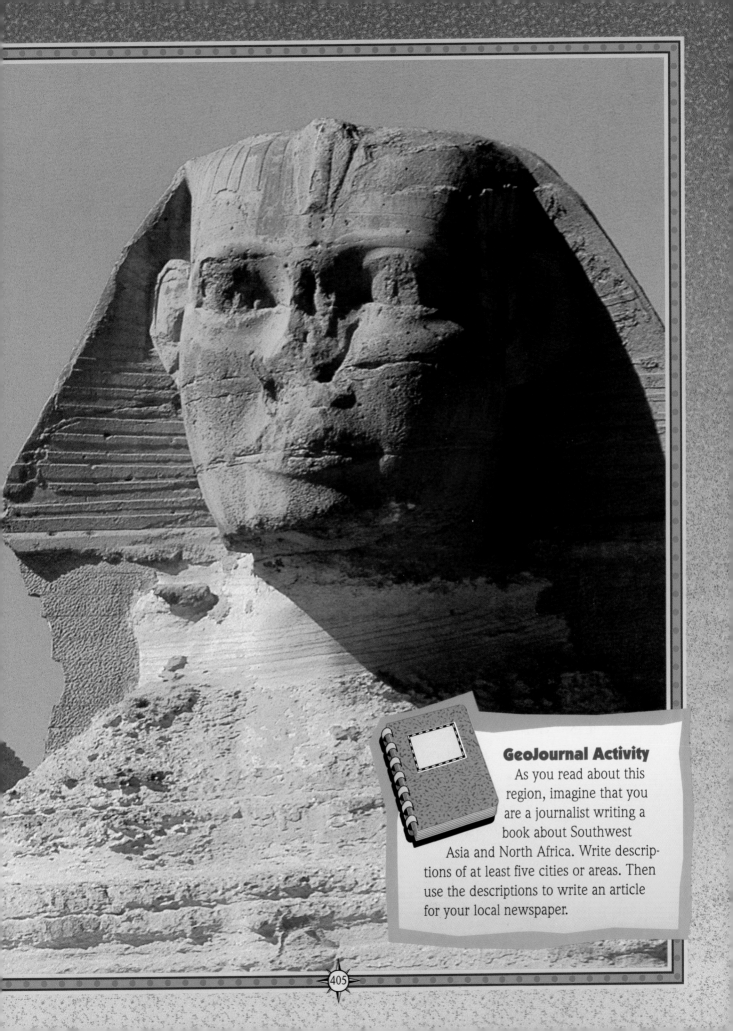

GeoJournal Activity

As you read about this region, imagine that you are a journalist writing a book about Southwest Asia and North Africa. Write descriptions of at least five cities or areas. Then use the descriptions to write an article for your local newspaper.

UNIT 6 ATLAS

NATIONAL
GEOGRAPHIC
SOCIETY

IMAGES
of the
WORLD

1. **Portrait of a child, Turkey**
2. **Boy in a poppy field, Tunisia**
3. **Dome of the Rock, Jerusalem**
4. **Hobbled camels, Egypt**
5. **Woman and children, Saudi Arabia**
6. **Pyramid, Egypt**
7. **Fishermen with their catch, Yemen**

All photos viewed against a desert landscape, Tunisia.

2

3

4

5

6

407

Regional Focus

Southwest Asia and North Africa lie where the continents of Asia, Africa, and Europe meet. You will find the world's largest desert and part of the world's longest river in this region. Some of the world's earliest civilizations and three great world religions started here. Today this region is one of the world's major suppliers of oil.

Region
The Land

The region of Southwest Asia and North Africa covers about 5.5 million square miles (14.2 million sq. km)—about 10 percent of the earth's total land area. Look at the physical map on page 412. The region stretches from sandy beaches along the Atlantic Ocean on the west to the towering Hindu Kush on the east. North to south, the region reaches from the deep blue waters of the Mediterranean Sea to the Sahara.

Euphrates River in Iraq

Mountains Towering mountains rise over much of Southwest Asia and North Africa. The Taurus Mountains run east and west through the southern edge of the country of Turkey. Another range—the Zagros—stretches between Iran and Iraq. Other mountain chains are the Elburz Mountains of Iran and the Asir Mountains of Saudi Arabia. Farther west, in North Africa, stretch the Atlas Mountains—Africa's longest mountain range.

A thick stand of palm trees lines the banks of the Euphrates River.
REGION: Why do you think most people in Iraq live near the Tigris and Euphrates rivers?

Deserts Mountains and prevailing winds have created vast deserts in many parts of Southwest Asia and North Africa. The Rubal Khali, or Empty Quarter, of the Arabian Peninsula is made up of shifting sand dunes. The Sahara—the largest desert in the world—covers much of North Africa.

Water Several bodies of water border the region of Southwest Asia and North Africa. These include the Mediterranean Sea, the Black and Caspian seas, the Persian Gulf, and the Arabian Sea. Freshwater, however, is scarce. Land near rivers and underground springs is green and fertile. With the help of irrigation, crops grow in these areas.

The Nile River, more than 4,000 miles (6,400 km) long, flows north through Egypt to the Mediterranean Sea. It is the world's longest river. Two other major rivers—the Tigris and the Euphrates—flow through southeastern Turkey, Syria, and Iraq into the Persian Gulf.

Natural Resources Oil and natural gas are the most important natural resources in Southwest Asia and North Africa. You will find these minerals in the countries of North Africa and those bordering the Persian Gulf. Southwest Asia and North Africa are also rich in iron ore, copper, lead, manganese, zinc, and phosphate. Phosphate is used for making fertilizers.

Region
Climate and Vegetation

The many mountains of Southwest Asia and North Africa block the flow of rain clouds to the inland side of the region. Only coastal areas enjoy regular and adequate rainfall. Rainfall averages about 10 inches (25 cm) or less each year. This amount is inadequate to grow most food crops, and irrigation is necessary.

Desert and steppe climates cover much of Southwest Asia and North Africa. During the day, temperatures in the desert may soar above 100°F (38°C). In steppe areas, enough rain falls for grasses to grow. This allows farmers to raise livestock. A Mediterranean climate of hot, dry summers and cool, rainy winters is found on coastal plains.

Human/Environment Interaction
Economy

Economies differ from country to country in Southwest Asia and North Africa. The people living in countries that have oil, manufacturing, and trade generally enjoy a high standard of living. People living in countries where the economies are based on farming have a low standard of living.

Agriculture Most people in Southwest Asia and North Africa are farmers or herders. Cereals, citrus fruits, grapes, and dates grow in river valleys and coastal areas. Another source of food for the people of the region is livestock—mostly cattle and sheep. Farmers in river valleys or in irrigated areas also grow cotton, one of the region's major exports.

Industrial Growth Oil and natural gas are important sources of wealth for many Southwest Asian and North African countries. These resources are major exports and have allowed industries to develop. Factories in the region produce textiles, fertilizers, medicines, plastics, and paints. Service industries such as banking, insurance, and tourism have also grown in recent years.

Transportation and Communication In the past, mountains and deserts made transportation costly in the region. Today roads and railroads link cities, oil fields, and seaports. Inland waterways such as the Nile River and the Suez Canal also move people and goods.

Damascus, Syria

People gather in marketplaces to shop for items made by local workers.
PLACE: What mineral is an important source of wealth for many countries in this region?

Place

The People

For centuries Southwest Asia and North Africa have served as the meeting place for the peoples of Asia, Africa, and Europe. The region today has people from many different ethnic backgrounds.

History and Culture Southwest Asia and North Africa have a rich culture and history. Centuries ago the region's farmers were the first to raise many of the grains, vegetables, and animals still used as basic foods in much of the world. Some of the world's oldest civilizations developed in the Nile and Tigris-Euphrates river valleys. In Egypt you can still see the huge pyramids and temples left by the ancient Egyptians.

The religions of Judaism, Christianity, and Islam began in Southwest Asia. All of them share the belief in one God. From the 600s to the 1500s, Islamic empires flourished in Southwest Asia and North Africa and passed on much of their knowledge to other parts of the world. By the 1800s, Europeans ruled most of the region. After World War II, the peoples of Southwest Asia and North Africa set up independent states.

Ethnic Groups Most of the people of Southwest Asia and North Africa are Arabs. About 90 percent are Muslims who practice the religion of Islam. The Arab culture, especially the Arabic language, has had a lasting influence on the region. Two other groups—the Iranians and the Turks—have contributed to the region's cultures. Neither group is Arab, but many in each group are Muslims. Living among the Turks, Iranians, and Arabs are two smaller ethnic groups—Armenians and Kurds. Most people in the country of Israel are Jewish. Israel was founded as a Jewish state in 1948. For many years conflicts have taken place between Jews and Arabs. Today, however, peace efforts are underway between Israeli and Arab leaders.

Population About 400 million people live in Southwest Asia and North Africa. Because of deserts, most people live in rural areas along seacoasts or rivers, or near highlands. The environment in these areas makes it possible to grow crops and raise animals. For centuries the people of Southwest Asia and North Africa lived in rural areas. Today many of them are moving to large cities such as Cairo or Tehran. Increasing population has raised concerns about food and housing shortages as well as air and water pollution.

Ancient Thebes

Giant stone figures guard the 3,000-year-old Temple of Luxor.
LOCATION: In what country can you see ancient pyramids?

NATIONAL GEOGRAPHIC SOCIETY

Picture Atlas of the World

Cultural Differences

Using the CD-ROM People of many different ethnic backgrounds and religions make up the human environment of Southwest Asia and North Africa. Put together a cultural reference file on the region. (See the User's Guide on how to use the Collector button.) Collect photographs on the CD-ROM for the following countries: Afghanistan—nomads and Kirghiz tribespeople; Iraq—Bedouins and a Kurdish family; Israel—the Dome of the Rock and a Palestinian man; Saudi Arabia—Saudi women and Muslim pilgrims. Read the photo captions and answer the following:

1. Describe the life of nomads in Afghanistan.
2. Why do Kurds live at the mercy of often hostile neighbors?
3. To which three religions is the Dome of the Rock sacred?
4. How do women in Saudi Arabia show their devotion to Islam?

Surfing the "Net"

Libya's Need for Water

Most of Libya lies in the Sahara, which makes it one of the driest countries in the world. Thus, there are very few areas in the country that are suitable for farming. However, in 1996 the Libyan government opened a series of long irrigation pipelines to carry water from underground, water-bearing layers of rock. These aquifers in the Sahara will bring water to areas along the coast. To find out more about this recent development, search the Internet.

Getting There

Follow these steps to gather information on Libya's new irrigation project.

1. Use a search engine. Type in the word *Libya*.
2. After typing *Libya*, enter words like the following to focus your search: *environment, agriculture, water, irrigation,* and *pipeline.*
3. The search engine will provide you with a number of links to follow.

What To Do When You Are There

Click on the links to navigate through the pages of information. Find information about the location of aquifers in the Sahara and the routes taken by the pipelines north to the coastal areas. Then use a large wall map of North Africa to trace the routes of the pipelines. Place pins on the map to represent the location of cities and towns to which the pipelines will deliver water. Write a paragraph explaining how this new development will help change the Libyan landscape.

Physical Geography

SOUTHWEST ASIA AND NORTH AFRICA: Physical

ELEVATIONS

Feet	Meters
10,000	3,000
5,000	1,500
2,000	600
1,000	300
0	0

▲ Mountain peak

Mercator projection

Map Study

1. **REGION** What desert covers most of North Africa?
2. **PLACE** What body of water lies between Iran and the Arabian Peninsula?

ELEVATION PROFILE: Southwest Asia and North Africa

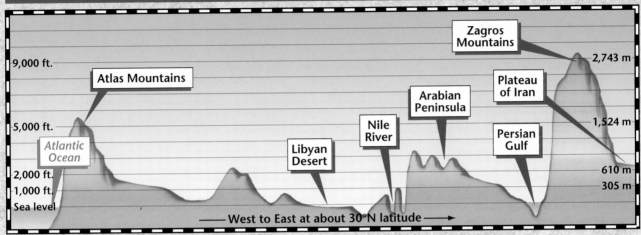

Source: *Goode's World Atlas*, 19th edition

GeoFacts

Highest point: Nowshak (Afghanistan) 24,557 ft. (7,485 m) high

Lowest point: Dead Sea (Israel-Jordan) 1,312 ft. (400 m) below sea level

Longest river: Nile River (Africa) 4,160 mi. (6,693 km) long

Largest lake: Caspian Sea (Europe-Asia) 143,244 sq. mi. (371,002 sq. km)

Largest desert: Sahara (Northern Africa) 3,500,000 sq. mi. (9,065,000 sq. km)

SOUTHWEST ASIA/NORTH AFRICA and the UNITED STATES: Land Comparison

Graphic Study

1. **HUMAN/ENVIRONMENT INTERACTION** How might elevation affect the population in the Zagros and Atlas mountains?
2. **PLACE** How would you describe the physical size of the United States compared to the combined sizes of Southwest Asia and North Africa?

Cultural Geography

SOUTHWEST ASIA AND NORTH AFRICA: Political

EUROPE

ASIA

Black Sea

Caspian Sea

10°W 0° 10°E 20°E 30°E 40°E 50°E

40°N

Ankara ⊛

TURKEY

ATLANTIC OCEAN

Tunis ⊛

Algiers ⊛

Mediterranean Sea

⊛ Tehran

Kabul ⊛

⊛ Rabat

TUNISIA

SYRIA

Damascus ⊛

Baghdad ⊛

AFGHANISTAN

MOROCCO

⊛ Tripoli

Beirut ⊛

LEBANON

Jerusalem ⊛

Amman ⊛

IRAQ

IRAN

KUWAIT

30°N

Cairo ⊛

ISRAEL

JORDAN

Kuwait ⊛

BAHRAIN (Manama)

ASIA

WESTERN SAHARA (Disputed Territory)

ALGERIA

LIBYA

EGYPT

SAUDI ARABIA

Riyadh ⊛

Abu Dhabi ⊛

Persian Gulf

Tropic of Cancer

Red Sea

QATAR

Doha ⊛

Muscat ⊛

Gulf of Oman

20°N

UNITED ARAB EMIRATES

OMAN

AFRICA

10°N

San'a ⊛

YEMEN

Gulf of Aden

Arabian Sea

— National boundary
⊛ National capital

Mercator projection

0   250   500 mi.

0   250   500 km

Map Study

1. **LOCATION** What country lies north of Syria?

2. **PLACE** What is the capital of Algeria?

SOUTHWEST ASIA AND NORTH AFRICA: Largest Urban Areas

Tehran, Iran

Cairo, Egypt

Istanbul, Turkey

Baghdad, Iraq

Alexandria, Egypt

Casablanca, Morocco

Ankara, Turkey

= 1,000,000

Source: *The World Almanac, 1998*

COMPARING POPULATION:
Southwest Asia/North Africa and the United States

Southwest Asia/ North Africa

United States

= 50,000,000

Source: *Population Reference Bureau, 1998*

GeoFacts

Biggest country (land area): Algeria
919,590 sq. mi.
(2,381,738 sq. km)

Smallest country (land area): Bahrain
266 sq. mi. (689 sq. km)

Largest city (population): Tehran
(1997) 11,681,000
(2015 projected) 14,000,000

Highest population density: Bahrain
2,387 people per sq. mi. (922 people per sq. km)

Lowest population density: Libya
8 people per sq. mi. (3 people per sq. km)

Graphic Study

1. **PLACE** About how many people live in Southwest Asia and North Africa?
2. **PLACE** What is the largest city in Southwest Asia and North Africa?

Countries at a Glance

Afghanistan

 Kabul

LANDMASS:
251,772 sq. mi./
652,089 sq. km

MONEY:
Afghani

MAJOR EXPORT:
Dried Fruits and Nuts

MAJOR IMPORT:
Machinery

CAPITAL:
Kabul

MAJOR LANGUAGE(S):
Pushtu, Dari Persian, Uzbek

POPULATION:
24,800,000

Algeria

Algiers

LANDMASS:
919,590 sq. mi./
2,381,738 sq. km

MONEY:
Dinar

MAJOR EXPORT:
Petroleum

MAJOR IMPORT:
Machinery

CAPITAL:
Algiers

MAJOR LANGUAGE(S):
Arabic, Berber

POPULATION:
30,200,000

Bahrain

Manama

LANDMASS:
266 sq. mi./
689 sq. km

MONEY:
Dinar

MAJOR EXPORT:
Petroleum Products

MAJOR IMPORT:
Petroleum Products

CAPITAL:
Manama

MAJOR LANGUAGE(S):
Arabic, Farsi, Urdu

POPULATION:
600,000

Egypt

Cairo

LANDMASS:
384,344 sq. mi./
995,450 sq. km

MONEY:
Pound

MAJOR EXPORT:
Petroleum

MAJOR IMPORT:
Machinery

CAPITAL:
Cairo

MAJOR LANGUAGE(S):
Arabic, English

POPULATION:
65,500,000

Iran

Tehran

LANDMASS:
631,660 sq. mi./
1,635,999 sq. km

MONEY:
Rial

MAJOR EXPORT:
Petroleum

MAJOR IMPORT:
Motor Vehicles

CAPITAL:
Tehran

MAJOR LANGUAGE(S):
Farsi, Turkish, Kurdish, Arabic

POPULATION:
64,100,000

Iraq

 Baghdad

LANDMASS:
168,870 sq. mi./
437,373 sq. km

MONEY:
Dinar

MAJOR EXPORT:
Fuels

MAJOR IMPORT:
Machinery

CAPITAL:
Baghdad

MAJOR LANGUAGE(S):
Arabic, Kurdish

POPULATION:
21,800,000

Israel

Jerusalem

LANDMASS:
7,961 sq. mi./
20,619 sq. km

MONEY:
Shekel

MAJOR EXPORT:
Machinery, Polished Diamonds

MAJOR IMPORT:
Rough Diamonds

CAPITAL:
Jerusalem

MAJOR LANGUAGE(S):
Hebrew, Arabic

POPULATION:
6,000,000

Jordan

Amman

LANDMASS:
34,336 sq. mi./
88,930 sq. km

MONEY:
Dinar

MAJOR EXPORT:
Phosphate Fertilizers

MAJOR IMPORT:
Food and Live Animals

CAPITAL:
Amman

MAJOR LANGUAGE(S):
Arabic

POPULATION:
4,600,000

Kuwait

Kuwait

LANDMASS:
6,880 sq. mi./
17,819 sq. km

MONEY:
Dinar

MAJOR EXPORT:
Petroleum

MAJOR IMPORT:
Machinery

CAPITAL:
Kuwait

MAJOR LANGUAGE(S):
Arabic

POPULATION:
1,900,000

Lebanon

Beirut

LANDMASS:
3,950 sq. mi./
10,231 sq. km

MONEY:
Pound

MAJOR EXPORT:
Jewelry

MAJOR IMPORT:
Machinery

CAPITAL:
Beirut

MAJOR LANGUAGE(S):
Arabic, French

POPULATION:
4,100,000

Countries not drawn to scale.

Libya

CAPITAL:
Tripoli
MAJOR LANGUAGE(S):
Arabic
POPULATION:
5,700,000

LANDMASS:
679,360 sq. mi./
1,759,542 sq. km
MONEY:
Dinar
MAJOR EXPORT:
Petroleum
MAJOR IMPORT:
Food

Morocco*

CAPITAL:
Rabat
MAJOR LANGUAGE(S):
Arabic, Berber
POPULATION:
28,600,000

LANDMASS:
172,320 sq. mi./
446,309 sq. km
MONEY:
Dirham
MAJOR EXPORT:
Food
MAJOR IMPORT:
Crude Oil

Oman

CAPITAL:
Muscat
MAJOR LANGUAGE(S):
Arabic
POPULATION:
2,500,000

LANDMASS:
82,030 sq. mi./
212,458 sq. km
MONEY:
Rial
MAJOR EXPORT:
Petroleum
MAJOR IMPORT:
Machinery

Qatar

CAPITAL:
Doha
MAJOR LANGUAGE(S):
Arabic, English
POPULATION:
500,000

LANDMASS:
4,250 sq. mi./
11,008 sq. km
MONEY:
Riyal
MAJOR EXPORT:
Petroleum
MAJOR IMPORT:
Machinery

Saudi Arabia

CAPITAL:
Riyadh
MAJOR LANGUAGE(S):
Arabic
POPULATION:
20,200,000

LANDMASS:
830,000 sq. mi./
2,149,700 sq. km
MONEY:
Riyal
MAJOR EXPORT:
Petroleum
MAJOR IMPORT:
Machinery

Syria

CAPITAL:
Damascus
MAJOR LANGUAGE(S):
Arabic, Kurdish,
Armenian, Turkish
POPULATION:
15,600,000

LANDMASS:
70,958 sq. mi./
183,781 sq. km
MONEY:
Pound
MAJOR EXPORT:
Petroleum
MAJOR IMPORT:
Food Products

Tunisia

CAPITAL:
Tunis
MAJOR LANGUAGE(S):
Arabic, French
POPULATION:
9,500,000

LANDMASS:
59,980 sq. mi./
155,348 sq. km
MONEY:
Dinar
MAJOR EXPORT:
Clothing
MAJOR IMPORT:
Textiles

Turkey

CAPITAL:
Ankara
MAJOR LANGUAGE(S):
Turkish, Kurdish,
Arabic, Greek
POPULATION:
64,800,000

LANDMASS:
297,150 sq. mi./
769,619 sq. km
MONEY:
Lira
MAJOR EXPORT:
Textiles
MAJOR IMPORT:
Machinery

United Arab Emirates

CAPITAL:
Abu Dhabi
MAJOR LANGUAGE(S):
Arabic
POPULATION:
2,700,000

LANDMASS:
32,280 sq. mi./
83,605 sq. km
MONEY:
Dirham
MAJOR EXPORT:
Petroleum
MAJOR IMPORT:
Machinery

Yemen

CAPITAL:
San'a
MAJOR LANGUAGE(S):
Arabic
POPULATION:
15,800,000

LANDMASS:
203,850 sq. mi./
527,972 sq. km
MONEY:
Rial (also the Dinar)
MAJOR EXPORT:
Coffee
MAJOR IMPORT:
Food and Live Animals

* Morocco claims the Western Sahara area but
other countries do not accept this claim.

Chapter 16 Southwest Asia

National capital
Other city
Mercator projection

Black Sea
30°E
40°E
50°E
60°E
70°E
40°N
Istanbul
Ankara
Izmir
TURKEY
Caspian Sea
ASIA
Aleppo
Mediterranean Sea
SYRIA
Beirut
Damascus
Tehran
LEBANON
Baghdad
Isfahan
Kabul
Tel Aviv-Yafo
Amman
IRAQ
IRAN
AFGHANISTAN
Jerusalem
30°N
ISRAEL
JORDAN
Basra
KUWAIT
Kuwait
AFRICA
SAUDI ARABIA
BAHRAIN
(Manama)
Tropic of Cancer
Madinah
Riyadh
Persian Gulf
Abu Dhabi
QATAR
Doha
Gulf of Oman
Jiddah
UNITED ARAB
Muscat
Arabian Sea
20°N
Makkah
EMIRATES
OMAN
San'a
YEMEN
0   250   500 mi.
0   250   500 km
Aden
Gulf of Aden

N
W   E
S

MAP STUDY ACTIVITY

As you read Chapter 16, you will learn about Southwest Asia. The countries in this region lie in the southwest corner of Asia.

1. How many countries make up Southwest Asia?
2. What are the two largest countries?
3. Which country connects Europe to Asia?

Turkey

PREVIEW

Words to Know
- mosque
- migrate

Places to Locate
- Turkish Straits
- Anatolian Plateau
- Pontic Mountains
- Taurus Mountains
- Istanbul
- Ankara

Read to Learn . . .
1. how Turkey's location has affected its history and development.
2. how Turkey blends its ancient heritage with modern ways.

Flocks of grazing sheep and goats are common sights in Turkey and other Southwest Asian countries. This shepherd watches a flock of sheep in

Turkey, one of the largest countries in Southwest Asia.

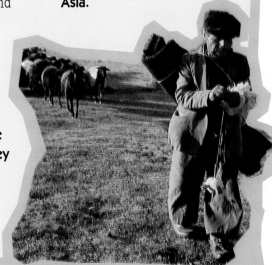

A little larger than the state of Texas, Turkey has a unique location—it lies on two continents: Europe and Asia. Because of its location, Turkey has links to both Asian and European cultures.

Location
The Land

The European and Asian parts of Turkey are separated by three important waterways—the Bosporus (BAHS•puh•ruhs), the Sea of Marmara (MAHR•muh•ruh), and the Dardanelles (DAHR•duhn•EHLZ). Together, these waterways are known as the Turkish Straits. The Turkish Straits join the Black Sea and the Mediterranean Sea. Find these waterways on the map on page A20.

The Land and Climate Highlands and plateaus cover much of Turkey. The heart of Turkey is the Anatolian (A•nuh•TOH•lee•uhn) Plateau. Mountain ranges surround this broad sweep of dry highlands. The Pontic Mountains border the plateau on the north. The Taurus Mountains tower over it on the south.

Grassy plains cover the northern part of Turkey along the Black Sea. On the western coast, you find broad, fertile river valleys running inland from the Aegean Sea. In the south, coastal plains extend along the Mediterranean Sea.

MAP STUDY

Mountains cover much of Southwest Asia.

LOCATION: What plateau covers central Turkey?

ELEVATIONS

Feet	Meters
10,000	3,000
5,000	1,500
2,000	600
1,000	300
0	0

▲ Mountain peak

Mercator projection

The map on page 424 shows you that Turkey's climate varies throughout the country. If you lived on the Anatolian Plateau, you would experience the hot, dry summers and cold, snowy winters of the steppe climate. The coastal areas enjoy a Mediterranean climate—hot, dry summers and mild, rainy winters.

Human/Environment Interaction
The Economy

Agriculture plays an important role in Turkey's economy. Wheat and livestock are the country's leading farm products. The best farmlands are found in the coastal areas. In recent years, Turkish industry has grown tremendously, especially in the making of textiles. The map on page 429 shows that Turkey is rich in mineral deposits, including iron ore, coal, and copper.

Region
The People

Most of Turkey's 65 million people live in the northern part of the Anatolian Plateau, on coastal plains, or in valleys. Turkish is the major language, but Arabic, Greek, and Kurdish are also spoken. About 98 percent of the Turkish people are Muslims. They follow Islam, a religion that teaches belief in one God. Islam is the major faith of most of Southwest Asia. Turkey also has small groups of Christians and Jews.

City and Country About 64 percent of Turkey's people live in cities or towns. Ahmed ul-Hamid, a 14-year-old Turkish student, lives among the 8 million people of Istanbul (IHS•tuhn•BOOL), Turkey's largest city. Istanbul is the only city in the world located on two continents. Ahmed has the opportunity to visit Istanbul's beautiful palaces, museums, and **mosques**, or Muslim places of worship. Only once has Ahmed visited Turkey's capital and second-largest city, Ankara (ANG•kuh•ruh). It has about 2.8 million people and is located on the Anatolian Plateau.

Roughly 35 percent of Turkey's people live on farms or in small villages. Since the mid-1900s, hundreds of thousands of people have left their villages to seek work in the cities. The cities, however, can't supply enough jobs for everyone. This results in many searching for work in other parts of Southwest Asia and in western Europe and Australia.

Istanbul, Turkey

Domed roofs and graceful towers, called minarets, rise above the many mosques of Istanbul.
PLACE: What is the major religion of Turkey?

Influences of the Past Most of Turkey's people are descendants of an Asian people called Turks who **migrated**, or moved, to the Anatolian Plateau during the A.D. 900s. One group of Turks—the Ottomans—established a Muslim empire centered in Turkey.

During World War I, the Ottomans were defeated. Kemal Atatürk, a military hero, became the first president of the new country—the modern republic of Turkey. Atatürk introduced many political and social changes to the country.

Turkey soon began to consider itself European as well as Asian. Modern Turkish people, however, remain proud of their Muslim faith. In the 1990s the Muslim party played an important role in Turkey's government.

SECTION 1 ASSESSMENT

REVIEWING TERMS AND FACTS
1. **Define the following:** mosque, migrate.
2. **LOCATION** What makes Turkey's location unique?
3. **PLACE** What areas of Turkey are best for farming?
4. **MOVEMENT** Where do Turkish workers move to find work?

MAP STUDY ACTIVITIES
5. Look at the physical map on page 420. What feature dominates central Turkey?
6. Turn to the political map on page 418. About how far is Ankara from Istanbul?

BUILDING GEOGRAPHY SKILLS

Reading a Time Zone Map

Earth's surface is divided into 24 time zones. The 0° line of longitude—the Prime Meridian—is the starting point for figuring out time around the world.

To read a time zone map, follow these steps:

- Locate a place where you know what time it is and select another place where you wish to know the time.

- Notice the time zones you cross between these places.

- If the second place lies east of the first, add an hour for each time zone. If it lies west, subtract an hour for each zone. If you must cross the International Date Line—the 180° meridian—add or subtract one day.

Glencoe's **Skillbuilder Interactive Workbook, Level 1** provides instruction and practice in key social studies skills.

World Time Zones

| Nonstandard time |
| *Mercator projection* |

60° 75° 90° 105° 120° 135° 150° 165° 180° 165° 150° 135° 120° 105° 90° 75° 60° 45°W 30° 15° 0° 15° 30° 45°E 60°

9 am 11 am

Prime Meridian

International Date Line

- Anchorage
- Moscow
- London
- Beijing
- Tokyo
- Denver
- New York
- Rome • Istanbul
- Los Angeles
- Memphis
- Honolulu
- Austin
- Mumbai (Bombay)
- Mexico City
- Rio de Janeiro
- Cape Town
- Sydney

N
W—E
S

4 pm | 5 pm | 6 pm | 7 pm | 8 pm | 9 pm | 10 pm | 11 pm | 12 am | 1 am | 2 am | 3 am | 4 am | 5 am | 6 am | 7 am | 8 am | 9 am | 10 am | 11 am | 12 pm | 1 pm | 2 pm | 3 pm | 4 pm

Geography Skills Practice

1. If it is 7 A.M. in New York City, New York, what time is it in Istanbul, Turkey?

2. If it is 6 A.M. on Wednesday in Mumbai, India, what day and time is it in Rio de Janeiro, Brazil?

SECTION 2 Israel

Words to Know
- potash
- phosphate
- monotheism
- Holocaust

Places to Locate
- Mediterranean Sea
- Sea of Galilee
- Dead Sea
- Negev
- Tel Aviv

Read to Learn . . .
1. how Israelis have developed their resources.
2. what groups of people live in Israel.
3. how the past affects Israel today.

Israel is the only Jewish nation in the world. Established as a nation in 1948, Israel celebrates its Independence Day just as Americans do—with parades and flag-waving.

Israel lies at the eastern end of the Mediterranean Sea. It is 256 miles (412 km) long from north to south and only 68 miles (109 km) wide from east to west. An hour's drive takes you from the eastern boundary of the country almost to the Mediterranean Sea.

Place
The Land

Israel's landscape includes plains, deserts, and highlands. In Israel's far north lie the mountains of Galilee. East of these mountains is a plateau called the Golan Heights. The Judean (ju•DEE•uhn) Hills lie south.

The Dead Sea lies between Israel and Jordan. At 1,312 feet (400 m) *below* sea level, the rim of the Dead Sea is the lowest place on the earth! It is also the saltiest body of water in the world—about 9 times as salty as the ocean. A desert landform, the Negev (NEH•gehv) in southern Israel, covers almost one-half of the country. It is a triangular area of dry hills, valleys, and plains. Not all of southern Israel is desert, however. A narrow fertile plain—only 20 miles

MAP STUDY

Steppe climate regions do not receive much rain.

PLACE: What type of climate occurs throughout most of Israel?

CLIMATE

Mid-Latitude
- Mediterranean
- Highland

Dry
- Steppe (partly dry)
- Desert

Mercator projection

(33 km) wide at its widest point—lies along Israel's Mediterranean coast. To the east, the Jordan River cuts through the floor of a long, narrow valley. The longest of Israel's few rivers, the Jordan flows south into the Dead Sea.

The Climate As you can see on the map above, Israel's climate varies from north to south. Northern Israel has a Mediterranean climate with hot, dry summers and mild winters. About 40 inches (100 cm) of rain fall in the north each year. Southern Israel has a desert climate, with summer temperatures soaring to 120°F (49°C) or higher. Less than 1 inch of rain (2.5 cm) falls in the south.

Place
The Economy

Israel has limited farmland and natural resources. Israelis, however, make good use of their few resources and have built a strong economy. A developing system of transportation and communication supports this economy.

Mining and Manufacturing Israel is the most industrialized country in Southwest Asia. Its factories produce food products, clothing, chemicals, building materials, electronic appliances, and machinery. Diamond cutting is also a major Israeli industry. Tel Aviv is Israel's largest manufacturing center.

Mining is important to Israel's economy. The Dead Sea area is rich in deposits of **potash**, a type of mineral salt. Potash and other minerals support a growing chemical industry in Israel. The Negev area is also a source of copper and **phosphate**, a mineral used in making fertilizer.

Agriculture The Israelis have drained swamps, built irrigation systems, and used fertilizers to improve their soil. Israel's major farming area, which produces citrus fruits such as oranges, grapefruits, and lemons, is the coastal plain. Citrus fruits are Israel's chief farm export. Farming also occurs in parts of the Negev but only with the help of irrigation.

Place
The People

A single Israeli law—The Law of Return—increased the country's population more than any other factor. Passed in 1950, the law states that settlement in Israel is open to all Jews from anywhere in the world. Today Israel has about 6 million people. About 80 percent of Israel's population are Jews, but Israel's people also include Muslims and Christian Arabs. Most of Israel's Arabs are part of a group called the Palestinians. Both Israeli Jews and Arabs trace their roots to groups that lived in the area centuries ago.

Because of their country's industrial growth, about 90 percent of Israelis live in urban areas. The largest cities are Tel Aviv and the neighboring cities of Jerusalem, Yafo (yah•FOH), and Haifa (HY•fuh).

Jerusalem is a holy city for Jews, Christians, and Muslims, whose religions began in Southwest Asia centuries ago. All three groups practice **monotheism**, or a belief in one God.

Teen Scene

A Special Birthday

If you see a look of pride on Shamir Mazar's face, it comes from his many days of preparation for his bar mitzvah. A bar mitzvah is a special ceremony for Jewish boys when they turn 13. A similar ceremony called a bat mitzvah is held for girls at the same age. At this time young people are accepted as members of the Jewish community. Dressed in a traditional prayer shawl and cap, Shamir carried the scrolls of the Torah, the Jewish holy book. As part of the ceremony, he read a passage from the scrolls.

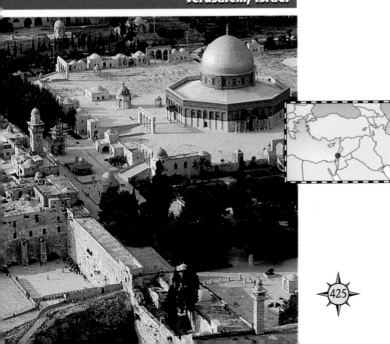

Jerusalem, Israel

The Muslim Dome of the Rock and the Jewish Western Wall are holy sites in Jerusalem's old city.
PLACE: Jerusalem is considered a holy city for followers of what three religions?

Benjamin Netanyahu (right) became Israel's leader in 1996. He firmly defended Israeli interests but was willing to meet with Palestinian leader Yasir Arafat (left) and sign a historic agreement in 1998. **REGION: What happened to Israel and the Arab countries between 1948 and 1974?**

Early History Many Israeli Jews today come from such places as Europe, North Africa, and the Americas. They trace their origins, however, to the Hebrews who set up a kingdom with its capital at Jerusalem in about 1000 B.C. By 922 B.C. the Hebrew kingdom had split into two states—Israel and Judah. The people of Judah were known as Jews. Israel and Judah were eventually destroyed by invaders.

Over time, the area that is now Israel was ruled by a series of peoples—Greeks, Romans, Byzantines, Arabs, and Ottoman Turks. Under the Romans, Israel and Judah became the country of Palestine. In the late 1800s, the people in Palestine included Arabs and a small community of Jews. At that time many Jews from Europe moved to Palestine. These Jewish settlers, known as Zionists, wanted to set up a homeland for Jews.

Modern Israel After World War I, Palestine came under British control. During World War II, millions of Jews in Europe were killed by German Nazis. This mass slaughter known as the **Holocaust** brought worldwide attention to the Zionist cause. In 1947 the United Nations voted to divide Palestine into a Jewish and an Arab state. In 1948 the Jews of Palestine proclaimed an independent republic called the State of Israel. The Arabs of Palestine, however, rejected this action.

A series of Arab-Israeli wars in which Israel gained Arab land were fought between 1948 and 1974. A 1978 treaty between Israel and Egypt was a first step toward peace. Agreements made in 1993 and 1994 between Israel and Palestinian Arab leaders and between Israel and Jordan also gave hope that peace may come to the region.

SECTION 2 ASSESSMENT

REVIEWING TERMS AND FACTS

1. Define the following: potash, phosphate, monotheism, Holocaust.

2. LOCATION Where is most of Israel's industry located?

3. PLACE What is Israel's major crop?

4. MOVEMENT Why do people around the world visit Jerusalem?

MAP STUDY ACTIVITIES

5. Turn to the map on page 424. What body of water borders Israel on the west?

6. Look at the same map on page 424. What climates are found in Israel?

426

UNIT 6

MAKING CONNECTIONS

| MATH | SCIENCE | **HISTORY** | LITERATURE | TECHNOLOGY |

Your friend Bashir from Southwest Asia has invited you to dinner. Some of the foods you're served look familiar. The table holds dates and other fruit, a bowl of rice, and the pita bread your own mother buys to make sandwiches. Whether you are eating Israeli matzo bread or Lebanese pita bread, you are enjoying the foods of Southwest Asia.

ANCIENT ORIGINS The foods of this region date to ancient times. Olives—a key ingredient in the olive oil used in the region's foods—have always grown well in a Mediterranean climate. About 5,000 years ago the Phoenicians taught the Greeks to burn olive oil in their clay lamps. The Greeks quickly learned to cook with the oil. Date palms were also cultivated in the region as early as 400 B.C. Wheat was grown in the Fertile Crescent by the earliest known civilizations. Oranges and spices came to the region from India in the 1200s.

SHARED REGIONAL FOODS The foods common to all of Southwest Asia include dishes made from wheat, fruits and vegetables, and flavorful spices. Dishes prepared

A family meal in Jordan

with eggplant, chickpeas and other legumes, celery, tomatoes, onions, chicken, and lamb appear in most countries. A generous dash of saffron, cinnamon, cardamom, cumin, or cilantro adds flavor. Fruits such as dates, raisins, lemons, figs, pomegranates, and apricots are also popular, especially as desserts.

Lack of refrigeration in some places led people to develop a taste for yogurt—fermented camel's milk—rather than fresh milk products. In your friend's home you might be offered fruit juices or tea to end your meal.

Making the Connection ▼ ▲

1. What are some of the oldest foods grown in the Southwest Asian region?
2. Of the foods described here, which have you tasted? How did you like them?

Syria, Lebanon, and Jordan

PREVIEW

Words to Know
- Bedouin
- civil war
- constitutional monarchy

Places to Locate
- Syria
- Lebanon
- Syrian Desert
- Damascus
- Beirut
- Jordan
- Jordan River
- Amman

Read to Learn . . .
1. what landforms make up Syria.
2. why Lebanon was torn by a fierce civil war.
3. how Jordan is governed.

From the sight of modern buildings in busy Amman, Jordan, you might not guess that the city is more than 3,500 years old. Today Amman is the capital and major economic center of Jordan, a small country that lies east of Israel in Southwest Asia.

Syria, Lebanon, and Jordan share a stretch of fertile land in the middle of Southwest Asia's mountains and deserts. This area is called the Fertile Crescent, because it is shaped like a half-moon. The Fertile Crescent runs from the Mediterranean coast in the west to the Persian Gulf in the east.

Place
Syria

Syria lies at the eastern end of the Mediterranean Sea and has been a center of commerce and trade for centuries. Throughout its early history, Syria was a part of many empires, but in 1946 it became an independent republic.

The Land and Economy Syria's land includes fertile coastal plains and valleys along the Mediterranean Sea. Inland mountains running north and south keep moist sea winds from reaching the eastern part of Syria. The map on page 420 shows that the vast Syrian Desert covers this region.

Agriculture is Syria's major economic activity. Syrian farmers raise mostly cotton and wheat in the rich soil of mountain valleys and coastal plains. In

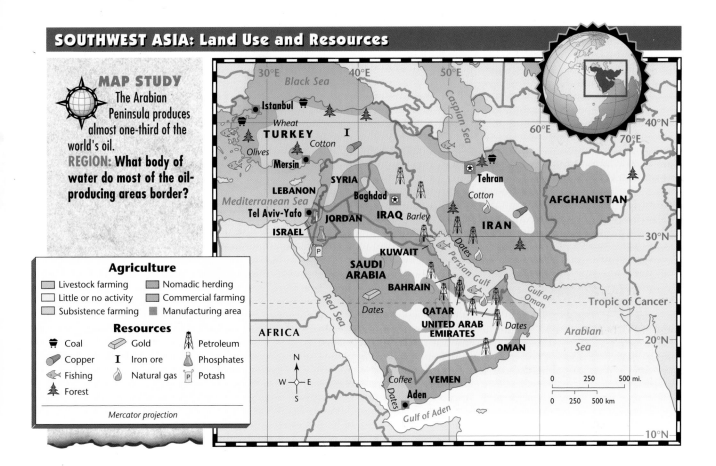

SOUTHWEST ASIA: Land Use and Resources

MAP STUDY
The Arabian Peninsula produces almost one-third of the world's oil.
REGION: What body of water do most of the oil-producing areas border?

Agriculture

- Livestock farming
- Little or no activity
- Subsistence farming
- Nomadic herding
- Commercial farming
- Manufacturing area

Resources

- Coal
- Copper
- Fishing
- Forest
- Gold
- Iron ore
- Natural gas
- Petroleum
- Phosphates
- Potash

Mercator projection

many dry areas, farmers rely on irrigation to grow crops. Syria's primary industry is textile making. Syrian cloth and fabrics have been highly valued since ancient times. The country also produces cement, chemicals, and glass.

The People About half of Syria's 15.6 million people live in rural areas, and a few are **Bedouins**, or people who move through the deserts. The word *bedouin* is Arabic for "desert dweller." The other half of the population live in cities. The city of Damascus, Syria's capital, is home to more than 2 million people. It was founded more than 5,000 years ago as a trading center.

Place

Lebanon

Lebanon, one of the smallest countries of Southwest Asia, lies west of Syria on the eastern coast of the Mediterranean Sea. Its land area is slightly smaller than the land area of the state of Connecticut.

The Land and Economy Lebanon consists of plains and mountains. Sandy beaches and a narrow plain run along the Mediterranean coast. Rugged mountains rise east of the plain and along Lebanon's eastern border. A fertile valley lies between the two mountain ranges. People living on the coast enjoy a mild, humid climate. Inland areas receive less rainfall and have lower winter and higher summer temperatures.

Service industries such as banking are Lebanon's major source of income. Lebanon's chief manufactured products include cement, chemicals, electric appliances, and textiles. If you were a Lebanese farmer, you might grow apples, oranges, grapes, potatoes, or olives.

The People Almost 70 percent of Lebanon's 4.1 million people are Muslims, while most of the rest are Christians. About 86 percent of Lebanon's people live in urban areas. Beirut (bay•ROOT), located on the coast, is the nation's capital and largest city.

From 1975 to 1991, groups of Muslims and Christians in Lebanon fought a **civil war,** or a conflict among different groups within a country. Many lives were lost, and the nation's economy was almost destroyed.

Place

Jordan

Jordan is slightly larger in size than the state of Kentucky. Before 1967 Jordan also held land west of the Jordan River. This area—the West Bank—came under Israeli control during the 1967 Arab-Israeli war. Today the West Bank is home to more than 1.8 million Palestinian Arabs.

The Land and Economy A land of contrasts, Jordan reaches from the fertile Jordan River valley in the west to dry, rugged country in the east. The northern and western parts of Jordan have mild, rainy winters and dry, hot summers. Southern and eastern parts of the country have a hot, dry climate year-round.

Most workers in Jordan are employed in agriculture and manufacturing. The leading manufactured goods are cement, chemicals, and petroleum products. Jordan's farmers in the Jordan River valley grow citrus fruits, tomatoes, and melons.

The People Most of Jordan's 4.6 million people are Arab Muslims and Christians. They include about 1 million Palestinian Arabs who fled Israel or the West Bank during the Arab-Israeli wars. Amman, with 1.2 million people, is the leading city and capital. Jordan is a **constitutional monarchy**, a form of government in which the monarch shares power with elected officials.

Ancient Cedars

The stately cedar tree is Lebanon's national symbol and appears on its flag, coins, and stamps.
LOCATION: How would you describe the landscape where these trees grow?

SECTION 3 ASSESSMENT

REVIEWING TERMS AND FACTS

1. Define the following: Bedouin, civil war, constitutional monarchy.

2. PLACE What city in Syria is considered one of the oldest cities in the world?

3. PLACE How has civil war affected Lebanon?

MAP STUDY ACTIVITIES

4. Look at the map on page 429. What is the primary economic activity of Syria?

5. Look at the same map on page 429. What countries border Lebanon?

The Arabian Peninsula

PREVIEW

Words to Know
- oasis
- *hajj*

Places to Locate
- Saudi Arabia
- Kuwait
- Bahrain
- United Arab Emirates
- Qatar
- Yemen
- Oman
- Makkah
- Riyadh

Read to Learn . . .
1. why Saudi Arabia is important to the world's Muslims.
2. how oil affects the lives of the people of the Arabian Peninsula.

The hot desert sun rises and sets over the Arabian Peninsula. Under these windswept dunes, oil constantly flows through the country's network of pipelines.

The Arabian Peninsula is like a giant platform that tilts toward the east and the north. Its highest elevations are in the south. The mostly desert land in the north slopes toward flat, sandy beaches along the Persian Gulf. The country of Saudi Arabia takes up about 80 percent of the Peninsula.

Place
Saudi Arabia

Saudi Arabia, the largest country in Southwest Asia, is about the size of the eastern half of the United States. Saudi Arabia holds a major share of the world's oil. The graph on page 432 compares the amount of oil that Southwest Asia pumps to that of other oil-producing nations.

The Land Vast deserts cover Saudi Arabia. The largest desert is the Empty Quarter in the southern part of the country. The Empty Quarter has mountains of sand that reach heights of more than 1,000 feet (305 m). In the west, highlands stretch along the Red Sea. Valleys among these highlands provide fertile farmland. Eastern Saudi Arabia is a coastal plain along the Persian Gulf.

GRAPHIC STUDY

Southwest Asia has more oil than all other regions of the world combined.
REGION: What is the total percentage of oil found in all other regions of the world?

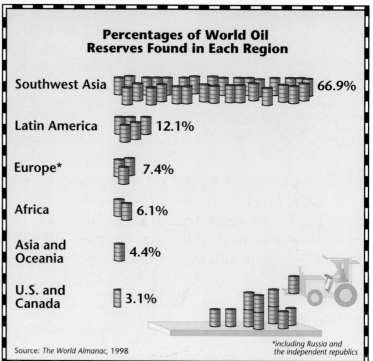

Percentages of World Oil Reserves Found in Each Region

Southwest Asia   66.9%

Latin America   12.1%

Europe*   7.4%

Africa   6.1%

Asia and Oceania   4.4%

U.S. and Canada   3.1%

Source: *The World Almanac*, 1998

*including Russia and the independent republics

The Economy The economy of Saudi Arabia is based on oil. Money from oil exports has built schools, hospitals, roads, and airports. Agriculture is less important than oil because of the limited amount of water and farmland. To meet the need for freshwater, the country's engineers have built industrial plants to remove salt from the seawater of the Persian Gulf and the Red Sea.

The People The people of Saudi Arabia once were divided into numerous family groups. In 1932 a monarchy led by the Saud family unified the country. The Saud family still rules Saudi Arabia today.

Most of the 20.2 million Saudi Arabians live in towns and villages. These are found along the oil-rich Persian Gulf coast or around **oases**—lush, green places in dry areas that have enough water for crops to grow. Some of the oases have grown into large cities such as Riyadh (ree•YAHD).

The Islamic religion affects almost all parts of life in Saudi Arabia—from government to the everyday lives of the people. The holy city of Makkah (MAH•kah) was very important in the life of Muhammad (moh•HA•muhd), the man who brought Islam to the Arabs in the A.D. 600s. Today hundreds of thousands of Muslims from around the world visit Makkah each year. Each Muslim tries to make a *hajj,* or religious journey to Makkah, at least once.

Saudi Women at Work

A female doctor in Saudi Arabia examines her patient.
PLACE: Income from what resource has helped build Saudi Arabia's hospitals?

Other Arabian Peninsula Nations

Saudi Arabia shares the Arabian Peninsula with six other Arab Muslim countries. They are Kuwait (ku•WAYT), Bahrain (bah•RAYN), Qatar (KAH•tuhr), the United Arab Emirates, Oman (oh•MAHN), and Yemen (YEH•muhn).

Persian Gulf States Kuwait, Bahrain, Qatar, and the United Arab Emirates are located along the Persian Gulf. Beneath their flat deserts and offshore areas lie vast deposits of oil. The Persian Gulf states have used oil profits to build prosperous economies. Their people—for the most part—enjoy a high standard of living with excellent health care, education, and housing. Many workers from other countries have settled in the Persian Gulf countries to work in the modern cities and oil fields.

The Kaaba, the most sacred Islamic shrine, is in the courtyard of Makkah's Grand Mosque.
PLACE: Who brought the Islamic religion to the Arabs?

Oman and Yemen At the southern end of the Arabian Peninsula are the countries of Oman and Yemen. Oman is largely desert, but its bare land yields oil—the basis of the country's economy. Most of the people of Oman live in rural villages. The oil industry, however, has drawn many rural dwellers as well as foreigners to Oman's growing urban areas.

The country of Yemen is made up of a narrow coastal plain and inland mountains. It has almost no natural mineral resources, and most of the people are farmers or herders of sheep and cattle. They live in the high fertile interior where the capital, San'a (sa•NAH), is located. Farther south lies Aden (AH•duhn), a major port for ships traveling between the Arabian and Red seas.

SECTION 4 ASSESSMENT

REVIEWING TERMS AND FACTS
1. **Define the following:** oasis, *hajj.*
2. **PLACE** What country takes up most of the Arabian Peninsula?
3. **LOCATION** Where is the Empty Quarter located?
4. **MOVEMENT** Why is the port of Aden important to Yemen?

GRAPHIC STUDY ACTIVITIES
5. Turn to the graph on page 432. What region comes closest to matching Southwest Asia's oil production?
6. Look at the graph on page 432. What two regions together produce about as much oil as Europe does?

Iraq, Iran, and Afghanistan

PREVIEW

Words to Know
- alluvial plain
- shah
- ethnic group

Places to Locate
- Iraq
- Baghdad
- Iran
- Caspian Sea
- Tehran
- Afghanistan
- Hindu Kush Mountains
- Kabul

Read to Learn . . .
1. why the Tigris and Euphrates rivers are important to the people of Iraq.
2. how a religious government came to power in Iran.

Poems, stories, and songs describe the ancient beauty of Baghdad—the heart of Iraq. Today Baghdad boasts modern buildings as well as old neighborhoods and busy marketplaces.

Baghdad, with a population of about 4.3 million, is one of the largest cities in Southwest Asia. It is the capital of Iraq, a country in the northern part of Southwest Asia. The other countries in this region are Iran and Afghanistan.

Location

Iraq

Iraq lies at the head of the Persian Gulf and north of the Arabian Peninsula. Some of the world's oldest civilizations developed there between the Tigris and Euphrates rivers in an area called Mesopotamia. As a nation, however, modern Iraq has been in existence only since the early 1900s. Today it is one of the important oil-producing countries of Southwest Asia.

The Land The Tigris and Euphrates rivers are the major geographic features of Iraq. They flow through Iraq's northern highlands and central plain before joining to enter the Persian Gulf. West of the Tigris-Euphrates area, the landscape is mostly desert. What types of climates can you find in Iraq on the map on page 424?

434

UNIT 6

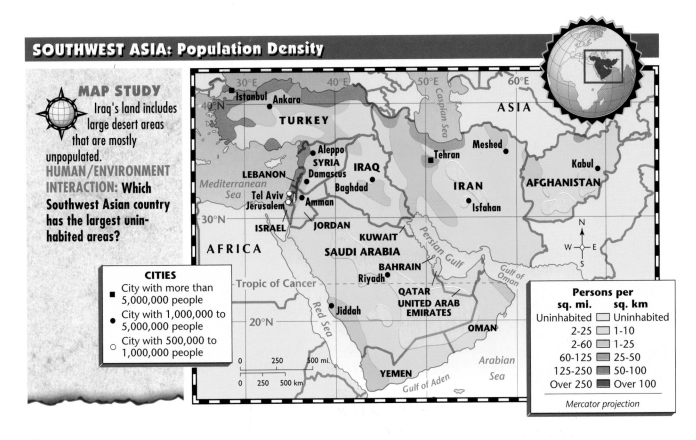

MAP STUDY Iraq's land includes large desert areas that are mostly unpopulated. **HUMAN/ENVIRONMENT INTERACTION: Which Southwest Asian country has the largest uninhabited areas?**

CITIES
- City with more than 5,000,000 people
- City with 1,000,000 to 5,000,000 people
- City with 500,000 to 1,000,000 people

Persons per	
sq. mi.	sq. km
Uninhabited	Uninhabited
2-25	1-10
2-60	1-25
60-125	25-50
125-250	50-100
Over 250	Over 100

Mercator projection

The Economy Iraq's economy is based on oil and agriculture as you can see on the map on page 429. Oil is the country's major export. Manufacturing also has developed in recent years, with Iraqi factories making food products, cloth, soap, and leather goods.

Most farming in Iraq takes place near the Tigris and Euphrates rivers. Find this area on the map on page 420. The plain between the rivers is called an **alluvial plain** because it is built up by rich fertile soil left by river floods. Iraq's farmers grow crops such as barley, dates, grapes, melons, citrus fruits, and wheat.

The People The land lined with date palms along the Tigris and Euphrates rivers is home to most of Iraq's 21.8 million people. About 70 percent live in urban areas such as Baghdad. Muslim Arabs make up the largest group in Iraq's population. A Muslim people, Kurds, are the second-largest group. The Kurds have their own culture and live in the mountains of northeast Iraq. Many Kurds in Iraq and in neighboring Turkey want to form their own independent country.

Past and Present Throughout the centuries, many empires have risen and fallen on the Tigris-Euphrates plain. From the A.D. 700s to 1200s, Baghdad was the center of a large Muslim empire that made many advances in the arts and sciences. Modern Iraq, with its wealth in oil, seeks to become a leading power in Southwest Asia. Over the past few years, Iraq has fought wars with some of its neighbors to gain more territory.

In 1990 Iraqi armies invaded Kuwait, Iraq's southern neighbor. In early 1991 a United Nations force led by the United States launched air and missile attacks on Iraq and its forces in Kuwait. The war against Iraq became known as the Persian Gulf War. Iraqi forces were forced to withdraw from Kuwait, but not before they set afire hundreds of Kuwait's oil wells. Oil spilling from the wells created huge, explosive lakes of petroleum and fires and smoke that threatened much of the Persian Gulf's plant and animal life.

Since the conflict, Iraq's people have faced many hardships. Iraq's government continues to threaten to invade its neighbors. In response many foreign nations, including the United States, refuse to trade with Iraq. This has severely damaged Iraq's economy, which depends on selling oil to other parts of the world.

Location
Iran

Iran lies east of Iraq and northeast of the Arabian Peninsula. Zapha, a 14-year-old schoolgirl in modern Iran, knows she lives in one of the world's oldest countries. In school she learned that her country even had a different name at one time—Persia. What has not changed is the land of Iran itself.

The Land Iran is about the size of the state of Alaska. A central, dry plateau stretches across most of Iran. Two vast mountain ranges—the Elburz and the Zagros—surround most of this plateau. Coastal plains lie outside the mountains along the shore of the Caspian Sea in the north and along the Persian Gulf coast in the south.

Iran has a variety of climates. Mountainous areas experience severely cold winters and mild summers. Most of the central plateau has a dry climate, with cold winter temperatures and mild to hot summers.

A Science Lesson in an Iranian School

Iranian students and their teacher work in an all-male science class.
PLACE: How is this science classroom similar to science classrooms in the United States?

The Economy Iran is one of the world's leading oil-producing countries. A major part of its income results from the sale of oil to foreign countries. In recent years, however, the falling price of oil on world markets has brought less money into Iran. Other Iranian industries produce a variety of goods, including leather goods, machine tools, and tobacco products.

As in much of Southwest Asia, water is scarce in Iran. Less than 12 percent of Iran's land can be used for farming. In dry areas, you see Iranian farmers bringing water to their fields from wells or through underground tunnels. Iran's chief agricultural products are wheat, barley, corn, cotton, dates, nuts, tea, and tobacco.

Tehran, Iran

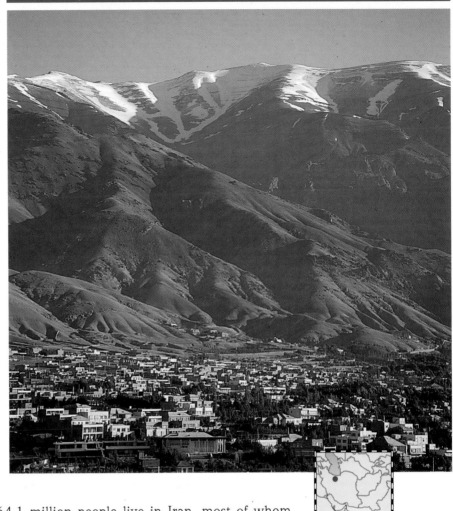

Iran's capital and largest city, Tehran, lies at the base of the majestic Elburz Mountains.
MOVEMENT: Why are many Iranians moving from rural areas to the cities?

The People Today about 64.1 million people live in Iran, most of whom speak Persian, or Farsi, a language that is different from Arabic. About 98 percent of Iranians are Muslims who belong to a group within Islam known as Shiites (SHEE•YTES). Most of the world's Muslims belong to another group known as Sunnis (SU•NEES).

About 61 percent of Iran's people live in urban areas. In recent years towns and cities have grown tremendously because many people from rural areas have moved to urban areas in search of jobs. Find Tehran, Iran's capital and largest city, on the map on page 435. It has a population of about 11.7 million.

Iran was part of the powerful Persian Empire about 3,500 years ago. The descendants of ancient Persians make up the majority of Iran's population today. For hundreds of years Iran was ruled by kings known as **shahs**. Mohammed Reza Pahlavi (PA•luh•vee) became shah during World War II. In the 1960s and 1970s, he used money from oil sales to promote industry and to build Iran's military forces. The shah, however, was accused of ruling harshly, and many Iranians turned against him. In 1979 a revolution forced the shah out of Iran. In place of the shah's government, the Iranians set up a government run by religious leaders. Iran's Muslim government has placed strict laws on the country, and many non-Muslim customs are now forbidden.

Place

Afghanistan

Afghanistan is the easternmost country in Southwest Asia. It is a land of rugged landscapes and has no seacoast. Because of these geographic features, Afghanistan has had difficulty developing its resources.

The Land The Hindu Kush range covers most of Afghanistan. It has peaks as high as 25,000 feet (7,620 m). The Khyber (KY•buhr) Pass, which cuts through the Hindu Kush, for centuries has been used as a major trade route linking Southwest Asia with other parts of Asia. Rolling grasslands and low deserts make up the nonmountainous areas of Afghanistan. Highland and desert climates prevail in most of the country.

The Economy Afghanistan's major economic activity is farming. You see such crops as wheat, barley, corn, cotton, nuts, fruits, and vegetables growing there. Afghanistan is rich in minerals, but it has little industry. A few mills produce textiles, and skilled craftspeople produce beautiful rugs and jewelry in their homes.

The People The 24.8 million people of Afghanistan are divided into about 20 different **ethnic groups,** with each group having its own ancestry, language, and culture. The two largest ethnic groups are the Pushtuns (PUHSH•TOONZ) and the Tajiks (tah•JIHKS). Afghanistan's people practice Islam and live in the fertile valleys of the Hindu Kush range. The capital city, Kabul, is located in one of these valleys.

Afghanistan has had a long and troubled history. From ancient times to the present, a series of foreign powers have won or tried to win control of the country. The country also has been torn apart by continuing civil wars among its many ethnic groups.

SECTION 5 ASSESSMENT

REVIEWING TERMS AND FACTS

1. **Define the following:** alluvial plain, shah, ethnic group.

2. **HUMAN/ENVIRONMENT INTERACTION** How did the Persian Gulf War affect the environment of the Persian Gulf area?

3. **PLACE** What type of government rules Iran today?

4. **PLACE** What is the major landform of Afghanistan?

MAP STUDY ACTIVITIES

5. Using the map on page 435, name the large body of water that lies southeast of Iraq and south of Iran.

6. Look at the map on page 435. Around what body of water do most Iranians live?

Chapter 16 Highlights

Important Things to Know About Southwest Asia

SECTION 1 TURKEY

- Turkey is located in both Europe and Asia.
- Highlands and plateaus make up most of Turkey's land area.
- Most of Turkey's people live in cities and towns.

SECTION 2 ISRAEL

- Israel is the only Jewish nation in the world.
- Despite its small size, Israel has a well-developed economy.
- Israel and its Arab neighbors are moving toward peace after a long period of tension and warfare.

SECTION 3 SYRIA, LEBANON, AND JORDAN

- Syria has a coastal plain, mountains, and deserts.
- Lebanon is one of the smallest countries of Southwest Asia.
- Jordan's farmers grow crops in the rich Jordan River valley.

SECTION 4 THE ARABIAN PENINSULA

- Oil-rich Saudi Arabia is the largest country of Southwest Asia.
- Most of Saudi Arabia's people live in coastal areas.
- Persian Gulf countries have strong economies based on oil.

SECTION 5 IRAQ, IRAN, AND AFGHANISTAN

- Iraq has recently fought wars to increase its power in Southwest Asia.
- Iran is governed by Muslim religious leaders.
- Afghanistan's land area is largely mountainous.

A market in San'a, Yemen ▶

REVIEWING KEY TERMS

Match the numbered terms in Set A with their lettered definitions in Set B.

A

1. potash
2. Bedouin
3. *hajj*
4. shah
5. monotheism
6. oasis
7. alluvial plain

B

A. area of fertile soil left by river floods
B. mineral used in making fertilizer
C. Muslim pilgrimage to Makkah
D. area in dry places that has enough water to grow crops
E. Iranian king
F. nomadic desert people
G. belief in one God

REVIEWING THE MAIN IDEAS

Mental Mapping Activity

Draw a freehand map of the Arabian Peninsula. Label the following:
- Persian Gulf
- Kuwait
- Saudi Arabia
- Yemen
- Red Sea

Section 1

1. LOCATION In what part of Turkey is the Anatolian Plateau?
2. PLACE What is a major industrial product of Turkey?

Section 2

3. LOCATION What river flows into the Dead Sea?
4. HUMAN/ENVIRONMENT INTERACTION How have Israelis made their land suitable for farming?

Section 3

5. PLACE What kind of climate does Lebanon have?
6. LOCATION Where is Jordan's major farming region?

Section 4

7. PLACE What is the major industry of Saudi Arabia?
8. MOVEMENT What has drawn foreigners to Oman's cities?

Section 5

9. PLACE What major rivers flow through Iraq?
10. LOCATION What Southwest Asian country is located east of Iran?

CRITICAL THINKING ACTIVITIES

1. **Making Inferences** From what you know about a desert climate, what could you expect to be true about farming in the Negev region of Israel?
2. **Determining Cause and Effect** How has the discovery of oil changed the lives of people living on the Arabian Peninsula?

CONNECTIONS TO ECONOMICS

Cooperative Learning Activity Working in a small group, select a country of Southwest Asia and research how the people have adapted their environment to help develop their country's economy. Each person in your group can research a different part of the economy and then share findings with the group. Prepare charts, storyboards, and posters that will illustrate your presentation to the rest of the class.

GeoJournal Writing Activity

In this chapter on Southwest Asia, you were introduced to several important cities. Review the chapter to see how these cities are similar and how they are different. Write a short story or letter describing a trip to two of these cities.

TECHNOLOGY ACTIVITY

Using the Internet Search the Internet for an on-line newspaper with current articles about Southwest Asia. Find a recent article about a Southwest Asian country that relates to its geography. Write a brief summary of the article, noting the source of the information. Then write a statement about how the issue described in the article might affect life in your community.

PLACE LOCATION ACTIVITY: SOUTHWEST ASIA

Match the letters on the map with the places in Southwest Asia. Write your answers on a separate sheet of paper.

1. Zagros Mountains
2. Arabian Sea
3. Istanbul
4. Persian Gulf
5. Afghanistan
6. Tel Aviv
7. Euphrates River
8. Makkah
9. Tehran
10. Saudi Arabia

GeoLab ACTIVITY

From the classroom of Eleanor Bloom, Bloom-Carroll Schools, Lithopolis, Ohio

SUNDIALS: Shadow Time

Background

The Chinese used water clocks to measure time more than 3,000 years ago. Egyptians also made water clocks, in which water spilled from one vessel to another. Early civilizations in Southwest Asia and North Africa measured time, too, but instead of water they used the sun as their timekeeper. Sundials measure the shadows an object casts as the sun moves from east to west during the day. Find out more about how these early civilizations measured time by making your own sundial.

Modern Sundial

In the 1300s Henry de Vick invented a clock that contained many of the parts that modern clocks have. Atomic clocks are the world's most accurate timepieces today, gaining or losing only a few seconds every 100,000 years!

A white or light-colored paper plate makes the best base for your sundial.

Materials

- 1 empty thread spool
- 1 ruler
- 1 paper plate
- 1 marker
- glue
- 1 new, sharpened pencil

What To Do

A. Glue the spool to the center of the paper plate.

B. Stand the pencil, with the point up, in the top hole of the spool.

C. Draw an arrow on the paper plate.

D. Place your sundial in a sunny window where it gets sunlight all day long. Make sure the arrow is pointing south.

E. Every hour, trace a line along the shadow's line. Use pictograms or Roman numerals to mark the hours.

Lab Activity Report

1. Are the shadow lines you made an equal distance apart?

2. As you made your shadow lines, did the same thing happen every hour?

3. What are the advantages and disadvantages of using a sundial to measure time?

4. **Drawing Conclusions** Does the space between the shadow lines have anything to do with telling time? Explain.

Go A Step Further!

Activity
Invent a new way to tell time. Think of using everyday items and materials that you usually do not associate with telling time. Write a news report explaining your new invention.

Cultural HERITAGE:
SOUTHWEST ASIA AND NORTH AFRICA

CALLIGRAPHY ▶ ▶ ▶ ▶

A page from the Quran, the Islamic holy book, shows the flowing curves of Arabic script called calligraphy. Artists and architects use calligraphy to decorate the walls of buildings, metalware, and pottery.

◀ ◀ ◀ ◀ RELIGIOUS ART

Religion is a common subject in this region's artwork. This stained glass window in Israel shows the 12 original Hebrew tribes. The window was created by world-famous painter Marc Chagall, a Russian Jew born in 1887.

ARTIFACTS ▶ ▶ ▶ ▶

The burial tomb of Tutankhamen, discovered in Egypt in 1922, was filled with jewelry, statues, clothing, and even toys. This funeral mask is pure gold and inlaid with semiprecious stones.

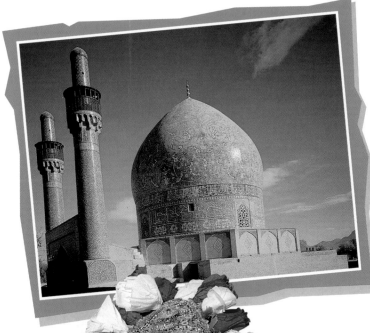

◄ ◄ ◄ ◄ ARCHITECTURE

A blue-domed mosque in Isfahan, Iran, shows typical calligraphy and geometric patterns. Most mosques have a *mihrab*—an arch or other structure that marks the wall closest to the holy city of Makkah.

MUSIC ▲ ▲ ▲ ▲

An Egyptian musician draws a bow across this instrument called a *kamanja.* The music of North Africa and Southwest Asia is most often played on stringed instruments, flutes, drums, and tambourines.

JEWELRY ▲ ▲ ▲ ▲

This elaborate head covering is called a *gargush.* It is made by knitting tiny silver wires together with multicolored beads. Some Jewish women of Yemen still wear this traditional headdress.

APPRECIATING CULTURE

1. What does the mask of Tutankhamen tell us about the king and the time in which he lived?

2. In what ways is calligraphy used as art in our country?

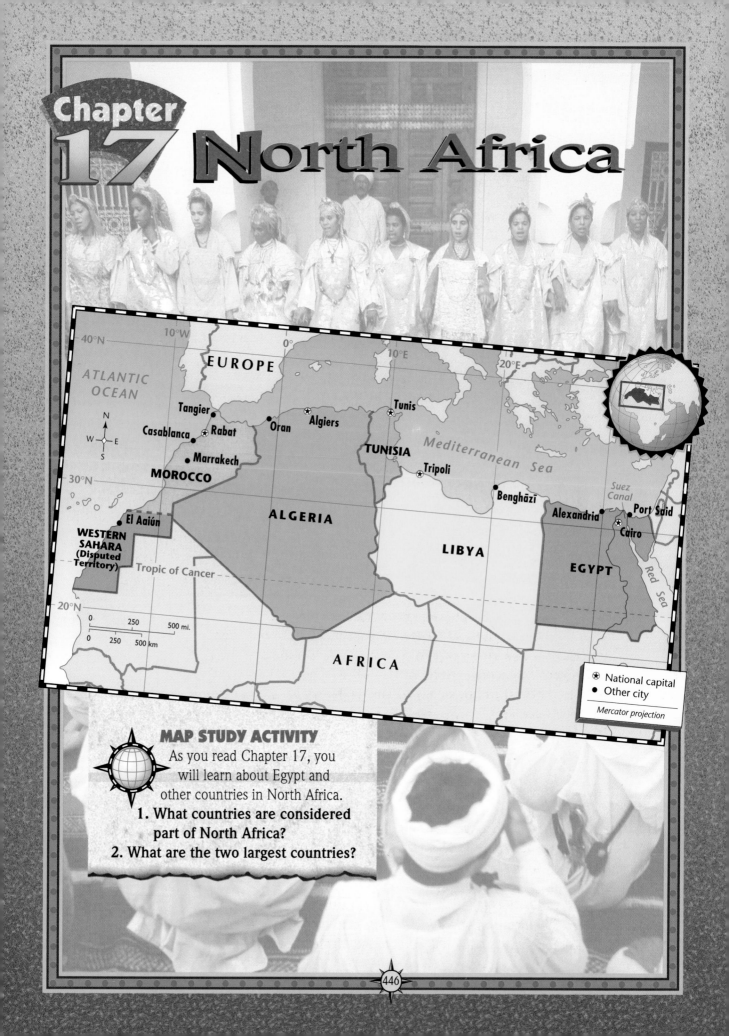

Chapter 17 North Africa

MAP STUDY ACTIVITY

As you read Chapter 17, you will learn about Egypt and other countries in North Africa.

1. What countries are considered part of North Africa?
2. What are the two largest countries?

Map labels

EUROPE

ATLANTIC OCEAN

Tangier
Casablanca
Rabat
Marrakech
Oran
Algiers
Tunis
TUNISIA
Tripoli
Benghāzi
MOROCCO
El Aaiún
WESTERN SAHARA (Disputed Territory)
Tropic of Cancer
ALGERIA
LIBYA
Alexandria
Port Said
Cairo
Suez Canal
EGYPT
Red Sea
Mediterranean Sea
AFRICA

National capital
Other city

Mercator projection

0 250 500 mi.
0 250 500 km

Egypt

PREVIEW

Words to Know
- silt
- delta
- hydroelectric power
- consumer goods
- *fellahin*
- bazaar
- hieroglyph

Places to Locate
- Nile River
- Sinai Peninsula
- Suez Canal
- Libyan Desert
- Arabian Desert
- Cairo
- Alexandria

Read to Learn . . .
1. why the Nile River is important to Egypt's people.
2. how the Aswan High Dam has affected Egypt's environment.

You live along the lush, green banks of the longest river in the world. Where are you living? You live along the Nile River in the North African country of Egypt.

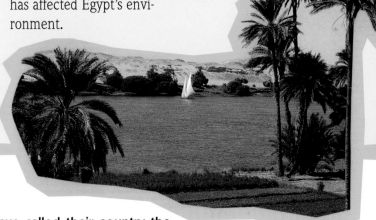

For centuries the people of Egypt have called their country the "gift of the Nile." The river gives them water, fertile soil, and transportation. Egypt receives little rain, and almost all of it is desert. Deserts also cover most of the lands of Egypt's neighbors in North Africa—Libya, Tunisia, Algeria, and Morocco. Egypt has the most people of any country in the region. Look at the graph on page 451 to see how Egypt's population compares with the population of the United States.

Place
The Land

Egypt has three major land areas. They are the Nile River valley, the Sinai (SY•NY) Peninsula, and desert areas. Most of Egypt has a desert climate, with hot summers and mild winters.

Nile River Valley The lifeline of Egypt is the Nile River, which supplies 85 percent of the country's water. The Nile River begins in east Africa. It flows north through the countries of Sudan and Egypt to the Mediterranean Sea. The

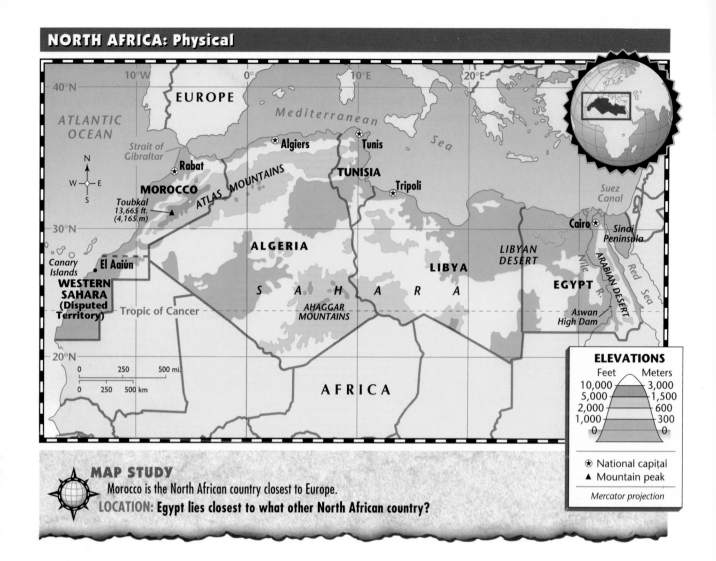

MAP STUDY
Morocco is the North African country closest to Europe.
LOCATION: Egypt lies closest to what other North African country?

Nile River's length of 4,180 miles (6,690 km) far surpasses the second-longest river in the world—the Amazon—which is 3,912 miles long (6,296 km).

Imagine you are looking down on Egypt from an airplane flying from south to north. Below you the Nile River and its banks appear as a narrow, green ribbon cutting through the vast desert.

Flood Control The Nile River valley has rich soils formed by **silt,** or particles of earth deposited by the river. In ancient times, floodwaters left heavy deposits of silt every summer. Today dams control the river's flow, and flooding no longer occurs regularly.

As you continue your flight, you can see the Nile River spread out into a broad wedge of farmland about 150 miles (240 km) from the Mediterranean Sea. You are viewing a **delta,** or triangle-shaped area of land at a river's mouth.

Sinai Peninsula The Sinai Peninsula lies southeast of the Nile Delta. This section of Egypt is not in Africa but is actually part of Southwest Asia. If you look at the map above, you can see why this area is a major crossroads between these two continents.

A human-made waterway called the Suez Canal separates the Sinai Peninsula from the rest of Egypt. Egyptians and Europeans built this important canal in the mid-1860s to allow ships to pass between the Red and the Mediterranean seas.

Deserts From the airplane you can see that most of Egypt is desert. West of the Nile River lies the Libyan (LIH•bee•uhn) Desert. It covers two-thirds of Egypt's land area. Oases are found throughout the Libyan Desert. East of the Nile River and west of the Red Sea is the Arabian Desert.

The Libyan and Arabian deserts are parts of the Sahara—one of the largest deserts in the world. *Sahara* is from the Arabic word meaning "desert." The Sahara—about the size of the United States—runs from Egypt westward through North Africa to the Atlantic Ocean.

Human/Environment Interaction
The Economy

Egypt has a developing economy that has grown considerably in recent years. Since the 1950s government and business leaders have started many new industries. Agriculture, however, remains Egypt's main economic activity.

Agriculture Only about 4 percent of Egypt's land is used for farming. The map on page 450 shows that Egypt's best farmland lies in the fertile Nile River valley. Most Egyptian farmers tend small plots and grow cotton, dates, vegetables, sugarcane, and wheat. They use irrigation, modern tools, and farming methods developed by their ancestors. Cotton is Egypt's leading agricultural export.

Aswan High Dam Until the 1960s Egyptian farmers could plant only once a year—after the Nile River finished flooding in the summer. In 1968 engineers completed the construction of the Aswan High Dam. It holds back the Nile's floodwater. Now Egyptian farmers plant crops two or three times a year.

The Aswan High Dam brings problems as well as blessings. Why? It now stops much of the rich silt flow that fertilized Egypt's fields each year. Egypt's farmers must rely on expensive artificial fertilizers. The dam also restricts the flow of water into the river valley and the Mediterranean Sea. Salty seawater now moves farther inland into the delta.

Industry The Aswan High Dam provides **hydroelectric power,** or electric energy from moving water, to Egypt's growing industries. The largest industrial centers are the capital city of Cairo and the seaport of Alexandria. Egyptian factories there produce mainly food products, textiles, and **consumer goods,** or household goods, clothing, and shoes that people buy.

Harvesting Cotton in Egypt

An Egyptian woman gathers cotton, Egypt's most valuable crop.
LOCATION: Where do you think most of Egypt's cotton fields are located?

Egyptian Music

Can you imagine keeping an orchestra in your home? In ancient Egypt, some wealthy households had their own household orchestras. Ancient Egyptians also put musical instruments in tombs. They believed that this would guarantee them entertainment in their lives after death.

Oil ranks as the country's most important natural resource and a major export. The map below shows that many of Egypt's oil wells are in and around the Red Sea. Another growing industry is tourism.

Place

The People

Most Egyptians live within 20 miles (33 km) of the Nile River. This means that 99 percent of Egypt's population live on only 3.5 percent of the land. Look at the population density map on page 457. You can see that the Nile River valley is one of the most densely populated areas in the Southwest Asia/North Africa region. It is also one of the most densely populated areas in the world.

Rural Life About 43 percent of Egypt's people live in rural areas. Most rural Egyptians are farmers called *fellahin* (FEHL•uh•HEEN). They live in villages and work on small plots of land rented from landowners. Many *fellahin* raise only

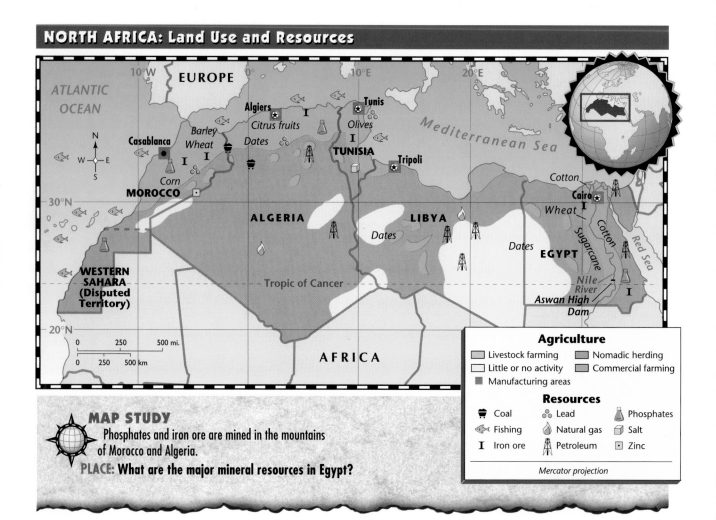

NORTH AFRICA: Land Use and Resources

Agriculture
- ☐ Livestock farming
- ☐ Little or no activity
- ■ Manufacturing areas
- ☐ Nomadic herding
- ☐ Commercial farming

Resources
- Coal
- Fishing
- I Iron ore
- Lead
- Natural gas
- Petroleum
- Phosphates
- Salt
- Zinc

Mercator projection

MAP STUDY

Phosphates and iron ore are mined in the mountains of Morocco and Algeria.

PLACE: What are the major mineral resources in Egypt?

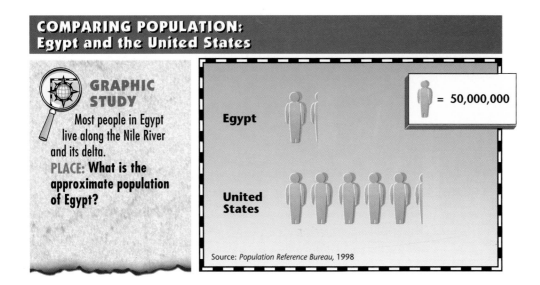

COMPARING POPULATION: Egypt and the United States

GRAPHIC STUDY

Most people in Egypt live along the Nile River and its delta.

PLACE: What is the approximate population of Egypt?

Egypt

United States

= 50,000,000

Source: *Population Reference Bureau, 1998*

enough crops to feed their families. Any food left over is sold in towns at a **bazaar,** or marketplace.

City Life Egypt's large cities offer a different kind of life. Skilled and unskilled workers make up the largest groups of Egyptians in cities. Cairo is a huge and rapidly growing city, with more than 11 million people. It is the largest city in Egypt as well as in Africa. Cairo's mosques, schools, and universities make it a leading center of the Muslim world.

Why is Cairo's population increasing? First, Egypt is a country with a high birthrate. Second, many *fellahin* from rural areas have moved into Cairo to find work. As Cairo's population grows, the city cannot provide enough living space for all of its people. If you were a student in one of Cairo's schools, you might attend crowded classes on a split shift.

Influences of the Past What do you think of when you hear the word "Egypt"? Pyramids? Pharaohs and kings? Egypt has a long and fascinating history. One of the ancient world's most advanced civilizations developed along the Nile River. Ancient Egyptians used **hieroglyphs,** or picture symbols, for writing. One of the first civilizations to make paper from the reedlike papyrus plant, the Egyptians also created a calendar to keep track of the growing season. They became skilled in building such lasting monuments as the Great Sphinx and the Pyramids.

In later centuries, Egypt was ruled by outsiders—Romans, Persians, Arabs, Turks, and the British. Under Arab rule, Islam—its followers are called Muslims—and the Arabic language came to Egypt. Both Islam and Arabic have been an important part of Egyptian life ever since. Today almost 90 percent of Egyptians are Muslims and about 10 percent are Christians.

Government Egypt became a republic in 1953. Gamal Abdel Nasser was president of Egypt from 1954 to 1970. Under Nasser, Egypt became the most powerful country in the Arab world. Nasser, supported by other Arab countries,

Wide avenues wind through
modern Cairo.
**PLACE: Why is Cairo so
densely populated?**

opposed Israel. He also angered many Europeans by taking control of the British-run Suez Canal, which was vital to European trade.

To regain control of the canal, Britain, France, and Israel invaded Egypt in 1956. The United Nations persuaded the Europeans and the Israelis to withdraw their troops. Tensions between the countries remained, however. In the 1970s Egypt and Israel decided to settle their differences. In recent years, Egypt has also strengthened its ties with the United States.

SECTION 1 ASSESSMENT

REVIEWING TERMS AND FACTS

1. **Define the following:** silt, delta, hydroelectric power, consumer goods, *fellahin,* bazaar, hieroglyph.

2. **PLACE** Why is Egypt called "the gift of the Nile"?

3. **HUMAN/ENVIRONMENT INTERACTION** How has the Aswan High Dam affected the lives of Egyptians?

4. **LOCATION** Where is Cairo located?

MAP STUDY ACTIVITIES

5. Turn to the physical map of North Africa on page 448. Where is the Aswan High Dam located?

6. Look at the political map of North Africa on page 446. (a) What direction is Alexandria from Cairo? (b) About how many miles (km) separate the two cities?

BUILDING GEOGRAPHY SKILLS

Using Technology

Using an Electronic Spreadsheet

A spreadsheet is an electronic worksheet that can manage numbers quickly and easily. Spreadsheets are powerful tools because you can change or update information and the spreadsheet automatically performs the calculations.

All spreadsheets follow a basic design of rows and columns. Each column is assigned a letter and each row is assigned a number. Each point where a column and a row intersect is called a *cell*. The cell's position on the spreadsheet is labeled according to its corresponding column and row—*A1* in column A, row 1; *B2* in column B, row 2, and so on. The formula (C1+C2) tells the spreadsheet to add the numbers in cells C1 and C2.

Spreadsheets are important tools for geographers. For example, a geographer might want to compare how much oil North African countries have produced over time.

Use these steps to create a spreadsheet that will provide this information.

1. In cells B1 and C1, type the years 1980 and 1994. In cell D1, type the word *total*.
2. In cells A2–A6, type the names of North Africa's countries. In cell A7, type the word *total*.
3. In row 2, enter the number of metric tons of oil produced in 1980 and 1994 by the country named in cell A2.
4. Repeat step 3 in rows 3–6. You can find the information you need for each country in a world almanac or encyclopedia.

	A	B	C	D
1		1980	1994	total
2	Algeria			
3	Egypt			
4	Libya			
5	Morocco			
6	Tunisia			
7	total			

5. Create a formula that tells which cells (B2+C2) to add together so the computer can calculate the number of tons of oil for that country.
6. Copy the formula down in the cells for the other four countries.
7. Use the process in steps 5 and 6 to create and copy a formula to calculate the total amount of oil produced each year.

Technology Skills Practice

For additional practice in using an electronic spreadsheet, follow the steps listed above to create a spreadsheet that tracks the number of students in your school over time. Find out the number of students in each grade in your school in the years 1995 and 2000 and enter these numbers in your spreadsheet. After you have completed the spreadsheet, write a conclusion about how the numbers changed between 1995 and 2000.

SECTION 2

Other North African Countries

PREVIEW

Words to Know
- dictatorship
- erg
- *casbah*

Places to Locate
- Sahara
- Libya
- Tunisia
- Atlas Mountains
- Maghreb
- Algeria
- Morocco
- Casablanca

Read to Learn . . .
1. what natural resources are found in North Africa.
2. why most people in North Africa live in coastal areas.
3. how urban and rural life differ in North Africa.

The busy sounds of this modern oil-refining plant echo across the Sahara in the country of Libya. You probably think the Sahara is nothing but miles and miles of shifting sand. The Sahara covers major oil reserves.

Like Egypt, the other countries of North Africa—Libya, Tunisia, Algeria, and Morocco—have established economies based on oil and other natural resources found in the Sahara. Look at the map on page 448. You see that the vast stretches of the Sahara lie to the south of North Africa, and the deep blue waters of the Mediterranean Sea lie to the north.

Place

Libya

Libya is a huge country about one-fifth the size of the United States. Until the mid-1900s Libya was a poor country with few natural resources. The discovery of oil in 1959 brought Libya great wealth.

The Land More than 90 percent desert, Libya is one of the world's driest countries. Its need for water increases as its population grows. In 1996 the Libyan government opened a long irrigation pipeline to bring water to coastal areas from aquifers in the south.

454

UNIT 6

The Economy Although most of Libya's land is too dry for farming, Libya is the richest country in North Africa. It earns an enormous income from its oil exports. A Libyan oil worker earns more in one month than could be earned in one year of farming. The government uses profits from oil to improve farming and to build new schools, houses, and hospitals.

The People The 5.7 million people of Libya are of mixed Arab and Berber ancestry. The Berbers were the first people known to live in North Africa. During the A.D. 600s, the Arabs brought Islam and the Arabic language to North Africa, including Libya.

If you lived in Libya today, you would probably live in an urban area along the Mediterranean coast, as about 86 percent of Libyans do. Most live in two modern cities—Tripoli, which is the capital, and Benghazi.

For many centuries Libya was a part of either Muslim or European empires. It finally became an independent country in 1951 under a monarchy. In 1969 a military officer named Muammar al-Qaddhafi (kuh•DAH•fee) came to power. He set up a **dictatorship**, or a government under the control of one all-powerful leader.

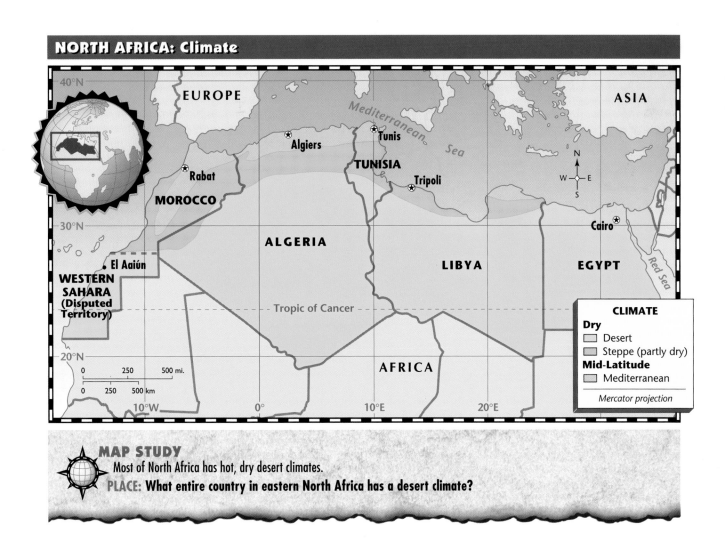

NORTH AFRICA: Climate

CLIMATE
Dry
Desert
Steppe (partly dry)
Mid-Latitude
Mediterranean

Mercator projection

MAP STUDY
Most of North Africa has hot, dry desert climates.
PLACE: What entire country in eastern North Africa has a desert climate?

Shepherds tend their flocks on the rocky slopes of North Africa's Atlas Mountains.
LOCATION: Through what three countries do the Atlas Mountains extend?

Region
Tunisia

Tunisia and two other western North African countries—Algeria and Morocco—form a region known as the Maghreb (MAH•gruhb). *Maghreb* means "the West" in Arabic. These three countries form the westernmost region of the Arab-Islamic world.

The Land About the size of the state of Missouri, Tunisia is North Africa's smallest country. Like other countries of North Africa, Tunisia includes large areas of the Sahara.

Two branches of the rugged Atlas mountain range sweep into the northern part of Tunisia. The Atlas Mountains stretch from western Morocco to northeastern Tunisia.

The Economy Tunisia depends on mining and agriculture for its income. It exports phosphates and oil. If you were a Tunisian farmer, you would probably grow wheat, barley, olives, and grapes—the country's major farm products. Most of Tunisia's farms are located along the fertile east coast. As the map on page 455 shows, this coastal area has a mild Mediterranean climate that favors the growing of crops.

The People Almost all of Tunisia's 9.5 million people are of Arab and Berber ancestry and speak Arabic. Look at the population density map on page 457.

Notice that most Tunisians live in the northern and eastern areas of the country. About 60 percent of Tunisia's people live in urban areas. Tunis, with a population of about 1 million, is the capital and largest city.

In ancient times the city of Carthage arose in the area that is now Tunisia. Carthage fought unsuccessfully with Rome for control of the Mediterranean world. In modern times France ruled Tunisia as a colony. Although Tunisia became an independent republic in 1956, French influences can still be seen.

Place
Algeria

Crossing Algeria is no quick trip. Algeria is the largest country in the region of Southwest Asia and North Africa. It is more than three times bigger than the state of Texas.

The Land The landscape of Algeria varies from plains to mountains to deserts. Along the Mediterranean coast is a narrow strip of land known as the Tell. The word *tell* is an Arabic term meaning "hill." The hills and plains of the

Praying in Tunisia

Muslims gather at a mosque for daily prayers.
REGION: What is the major religion of Tunisia?

NORTH AFRICA: Population Density

CITIES
- ■ City with more than 5,000,000 people
- ● City with 1,000,000 to 5,000,000 people
- ○ City with 500,000 to 1,000,000 people

Persons per

sq. mi.	sq. km
Uninhabited	Uninhabited
Under 2	Under 1
2-60	1-25
60-125	25-50
125-250	50-100
Over 250	Over 100

Mercator projection

EUROPE

Mediterranean Sea

Oran • Algiers • Tunis
Rabat •
Casablanca •
MOROCCO
TUNISIA
Tripoli ○
Alexandria ■
Giza ● Cairo ■
WESTERN SAHARA (Disputed Territory)
ALGERIA
LIBYA
EGYPT
Red Sea
Tropic of Cancer
AFRICA

0   250   500 mi.
0   250 500 km

MAP STUDY
Most people in North Africa live near the Mediterranean coast and in river valley areas where water is available.
HUMAN/ENVIRONMENT INTERACTION: What North African country has the highest population density?

Tell contain Algeria's best farmland. A Mediterranean climate with hot, dry summers and mild, rainy winters helps crops grow.

South of the Tell are the Atlas Mountains. In Algeria the Atlas Mountains form two major chains with an average height of about 7,000 feet (2,134 m). Another mountain range known as the Ahaggar (uh•HAH•guhr) lies in southern Algeria. Between the Atlas and Ahaggar mountains are parts of the Sahara known as **ergs,** huge areas of shifting sand dunes. You find a hot, dry climate in most parts of Algeria south of the Tell.

The Economy Agriculture, manufacturing, and mining are the basis of Algeria's developing economy. Algeria has large deposits of natural gas and petroleum. These two natural resources make up 30 percent of the country's income.

The People About 30 million people live in Algeria. Like Libya and Tunisia, Algeria has a population of mixed Arab and Berber ancestry. Most Algerians practice Islam and speak Arabic. People in the countryside raise livestock or farm small pieces of land. Algiers, the capital and largest city, has about 1.5 million people.

What is it like to be a teenager living in Algiers? Fatimah Malek is an Algerian teen who enjoys visiting the old areas of Algiers called **casbahs.** In these sections, shops, mosques, bazaars, and homes line narrow streets. Fatimah lives in a new section of Algiers that has broad streets and modern buildings.

In school Fatimah has learned about her country's independent spirit. Algeria came under French rule in the 1800s. The Algerians never accepted French control of their country, however. In 1962 Algeria became an independent republic. Since the early 1990s, Fatimah and other Algerians have faced hardships as a result of a conflict between the Algerian government and opposing political groups.

Location
Morocco

The country of Morocco lies in the northwestern corner of Africa. Its long seacoast is bordered by the Mediterranean Sea on the north and the Atlantic Ocean on the west. The northern tip of Morocco meets the Strait of Gibraltar.

The Land Morocco's landforms are similar to those of neighboring Algeria. A fertile coastal plain borders the Mediterranean Sea and the Atlantic Ocean. This

It's Festival Time!

Amineh and Jamila are wearing their nicest *caftans* and head scarves. Tonight, the Berber folklore festival will begin. Dancers, singers, and acrobats from all over Morocco come to entertain the large crowds. The 15-day folklore festival takes place every year in May. Amineh and Jamila like to share in all the activities, but their favorite part is meeting new people from other Berber villages.

area has a Mediterranean climate of hot, dry summers and mild, rainy winters. Farther inland rise the Atlas Mountains. You can see from the map on page 448 that the Sahara lies east and south of the Atlas Mountains.

The Economy The major economic activities of Morocco are agriculture, mining, fishing, and tourism. Morocco's farms produce citrus fruits, potatoes, olives, sugar beets, and wheat. The country's mines yield many resources, such as phosphates, iron ore, lead, and natural gas. Morocco leads the world in the export of phosphate rock and is a leading producer of phosphates. Tourism ranks as one of the country's major service industries.

The People Morocco has a population of about 29 million. Most Moroccans are Muslims of mixed Arab and Berber ancestry. They speak the Arabic language or one of several Berber dialects.

About half of Morocco's population live in rural areas. Some live in villages and farm the land; others are herders in desert areas. The rest live in cities. Rabat, with a population of more than 1 million, is Morocco's capital.

The country's largest city and port is Casablanca (KA•suh•BLANG•kuh), home to more than 3 million people. Both Rabat and Casablanca are located on the Atlantic coast. Moroccan cities face the challenge of rapidly growing populations.

History From the A.D. 1000s to the early 1900s, Morocco was a Muslim kingdom that ruled much of northwestern Africa. France and Spain, however, gained control of Morocco's affairs at the beginning of this century. In 1956 Morocco became an independent kingdom once again. At this time, the Moroccan government laid claim to Western Sahara, a large stretch of African territory south of Morocco. Many countries, however, do not recognize this claim.

SECTION 2 ASSESSMENT

REVIEWING TERMS AND FACTS
1. **Define the following:** dictatorship, erg, *casbah.*
2. **PLACE** Where do most of Libya's people live?
3. **LOCATION** What body of water lies north and east of Tunisia?
4. **MOVEMENT** What is Morocco's major export?

MAP STUDY ACTIVITIES
5. Look at the population map of North Africa on page 457. What is the population density around Algiers, Algeria?
6. Using the climate map on page 455, name the North African countries that have both steppe and Mediterranean climates.

MAKING CONNECTIONS

By A.D. 750 Arabs united by the religion of Islam had created a huge empire. Their empire's territory stretched across Southwest Asia and North Africa. The Arabs came into contact with Persian, Indian, Christian, and Jewish scholars living within their empire.

From the A.D. 700s to the 1200s, the city of Baghdad was the Muslim empire's center of learning. The Arabs not only learned Persian astronomy, Indian mathematics, and Greek science, but also added new knowledge to these subjects. Indeed, Muslim mathematicians gave the Western world two kinds of mathematics: algebra and trigonometry.

ALGEBRA About A.D. 825 al-Khwarizmi (ahl•KWAHR•eez•mee), a teacher of mathematics in Baghdad, wrote a book titled *Kitab al-jabr wa al-muqabalah.* His work was a presentation of what was known about algebra at the time. The Arab mathematician improved and expanded algebra, the mathematics that uses symbols to solve complex mathematical problems. Al-Khwarizmi—and readers of his book—invented so many things that scholars consider algebra an Arab creation. Even the name *algebra* comes from part of the title of al-Khwarizmi's book—*al-jabr wa.*

TRIGONOMETRY During the A.D. 900s Muslim mathematicians developed trigonometry, a type of mathematics that deals with the measurements of triangles. They studied and described the spheres in which the sun, moon, and planets were thought to move. Their studies led them to invent the basic ratios, or comparisons, that allow engineers and scientists to measure triangles and distances.

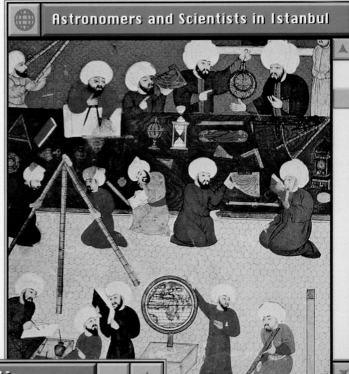

Astronomers and Scientists in Istanbul

Making the Connection

1. From whom did the Arabs learn basic science and mathematics?

2. What contributions did Muslim mathematicians make to Western culture?

Chapter 17 Highlights

Important Things To Know About North Africa

SECTION 1 EGYPT

- The Libyan Desert covers two-thirds of Egypt's land area.
- The Aswan High Dam holds back the Nile's floodwater. The dam provides hydroelectric power to Egypt's growing industries.
- Most of Egypt's people live near the Nile River and depend on it for water and transportation.
- About 43 percent of Egypt's people live in rural areas and farm small plots of land.
- Cairo, Egypt's capital, is the largest city in Africa and a leading center of the Muslim world.
- One of the ancient world's most advanced civilizations developed in the Nile River valley.
- Today Egypt is a republic. Almost 90 percent of Egyptians are Muslims and about 10 percent are Christians.

SECTION 2 OTHER NORTH AFRICAN COUNTRIES

- North Africa also includes the countries of Libya, Tunisia, Algeria, and Morocco. The people of all four countries are of mixed Arab and Berber ancestry.
- The landscape of North Africa is mostly desert or mountains.
- The region's people live on fertile coastal plains or near oases.
- Oil, natural gas, and phosphate rock are among the most important natural resources of North Africa.
- All countries of the region border on the Mediterranean Sea or Atlantic Ocean. This affects climate.

A *casbah* near Duarzazate, Morocco ▶

REVIEWING KEY TERMS

Match the numbered terms in Set A with their lettered definitions in Set B.

A

1. delta
2. *fellahin*
3. hydroelectric power
4. hieroglyphs
5. bazaar
6. consumer goods
7. dictatorship
8. erg
9. *casbah*

B

A. picture symbols
B. government ruled by one all-powerful leader
C. Egyptian farmers
D. sand dune
E. broad swampy triangle where a river runs into an ocean or sea
F. old section of a North African city
G. household products, clothes, and shoes that people buy
H. energy produced from moving water
I. marketplace

Mental Mapping Activity

Draw a freehand map of North Africa. Label the following:

• Egypt
• Nile River
• Cairo
• Libya
• Sahara
• Atlas Mountains

REVIEWING THE MAIN IDEAS

Section 1

1. LOCATION Where is Egypt located?
2. HUMAN/ENVIRONMENT INTERACTION Why did the Egyptians build the Aswan High Dam?
3. PLACE In what direction does the Nile River flow?

Section 2

4. LOCATION Which North African countries border Libya?
5. PLACE What landforms are found in the Sahara?
6. REGION What region includes Tunisia, Morocco, and Algeria?
7. HUMAN/ENVIRONMENT INTERACTION How does Morocco's location help it have a prosperous fishing industry?

CRITICAL THINKING ACTIVITIES

1. **Determining Cause and Effect** Why do you think an early Egyptian civilization developed in a river valley?
2. **Analyzing Information** How have the people of North Africa adapted to their desert environment?

CONNECTIONS TO WORLD HISTORY

Cooperative Learning Activity Work in small groups to discover what life was like in ancient Egypt. Different groups can research the pharaohs, the building of the pyramids, and the daily lives of people. Collect photographs, posters, or real objects to represent what you discover. Put all information together to make a visual presentation of "Life in Ancient Egypt."

GeoJournal Writing Activity

Imagine that you are taking a boat trip along the Nile River. Write a daily diary for seven days, describing what you see and telling about your experiences.

TECHNOLOGY ACTIVITY

Using the Internet Search the Internet for information on the hydroelectric power provided by Egypt's Aswan High Dam. Based on the information, write an article for the school newspaper or magazine about your topic. Be sure to provide a diagram, including labels, of the dam and power plant to explain how power is produced.

PLACE LOCATION ACTIVITY: NORTH AFRICA

Match the letters on the map with the places and physical features of North Africa. Write your answers on a separate sheet of paper.

1. Tripoli
2. Sinai Peninsula
3. Tunis
4. Atlas Mountains
5. Libya
6. Strait of Gibraltar
7. Mediterranean Sea
8. Morocco
9. Cairo

Water: A Precious Resource

PROBLEM

Most of the usable water in **Southwest Asia and North Africa** comes from aquifers and from three river basins: the Jordan, the Tigris-Euphrates, and the Nile. Despite these large river systems, water is scarce. Each of the rivers and its tributaries flows through several countries—and each country's needs are growing. Drought, industrialization, irrigation needs, and mushrooming populations—all strain the limited water supply.

SOLUTIONS

● To resolve water-rights issues, Israel is negotiating with Jordan and the Palestinians over rights to the Jordan River and West Bank aquifers.

● To promote conservation, Tunisia is introducing higher prices for water used for irrigation.

● A recycling project in Tel Aviv, Israel, generates enough recycled wastewater to cultivate 20,000 acres (8,100 hectares) of farmland.

● Advances in technology have lowered the cost of converting seawater to freshwater.

● Cooperative measures, such as Turkey's plans for a Peace Pipeline, may carry water from water-rich countries to water-poor countries.

Drip irrigation, which minimizes water loss, delivers a precise drink of water to a seedling in the desert. Drip irrigation may use 25 percent less water than sprinkler systems.

WATER FACT BANK

🍃 By the year 2015, most of the nations of North Africa will not have enough water to meet basic human needs.

🍃 Crops growing in the desert require huge amounts of water. It takes 3 cubic meters of water (780 gallons) to produce about 2 pounds (1 kilogram) of wheat.

🍃 Turkey's Atatürk Dam, on the Euphrates River, holds back water that once reached other nations downstream. Soon, Syria's share of the Euphrates will shrink by 40 percent, and Iraq's share by 80 percent.

🍃 Saudi Arabia leads the world in producing freshwater from salt water. Its 22 desalination plants produce 30 percent of all the desalinated water in the world.

TEEN TRIBUTE

Hamidreza Modaberi, age 12, lives in the desert country of Iran. In a letter to an environmental publication, she wrote: "I dreamed the whole world had changed. All these dry lands had been turned into a beautiful nature full of trees, full of rivers ... war and bloodshed had ended.... I wish the world would be like my dream."

environmental activities

good planets are hard to find

TAKE A CLOSER LOOK

1 What sources provide Southwest Asia and North Africa with water?

2 What human activities have caused water shortage problems in this region?

WHAT CAN YOU DO?

🍃 Put "Water Watch" posters around your school giving tips about conserving water.

🍃 Improve your own water-saving habits and avoid using products that are polluters.

🍃 Write a letter to the editor of your local newspaper to protest industrial pollution in your community.

🍃 Educate yourself – find out where your water comes from and what is being done to protect that source.

🍃 Fix that dripping faucet!

All's well—as long as the well water flows. This Tunisian farmer bought a pump with a government loan to lift well water to his thirsty fields. Tunisian farms have been irrigated since Roman times.

Unit 7

Africa South of the Sahara

What Makes Africa South of the Sahara a Region?

Most people share...

- a location almost entirely in the tropics.

- the world's fastest-growing and youngest population.

- challenges to the environment, especially natural resources and wildlife.

- a struggle to improve the quality of life.

To find out more about Africa south of the Sahara, see the Unit Atlas on pages 468–483.

Cape Town, Republic of South Africa

EXPLORING THE INTERNET

To learn more about Africa south of the Sahara, visit the Glencoe Social Studies Web site at **www.glencoe.com** for information, activities, and links to other sites.

GeoJournal Activity

As you read this unit, think about why many geographers call Africa an unopened treasure chest.

In your journal, choose the three most important treasures you think Africa has to share with the rest of the world.

UNIT 7 ATLAS

NATIONAL
GEOGRAPHIC
SOCIETY

IMAGES
of the
WORLD

1. African elephant, Kenya
2. Woman in Tombouctou, Mali
3. Victoria Falls, Zimbabwe
4. Shoppers at a market, Madagascar
5. Mosque at Omdurman, Sudan
6. Storefronts, Kenya
7. Oil company supervisor, off Gabon

All photos viewed against a village in
the Tibesti Mountains, Chad.

3

4

2

5

6

Regional Focus

Africa south of the Sahara covers the central and southern parts of the continent. With the Equator crossing its middle, Africa south of the Sahara is the only region in the world that lies almost entirely in the tropics.

Region

The Land

The region of Africa south of the Sahara is about 9.5 million square miles (24.6 sq. km) in size. Its center is mostly made up of large, rolling plateaus. Narrow coastal plains run along the Atlantic and Indian oceans.

Plateaus The region's plateaus rise from west to east like a stairway. Because of these plateaus, Africa has a higher average elevation than any other continent in the world. The map on page 474 shows you that the average elevation in Africa is more than 2,000 feet (610 m) above sea level. Separating the plateaus are steep cliffs. Rivers often spill over the cliffs in thundering waterfalls. The cliffs and waterfalls make land and river travel difficult in many parts of Africa.

Mountains and Valleys Even with its high elevation, Africa south of the Sahara has few tall mountains. Wind and water wore away many of them over millions of years. At 19,340 feet (5,895 m) high, Kilimanjaro is the tallest peak in Africa.

Crossing the plateaus is the Great Rift Valley. This long, narrow break in the earth's surface runs more than 3,000 miles (4,800 km) through eastern Africa. Movements of the earth's crust formed the Great Rift Valley millions of years ago. A chain of deep lakes lies in the Great Rift Valley near the Equator.

A Herder in Burkina Faso

Most people in the country of Burkina Faso make their living by herding cattle.
PLACE: What is the average elevation of land in Africa?

Rivers Four great rivers slice through Africa: the Nile, the Congo, the Niger, and the Zambezi. The largest river system in Africa south of the Sahara is the Congo. It twists and turns for almost 2,800 miles (4,505 km) through the region. A number of small rivers flow into the Congo and the other three large rivers. Africa's major river systems are important means of transportation that link inland areas with oceans.

Region
Climate and Vegetation

Africa south of the Sahara has many types of climate and vegetation. Differences in elevation create much of this variety. If you travel in Africa toward the Equator from either the north or the south, you will find four main climate regions: desert, steppe, tropical savanna, and tropical rain forest. Only the highlands in eastern Africa and the southern tip of Africa have moderate climates.

More of Africa is covered by deserts than any other continent. This occurs because many high plateaus block rain clouds from reaching inland areas. The largest African deserts are the Sahara in the north and the Namib and Kalahari in the south. Around Africa's deserts stretch steppe areas, or partly dry grasslands. Because of drought and human activity, the Sahel steppe area in western Africa is gradually becoming a desert.

South of the Sahara, much of Africa is made up of savannas—tropical grasslands with scattered trees. A wide variety of animal life live in the savannas. Steamy rain forests, however, cover land near the Equator. They have many hardwood trees that provide timber.

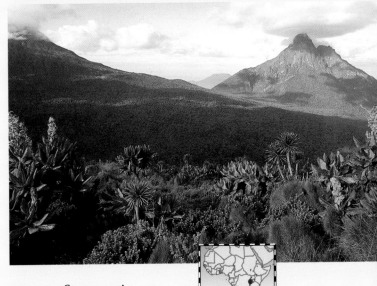

Volcanoes National Park, Rwanda

Volcanic peaks tower over the vast plateaus of northwestern Rwanda.
HUMAN/ENVIRONMENT INTERACTION: What do Africa's rain forests provide?

Human/Environment Interaction
The Economy

The economy of Africa south of the Sahara depends mainly on farming. Another important economic activity is the mining and export of mineral resources.

Agriculture and Mining Farming and herding are Africa's leading economic activities. Some Africans grow only enough food to feed their families. Others work on plantations that grow crops for export. Africa is a major producer of cacao, sweet potatoes, coffee, bananas, cotton, peanuts, tea, and sugar.

Africans also work in mining. In central and southern Africa, miners work some of the world's largest deposits of gold, diamonds, and copper. Oil is found in western and central Africa.

Manufacturing In spite of many resources, manufacturing plays only a small role in Africa's economy. In the past, European nations ruled most of the continent. Today many countries in Africa south of the Sahara are building industries and improving transportation. Few paved roads exist outside of urban areas. Railroads and airplanes are best for traveling long distances in the region.

UNIT 7 ATLAS

Region
The People

South of the Sahara, Africa is divided into 48 nations. Each nation has many ethnic groups, languages, religions, and customs.

Population More than 625 million people live in this region, which is growing rapidly in population. Because so much of Africa is desert or partly dry grasslands, most people live along coasts. Some African governments have encouraged their people to move from the crowded coasts to inland areas. Three countries—Côte d'Ivoire, Nigeria, and Tanzania—have moved or will move their capitals from coastal cities to newly built inland cities.

About 73 percent of Africans south of the Sahara live in rural villages. Economic hardships and the desire for a better life, however, are drawing many people to the cities. African cities are among the fastest-growing urban areas. The three largest cities are Lagos in Nigeria, Kinshasa in the Democratic Republic of the Congo, and Abidjan in Côte d'Ivoire.

Culture People in this region are devoted to family life. Households often are made up of extended families—grandparents and other relatives as well as parents and children. Africans also have close ties to their ethnic groups. In many countries, loyalty to an ethnic group is more important than loyalty to the national government.

History Early Africa saw the rise of powerful empires and city-states that became important cultural centers. From the 1500s to the 1800s, Europeans explored the continent, enslaved many Africans, and sent them to other parts of the world. By 1914, Europeans had divided nearly all of Africa among themselves. They set up borders without regard to the different peoples living in the area.

In many parts of Africa, however, Africans resisted European rule. By the 1960s, most of Africa was made up of independent nations. Descendants of European settlers, however, continued to rule the country of South Africa. They withheld many rights from black Africans and other non-Europeans. In the early 1990s, South Africa extended its democratic form of government to all of its citizens.

The Arts Africans have developed many art forms. African artists are known for their decorative cloth weavings, wooden sculptures, metal jewelry, and pottery. Through the centuries African storytellers have passed down myths, history, and poems from early ancestors. African authors today blend these traditions with modern writing styles. African music has influenced popular music throughout the world.

Johannesburg, South Africa

Johannesburg is South Africa's largest urban area and most important industrial and commercial center.
PLACE: About how many people live in Africa south of the Sahara?

Multimedia Unit 7 Activities

NATIONAL GEOGRAPHIC SOCIETY

Picture Atlas of the World

Population Geography

Using the CD-ROM Calculate the population density of countries in Africa south of the Sahara. Population density refers to the number of people per square mile (or kilometer). To do this you must first go to the *Country* screen. Select 10 African nations. Then calculate the population density for each country by dividing the country's total population by its area. Record your findings on a chart and discuss the following questions:

1. Is the most populous country also the most densely populated country? If not, determine the most densely populated country.

2. How do the following characteristics affect population density?

climate	literacy rate
access to water	fertility rate
elevation	population growth rate

3. What might be the advantages and disadvantages of living in a densely populated city?

Surfing the "Net"

Snapshot of Africa

Imagine that you are a journalist and your editor has assigned you to prepare a feature story on a country of Africa. Your article will focus on the politics, climatic changes, tourist sites, and/or recent events of an African nation you choose. The theme of your feature story should be the changing face of Africa. The article should describe how traditions, popular culture, and the modern world meet in the nations of Africa today.

Getting There

Follow these steps to gather information on African nations:

1. Use a search engine. Type in *Africa*.

2. Enter names of individual African nations and words like the following to focus your search: *politics, news, culture, history*.

3. The search engine will provide you with a number of links to follow.

What To Do When You Are There

Begin your assignment by selecting one African nation. This will be the topic of your feature article. Devise a plan by determining an aspect of this nation on which to focus your article. Create an outline for your article. Navigate through the Web pages to collect information to build your feature story. Prepare your outline along with headline and photo ideas to present to your editor (your teacher) for approval. Once your outline is approved, work to complete your feature story. Share the final article with the class.

Physical Geography

AFRICA SOUTH OF THE SAHARA: Physical

ELEVATIONS

Feet	Meters
10,000	3,000
5,000	1,500
2,000	600
1,000	300
0	0

▲ Mountain peak

Azimuthal Equal-Area projection

Map Study

1. **PLACE** Name three countries crossed by the Sahel.
2. **REGION** In what part of Africa are the three highest mountain peaks located?

ELEVATION PROFILE: Africa

18,000 ft.	
14,000 ft.	4,267 m
10,000 ft.	3,048 m
5,000 ft.	1,524 m
2,000 ft.	610 m
1,000 ft.	305 m
Sea level	Sea level

Mt. Kenya

Great Rift Valley

Ruwenzori Mountains

Lake Victoria

Atlantic Ocean

Indian Ocean

Congo Basin

← West to East at 0° latitude →

Source: *Goode's World Atlas*, 19th edition

GeoFacts

Highest point: Kilimanjaro (Tanzania) 19,340 ft. (5,895 m) high

Lowest point: Lake Assal (Djibouti) 512 ft. (156 m) below sea level

Longest river: Nile River 4,160 mi. (6,693 km) long

Largest lake: Lake Victoria (Uganda/Tanzania) 26,828 sq. mi. (69,485 sq. km)

Largest desert: Sahara 3,500,000 sq. mi. (9,065,000 sq. km)

AFRICA SOUTH OF THE SAHARA AND THE UNITED STATES: Land Comparison

Graphic Study

1. PLACE What is the elevation of Lake Victoria?

2. REGION About how many times larger than the continental United States is Africa south of the Sahara?

Cultural Geography

AFRICA SOUTH OF THE SAHARA: Political

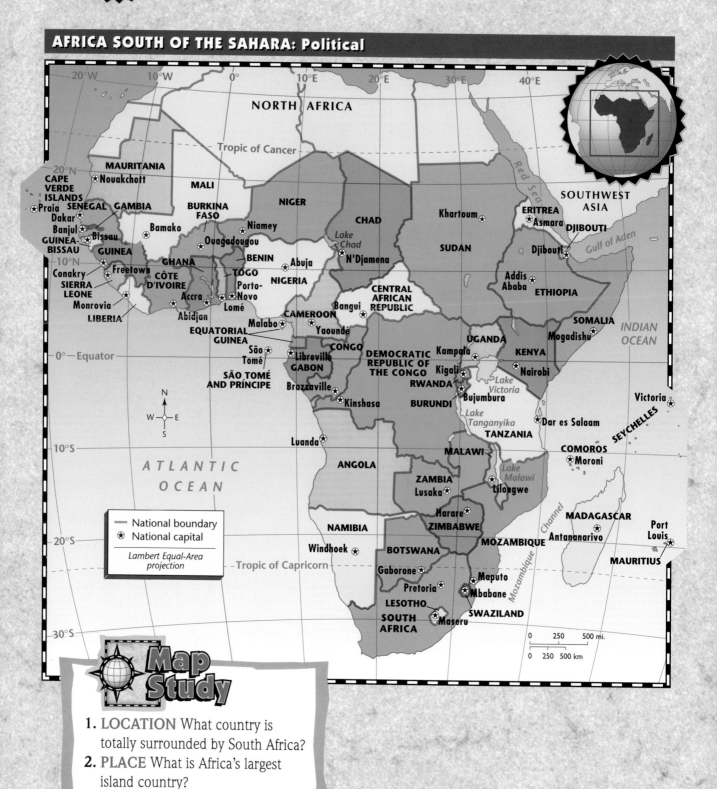

NORTH AFRICA

Tropic of Cancer

MAURITANIA
⊛ Nouakchott

CAPE
VERDE
ISLANDS
⊛ Praia   SENEGAL   GAMBIA
Dakar ⊛
Banjul ⊛
GUINEA- ⊛ Bissau
BISSAU   GUINEA
Conakry ⊛   ⊛ Freetown
SIERRA
LEONE
Monrovia ⊛
LIBERIA

MALI
Bamako ⊛

BURKINA
FASO
⊛ Ouagadougou

Niamey ⊛

GHANA
CÔTE
D'IVOIRE
Accra ⊛
Abidjan ⊛

BENIN
TOGO
Porto-
Novo ⊛
Lomé ⊛

NIGERIA
Abuja ⊛

NIGER

CHAD
Lake
Chad
N'Djamena ⊛

CAMEROON
Bangui ⊛
Malabo ⊛   Yaoundé ⊛
EQUATORIAL
GUINEA
São
Tomé ⊛   Libreville ⊛
GABON
SÃO TOMÉ
AND PRÍNCIPE   Brazzaville ⊛

CONGO
DEMOCRATIC
REPUBLIC OF
THE CONGO

CENTRAL
AFRICAN
REPUBLIC

Khartoum ⊛

SUDAN

Red Sea

ERITREA
⊛ Asmara   DJIBOUTI
⊛ Djibouti
Gulf of Aden

Addis
Ababa ⊛
ETHIOPIA

SOUTHWEST
ASIA

SOMALIA
Mogadishu ⊛

INDIAN
OCEAN

UGANDA
Kampala ⊛
Kigali ⊛
RWANDA
Bujumbura ⊛
BURUNDI
Lake
Tanganyika

KENYA
Nairobi ⊛

Lake
Victoria

Dar es Salaam ⊛
TANZANIA

Victoria ⊛
SEYCHELLES

0° — Equator

Kinshasa ⊛
Luanda ⊛

ATLANTIC
OCEAN

ANGOLA

ZAMBIA
Lusaka ⊛

MALAWI
Lake
Malawi
Lilongwe ⊛

COMOROS
⊛ Moroni

— National boundary
⊛ National capital

Lambert Equal-Area
projection

N
W · E
S

Harare ⊛
ZIMBABWE
NAMIBIA

MOZAMBIQUE

Mozambique Channel

MADAGASCAR
Antananarivo ⊛

Port
Louis ⊛

MAURITIUS

Windhoek ⊛

BOTSWANA
Gaborone ⊛

Tropic of Capricorn

Pretoria ⊛
Maputo ⊛
Mbabane ⊛
LESOTHO
Maseru ⊛
SOUTH
AFRICA
SWAZILAND

0   250   500 mi.
0   250 500 km

Map Study

1. **LOCATION** What country is
   totally surrounded by South Africa?
2. **PLACE** What is Africa's largest
   island country?

UNIT 7

AFRICA SOUTH OF THE SAHARA:
Selected Rural and Urban Populations

	Rural	Urban
WEST AFRICA		
Niger	85%	15%
Cape Verde	56%	44%
CENTRAL AFRICA		
Angola	58%	42%
Central African Republic	61%	39%
EAST AFRICA		
Rwanda	95%	5%
Djibouti	19%	81%
SOUTHERN AFRICA		
Lesotho	84%	16%
South Africa	43%	57%

Source: *Population Reference Bureau, 1998*

GeoFacts

Biggest country (land area): Sudan 917,375 sq. mi. (2,376,000 sq. km)

Smallest country (land area): Seychelles 174 sq. mi. (451 sq. km)

Largest city (population): Lagos (1997) 10,287,000; (2015 projected) 24,600,000

Highest population density: Mauritius 1,483 people per sq. mi. (573 people per sq. km)

Lowest population density: Namibia 5 people per sq. mi. (2 people per sq. km)

COMPARING POPULATION:
Africa South of the Sahara and the United States

Africa South of the Sahara

United States

= 50,000,000

Source: *Population Reference Bureau, 1998*

Graphic Study

1. **PLACE** About how many people live in Africa south of the Sahara?
2. **REGION** What countries in Africa south of the Sahara have a greater urban population than a rural population?

Countries at a Glance

Angola

Luanda

CAPITAL:
Luanda

MAJOR LANGUAGE(S):
Portuguese, Bantu languages

POPULATION:
12,000,000

LANDMASS:
481,350 sq. mi./
1,246,697 sq. km

MONEY:
New Kwanza

MAJOR EXPORT:
Mineral Fuels

MAJOR IMPORT:
Transport Equipment

Benin

Porto-Novo

CAPITAL:
Porto-Novo

MAJOR LANGUAGE(S):
French, Fon, Yoruba, Somba

POPULATION:
6,000,000

LANDMASS:
42,710 sq. mi./
110,619 sq. km

MONEY:
CFA Franc

MAJOR EXPORT:
Cotton

MAJOR IMPORT:
Yarn and Fabric

Botswana

Gaborone

CAPITAL:
Gaborone

MAJOR LANGUAGE(S):
English, Setswana

POPULATION:
1,400,000

LANDMASS:
218,810 sq. mi./
566,718 sq. km

MONEY:
Pula

MAJOR EXPORT:
Diamonds

MAJOR IMPORT:
Transport Equipment

Burkina Faso

Ouagadougou

CAPITAL:
Ouagadougou

MAJOR LANGUAGE(S):
French, Sudanic languages

POPULATION:
11,300,000

LANDMASS:
105,637 sq. mi./
273,763 sq. km

MONEY:
CFA Franc*

MAJOR EXPORT:
Cotton

MAJOR IMPORT:
Machinery

Burundi

Bujumbura

CAPITAL:
Bujumbura

MAJOR LANGUAGE(S):
Rundi, French

POPULATION:
5,500,000

LANDMASS:
9,900 sq. mi./
25,641 sq. km

MONEY:
Burundi Franc

MAJOR EXPORT:
Coffee

MAJOR IMPORT:
Machinery

Cameroon

Yaoundé

CAPITAL:
Yaoundé

MAJOR LANGUAGE(S):
English, French

POPULATION:
14,300,000

LANDMASS:
179,690 sq. mi./
465,397 sq. km

MONEY:
CFA Franc*

MAJOR EXPORT:
Petroleum

MAJOR IMPORT:
Machinery

Cape Verde Islands

Praia

CAPITAL:
Praia

MAJOR LANGUAGE(S):
Portuguese

POPULATION:
400,000

LANDMASS:
1,560 sq. mi./
4,040 sq. km

MONEY:
Escudo

MAJOR EXPORT:
Bananas

MAJOR IMPORT:
Food

Central African Republic

Bangui

CAPITAL:
Bangui

MAJOR LANGUAGE(S):
French, ethnic languages

POPULATION:
3,400,000

LANDMASS:
240,530 sq. mi./
622,973 sq. km

MONEY:
CFA Franc*

MAJOR EXPORT:
Diamonds

MAJOR IMPORT:
Food Products

Chad

N'Djamena

CAPITAL:
N'Djamena

MAJOR LANGUAGE(S):
French, Arabic

POPULATION:
7,400,000

LANDMASS:
486,180 sq. mi./
1,259,206 sq. km

MONEY:
CFA Franc*

MAJOR EXPORT:
Cotton

MAJOR IMPORT:
Petroleum Products

Comoros

Moroni

CAPITAL:
Moroni

MAJOR LANGUAGE(S):
Arabic, French

POPULATION:
500,000

LANDMASS:
860 sq. mi./
2,227 sq. km

MONEY:
CFA Franc*

MAJOR EXPORT:
Vanilla

MAJOR IMPORT:
Rice

Countries not drawn to scale.

Congo

CAPITAL:
Brazzaville
MAJOR LANGUAGE(S):
French, Kongo, Teke
POPULATION:
2,700,000

LANDMASS:
131,850 sq. mi./
341,492 sq. km
MONEY:
CFA Franc*
MAJOR EXPORT:
Petroleum
MAJOR IMPORT:
Machinery

Congo, Democratic Republic of the

CAPITAL:
Kinshasa
MAJOR LANGUAGE(S):
French, Kongo, Luba, Mongo
POPULATION:
49,000,000

LANDMASS:
875,309 sq. mi./
2,267,050 sq. km
MONEY:
Congolese Franc
MAJOR EXPORT:
Copper
MAJOR IMPORT:
Machinery

Côte d'Ivoire

ADMINISTRATIVE CAPITAL:
Abidjan
MAJOR LANGUAGE(S):
French, Akan, Kru, Voltaic
POPULATION:
15,600,000

LANDMASS:
122,780 sq. mi./
318,000 sq. km
MONEY:
CFA Franc*
MAJOR EXPORT:
Food Products
MAJOR IMPORT:
Petroleum

Djibouti

CAPITAL:
Djibouti
MAJOR LANGUAGE(S):
French, Arabic
POPULATION:
700,000

LANDMASS:
8,950 sq. mi./
23,181 sq. km
MONEY:
Franc
MAJOR EXPORT:
Live Animals
MAJOR IMPORT:
Food and Beverages

Equatorial Guinea

CAPITAL:
Malabo
MAJOR LANGUAGE(S):
Spanish, Fang, Bubi
POPULATION:
400,000

LANDMASS:
10,830 sq. mi./
28,050 sq. km
MONEY:
CFA Franc*
MAJOR EXPORT:
Food and Live Animals
MAJOR IMPORT:
Food and Beverages

Eritrea

CAPITAL:
Asmara
MAJOR LANGUAGE(S):
Tigrinya, Tigre
POPULATION:
3,800,000

LANDMASS:
38,996 sq. mi./
101,000 sq. km
MONEY:
Birr
MAJOR EXPORT:
Food Products
MAJOR IMPORT:
Machinery

Ethiopia

CAPITAL:
Addis Ababa
MAJOR LANGUAGE(S):
Amharic, Tigre, Oromo
POPULATION:
58,400,000

LANDMASS:
386,100 sq. mi./
1,000,000 sq. km
MONEY:
Birr
MAJOR EXPORT:
Coffee
MAJOR IMPORT:
Machinery

Gabon

CAPITAL:
Libreville
MAJOR LANGUAGE(S):
French, Bantu languages
POPULATION:
1,200,000

LANDMASS:
99,490 sq. mi./
257,679 sq. km
MONEY:
CFA Franc*
MAJOR EXPORT:
Petroleum
MAJOR IMPORT:
Machinery

Gambia

CAPITAL:
Banjul
MAJOR LANGUAGE(S):
English, Mandinka, Wolof
POPULATION:
1,200,000

LANDMASS:
3,860 sq. mi./
9,997 sq. km
MONEY:
Dalasi
MAJOR EXPORT:
Peanuts
MAJOR IMPORT:
Food

Ghana

CAPITAL:
Accra
MAJOR LANGUAGE(S):
English, Akan, Mossi, Ewe
POPULATION:
18,900,000

LANDMASS:
87,583 sq. mi./
226,840 sq. km
MONEY:
Cedi
MAJOR EXPORT:
Cocoa
MAJOR IMPORT:
Machinery

* Communauté Financière Africaine
(African Financial Community)

Countries at a Glance

Guinea

Conakry

LANDMASS:
94,873 sq. mi./
245,721 sq. km
MONEY:
Franc
MAJOR EXPORT:
Bauxite
MAJOR IMPORT:
Petroleum

CAPITAL:
Conakry
MAJOR LANGUAGE(S):
French, Peul, Mande
POPULATION:
7,500,000

Madagascar

Antananarivo

LANDMASS:
224,530 sq. mi./
581,533 sq. km
MONEY:
Franc
MAJOR EXPORT:
Coffee
MAJOR IMPORT:
Machinery

CAPITAL:
Antananarivo
MAJOR LANGUAGE(S):
Malagasy, French
POPULATION:
14,000,000

Guinea-Bissau

Bissau

LANDMASS:
10,860 sq. mi./
28,127 sq. km
MONEY:
Peso
MAJOR EXPORT:
Cashews
MAJOR IMPORT:
Transport Equipment

CAPITAL:
Bissau
MAJOR LANGUAGE(S):
Portuguese, Crioulo,
ethnic languages
POPULATION:
1,100,000

Malawi

Lilongwe

LANDMASS:
36,320 sq. mi./
94,069 sq. km
MONEY:
Kwacha
MAJOR EXPORT:
Tobacco
MAJOR IMPORT:
Machinery

CAPITAL:
Lilongwe
MAJOR LANGUAGE(S):
English, Chewa,
Lomwe, Yao
POPULATION:
9,800,000

Kenya

Nairobi

LANDMASS:
219,745 sq. mi./
569,139 sq. km
MONEY:
Shilling
MAJOR EXPORT:
Tea
MAJOR IMPORT:
Machinery

CAPITAL:
Nairobi
MAJOR LANGUAGE(S):
Swahili, English, Kikuyu,
Luhya
POPULATION:
28,300,000

Mali

Bamako

LANDMASS:
471,120 sq. mi./
1,220,201 sq. km
MONEY:
CFA Franc*
MAJOR EXPORT:
Cotton Products
MAJOR IMPORT:
Machinery

CAPITAL:
Bamako
MAJOR LANGUAGE(S):
French, Bambara, Senufo
POPULATION:
10,100,000

Lesotho

Maseru

LANDMASS:
11,720 sq. mi./
30,355 sq. km
MONEY:
Loti
MAJOR EXPORT:
Machinery
MAJOR IMPORT:
Clothing

CAPITAL:
Maseru
MAJOR LANGUAGE(S):
English, Sotho
POPULATION:
2,100,000

Mauritania

Nouakchott

LANDMASS:
395,840 sq. mi./
1,025,226 sq. km
MONEY:
Ouguiya
MAJOR EXPORT:
Fish
MAJOR IMPORT:
Machinery

CAPITAL:
Nouakchott
MAJOR LANGUAGE(S):
Arabic, French,
Hassanya Arabic
POPULATION:
2,500,000

Liberia

Monrovia

LANDMASS:
37,190 sq. mi./
96,322 sq. km
MONEY:
Dollar
MAJOR EXPORT:
Iron Ore
MAJOR IMPORT:
Machinery

CAPITAL:
Monrovia
MAJOR LANGUAGE(S):
English, ethnic languages
POPULATION:
2,800,000

Mauritius

Port Louis

LANDMASS:
784 sq. mi./
2,030 sq. km
MONEY:
Rupee
MAJOR EXPORT:
Clothing and Textiles
MAJOR IMPORT:
Machinery

CAPITAL:
Port Louis
MAJOR LANGUAGE(S):
English, French Creole,
Bhojpuri
POPULATION:
1,200,000

Countries not drawn to scale.

Mozambique

CAPITAL:
Maputo
MAJOR LANGUAGE(S):
Portuguese, Makua, Malawi
POPULATION:
18,600,000
LANDMASS:
302,740 sq. mi./
784,097 sq. km
MONEY:
Metical
MAJOR EXPORT:
Shrimp
MAJOR IMPORT:
Food

Namibia

CAPITAL:
Windhoek
MAJOR LANGUAGE(S):
Afrikaans, English
POPULATION:
1,600,000
LANDMASS:
317,870 sq. mi./
823,283 sq. km
MONEY:
South African Rand
MAJOR EXPORT:
Minerals
MAJOR IMPORT:
Petroleum Products

Niger

CAPITAL:
Niamey
MAJOR LANGUAGE(S):
French, Hausa, Fulani
POPULATION:
10,100,000
LANDMASS:
489,070 sq. mi./
1,266,691 sq. km
MONEY:
CFA Franc*
MAJOR EXPORT:
Uranium
MAJOR IMPORT:
Machinery

Nigeria

CAPITAL:
Abuja
MAJOR LANGUAGE(S):
English, Hausa,
Yoruba, Ibo
POPULATION:
121,800,000
LANDMASS:
351,650 sq. mi./
910,774 sq. km
MONEY:
Naira
MAJOR EXPORT:
Petroleum
MAJOR IMPORT:
Machinery

Rwanda

CAPITAL:
Kigali
MAJOR LANGUAGE(S):
French, Rwanda
POPULATION:
8,000,000
LANDMASS:
9,525 sq. mi./
24,670 sq. km
MONEY:
Franc
MAJOR EXPORT:
Coffee and Tea
MAJOR IMPORT:
Machinery

São Tomé and Príncipe

CAPITAL:
São Tomé
MAJOR LANGUAGE(S):
Portuguese
POPULATION:
200,000
LANDMASS:
293 sq. mi./
759 sq. km
MONEY:
Dobra
MAJOR EXPORT:
Cocoa
MAJOR IMPORT:
Food

Senegal

CAPITAL:
Dakar
MAJOR LANGUAGE(S):
French, Wolof, Serer, Peul
POPULATION:
9,000,000
LANDMASS:
74,340 sq. mi./
192,541 sq. km
MONEY:
CFA Franc*
MAJOR EXPORT:
Peanut Oil
MAJOR IMPORT:
Machinery

Seychelles

CAPITAL:
Victoria
MAJOR LANGUAGE(S):
English, French
POPULATION:
100,000
LANDMASS:
174 sq. mi./
451 sq. km
MONEY:
Rupee
MAJOR EXPORT:
Food Products
MAJOR IMPORT:
Machinery

Sierra Leone

CAPITAL:
Freetown
MAJOR LANGUAGE(S):
English, ethnic languages
POPULATION:
4,600,000
LANDMASS:
27,650 sq. mi./
71,614 sq. km
MONEY:
Leone
MAJOR EXPORT:
Food Products, Diamonds
MAJOR IMPORT:
Food and Live Animals

Somalia

CAPITAL:
Mogadishu
MAJOR LANGUAGE(S):
Somali, Arabic
POPULATION:
10,700,000
LANDMASS:
242,220 sq. mi./
627,350 sq. km
MONEY:
Shilling
MAJOR EXPORT:
Live Animals
MAJOR IMPORT:
Petroleum

* **Communauté Financière Africaine**
(African Financial Community)

Countries at a Glance

South Africa

Pretoria

LANDMASS:
471,440 sq. mi./
1,221,030 sq. km
MONEY:
Rand
MAJOR EXPORT:
Gold
MAJOR IMPORT:
Machinery

ADMINISTRATIVE CAPITAL:
Pretoria
MAJOR LANGUAGE(S):
Afrikaans, English, Nguni
POPULATION:
38,900,000

Sudan

Khartoum

LANDMASS:
917,375 sq. mi./
2,376,000 sq. km
MONEY:
Dinar
MAJOR EXPORT:
Cotton
MAJOR IMPORT:
Machinery

CAPITAL:
Khartoum
MAJOR LANGUAGE(S):
Arabic, Dinka, Nubian,
Nuer
POPULATION:
28,500,000

Swaziland

Mbabane

LANDMASS:
6,640 sq. mi./
17,198 sq. km
MONEY:
Lilangeni
MAJOR EXPORT:
Sugar
MAJOR IMPORT:
Machinery

CAPITAL:
Mbabane
MAJOR LANGUAGE(S):
Swazi, English
POPULATION:
1,000,000

Tanzania

Dar es Salaam

LANDMASS:
341,154 sq. mi./
883,588 sq. km
MONEY:
Shilling
MAJOR EXPORT:
Coffee
MAJOR IMPORT:
Machinery

CAPITAL:
Dar es Salaam (seat of govt.)
Dodoma (capital designate)
MAJOR LANGUAGE(S):
Swahili, English
POPULATION:
30,600,000

Togo

Lomé

LANDMASS:
21,000 sq. mi./
54,390 sq. km
MONEY:
CFA Franc*
MAJOR EXPORT:
Calcium Phosphates
MAJOR IMPORT:
Machinery

CAPITAL:
Lomé
MAJOR LANGUAGE(S):
French, Gur & Kwa
languages
POPULATION:
4,900,000

Uganda

Kampala

LANDMASS:
77,085 sq. mi./
199,650 sq. km
MONEY:
Shilling
MAJOR EXPORT:
Coffee
MAJOR IMPORT:
Sugar

CAPITAL:
Kampala
MAJOR LANGUAGE(S):
English, Luganda, Swahili
POPULATION:
21,000,000

Zambia

Lusaka

LANDMASS:
287,020 sq. mi./
743,382 sq. km
MONEY:
Kwacha
MAJOR EXPORT:
Copper
MAJOR IMPORT:
Machinery

CAPITAL:
Lusaka
MAJOR LANGUAGE(S):
English, Bantu languages
POPULATION:
9,500,000

Zimbabwe

Harare

LANDMASS:
149,363 sq. mi./
386,850 sq. km
MONEY:
Dollar
MAJOR EXPORT:
Tobacco
MAJOR IMPORT:
Machinery

CAPITAL:
Harare
MAJOR LANGUAGE(S):
English, Shona, Sinde bele
POPULATION:
11,000,000

Countries not drawn to scale.

* **Communauté Financière Africaine**
(African Financial Community)

The Sahel

A dust storm kicks up a huge wall of sand on the Sahel in northern Burkina Faso.

Bringing in the Nets in Accra, Ghana

A fisher pulls in his fishing nets from a harbor in Accra, Ghana's capital.

Drilling for Gold in South Africa

South African gold miners work with large drills and dynamite to extract gold ore.

ATLANTIC OCEAN

Tropic of Cancer

NORTH AFRICA

30°N

CAPE VERDE ISLANDS

MAURITANIA

★ Nouakchott

★ Praia

Dakar

MALI

NIGER

20°N

★ SENEGAL

Banjul ★

GAMBIA

★ Bissau

★ Bamako

BURKINA FASO

Niamey ★

CHAD

GUINEA-BISSAU

GUINEA

★ Ouagadougou

Lake Chad

Conakry ★

★ Freetown

CÔTE D'IVOIRE

BENIN

★ Abuja

★ N'Djamena

SIERRA LEONE

GHANA

TOGO

NIGERIA

10°N

Monrovia ★

LIBERIA

★ Accra

Abidjan

Lomé

Porto-Novo

--- Disputed boundary
— National boundary
★ National capital
● Other city

Lambert Equal-Area projection

Gulf of Guinea

Equator

N
W ✦ E
S

CENTRAL AFRICA

0°

0   250   500 mi.
0 250 500 km

20°W   10°W   0°   10°E   20°E

MAP STUDY ACTIVITY

In this chapter you will read about Nigeria and the other countries of West Africa.

1. How many countries make up West Africa?
2. What West African country is made up of islands?
3. What body of water do the coastal countries border?

SECTION 1
Nigeria

PREVIEW

Words to Know
- mangrove
- savanna
- harmattan
- cacao
- ethnic group
- compound

Places to Locate
- Nigeria
- Gulf of Guinea
- Niger River
- Lagos
- Abuja

Read to Learn . . .
1. what landforms are found in Nigeria.
2. what mineral supports Nigeria's economy.
3. why Nigeria has many ethnic groups.

The mighty Niger River flows about 2,600 miles (4,180 km) through the western part of Africa. It is the third-longest river in Africa and drains an area larger than the state of Alaska! The Niger River is a major "highway" for those who live along it.

The West African country of Nigeria takes its name from the Niger River, which flows through western and central Nigeria. One of the largest nations in Africa, Nigeria covers 351,650 square miles (910,774 sq. km). It is more than twice the size of the state of California.

Place
The Land

Imagine taking a trip through Nigeria from south to north. Nigeria has a long coastline on the Gulf of Guinea. The map on page 484 shows you that this gulf is part of the Atlantic Ocean. Along Nigeria's coast, the land is laced with many rivers and creeks and covered with mangrove swamps. A **mangrove** is a tropical tree with roots extending above and beneath the water.

As you travel north, the land becomes a vast tropical rain forest. Small villages and farms appear in only a few clearings. The forests gradually thin into woodlands and savannas in central Nigeria. **Savannas** are tropical grasslands with scattered trees. Highlands and plateaus also blanket this area. Farther north, a stretch of partly dry grasslands lies on the edge of the vast Sahara.

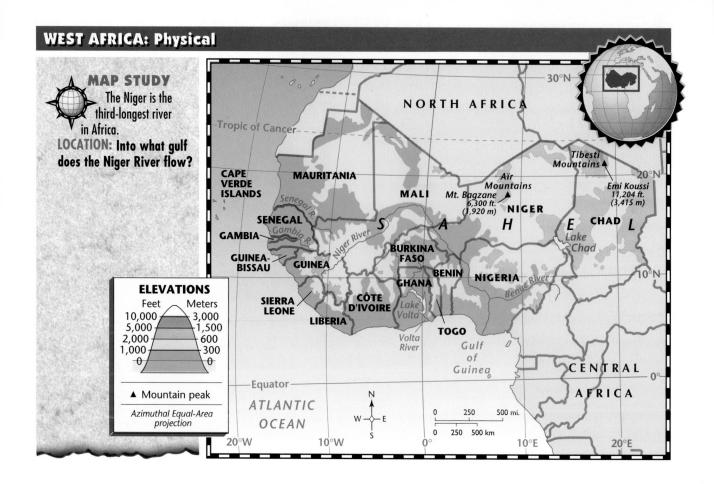

MAP STUDY
The Niger is the third-longest river in Africa.
LOCATION: Into what gulf does the Niger River flow?

ELEVATIONS

Feet	Meters
10,000	3,000
5,000	1,500
2,000	600
1,000	300
0	0

▲ Mountain peak

Azimuthal Equal-Area projection

The Climate The map on page 491 shows you that Nigeria has several climate regions. Most of the country, however, is tropical with high average temperatures. Tropical areas in the south receive plenty of rainfall year-round. Steppe regions to the north have a distinct dry season. In the winter months, a dry, dusty wind called the **harmattan** blows south from the Sahara.

Human/Environment Interaction
The Economy

Nigeria has a developing economy based on mining and farming. It is one of the world's major oil-producing countries and one of the few industrialized African countries. In recent years oil has become the leading source of income for the government. The Nigerian government has used money from oil exports to build factories that turn out textiles, food products, and chemicals. Coal and tin deposits also help boost the country's industrial growth.

Boom and Bust In the 1980s Nigeria's oil-rich economy faced hard times. World oil prices fell, and Nigeria's income declined. Nigerians also realized that, in focusing on industry, they had neglected agriculture. Many farmers had left their farms in search of jobs in the cities. Food production fell so much that Nigeria had to import food. Today Nigeria is using income from oil to improve farming and to raise more food products.

Agriculture If you like chocolate, you may have Nigeria to thank. Nigeria's major crops include peanuts, cotton, rubber, palm products, and **cacao.** Beans from the cacao, or cocoa, pod are used to make chocolate. Despite their country's mineral riches, most Nigerians earn their livings as farmers. More than one-half of Nigeria's land is good for farming. Some Nigerian farmers grow subsistence crops, or crops only for their own use. Others produce cash crops, or crops to sell for export.

Place
The People

Like many African countries, Nigeria has a high birthrate and a rapidly growing population. About 98 million people live in Nigeria—more people than in any other country in Africa.

Ethnic Groups Nigeria's people belong to more than 250 ethnic groups. An **ethnic group** is a group of people that has a common language, culture, and history. The four largest ethnic groups are the Hausa (HOW•suh), Fulani (FOO•LAH•nee), Yoruba (YAWR•uh•buh), and Ibo (EE•boh).

Nigerians speak many different African languages. They use English, however, in business and government affairs. About half of Nigeria's people are Muslims and another 40 percent are Christians. The remaining 10 percent practice traditional African religions.

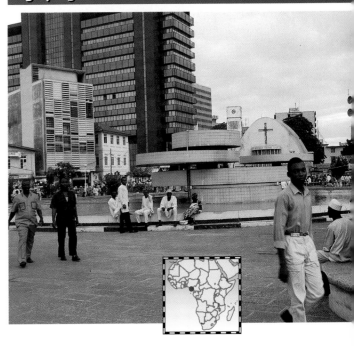

Lagos, Nigeria

Lagos is Nigeria's chief port and commercial center.
PLACE: What language do most Nigerians use when conducting business?

Leading Cocoa-Producing Countries

GRAPHIC STUDY

Half of the world's top cocoa-producing countries are in Africa south of the Sahara.
PLACE: What African country leads the world in cocoa production?

 = 200,000 metric tons

Cocoa Beans Produced in One Year

Thousands of metric tons: 0, 100, 200, 300, 400, 500, 600, 700, 800, 900, 1000
Thousands of short tons: 0, 110, 220, 331, 441, 551, 661, 771, 882, 992, 1102

Côte d'Ivoire, Ghana, Indonesia, Brazil, Nigeria, Malaysia

Source: FAO Production Yearbook, 1997

Influences of the Past The history of Nigeria reaches farther back than that of almost any other in Africa. About 500 B.C., the Nok people hammered iron into tools and made baked clay sculptures. During the following centuries, powerful city-states and kingdoms arose throughout the region and became centers of trade and the arts. Territories in the north came under the influence of Islamic cultures from North Africa. Peoples in the south developed cultures based on traditional African religions.

Europeans looking for gold and slave labor arrived in Africa in the 1400s. They set up trading forts in Nigeria as early as 1498. By the early 1900s, the British controlled the area that is now Nigeria. The many ethnic groups there resisted British rule. On October 1, 1960, the colony of Nigeria finally became an independent nation. The ethnic differences that intensified during the time of European rule later erupted in civil war. Today Nigeria is moving from harsh military rule to democracy.

Ways of Life About 84 percent of Nigeria's population live in rural villages. Fourteen-year-old Elizabeth Tofa lives in a small village in western Nigeria. Like most rural Nigerians, Elizabeth and her family live in a **compound,** or a group of houses surrounded by walls. Every four days there is a market in her village. Run by women, markets are important in Nigeria and the rest of Africa. They not only provide a variety of goods but also a chance for friends to meet. Elizabeth, her mother, and her sisters sell meat, palm oil, cloth, yams, and nuts.

Nigeria has several large cities bustling with activity. Lagos, located on the coast, is the largest city and commercial center. Other cities—such as Ibadan (ih•BAH•duhn) and Abuja (ah•BOO•jah), the national capital—lie inland.

Nigerians take pride in their art. They make elaborate wooden masks, metal sculptures, and colorful cloth. Playing drums, horns, and other instruments, musicians create rhythms with two or more patterns going at once. In the past, Nigerians passed on stories, proverbs, and riddles by word of mouth from one generation to the next. During the mid-1900s, however, many Nigerian authors began to publish novels, stories, and poetry. In 1986 Nigerian writer Wole Soyinka (WAH•lay shaw•YIHNG•kah) became the first African to win the Nobel Prize for literature.

SECTION 1 ASSESSMENT

REVIEWING TERMS AND FACTS
1. Define the following: mangrove, savanna, harmattan, cacao, ethnic group, compound.
2. PLACE How does Nigeria's landscape change from south to north?
3. HUMAN/ENVIRONMENT INTERACTION What is Nigeria's most important mineral resource?
4. PLACE Why are village markets important in Nigeria?

MAP STUDY ACTIVITIES
5. Turn to the political map on page 484. What is Nigeria's capital?
6. Look at the physical map on page 486. Most of northern Nigeria lies at what elevation?

BUILDING GEOGRAPHY SKILLS

Interpreting a Diagram

Have you ever tried to put something together without directions or even a picture to follow? A diagram can be very helpful in cases like this. A *diagram* is a drawing that shows how something works or how its parts fit together.

In most diagrams, labels point out parts or steps in a process. Labels such as words, letters, colors, or numbers identify different parts. Arrows sometimes show the order in which steps follow one another or the direction of an object's movement.

To interpret a diagram, apply the following steps:

• Read the title or caption to find out what the diagram shows.

• Read all labels to determine their meanings.

• Look for arrows that show movement or the order of the steps to be completed.

Glencoe's **Skillbuilder Interactive Workbook, Level 1** provides instruction and practice in key social studies skills.

GO TO

A Saharan Landscape

Mountains

Desert Pavement (gravel plain)

Hammada (rocky plateau)

Erg (windblown sand dune)

Wadi (dry streambed)

Oasis

Sahel

Geography Skills Practice

1. What is the title of this diagram?

2. What labels are used?

3. What do the arrows in the diagram show?

4. According to the diagram, how is the Sahel landscape different from the desert landscape?

SECTION 2

The Sahel Countries

PREVIEW

Words to Know
- drought
- desertification

Places to Locate
- the Sahel
- Niger River
- Mauritania
- Mali
- Niger
- Burkina Faso
- Chad

Read to Learn . . .
1. where the Sahel is located.
2. why Sahel grasslands are turning into desert areas.
3. how people in the Sahel countries live.

Slowly but surely, the desert is creeping into grassy inland areas of West Africa north of Nigeria. Over the past 100 years, a stretch of the Sahara more than 93 miles (150 km) wide has swallowed parts of countries in West Africa. This growing desert is like an invading army slowly taking over the countries.

What countries lie in the path of the creeping Sahara? Mauritania (MAWR•uh•TAY•nee•uh), Mali (MAH•lee), Niger (NY•juhr), Chad, and Burkina Faso (bur•KEE•nuh FAH•soh) are located in an area known as the Sahel. *Sahel* comes from an Arabic word that means "border." The map on page 486 shows you that the Sahel forms the border between the Sahara to the north and the fertile, humid lands to the south.

Human/Environment Interaction
The Growing Desert

The Sahel receives little rainfall, so only short grasses and small trees are able to grow here. As you might guess, this type of vegetation is good for grazing animals. Most people in the Sahel are livestock herders. Their flocks, unfortunately, have overgrazed the land, stripping areas so bare that plant life does not grow back. Without plants, the bare soil is blown away by winds.

To make matters worse, the Sahel has entered a period of **drought.** A drought is an extreme shortage of water. Droughts are common in the Sahel,

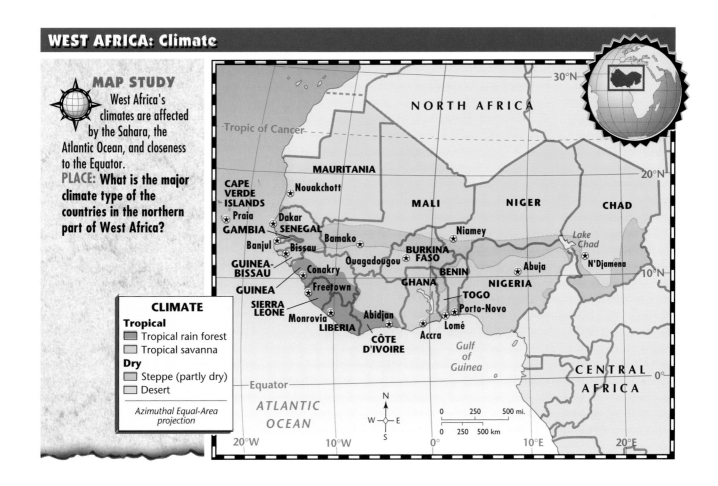

West Africa's climates are affected by the Sahara, the Atlantic Ocean, and closeness to the Equator.

PLACE: What is the major climate type of the countries in the northern part of West Africa?

CLIMATE

Tropical
- Tropical rain forest
- Tropical savanna

Dry
- Steppe (partly dry)
- Desert

Azimuthal Equal-Area projection

where dry and wet periods regularly follow each other. The latest period of drought began in the 1980s. Since then rivers have dried up, crops have failed, and millions of cattle and other animals have died. Thousands of people have died of hunger. Millions more have fled to fertile southern areas in search of food.

Over the years, both overgrazing and drought have ruined once-productive areas of the Sahel. Many grassland areas have become desert—a change called **desertification.** Scientists believe that the increasing human use of land in the Sahel will only increase the spread of desert. You can read more about desertification south of the Sahara on page 568.

Place

People of the Sahel

The countries of the Sahel are large in size but have small populations. Look at the population density map on page 496. It shows you that most people live in the southern areas of these countries. Can you guess why? Rivers flow here, and the land can be farmed or grazed. Even these areas do not have enough water and fertile land to support large numbers of people, however.

WHAT IN THE WORLD?

The Wet Sahara?
The Sahara was not always a desert. Many caves in Mali have paintings that date back 10,000 years. The paintings show hippos, rhinos, giraffes, crocodiles, and even fish. These drawings suggest that at least the southern part of the Sahara had a wet climate in the distant past.

Djenné, Mali

Villagers set up shop at a street market outside the Great Mosque in Djenné.
MOVEMENT: How is the Arab influence in Mali shown in this photo?

Influences of the Past You may be surprised to learn that the Sahel was an early trading and cultural area. At a time when the climate was favorable, three great African empires—Ghana (GAH•nuh), Mali, and Songhai (SONG•hy)—arose in the Sahel. From the A.D. 300s to the 1500s, these empires controlled the trade in gold, salt, and other resources between West Africa and the Arab lands of the Mediterranean. The city of Tombouctou (tohn•book•too) on the Niger River was a leading center of learning, drawing students from Europe, Asia, and Africa.

During the 1800s, the countries of the Sahel came under French rule. They finally won their independence in 1960.

A Rural Population Most people in the Sahel live in small towns and villages. They raise only enough food for their own use. Porridges made with sorghum, millet, and other grains are popular dishes.

For years, nomadic groups such as the Tuareg (TWAH•REHG) and Fulani crossed northern desert areas with herds of camels, cattle, goats, and sheep. The recent droughts, however, have forced many of them to give up their traditional way of life and move to the towns and villages.

The people of the Sahel practice a mix of African, Arab, and European traditions. Most follow the religion of Islam. They speak Arabic as well as a variety of African languages. French is also spoken in such cities as Nouakchott (nu•AHK•SHAHT) in Mauritania, Bamako (BAH•muh•KOH) in Mali, and Niamey (nee• AH•MAY) in Niger.

SECTION 2 ASSESSMENT

REVIEWING TERMS AND FACTS
1. **Define the following:** drought, desertification.
2. **LOCATION** Where is the Sahel located?
3. **HUMAN/ENVIRONMENT INTERACTION** How have humans affected the spread of desert in the Sahel?
4. **PLACE** How do most people make their livings in the Sahel countries?

MAP STUDY ACTIVITIES
5. Look at the climate map on page 491. What climates do you find in the Sahel countries?

MAKING CONNECTIONS

MATH   **SCIENCE**   **HISTORY**   **LITERATURE**   **TECHNOLOGY**

Wole Soyinka of Nigeria is perhaps Africa's best-known playwright and writer. In this excerpt from *The Interpreters,* friends talk as they journey in their canoe. They discuss how the landscape makes them feel.

Two paddles clove [moved through] the still water of the creek, and the canoe trailed behind it a silent groove, between gnarled tears of mangrove; it was dead air, and they came to a spot where an old rusted cannon showed above the water. . . . The paddlers slowed down and held the boat against the cannon. Egbo put his hand in the water and dropped his eyes down the brackish stillness, down the dark depths to its bed of mud.

. . . The canoe began to move off.

. . . From the receding cannon a quizzical crab emerged, seemed to stretch its claws in the sun and slipped over the edge, making a soft hole in the water. The mangrove arches spread seemingly endless and Kola broke the silence saying, 'Mangrove depresses me.'

'Me too,' said Egbo. . . . I remember when I was in Oshogbo I loved [the] grove and would lie there for hours listening at the edge of the water. It has a quality of this part of the creeks, peaceful and comforting. . . .' He

trailed his hand in the water as he went, pulling up lettuce and plaiting [braiding] the long whitened root-strands.

Mangrove Trees

'That was only a phase of course, but I truly yearned for the dark. I loved life to be still, mysterious. I took my books down there to read, during the holidays. But later, I began to go further, down towards the old suspension bridge where the water ran freely, over rocks and white sand. And there was sunshine. . . . It was so different from the grove where depth swamped me. . . .

From Wole Soyinka's *The Interpreters.* Copyright © 1965 by Wole Soyinka, New York, N.Y.: Africana Publishing Corporation.

Making the Connection

1. What type of physical environment surrounds Kola and Egbo?

2. How do they feel when they are in this area?

SECTION 3

Coastal Countries

PREVIEW

Words to Know
- cassava
- bauxite

Places to Locate
- Senegal
- Dakar
- Cape Verde Islands
- Liberia
- Côte d'Ivoire
- Abidjan
- Ghana

Read to Learn . . .
1. what climates are found in coastal West Africa.
2. how people earn their livings in this region.
3. how coastal West African countries won their independence.

Do you like peanuts? The next time you bite into a peanut butter sandwich, think about West Africa. Workers in the West African country of Gambia dry peanuts to send to other countries. Gambia began exporting peanuts in the 1800s. Today it depends on this one crop for about 95 percent of its income.

Besides Nigeria and the Sahel countries, West Africa includes 11 coastal countries. One—Cape Verde—is a group of 15 islands in the Atlantic Ocean. The other countries spread along West Africa's Atlantic bend, north of the Equator, from Senegal in the west along the coast to Benin. Find these countries on the map on page 484.

Human/Environment Interaction
The Land

Coastal lowlands sweep along the Atlantic shore of West Africa's coastal countries. Sandy beaches, rain forests, and thick mangrove swamps cover most of this area. Inland from the coast lie highland areas with grasses and trees. Several major rivers—the Senegal, Gambia, Volta, and Niger—flow from these highlands to the coast. You won't see many ships on these rivers. Why? Rapids and shallows prevent ships from traveling far into inland areas.

The Climate Because they border the ocean, the coastal countries of West Africa receive plenty of rainfall. Warm currents in the Gulf of Guinea create a moist, tropical climate in the coastal lowlands year-round. Some coastal areas receive more than 170 inches (432 cm) of rain a year! Farther inland, rainfall is not as plentiful. These highland areas have a tropical savanna climate with dry and wet seasons.

The Economy Because of the wet climate, most people in coastal West Africa are farmers. On small plots of land, farmers grow yams, corn, rice, cassava, and other foods for their families. **Cassava** is a plant root that looks like a potato. It is used to make flour for bread.

West Africa also has large plantations that grow coffee, rubber, cacao, palm oil, and kola nuts for export. Can you guess what the kola nut is used for? This sweet-tasting nut is used in making soft drinks. Until industries become more developed in the region, these cash crops will continue to be the major source of income.

Region
The People

West Africa's coastal countries have a long and rich history. In early times, powerful kingdoms such as the Ashanti and Benin ruled the region. These kingdoms were centers of trade, learning, and the arts.

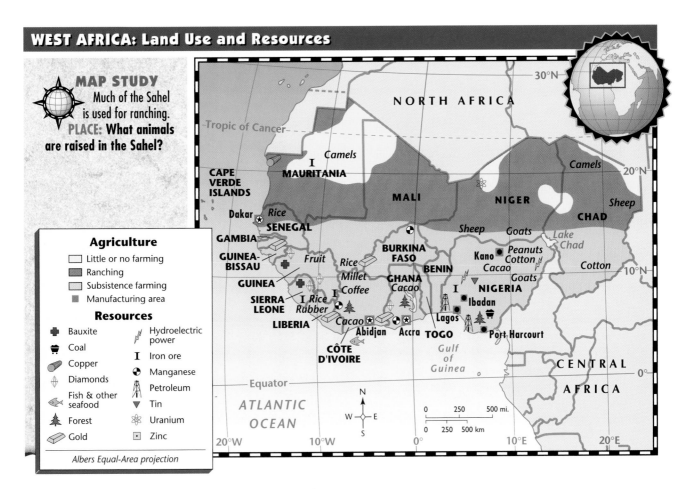

WEST AFRICA: Land Use and Resources

MAP STUDY
Much of the Sahel is used for ranching.
PLACE: What animals are raised in the Sahel?

Agriculture
☐ Little or no farming
■ Ranching
☐ Subsistence farming
■ Manufacturing area

Resources
✚ Bauxite
⛏ Coal
▬ Copper
◈ Diamonds
🐟 Fish & other seafood
🌲 Forest
▭ Gold
⚡ Hydroelectric power
I Iron ore
◐ Manganese
⛏ Petroleum
▼ Tin
☢ Uranium
⊡ Zinc

Albers Equal-Area projection

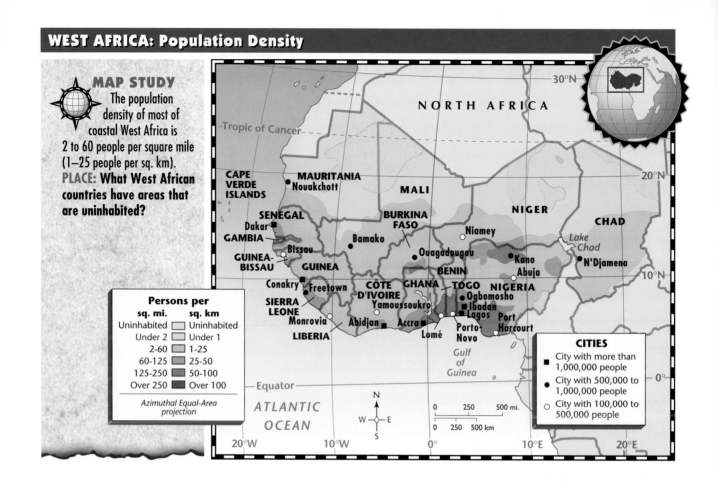

MAP STUDY The population density of most of coastal West Africa is 2 to 60 people per square mile (1–25 people per sq. km).

PLACE: What West African countries have areas that are uninhabited?

Persons per

sq. mi.	sq. km
Uninhabited	Uninhabited
Under 2	Under 1
2-60	1-25
60-125	25-50
125-250	50-100
Over 250	Over 100

Azimuthal Equal-Area projection

CITIES

■ City with more than 1,000,000 people

● City with 500,000 to 1,000,000 people

○ City with 100,000 to 500,000 people

The Arrival of Europeans From the late 1400s to the early 1800s, Europeans set up trading posts along the West African coast. From these posts they traded with Africans for gold, ivory, and other goods that people in Europe wanted. They also traded enslaved Africans. The traders shipped millions of enslaved Africans to the Americas. This trade in human beings finally ended in the 1800s.

Toward Freedom The British, French, and Portuguese eventually set up colonies in coastal West Africa. They brought Christianity and European culture to the region. After several decades of European rule, the peoples of West Africa began to demand independence. In 1957 Ghana became the first country in West Africa to become independent. By the late 1970s, all of the countries in the region had won their independence.

Ways of Life The cultures of West Africa show European influences. Many West Africans practice traditional African religions, but some are Christians or Muslims. Most people in West Africa speak African languages but often use French, English, or Portuguese in business or government activities.

Cities in coastal West Africa are modern and growing. If you visited a city like Ghana's capital—Accra (uh•KRAH)—or Côte d'Ivoire's capital—Abidjan (A•bih•JAHN)—you would find downtown areas with modern government and office buildings. You would also see people dressed in business clothes or in traditional African clothing and wide streets with busy traffic. In rural areas, people live in small villages. Many village homes have mud walls and straw or metal roofs. People here follow many of their ancestors' traditions.

Region
Country Profiles

The 11 countries of coastal West Africa have many things in common. Each country, however, has certain features that make it stand out from the others.

Senegal, Gambia, and Guinea These countries all depend on farming as their major source of income. The map on page 495, however, shows that Guinea is rich in **bauxite**—a mineral from which we make aluminum—and other mineral resources.

Senegal has more city dwellers than either Gambia or Guinea. About 42 percent of Senegal's people live in urban areas. Dakar (DA•KAHR), Senegal's capital and largest city, also is a major port on the Atlantic Ocean.

Village Life

Iyabo Ayinde lives in a small village outside Abidjan. The people in her village are related, and each family has its own group of dwellings. Her family's homes have cone-shaped thatched roofs. Villagers share a small plot of land where they raise corn and yams. Today after school, Iyabo will meet her cousins in the central square of her village to plan a trip to Abidjan. Iyabo's cousins want to go to the art museum. Iyabo has another idea. "Let's go to the ice skating rink!" she says.

Guinea-Bissau and Cape Verde Guinea-Bissau lies between Senegal and Guinea. The islands of Cape Verde are located about 375 miles (600 km) offshore in the Atlantic Ocean. Guinea-Bissau and Cape Verde were Portuguese colonies until they won independence in 1975. Portuguese influences are widespread in the languages and cultures of both countries. Most of the people here make their livings by farming or fishing.

Liberia and Sierra Leone At the "bend" of Africa's west coast are Liberia and Sierra Leone. Liberia is the only West African country that was never a colony. African Americans freed from slavery founded Liberia in 1822. Monrovia, Liberia's capital and largest city, was named for James Monroe—American President when Liberia was founded. From 1989 to 1996, fighting among Liberian political groups cost many lives and left thousands homeless.

Like Liberia, Sierra Leone was established as a home for people freed from enslavement. The British ruled Sierra Leone from 1787 until 1961, when Sierra Leone became independent. Most of the country's land is used for agriculture, but minerals also provide wealth.

Côte d'Ivoire and Ghana Côte d'Ivoire was a French colony until winning its independence in 1960. Many ethnic groups live in Côte d'Ivoire's rural

The modern port of Abidjan handles many of the imports and exports of West Africa. **PLACE: What European country controlled Côte d'Ivoire until 1960?**

villages. They cultivate coffee, cacao, and forest products for export. In recent years some farmers have moved from their villages to find factory jobs in Abidjan and other cities.

Ghana—like Côte d'Ivoire—produces cacao and forest products for export. Ghana's people belong to about 100 different ethnic groups. The Ashanti and the Fante are the largest groups. About 35 percent of Ghanaians live in cities. Accra, located on the coast, is the capital and largest city.

Togo and Benin The countries of Togo and Benin lie between Ghana and Nigeria. The map on page 484 shows you that both countries are long and narrow. Togo and Benin—once French colonies—became independent in 1960. Many ethnic groups whose dress, language, and other ways of life differ a great deal make up the cultures of Togo and Benin.

SECTION 3 ASSESSMENT

REVIEWING TERMS AND FACTS
1. Define the following: cassava, bauxite.
2. LOCATION Where is Cape Verde located?
3. HUMAN/ENVIRONMENT INTERACTION What food crops are grown in coastal West Africa?
4. REGION How did the arrival of Europeans influence life in coastal West Africa?

MAP STUDY ACTIVITIES
5. Study the population density map on page 496. Where do most people in coastal West Africa live?

Chapter 18 Highlights

Important Things to Know About West Africa

SECTION 1 NIGERIA

- Nigeria's major landforms are coastal lowlands, savanna highlands, and partly dry grasslands.
- Most Nigerians farm the land, but oil is Nigeria's major export.
- Many different ethnic groups live in Nigeria.
- Nigeria is the most highly populated African country.

SECTION 2 THE SAHEL COUNTRIES

- The Sahel countries are Mauritania, Mali, Niger, Chad, and Burkina Faso.
- The Sahel lies between the Sahara in the north and fertile, humid lands in the south.
- Most people in the Sahel countries are herders or farmers.
- Desertification has destroyed much of the Sahel's most productive land.

SECTION 3 COASTAL COUNTRIES

- The 11 countries that make up coastal West Africa are Senegal, Gambia, Guinea, Guinea-Bissau, Cape Verde, Liberia, Sierra Leone, Ghana, Côte d'Ivoire, Togo, and Benin.
- Because of the wet climate, farming is the major economic activity in coastal West Africa.
- Most people in the coastal countries of West Africa live in the coastal lowlands.
- People freed from slavery helped establish the countries of Liberia and Sierra Leone.

Rain forest in Liberia ▶

REVIEWING KEY TERMS

Match the numbered terms in Set A with their lettered definitions in Set B.

A

1. cassava
2. savanna
3. mangrove
4. cacao
5. desertification
6. harmattan
7. bauxite

B

A. change of grasslands to desert
B. dusty wind blowing south from the Sahara
C. plant root used in making flour
D. tropical grassland with scattered trees
E. mineral from which aluminum is made
F. beans used in making chocolate
G. tropical tree with roots above and below water

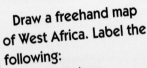

Mental Mapping Activity

Draw a freehand map of West Africa. Label the following:
- Gulf of Guinea
- Atlantic Ocean
- Lagos
- Senegal River
- Gambia
- Sahara

REVIEWING THE MAIN IDEAS

Section 1

1. HUMAN/ENVIRONMENT INTERACTION What challenges has Nigeria faced because of its dependence on oil?
2. MOVEMENT Why are Nigeria's cities growing?

Section 2

3. HUMAN/ENVIRONMENT INTERACTION Why is farming difficult in the Sahel?
4. PLACE Why was the city of Tombouctou important?
5. REGION What is the major religion in the Sahel countries?

Section 3

6. REGION Why does the coastal strip in coastal West Africa receive plenty of rainfall?
7. PLACE What West African country was the first to win independence?

CRITICAL THINKING ACTIVITIES

1. **Drawing Conclusions** Why do you think people in many areas of the Sahel have followed a nomadic way of life?
2. **Determining Cause and Effect** How has location on the coast affected the history and culture of coastal West Africa?

CONNECTIONS TO WORLD CULTURES

Cooperative Learning Activity Work in a group of three to learn more about the arts of West Africa. As a group, choose one country in West Africa. Each member in the group will then research that country's sculpture, music, or dance. After your research is complete, share your information with your group. Present your country's art to the class as a whole.

GeoJournal Writing Activity

Imagine that you are on a journey down the Niger River. Write several entries in a diary describing how the landscape changes as you travel down the river from inland areas to the coast.

TECHNOLOGY ACTIVITY

Using a Computerized Card Catalog

Choose a West African country to research, then use a computerized card catalog to find information about its early history to the present. Create a bulletin board display about that country, including an illustrated time line of significant events in the country's history. Be sure to include current information about natural resources and environmental concerns in your display.

PLACE LOCATION ACTIVITY: WEST AFRICA

Match the letters on the map with the places and physical features of West Africa. Write your answers on a separate sheet of paper.

1. Côte d'Ivoire
2. Monrovia
3. Tibesti Mountains
4. Senegal
5. Mali
6. Gulf of Guinea
7. Lake Chad
8. Niger River
9. Cape Verde Islands
10. Lagos

Cultural HERITAGE:
AFRICA SOUTH OF THE SAHARA

◀ ◀ ◀ ◀ MASKS

Many of Africa's ethnic groups can be identified by the types of masks they create. Masks are usually worn by African dancers in social and religious ceremonies.

SCULPTURE ▶ ▶ ▶ ▶

Europeans often paid African artists to create intricate carvings for their personal collections. Skilled ivory carvers created this salt container from a single elephant tusk in the 1600s.

◀ ◀ ◀ ◀ DANCE

Many African ethnic groups use dance to mark important events in their lives. The rhythms in African music are reproduced by dancers' bodies. Their heads may be moving to one rhythm, their shoulders to another, and their arms and feet to yet another.

◄ ◄ ◄ ◄ ARCHITECTURE

Much of the architecture in Africa reflects the influence of the Arab world. This modern mosque with its towering minarets is located in Nigeria.

MUSIC ► ► ► ►

African music can have as many as 5 to 12 different rhythms. The complicated rhythms are often produced on drums, horns, and trumpets made from natural materials. Jazz and other music popular in the United States have been greatly influenced by African music.

JEWELRY ▲ ▲ ▲ ▲

The gold trade in the Ashanti empire in the 1600s brought great riches to the Ashanti kings. Many kings even had their own goldsmiths. This breast ornament was made by twisting delicate gold wire into lacelike patterns.

APPRECIATING CULTURE

1. How would you describe this African mask to someone who had not seen it?

2. What are some characteristics of African music?

3. Why do you think gold was a symbol of power and status in the Ashanti empire?

Chapter 19 Central Africa

WEST AFRICA

10°N

Garoua

CAMEROON

CENTRAL AFRICAN REPUBLIC

EQUATORIAL GUINEA

Malabo
Douala
Yaoundé
Bangui

SÃO TOMÉ AND PRÍNCIPE

São Tomé
Libreville

0°

GABON

CONGO

Kisangani

DEMOCRATIC REPUBLIC OF THE CONGO

Equator

Brazzaville

Pointe-Noire

Kinshasa

Cabinda (ANGOLA)

Kikwit

ATLANTIC OCEAN

10°S

Kolwezi

SOUTHERN AFRICA

| 0 | 150 | 300 mi. |
| 0 | 150 | 300 km |

— National boundary
⊛ National capital
● Other city

Azimuthal Equal-Area projection

N W E S

MAP STUDY ACTIVITY

As you read Chapter 19, you will learn about the countries of Central Africa.

1. How many countries are in Central Africa?
2. What is the largest country in Central Africa?
3. What is the capital of Gabon?

Democratic Republic of the Congo

PREVIEW

Words to Know
- canopy
- hydroelectricity

Places to Locate
- Congo River
- Kinshasa
- Lake Tanganyika

Read to Learn . . .
1. why the Congo River is a highway for the Democratic Republic of the Congo's people.
2. about the potential wealth of the Democratic Republic of the Congo.
3. how large movements of people have shaped the history of the Democratic Republic of the Congo.

This lush countryside lies in the Democratic Republic of the Congo, one of the countries in the region of Central Africa. Water is abundant in the rainy and green stretches of this region.

Central Africa's many rivers are a source of life for the people of the region. Africa's second-longest river—the Congo—flows through the Democratic Republic of the Congo. This country is located on the Equator in the very heart of Africa. A large country, this republic is bordered by nine other African countries.

Place
The Land

The Democratic Republic of the Congo covers an area of 875,309 square miles (2,267,050 sq. km)—about one-fourth the size of the United States. In Africa, only Sudan and Algeria are larger. The Democratic Republic of the Congo encompasses many landscapes, including rain forests, savannas, and highlands. Its only coastline is a 25-mile (41-km) strip on the Atlantic Ocean.

Rain Forests Vast tropical rain forests cover about one-third of the Democratic Republic of the Congo. It is one of the largest rain forest areas in the world. The treetops of the rain forests form a **canopy,** or umbrella-like forest covering. This canopy is so thick that sunlight seldom reaches parts of the forest

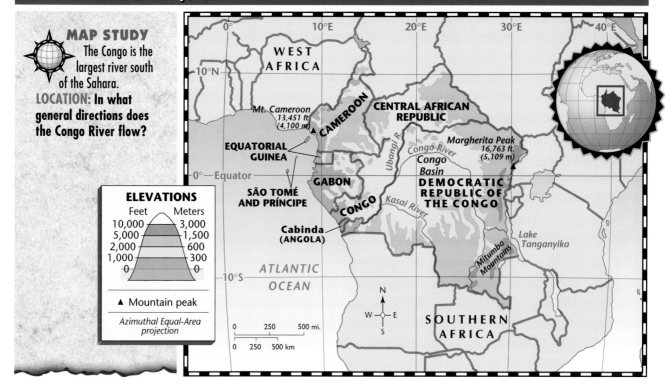

MAP STUDY
The Congo is the largest river south of the Sahara.
LOCATION: In what general directions does the Congo River flow?

ELEVATIONS

Feet	Meters
10,000	3,000
5,000	1,500
2,000	600
1,000	300
0	0

▲ Mountain peak

Azimuthal Equal-Area projection

floor, which is almost clear of plants. Many monkeys, snakes, birds, and other small animals spend their entire lives in the canopy.

More than 750 different kinds of trees grow in the rain forests. Mahogany, ebony, and other woods prized by furniture makers are harvested in abundance. Like South America's Amazon rain forest, Central Africa's rain forests are being destroyed at a fast rate.

Highlands and Savannas Spectacular mountains rise along the eastern border of the Democratic Republic of the Congo. Savannas cross the northern and southern parts of the country. These vast open grasslands are home to some of the country's most valuable natural resources—its wildlife. Antelopes, leopards, lions, rhinoceroses, zebras, and giraffes roam freely on government preserves. An animal similar to a giraffe—the okapi—is found only in the Democratic Republic of the Congo and is the country's national symbol.

Rivers and Lakes The mighty Congo River—above 2,800 miles (4,505 km) long—courses its way through the rain forests of Central Africa to the Atlantic Ocean. Many smaller rivers branch out from the Congo River.

One of the world's longest rivers, the Congo River is the country's highway for trade and travel. Dugout canoes, steamers carrying passengers to various port cities, and cargo ships travel the river to the Atlantic Ocean.

WHAT IN THE WORLD?

That's a Strong River!
The Congo River doesn't stop when it meets the Atlantic Ocean. The river's current carries water about 100 miles (161 km) into the ocean. The force of the current has gouged a 4,000-foot (1,200-m) canyon into the ocean floor!

In the eastern mountainous region of the Democratic Republic of the Congo, you will find Lake Albert, Lake Edward, Lake Kivu, and Lake Tanganyika (TAN•guh•NYEE•kuh). Lake Tanganyika is the world's longest freshwater lake and the second-deepest, after Lake Baikal in Russia.

The Climate Because of its location on the Equator, the Democratic Republic of the Congo generally has a tropical climate. Rain forest areas are hot and humid all year. Average daytime temperatures here reach about 90°F (32°C). Heavy rainstorms bring 80 inches (203 cm) or more of rain each year. Savanna and highland areas are cooler and drier.

Human/Environment Interaction
The Economy

The Democratic Republic of the Congo has the potential to become wealthy. The map on page 512 shows you its mineral resources. Mining is the major economic activity. The Congolese are among world leaders in copper production. They also lead the rest of Africa in the mining of industrial diamonds, which are used in precision tools.

Energy Sources The Democratic Republic of the Congo has oil and natural gas deposits, but rivers provide the main source of energy. Experts believe that the country's rivers have the ability to produce about 13 percent of the world's **hydroelectricity**, electricity created by moving water. The Congo River carries

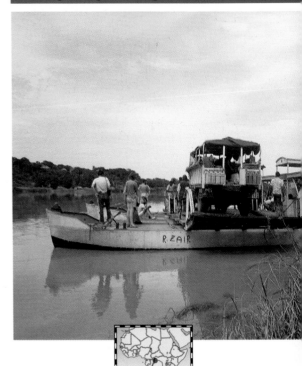

A ferry shuttles passengers and vehicles across the Congo River.
HUMAN/ENVIRONMENT INTERACTION: What is hydroelectricity?

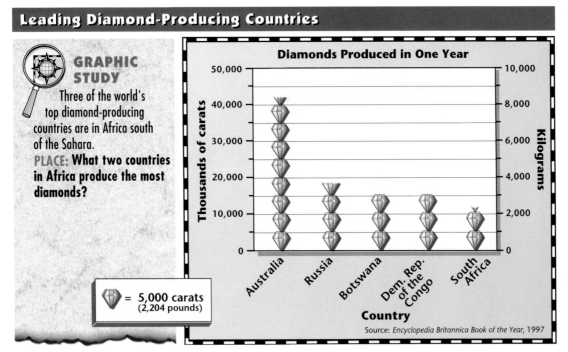

Leading Diamond-Producing Countries

GRAPHIC STUDY
Three of the world's top diamond-producing countries are in Africa south of the Sahara.
PLACE: What two countries in Africa produce the most diamonds?

Diamonds Produced in One Year

Thousands of carats — Kilograms

Country: Australia, Russia, Botswana, Dem. Rep. of the Congo, South Africa

= 5,000 carats (2,204 pounds)

Source: *Encyclopedia Britannica Book of the Year, 1997*

more water than any other river in the world except the Amazon. About 10 million gallons (38 million l) of water rush down the Congo River every second!

Farming Despite rich resources, most people in the Democratic Republic of the Congo make a living by subsistence farming. Farmers grow crops such as corn, rice, and cassava for their families. Coffee, cotton, and palm oil are grown to sell. Along with farming, the Congolese also hunt wild animals in the forests and fish in the rivers, sometimes with traps woven from vines.

Movement
The People

The Democratic Republic of the Congo has a population of about 49 million. Like other African countries, it is made up of different ethnic groups with their own separate languages. At times, tensions between ethnic groups have led to fighting. In recent years, the country has been torn apart by warfare that has cost many lives.

Influences of the Past Groups of people began moving into the Congo region from other parts of Africa about 2,000 years ago. Before the A.D.1400s, several powerful kingdoms developed in the savanna area south of the rain forests. The largest kingdom was the Kongo.

In the late 1400s, Portuguese and other European traders arrived in Central Africa. During the next 300 years, they enslaved thousands of Central Africans, shipping them to the Americas.

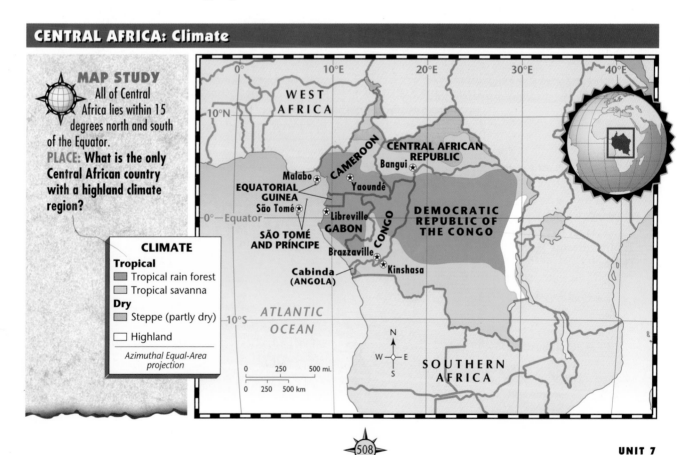

CENTRAL AFRICA: Climate

MAP STUDY
All of Central Africa lies within 15 degrees north and south of the Equator.
PLACE: What is the only Central African country with a highland climate region?

CLIMATE
Tropical
- Tropical rain forest
- Tropical savanna
Dry
- Steppe (partly dry)
- Highland

Azimuthal Equal-Area projection

0   250   500 mi.
0   250   500 km

In 1878 Belgium's King Leopold II took over a large area of Central Africa. He considered the entire region his own plantation and treated the people harshly. When these outrages were publicized in 1908, the Belgian government took control of the colony and named it the Belgian Congo. In 1960 the Belgian Congo became an independent nation known as Congo. Nine years later, the country changed its name to Zaire. In 1997, Congolese troops overthrew longtime leader Mobutu Sese Seko. The new military government then renamed the country the Democratic Republic of the Congo.

Ways of Life The culture of the Democratic Republic of the Congo is largely African with European influences. More than 75 percent of the Congolese are Christians. Most of these are Roman Catholics. Other people in the country practice traditional African religions.

About 70 percent of the Congolese live in rural villages. Since the 1960s, however, many of them have migrated to cities in search of jobs. This movement of people has turned Kinshasa, the capital, into a city of about 4.2 million people. Kinshasa is a major port on the Congo River.

Fifteen-year-old Kilundu Basese lives in Kinshasa. During his free time, Kilundu strolls along Kinshasa's streets lined with trees, elegant shops, and outdoor cafés. Many areas of the city are crowded with new residents looking for work.

Market Day

Masika Mbwana lives in a village on the banks of the Congo River. This morning, with other girls from her village, she will walk to the market in a nearby town. Masika's family grows its own food. Any extra food is gathered to sell at the market. Today Masika has a basket of cassava roots to sell. The meal made from ground cassava is mixed with corn or rice and is the main food of most Congolese.

SECTION 1 ASSESSMENT

REVIEWING TERMS AND FACTS

1. **Define the following:** canopy, hydroelectricity.
2. **PLACE** Why is the Congo River important to the Congolese people?
3. **HUMAN/ENVIRONMENT INTERACTION** The Democratic Republic of the Congo is among world leaders in the production of what mineral resource?
4. **MOVEMENT** How was the Congo region settled?

MAP STUDY ACTIVITIES

5. Turn to the physical map on page 506. What large body of water forms part of the southeast boundary of the Democratic Republic of the Congo?
6. Look at the climate map on page 508. What climates are found in Central Africa?

BUILDING GEOGRAPHY SKILLS

Reading a Bar Graph

You want to compare your running time in the 100-yard dash to that of the other sprinters on your team. Putting your running times on a bar graph would allow you to visually compare all the runners' times at once.

A *bar graph* presents numerical information in a visual way. Bars of various lengths stand for different quantities. Bars may be drawn vertically—up and down—or horizontally—left to right. Labels along the axes, or the left side and bottom of the graph, explain what the bars represent. Some bar graphs show changes over time. Others compare quantities during the same time period, but in different locations. To read a bar graph, apply these steps:

- Read the title to find out what the graph is about.
- Study the information on both axes to figure out what the bars represent.
- Compare the lengths of the bars to draw conclusions about the graph's topic.

Glencoe's **Skillbuilder Interactive Workbook, Level 1** provides instruction and practice in key social studies skills.

Literacy Rate in Selected African Countries

Country (vertical axis):
- Angola
- Cameroon
- Central African Republic
- Chad
- Congo
- Democratic Republic of the Congo
- Equatorial Guinea
- Gabon
- São Tomé and Príncipe

Horizontal axis: 0, 10, 20, 30, 40, 50, 60, 70, 80, 90, 100

Percentage of people who can read and write

Source: *The World Almanac, 1998*

Geography Skills Practice

1. Which countries are compared on this graph?

2. What quantities appear on the horizontal axis? The vertical axis?

3. Which country has the highest literacy rate? Which has the lowest?

Other Countries of Central Africa

PREVIEW

Words to Know
- basin
- tsetse fly

Places to Locate
- Central African Republic
- Cameroon
- Gabon
- Congo
- Equatorial Guinea
- São Tomé and Príncipe

Read to Learn . . .
1. where the Central African Republic and Cameroon are located.
2. what resources are found in Gabon and Congo.
3. how people in Equatorial Guinea and São Tomé and Príncipe make their livings.

The sound of buzz saws rings through Gabon's rain forests. These rain forests hold vast resources, including the ebony trees shown here.

Ebony and mahogany hardwoods provide Central Africa with one of its most valuable sources of income.

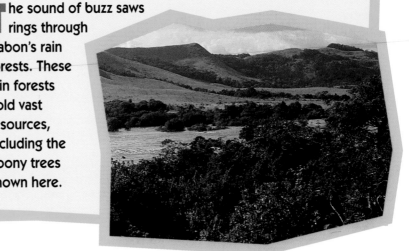

In addition to the Democratic Republic of the Congo, Central Africa includes Gabon (ga•BOHN), the Central African Republic, Cameroon, Congo, Equatorial Guinea, and São Tomé (SOWN tuh•MAY) and Príncipe (PRIHN•suh•puh). All of these countries are only beginning to develop their natural resources.

Location

The Central African Republic and Cameroon

The Central African Republic and Cameroon became independent from France in 1960. Both countries are working to develop their economies. Cameroon, with a coastline on the Gulf of Guinea, enjoys greater natural advantages than the landlocked Central African Republic.

The Land The Central African Republic lies deep in the middle of Africa, just north of the Equator. Most of the country lies on a vast plateau bordered on both sides by basins. A **basin,** you will remember, is a broad flat valley. Savannas cover most of the plateau, but tropical rain forests are found in the

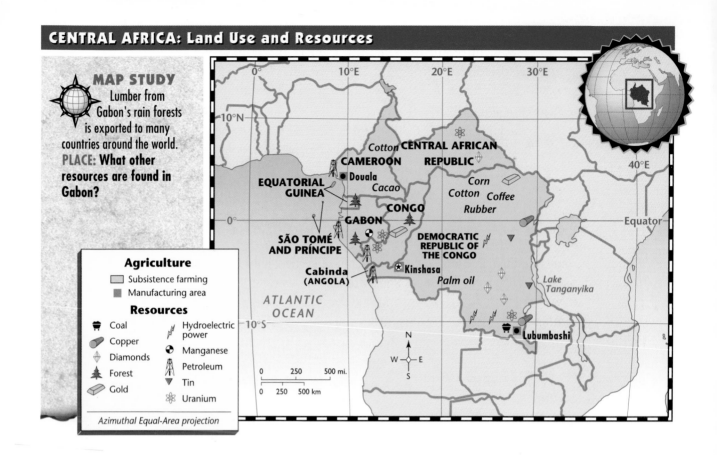

MAP STUDY
Lumber from Gabon's rain forests is exported to many countries around the world.
PLACE: What other resources are found in Gabon?

Agriculture

- ▢ Subsistence farming
- ◼ Manufacturing area

Resources

⛏ Coal		⚡	Hydroelectric power
🪵 Copper		◉	Manganese
◈ Diamonds		⛽	Petroleum
🌲 Forest		▽	Tin
▭ Gold		✴	Uranium

Azimuthal Equal-Area projection

southwestern part of the country. The map on page 508 shows you that the Central African Republic has a tropical savanna climate and a steppe climate.

Cameroon lies on the west coast of Central Africa. In the south hot, humid lowlands stretch along the Gulf of Guinea. The central part of Cameroon is a forested plateau with cooler temperatures and less rainfall. To the north lies a partly dry grasslands area. Mountains and hills run along Cameroon's western border.

The Economy Most people in the Central African Republic and Cameroon depend on farming for a living. In the Central African Republic, most farmers grow only enough food to feed their families. A few large plantations raise coffee, cotton, and rubber for export. Farmers in Cameroon raise cassava, corn, millet, and yams. The chief cash crops are bananas, cacao, coffee, cotton, and peanuts.

The Central African Republic and Cameroon are only beginning to industrialize. Cameroon, however, has had greater success in this effort. It has coastal ports and many natural resources such as petroleum, bauxite, and forest products. With no seaports and limited resources, the Central African Republic can claim only diamond mining as an important industry.

Some people in these two countries herd livestock. They raise their animals in regions that are safe from tsetse flies. The bite of the **tsetse fly** causes a deadly disease called sleeping sickness in cattle. Tsetse flies can also spread this disease to humans.

The People Most of the people in the Central African Republic and Cameroon live in rural areas. In recent years, however, many people from the countryside have moved to cities such as Yaoundé (yown•DAY) in Cameroon and Bangui (bahn•gee) in the Central African Republic in search of work.

Many languages are spoken in these cities. The people of the Central African Republic and Cameroon belong to many ethnic groups. In both countries, most people follow traditional African religions. Smaller numbers are Christians or Muslims.

Place

Gabon and Congo

Gabon and Congo—once French colonies—became independent countries in 1960. Both have many natural resources and excellent waterways. The map on page 508 shows you that Gabon and Congo lie on the Equator along the west coast of Central Africa. Because of this location, both countries have hot, humid climates.

The Land Although they share the same type of climate, Gabon and Congo have different landforms. In Gabon, palm-lined beaches and swamps run along the Gulf of Guinea. As you move inland, you see that the land rises to become rolling hills and low mountains. Thick rain forests crossed by rivers cover most of Gabon.

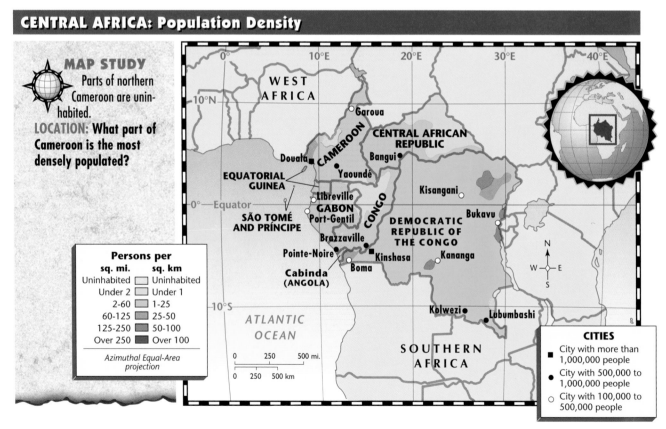

CENTRAL AFRICA: Population Density

MAP STUDY Parts of northern Cameroon are uninhabited.

LOCATION: What part of Cameroon is the most densely populated?

Persons per	
sq. mi.	sq. km
Uninhabited	Uninhabited
Under 2	Under 1
2-60	1-25
60-125	25-50
125-250	50-100
Over 250	Over 100

Azimuthal Equal-Area projection

CITIES
- ■ City with more than 1,000,000 people
- ● City with 500,000 to 1,000,000 people
- ○ City with 100,000 to 500,000 people

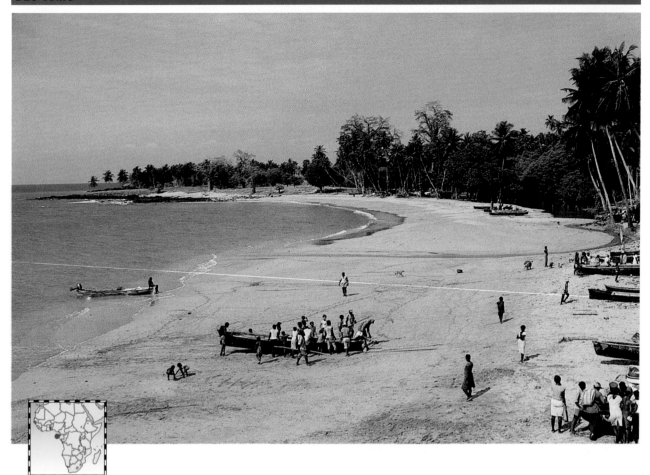

Boats are used for fishing and transportation in the island country of São Tomé and Príncipe.
PLACE: Why does the nation of São Tomé and Príncipe have such fertile soil?

In Congo, a low treeless plain stretches along the Atlantic coast. Just inland from this coastal plain, you will find low mountain ranges and plateaus. To the north a large swampy area lies along the Ubangi River. Farther south flows the Congo River, Congo's major waterway.

The Economy Gabon and Congo have economies based on agriculture and mining. Gabon's farmers cultivate cacao and coffee for export. Throughout Congo subsistence farmers grow food crops such as cassava and yams.

Gabon is rich in natural resources. Its rain forests provide high-quality lumber that is exported throughout the world. Gabon also has oil reserves on the mainland and off the coast. The map on page 512 shows you that Gabon also has valuable deposits of manganese and uranium. Congo has fewer natural resources than Gabon. Petroleum and lumber are its main exports.

The People Gabon and Congo have relatively few people. Only 1.2 million people live in Gabon—mainly in villages along rivers or on the coast at the capital, Libreville. Most of Congo's 2.7 million people live along the Atlantic coast or near Brazzaville, the capital.

The cultures of both countries are made up of many ethnic groups. In Gabon the Fang group controls the national government. Two groups—the Kongo and

514

the Bateke (bah•TEH•keh)—make up most of Congo's population. Most Kongo farm for a living. The Bateke are primarily hunters and fishers.

Place
The Island Countries

The map on page 504 shows you that Equatorial Guinea and São Tomé and Príncipe are island nations. Equatorial Guinea includes mainland territory on the west coast of Africa, plus five offshore islands. São Tomé and Príncipe lies in the Gulf of Guinea, about 180 miles (290 km) west of the Central African coast. This country consists of two main islands and several tiny islands.

Equatorial Guinea Equatorial Guinea was a Spanish colony until 1968. Today the country is home to about 400,000 people from different ethnic groups. Most of Equatorial Guinea's people live on the mainland. They live in rural areas where they grow bananas and coffee. They also harvest timber from the country's thick rain forests. Equatorial Guinea's largest island, Bioko (bee•OH•koh), lies in the Gulf of Guinea. Farmers grow cacao in Bioko's rich volcanic soil. Malabo, the nation's capital and largest city, is on Bioko.

São Tomé and Príncipe At one time a Portuguese colony, the island country of São Tomé and Príncipe became independent in 1975. The Portuguese first settled the islands in 1470. At that time, the islands had no humans living on them. Today São Tomé and Príncipe has about 200,000 people. Most are of mixed African and Portuguese ancestry. Nearly all of the population live on São Tomé, the largest island.

São Tomé and Príncipe lies on a chain of inactive volcanoes, which no longer erupt. Over the years, volcanic ash formed deep layers of fertile soil. Today plantation workers make use of this rich soil to grow bananas, cacao, coconuts, and coffee for export.

SECTION 2 ASSESSMENT

REVIEWING TERMS AND FACTS
1. Define the following: basin, tsetse fly.
2. LOCATION What Central African country is landlocked?
3. HUMAN/ENVIRONMENT INTERACTION What is Gabon's most important natural resource?
4. HUMAN/ENVIRONMENT INTERACTION How do most people in Equatorial Guinea and São Tomé and Príncipe make their livings?

MAP STUDY ACTIVITIES
5. Turn to the land use map on page 512. What natural resources are found in Congo?
6. Look at the population density map on page 513. What is the population density of most of Central Africa?

MAKING CONNECTIONS

Around 500 B.C., a people known as the Bantu lived in West Africa. Bantu, meaning "the people," is the name of a major African language group. The Bantu lived simply—farming, hunting, and fishing—probably in the Benue Valley of Nigeria. Within 500 years the Bantu had learned to mine and to work metals.

POPULATION GROWTH The development of metalworking allowed Bantu farmers to make iron tips for their tools and Bantu hunters to fashion weapons. These advancements made farming easier and hunting more successful. As food supplies increased, more people could be supported. The population in Bantu settlements thrived and grew.

By about 2,000 years ago, the Bantu population had increased so much that most settlements could no longer feed all their members. As a result, small groups split off to search for new land.

CENTURIES OF MOVEMENT Anthropologists have come to believe that Bantu-speaking groups gradually spread throughout central, eastern, and southern Africa. As they pushed into new areas, the Bantu shared their farming and metalworking knowledge—

as well as their language—with other African groups.

The Spread of Ironworking

→ Spread of iron-working, 900–600 B.C.
→ Spread of iron-working, 600–0 B.C.
→ Spread of iron-working, A.D. 0–500
▨ Area for Bantu migrations into southern and eastern Africa

0 500 1000 mi.
0 500 1000 km

Azimuthal Equal-Area projection

By A.D. 1500, nearly 15 centuries of migration had produced hundreds of ethnic groups, each culturally different from the others. Today between 60 and 80 million African people speak Bantu languages.

Making the Connection

1. Why did Bantu-speaking settlements increase in population?
2. To where did Bantu groups migrate?

Chapter 19 Highlights

Important Things to Know About Central Africa

SECTION 1 DEMOCRATIC REPUBLIC OF THE CONGO

- The land area of the Democratic Republic of the Congo is about one-fourth the size of the United States.
- The Congo River is the major "highway" for the Congo region.
- The Democratic Republic of the Congo has one of the largest tropical rain forest areas in the world.
- Vast savannas in the Congo region are home to valuable natural resources—antelopes, leopards, lions, zebras, giraffes, and other wildlife.
- Because of its location on the Equator, the Democratic Republic of the Congo generally has a tropical climate.
- Many important mineral resources, including copper and industrial diamonds, are found in the Democratic Republic of the Congo.
- The 49 million people of the Democratic Republic of the Congo belong to many different ethnic groups.

SECTION 2 OTHER COUNTRIES OF CENTRAL AFRICA

- The Central African Republic's landlocked location makes economic development difficult.
- Cameroon's coastal location has boosted its economic growth.
- Gabon and Congo export lumber and petroleum.
- Most of the people in Equatorial Guinea live on the mainland where they farm and harvest wood from the rain forests.
- São Tomé and Príncipe is an island nation with rich volcanic soil good for farming.

A market in the Democratic Republic of the Congo ▶

Chapter 19 Assessment and Activities

REVIEWING KEY TERMS

Match the numbered terms in Set A with their lettered definitions in Set B.

A

1. hydroelectricity
2. tsetse fly
3. basin
4. canopy

B

A. forest covering
B. insect that spreads tropical diseases to humans and animals
C. power developed from the force of moving water
D. broad, flat valley

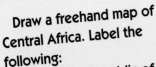

Mental Mapping Activity

Draw a freehand map of Central Africa. Label the following:
- Democratic Republic of the Congo
- Congo River
- Gulf of Guinea
- Gabon
- Central African Republic
- Cameroon
- Congo

REVIEWING THE MAIN IDEAS

Section 1

1. **HUMAN/ENVIRONMENT INTERACTION** What challenges to the environment does the Democratic Republic of the Congo face?
2. **PLACE** How do the many ethnic groups in the Democratic Republic of the Congo affect its national unity?
3. **REGION** Why are the savannas of the Democratic Republic of the Congo important?

Section 2

4. **LOCATION** Describe how the locations of the Central African Republic and Cameroon have influenced their economic development.
5. **PLACE** What mineral resources are found in Gabon?
6. **PLACE** What Central African nation is made up entirely of islands?

CRITICAL THINKING ACTIVITIES

1. **Determining Cause and Effect** How do you think the presence of thick rain forests has affected the development of Central Africa?
2. **Drawing Conclusions** As the nations of Central Africa make use of their resources, what challenges do they face in developing their economies?

CONNECTIONS TO WORLD HISTORY

Cooperative Learning Activity Work in groups of three to learn about the colonial history of one of the Central African countries. Then create a documentary showing your findings. Each group should choose one country and do research for a documentary. Your findings should be presented in storyboard form—showing still pictures and dialogue that go together to form the documentary. Research as a group, then assign the following individual roles: (a) author, (b) editor, and (c) critic.

GeoJournal Writing Activity

Imagine that you work in a large corporation. You have been sent by your company to open a branch office in Kinshasa. Write a letter to your employer back in the United States describing how life in the Democratic Republic of the Congo is different from and similar to life in the United States.

TECHNOLOGY ACTIVITY

Using a Database Create a database about countries in Africa south of the Sahara. Your database should have a separate record for each country. Each record should have a separate field for the following: capital, languages, religions, population, land area, principal export, and principal import. After you have completed the database, write a short summary pointing out the similarities and differences among the countries.

PLACE LOCATION ACTIVITY: CENTRAL AFRICA

Match the letters on the map with the places and physical features of Central Africa. Write your answers on a separate sheet of paper.

1. Congo
2. Lake Tanganyika
3. Libreville
4. Cameroon
5. São Tomé and Príncipe
6. Kinshasa
7. Congo River

Map

20°E
Tropic of Cancer
30°E
40°E
50°E

SOUTHWEST
ASIA

20°N

Port
Sudan

Red Sea

Omdurman
Khartoum

SUDAN

ERITREA
Asmara

DJIBOUTI

10°N

Djibouti
Gulf of Aden

ETHIOPIA
Addis Ababa

CENTRAL

AFRICA

SOMALIA

N
W   E
S

INDIAN
OCEAN

Mogadishu

UGANDA   KENYA
0°   Equator   Kampala
Kisumu

RWANDA   Kigali
Nairobi

BURUNDI   Mwanza
Bujumbura   Lake Victoria

National boundary
National capital
Other city

Azimuthal Equal-Area
projection

Lake
Tanganyika

Mombasa

0   250   500 mi.
0   250   500 km

Dodoma
TANZANIA

Victoria

Dar es Salaam

SEYCHELLES

10°S

MAP STUDY ACTIVITY

As you read Chapter 20, you will learn about Kenya and the other countries in East Africa.

1. What East African countries border the Red Sea?
2. What is the largest East African country?
3. What country east of the African mainland is made up of islands?

Kenya

PREVIEW

Words to Know
- coral
- reef
- fault
- escarpment
- poacher

Places to Locate
- Kenya
- Great Rift Valley
- Indian Ocean
- Nairobi
- Mombasa

Read to Learn . . .
1. what landforms are found in Kenya.
2. why most Kenyans live in highland areas.
3. what languages are spoken in Kenya.

The Great Rift Valley cuts a deep gash through East Africa. In places, the valley's sides are about 1 mile (1.6 km) high, and the valley floor is more than 50 miles (80 km) wide. The Great Rift Valley was formed when two of the plates that make up the earth's crust moved apart millions of years ago.

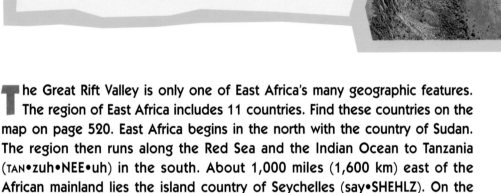

The Great Rift Valley is only one of East Africa's many geographic features. The region of East Africa includes 11 countries. Find these countries on the map on page 520. East Africa begins in the north with the country of Sudan. The region then runs along the Red Sea and the Indian Ocean to Tanzania (TAN•zuh•NEE•uh) in the south. About 1,000 miles (1,600 km) east of the African mainland lies the island country of Seychelles (say•SHEHLZ). On the mainland, Kenya lies close to the center of East Africa.

Region
The Land

Kenya's land area of 219,745 square miles (569,139 sq. km) makes it slightly smaller than the state of Texas. Like Texas's landforms, Kenya's landforms include coastal areas, plains, and highlands.

The Coast The blue Indian Ocean borders Kenya on the east. Kenya's long coastline has stretches of white beaches lined with palm trees. Not far offshore is a coral reef. **Coral** is a hard, rocklike material made of the skeletons of small

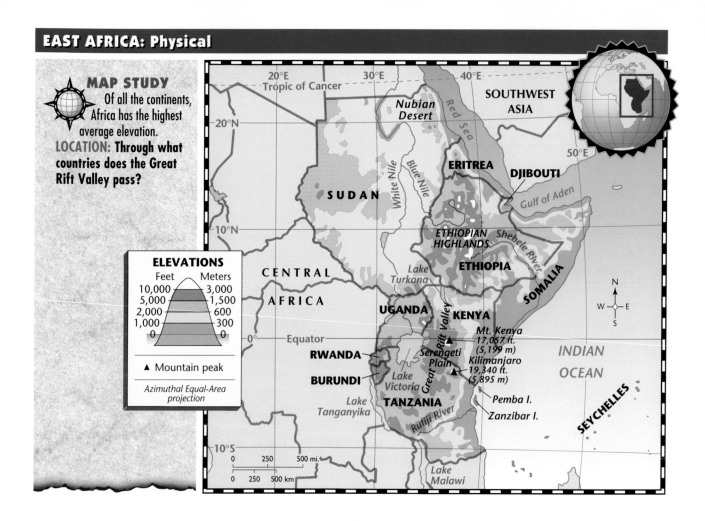

MAP STUDY
Of all the continents, Africa has the highest average elevation.
LOCATION: Through what countries does the Great Rift Valley pass?

ELEVATIONS

Feet	Meters
10,000	3,000
5,000	1,500
2,000	600
1,000	300
0	0

▲ Mountain peak

Azimuthal Equal-Area projection

sea animals. A **reef** is a narrow ridge of coral, rock, or sand at or near the water's surface. Beaches near Kenya's coral reef area draw tourists from around the world.

Plains If you traveled about 20 miles (32 km) inland, you would find a vast plains area covering about three-fourths of Kenya. Bushes, shrubs, and low thorn trees thrive on the plains. Except for groups of nomads who herd their cattle through the region, few people make their homes here. Many animals, however, roam these vast plains. These include antelopes, water buffaloes, elephants, giraffes, lions, zebras, and other animals.

Highlands Southwestern Kenya is a highlands area made up of mountains, valleys, and plateaus. Forests and grasslands sweep through the highlands. This region, which boasts Kenya's most fertile soil, is home to about 75 percent of Kenya's people.

Look at the map above. You see that the Great Rift Valley **fault,** or crack in the earth, divides Kenya's highlands into eastern and western areas. Mountain ranges and **escarpments,** or steep cliffs, tower over both sides of the valley. Mount Kenya—Kenya's highest peak—rises 17,057 feet (5,199 m) in the eastern highlands. Many lakes are found in the western highlands.

522

The Climate The map on page 528 shows you that the Equator passes through the middle of Kenya. Almost all of Kenya has a savanna or steppe climate with hot or warm temperatures. The coast is hot and humid year-round. This area gets enough rain to support a few small rain forests. The plains region is the driest part of Kenya and has a desert climate.

In the highlands, the climate is mild with plenty of rainfall. Temperatures here average about 67°F (19°C), and rainfall may reach about 50 inches (130 cm) each year. The mild climate and fertile soil make the highlands Kenya's most important farming area.

Human/Environment Interaction
The Economy

Kenya has a developing economy based on free enterprise. Its chief economic activity is farming. About 50 percent of Kenya's farm products are subsistence food crops, the most important of which is corn. Kenyans grind corn into a porridge and mix it with vegetables to make a stew. Other subsistence food crops include bananas, beans, and cassava.

Cash Crops The other half of Kenya's farm products are cash crops cultivated for export. The country's leading cash crops—coffee and tea—are Kenya's main source of income. You can find both of these products growing on the slopes of the highlands.

Industries Although Kenya has no major mineral deposits to develop, the government has encouraged the growth of manufacturing in recent years. Kenya's chief factory-made products are cement, chemicals, light machinery, and household appliances.

Tourism adds to Kenya's treasury. Thousands of tourists visit Kenya each year to take trips called safaris. On safaris, visitors tour through national parks to see the country's spectacular wildlife in natural surroundings. The government has set up these parks to protect endangered animals from **poachers,** or people who hunt and kill animals illegally.

Tsavo National Park, Kenya

Elephants and other animals roam the vast plains in Kenya's parks and game reserves.
REGION: What is the climate of Kenya's plains region?

Place
The People

Harambee, which means "pulling together," is an important word in Kenya. Kenyans come from many different ethnic groups and speak many languages. Since their independence, Kenyans have tried to strengthen their country by working together. *Harambee,* however, is being tested as ethnic disputes become more frequent.

Impact of the Past Scientists have found some of the earliest-known remains of humans in the Great Rift Valley. About 3,000 years ago, people from other parts of Africa began to move into Kenya. These people farmed and herded animals in the highlands. They became the ancestors of today's Kenyans.

In the A.D. 700s, Arabs from Southwest Asia set up trading settlements along Kenya's coast. Some of these Arabs married Africans. From these marriages came a new people, culture, and language known as Swahili.

In the late 1800s, Kenya came under British control. Many British people moved to Kenya's highlands because of the mild climate and fertile soil. They took land away from Africans and established their own farms on that land. By the 1940s Kenya's African population had organized to reclaim their land. They opposed the British until Kenya finally won its independence in 1963.

After independence, Kenya became the political and economic leader of East Africa. Since the late 1970s, Kenya has struggled to overcome ethnic conflicts and to build a strong and lasting democracy.

Kenyans Today Kenya's population of 28.3 million people is growing rapidly. Kenya has a high population growth rate—over 2 percent a year. Experts predict that the Kenyan population will reach about 33 million by the year 2015. One of the biggest challenges Kenya faces is providing enough food and jobs for its people.

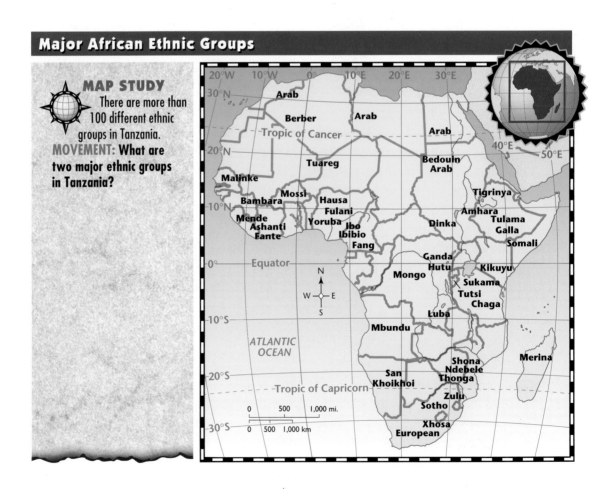

Major African Ethnic Groups

MAP STUDY
There are more than 100 different ethnic groups in Tanzania.
MOVEMENT: **What are two major ethnic groups in Tanzania?**

About 40 different ethnic groups are found in Kenya. The map on page 524 shows several of the many ethnic groups of Africa. The largest of Kenya's ethnic groups is the Kikuyu (kee•KOO• yoo), who live mostly in the highlands. What other major groups are found in East Africa?

Although Kenya's many ethnic groups speak many different African languages, Swahili—a blend of African languages and Arabic—is the most widely spoken. About 65 percent of Kenya's population are Christians, while another 25 percent of the people practice traditional African religions.

Most Kenyans—about 73 percent— live in rural villages. Only 27 percent of the population live in cities such as Nairobi (ny•ROH•bee)—Kenya's modern capital— and the Indian Ocean port of Mombasa (mahm•BAH•suh). Find these cities on the map on page 520.

In recent years, many Kenyans have moved from the countryside to the cities. Lucy Ombasa, a Nairobi teenager, and her family recently moved to the city from their village in western Kenya. Their village specialized in stone carvings of animals, fish, and birds. Lucy's parents and sister now sell carvings to tourist shops in the Kenyan capital.

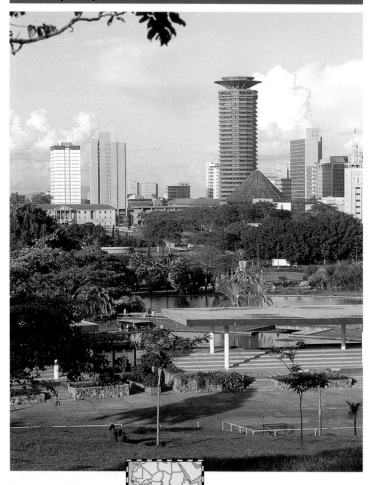

Nairobi, Kenya

Kenya's capital and largest city has many parks and modern office buildings.
MOVEMENT: Why do you think many rural Kenyans have moved to cities?

SECTION 1 ASSESSMENT

REVIEWING TERMS AND FACTS
1. Define the following: coral, reef, fault, escarpment, poacher.
2. LOCATION Where is Kenya's most important farming area?
3. HUMAN/ENVIRONMENT INTERACTION What draws tourists to Kenya?
4. PLACE What is the most widely spoken language in Kenya?

MAP STUDY ACTIVITIES
5. Turn to the physical map on page 522. What large lake lies entirely within Kenya?
6. Look at the political map on page 520. About how far is Kenya's capital from the Ugandan border?

BUILDING GEOGRAPHY SKILLS

Reading a Line Graph

A **line graph** is a good way to show how things change. On a line graph, time intervals appear on the bottom of the graph—the horizontal axis. The information being compared usually appears on the left side of the graph—the vertical axis. Dots or other symbols mark specific quantities. These dots are connected with a line to show relationships and trends. To read a line graph, apply these steps:

Glencoe's **Skillbuilder Interactive Workbook, Level 1** provides instruction and practice in key social studies skills.

- Read the title to find out the subject of the graph.
- Familiarize yourself with the information on both axes.
- Examine where the dots are placed on the graph.
- Determine what the lines or curves mean.

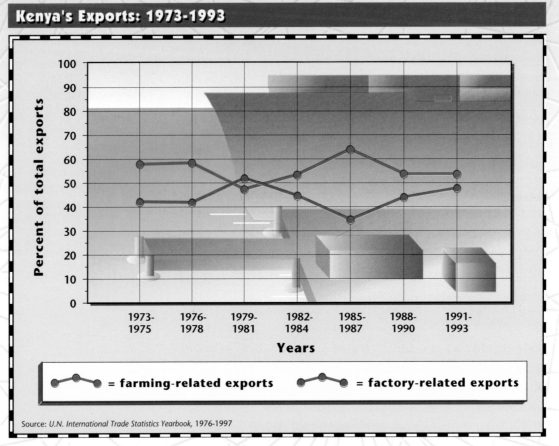

Kenya's Exports: 1973-1993

Years

● = farming-related exports   ● = factory-related exports

Source: *U.N. International Trade Statistics Yearbook, 1976-1997*

Geography Skills Practice

1. What is measured on this graph? Over what time period?

2. In what years did Kenya have the fewest farming-related exports?

3. In what years did Kenya have the most factory-related exports?

Tanzania

PREVIEW

Words to Know
- sisal
- cloves

Places to Locate
- Tanzania
- Lake Victoria
- Lake Tanganyika
- Dar es Salaam
- Zanzibar
- Dodoma

Read to Learn . . .
1. how many ethnic groups make up Tanzania's population.
2. how most people in Tanzania earn a living.

The gleaming, snow-capped peak of Kilimanjaro towers 19,340 feet (5,895 m) over grassy plains in northern Tanzania. For centuries, Africans have gazed at Africa's tallest mountain with awe and wonder. An old African story says that God built Kilimanjaro as a throne from which to view the world.

Kilimanjaro is probably the best-known sight in Tanzania. One of the largest countries in East Africa, Tanzania has a land area of 341,154 square miles (883,588 sq. km). Look at the map on page 520. You see that Tanzania lies south of Kenya and below the Equator.

Place
The Land

Most of Tanzania lies on the mainland of East Africa. The country also includes several small coral islands just off the coast, in the Indian Ocean. The largest of these islands is called Zanzibar.

Coast, Plateaus, and Lakes Like the coast of Kenya, Tanzania's coastline boasts white beaches and palm trees. As you travel inland, the country's elevation rises gradually from humid lowlands to partially dry plateaus. Huge grasslands with patches of trees and shrubs cover the plateaus. To the north, near the Kenyan border, lies a mountainous area that includes Kilimanjaro.

Much of western Tanzania is part of the Great Rift Valley. A number of lakes lie in this area, including Lake Victoria and Lake Tanganyika. Lake Victoria is the largest lake in Africa. Lake Tanganyika's floor is the deepest point on the African continent. Unusual fish found nowhere else in the world live in Lake Tanganyika's deep, dark waters.

Wildlife Like Kenya, Tanzania has many kinds of animals. The Tanzanian government has set aside thousands of square miles to protect its wildlife. Serengeti National Park covers about 5,600 square miles (14,500 sq. km). It is home to many lions and huge herds of antelopes and zebras. During the dry season, thousands of animals roam the plains in search of water.

Place
The Economy and People

Tanzania has a developing economy based on agriculture. Service industries are growing, but manufacturing plants are still small. Tanzania is rich in mineral resources such as gold and diamonds. These riches, however, have not yet been developed.

Most Tanzanians raise livestock or farm small plots of land. Farmers grow only enough bananas, cassava, corn, millet, and rice to feed their families. Large, government-run farms grow many of the crops that Tanzania exports. These cash crops include coffee, cotton, tea, and tobacco.

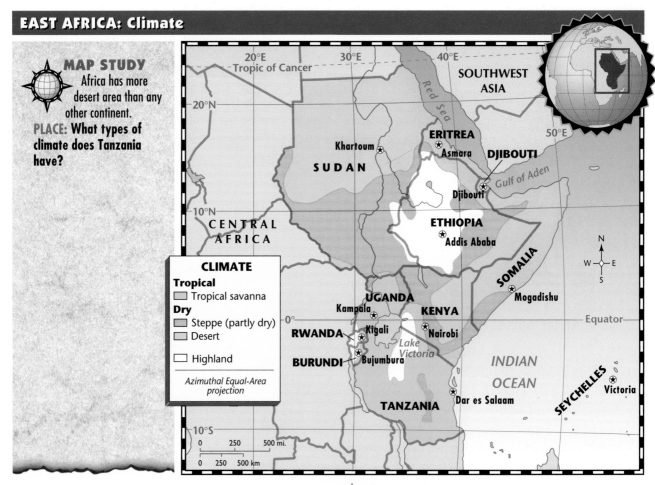

EAST AFRICA: Climate

MAP STUDY
Africa has more desert area than any other continent.
PLACE: What types of climate does Tanzania have?

CLIMATE
Tropical
☐ Tropical savanna
Dry
☐ Steppe (partly dry)
☐ Desert
☐ Highland
Azimuthal Equal-Area projection

Tanzania is the world's largest producer of **sisal,** a plant fiber used in making rope and twine. Farmers on the island of Zanzibar raise the world's largest supply of **cloves,** a spice made from the buds of clove trees.

National Unity About 31 million people live in Tanzania. Most of the population belong to one of about 120 African ethnic groups. A small number of the country's people are Asians or Europeans. Although each ethnic group has its own language, many people speak Swahili, the national language. The population is about evenly divided among Christian, Muslim, and traditional African religions. Because there are so many ethnic groups and religions in Tanzania, no single group controls the country. This ethnic and religious balance has helped Tanzania achieve national unity.

The Past and Present Scientists have found the remains of some of the earliest human settlements in Tanzania. By about A.D. 500, Bantu-speaking peoples had settled in this area. Nearly 600 years later, Arabs from Southwest Asia set up major trading centers on Zanzibar and other islands. The region that is now Tanzania came under European control beginning in the early 1500s. After periods of Portuguese and German rule, the area came under British control following World War I. In the early 1960s, the Tanzanians finally won their independence as the United Republic of Tanzania.

Today about 80 percent of Tanzania's people live in rural villages. Dar es Salaam, on the Indian Ocean, is Tanzania's capital, largest city, and major port. The central area of Tanzania has few people. In an effort to encourage people to move there, the Tanzanian government is planning to build a new national capital—Dodoma—in the area.

Teen Scene

Olympic Hopeful

Sadiki Abasi hopes to be in the Olympics someday. Soccer is his favorite hobby, but his real talent is running. Sadiki is competing with long-distance runners from all over Tanzania for a spot on the national team. He thinks he's got a chance. "I started running with my uncle when I was seven," Sadiki says. "I try to run at least 100 miles a week to stay competitive." Sadiki's uncle, a former national champion, is Sadiki's coach.

SECTION 2 ASSESSMENT

REVIEWING TERMS AND FACTS

1. **Define the following:** sisal, cloves.

2. LOCATION In what area of Tanzania is Kilimanjaro located?

3. PLACE What agricultural products does Tanzania export?

4. MOVEMENT Why will Tanzania move its capital from Dar es Salaam to Dodoma?

MAP STUDY ACTIVITIES

5. Turn to the climate map on page 528. What type of climate is found in southern Tanzania?

MAKING CONNECTIONS

A REMARKABLE FIND

| MATH | SCIENCE | HISTORY | LITERATURE | TECHNOLOGY |

On July 17, 1959, archaeologist Mary Leakey discovered fossils of teeth buried in the ground. An expert on prehistoric bones, she had never seen teeth quite like these before. Hopeful and excited, Mary Leakey ran to tell her husband, Louis, also an archaeologist.

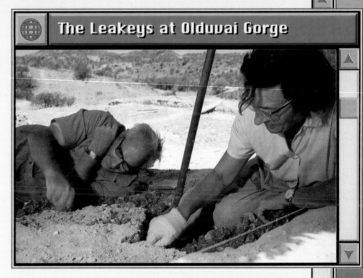

The Leakeys at Olduvai Gorge

EARLY DIGS Louis and Mary Leakey worked at the Olduvai (OHL•duh•vy) Gorge in northern Tanzania. The Gorge—a 25-mile-long (41km) canyon—had proven to be a rich treasure of human and animal fossils. The Leakeys had been digging at various places along the Gorge since the early 1930s. They had already unearthed thousands of remains.

In 1948 Mary Leakey had found a fossilized skull and other bones. These remains were between 25 and 40 million years old. Putting the bones together, the Leakeys produced a creature that had human-like jaws and walked upright on hind legs. It was the first significant evidence that the human race may have started in Africa rather than in Asia, as most archaeologists believed. As the Leakeys ran back to excavate the teeth on that July day in 1959, they thought the teeth might provide further evidence of humankind's beginnings in Africa.

TWICE AS OLD With dental picks and brushes, the Leakeys slowly uncovered the teeth, which turned out to be part of an almost-complete human skull. When dated, the skull proved to be about 1.75 million years old. It was twice as old as scientists had judged the human race to be.

The skull and other Leakey finds forced archaeologists to change their search for human origins from Asia to Africa. In addition, scientists were forced to hypothesize that the development of human beings took much longer than previously thought.

Making the Connection

1. Where is Olduvai Gorge?
2. How did the Leakeys' discoveries change scientists' thinking about human origins?

SECTION 3 Inland East Africa

PREVIEW

Words to Know
- autonomy
- watershed
- civil war
- refugee

Places to Locate
- Uganda
- Rwanda
- Burundi
- Lake Victoria
- Nile River
- Kampala

Read to Learn . . .
1. why inland East Africa has a mild climate.
2. what farm products are grown in inland East Africa.
3. how conflict between ethnic groups has divided the people of inland East Africa.

The sparkling waters of Lake Victoria

cover 26,828 square miles (69,485 sq. km). About half of this magnificent lake lies inside the landlocked East African country of Uganda. Large lakes are also found in two other inland countries of East Africa—Rwanda and Burundi.

Great lakes, snow-covered mountains, deep tropical valleys, and thundering rivers are all found in Uganda, Rwanda, and Burundi. Each of these three countries of inland East Africa is also home to many different peoples.

Place
Uganda

Uganda lies in the highlands region of East Africa. Uganda's 77,085 square miles (199,650 sq. km) make it slightly smaller than Oregon. A plateau covers most of northern Uganda. In the center of the country is a large area of marshes and lakes. Here, waters flowing out of Lake Victoria gather to form a source of the Nile River. In southern Uganda, thick forests spread across the landscape. To the east and west, mountains form Uganda's borders with Kenya and the Democratic Republic of the Congo.

The Equator crosses southern Uganda. The country's generally high elevation, however, keeps temperatures mild. In most areas, at least 40 inches (100 cm) of rain falls each year.

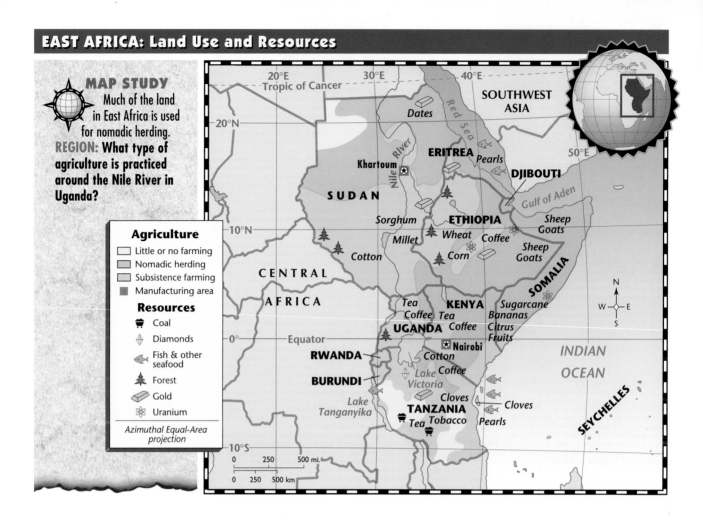

MAP STUDY
Much of the land in East Africa is used for nomadic herding.
REGION: What type of agriculture is practiced around the Nile River in Uganda?

Agriculture

- ☐ Little or no farming
- ▨ Nomadic herding
- ▨ Subsistence farming
- ■ Manufacturing area

Resources

- ⛏ Coal
- ◈ Diamonds
- 🐟 Fish & other seafood
- 🌲 Forest
- ▱ Gold
- ❋ Uranium

Azimuthal Equal-Area projection

The Economy Agriculture is the most important economic activity in Uganda. Fertile soil and a mild climate help crops to grow well. The most productive areas lie along the western and northern sides of Lake Victoria and in the western highlands.

Uganda's farmers grow bananas, beans, cassava, corn, and sweet potatoes to feed their families. They sell any extra food at local markets. Coffee is Uganda's leading export crop. Cotton, sugarcane, and tea are valuable exports, too. These cash crops support Uganda's economy.

The People Uganda has about 21 million people. You will find almost two-thirds of Uganda's people living in the fertile south. There you will find Kampala, the capital, on the shores of Lake Victoria.

The people of Uganda belong to more than 20 different ethnic groups. The Ganda are the largest and most prosperous group. Until 1967 the Ganda enjoyed local **autonomy,** or self-government. Today they are part of a united Uganda.

For most of this century, the British ruled Uganda. After Uganda won its independence in 1962, fighting broke out between ethnic groups in the north and the south. Ethnic conflict, plus a period of cruel dictatorship, hurt Uganda throughout much of the 1980s. Today Ugandans are making great strides in rebuilding their country after this time of suffering and warfare.

Place
Rwanda and Burundi

Rwanda and Burundi are located deep in inland East Africa. Although these two countries lie just south of the Equator, high altitudes give them a mild climate. They also lie on the ridge that separates the Nile and Congo **watersheds.** A watershed is an area drained by a river. To the west of the ridge, waters eventually run into the Congo River watershed. To the east, they run into the Nile watershed.

The Economy Most people in Rwanda and Burundi are farmers. They grow tea, coffee, beans, bananas, cotton, and grains on gently rolling plateaus. In both countries, some people raise livestock. Along lakes, such as Lake Tanganyika and Lake Kivu, fishing is an important economic activity. Some tin mining takes place in mountainous areas, but neither country has valuable minerals.

Because Burundi and Rwanda are landlocked, they have trouble getting their exports to foreign buyers. There are few paved roads and no railroads. Most goods must be transported by road to Lake Tanganyika, where boats take them to Tanzania and the Democratic Republic of the Congo. Another route is by dirt road to Tanzania and then by rail to Dar es Salaam.

Ethnic Conflict Burundi and Rwanda are two of the smallest and most crowded nations in Africa. Rwanda, for example, has an average of 835 persons per square mile (322 persons per sq. km). This density is about 13 times as great

WHAT IN THE WORLD?

Glaciers in Africa?

"Impossible!" thought British geographers in the mid-1800s. They were proved wrong in 1889, when British explorer Henry Morton Stanley saw glaciers in the Ruwenzori (ROO•uhn•ZOHR•ee) Mountains. The Ruwenzori range lies between Uganda and the Democratic Republic of the Congo. Even harder to believe is the fact that the Nile—the river that flows through rain forests and deserts—begins as a trickle in these frozen cliffs.

Volcanoes National Park, Rwanda

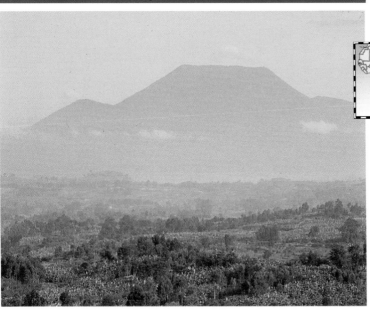

A small village sits in the shadow of one of several inactive volcanoes in Rwanda.
MOVEMENT: How does the lack of a coastline affect the economy of Rwanda?

A Field of Tea in Ijenda, Burundi

Tea pickers gather leaves in the highland plantations of Burundi.
PLACE: What is the occupation of most people in Burundi?

as Africa's population density as a whole! Less than 10 percent of these people live in towns. Most live in villages surrounded by their fields.

The majority of the population in Rwanda and Burundi belong to two ethnic groups—the Hutu and the Tutsi. The Hutu are the largest group in both countries. The Tutsi, however, have controlled the countries' governments and economies. Since Rwanda's and Burundi's independence from Belgium in 1962, the Hutu have tried to gain part of this control.

In 1994 **civil war,** or fighting within a country, broke out in Rwanda between the Hutu and the Tutsi. About 500,000 people were killed. More than 2 million refugees fled Rwanda and settled in camps on the borders of neighboring countries. A **refugee** is a person who must flee his or her home and seek safety elsewhere. In 1996, many refugees returned to Rwanda. By this time, however, the ethnic conflict had spread to Burundi.

SECTION 3 ASSESSMENT

REVIEWING TERMS AND FACTS
1. **Define the following:** autonomy, watershed, civil war, refugee.
2. **PLACE** How does elevation affect climate in inland East Africa?
3. **HUMAN/ENVIRONMENT INTERACTION** What is Uganda's most important economic activity?
4. **PLACE** What two major ethnic groups live in Rwanda and Burundi?

MAP STUDY ACTIVITIES
5. Turn to the land use map of East Africa on page 532. What type of farming takes place in Rwanda and Burundi?

The Horn of Africa

Words to Know
- drought
- clan

Places to Locate
- Sudan
- Ethiopia
- Eritrea
- Somalia
- Djibouti
- Gulf of Aden
- Indian Ocean

Read to Learn . . .
1. what ethnic groups live in Sudan.
2. why Ethiopia has been independent for thousands of years.
3. how civil war has affected countries in the Horn of Africa.

Fierce desert winds often blow through the streets of Khartoum (kahr•TOOM), the capital of Sudan. Yet water flows nearby. Two branches of the Nile River meet at Khartoum. As in Egypt, the Nile River is the giver of life to people in Sudan and other countries of northeastern Africa.

A large area of northeastern Africa is called the Horn of Africa. The map on page 520 shows you how this region got its name. The land is shaped like a horn as it juts out into the Indian Ocean. The countries that lie in the Horn of Africa region are Sudan, Ethiopia, Eritrea (EHR•uh•TREE•uh), Somalia, and Djibouti (juh•BOO•tee).

Place
Sudan

Sudan is the largest country in Africa. Its 917,375 square miles (2,376,000 sq. km) cover an area about one-third the size of the contiguous United States.

Northern Sudan is mostly a desert of bare rocks or sand dunes. Grassy plains cross the central part of Sudan. Here, two great branches of the Nile River—the Blue Nile and the White Nile—meet. This area is the most fertile part of the country. To the south, Sudan has humid tropical rain forests and swamps.

Sudan is one of the world's leading producers of cotton. Most of Sudan's 28.5 million people live along the Nile River or one of its branches. They use water from the Nile to irrigate huge fields of cotton. Some work on large farms owned by the government.

The People If you visited Sudan, you would find that the people differ greatly from north to south. Most people who live in the northern two-thirds of the country are Muslim Arabs. People who live in the south come from several different African ethnic groups. They are Christians or practice traditional African religions.

Since its independence in 1956, Sudan has been torn by civil war between the north and the south. The fighting has disrupted food production and caused widespread hunger. In the early 1990s, a **drought**—an extended dry period—occurred in Sudan and caused even more suffering.

Place
Ethiopia

To the east of Sudan lies Ethiopia. If you look at the map on page 522, you will see that Ethiopia is a rugged, landlocked, mountainous country with a high plateau. The Great Rift Valley cuts through this plateau, forming deep river gorges and sparkling waterfalls. Mild temperatures and fertile soil make areas of the plateau excellent for farming. Ethiopia's farmers, however, cannot always depend on regular rainfall. Drought often occurs, destroying crops and bringing famine. This has happened several times since the 1970s.

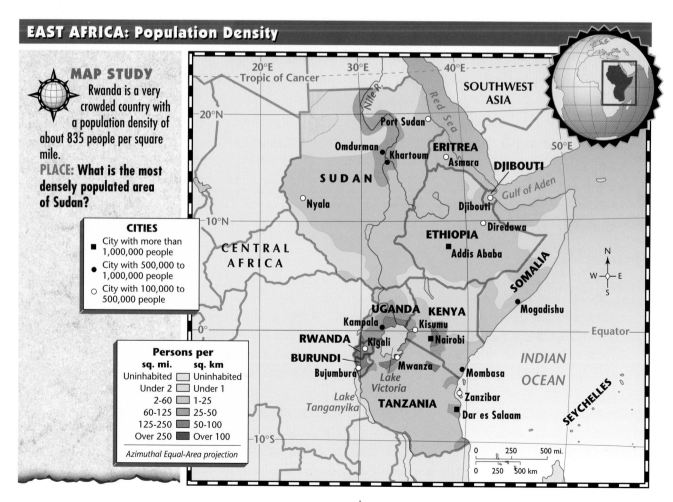

EAST AFRICA: Population Density

MAP STUDY Rwanda is a very crowded country with a population density of about 835 people per square mile.
PLACE: What is the most densely populated area of Sudan?

CITIES
■ City with more than 1,000,000 people
● City with 500,000 to 1,000,000 people
○ City with 100,000 to 500,000 people

Persons per	
sq. mi.	sq. km
Uninhabited	Uninhabited
Under 2	Under 1
2-60	1-25
60-125	25-50
125-250	50-100
Over 250	Over 100

Azimuthal Equal-Area projection

Most Ethiopians live on the high plateau and grow wheat, corn, and other grains on subsistence farms. Some farmers grow coffee to sell. Others also raise livestock.

The People Ethiopia—one of the world's oldest countries—sent government representatives to meet Egyptian pharaohs centuries ago. Ethiopia's mountains kept it isolated and independent for thousands of years. During most of its history, emperors and empresses ruled. In 1974, military leaders overthrew the last emperor. Today Ethiopia is struggling to build a democracy.

About 58.4 million people live in Ethiopia. Only 16 percent of them live in urban areas. Addis Ababa (A•duhs A•buh•buh) is Ethiopia's capital and largest city. About 70 different languages are spoken in Ethiopia. Amharic, similar to Hebrew and Arabic, is the official language. Most Ethiopians are either Christians or Muslims. A smaller number practice traditional African religions.

The walls and ceiling of this church tell the story of Ethiopian Christianity *(left)*. Many residents of Ethiopia's capital live and work in modern buildings *(right)*.
PLACE: What are the two main religions of Ethiopia?

Place
Eritrea

Ethiopia is one of the oldest countries in Africa, and Eritrea is the newest! In 1993, after 30 years of war, Eritrea won its independence from Ethiopia.

Look at the map on page 522. It shows you that Eritrea lies on the Red Sea. Along this Red Sea coast runs a wide plain—one of the hottest and driest areas in Africa. As you travel inland, you will discover that mountains cover the rest of Eritrea.

Most of Eritrea's 3.8 million people farm the land, although farming is uncertain in this dry land. Eritrea's long war with Ethiopia has also made farming difficult. Soldiers cut down the forests, which led to soil erosion. Now that an unstable peace prevails, Eritreans are rebuilding their country.

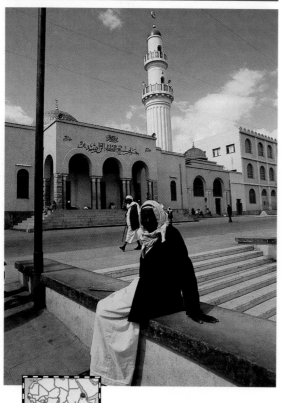

The Central Mosque in Asmara, Eritrea

Asmara is one of the few large cities in the tiny country of Eritrea.
PLACE: What country was Eritrea a part of until 1993?

Place
Somalia

Like Eritrea, Somalia is a hot, dry country. Grassy plains cover most of Somalia. About half of the country's 10.7 million people are nomads. Southern Somalia, however, has rivers that provide water for irrigation. Farmers there grow sugarcane and citrus fruits.

The People Nearly all Somalis are Muslims and speak either Somali or Arabic. Yet they are deeply divided. They belong to **clans,** groups of people related to one another. In the late 1980s, clan disputes led to civil war. When a drought struck a few years later, hundreds of thousands of Somalis starved. Other countries sent food, but the fierce fighting kept much of the food from reaching the starving people.

In 1992 the United States and other countries sent troops to protect food supplies. The troops withdrew in 1995 after the worst of the famine ended. Armed Somali groups, however, still control parts of the country.

Place
Djibouti

Djibouti is a tiny land wedged between Eritrea and Somalia. Djibouti's 700,000 people are mostly Muslims who, in the past, lived a nomadic life. Now many of them have settled permanently in the capital city, also called Djibouti.

Almost all of the country's income derives from shipping. Farming is difficult on its dry lands. The city of Djibouti on the Gulf of Aden is an important port. A railroad line connecting it to Ethiopia makes Djibouti an important outlet for Ethiopia's products.

SECTION 4 ASSESSMENT

REVIEWING TERMS AND FACTS
1. **Define the following:** drought, clan.
2. **PLACE** Where do most of Sudan's people live?
3. **PLACE** What is the newest country in Africa?
4. **HUMAN/ENVIRONMENT INTERACTION** What challenges do farmers face in the Horn of Africa?

MAP STUDY ACTIVITIES
5. According to the population density map on page 536, what country in the Horn of Africa is the most densely populated?

Chapter 20 Highlights

Important Things to Know About East Africa

SECTION 1 KENYA

- Kenya has coastal lowlands as well as inland plains and highlands.
- The Great Rift Valley is a huge gash in the earth that runs through most of East Africa.
- Two important economic activities in Kenya are farming and tourism.
- Coffee and tea exports are Kenya's main source of income.
- Kenya's population of about 28 million is growing rapidly.

SECTION 2 TANZANIA

- Tanzania is made up of a mainland area and a group of offshore islands.
- Kilimanjaro, Africa's tallest mountain, lies in the northern area of Tanzania.
- Serengeti National Park in Tanzania is home to many animal species, including lions, antelopes, and elephants.
- Tanzania's population consists of about 120 ethnic groups.

SECTION 3 INLAND EAST AFRICA

- Uganda has a fertile plateau that is good for farming.
- Uganda, Rwanda, and Burundi lie close to the Equator, but their generally high elevation keeps their temperatures mild.
- The two main ethnic groups in Rwanda and Burundi are the Hutu and the Tutsi.

SECTION 4 THE HORN OF AFRICA

- Most of Sudan's people live along the Nile River and farm for a living.
- Ethiopia has been an independent country for thousands of years.
- Eritrea, Somalia, and Djibouti are hot, dry countries where farming is difficult.

Goma cane dancers in Kenya ▶

Chapter 20 Assessment and Activities

REVIEWING KEY TERMS

Match the numbered terms in Set A with their lettered definitions in Set B.

A

1. clan
2. poacher
3. autonomy
4. refugee
5. civil war
6. cloves
7. reef
8. sisal

B

A. person who kills animals illegally
B. plant fiber used to make rope
C. person who flees home for safety elsewhere
D. sea ridge rising above or below the water's surface
E. spice made from dried flower buds
F. self-government
G. conflict within a country
H. large group of related people

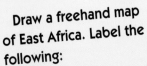

Mental Mapping Activity

Draw a freehand map of East Africa. Label the following:

- Kenya
- Lake Tanganyika
- Rwanda
- Nairobi
- Eritrea
- Indian Ocean
- Somalia

REVIEWING THE MAIN IDEAS

Section 1

1. **MOVEMENT** What group of people set up trading settlements along East Africa's coast?
2. **HUMAN/ENVIRONMENT INTERACTION** What major challenge does Kenya face today?

Section 2

3. **PLACE** What is the largest lake in Africa?
4. **PLACE** Where are cloves grown in Tanzania?

Section 3

5. **LOCATION** In what part of Uganda do most Ugandans live?
6. **MOVEMENT** Why did more than 2 million refugees flee Rwanda during the early 1990s?

Section 4

7. **MOVEMENT** Why were troops sent to Somalia in the early 1990s?
8. **LOCATION** How does Djibouti's location affect its economy?

CRITICAL THINKING ACTIVITIES

1. **Identifying Central Issues** How do ethnic differences create problems for the countries of the East African region?
2. **Predicting Consequences** What effect do you think moving from the countryside to cities has on the way people live in East Africa?

CONNECTIONS TO WORLD CULTURES

Cooperative Learning Activity Work in a group of four to learn about an ethnic group in East Africa. Choose one ethnic group, then have each student research one of the following topics: (a) family life; (b) education; (c) way of earning a living; or (d) the arts. After your research is complete, share your information with your group. Brainstorm ways to present your ethnic group to the entire class.

GeoJournal Writing Activity

Imagine you have been sent to Somalia, Sudan, or Rwanda as part of a relief agency such as the American Red Cross, CARE, or Doctors Without Borders. Write a short article for your hometown newspaper describing your experience.

TECHNOLOGY ACTIVITY

Using the Internet Search the Internet to find information about organizations dedicated to the preservation of animals in Africa south of the Sahara. Choose one organization and then research and write a report about the organization and what it is currently doing to protect endangered animals. Include photographs, clip art, and a map in your report.

PLACE LOCATION ACTIVITY: EAST AFRICA

Match the letters on the map with the places and physical features of East Africa. Write your answers on a separate sheet of paper.

1. Zanzibar
2. Tanzania
3. Lake Victoria
4. Nile River
5. Mogadishu
6. Red Sea
7. Khartoum
8. Uganda
9. Ethiopia

GeoLab ACTIVITY

From the classroom of
Carole Mayrose
Clay City, Indiana

LANDFORMS: Contour Mapping

Background

Africa south of the Sahara rises from west to east in a series of plateaus. How can you show plateaus or a rise in elevation on a map? In this activity you will create a contour map by drawing lines that follow the shape of a landform at different elevations.

WEST KENYA: Contour Map

Lake Kyoga

1000
1500
1000
2000
1500
1500
3000
1500
2000
1000
1500

Equator 0°

N
W E
S

Lake Victoria

1500

2000

3000

2000

Mt. Kenya
17,057 ft.
(5,199 m)

2000

1500

0   25   50 mi.

0   25   50 km

1500
2000

35°E

Contour intervals in meters
_____
*Lambert Equivalent
Azimuthal projection*

Believe it or NOT!

Most of the African continent is a plateau, with the exception of the Great Rift Valley, which slices through eastern Africa. This valley has sides up to 1 mile (1.6 km) high and a floor up to 50 miles (80 km) wide. The Great Rift Valley is like a huge scar on the earth—and can be seen from space.

Materials

- a metric ruler
- 1 clear plastic box and lid
- modeling clay
- a beaker of water
- 1 transparency (clear plastic)
- a transparency marker
- tape

542

What To Do

A. Using the ruler and the transparency marker, measure and mark 1-cm lines up the side of the box. (The bottom of the box will be zero elevation, or sea level.)

B. Tape the transparency to the top of the box lid.

C. With the modeling clay, mold a landform with mountains, plateaus, and valleys.

D. Place the model in the box.

E. Using the beaker, pour water into the box to a height of 1 cm. Place the lid on the box.

F. Looking down through the transparency on top of the box, use the marker to trace the top of the water line as it surrounds the landform.

G. Using the scale 1 cm=5 feet, mark the elevation on the line.

H. Repeat steps D through F, adding water to the next 1-cm level and tracing until you have mapped the landform by means of contour lines.

I. Transfer the tracing of the contours of the landform onto paper.

Lab Activity Report

1. What is the difference in elevation between each contour line on your map?

2. What is the average elevation of your landform?

3. **Making Comparisons** How would the number of contour lines on an area of steep mountains compare with the number on an area of flat plains?

Go A Step Further!

Activity

Describe the kind of landform you think occurs where the contour lines are close together. What kind of landform occurs where the lines are far apart?

Chapter 21 South Africa and Its Neighbors

MAP STUDY ACTIVITY

As you read Chapter 21, you will learn about South Africa and its neighbors.

1. What three island countries lie off Africa's southeastern coast?

2. What country forms the southern tip of the African continent?

3. Through what countries does the Tropic of Capricorn pass?

SECTION 1

Republic of South Africa

PREVIEW

Words to Know
- enclave
- high veld
- escarpment
- apartheid
- township

Places to Locate
- Republic of South Africa
- Cape Town
- Drakensberg Mountains
- Johannesburg
- Durban
- Pretoria

Read to Learn . . .
1. what landscapes are found in South Africa.
2. what mineral resources South Africa has.
3. what changes have occurred recently in South Africa's government.

This huge natural wonder is called Table Mountain. It looms over the city of Cape Town—a major port in the Republic of South Africa.

The Republic of South Africa spreads across the southern end of Africa. It is a land of breathtaking scenery and great mineral wealth. It is also a land of great change. In recent years, South Africa's people have gone through many changes in their lives and their government.

Region

The Land

South Africa sprawls across 471,440 square miles (1,221,030 sq. km)—an area nearly three times the size of California. South Africa has many different landscapes: winding coastlines, tall mountains, deep valleys, and a high plateau. The map on page 544 shows you that South Africa's large land area also swallows up two small independent African nations—Lesotho (luh•SOH•toh) and Swaziland. These are **enclaves,** or small countries surrounded or nearly surrounded by a larger country.

Coasts The west coast of South Africa borders the Atlantic Ocean, and the south and east coasts border the Indian Ocean. Northwest along the Atlantic coast stretches the vast Namib Desert. Farther south lies the Cape of Good Hope, the southernmost point of Africa. A group of long, narrow mountain ranges runs through this southwestern area. Between the ranges lies a dry, flat land called the Great Karroo. Farther east, along the Indian Ocean, are high cliffs, sandy beaches, rolling hills, and a lowland plain.

A Plateau and Mountains A large plateau spreads through the center of South Africa. It ranges from about 2,000 to 8,000 feet (610 to 2,440 m) above sea level. Part of the South African plateau is made up of flat, grass-covered plains called the **high veld.** Isolated rocky hills rise as high as 100 feet (30 m) above the surrounding land.

A group of mountains and cliffs circle the plateau and divide it from the coastal areas. They are known as the Great Escarpment. An **escarpment,** you will recall, is a steep cliff or slope that divides high and low ground. The Great Escarpment rises to its highest elevations in the eastern Drakensberg Mountains. Many peaks in this range are more than 10,000 feet (3,000 m) high.

The Climate South Africa lies south of the Equator. Its seasons are opposite those in the Northern Hemisphere. When it is winter north of the Equator, it is summer south of the Equator. In winter the South African plateau is cool and sunny—with some rainfall—during the day. Temperatures sometimes drop below freezing at night. Summers are mild because of the high elevation.

Cape Town—a major port city—has a Mediterranean climate of cool, rainy winters and hot, often dry summers. Along the eastern coast warm winds from the Indian Ocean bring a humid subtropical climate.

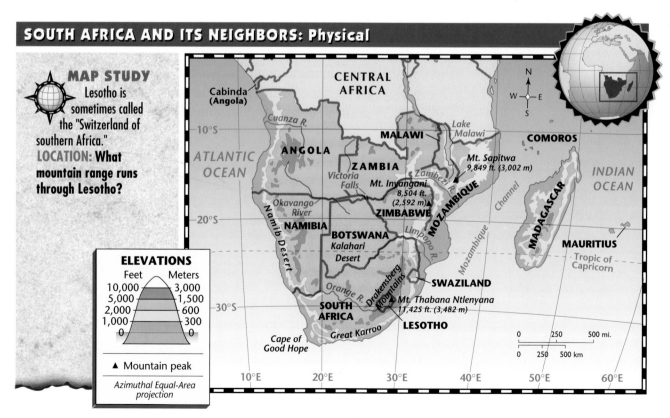

SOUTH AFRICA AND ITS NEIGHBORS: Physical

MAP STUDY
Lesotho is sometimes called the "Switzerland of southern Africa."
LOCATION: What mountain range runs through Lesotho?

ELEVATIONS
Feet	Meters
10,000	3,000
5,000	1,500
2,000	600
1,000	300
0	0

▲ Mountain peak

Azimuthal Equal-Area projection

Cabinda (Angola)
CENTRAL AFRICA
Cuanza R.
ATLANTIC OCEAN
ANGOLA
MALAWI
Lake Malawi
COMOROS
ZAMBIA
Zambezi R.
Mt. Sapitwa 9,849 ft. (3,002 m)
INDIAN OCEAN
Victoria Falls
Mt. Inyangani 8,504 ft. (2,592 m)▲
MOZAMBIQUE
MADAGASCAR
Okavango River
ZIMBABWE
Mozambique Channel
NAMIBIA
BOTSWANA
Limpopo R.
MAURITIUS
Namib Desert
Kalahari Desert
Mozambique
Tropic of Capricorn
Orange R.
Drakensberg Mountains
SWAZILAND
SOUTH AFRICA
Mt. Thabana Ntlenyana 11,425 ft. (3,482 m)
Cape of Good Hope
Great Karroo
LESOTHO

0 250 500 mi.
0 250 500 km

10°S 20°S 30°S
10°E 20°E 30°E 40°E 50°E 60°E

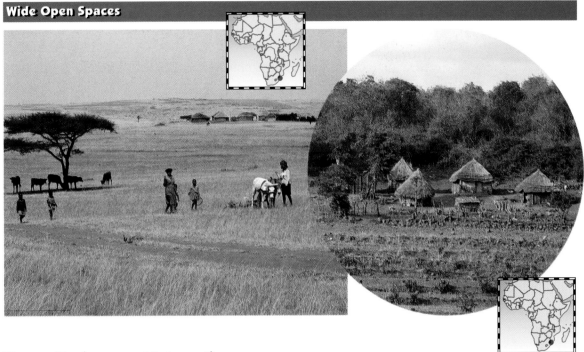

Human/Environment Interaction
The Economy

South Africa has the most developed economy in Africa. Its workers mine one-half of Africa's minerals and produce two-fifths of Africa's manufactured goods. South Africa is also the continent's largest exporter of farm products.

Not all South African workers take part in this prosperous economy. Workers in modern industries and businesses live in urban areas. Yet many people in rural South Africa are poor and depend on subsistence farming.

Many people raise livestock in South Africa's high veld *(left)* and in the small enclave of Swaziland *(right)*.
PLACE: What is an enclave?

Land of Gold and Diamonds In terms of mineral wealth, South Africa is one of the richest countries in the world. South Africa produces about one-third of all the gold mined in the world each year. The Witwatersrand (WIHT•WAW•tuhrz•RAND)—an area around the city of Johannesburg—holds the world's largest and richest goldfield. South Africa also has the world's largest deposits of diamonds.

Manufacturing and Farming South Africa's industrial workers produce many manufactured goods. Many of the products South Africans use are made in their own factories. South Africa also exports metal products, chemicals, clothing, and processed foods.

Most of South Africa is either too dry or too hilly to farm. On the land that is available, South Africa's farmers grow enough food for the country's needs and for export. Among the crops they cultivate are corn, fruits, potatoes, and wheat. Herding sheep and livestock is a major economic activity on the plateau.

WHAT IN THE WORLD?

The Biggest Diamond

The largest diamond ever found was dug from Premier Mine near the city of Pretoria in South Africa. It was about the size of a person's fist and weighed 3,106 carats—about 1.4 pounds (.64 kg). When it was cut, it made 9 large jewels and more than 100 smaller ones. The largest jewel became known as the Star of Africa.

Place
Influences of the Past

About 39 million people live in South Africa. African ethnic groups make up 74 percent of South Africa's population. Africans of European origin represent 14 percent, and Asians 3 percent. People of mixed European, African, and Asian backgrounds make up the remaining 9 percent.

Africans Most Africans in South Africa trace their ancestry to Bantu-speaking peoples that settled throughout Africa between A.D. 100 and 1000. The largest ethnic groups in South Africa today are the Sotho, Zulu, and Xhosa (KOH•suh).

Europeans In the 1600s the Dutch became the first Europeans to settle in South Africa. Over time German and French settlers joined them. Together these European groups came to speak their own language—Afrikaans (A•frih•KAHNS). The Afrikaners pushed Africans off the best land and set up farms.

The British settled in South Africa in the early 1800s. By the end of the century, diamonds and gold drew many British people to South Africa. War broke out between the British and the Afrikaners in 1899. After three years of fighting, the British won the conflict.

African Independence Dates

MAP STUDY All of the countries in Africa, except Ethiopia and Liberia, have been controlled by one European country or another. **PLACE: In what year did Angola gain its independence?**

A New Nation In 1910 Afrikaner and British territories united into one country—the Union of South Africa—within the British Empire. Black South Africans founded the African National Congress in 1912 in hopes of gaining power. In 1931 the United Kingdom gave South Africa full independence.

In 1948 the Afrikaners set up **apartheid**—"apartness"—or practices that separated South Africans of different ethnic groups. For example, laws forced black South Africans to live in separate areas and attend different schools from European South Africans. People of non-European background could not vote. They had virtually no political rights enjoyed by those of European ancestry.

For more than 40 years, people inside and outside South Africa protested against the practice of apartheid. In 1991, the South African government finally agreed to end apartheid. In April 1994, South Africa had its first-ever election in which people of all ethnic groups could vote. South Africans elected their first black African president, Nelson Mandela.

In 1994, for the first time, South Africa's elections were open to all races *(left)*. Nelson Mandela became the country's first black president *(right)*.
PLACE: What group of people were favored under apartheid?

COMPARING POPULATION:
South Africa and the United States

GRAPHIC STUDY
Cape Town is South Africa's largest city.
PLACE: What is South Africa's total population?

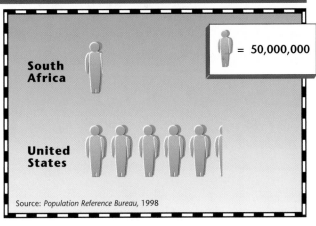

= 50,000,000

South Africa

United States

Source: *Population Reference Bureau, 1998*

Creating History

Mosi Faraji feels lucky to be living in South Africa right now. Someday he will tell his children about what it was like to live under apartheid. Now he is allowed to attend schools that were once all-white. The history books in his classes finally include the story of his nation's black people. Many restaurants and theaters that served only whites are now open to everyone. Even sports teams can now be mixed.

Place
The People

About 57 percent of South Africans live in urban areas. The map on page 562 shows you that South Africa has five large cities with more than 500,000 people. These cities are Johannesburg, Cape Town, Durban, Soweto, and Pretoria. Cape Town and Durban are port cities. Johannesburg is an inland industrial and commercial center. North of Johannesburg is Pretoria, which is one of the national capitals along with Cape Town and Bloemfontein (BLOOM•fuhn•TAYN).

One of the challenges facing South Africa is to develop a better standard of living for all of its people. Most European South Africans live in modern homes or apartments, own cars, and enjoy foods similar to those common in the United States and Europe. Most African, Asian, and mixed-group South Africans, however, have a much harder life. Many live in crowded **townships,** or neighborhoods outside cities. Others live in rural areas where the land is difficult to farm.

The arts in South Africa reflect the country's long struggle for justice and equality. In recent years, African musicians have combined traditional African dance rhythms and modern rock music. This style of music has become popular in many countries, especially the United States. You may be familiar with South African groups such as Mahlathini and the Mahotella Queens and Ladysmith Black Mambazo.

SECTION 1 ASSESSMENT

REVIEWING TERMS AND FACTS
1. **Define the following:** enclave, high veld, escarpment, apartheid, township.
2. **PLACE** What landform covers most of inland South Africa?
3. **HUMAN/ENVIRONMENT INTERACTION** What are South Africa's two main mineral resources?
4. **PLACE** How did South Africa's government change in the early 1990s?

MAP STUDY ACTIVITIES
5. Look at the political map on page 544. About how far is Cape Town from Pretoria?
6. Turn to the physical map on page 546. At what elevation does Lesotho lie?

BUILDING GEOGRAPHY SKILLS

Using Technology

Developing Multimedia Presentations

You have been assigned a research report to present to your class. You want to make your presentation informative, but also interesting and fun. How can you do this? One way is to combine several types of media into a multimedia presentation.

Suppose you plan to give a multimedia presentation on life in South Africa. You might show photographs of the country, play a recording of local music, or present a video showing the people at work and at play. You could also develop your multimedia presentation on a computer. Computer multimedia programs can allow you to combine text, video, audio, graphics, and other media to create dynamic presentations.

In order to create multimedia presentations on a computer, you need to have certain tools. These may include computer graphics tools and drawing programs, animation programs that make certain images move, and presentation programs that tie everything together. Your computer manual will tell you which programs your computer supports.

Ask questions like the following to develop a multimedia presentation:

- Which forms of media do I want to include: Video? Sound? Animation? Photographs? Graphics? Other media?

- Which of these media forms does my computer support?

- What kind of software programs do I need?

- Is there a "do-it-all" program that I can use to develop the kind of presentation I want?

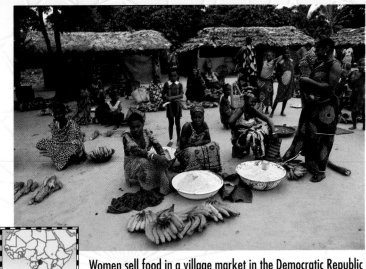

Women sell food in a village market in the Democratic Republic of the Congo. Most farming in this country centers around small family plots. People produce food for their own needs, as well as food to sell and trade for other products.

Technology Skills Practice

For additional practice in developing multimedia presentations, use the questions above to help you develop a presentation on life in one of the African countries you have studied in this unit. Write a plan describing a multimedia presentation you would like to develop. Indicate what tools you will need and what steps you must take to make the presentation a reality.

Atlantic Countries

PREVIEW

Words to Know
- exclave

Places to Locate
- Namibia
- Angola
- Windhoek
- Luanda
- Namib Desert
- Kalahari Desert

Read to Learn . . .
1. what landforms Angola and Namibia share.
2. why Portuguese is the official language of Angola.
3. why Namibia has difficulty feeding its people.

You would not want to get a flat tire on the vast Namib Desert! This empty stretch of sand and rock is one of the loneliest places on the earth. The Namib Desert stretches north to south about 1,200 miles (1,931 km) through southwestern Africa.

The Namib Desert extends most of the length of the country of Namibia. In addition to desert, Namibia and its northern neighbor—Angola—have long coastlines on the Atlantic Ocean. For this reason, they are known as southern Africa's Atlantic countries.

Place

Angola

Angola is a huge, nearly square mass of land. It covers 481,350 square miles (1,246,697 sq. km)—an area larger than Texas and California put together. Angola also includes a tiny exclave called Cabinda. An **exclave** is a tiny area of a country that is separated from the main part. The map on page 544 shows you that Cabinda is separated from Angola.

The Land Most of Angola is part of the same huge inland plateau that sweeps through the Republic of South Africa. Many rivers cross this area in Angola. Some flow into the Congo River in the north; others flow into the Atlantic Ocean or the Indian Ocean.

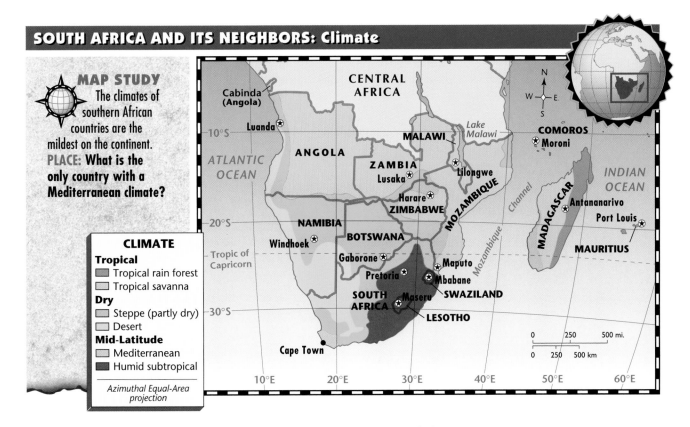

MAP STUDY The climates of southern African countries are the mildest on the continent. **PLACE: What is the only country with a Mediterranean climate?**

CLIMATE

Tropical
- ▓ Tropical rain forest
- ░ Tropical savanna

Dry
- ▒ Steppe (partly dry)
- ░ Desert

Mid-Latitude
- ▒ Mediterranean
- ▓ Humid subtropical

Azimuthal Equal-Area projection

Hilly grasslands cover northern Angola. The southern part of the country, however, is a rocky desert. A low strip of land winds along the 900-mile (1,448-km) Atlantic coastline. This lowland area has little natural vegetation, except for a few rain forests in the north.

If you traveled across Angola, you would experience three kinds of climates. The map above shows you that coastal areas have a steppe or desert climate. The inland plateau has a tropical savanna climate of wet and dry seasons. This area receives enough rainfall for farming.

The Economy Angola's major economic activity is agriculture. Nearly 58 percent of Angola's 12 million people live in the countryside. Subsistence farmers there grow corn, cotton, and sugarcane. Coffee is the leading export crop. Some Angolans also herd cattle, sheep, and goats.

Oil and mining, however, provide most of Angola's income. Look at the map on page 558. It shows you that Angola is rich in diamonds, iron ore, manganese, and petroleum. Oil is the country's leading export. Most of the oil deposits are located off the shore of Cabinda.

Influences of the Past Most of Angola's people are Africans who belong to several ethnic groups. They trace their ancestry to the ancient Bantu-speaking peoples. In the 1400s the Kongo kingdom ruled a large part of northern Angola.

From the 1500s until its independence in 1975, Angola was a colony of Portugal. Portuguese influence still remains strong in Angola. Although African languages are spoken, Portuguese is the official language. Almost 70 percent of Angolans practice the Roman Catholic faith brought to Angola by Portuguese missionaries.

Angola's capital and major port is located on the country's long coastline.
LOCATION: What is the name of Angola's exclave?

After independence, civil war among different political and ethnic groups broke out in Angola. The fighting brought great suffering to Angola's people. Today the fighting has diminished, but rebuilding Angola will be a very difficult task.

Place
Namibia

South of Angola lies Namibia, one of Africa's newest countries. Namibia became independent in 1990 after 75 years of South African rule. The map on page 548 shows you the dates of independence for other African countries.

A Plateau and Deserts Namibia has a land area of 317,870 square miles (823,283 sq. km)—about one-half the size of Alaska. If you look at the map on page 546, you will see that a large plateau runs through the center of Namibia. It is the most populated area of the country. The rest of Namibia is made up of deserts. The Namib Desert runs almost the entire length of Namibia's Atlantic coast. The Kalahari Desert stretches across the southeastern part of the country. As you might guess, most of Namibia has a hot, dry climate.

The Economy Namibia's economy depends on the export of minerals. The country has rich deposits of diamonds, manganese, copper, silver, and zinc. Many Namibians work in the country's mines.

Because of the desert environment, Namibia has difficulty feeding its people. Farmers in the plateau region receive barely enough rainfall to grow corn. Most Namibians are herders who raise cattle, goats, and sheep.

Land of Few People Only 1.6 million people live in Namibia—one of the most sparsely populated countries in Africa. Most Namibians belong to African ethnic groups. A small number are of European ancestry. English and Afrikaans are the official languages, but most Namibians speak African languages.

SECTION 2 ASSESSMENT

REVIEWING TERMS AND FACTS
1. Define the following: exclave.
2. HUMAN/ENVIRONMENT INTERACTION What is Angola's most important mineral export?
3. PLACE What European country once ruled Angola?
4. LOCATION Where do most Namibians live?

MAP STUDY ACTIVITIES
5. Turn to the climate map on page 553. What climate regions are found in Angola and Namibia?

GREAT ZIMBABWE

| MATH | SCIENCE | **HISTORY** | LITERATURE | TECHNOLOGY |

Long before Europeans arrived on Africa's shores, inland African kingdoms were wealthy from the gold trade. Between A.D. 1000 and 1500, a Bantu-speaking people—the Shona—built nearly 300 stone-walled fortresses throughout southern Africa. The largest fortress was called Great Zimbabwe (zihm•BAH•bwee)—meaning "house of stone." It was the religious and trading center of the Shona kingdom.

A GIGANTIC CAPITAL Great Zimbabwe included fortress walls, temples, marketplaces, and homes spread out on a fertile, gold-rich plateau south of the Zambezi River. The city was the capital of the Shona kingdom and displayed the wealth and power of its kings. Its shape was oval, and its buildings were made of stone. This made the city stand out from the traditional circular mud-and-thatch villages.

The most impressive part of the city was an area called the Great Enclosure. The Great Enclosure's outer wall was 16.5 feet (5 m) thick and 32 feet (9.8 m) high. It was built of 900,000 granite stones fitted together without mortar. Enclosed within this wall, a maze of interior walls and hidden passages pro-

tected the circular house of the king, the Great Temple, and other religious buildings.

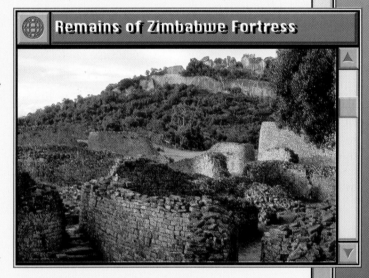

Remains of Zimbabwe Fortress

INTERNATIONAL TRADE During the A.D.1400s, Shona kings controlled the trade routes between inland goldfields and seaports on the Indian Ocean coast. Civil wars and attacks from European invaders brought an end to the empire. Archaeologists in the late 1800s concluded that Great Zimbabwe, however, enjoyed a profitable trade with overseas lands. In Great Zimbabwe's ruins, they uncovered articles from India, China, and Asia.

Making the Connection

1. Why did Great Zimbabwe become so powerful?
2. With whom did Great Zimbabwe trade?

PREVIEW

Words to Know
- copper belt
- sorghum

Places to Locate
- Zambia
- Malawi
- Zimbabwe
- Botswana
- Zambezi River
- Harare

Read to Learn . . .
1. what Zambia's most important natural resource is.
2. how Zimbabwe's recent history is similar to South Africa's.
3. why most of Botswana's people live in the eastern part of the country.

So much mist and noise rise from this waterfall that people in the area call it the "smoke that thunders." You are looking at the waters of the Zambezi River as they plunge 350 feet (107 m) to the bottom of a deep gorge. They form Victoria Falls, one of Africa's great natural wonders.

The Zambezi (zam•BEE•zee) River is one of southern Africa's longest rivers. For part of its journey, the Zambezi forms the border between two inland countries in southern Africa—Zambia and Zimbabwe. Two other countries—Malawi (muh•LAH•wee) and Botswana (baht•SWAH•nuh)—are also located in this region.

Place
Zambia

Zambia is a landlocked country of 287,020 square miles (743,382 sq. km). Zambia—slightly larger than the state of Texas—lies near the Equator. Zambia's high elevation gives most of the country a mild climate.

The map on page 546 shows you that a high plateau covers much of Zambia. Several rivers, including the Zambezi, cross the country. Kariba Dam—one of Africa's largest hydroelectric projects—spans the Zambezi River.

The Economy Zambia is one of the world's largest producers of copper. This resource provides more than 80 percent of Zambia's income. You will find a copper belt, a large area of copper mines, in northern Zambia near the border with the Democratic Republic of the Congo.

Because copper is so valuable, Zambians have paid less attention to developing agriculture. As a result, Zambia must import much of its food. Railroads link landlocked Zambia to ports in neighboring countries, such as Mozambique, Angola, and Tanzania.

The People Zambia's 9.5 million people belong to more than 70 different ethnic groups. They speak 8 major African languages. Once a British colony, Zambia became independent in 1964. Because of the British influence, many Zambians today also speak English.

About 40 percent of Zambia's population live in urban areas. Lusaka is the capital and largest city. Many urban dwellers work in mining and service industries. The rest of Zambia's people live in rural villages. They grow corn and other subsistence food crops for their families.

Place
Malawi

East of Zambia lies Malawi, a small, narrow country of only 36,320 square miles (94,069 sq. km). In some places, Malawi is no more than 50 miles (81 km) wide! Green plains and savanna grasslands cover western Malawi. Part of the Great Rift Valley runs through the country from north to south. In the middle of the valley lies beautiful Lake Malawi. High plateaus and tall mountains rise on both sides of the lake. Malawi lies in the tropics, but its plateaus and mountains give it a mild climate.

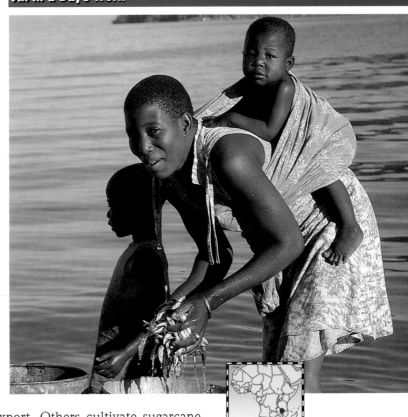

All in a Day's Work

The Economy Because of its mountains, only one-third of the land in Malawi is suitable for farming. Agriculture, however, is the country's major economic activity. Some of Malawi's farmers work on large commercial farms that grow tea for export. Others cultivate sugarcane, corn, cotton, peanuts, and **sorghum** for local use on small family plots. Sorghum is a tall grass with seeds like corn. People in Malawi also fish and herd livestock.

Fish from Lake Malawi are an important part of the diet of local residents.
REGION: Why does the tropical country of Malawi have a mild climate?

The People Look at the map on page 562. It shows you that Malawi is one of the most densely populated countries in Africa. Malawi has about 269 people per square mile (104 people per sq. km). Most of its 9.8 million people belong to many different African ethnic groups and live in small villages.

Place
Zimbabwe

South of Zambia lies the country of Zimbabwe. With 149,363 square miles (386,850 sq. km), Zimbabwe is a little larger than the state of Montana. Like other countries in southern Africa, most of Zimbabwe occupies a high plateau. North and south of the plateau are lowlands. The Zambezi River crosses the northern lowlands. The Limpopo River winds through the southern lowlands.

Most of Zimbabwe has a tropical savanna climate of wet and dry seasons. High elevations, however, keep temperatures cool and pleasant in many parts of the country.

The Economy Gold, asbestos, and copper are three of the most important minerals mined in Zimbabwe. Although mining provides most of Zimbabwe's income, a majority of its people are farmers. About half of Zimbabwe's land is fertile enough for farming. Farmers grow corn and herd cattle and livestock. Some people also work on large commercial farms that grow coffee and tobacco for export.

The People Zimbabwe has about 11 million people. Most of the people belong to two African ethnic groups—the Shona and the Ndebele (ehn•duh•BEH•leh). The country takes its name from the famous trading center—Great Zimbabwe—built by the Shona in the A.D. 1400s.

In the 1890s the British began to rule the area that is now Zimbabwe. As in South Africa, Europeans ran the government and owned all the best farmland.

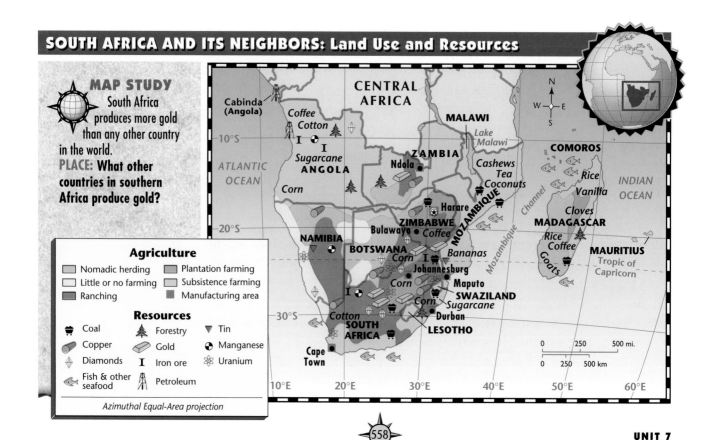

SOUTH AFRICA AND ITS NEIGHBORS: Land Use and Resources

MAP STUDY South Africa produces more gold than any other country in the world.
PLACE: What other countries in southern Africa produce gold?

Agriculture
- Nomadic herding
- Little or no farming
- Ranching
- Plantation farming
- Subsistence farming
- Manufacturing area

Resources
- Coal
- Copper
- Diamonds
- Fish & other seafood
- Forestry
- Gold
- Iron ore
- Petroleum
- Tin
- Manganese
- Uranium

Azimuthal Equal-Area projection

The Kariba Dam harnesses the power of the mighty Zambezi River.
LOCATION: The Zambezi forms the border between Zambia and what other country?

They refused to share power with the Africans. The Africans, in turn, resisted European rule. Peace talks finally led to a settlement. In 1980 free elections brought an independent African government to power.

Today about 70 percent of the population live in rural villages. A growing number, however, are moving to cities to find factory jobs. The largest city is Harare, the national capital. One of Harare's residents is fifteen-year-old Moses Katiyo. He and his family live in a crowded township in the suburbs. When school is not in session, Moses and his older brother take the train to Bulawayo (BOO•luh•WAY•oh), a city in the south. From there they often visit the Khami Ruins. These are the remains of stone buildings built hundreds of years ago by Moses' Bantu-speaking ancestors.

Place

Botswana

Botswana is the most isolated country in inland southern Africa. Desert covers much of its land area of 218,810 square miles (566,718 sq. km). If you look at the map on page 546, you will see that the vast Kalahari Desert spreads over southwestern Botswana. The Kalahari Desert is hot and dry, but parts of it have some vegetation. In eastern Botswana the land rises to a savanna region of grasses, bushes, and trees. The Okavango River flows through northwestern Botswana. There it forms one of the largest swamp areas in the world.

Celebrating National Day in Harare, Zimbabwe

On National Day in Zimbabwe, a flame is lit to mark the country's independence from the United Kingdom.
PLACE: What industry generates the most income for Zimbabwe?

The Economy Like its neighbors, Botswana is rich in mineral resources. Among its treasures are diamonds, copper, and uranium. Mining, however, provides jobs for only a small number of Botswana's people. Most raise livestock or farm the land, but growing crops is difficult in Botswana. During the 1980s a severe drought brought hardships to many of Botswana's farmers. To earn a living, many young people work in the Republic of South Africa for several months a year.

The People The map on page 562 shows you that Botswana has few people for its large size. Most of the 1.4 million people live in eastern Botswana, where the land is most fertile. About 75 percent of the people live in rural areas, but thousands of them move to the cities each year. Gaborone is the capital and largest city.

SECTION 3 ASSESSMENT

REVIEWING TERMS AND FACTS
1. **Define the following:** copper belt, sorghum.
2. **HUMAN/ENVIRONMENT INTERACTION** What is Zambia's most abundant natural resource?
3. **PLACE** What lake lies in Malawi's Great Rift Valley?
4. **REGION** Why do many young people from Botswana go to the Republic of South Africa?

   MAP STUDY ACTIVITIES
   5. Look at the land use map on page 558. What are the major resources of Zambia?

Indian Ocean Countries

PREVIEW

Words to Know
- slash-and-burn farming

Places to Locate
- Mozambique
- Madagascar
- Comoros
- Mauritius
- Indian Ocean

Read to Learn . . .
1. why Mozambique's ports are so valuable.
2. why Madagascar has unusual plants and animals.
3. how the islands of Comoros and Mauritius were formed.

Modern buildings rise along the tree-lined streets of Maputo, capital of the country of Mozambique (MOH•zuhm•BEEK). Maputo is a port city near the Indian Ocean. It provides a link to the outside world for the landlocked countries of southern Africa.

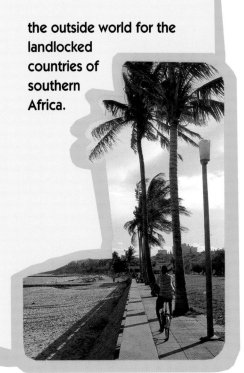

Mozambique is a large country in southern Africa that borders the Indian Ocean. Three island countries—Madagascar (MA•duh•GAS•kuhr), Comoros (KAH•muh•ROHS), and Mauritius (maw•RIH•shuhs)—also form part of southern Africa's Indian Ocean region.

Place

Mozambique

The map on page 544 shows you that Y-shaped Mozambique stretches along the Indian Ocean. Its landscapes include sandy lowlands, high plateaus, and tall mountains. Sand dunes, swamps, and fine natural harbors line Mozambique's Indian Ocean coast. In the center of the country lies a flat plain covered with grasses and tropical forests. Beyond the plain, the land slowly rises to form high plateaus and mountains along Mozambique's border with Malawi.

A number of rivers cross the northern and central parts of Mozambique. The most important river is the Zambezi. The Cabora Bassa Dam on the Zambezi provides electric power for much of the country. The map on page 553 shows you that most of Mozambique has a tropical savanna climate with wet and dry seasons. Rainfall is heaviest in the north. Much of the southwest is dry.

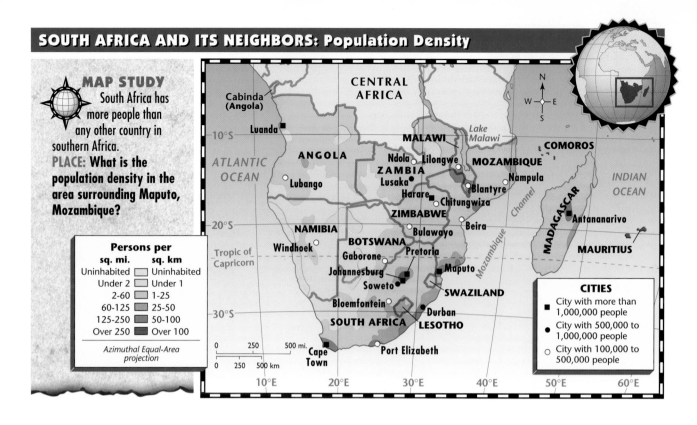

MAP STUDY
South Africa has more people than any other country in southern Africa.
PLACE: What is the population density in the area surrounding Maputo, Mozambique?

The Economy Most people in Mozambique are farmers. Some of them practice **slash-and-burn farming.** This means they cut and burn forest trees to clear areas for planting. Mozambique's major crops are cashews, coconuts, tea, sugarcane, and bananas. Fishing provides an income for people living along the Indian Ocean.

Mozambique's major source of income, however, comes from its seaports. South Africa, Zimbabwe, Swaziland, and Malawi pay Mozambique to use docks at Maputo and other ports.

During the 1980s and early 1990s, a fierce civil war slowed industrial growth in Mozambique. Although the fighting has ended, the country's economy still cannot provide enough jobs. In order to earn their livings, many people from Mozambique work in the Republic of South Africa.

The People About 18.6 million people live in Mozambique. Nearly all of them belong to African ethnic groups. Most live in the southern part of the country around Maputo, the capital. Portugal governed Mozambique from the early 1500s until 1975, when Mozambique became independent. Portuguese is still the official language. Most of the people, however, speak African languages.

Place

Madagascar

Madagascar is an island nation in the Indian Ocean. Look at the map on page 546. It shows you that Madagascar lies about 250 miles (400 km) southeast of the African mainland. Cool highland areas cross the middle of

Madagascar. Most coastal areas have warm, humid plains and fertile river valleys. Partly dry grasslands cover southern Madagascar.

In the past, Madagascar's island location kept it isolated from other parts of the world. Today Madagascar has many plants and animals that are not found elsewhere on the earth. One of these unusual animals is the lemur, which looks like a monkey. Lemurs have large eyes that appear to glow at night as they leap from tree to tree in the forests.

The Economy Agriculture is the chief economic activity in Madagascar. Farmers grow food crops—mainly rice—and herd cattle. Coffee is the leading export. If you like vanilla ice cream, thank Madagascar! It produces most of the world's vanilla beans.

The People About 14 million people live in Madagascar. Most trace their ancestry to Southeast Asian and African groups that settled the island centuries ago. Malagasy, the major language, is similar to languages spoken in Southeast Asia. French is also spoken in Madagascar's cities. Madagascar was a colony of France from the 1890s until it gained its independence in 1960.

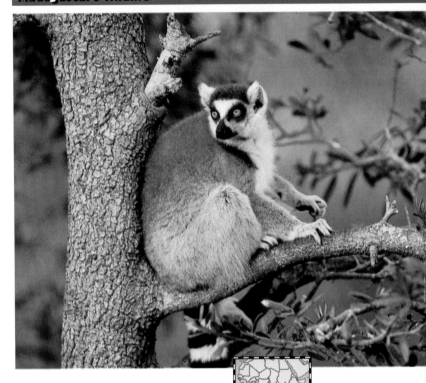

Madagascar's Wildlife

The ring-tailed lemur is one of the many unusual species of animals that live in Madagascar.
LOCATION: Why does Madagascar have so many unusual plants and animals?

Place
Small Island Countries

Far from Africa in the Indian Ocean are two other island republics—Comoros and Mauritius. The people of both countries have many different backgrounds.

Comoros Comoros is a group of four mountainous islands that lie between mainland Africa and Madagascar. Volcanoes formed all four islands thousands of years ago. Thick tropical forests cover Comoros today. At one time a French territory, Comoros became independent in 1975.

Most of Comoros's 500,000 people are farmers. They grow rice, cassava, corn, vanilla, sugarcane, and coffee. The people of Comoros are a mixture of Arabs, Africans, and people from Madagascar. They speak Arabic and Swahili, and most practice the religion of Islam.

Mauritius The island republic of Mauritius lies about 500 miles (800 km) east of Madagascar in the Indian Ocean. Mauritius includes one major island and a number of smaller islands, which are territories. Mauritius gained its freedom from the United Kingdom in 1968.

Horse-drawn wagons share the streets with cars in Madagascar's capital.
PLACE: What flavoring is Madagascar known for?

Like Comoros, the islands of Mauritius were formed by volcanoes. Bare, black peaks rise sharply above green fields, and palm-dotted white beaches line the coasts. The climate is subtropical. Because Mauritius has few natural resources, its economy depends on agriculture. Sugar and sugar products are the island country's major exports.

Mauritius has about 1.2 million people who come from many different backgrounds. About 70 percent are descendants of settlers from India. The rest are of African, European, or Chinese ancestry. The population of Mauritius is increasing rapidly. Providing food, jobs, and housing for more people will be a major challenge for Mauritius in the years ahead.

SECTION 4 ASSESSMENT

REVIEWING TERMS AND FACTS

1. **Define the following:** slash-and-burn farming.

2. **HUMAN/ENVIRONMENT INTERACTION** What is Mozambique's major source of income?

3. **LOCATION** Where is Madagascar located?

4. **MOVEMENT** What major groups settled in Madagascar?

MAP STUDY ACTIVITIES

5. According to the population density map on page 562, where are Mozambique's most densely populated areas?

Chapter 21 Highlights

Important Things to Know About South Africa and Its Neighbors

SECTION 1 REPUBLIC OF SOUTH AFRICA

- Most of inland South Africa is a high plateau.
- Because of its mineral resources, South Africa has the most developed economy in Africa.
- In recent years, South Africa has given equality to citizens of all ethnic groups and is struggling to become a more complete democracy guaranteeing the rights of all its citizens.

SECTION 2 ATLANTIC COUNTRIES

- Angola has large deposits of oil, diamonds, and iron ore.
- Two major deserts cross Namibia. This harsh landscape limits agriculture in Namibia.

SECTION 3 INLAND SOUTHERN AFRICA

- Zambia is one of the world's largest producers of copper.
- Tiny, mountainous Malawi has a large lake running almost the entire length of its eastern border.
- Zimbabwe has many mineral resources and good farmland.
- Desert covers a large part of Botswana.

SECTION 4 INDIAN OCEAN COUNTRIES

- Mozambique's ports on the Indian Ocean are used by landlocked countries in southern Africa.
- Madagascar's people trace their ancestry to African and Southeast Asian settlers.

Celebrating South Africa National Independence Day ▶

Chapter 21 Assessment and Activities

REVIEWING KEY TERMS

Match the numbered terms in Set A with their lettered definitions in Set B.

A
1. exclave
2. high veld
3. sorghum
4. enclave
5. township
6. apartheid

B

A. flat, grass-covered plains in South Africa

B. official system of racial separation in South Africa

C. crowded African neighborhood outside a city

D. part of a country separated from the main part

E. tall grass with seeds like corn

F. small country surrounded by another country

REVIEWING THE MAIN IDEAS

Mental Mapping Activity

Draw a freehand map of South Africa and its neighbors. Label the following:
- South Africa
- Indian Ocean
- Angola
- Zambia
- Zimbabwe
- Johannesburg

Section 1
1. PLACE What oceans border South Africa?
2. MOVEMENT How did the coming of Europeans affect life for Africans in South Africa?

Section 2
3. LOCATION Describe Namibia's coast.
4. HUMAN/ENVIRONMENT INTERACTION What is Angola's main agricultural export?

Section 3
5. PLACE How does the population density of Malawi compare with populations in other African countries?
6. MOVEMENT What two African ethnic groups are found in Zimbabwe?

Section 4
7. LOCATION Why has industrial development been slow in Mozambique?
8. REGION How were Comoros and Mauritius formed?

CRITICAL THINKING ACTIVITIES

1. **Formulating Questions** Write three questions you would ask a South African about his or her way of life and recent changes there.
2. **Identifying Central Issues** What are some of the challenges faced by countries in southern Africa as they try to develop their economies?

CONNECTIONS TO GOVERNMENT

Cooperative Learning Activity Work in small groups to learn more about democracy in southern Africa today. Each group will choose one country and research the following topics: (a) form of government before independence; (b) present form of government; or (c) current political challenges faced by the government. As a group, create a skit or news broadcast to share with the class.

GeoJournal Writing Activity

Choose a country in southern Africa and imagine that you are a travel writer visiting the place. Write a short article about the country. You may want to describe its major natural attractions or its cities, or give interesting information about its people.

TECHNOLOGY ACTIVITY

Developing Multimedia Presentations

Use the Internet, as well as other reference works, to research the kingdom of the Shona and its capital city of Great Zimbabwe. Then, imagine that you are a tour guide. Create a short multimedia presentation about the political and religious center of the Shona kingdom. Incorporate photographs, drawings, maps, music, and video, if possible, into your presentation.

PLACE LOCATION ACTIVITY: SOUTH AFRICA AND ITS NEIGHBORS

Match the letters on the map with the places of South Africa and its neighbors. Write your answers on a separate sheet of paper.

1. Mauritius
2. Lake Malawi
3. Drakensberg Mountains
4. Botswana
5. Cape Town
6. Luanda
7. Kalahari Desert
8. Zambezi River
9. Madagascar
10. Mozambique

Africa South of the Sahara

DESERTIFICATION

PROBLEM

Desertification, or the "making of deserts," is occurring in parts of Africa south of the Sahara. Poor conservation methods lead to soil erosion and dried-up wells and water holes. Trees and shrubs are cut down and used as fuel. Vegetation dies out as herds of goats and cattle overgraze fragile lands. Dry winds and fierce sandstorms blow away the naked topsoil and cover once-productive fields with sheets of sand. Marching dunes bury fields, roads, and entire villages. And so the desert advances.

SOLUTIONS

● Farmers in some areas confine grazing animals to fenced areas and bring food to the animals.

● To help save rapidly dwindling forests, Mali, Niger, and Burkina Faso have started national campaigns to place more efficient clay or metal cookstoves in every household.

● In Niger, more than 435 miles of windbreaks have been planted to slow advancing sand and protect fragile seedlings.

● In Ethiopia, communities are planting hundreds of trees, and in Kenya, people are terracing farmland to control erosion.

DESERTIFICATION FACT BANK

🍃 Thirty-four percent of Africa's land is at risk from desertification.

🍃 The Sahel, a fragile belt of grasses and forests that stretches 3,000 miles across Africa, has lost 30 percent of its trees in the last 20 years.

🍃 Once 40 percent of Ethiopia was forested; in 1990 less than 4 percent of the forests remained.

🍃 In Mali, the Sahara has spread more than 400 miles in 20 years.

🍃 During the last 20 years, many villages in the Sahel have lost as much as one-half of their farmland to desertification.

568

Dwellings nestle in a sandy area of trees and shrubs in Kenya. Drought and overuse could easily turn a semiarid region into desert.

TEEN TRIBUTE

Eleven-year-old George Otieno lives on a farm in Kenya. George's family could not grow enough food to feed themselves because the soil on their farm was so poor. Then at school George learned that planting trees can help reverse desertification. George planted several hundred seedlings he received from CARE, an environmental relief group. The trees restored nutrients to the soil—and improved the family's harvest and their standard of living.

environmental activities

TAKE A CLOSER LOOK

1 What is desertification?

2 What are the main causes of desertification in Africa south of the Sahara?

BE NICE TO TREES

WHAT CAN YOU DO?

🍃 Adopt a piece of land in your own neighborhood. Clean it up, plant flowers, and put up a No Littering sign.

🍃 Conserve water—cut your shower water use by half by a using a low-flow shower head.

🍃 Volunteer at your local zoo. Help with programs to save endangered species.

🍃 Support agencies that help African countries to reforest empty land.

Men on camels herd cattle in Chad. As livestock strip away vegetation, soil blows away, and bare patches become desert.

Asia

What Makes Asia a Region?

The people share . . .

- high population densities.
- deadly natural hazards—typhoons, floods, volcanic activity.
- expanding economies.
- rich natural resources.
- ancient religions and cultures.

To find out more about Asia, see the Unit Atlas on pages 572–585.

Bali Island, Indonesia

EXPLORING THE INTERNET

To learn more about Asia, visit the Glencoe Social Studies Web site at **www.glencoe.com** for information, activities, and links to other sites.

GeoJournal Activity
As you read about Asia, follow news reports about the region either on television or in newspapers and magazines. Organize your information in your journal under the following categories: Environment, Culture and Daily Life, and Economy.

NATIONAL
GEOGRAPHIC
SOCIETY

IMAGES *of the* WORLD

1. **Horse breeder, Mongolia**
2. **Traffic in the heart of the city, Hong Kong**
3. **Harvesting coffee, Indonesia**
4. **Mosque in a rainstorm, Indonesia**
5. **Girl holding the Quran, Indonesia**
6. **Father and son readying their boat, Indonesia**
7. **Pilgrims bathing in the Ganges River, India**

All photos viewed against snow-covered peaks in the Karakoram Range, Pakistan.

Regional Focus

Asia is both a continent and a region. The *continent* of Asia covers the eastern part of the large landmass called Eurasia. The *region* of Asia is a smaller part of the Asian continent. As a region, Asia reaches from the rugged mountains of Pakistan in the west to the volcanic islands of the Philippines in the east. From north to south, the region of Asia stretches from the cool highlands of northeastern China to the tropical islands of Indonesia.

Region
The Land

The Gobi

The Gobi stretches across southern Mongolia and northern China. It is colder and farther north than any other desert in the world.
PLACE: What other desert lies in central Asia?

The region of Asia covers about 7.8 million square miles (20.2 million sq. km). Look at the physical map on page 578. Asia's winding coastlines touch the Indian and Pacific oceans as well as many seas. Within Asia's vast land area are mountains, deserts, plains, and great rivers.

Mountains Rugged mountain ranges sweep through central Asia. The best known are the Himalayas. Their highest peak—Mount Everest—is the world's tallest mountain. Mountains also cross northeastern China, the Korean Peninsula, and Southeast Asia. Off Asia's coasts you will find mountainous groups of islands, such as Japan, the Philippines, and Indonesia. They lie in the Ring of Fire, a Pacific area known for its earthquakes and active volcanoes.

Deserts and Plains Large deserts—the Taklimakan (tah•kluh•muh•KAHN) and the Gobi—stretch across inland parts of central Asia. Fertile plains lie in northern India, eastern China, and mainland Southeast Asia. Many of Asia's rivers flow through these plains to the ocean or sea. The most important rivers are the Indus in Pakistan; the Ganges and Brahmaputra in India; the Mekong in Southeast Asia; and the Chang Jiang and Huang He in China.

Region
Climate and Vegetation

Because of its vast size, Asia has diverse climates. They include cold highlands and hot deserts in north and central Asia, mild climates in the east, and tropical climates in the south.

Monsoons Winds called monsoons affect climate in much of Asia. In winter, monsoons from the north bring cool, dry weather. In summer, the winds reverse direction and blow from the seas that lie south of Asia. The summer monsoons bear hot, humid weather. Wet monsoons often bring heavy rains and floods.

Vegetation Dry areas in central Asia have little plant life, except for grasses. These grasses provide food for livestock. You will find many trees and plants in eastern Asia, which gets plenty of rain. The warm, wet climate of Southeast Asia favors tropical vegetation. Many Southeast Asian exports are hardwoods from rain forests.

Place
The Economy

Asia is made up of 23 countries. Economies differ from country to country, although agriculture is the major economic activity. Important crops include rice, wheat, cotton, rubber, and tea. Because of Asia's mountainous areas and large populations, farmers try to produce as much food as they can on small areas of land, including terraced mountain slopes.

Mining and Industry Asia is rich in mineral resources. Coal, iron ore, manganese, and mica come from India and China. Southeast Asia is a major supplier of tin, oil, and bauxite. Most of Asia's manufacturing takes place in Japan, South Korea, Taiwan, China, and India. Factories in these countries produce cars, electronic equipment, ships, and textiles. In other parts of Asia, industry is less developed. Governments in these areas, however, are trying to create new industries and improve old ones.

Transportation Industrial growth in Asia has led to better means of transportation. Roads and railroads link major urban areas. In Asian cities you can see modern buses, trains, and cars. In rural areas people often travel by foot or use carts pulled by animals. People living along rivers rely on small boats for traveling and transporting goods.

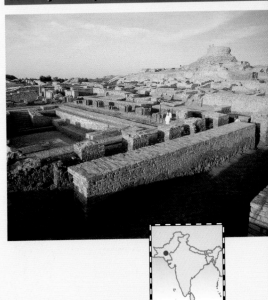

Mohenjo-Daro, Pakistan

Ruins of one of the world's first civilizations were discovered in the Indus River Valley in Pakistan.
PLACE: What forms of transportation might have been used by these early people?

575

Movement

The People

About 3.3 billion people live in Asia. China, India, Indonesia, Bangladesh, and Japan are among the world's most heavily populated countries. Most Asians make their homes in river or mountain valleys or near seacoasts. Among the most crowded areas of Asia are Bangladesh, eastern China, northern India, southern Japan, and the island of Java in Indonesia.

Population People are not evenly distributed throughout Asia. Few Asians live in the mountains or desert areas. Only about 34 percent of them live in urban areas. However, Asian cities such as Calcutta (India), Shanghai (China), Tokyo (Japan), and Seoul (South Korea) are rapidly growing. Many are over-crowded, and some show great contrasts of wealth and poverty.

Ethnic Groups and Religions Japan and the Koreas each have one main ethnic group. China also has one, but many small non-Chinese groups live on the edges of the country. India and Southeast Asia, however, have many ethnic groups with different languages and cultures.

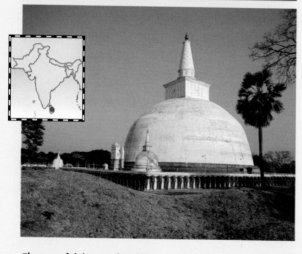

Anuradhapura, Sri Lanka

Religion has strongly influenced the arts and cultures of Asia. Hinduism is the primary religion of the region. Hindus generally live in India, where the religion began thousands of years ago. Islam—Asia's most widespread faith—began in Southwest Asia and later reached India, western China, and Southeast Asia. Buddhism, which started in India, is now a major religion of Southeast Asia, China, Korea, and Japan. Smaller numbers of Asians practice Christianity or local religions.

The graceful domes of Buddhist temples are a common sight in the island country of Sri Lanka. **PLACE: What religion is practiced by more Asians than any other religion?**

History Some of the world's oldest civilizations arose in Asia. Until the 1500s, Asia was more advanced than Europe in culture and technology. Early Asians founded cities, set up states, and carved out trade routes.

Europeans arrived in Asia around 1500. By the early 1800s many Asian lands had fallen under European control. The Europeans brought Western ideas to Asia. In the early 1900s, Japan became the world's leading Asian power. World War II led to Japan's defeat, but it also ended Europe's hold on Asia. Nearly all of the Asian lands ruled by foreigners became independent in the mid-1900s.

From the late 1940s to the 1970s, Asia was caught in the global struggle between communist and noncommunist countries. Today communist governments still rule in China, Vietnam, and North Korea. Other Asian nations, however, are governed by monarchs (Nepal), military leaders (Myanmar), or democratic systems (India, Japan, and the Philippines).

Multimedia Unit 8 Activities

NATIONAL GEOGRAPHIC SOCIETY

Picture Atlas of the World

Asian Ethnic Groups, Religions, and Languages

Using the CD-ROM Asia is a land of many languages, ethnic groups, and religions. Japan and the Koreas each have one main ethnic group, as does the populous country of China. In addition, many small non-Chinese groups live throughout China. India and the countries of Southeast Asia claim a variety of ethnic groups, which practice different religions and speak various languages. Develop a cultural distribution map of Asia, which marks the locations of the major religions, languages, and ethnic groups. Follow these steps to create your map:

1. Access the *World Globe* and click on the continent of Asia.
2. Then click on the individual countries of Asia.
3. Note the major religions and languages of each country. Use an encyclopedia or other reference work to find the major ethnic groups of each country.
4. On a blank map of Asia, indicate the major religions, languages, and ethnic groups of each Asian country. Be sure to include a map legend.

Surfing the "Net"

The Past, Present, and Future of Asia

The last several years have brought great change to Asia. Japan, once admired for its strong economy, experienced a slowed economic growth rate in the 1990s. At the same time, several other Asian countries were experiencing rapid industrialization. In China, Communists held tightly to their control of the government despite a movement for democracy. To find out more about the recent history of Asia, search the Internet.

Getting There

Follow these steps to gather information on Asia's past and present:
1. Use a search engine. Type in *Asia*.
2. Enter the names of individual Asian countries and words like the following to focus your search: *history, economy, news,* and *culture.*
3. The search engine will provide you with a number of links to follow.

What To Do When You Are There

Organize the class into groups of three to four students. Each group should focus on one Asian country and work to compile information on the country's past and present, and also make predictions for the future. Groups should present their information to the rest of the class. As a class, determine whether each group's "predictions" for their country's future seem likely to occur.

UNIT 8 ATLAS

Physical Geography

ELEVATIONS
Feet — Meters
10,000 — 3,000
5,000 — 1,500
2,000 — 600
1,000 — 300
0 — 0

▲ Mountain peak

Azimuthal Equal-Area projection

Map Study

1. **LOCATION** What desert extends across northern China and southern Mongolia?

2. **PLACE** What mountain range forms a natural border between India and China?

ELEVATION PROFILE: South Asia

25,000 ft.		7,620 m
Himalayas	Plateau of Tibet	
20,000 ft.		6,096 m
15,000 ft.		4,572 m
10,000 ft.	North China Plain / East China Sea	3,048 m
Pakistan / Indus River		1,524 m
5,000 ft.		
2,000 ft.		610 m
1,000 ft.		305 m / Sea level

⟵ West to East at 35°N latitude ⟶

Source: *Goode's World Atlas*, 19th edition

GeoFacts

Highest point: Mount Everest (Nepal-Tibet) 29,028 ft. (8,848 m) high

Longest river: Chang Jiang (China) 3,964 mi. (6,378 km) long

Largest desert: Gobi (Mongolia and China) 500,000 sq. mi. (1,300,000 sq. km)

Highest waterfall: Jog (Gersoppa) Falls (India) 830 ft. (253 m) high

ASIA AND THE UNITED STATES: Land Comparison

Graphic Study

1. **PLACE** What is the average elevation of the Himalayas?
2. **PLACE** What is the difference in elevation between the Plateau of Tibet and the North China Plain?

UNIT 8 ATLAS

Cultural Geography

ASIA

60°E

40°N

80°E

100°E

120°E

140°E

160°E

Ulan Bator

MONGOLIA

NORTH KOREA

Sea of Japan

Pyongyang

Beijing

Seoul

SOUTH KOREA

Tokyo

Islamabad

CHINA

Yellow Sea

JAPAN

Tropic of Cancer

PAKISTAN

New Delhi

NEPAL

Kathmandu

BHUTAN

Thimphu

East China Sea

Taipei

TAIWAN

INDIA

Dhaka

Hanoi

Hong Kong

20°N

Arabian Sea

BANGLADESH

MYANMAR

LAOS

Vientiane

Macao

South China Sea

PACIFIC OCEAN

Philippine Sea

Bay of Bengal

Yangon

THAILAND

Bangkok

CAMBODIA

VIETNAM

Manila

PHILIPPINES

Phnom Penh

0   300   600 mi.

MALDIVES

Colombo

SRI LANKA

0   300   600 km

Male

INDIAN OCEAN

Kuala Lumpur

BRUNEI

Bandar Seri Begawan

0°

Equator

Singapore

MALAYSIA

SINGAPORE

INDONESIA

— National boundary
★ National capital

Azimuthal Equal-Area projection

N
W   E
S

Jakarta

Map Study

1. **LOCATION** What country lies at the southern tip of mainland Malaysia?

2. **PLACE** What country borders northwestern India?

COMPARING POPULATION: Asia and the United States

Asia

United States

= 100,000,000

Source: *Population Reference Bureau, 1998*

Biggest country (land area): China 3,600,930 sq. mi. (9,326,409 sq. km)

Smallest country (land area): Maldives 116 sq. mi. (300 sq. km)

Largest urban area (population): Tokyo (1995) 28,447,000; (2015 projected) 30,000,000

Highest population density: Singapore 16,415 people per sq. mi. (6,338 people per sq. km)

Lowest population density: Mongolia 4 people per sq. mi. (2 people per sq. km)

Asian Population

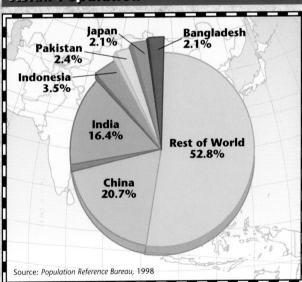

Japan 2.1%

Bangladesh 2.1%

Pakistan 2.4%

Indonesia 3.5%

India 16.4%

Rest of World 52.8%

China 20.7%

Source: *Population Reference Bureau, 1998*

1. **PLACE** About how many times more people live in Asia than live in the United States?
2. **REGION** What two Asian countries have the largest populations?

UNIT 8 ATLAS

Countries at a Glance

Bangladesh

CAPITAL:
Dhaka
MAJOR LANGUAGE(S):
Bengali, Chakma, Magh
POPULATION:
123,400,000

LANDMASS:
50,260 sq. mi./
130,173 sq. km
MONEY:
Taka
MAJOR EXPORT:
Garments
MAJOR IMPORT:
Textile Yarn

Bhutan

CAPITAL:
Thimphu
MAJOR LANGUAGE(S):
Dzongkha, Nepali and
Tibetan dialects
POPULATION:
800,000

LANDMASS:
18,150 sq. mi./
47,009 sq. km
MONEY:
Ngultrum
MAJOR EXPORT:
Electricity
MAJOR IMPORT:
Petroleum

Brunei

CAPITAL:
Bandar Seri Begawan
MAJOR LANGUAGE(S):
Malay, English, Chinese
POPULATION:
300,000

LANDMASS:
2,035 sq. mi./
5,271 sq. km
MONEY:
Brunei Dollar
MAJOR EXPORT:
Petroleum
MAJOR IMPORT:
Machinery

Cambodia

CAPITAL:
Phnom Penh
MAJOR LANGUAGE(S):
Khmer, French
POPULATION:
10,800,000

LANDMASS:
68,154 sq. mi./
176,519 sq. km
MONEY:
Riel
MAJOR EXPORT:
Rubber
MAJOR IMPORT:
Machinery

China

CAPITAL:
Beijing
MAJOR LANGUAGE(S):
Mandarin, Yue,
Wu Hakka, Xiang
POPULATION:
1,242,500,000

LANDMASS:
3,600,930 sq. mi./
9,326,409 sq. km
MONEY:
Yuan
MAJOR EXPORT:
Textile Products
MAJOR IMPORT:
Machinery

India

CAPITAL:
New Delhi
MAJOR LANGUAGE(S):
Hindi, English
POPULATION:
988,700,000

LANDMASS:
1,147,950 sq. mi./
2,973,191 sq. km
MONEY:
Rupee
MAJOR EXPORT:
Diamonds
MAJOR IMPORT:
Fuels

Indonesia

CAPITAL:
Jakarta
MAJOR LANGUAGE(S):
Bahasa Indonesia
(Malay), Javanese
POPULATION:
207,400,000

LANDMASS:
705,190 sq. mi./
1,826,442 sq. km
MONEY:
Rupiah
MAJOR EXPORT:
Petroleum
MAJOR IMPORT:
Machinery

Japan

CAPITAL:
Tokyo
MAJOR LANGUAGE(S):
Japanese
POPULATION:
126,400,000

LANDMASS:
145,370 sq. mi./
376,508 sq. km
MONEY:
Yen
MAJOR EXPORT:
Motor Vehicles
MAJOR IMPORT:
Fuels

Laos

CAPITAL:
Vientiane
MAJOR LANGUAGE(S):
Lao
POPULATION:
5,300,000

LANDMASS:
89,110 sq. mi./
230,795 sq. km
MONEY:
New Kip
MAJOR EXPORT:
Wood
MAJOR IMPORT:
Food Products

Malaysia

CAPITAL:
Kuala Lumpur
MAJOR LANGUAGE(S):
Malay, English, Chinese,
Indian languages
POPULATION:
22,200,000

LANDMASS:
126,850 sq. mi./
328,542 sq. km
MONEY:
Ringgit
MAJOR EXPORT:
Machinery
MAJOR IMPORT:
Machinery

Countries not drawn to scale.

Maldives

CAPITAL:
Male
MAJOR LANGUAGE(S):
Divehi (Sinhalese dialect)
POPULATION:
300,000

Male

LANDMASS:
116 sq. mi./
300 sq. km
MONEY:
Rufiyaa
MAJOR EXPORT:
Clothing
MAJOR IMPORT:
Food and Beverages

Mongolia

Ulan Bator

CAPITAL:
Ulan Bator
MAJOR LANGUAGE(S):
Khalkha, Mongolian
POPULATION:
2,400,000

LANDMASS:
604,825 sq. mi./
1,566,500 sq. km
MONEY:
Tugrik
MAJOR EXPORT:
Minerals and Metals
MAJOR IMPORT:
Machinery

Myanmar

Yangon

CAPITAL:
Yangon
MAJOR LANGUAGE(S):
Burmese, Karen, Shan
POPULATION:
47,100,000

LANDMASS:
253,880 sq. mi./
657,549 sq. km
MONEY:
Kyat
MAJOR EXPORT:
Agricultural Products
MAJOR IMPORT:
Machinery

Nepal

Kathmandu

CAPITAL:
Kathmandu
MAJOR LANGUAGE(S):
Nepali
POPULATION:
23,700,000

LANDMASS:
52,820 sq. mi./
136,804 sq. km
MONEY:
Rupee
MAJOR EXPORT:
Food and Live Animals
MAJOR IMPORT:
Machinery

North Korea

Pyongyang

CAPITAL:
Pyongyang
MAJOR LANGUAGE(S):
Korean
POPULATION:
22,200,000

LANDMASS:
46,490 sq. mi./
120,409 sq. km
MONEY:
Won
MAJOR EXPORT:
Minerals
MAJOR IMPORT:
Petroleum

Pakistan

Islamabad

CAPITAL:
Islamabad
MAJOR LANGUAGE(S):
Urdu, Punjabi, Sindhi,
Pushtu
POPULATION:
141,900,000

LANDMASS:
297,640 sq. mi./
770,888 sq. km
MONEY:
Rupee
MAJOR EXPORT:
Textile Fabrics
MAJOR IMPORT:
Petroleum

Philippines

Manila

CAPITAL:
Manila
MAJOR LANGUAGE(S):
Pilipino, English,
Cebuano, Bicol
POPULATION:
75,300,000

LANDMASS:
115,120 sq. mi./
298,161 sq. km
MONEY:
Peso
MAJOR EXPORT:
Food and Live Animals
MAJOR IMPORT:
Machinery

Singapore

Singapore

CAPITAL:
Singapore
MAJOR LANGUAGE(S):
Chinese, Malay,
Tamil, English
POPULATION:
3,900,000

LANDMASS:
236 sq. mi./
611 sq. km
MONEY:
Dollar
MAJOR EXPORT:
Office Machines
MAJOR IMPORT:
Petroleum

South Korea

Seoul

CAPITAL:
Seoul
MAJOR LANGUAGE(S):
Korean
POPULATION:
46,400,000

LANDMASS:
38,120 sq. mi./
98,731 sq. km
MONEY:
Won
MAJOR EXPORT:
Machinery
MAJOR IMPORT:
Machinery

Sri Lanka

Colombo

CAPITAL:
Colombo
MAJOR LANGUAGE(S):
Sinhalese, Tamil
POPULATION:
18,900,000

LANDMASS:
24,950 sq. mi./
64,621 sq. km
MONEY:
Rupee
MAJOR EXPORT:
Food and Live Animals
MAJOR IMPORT:
Machinery

Countries at a Glance

Taiwan

Taipei

LANDMASS:
13,970 sq. mi./
36,182 sq. km
MONEY:
New Taiwan Dollar
MAJOR EXPORT:
Machinery
MAJOR IMPORT:
Machinery

CAPITAL:
Taipei
MAJOR LANGUAGE(S):
Mandarin Chinese,
Taiwanese, Hakka
POPULATION:
21,700,000

Thailand

Bangkok

LANDMASS:
197,250 sq. mi./
510,878 sq. km
MONEY:
Baht
MAJOR EXPORT:
Machinery
MAJOR IMPORT:
Machinery

CAPITAL:
Bangkok
MAJOR LANGUAGE(S):
Thai, Chinese, Malay,
regional dialects
POPULATION:
61,100,000

Vietnam

Hanoi

LANDMASS:
125,670 sq. mi./
325,485 sq. km
MONEY:
Dong
MAJOR EXPORT:
Fuels
MAJOR IMPORT:
Machinery

CAPITAL:
Hanoi
MAJOR LANGUAGE(S):
Vietnamese, Chinese
POPULATION:
78,500,000

Thimphu, Bhutan

Bhutan's king rules from this fortified hillside monastery in Bhutan's capital.

Guangxi Province, China

These unusual cone-shaped hills in southern China were formed by erosion and weathering.

Countries not drawn to scale.

Angkor Wat, Cambodia

This elaborate stone temple was built almost 900 years ago to honor a Hindu king.

World's Tallest Mountains

GRAPHIC STUDY

Kilimanjaro is the highest mountain peak in Africa.

PLACE: What is the highest mountain peak in the world?

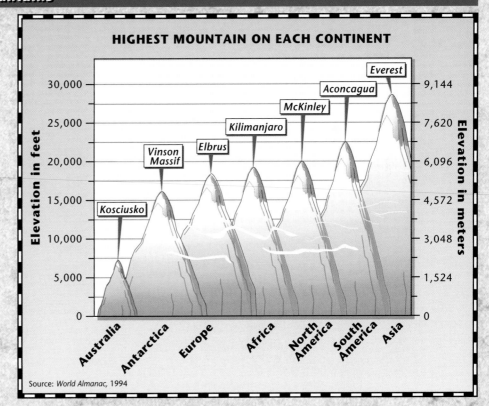

HIGHEST MOUNTAIN ON EACH CONTINENT

Elevation in feet: 0, 5,000, 10,000, 15,000, 20,000, 25,000, 30,000

Elevation in meters: 0, 1,524, 3,048, 4,572, 6,096, 7,620, 9,144

Kosciusko — Australia
Vinson Massif — Antarctica
Elbrus — Europe
Kilimanjaro — Africa
McKinley — North America
Aconcagua — South America
Everest — Asia

Source: *World Almanac*, 1994

Map Legend
— National boundary
⊛ National capital
● Other city

Lambert Conical projection

60°E · 70°E · 80°E · 90°E

ASIA

Peshawar · Islamabad · Rawalpindi · Faisalabad · Amritsar · Lahore

PAKISTAN

30°N

Delhi · New Delhi · Lucknow · NEPAL · Kathmandu · BHUTAN · Thimphu

Karachi · Hyderabad · Jaipur · Agra · BANGLADESH · Dhaka

Tropic of Cancer

Ahmadabad · INDIA · Calcutta · Chittagong

20°N

Arabian Sea

Bay of Bengal

Mumbai (Bombay)

Chennai (Madras) · Andaman Islands (INDIA)

10°N

Laccadive Islands (INDIA) · Coimbatore

INDIAN OCEAN

SRI LANKA · Colombo · Nicobar Islands (INDIA)

Male · MALDIVES

0   150   300 mi.
0   150   300 km

MAP STUDY ACTIVITY

As you read Chapter 22, you will learn about India and the other countries in South Asia.

1. What is the largest country in South Asia?

2. What two island countries lie off the coast of southern India?

3. What is the capital of India?

SECTION 1

India

PREVIEW

Words to Know
- subcontinent
- monsoon
- jute
- cottage industry

Places to Locate
- India
- Himalayas
- Ganges River
- Deccan Plateau
- Calcutta
- Mumbai (Bombay)
- New Delhi

Read to Learn . . .
1. what a subcontinent is.
2. how seasonal winds affect India's climate.
3. what religions India's people follow.

This is the Ganges River in the South Asian country of India.

Hindus—the largest religious group in India—consider the Ganges a holy river. About 1 million Hindus from all areas of India pray and bathe in this river each year.

India and several other countries—Pakistan, Bangladesh (BAHN•gluh•DEHSH), Nepal, Bhutan, Sri Lanka, and the Maldives—make up the area known as South Asia. South Asia is often called a **subcontinent,** or a landmass that is like a continent, only smaller. The map on page 588 shows you that towering mountains in the north separate South Asia from the rest of the continent of Asia. Bordering South Asia are three large bodies of water: the Indian Ocean, the Arabian Sea, and the Bay of Bengal.

Location

The Land

India takes up about 75 percent of the land area of South Asia. India covers 1,147,950 square miles (2,973,191 sq. km)—about one-third the area of the United States. The map on page 588 shows you that mountains run along three sides and through the middle of the country. Plateaus and desert plains run through the rest of the country.

Mountains Two huge walls of mountains—the Karakoram (KAR•uh•KOHR•uhm) Range and the Himalayas (HIH•muh•LAY•uhs)—form India's northern border. The Himalayas—made up of several ranges—stretch more than 1,500 miles (2,414 km) across northern South Asia. They are the tallest mountains in the world. Their snowcapped peaks average more than 5 miles (8 km) in height!

In the center of India lies another mountain range—the Vindhya (VIHN•dyuh) Mountains. These low mountains divide India in half. They have helped create two very different cultures in northern India and southern India.

Two chains of hills and mountains called the Eastern Ghats (GAHTS) and Western Ghats edge the southern coasts of India. These mountain chains lie just inland from the Bay of Bengal and the Arabian Sea.

Plains and Plateaus Sweeping through northern India between the Himalaya and Vindhya ranges is the Ganges Plain. It boasts some of the most fertile soil in the country. Look at the map below. You see that the Ganges River begins in the Himalayas and flows through the Ganges Plain to the Bay of Bengal. At the western edge of the Ganges Plain lies the Thar (TAHR) Desert. It is about 500 miles (804 km) long and 275 miles (442 km) wide.

The Deccan Plateau is located south of the Vindhya Mountains. This triangle-shaped landmass makes up the southern two-thirds of India. Forests, fertile farmland, and rich deposits of minerals make the Deccan Plateau a valuable region.

SOUTH ASIA: Physical

MAP STUDY The largest river delta in the world is found in Bangladesh. **LOCATION: What rivers flow through India?**

ELEVATIONS

Feet	Meters
10,000	3,000
5,000	1,500
2,000	600
1,000	300
0	0

▲ Mountain peak

Lambert Conical projection

0   150   300 mi.
0   150 300 km

The Thar Desert is one of the most sparsely populated areas of India *(left)*. In contrast, Calcutta is one of the most crowded cities in the world *(right)*.
LOCATION: In what part of India is Calcutta located?

Climate Most places in India are warm or hot most of the year. The people of India can thank the Himalayas for their warm climate. These mountains block cold northern air from entering India. The map on page 595 shows you the climate regions of India.

The **monsoons,** or seasonal winds, are another important influence on India's climate. Most of India has three seasons—cool, hot, and rainy. During the cool season—November through February—and the hot season—March through April—monsoon winds from the north bring dry air. During the rainy season—May through October—monsoon winds reverse direction and bring moist air from the Indian Ocean.

Human/Environment Interaction
The Economy

Agriculture and industry are equally important to India's economy. The government of India has set up plans to increase the production of farm and industrial goods. The goal is to develop India's resources and to improve the standard of living for India's people.

Agriculture Most of India's best farmland lies in the Ganges Plain and the Deccan Plateau. In both places you will see many farmers work small plots of land. India is the world's second-largest producer of rice. Other important crops are tea, sugarcane, wheat, barley, cotton, and jute. **Jute** is a plant fiber used in making rope, twine, and burlap bags.

Industry and Mining Huge factories in India turn out cotton textiles and produce iron and steel. Oil and sugar refineries loom over the industrial landscape

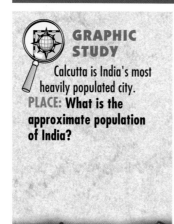

GRAPHIC STUDY

Calcutta is India's most heavily populated city. **PLACE: What is the approximate population of India?**

India

United States

= 50,000,000

Source: *Population Reference Bureau, 1998*

of many cities. Other factories produce locomotives, cars, cement, and chemical products. India's mica mines produce much of the world's supply of this mineral.

Cottage industries are also the source of many Indian products. A **cottage industry** is based in a rural village where family members use their own equipment. Goods produced in cottage industries include cotton cloth, silk cloth, rugs, leather products, and metalware.

Human/Environment Interaction
The People

India has more than 988 million people. It is the world's second-largest country in population. Only China is larger. The graph above shows you how India's population compares with that of the United States. The people of India speak 14 major languages and more than 1,000 other languages and dialects. Hindi is India's official language, but English is commonly spoken in government and business.

Influences of the Past About 4,000 years ago, the first Indian civilization built well-planned cities in present-day Pakistan. About 1500 B.C. warriors known as Aryans (AR•ee•uhnz) entered the subcontinent from central Asia. They set up kingdoms in northern India, forcing many of the earlier Indian peoples to move southward. The Aryans brought the religious teachings of Hinduism and the traditional system of social groups to India's culture.

Many other groups came later to the area that is now India. Beginning in the A.D. 700s, Muslims from Southwest Asia brought Islam to India. In the 1500s they founded the Mogul (MOH•guhl) Empire, which lasted more than 200 years.

The British ruled large areas of India from the 1700s to the mid-1900s. They built roads, railroads, and seaports. They also made large profits from the plantations, mines, and factories they set up in India. An Indian leader named Mohandas Gandhi (moh•HAHN•das GAHN•dee) led a movement that brought

India independence from the United Kingdom in 1947. Since independence India has been a democracy.

Religion About 80 percent of India's people are Hindus. Hindus believe that all living things have souls that belong to one eternal spirit. After the body dies, the soul is reborn and returns to the earth. This process is repeated many times until the soul reaches perfection in a higher state of existence.

Islam also claims many followers in India. India's 140 million Muslims form one of the largest Muslim populations in the world. Other religions in India are Buddhism, Sikhism (SEE•KIH•zuhm), Jainism (JY•NIH•zuhm), and Christianity.

The Arts Religion has influenced the arts of India. Ancient Hindu builders constructed temples with tall, elaborately carved towers. Hindu writers left stories, poems, and legends. Hindu artists developed dances and music that are still performed today.

Muslims also have added to India's artistic heritage. One of the finest Muslim buildings in India is the Taj Mahal. A ruler in the mid-1600s built the Taj Mahal as a monument to a beloved wife. By the 1800s European influences affected the arts of India. Today Indian arts reflect a blend of both East and West, old and new.

WHAT IN THE WORLD?

Where's Mumbai?

In 1996 Bombay became known as Mumbai to English speakers. The word "Mumbai" comes from the name of a Hindu goddess.

Movie-Mania in New Delhi, India

A large billboard advertises a popular movie—one of hundreds produced every year in India.
PLACE: What other forms of entertainment are popular in India?

Daily Life About 74 percent of India's people live in rural villages. Some villagers have brick homes. Others live in mud-and-straw shelters. Both men and women work in nearby fields. The Indian government tries to provide electricity, drinking water, better schools, and paved roads for many villages. Life is still difficult, however, for many Indian villagers. In recent years large numbers of people from the countryside have moved to urban areas.

India's cities today are very crowded. Delhi, Calcutta, and Mumbai are among the cities in India that have more than 5 million people each. Modern high-rise apartment and office buildings rise above the skyline. Next to these modern buildings stand slum areas of poverty. Bicycles, carts, animals, and people fill the narrow streets lined by small family-owned shops.

Fifteen-year-old Rajinder Swarup lives in Mumbai. Like many Indians, he wears a mix of traditional and modern clothing. He favors light, loose clothes because of India's hot climate. Like you, Rajinder loves going to the movies. Filled with action, adventure, and romance, movies are the most popular form of entertainment in India today. India makes more movies than any other country in the world. Rajinder also enjoys sports such as rugby and soccer. His favorite holiday is Diwali—the festival of lights. It is a Hindu festival marking the coming of winter and the victory of good over evil.

Teen Scene

A Typical Morning in New Delhi

Rani Singh lives in a two-room apartment in New Delhi with her parents, grandparents, and uncles. Before school each day Rani and her grandmother walk to the bazaar in their neighborhood to buy food for that day's meals. Rani has chosen her favorite *sari* to wear today. A *sari* is a long piece of fabric that is draped over the shoulders and head. The round dot that Rani wears in the middle of her forehead is called a *kumkum*. It is worn as a decoration— much like lipstick or jewelry.

SECTION 1 ASSESSMENT

REVIEWING TERMS AND FACTS

1. Define the following: subcontinent, monsoon, jute, cottage industry.

2. LOCATION What two mountain ranges lie along India's northern border?

3. PLACE What kinds of landforms are found in India?

4. HUMAN/ENVIRONMENT INTERACTION What is India's leading food crop?

MAP STUDY ACTIVITIES

5. Look at the physical map on page 588. What three major bodies of water border India?

6. Turn to the political map on page 586. What is the capital of India?

BUILDING GEOGRAPHY SKILLS

Reading a Circle Graph

A **circle graph** is like a sliced pie. Often it is even called a pie chart. In a circle graph, the complete circle represents a whole group—or 100 percent. The circle is divided into "slices," or wedge-shaped sections representing parts of the whole.

Suppose, for example, that 25 percent of your friends watch five hours of television per day. On a circle graph representing hours of TV watching, 25 percent of the circle would represent friends who watch five hours. To read a circle graph, follow these steps:

- Read the title to find out what the subject is.
- Study the labels or key to determine what the parts or "slices" represent.
- Compare the parts to draw conclusions about the subject.

Glencoe's **Skillbuilder Interactive Workbook, Level 1** provides instruction and practice in key social studies skills.

Religions of South Asia

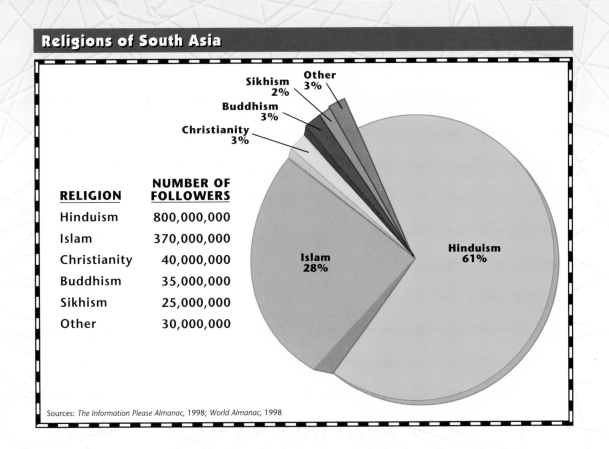

RELIGION	NUMBER OF FOLLOWERS
Hinduism	800,000,000
Islam	370,000,000
Christianity	40,000,000
Buddhism	35,000,000
Sikhism	25,000,000
Other	30,000,000

Hinduism 61%

Islam 28%

Christianity 3%

Buddhism 3%

Sikhism 2%

Other 3%

Sources: *The Information Please Almanac, 1998; World Almanac, 1998*

Geography Skills Practice

1. Which religion in Asia has the most followers?

2. What percentage of South Asians are Muslim?

3. What is the combined percentage of Buddhist and Christian followers?

Muslim South Asia

PREVIEW

Words to Know
- tributary
- delta
- cyclone
- teak

Places to Locate
- Pakistan
- Bangladesh
- Hindu Kush
- Brahmaputra River
- Indus River
- Karachi
- Islamabad
- Dhaka

Read to Learn . . .
1. where Pakistan and Bangladesh are located.
2. how people in Pakistan and Bangladesh earn their livings.
3. how Islam influences the cultures of Pakistan and Bangladesh.

This beautiful domed mosque soars above the city sky-line of Lahore, Pakistan. About 1,000 years old, Lahore boasts many buildings that reflect the religion of Islam.

Two countries in South Asia—Pakistan and Bangladesh—are largely Muslim. Although they share a religion, the peoples of these two countries have very different cultures. They also are separated from each other by more than 1,000 miles (1,610 km).

Location
Pakistan

Pakistan lies northwest of India. Its 297,640 square miles (770,888 sq. km) make it about the size of Texas. Pakistan is an independent country today because of religion. Its Muslim population did not want to be part of largely Hindu India. When British rule of India ended in 1947, the western and eastern parts of India became Pakistan. In 1971 the eastern section became Bangladesh.

Land and Climate Snow-topped mountains, high plateaus, fertile plains, and sandy deserts make up Pakistan. In the north you will find the Hindu Kush. Mountain passes cut through these rugged peaks. Centuries ago, the Khyber Pass was an important passage for people entering into South Asia from the north.

MAP STUDY
South Asia's coldest climates are found in the Himalayas.
PLACE: What two South Asian countries have desert climate regions?

CLIMATE

Tropical
- Tropical rain forest
- Tropical savanna

Dry
- Steppe (partly dry)
- Desert

Mid-Latitude
- Humid subtropical
- Highland

Lambert Conical projection

Plains cover most of eastern Pakistan. They are rich in fertile soil deposited by rivers. The major river system running through Pakistan's plains is the Indus River and its tributaries. A **tributary** is a small river that flows into a larger river or body of water. West of the Indus River valley, the land rises to form a plateau. A large part of this plateau is dry and rocky with little vegetation. Another vast barren area—the Thar Desert—sweeps east of the Indus River valley.

Pakistan has desert and steppe climates, with hot summers and cool winters. Rainfall in most regions is less than 10 inches (25 cm) a year. As in India, mountains in northern Pakistan block cold air from central Asia.

The Economy Many Pakistanis earn their livings by farming. Farmers use irrigation to grow wheat, cotton, and corn. They also raise cattle, goats, and sheep. Pakistan's factories manufacture cotton textiles for export. Other manufactured goods include cement, chemicals, fertilizer, and steel. Many craftworkers participate in cottage industries making metalware, pottery, and carpets.

The People Although 97 percent of Pakistanis are Muslim, the country's population includes many different ethnic and language groups. Among the major languages of Pakistan are Punjabi and Urdu. English is widely spoken in government and business.

Pakistani women prepare the evening meal while one of the men spins wool.
PLACE: What is the major religion of Pakistan?

About 72 percent of Pakistan's people live in rural villages. Most follow traditional customs and live in small homes of clay or sun-dried mud. In spite of its largely rural population, Pakistan has many large cities. Karachi, a seaport on the Arabian Sea, has about 9.3 million people. To the far north lies Islamabad, the national capital. It is a well-planned, modern city of 210,000 citizens. The government of Pakistan built Islamabad to draw people inland from crowded coastal areas.

Most people in Pakistan's cities are factory workers, shopkeepers, and craftworkers. They live in crowded neighborhoods. Many come from the countryside and keep close ties to their villages. Wealthier city dwellers live in modern homes and follow modern ways of life. In recent years, women in Pakistan have become active in politics. Benazir Bhutto served as prime minister of Pakistan during the late 1980s and the mid-1990s. She was the first woman to head a modern Muslim country.

Location
Bangladesh

The South Asian republic of Bangladesh has an area of 50,260 square miles (130,173 sq. km)—about the size of the state of Wisconsin. The map on page 586 shows that Bangladesh is nearly surrounded by India. Although Bangladesh is an Islamic nation, it shares many cultural features with eastern India.

From 1947 to 1971, Bangladesh was part of Pakistan, but separated from the rest of Pakistan by the nation of India. In 1971 Bangladesh gained its independence from Pakistan after a nine-month civil war.

The Land Flat, low plains cover most of Bangladesh. Two major rivers—the Brahmaputra (BRAH•muh•POO•truh) and the Ganges—flow through these plains. Find these rivers on the map on page 588. The people of Bangladesh depend on the rivers for transportation and for farming. The rivers often overflow their banks, leaving fertile soil. These deposits have formed a **delta,** or land formed by mud and sand at the mouth of a river. The largest river delta in the world has formed in Bangladesh where the Brahmaputra and Ganges rivers flow into the Indian Ocean.

Bangladesh has tropical and humid subtropical climates. As in India, the monsoons affect Bangladesh. During the summer monsoons, **cyclones** may cause flooding. A cyclone is an intense storm with high winds and heavy rains. Cyclones kill many people and animals and ruin crops.

The Economy Bangladesh's economy depends on farming. Farmers there raise rice, sugarcane, and jute in the wet, fertile soil. Bangladesh produces the world's largest supply of jute. Its thick forests provide **teak,** a wood used for

Almost 80 percent of the land in Bangladesh is part of a large delta.
HUMAN/ENVIRONMENT INTERACTION: What is the advantage and one disadvantage of living in a delta area?

shipbuilding and fine furniture. Although it has natural riches, Bangladesh is a struggling country. Its farmers have few modern tools and use outdated farming methods. The country often suffers from disastrous floods and food shortages.

The People Bangladesh—with about 123 million people—is one of the world's most densely populated countries. It has about 2,454 people per square mile (948 people per sq. km). About 86 percent of Bangladesh's people live in rural areas. Their homes are made of bamboo with thatched roofs. In recent years, many people have moved to crowded neighborhoods in urban areas to find work in factories. Their most common choice is Dhaka (DA•kuh), Bangladesh's capital and major port.

Most of Bangladesh's people speak the Bengali language, which is also spoken in neighboring India. About 87 percent of the people in Bangladesh are Muslim. Muslim influences are strong in the country's art, literature, and music.

SECTION 2 ASSESSMENT

REVIEWING TERMS AND FACTS

1. **Define the following:** tributary, delta, cyclone, teak.

2. **LOCATION** Describe the landforms of Pakistan.

3. **PLACE** How have rivers affected life in Bangladesh?

4. **REGION** What is the major religion of Pakistan and Bangladesh?

MAP STUDY ACTIVITIES

5. Turn to the climate map on page 595. What are the three major climate regions of Pakistan?

MAKING CONNECTIONS

MAKING IT COUNT

| MATH | SCIENCE | HISTORY | LITERATURE | TECHNOLOGY |

Have you ever stopped to think where the number system you use came from? Centuries ago, Hindu scholars in India made great discoveries in mathematics.

NUMBER SYSTEM As early as 300 B.C., Hindu scholars came up with a number system based on 10. This number system used just 9 symbols, or numerals: 1, 2, 3, 4, 5, 6, 7, 8, 9. The strength of their number system lay in the idea of *place value.* The same symbol could represent different amounts, depending on its place in a number. For example, the symbol "3" represents 3 ones in the number 13, and 30 ones in the number 31. The Hindu scholars discovered that an infinitely large number could be represented using only 9 symbols.

ZERO About A.D. 600, Hindu thinkers invented a tenth symbol, *sunya,* which means "empty." This symbol, which became known as zero, was used to fill an empty place in a number. Until the invention of *sunya,* Hindus wrote a word to show the place value of each numeral above 99. For example, the number we would write as 306 was written "3 *sata* 6."

Zero ended the need for written place names, so "3 *sata* 6" became "306."

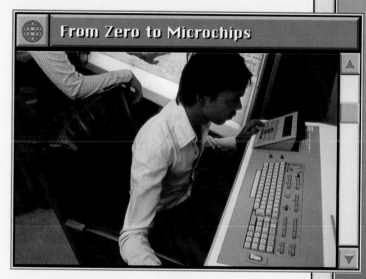

From Zero to Microchips

SPREAD OF NUMBERS For several centuries, only well-educated Hindus used the number system. Later, Arabs from Southwest Asia began using the Hindu system and found it much easier than their own. They adopted the system and eventually brought it to Europe. There it became known as the Arabic-Hindu number system. It replaced the long, clumsy system of numerals that had been used by the Romans.

Making the Connection

1. Hindu scholars developed 9 symbols and what special new symbol as part of their number system?
2. What people later used the Hindu number system?

The Himalayan Countries

Words to Know
- dzong

Places to Locate
- Nepal
- Bhutan
- Mount Everest
- Kathmandu
- Thimphu

Read to Learn . . .
1. why Nepal and Bhutan were historically isolated.
2. how the people of Nepal and Bhutan earn their livings.
3. what influence religion has on the Himalayan countries.

In the Himalayas, north and east of India, you will find two small kingdoms— Nepal and Bhutan. The people of these

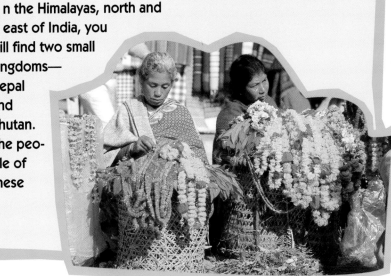

Himalayan countries visit street markets like this one every day to shop for food and visit with their neighbors.

Nepal and Bhutan both lie hidden among the towering peaks of the Himalayas. For centuries their mountain location kept them isolated. Today, airplanes and roads open up Nepal and Bhutan to the rest of the world.

Place
Nepal

A well-known myth of the Himalayas tells about a gigantic, apelike beast that roams the mountainous wilderness of Nepal. This "abominable snowman" seems almost too large for the country of Nepal, a small kingdom of only 52,820 square miles (136,804 sq. km)—an area about the size of North Carolina.

The Land The map on page 588 shows you that the Himalayas cover about 80 percent of Nepal's land area. The Himalayas are actually three mountain chains running side by side. Steep river valleys cut through the ice and snow of these mountains. You will find 8 of the 10 highest mountains in the world in the Himalayas of Nepal. Mount Everest is the highest peak at 29,028 feet (8,848 m).

Hills and valleys lie south of the Himalayas. Thick forests of trees and bamboo grasses grow in this region. A flat fertile river plain runs along Nepal's southern border with India. The plain includes farmland, rain forests, and swamps. Animals such as tigers and elephants roam these forests.

Differences in elevation affect Nepal's climate. Mountainous areas have long, harsh winters and short, cool summers. Valley areas have a cool climate with heavy summer rains. The plains in the south have a humid subtropical climate.

The Economy Nepal's economy depends almost entirely on farming. The farmers of Nepal grow enough wheat, barley, rice, and potatoes to feed themselves and their families. At markets farmers trade surplus crops for other items.

With few railroads or roads, Nepal carries on limited trade with the outside world. Herbs, jute, rice, spices, and wheat are exported to India. In return Nepal imports gasoline, machinery, and textiles. The country's rugged mountains, which attract thousands of climbers and hikers each year, have helped build a growing tourist industry.

The People Nepal has a population of 23.7 million. Most of its people are related to peoples in northern India and in Tibet to the north. One group in Nepal—the Sherpa—are known for their skills as mountain guides. About 90 percent of Nepal's people live in rural villages. A growing number of Nepal's people live in Kathmandu, the capital and largest city. Most Nepalese follow a form of Hinduism mixed with Buddhist practices.

SOUTH ASIA: Land Use and Resources

MAP STUDY
The Indus River and its tributaries have created a large area of fertile land in Pakistan.
PLACE: What resource is being developed in Bhutan?

Agriculture
- ☐ Little or no farming
- ☐ Nomadic herding
- ☐ Plantation farming
- ☐ Subsistence farming
- ■ Manufacturing area

Resources
- 🛒 Coal
- ▲ Chromite
- 🐟 Fish & other seafood
- 🌲 Forest
- ⚡ Hydroelectric power
- I Iron ore
- ⚬⚬ Lead
- ◕ Manganese
- 🜄 Natural gas
- ⛏ Petroleum
- Phosphates
- ▫ Zinc

Lambert Conical projection

Place
Bhutan

East of Nepal lies the even smaller kingdom of Bhutan. The map on page 586 shows you that a small part of India separates Bhutan from Nepal. Bhutan has a land area of about 18,150 square miles (47,009 sq. km)—about the size of New Hampshire and Vermont put together.

The Land and Economy As in Nepal, the Himalayas are the major landform of Bhutan. They rise more than 24,000 feet (7,320 m) in many places. Mountainous areas of the country have snow and ice all year. In the foothills of the Himalayas the climate is mild. Thick forests cover much of this area. To the south along Bhutan's border with India lies an area of subtropical plains and river valleys.

Most of Bhutan's people are subsistence farmers. They live in the fertile mountain valleys and grow barley, rice, and wheat. In the severe climate of the mountain areas people herd cattle and yaks, or longhaired oxen. With India's help, Bhutan is developing its economy. It has set up commercial farms and built hydroelectric plants.

The People Bhutan has about 800,000 people. Most of them speak the Dzongkha dialect. Many live in rural villages that dot valleys and plains in the southern part of the country. Thimphu, the national capital, is in this area.

Bhutan once was called the "hidden holy land." Bhutan's people are not as isolated as they used to be. They are deeply loyal to the Buddhist religion, which teaches that people can find peace from life's troubles by living simply, doing good deeds, and praying. An Indian holy man named Siddhartha Gautama first preached Buddhism in India in the 500s B.C. Buddhism later spread eastward and northward to other parts of Asia. In Bhutan, Buddhist centers of prayer and study called **dzongs** have shaped the country's art and culture.

The Sherpas of northern Nepal serve as guides in the Himalayas.
LOCATION: What is the highest peak in the Himalayas?

SECTION 3 ASSESSMENT

REVIEWING TERMS AND FACTS
1. Define the following: dzong.
2. PLACE What climate areas are found in Nepal?
3. LOCATION Where do most people in Nepal and Bhutan live?

MAP STUDY ACTIVITIES
4. Turn to the land use map on page 600. What natural resource is found in eastern Nepal?

SECTION 4
Island Countries

Words to Know
- atoll
- lagoon

Places to Locate
- Sri Lanka
- Maldives
- Colombo

Read to Learn . . .
1. where Sri Lanka and the Maldives are located.
2. what major products are grown in Sri Lanka.

3. what formed the islands of the Maldives.

Two countries of South Asia—Sri Lanka and the Maldives—are islands in the Indian Ocean. Sri Lanka's capital city, Colombo, is a major seaport. Most of its people are Buddhists.

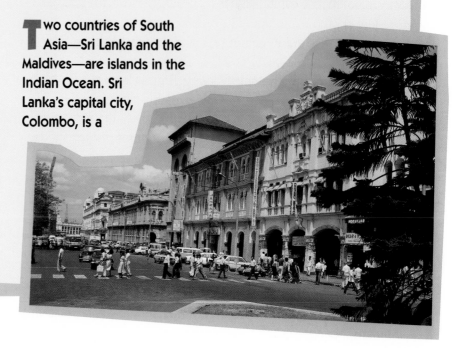

Sri Lanka and the Maldives lie south of India in the Indian Ocean. The sea affects the ways in which the peoples of both island countries live and earn their livings.

Place
Sri Lanka

Pear-shaped Sri Lanka lies about 20 miles (32 km) off the southeastern coast of India. Covering 24,950 square miles (64,621 sq. km), Sri Lanka is about the size of West Virginia. Sri Lanka, located on an important ocean route between Africa and Asia, became a natural stopping place for traders. Beginning in the 1500s, Sri Lanka—then known as Ceylon—came under the control of European countries. The British ruled the island from 1802 to 1948, when it became independent once again. In 1972 Ceylon took the name Sri Lanka, an ancient term meaning "brilliant land."

Sri Lanka is a land of white beaches and thick forests. Much of the country along the coast is rolling lowlands. Highlands cover the center. Rivers flow down the low mountains, providing irrigation for crops.

602

The Economy Farming is Sri Lanka's major economic activity. Many farmers grow rice and other food crops in lowland areas. Water buffaloes help to plow their fields. In higher elevations, tea, rubber, and coconuts grow on large plantations. Sri Lanka is one of the world's leading producers of tea and rubber.

Sri Lanka, rich in natural resources, is famous for its sapphires, rubies, and other gemstones. Sri Lanka's forests contain many valuable woods such as ebony and satinwood, and a variety of birds and animals. To protect wildlife, the government of Sri Lanka has set aside land for national parks.

Sri Lanka is developing its industrial economy. Factories in Sri Lanka's cities produce textiles, fertilizers, cement, leather products, and wood products for export. Colombo, the capital city, is a bustling port on the country's west coast.

The People About 19 million people live in Sri Lanka. They belong to two major ethnic groups, the Sinhalese (SIHN•guh•LEEZ) and the Tamils (TA•muhlz). Forming about 74 percent of the population, the Sinhalese live in the southern and western parts of the island. They speak Sinhalese and are Buddhists. The Tamils make up about 18 percent of the population. They live in the north and east, speak Tamil, and are Hindus. Some Tamils have fought to set up a separate country in northern Sri Lanka.

Whatever their ethnic background, people in Sri Lanka value their history and the arts—still visible in the remains of ancient cities. These remains hold

SOUTH ASIA: Population Density

MAP STUDY
In Bangladesh, there are about 2,500 people for every square mile of land.
PLACE: What is the general population density of most of Sri Lanka?

Persons per

sq. mi.	sq. km
Uninhabited	Uninhabited
Under 2	Under 1
2-60	1-25
60-125	25-50
125-250	50-100
Over 250	Over 100

Lambert Conical projection

CITIES
■ City with more than 3,000,000 people
● City with 1,000,000 to 3,000,000 people
○ City with 500,000 to 1,000,000 people

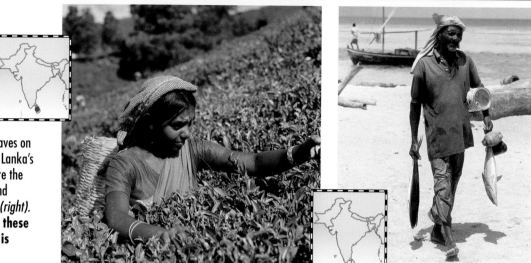

Workers harvest tea leaves on large plantations in Sri Lanka's highlands *(left)*. Fish are the most important food and export in the Maldives *(right)*. **LOCATION: Which of these two island countries is closer to India?**

many old palaces, temples, and statues of Buddha. Sri Lankan craftspeople also take pride in their carved wooden masks, brass work, and handmade cloth.

Region
Maldives

About 370 miles (595 km) south of India lie the Maldives, the smallest country of South Asia. The Maldives are made up of about 1,200 coral islands. Many of the islands are **atolls,** or low-lying islands that circle pools of water called **lagoons.** Only 200 islands have people living on them.

The climate of the Maldives is warm and humid throughout the year. Monsoons bring plenty of rain. Fish and tortoises fill the tropical waters around the islands. The people of the Maldives are skilled sailors, and fishing is their major economic activity. Fish and rice are the major foods. In recent years, the islands' palm-lined sandy beaches and coral formations have attracted tourists.

About 300,000 people live in the Maldives. Some 30,000 make their homes in Male, the capital. Most are Muslims. The islands, which came under British rule during the late 1800s, became independent in 1965.

SECTION 4 ASSESSMENT

REVIEWING TERMS AND FACTS
1. Define the following: atoll, lagoon.
2. PLACE What two major ethnic groups are found in Sri Lanka?
3. REGION What is the major economic activity of the Maldives?

MAP STUDY ACTIVITIES
4. Look at the population density map on page 603. What part of Sri Lanka has the highest population density?

Chapter 22 Highlights

Important Things to Know About South Asia

SECTION 1 INDIA

- India is the largest country of South Asia in size and population.
- The Himalayas and the monsoons, or seasonal winds, affect India's climate.
- India's economy is based on farming and industry.
- Although the peoples of India belong to many religious and language groups, most are Hindus.

SECTION 2 MUSLIM SOUTH ASIA

- Islam has shaped the cultures of Pakistan and Bangladesh.
- Pakistan is made up of mountains, deserts, and fertile river valleys.
- The Ganges and Brahmaputra rivers form a fertile delta area in Bangladesh.
- Monsoons bring plenty of rain to Bangladesh's low, fertile plains.

SECTION 3 THE HIMALAYAN COUNTRIES

- The Himalayas are the major landform of Nepal and Bhutan.
- Most people in Nepal and Bhutan are farmers or herders. They live in the southern parts of their countries.
- The Hindu and Buddhist religions have shaped the cultures of Nepal and Bhutan.

SECTION 4 ISLAND COUNTRIES

- Sri Lanka and the Maldives are island republics in the Indian Ocean.
- Sri Lanka is one of the world's major tea-producing countries.
- The Maldives are made up of about 1,200 coral islands. Only 200 are inhabited.

Festival market in Rajasthan, India ▶

Chapter 22 Assessment and Activities

REVIEWING KEY TERMS

Match the numbered terms in Set A with their lettered definitions in Set B.

A
1. cottage industry
2. tributary
3. jute
4. atoll
5. subcontinent
6. lagoon
7. teak
8. cyclone

B
A. landmass like a continent, only smaller
B. low-lying island circling a pool of water
C. small river that flows into a larger river
D. wood used for shipbuilding and fine furniture
E. where family members use their own equipment to create a product
F. seasonal wind
G. plant fiber used in making burlap bags
H. pool of water circled by an island

REVIEWING THE MAIN IDEAS

Mental Mapping Activity

Draw a freehand map of South Asia. Label the following:
- Calcutta
- Arabian Sea
- Hindu Kush
- Bay of Bengal
- Bhutan
- Deccan Plateau
- Indian Ocean

Section 1
1. LOCATION Where is the Deccan Plateau located?
2. REGION What major river flows through northern India?

Section 2
3. HUMAN/ENVIRONMENT INTERACTION What has helped increase food production in Pakistan?
4. MOVEMENT What is the major means of transportation in Bangladesh?

Section 3
5. PLACE What climates are found in Nepal?
6. PLACE Why was Bhutan once called the "hidden holy land"?

Section 4
7. HUMAN/ENVIRONMENT INTERACTION What agricultural products are grown on plantations in Sri Lanka?
8. PLACE What is the major religion of the Maldives?

CRITICAL THINKING ACTIVITIES

1. **Drawing Conclusions** Why do you think the description "brilliant island" applies to Sri Lanka?
2. **Cause and Effect** How have the environments of Nepal and Bhutan affected the way the countries' people live?

CONNECTIONS TO WORLD CULTURES

Cooperative Learning Activity Work in groups of three to learn more about the major religions of South Asia: Hinduism, Islam, and Buddhism. Choose one of the religions and research how it has affected one of the following areas: (a) the arts; (b) diet; and (c) family life. After your research is complete, share your information with your group. As a group, prepare a chart and a poster that present the group's findings.

GeoJournal Writing Activity

Imagine what it would be like to visit the Himalayas. Write about your experiences to a friend. Describe the types of transportation that you might use and the scenes that you might see on your journey.

TECHNOLOGY ACTIVITY

Using a Database Conduct research about the following religions of India: Buddhism, Hinduism, Jainism, Sikhism, Christianity, and Islam. Organize your research into a database with the following fields: number of followers, basic beliefs, and major leaders. Share your database with the rest of the class.

PLACE LOCATION ACTIVITY: SOUTH ASIA

Match the letters on the map with the places and physical features of South Asia. Write your answers on a separate sheet of paper.

1. Karachi
2. Himalayas
3. New Delhi
4. Ganges River
5. Mumbai (Bombay)
6. Bangladesh
7. Thar Desert
8. Sri Lanka
9. Indus River
10. Western Ghats

Chapter 23 China

80°E
90°E
100°E
110°E
120°E
130°E
140°E
50°N
40°N
30°N
20°N

RUSSIA

Ulan Bator ⊛
MONGOLIA

Harbin •

Kashi •

Shenyang •

Yinchuan •

Beijing ⊛
Dalian •

Xining •
Tianjin •
Jinan •
Qingdao •

Zhengzhou •

CHINA
Xi'an •
Zaozhuang •
Yellow Sea

Chengdu •
Nanjing •
Wuhan •
Shanghai •

Lhasa •

ASIA
Chongqing •
Hangzhou •

Tropic of Cancer
East China Sea

Kunming •
Fuzhou •
Taipei ⊛

Guangzhou •
Kaohsiung •
TAIWAN

Haikou •
Hong Kong
Macao

South China Sea

Sea of Japan

0   150   300 mi.
0   150   300 km

— National boundary
⊛ National capital
• Other city
Conic projection

MAP STUDY ACTIVITY

As you read Chapter 23, you will learn about China and its neighbors.

1. What area is an island?
2. What is the capital of China?
3. What is the capital of Mongolia?

SECTION 1

The Land

PREVIEW

Words to Know
- loess
- dike
- typhoon

Places to Locate
- China
- Plateau of Tibet
- Kunlun Shan
- Taklimakan
- Gobi
- Huang He
- Chang Jiang
- Xi

Read to Learn . . .
1. why the Plateau of Tibet is called the "Roof of the World."
2. where most of China's people live.
3. what climates are found in China.

The Great Wall of China is one of the wonders of the world. The longest structure ever built, the wall stretches about 4,000 miles (6,437 km). The Chinese built the wall centuries ago to keep out invaders.

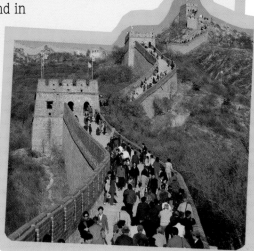

The People's Republic of China lies in the eastern part of Asia. It is a vast country that covers more than 3,600,930 square miles (9,326,409 sq. km). China is the world's third-largest country in area, after Russia and Canada.

Region

Landscapes

If you travel by train across China, you will be amazed by the many different landscapes and climates. Look at the map on page 610. You see that China has tall mountains, vast deserts, fertile plains, and mighty rivers.

Mountains Rugged mountains cover about one-third of China. They lie in the western part of the country. The Himalayan range sweeps across the south on the border between China and Nepal. The center of China's mountainous area holds the largest plateau in the world—the Plateau of Tibet. It is called the "Roof of the World" because its average height is about 13,000 feet (4,000 m) above sea level. Scattered shrubs and grasses cover the countryside. The eastern edge of the plateau is home to pandas, golden monkeys, and other rare animals.

CHAPTER 23

609

Deserts In the north of China, you notice that the mountain ranges circle desert basins. One of these deserts is the Taklimakan. It is an isolated region with some of the world's highest temperatures. Sandstorms there may last for days and create huge, shifting dunes.

Farther east lies another desert, called the Gobi. The Gobi is made up of rock and gravel instead of sand. Temperatures there can rise to 110°F (43°C) during summer days. Because the Gobi is far north and at a high altitude, its temperatures during winter nights can drop as low as –30°F (–34°C)!

Plains and Highlands Plains cover the eastern part of China. Look at the map below. You see that these plains run along the coasts of the South China and East China seas. This area has fertile land and is home to almost 90 percent of China's people.

The Northeast Plain lies in the center of Manchuria, a region in northeast China. To the east of the plain lies a heavily forested, hilly area near China's border with Korea. To the south is the wide, flat North China Plain. Other plains areas extend farther south near the coast.

Inland in the southeast, the land changes from plains to green highlands. This region is one of the most scenic areas in China. Many tourists come to see its many scattered limestone hills that rise 100 to 600 feet (30 to 182 m).

Rivers Three of China's major rivers—the Huang He (HWAHNG HUH), the Chang Jiang (CHAHNG jee•AHNG), and the Xi (SHEE)—flow through the

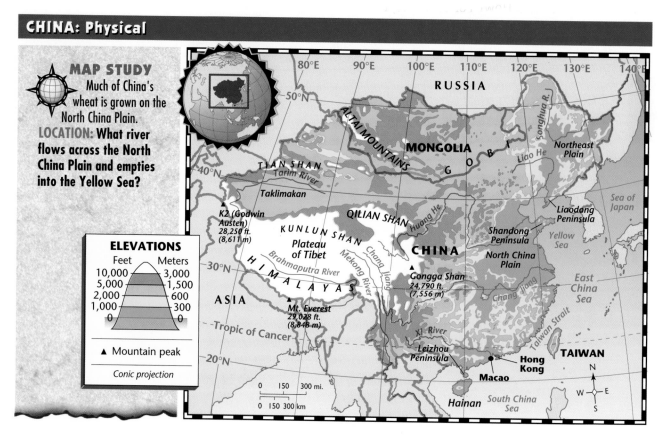

CHINA: Physical

MAP STUDY
Much of China's wheat is grown on the North China Plain.
LOCATION: What river flows across the North China Plain and empties into the Yellow Sea?

ELEVATIONS

Feet	Meters
10,000	3,000
5,000	1,500
2,000	600
1,000	300
0	0

▲ Mountain peak

Conic projection

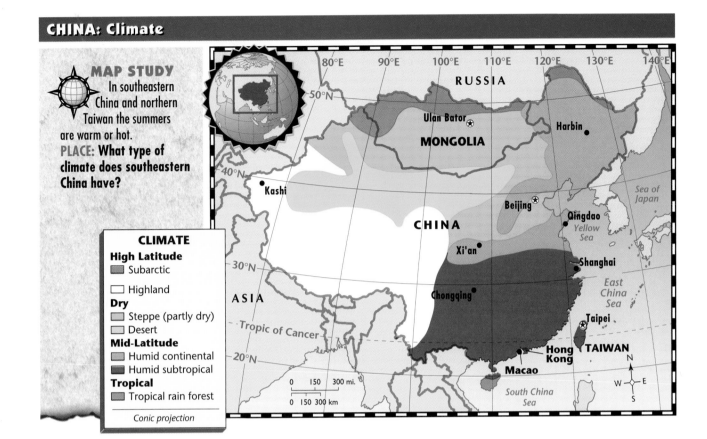

MAP STUDY
In southeastern China and northern Taiwan the summers are warm or hot.
PLACE: What type of climate does southeastern China have?

CLIMATE

High Latitude
- Subarctic
- Highland

Dry
- Steppe (partly dry)
- Desert

Mid-Latitude
- Humid continental
- Humid subtropical

Tropical
- Tropical rain forest

Conic projection

plains and southern highlands. They serve as important transportation routes and as a source of soil. How? For centuries, floodwaters have deposited rich soil to form flat river basins.

The Huang He basin is an important farming area. It is thickly covered with **loess,** a fertile, yellow-gray soil deposited by wind and water. The name *Huang He* means "yellow river," referring to the loess carried by the river.

The rivers of China have brought disasters as well as blessings. The Chinese, for example, call the Huang He "China's sorrow." In the past, its flooding cost hundreds of thousands of lives and caused much damage. To control floods, the Chinese have built dams and **dikes,** or high banks of soil, along the sides of this river. In the late 1990s work began on the Three Gorges Dam on the Chang Jiang. The dam—the world's largest construction project—will prevent serious flooding and provide electricity for industries.

Region
Climate

Like the United States, China has many different climate regions. The map above shows you the seven climate regions of China. Location, elevation, and wind currents affect the type of climate found in any particular area of the country. Southeastern China has a humid subtropical climate with hot, humid summers. The northeast has a humid continental climate with cold winters. In desert areas to the northwest, summers are hot and dry and winters are cold

Rice fields are a common sight in warm, humid southeastern China *(left)*. Beijing has a humid continental climate with cold, snowy winters *(right)*.
LOCATION: What are hurricanes in the Pacific Ocean called?

and windy. In the southwestern part of China, the high Plateau of Tibet has bitterly cold winters and cool summers.

Monsoons greatly affect China's climates. In winter cold, dry air flows from central Asia across China. In summer the monsoons blow in from the sea, bringing warm, moist air. The summer monsoons often bring typhoons to coastal areas in the south. **Typhoons**—called hurricanes in the Atlantic Ocean—are tropical storms with strong winds and heavy rains.

SECTION 1 ASSESSMENT

REVIEWING TERMS AND FACTS

1. **Define the following:** loess, dike, typhoon.

2. **LOCATION** Where is the Plateau of Tibet located?

3. **PLACE** How would you describe the landscape of southeastern China?

4. **REGION** How do monsoons affect China's climates?

MAP STUDY ACTIVITIES

5. Look at the physical map on page 610. What three major rivers flow through China?

6. Study the climate map on page 611. What are the three major climate regions of western China?

BUILDING GEOGRAPHY SKILLS

Comparing Two or More Graphs

Comparing two or more graphs gives you a better understanding of a topic. When comparing graphs, first see how they are related. Are they on the same topic? Are they the same kind of graph? Are the same units of measurement used? Then look for similarities and differences in the information on the graphs. To compare two or more graphs, apply these steps:

- Read the title and labels on each graph to see how they are related.

- Look for similarities and differences in the information given on each graph. Draw conclusions based on the comparison.

Glencoe's **Skillbuilder Interactive Workbook, Level 1** provides instruction and practice in key social studies skills.

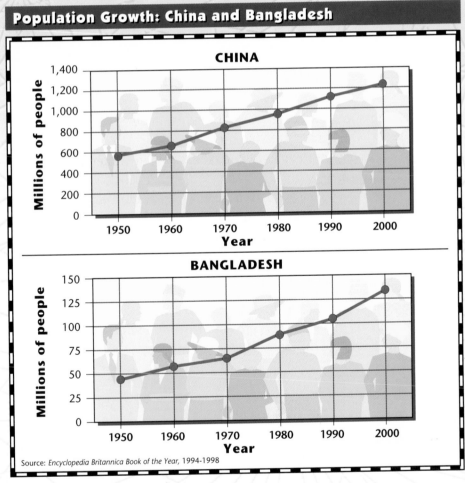

Population Growth: China and Bangladesh

CHINA

BANGLADESH

Source: *Encyclopedia Britannica Book of the Year, 1994-1998*

Geography Skills Practice

1. What is the subject of the graphs?
2. What was Bangladesh's population in 1960?
3. By how much did China's population increase from 1980 to 1990?
4. What conclusions can you draw from the information on these graphs?

The Economy

PREVIEW

Words to Know
- invest
- consumer goods
- tungsten
- terraced field

Places to Locate
- Shanghai
- Beijing
- Wuhan
- Guangzhou

Read to Learn . . .
1. how most Chinese earn their livings.
2. what the three economic regions of China are.
3. how China's economy has changed in recent years.

Shanghai is China's largest city and its major port. The name *Shanghai* means "on the water." Shanghai is a leader in trade and business. Because Shanghai is a port city, it has many contacts with the rest of the world.

China has a developing economy based on farming and industry. About 60 percent of the Chinese people farm the land. Because there are so many mountains and deserts, farmland is limited in China. Chinese farmers, however, are able to produce almost enough food to feed the entire country. China also has growing industries. It is among the world's ten leading countries in terms of the total value of products produced each year.

Region
A New Economy

Since 1949 China has been a communist country. Under communism, the government—not individuals or businesses—decides what crops are grown, what products are made, and what prices are charged for both. In recent years China's government has made many changes in the economy. Why? It hopes to make China a modern, industrialized nation. It also wants to increase trade with the United States and other Western countries. Without completely giving up communism, the government has allowed many features of free enterprise to develop in China.

Making a Living Since the 1980s, China has increased its ties with foreign countries. Eager to learn about new business methods, it has asked other countries to **invest,** or put money, in Chinese businesses. Many businesses in China are now jointly owned by Chinese and foreign businesspeople.

Instead of telling people what jobs they should have, the Chinese government now wants individuals to choose where to work and even to start their own businesses. Shop owners, dentists, and barbers are among the people competing for customers in China's major cities.

Changes have also come to China's countryside. Farmers once spent most of their time working on government farms. Now they grow extra crops on private plots of land. Farmers can keep the money they make from selling these crops.

Because of all these changes, farming, manufacturing, and trade are booming in China. Some Chinese now enjoy a good standard of living. They can afford **consumer goods,** or products such as television sets, cars, and motorcycles. Not everyone, however, finds it easy to adjust to the new economy. Many Chinese are finding that the prices of food and goods are rising faster than their incomes. Some Chinese are getting very rich, while others remain poor.

As China industrializes, it faces environmental problems. Many factories dump poisonous chemicals into rivers. Others, powered by coal, send out air-polluting smoke. The building of Three Gorges Dam also has raised concerns. About 2 million people will be moved before the dam's lake covers up farms, villages, and canyons. Critics claim that the project is destroying one of the world's most scenic areas, as well as centuries-old temples.

CHINA: Land Use and Resources

MAP STUDY Because of its location, Hong Kong is a center of world trade and manufacturing. **PLACE: What are three major manufacturing areas along China's east coast?**

Resources
- Bauxite
- Coal
- Copper
- Fish & other seafood
- Forest
- Hydroelectric power
- Iron ore
- Lead
- Manganese
- Petroleum
- Tin
- Tungsten
- Zinc

Conic projection

Agriculture
- Little or no farming
- Nomadic herding
- Commercial farming
- Subsistence farming
- Manufacturing area

Region
Economic Regions

The physical geography of China influences its economy. Many geographers divide China into three economic regions: the north, the south, and the west.

The North The north region includes the plains and highlands of northeastern China. It has a variety of economic activities, including manufacturing, mining, farming, and commercial fishing. Because of the partly dry, often cold climate, farmers in the region grow hearty grains such as wheat, cotton, and soybeans. In isolated grassland areas, nomads herd livestock.

The map on page 615 shows you that the north is rich in natural resources such as coal, petroleum, iron ore, and tungsten. **Tungsten** is a metal used in electrical equipment. China is a world leader in the mining of coal and iron ore. A number of large urban areas in the north manufacture many goods. Workers in these industrial centers produce textiles, chemicals, electronic equipment, farm machinery, airplanes, and other metal goods. Beijing (BAY•JIHNG), China's capital and major industrial city, is located in the north.

Fourteen-year-old Lai Sau Chun has lived in Beijing all of her life. She explains that, like many Chinese cities, Beijing is a blend of old and new. Many factories have been built near the city, but Sau Chun prefers the old Beijing. She takes visitors to the Imperial Palace in the heart of the city. Chinese rulers built it in the early 1400s. The palace was called "the forbidden city" because only the ruler's family and government officials were allowed to enter.

World's Leading Rice-Producing Countries

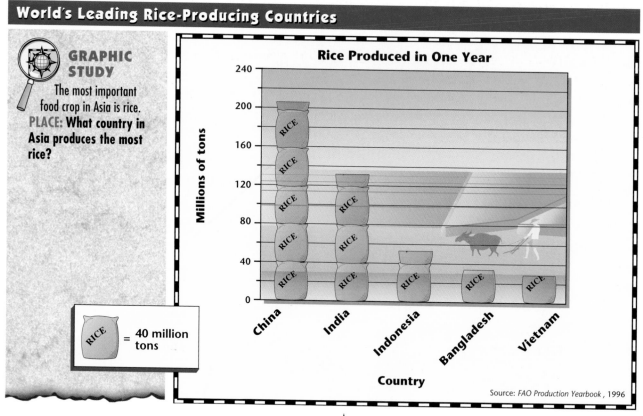

GRAPHIC STUDY

The most important food crop in Asia is rice.
PLACE: What country in Asia produces the most rice?

Rice Produced in One Year

Millions of tons

China · India · Indonesia · Bangladesh · Vietnam

Country

RICE = 40 million tons

Source: *FAO Production Yearbook*, 1996

616

UNIT 8

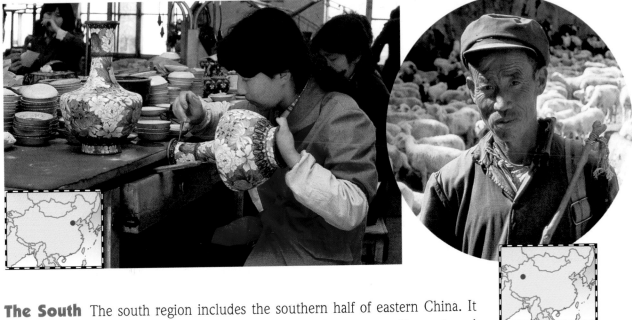

The South The south region includes the southern half of eastern China. It has fertile soil, a humid climate, and a long growing season. If you travel through hilly areas, you will see farmers growing crops on terraced fields. A **terraced field** has strips of land cut out of a hillside like stair steps. Rice is the south's major crop. Farmers also grow tea, jute, silk, fruits, and vegetables.

In addition to fertile soil, the south is rich in bauxite, iron ore, tin, and other minerals. It also has many urban manufacturing areas. Some cities, such as Shanghai, are located on or near the coast. Others, such as Wuhan (WOO•HAHN) or Guangzhou (GWAHNG•JOH), are on rivers. Workers in these industrial cities make ships, machinery, textiles, and electrical equipment.

A worker puts the finishing touches on a vase in a Beijing factory *(left)*. A sheepherder tends his flock in northwestern China *(right)*.
PLACE: What natural resources are found in northern China?

The West The west region takes up the part of China that is covered by mountains, deserts, and grasslands. The dry and cold Plateau of Tibet is not very good for farming. It provides only limited grazing for hardy animals such as yaks. In low-lying fertile areas, farmers are able to grow cotton, wheat, and other food crops. The west is also rich in petroleum, coal, and iron ore.

SECTION 2 ASSESSMENT

REVIEWING TERMS AND FACTS
1. **Define the following:** invest, consumer goods, tungsten, terraced field.
2. **PLACE** How do most Chinese earn their livings?
3. **HUMAN/ENVIRONMENT INTERACTION** How has China's economy been changing?
4. **REGION** What region is the major rice-producing area of China?

MAP STUDY ACTIVITIES

5. Look at the map on page 615. What minerals are found in northeastern China?
6. Where do you think oranges and other tropical crops grow in China?

CHINESE NATURE POETRY

MATH **SCIENCE** **HISTORY** **LITERATURE** **TECHNOLOGY**

Chinese poets aimed to create a certain mood and atmosphere in their works. Many of their poems describe brief moments of deep feelings, such as those expressed in these poems by Wang Wei.

NORTH HILL

North Hill stands out above the lake
Against thick evergreens gleams startlingly
    a vermilion [red-orange] gate.
Below, South River zig-zags toward the horizon,
Glistening, here and there, beyond the treetops of the
    blue forest.

SAILING ON THE RIVER TO CH'ING-HO

Sailing on the great river
The gathered waters reach to the very rim of heaven.
Suddenly the sky-high waves part,
Disclosing country of a thousand and cities of ten
    thousand roofs.
And sailing further, still other villages and
    market-towns appear
Mid mulberry trees and growing flax.
Looking back towards my native village . . .
The vast waters have joined the clouds.

Chinese Painting

From *Poems by Wang Wei,* translated by Chang Yin-nan and Lewis C. Walmsley. Copyright © 1958 by Charles E. Tuttle Co., Inc., Tokyo, Japan. Reprinted by permission.

Making the Connection

1. What geographic features are mentioned in these Chinese nature poems?
2. How does the poet describe the environment?

SECTION 3 — The People

PREVIEW

Words to Know
- dynasty
- calligraphy
- pagoda

Places to Locate
- Taiwan
- Beijing

Read to Learn . . .
1. what groups influenced the culture of China.
2. how city life differs from country life in China.
3. what arts and recreation the Chinese enjoy.

Along city streets in China, you will see many young people dressed as you are—in jeans. Western-style clothing is very popular. People are prepared to pay high prices for this clothing.

Crowded city streets are common in China. The country has more people than any other place in the world. About 1.2 billion people—one-fourth of the world's population—make China their home. The graph on page 620 shows you how China's population compares with that of the United States.

About 94 percent of China's people are Han Chinese. They have a unique culture, although they speak different dialects of the same Chinese language. The remaining 6 percent belong to 55 other ethnic groups. Most of these groups, such as the Tibetans, live in the western part of the country. For years the Tibetans have struggled to keep their culture and win their independence from China.

Place
Influences of the Past

Chinese civilization is more than 4,000 years old. For centuries **dynasties,** or ruling families, governed China. Each dynasty was made up of a line of rulers from the same family. Under the dynasties, China set up a strong government and enlarged its borders.

COMPARING POPULATION: China and the United States

GRAPHIC STUDY

Because China's population is so large, its government offers rewards to families that have only one child.

PLACE: About how many people live in China?

China

United States

Source: *Population Reference Bureau, 1998*

= 50,000,000

Ideas and Inventions The early Chinese developed a rich civilization. They believed that learning was a key to good behavior. A philosopher named Konfuzi, or Confucius, taught that people should be polite, honest, brave, and wise. Children were to obey their parents, and every person was to respect the elderly and obey the country's rulers. For more than 2,000 years, the Chinese followed the teachings of Confucius. They blended these teachings with those of Buddhism, which reached China from India about A.D. 100.

Did you know that the early Chinese were using paper and ink before people in other parts of the world? Early Chinese developed a number of outstanding inventions. Besides paper and ink, these inventions include the clock, the compass, the first printed book, and fireworks.

Modern China The Chinese tried to avoid contact with other parts of the world. In the 1700s and 1800s, however, European powers forced the Chinese to trade and tried to make them accept Western ways. This angered the Chinese.

In 1912 a national uprising overthrew the last dynasty, and China became a republic. Soon civil war divided the country. Nationalist forces, led by General Chiang Kai-shek (jee•AHNG KY•SHEHK), fought the Chinese Communists, led by Mao Zedong (MOW ZUH•DUNG). In 1949 the Communists won the civil war, driving Chiang's government to the offshore island of Taiwan.

Mainland China became the communist People's Republic of China. The Communists wanted to make China a modern, industrialized nation, but they denied freedoms to the Chinese people. In 1989 Chinese students in Beijing's Tiananmen Square called for democracy. The government answered their protest with gunfire, killing many and jailing others.

Meanwhile, the people of Tibet, a mountainous region of southwestern China, demanded more freedom and independence. Once a separate Buddhist kingdom, Tibet came under direct Chinese rule in the 1950s. The Dalai Lama, Tibet's spiritual leader, leads a worldwide movement for Tibetan rights from his place of exile in India.

Tiananmen Square, Beijing

In 1989 hundreds of students were killed here when they protested against the Chinese government.

PLACE: Why do you think the Chinese government would kill protesting students?

620

Rural Life About 70 percent of China's people live in rural areas. The map below shows you that most people are crowded into the fertile river valleys of eastern China. Families in the countryside work very hard in their fields. They often use simple hand tools because farming equipment is too expensive.

Village life, though, has improved in recent years. Most rural families live in three- or four-room houses. They have enough food and some modern appliances. Many villages have community centers where people can watch movies, read books, and play sports such as table tennis and basketball.

City Life More than 370 million Chinese—about 30 percent of the population—live in cities. China's cities are growing rapidly as people from the countryside move to cities hoping to find work. Living conditions are crowded, but most homes and apartments have heat, electricity, and running water. Many people now earn enough money to buy extra clothes and television sets. They also have more leisure time to attend concerts or Chinese operas, walk in parks, visit zoos, or talk with friends.

Region
The Arts

China is famous for its traditional arts. Chinese craftworkers make bronze bowls, jade jewelry, glazed pottery, and fine porcelain. The Chinese are also known for their painting, sculpture, and architecture.

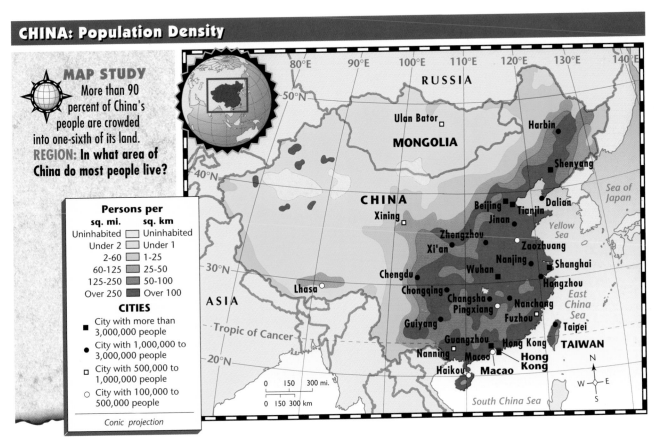

CHINA: Population Density

MAP STUDY More than 90 percent of China's people are crowded into one-sixth of its land. **REGION: In what area of China do most people live?**

Persons per

sq. mi.	sq. km
Uninhabited	Uninhabited
Under 2	Under 1
2–60	1–25
60–125	25–50
125–250	50–100
Over 250	Over 100

CITIES
- ■ City with more than 3,000,000 people
- ● City with 1,000,000 to 3,000,000 people
- □ City with 500,000 to 1,000,000 people
- ○ City with 100,000 to 500,000 people

Conic projection

Art The Chinese love of nature has influenced painting and poetry in China. Chinese artists paint on long panels of paper or silk. Artwork often shows scenes of mountains, rivers, and forests. Artists attempt to portray the harmony between nature and the human spirit.

Many Chinese paintings include a verse or poem written in **calligraphy,** the art of beautiful writing. Chinese writing is different from the print you are reading right now. It uses characters that represent words or ideas instead of sounds. There are more than 50,000 Chinese characters, but the average person recognizes only about 8,000.

Chinese pottery is famous for its painted decoration. The Chinese developed the world's first porcelain centuries ago. Porcelain is made from coal dust and a fine, white clay. Porcelain vases from early Chinese history are considered priceless today.

Architecture Most buildings in Chinese cities are modern in style, but a few traditional buildings stand. Some have large tiled roofs with edges that curve gracefully upward. Others are Buddhist temples with many-storied towers called **pagodas.** Large statues of the Buddha are found in these buildings.

Foods Cooking differs greatly from region to region in China. In coastal areas fish, crab, and shrimp dishes are common, while central China is famous for its spicy dishes. Most Chinese, however, eat very simply. A typical Chinese meal includes vegetables with bits of meat or seafood, soup, and rice or noodles.

Teen Scene

At Home in the Air

Acrobat Choi Hong See has been in training since she was three years old. Her family performs in Shanghai's Acrobatics Theater. She can walk on high wires, do triple somersaults, and balance on a human pyramid. Acrobatics have been popular in China for more than 2,000 years. Many acrobatic groups are supported by the government and are often invited to perform in Europe or the United States.

SECTION 3 ASSESSMENT

REVIEWING TERMS AND FACTS
1. Define the following: dynasty, calligraphy, pagoda.
2. PLACE How was early China governed?
3. MOVEMENT Why have many Chinese moved from the countryside to cities?
4. REGION How is life in urban China different from life in rural China?

MAP STUDY ACTIVITIES
5. Look at the population density map on page 621. Name the cities in the People's Republic of China that have more than 3 million people.

SECTION 4 China's Neighbors

PREVIEW

Words to Know
- empire
- yurt
- high-technology industry

Places to Locate
- Mongolia
- Taiwan
- Hong Kong
- Macao

Read to Learn . . .
1. how people live and earn their livings in Mongolia.
2. what products are made in Taiwan.
3. why Hong Kong is one of the world's busiest ports.

North of China lies Mongolia. If you flew to Mongolia, you would arrive in Ulan Bator (OO•LAHN BAH•TAWR), the capital and largest city. Ulan Bator began as a Buddhist community in the early 1600s. Today it is a modern cultural and industrial center.

The large inland territory of Mongolia and the island of Taiwan are two countries that border or lie close to the People's Republic of China. Throughout their history, the people of these lands have had close ties to China. Mongolia once had a communist government similar to China's. Many of Taiwan's people are Chinese who left the mainland and set up a noncommunist Chinese government on Taiwan. On China's southern coast are two other Chinese territories—Hong Kong and Macao. After years of European rule, Hong Kong and Macao in the late 1990s became part of the People's Republic of China.

Place
Mongolia

Mongolia lies in east central Asia between China and Russia. The map on page 608 shows you that Mongolia is a landlocked country. Its land area of 604,825 square miles (1,566,500 sq. km) is more than twice the size of Texas.

Centuries ago, Mongolia was the home of an Asian people called the Mongols. During the 1200s powerful Mongol armies carved out the largest land empire in history. An **empire** is a collection of territories under one ruler. The

Workers assemble electronic circuit boards in a Taiwan factory.
MOVEMENT: Why do the Republic of China and mainland China have different governments?

Mongol Empire reached from China to eastern Europe. Today Mongolia is smaller in size, but its people still honor their Mongol past.

The Land Rugged mountains and high plateaus cover most of Mongolia. In the southeast, river basins dot the mountainous landscape. The bleak desert landscape of the Gobi spreads through central and southeastern Mongolia. Most of the country receives only small amounts of rain, and temperatures are usually very cold or very hot.

The Economy Mongolia's economy relies on the raising of livestock. Many Mongolians herd sheep, goats, cattle, or camels on grasslands that cover large areas of the country. For centuries the people of Mongolia have been famous for their skills in raising and riding horses. In limited areas, farmers grow wheat, barley, and oats.

The People Nearly all of Mongolia's 2.4 million people are Mongols who speak the Mongol language. About 57 percent of them live in urban areas such as Ulan Bator. Mongolians in the countryside live on farms. A few still follow the nomadic way of their ancestors. These herder-nomads live in **yurts,** or large circle-shaped tents made of animal skins.

Mongolians traditionally followed a form of Buddhism. When Mongolia was under a rigid communist government from 1924 to 1990, however, the Communists discouraged religious practice. Now that Mongolia is independent, people are free to observe their Buddhist beliefs again.

Place
Taiwan

About 100 miles (161 km) off the southeast coast of China lies the island country of Taiwan. In 1949 the Chinese Communists conquered mainland China. The defeated Chinese government of Chiang Kai-shek moved to Taiwan and established the Republic of China. Today Taiwan is still governed separately from the communist-ruled mainland.

The Land Thickly forested mountains run through the center of Taiwan. A flat plain along the western coast is home to most of the island's people. Like southeastern China, Taiwan has a humid subtropical climate of mild winters and hot, rainy summers.

The Economy Taiwan has one of the world's most prosperous economies. Taiwan's wealth rests largely on high-technology industries, manufacturing, and trade with foreign countries. **High-technology industries** produce computers and other kinds of electronic equipment. Taiwanese workers produce many different products, including computers, clothing, furniture, ships, radios, and televisions. You have probably seen goods from Taiwan sold in stores in your community.

Taiwan's mountains limit available farmland. Farmers often terrace hills to provide more land for growing rice. Other crops grown in Taiwan include bananas, citrus fruits, corn, peanuts, sugar, tea, and vegetables.

The People About 75 percent of Taiwan's 21.7 million people live in urban areas. Taipei is the capital and largest city. Skyscrapers and busy streets are major features of Taipei, which has about 2.6 million people.

Taiwan is a modern country, but many of its people still follow Chinese traditions. About 95 percent of the people are Chinese and speak Chinese dialects. Buddhism is the leading religion of Taiwan.

WHAT IN THE WORLD?

Growing Land?
You've heard of growing crops, but have you heard of growing land? Hong Kong has many people, and there is no place to put them all. Therefore, workers are blasting the mountains on Hong Kong's Kowloon Peninsula. They dump the rock and dirt from the blastings onto the shore of the South China Sea—growing new land.

Place
Hong Kong and Macao

Big changes recently occurred in Hong Kong and Macao, which lie on the southeastern coast of China. Both are made up of hilly peninsulas and groups of islands. The United Kingdom ruled Hong Kong until 1997, when it returned to Chinese rule. Another European country—Portugal—governed Macao before the territory became part of China in 1999.

Hong Kong Souvenirs

Busy Port Hong Kong has a land area of about 382 square miles (990 sq. km). Natural harbors make Hong Kong one of the world's busiest ports and a major center of trade and business. It is also one of the world's most crowded places. About 6.7 million people live in Hong Kong. This means that the population density is about 16,383 people per square mile (6,325 per sq. km).

Nearly all the people of Hong Kong are Chinese. They live mostly in urban areas in crowded, high-rise apartments. Others make their homes on boats in harbors. Many of Hong Kong's people work in manufacturing, banking, government, foreign trade, and tourism.

A gift shop in Hong Kong sells souvenirs commemorating the territory's return to China.
PLACE: What country ruled Hong Kong before 1997?

At a Hindu wedding, the bride and groom dress in traditional clothing and sit in front of a sacred fire.
PLACE: How is this wedding different from or similar to the weddings you have attended?

Once A Bit of Portugal About 40 miles (64 km) west of Hong Kong lies the territory of Macao. The map on page 608 shows you that Macao covers about 8 square miles (20 sq. km). It has about 500,000 people, most of whom are Chinese. Most of the territory's food is imported from China. Macao's economy is based on industry, trade, and tourism.

Macao has an interesting mix of Chinese and Portuguese cultures. In the older sections of Macao, you will find Roman Catholic churches and old European-looking houses next to Chinese temples and Chinese-owned shops. Across town high-rise apartments and modern office buildings crowd the skyline. There is much new construction here in response to the political change in 1999.

SECTION 4 ASSESSMENT

REVIEWING TERMS AND FACTS

1. Define the following: empire, yurt, high-technology industry.

2. PLACE What desert area crosses Mongolia?

3. HUMAN/ENVIRONMENT INTERACTION What is the major economic activity of Mongolia?

4. PLACE Where do most of Taiwan's people live?

MAP STUDY ACTIVITIES

5. Look at the climate map on page 611. What is the major climate region of Mongolia?

6. Turn to the physical map on page 610. What body of water touches Taiwan, Hong Kong, and Macao?

Chapter 23 Highlights

Important Things to Know About China

SECTION 1 THE LAND

- China has more people than any other country in the world. It is the world's third-largest country in area, after Russia and Canada.
- Three important rivers—the Huang He, Chang Jiang, and Xi—flow through fertile river valleys in eastern China.
- The western part of China is largely mountains and deserts.
- China's climate is affected by monsoons.

SECTION 2 THE ECONOMY

- Modern China's communist leaders have moved China's economy toward free enterprise.
- Most of China's people are farmers. Rice is the major food crop in the south.
- China's largest urban areas lie near rivers or on the coast.

SECTION 3 THE PEOPLE

- China has one of the world's oldest civilizations.
- The early Chinese passed on many inventions to the rest of the world, including paper, ink, porcelain, and the first printed book.

SECTION 4 CHINA'S NEIGHBORS

- Mongolia has rugged mountains, plateaus, and desert.
- Taiwan has a prosperous economy based on high-technology industries, manufacturing, and trade.
- Hong Kong, once under British rule, became part of China in 1997. Macao, once a Portuguese colony, returned to Chinese rule in 1999.

Tiananmen Square, Beijing ▶

REVIEWING KEY TERMS

Match the numbered terms in Set A with their lettered definitions in Set B.

A

1. loess
2. typhoon
3. dike
4. terraced field
5. tungsten
6. yurt
7. high-technology industry
8. calligraphy

B

A. level strip of land cut out of a hillside
B. the art of beautiful writing
C. tent made of animal skins
D. production of computers and electronic equipment
E. yellow-gray soil deposited by the wind
F. tropical storm with strong winds and heavy rains
G. bank of earth built to prevent floods
H. metal used in electrical equipment

Mental Mapping Activity

Draw a freehand map of China and its neighbors. Label the following:
• Beijing
• Chang Jiang
• Gobi
• Taiwan
• Ulan Bator

REVIEWING THE MAIN IDEAS

Section 1
1. REGION How does China compare in size to other countries?
2. PLACE Why was the Huang He called "China's sorrow"?

Section 2
3. MOVEMENT Why has China made changes in its economy?
4. HUMAN/ENVIRONMENT INTERACTION How has the growth of industry affected China's economy?

Section 3
5. REGION What percent of China's people live in rural areas?
6. PLACE On what ideas did the ancient Chinese base their way of living?

Section 4
7. PLACE What religion is practiced in Mongolia?
8. PLACE Why does Taiwan have limited farmland?
9. PLACE What happened to Macao in 1999?

CRITICAL THINKING ACTIVITIES

1. **Determining Cause and Effect** How have recent changes in China's economy affected the Chinese people?
2. **Drawing Conclusions** How have landscape and climate affected where the Chinese people live?

CONNECTIONS TO WORLD HISTORY

Cooperative Learning Activity Work in a group of three to learn about the flags of China, Mongolia, and Taiwan. Each group will choose the flag of one country, and research the following: (a) flag symbols and their meanings; (b) flag colors and their meanings; or (c) the historical events related to the creation of the flags. Then prepare a group report describing the symbols, colors, and history of the flag.

GeoJournal Writing Activity

Imagine that you are a reporter traveling on one of the major rivers of China. Write a news story about the river and the people who live along it.

TECHNOLOGY ACTIVITY

Using a Computerized Card Catalog Use a computerized card catalog to locate sources of information about the Three Gorges Dam Project on the Chang Jiang in China. Write a report describing its size, how much electricity it generates, and how many villages and people it will ultimately displace. Summarize your report by explaining your opinion about the dam's development.

PLACE LOCATION ACTIVITY: CHINA

Match the letters on the map with the places and physical features of China and its neighbors. Write your answers on a separate sheet of paper.

1. Huang He
2. Mongolia
3. Taklimakan
4. Beijing
5. Hong Kong
6. Taipei
7. Shanghai
8. South China Sea
9. Tian Shan
10. Himalayas

GeoLab ACTIVITY

From the classroom of
Don Mendenhall,
Coleman Junior High,
Van Buren, Arkansas

EROSION: Saving the Soil

Background

Because of the enormous amount of rainfall in many Asian countries, growing crops has become very difficult. Too much rain erodes topsoil and results in the destruction of crops. In this activity, you will try various ways to solve the problem of erosion.

Terraced Fields

Monsoon rains drench Asia every year, bringing much-needed water. But they also cause serious flooding. In 1887 the Huang He overflowed its banks because of heavy rains and the spring thaw. About 1 million people died as a result—the greatest flood disaster in history.

Materials

- 5 aluminum 8- or 9-inch pans
- leaves or grass clippings
- 500-ml beaker
- water
- ruler
- newspaper
- pebbles
- potting soil
- watering can
- dishpan

What To Do

A. Fill each pan almost to the rim with soil. Pat the soil until the surface is firm and flat. Soak the soil by pouring 100 ml of water into each pan.

B. In one pan, cover the surface with a layer of grass clippings or leaves.

C. In the second pan, lay newspaper strips across the surface.

D. In the third pan, build a terrace by forming two small walls of pebbles.

E. In the fourth pan, use your finger to make curved grooves across the surface. This represents contour plowing.

F. Set the fifth pan aside.

G. Now follow this procedure with all five pans:

H. Measure 200 ml of water into the watering can.

I. Hold the pan so that one side dips slightly into the dishpan.

J. Slowly pour the water onto the soil at the top of the pan. Wait until the excess water runs across the soil and into the dishpan. **Note:** Be sure to hold the terracing and contour plowing pans so the water runs across the pebble walls and the grooves.

K. After repeating step J for each pan, pour the water and soil that ends up in the dishpan into the beaker. Measure the amount and record the results. When the soil settles to the bottom, measure and record its height in the beaker.

Lab Activity Report

1. Which pan had the least erosion?

2. Which pan had the most erosion?

3. **Drawing Conclusions** What did you learn about controlling erosion?

Go A Step Further

Activity

Experiment with different types of soils to see if soil composition—as well as soil covering—affects erosion. Mix potting soil with sand, clay, or flour. Which mixture best prevents erosion?

Chapter 24 Japan and the Koreas

MAP STUDY ACTIVITY

As you read Chapter 24, you will learn about Japan and the Koreas.

1. What is the capital of North Korea?
2. What sea lies between Japan and North Korea?
3. What is Japan's capital?

SECTION 1 Japan

PREVIEW

Words to Know
- archipelago
- tsunami
- intensive cultivation
- clan
- samurai
- shogun
- megalopolis

Places to Locate
- Japan
- Tokyo
- Honshu
- Hokkaido
- Kyushu
- Shikoku

Read to Learn . . .
1. where Japan is located.
2. why Japan has a strong economy.
3. what religions influenced the culture of Japan.

On a clear day in Tokyo, Japan, you can see beautiful Mount Fuji. Mount Fuji, Japan's highest peak, is an inactive volcano. During the summer thousands of Japanese make their way to the top of the mountain.

Love of nature is a major part of the Japanese way of life. The sun, the mountains, and the sea have always been important to the people of Japan. The map on page 632 shows you that Japan is an **archipelago,** or a chain of islands. The Japanese islands form a curve off the coast of eastern Asia between the Sea of Japan and the Pacific Ocean. Four main islands make up Japan. They are Hokkaido (hah•KY•doh), Honshu, Shikoku (shih•KOH•koo), and Kyushu (kee•OO•shoo). Thousands of smaller islands are also part of Japan.

Location
The Land

Japan has a land area of 145,370 square miles (376,508 sq. km)—slightly smaller than California. The Japanese islands are the peaks of a great mountain range rising 20,000 to 30,000 feet (6,000 to 9,000 m) from the floor of the Pacific Ocean. They lie in the Ring of Fire—an area surrounding the Pacific Ocean where the earth's crust often shifts. As a result, earthquakes and volcanic eruptions are common in Japan and other parts of the Ring of Fire.

MAP STUDY

Japan is made up of four main islands and thousands of smaller islands.

PLACE: What are the names of Japan's four main islands?

ELEVATIONS

Feet	Meters
10,000	3,000
5,000	1,500
2,000	600
1,000	300
0	0

▲ Mountain peak

Bonne projection

CHINA

RUSSIA

Hokkaido

Yalu R.

Sea of Japan

40°N NORTH KOREA

Taedong R.

Korean Peninsula

Taebaek Sanmaek Mountains

Shinano-Gawa R.

Honshu

Yellow Sea

Han R.

Nakdong R.

SOUTH KOREA

JAPAN

Kanto Plain

Korea Strait

Cheju

Shikoku

Mt. Fuji 12,388 ft. (3,776 m)

N W E S

Kyushu

Inland Sea

PACIFIC OCEAN

140°E

East China Sea

30°N

Ryukyu Islands

130°E

0 150 300 mi.
0 150 300 km

Earthquakes Japan experiences about 5,000 earthquakes a year. Most are minor and cause little damage. But every few years, severe earthquakes shake the land. One of the worst earthquakes took place in 1995, near the port city of Kobe (KOH•bee). Thousands of people died, and damage was estimated at $50 billion to $70 billion. People in Japan and other areas of the Ring of Fire also have to face **tsunamis.** These huge sea waves caused by undersea earthquakes are very destructive along Japan's Pacific coast.

Mountains The physical map above shows you that rugged mountains and steep hills cover most of Japan. Rocky gorges and narrow valleys cut through the mountains. Thick forests grow on the lower slopes. Swift, short rivers flow through the mountains in thundering waterfalls before running to the sea.

Sea and Plains No part of Japan is more than 70 miles (113 km) from the sea. Coastlines are rough and jagged. In bay areas along the coasts, you will find many fine harbors and ports. One of Japan's most important seacoast areas lies along a body of water called the Inland Sea. This sea winds its way among the islands of Honshu, Shikoku, and Kyushu.

Narrowly squeezed between the seacoast and the mountains are the plains areas of Japan. The largest is the Kanto Plain, on the east coast of Honshu where Tokyo and Yokohama are located. You will find most of Japan's cities, farms, and industries in the coastal plains.

UNIT 8

The Climate Ocean and wind currents affect Japan's climate. Look at the map below. You see that climate differs in northern and southern Japan. Hokkaido and northern Honshu have a humid continental climate. Cold ocean and wind currents from the Arctic area and Siberia result in cold winters here. Southern Honshu and the other two major islands have a humid subtropical climate. This climate is caused by a warm current flowing north from the Pacific Ocean.

Human/Environment Interaction
The Economy

Although Japan's land area is relatively small, the country is an economic giant. Japan is one of the world's major industrial powers. It makes use of every resource—people, technology, land, and sea. The Japanese people have one of the highest standards of living in the world.

Farming Farmland in Japan is very limited. Most of Japan's farms are small—about three acres (one ha). Japanese farmers, however, raise about 60 percent of their country's food on privately owned plots of land. How do they do this? Japanese farmers use fertilizers and modern machinery to produce high crop yields. They also practice **intensive cultivation** in which farmers grow crops on

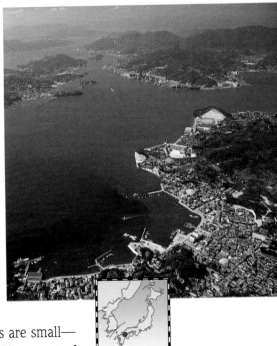
Inland Sea, Japan

The Inland Sea is an important waterway linking the Pacific Ocean and the Sea of Japan.
PLACE: What is a tsunami?

JAPAN AND THE KOREAS: Climate

MAP STUDY
In northern Japan, the winters are cold and snowy.
REGION: What type of climate is found in northern Japan and all of North Korea?

CHINA
RUSSIA
Sapporo
Chongjin
NORTH KOREA
Sea of Japan
40°N
Pyongyang
Yellow Sea
Seoul
SOUTH KOREA
JAPAN
Tokyo
Kobe
Osaka
PACIFIC OCEAN
140°E
East China Sea
30°N

CLIMATE
Mid-Latitude
Humid continental
Humid subtropical
Bonne projection

Ryukyu Islands

0   150   300 mi.
0   150 300 km

130°E

every available piece of land. If you visit Japan, you will see farmers growing rice on terraces cut into the hillsides. You will also see rows of crops growing between buildings and highways. Using these methods, Japanese farmers are able to plant and harvest three crops a year in the warmer regions of the country. They grow rice, wheat, fruit, vegetables, and tea.

The Japanese also rely on the sea for food. People who fish in Japan catch salmon, tuna, and snapper. Huge catches make Japan one of the world's leading fishing countries.

Cars Made in Japan

GRAPHIC STUDY

Japan produces about as many passenger cars as the United States does.
MOVEMENT: By how much did Japanese car production increase between 1965 and 1990?

Millions of cars

| | 1965 | 1970 | 1975 | 1980 | 1985 | 1990 | 1995 |

Year

Source: *The World Almanac, 1998*

Manufacturing Japan is known around the world for the variety and quality of its manufactured goods. It is a leader in manufacturing because of its use of high technology, including robots. Japan produces and exports steel, cars, ships, computers, cameras, televisions, and textiles. The graph above shows you car production in Japan since 1965. You probably own a piece of electronic equipment—TV, camera, or VCR—that was made in Japan or has Japanese parts.

In addition to the latest technology, Japan's economy has benefited from its highly skilled workers. The Japanese people value education, hard work, and cooperation. In recent years, however, Japan's economy has been hard hit by global economic troubles. Some Japanese banks have failed, industrial production has dropped, and an increasing number of Japanese workers have lost their jobs.

636

Trade Japan has limited mineral resources and must import oil, coal, iron ore, and other materials for manufacturing. In return, Japan exports manufactured goods to other countries. The chart on page 648 compares Japan's trade with that of other Asian countries in the Pacific Rim. The term "Pacific Rim" often refers to the economically important Asian countries that border the Pacific Ocean.

Environment Japan's industrial growth has created many environmental challenges. By the 1970s, waste products from factories had polluted the air and water. The Japanese government urged industries to prevent pollution. Today Japan's pollution-control laws are among the strictest in the world. Japan also leads the world in the development of advanced public transportation systems. You can read about Japan's famous bullet trains on page 641.

Movement
Influences of the Past

The heritage of the Japanese people is long and rich. The Japanese trace their ancestry to various **clans,** or groups of related families, that lived and ruled in Japan as early as the late A.D. 400s.

Early Japan The Japanese developed close ties with the Chinese on the Asian mainland. Ruled by emperors, Japan modeled its society on the Chinese way of life. The Japanese also borrowed the Chinese system of writing and accepted the Buddhist religion brought by Chinese missionaries.

Beginning in the 790s, the Japanese emperors' power declined. From the late 1100s to the 1860s, Japan was ruled by the **samurai**—the warrior class—and their leaders—the **shoguns.** Like China, Japan worked to keep out foreign countries that wanted to trade with them. In 1853 the United States government sent a fleet headed by Commodore Matthew Perry to Japan to demand trading privileges. On threat of war, the Japanese opened their country to the rest of the world.

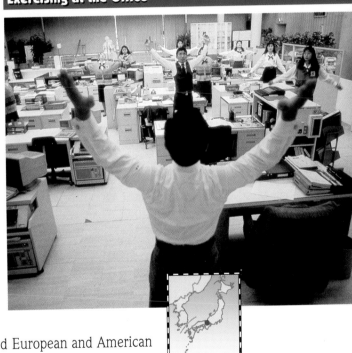
Exercising at the Office

Japanese office workers in Kyoto stand for their morning exercises.
MOVEMENT: How can Japan produce so many goods when it has so few natural resources?

Modern Japan In the late 1800s, Japan began to change into a modern country. Japanese leaders used European and American ideas to improve education and to set up industries. By the early 1900s, Japan had become the world's leading Asian power.

In the 1930s Japan needed more resources for its growing population. It began taking over land in China. In 1941 the Japanese attacked the American naval base at Pearl Harbor in Hawaii and began the Pacific conflict in World War II. The fighting between Japan and the United States and other countries ended in 1945 with Japan's defeat. After the war, many of Japan's cities lay in ruins.

The Japanese economy was near collapse. With help from the United States, Japan became a democracy and rebuilt its economy.

Movement

The People

Although only the size of California, Japan has about one-half the population of the entire United States. Look at the graph below to compare Japan's population of 126.4 million people with that of the United States. About 78 percent of Japan's people are crowded into urban areas on the coastal plains. More than one-third of these city dwellers live in four large cities located on the plains of Honshu. These four cities are Tokyo, Yokohama, Osaka, and Nagoya. They form a **megalopolis,** a huge supercity made up of several large cities and the smaller cities near them.

City Life Japanese cities are very modern. They are crowded with tall office buildings, busy streets, and freeways. Homes are small and close to one another. In the suburbs, you will find small apartment buildings and wooden houses with tiny gardens.

In Japan's cities, the past remains very much a part of urban life. Along the narrow side streets of most cities, small shops sell traditional items. Parks, gardens, and religious shrines are found close to modern neighborhoods. In Tokyo and other cities, it is common to see a person dressed in a traditional garment known as a kimono walking with another person wearing a T-shirt and jeans!

Country Life Only 22 percent of Japan's people live in rural areas. These people generally earn less than city dwellers, but their standard of living has improved in recent years. Most have a small house, a TV, and modern kitchen

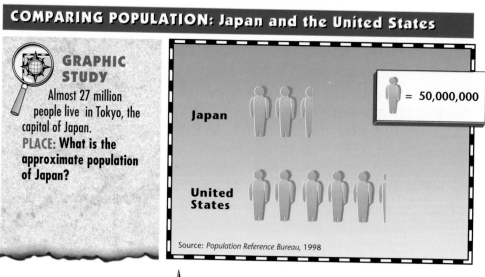

Paper Art
People in Japan make an art—called origami—out of folding paper. From paper they create decorative objects such as animals, fish, or flowers. There are about 100 traditional origami patterns. Each year new patterns are developed.

COMPARING POPULATION: Japan and the United States

GRAPHIC STUDY
Almost 27 million people live in Tokyo, the capital of Japan.
PLACE: What is the approximate population of Japan?

= 50,000,000

Japan

United States

Source: *Population Reference Bureau, 1998*

638

UNIT 8

appliances. In some rural areas, a small farmer might have three jobs. For example, a person might farm one day, fish or cut timber another day, and work occasionally in a factory.

Family Life In traditional Japan the family was the center of one's life. Each family member had to obey certain rules. Grandparents, parents, and children all lived in one house. In recent years much has changed. Family ties remain strong, but each family member is allowed more freedom. Today many Japanese also live in small family groups that consist only of parents and children.

Fifteen-year-old Michiko Wakita lives with her parents and older brother Naohiro in Tokyo. Michiko, like most Japanese teenagers, studies hard six days a week in school. After graduation from high school, she plans to study marine biology at a local university.

Despite Japan's strong emphasis on education, life is not all work for Michiko and other Japanese young people. She enjoys rock music, modern fashions, television, and movies. Her brother Naohiro likes motorcycles and comic books. When Michiko isn't watching game shows on television, Naohiro watches baseball and sumo, a Japanese form of wrestling. Judo is also popular. It is a form of martial arts that developed from ancient Asian fighting skills. Today martial arts are practiced for self-defense and for exercise. They are also very popular in the United States.

Teen Scene

Making the Grade

It's time for exams in Japan, and all eyes are turned toward middle school students. To get into high school, students must take very difficult entrance exams. Kin Toshiro has been studying every day and weekend for months. Exams are the main topic of conversation in his neighborhood and city. Even television shows give advice on how and what to study. After the exam, Kin and his mother will go to his school with hundreds of others to wait for the grades to be posted on the bulletin board. If Kin fails, he will have to go to a "cram school" and take the test again next year.

Place
Culture

Over the centuries the Japanese have developed many customs and art forms to express their delight in nature. They have passed on some of these traditions to the rest of the world. At the same time, the Japanese have accepted cultural practices from foreign countries. Many of Japan's people, for example, enjoy Western movies, hamburgers, and rock music.

Religion Japan has two major religions—Shinto and Buddhism. Shinto began in Japan centuries ago. It teaches a respect for nature, a love of simple things, and a concern for cleanliness and good manners. Buddhism came to Japan from China. It teaches respect for nature and the need for inner peace. Many Japanese practice both religions.

The people of Japan love baseball *(left)*. A colorful float used for puppet shows is part of a festival parade in Japan *(right)*. **PLACE: What are some other popular pastimes in Japan?**

The Arts You may sense a peaceful feeling of nature in Japanese painting, music, dance, and literature. Many paintings show scenes of the countryside and include verses in calligraphy. The Japanese enjoy traditional and modern forms of drama. Since the 1600s Japanese theatergoers have attended the historical plays of the Kabuki theater. Kabuki plays are set on colorful stages with actors wearing brilliantly colored costumes.

Japanese literature includes poetry and novels. Many scholars believe that the world's first novel came from Japan. This novel is called *The Tale of Genji* and was written by a noblewoman of the emperor's court about A.D. 1000. Haiku (HY•koo) is a well-known type of Japanese poetry that is written according to a very specific formula. A haiku has only 3 lines and 17 syllables.

SECTION 1 ASSESSMENT

REVIEWING TERMS AND FACTS

1. Define the following: archipelago, tsunami, intensive cultivation, clan, samurai, shogun, megalopolis.

2. PLACE What is the major landform of Japan?

3. HUMAN/ENVIRONMENT INTERACTION What are the main economic activities that take place in Japan?

4. MOVEMENT Where do most Japanese live?

MAP STUDY ACTIVITIES

5. Look at the physical map on page 634. About how many miles is Japan from north to south?

6. Study the climate map on page 635. What are Japan's two climate regions?

JAPANESE BULLET TRAINS

| MATH | SCIENCE | HISTORY | LITERATURE | TECHNOLOGY |

What travels almost as fast as a speeding bullet? Japan's famous bullet trains first whizzed across the Japanese countryside in 1964. The trains completely changed ground travel in Japan. They also became the model for public transport vehicles in other densely populated countries.

Speeding Along

FROM TOKYO TO OSAKA The first blue-and-ivory bullet-nosed train raced at 125 miles per hour (242 km per hour) between Tokyo and Osaka. These two cities lie 320 miles (515 km) apart. The new train gained instant popularity. The number of people riding the train daily grew by 300 percent during its first five years.

THE BULLETS INCREASE The bullet train became the first Japanese train to run at a profit. It was so successful that other trains were built in different parts of Japan. About 260 bullet trains run daily now, covering a distance equal to circling the earth three times. Lines stretch from Tokyo to cities north and south. Eventually a bullet train will run under the sea through a tunnel to Hokkaido, the northernmost Japanese island.

MEETING CHALLENGES The bullet trains carry 400,000 passengers every day—135 million each year—at speeds up to 170 miles per hour (274 km per hour). They have a 99 percent on-time record, and have never had a fatality.

The trains help the Japanese successfully overcome several challenges. They streamline transportation in tiny, crowded Japan. Most Japanese now prefer the comfort and speed of the trains to cars. As a result, the popular trains help to keep Japan's overseas oil purchases under control.

Making the Connection

1. How fast and how far do bullet trains travel daily?
2. What problems in Japan do the bullet trains help solve?

The Two Koreas

PREVIEW

Words to Know
- anthracite

Places to Locate
- North Korea
- South Korea
- Seoul
- Pyongyang

Read to Learn . . .
1. where the Korean Peninsula is located.
2. why the Koreas are divided.
3. how life in South Korea differs from life in North Korea.

Forests—often shrouded in mist—cover much of Korea. You feel a sense of peace and calm as you look at the mountainous Korean landscape. Because of its geography, Korea was once known as "land of the morning calm."

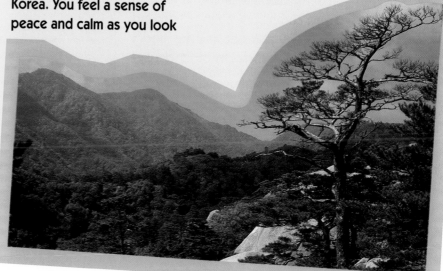

In modern times Korea has been anything but calm. Today it is divided into two nations—communist North Korea and noncommunist South Korea. The two governments of Korea are bitter enemies, although efforts are being made to bring them together.

Region
A Divided Country

Although Korea is now divided, it has a long history as a united country. The land of Korea lies on the Korean Peninsula. This peninsula juts out from northern China, between the Sea of Japan and the Yellow Sea.

The Korean Past The Koreans trace their ancestry to people who settled the Korean Peninsula thousands of years ago. From A.D. 668 to 935, a Korean kingdom called Silla united much of the peninsula for the first time under one government. Under Silla rulers, Korea enjoyed a period of cultural and scientific advances. For example, the Koreans built one of the world's earliest astronomical observatories in the A.D. 600s.

For centuries the Korean Peninsula was a bridge between Japan and the mainland of Asia. Trade and ideas went back and forth. China and Japan, however, wanted to control Korea. China ruled part of Korea from the 100s B.C. until the early A.D. 300s. Japan later governed Korea from 1910 until the end of World War II in 1945.

Division of Korea After Japan's defeat in World War II, troops from the communist Soviet Union took over the northern half of Korea. American troops occupied the southern half. Korea eventually divided along the 38th parallel. A noncommunist government ruled in what became South Korea, while a communist government governed what became North Korea.

The Korean War In 1950 North Korean armies attacked South Korea. Their plan was to bring all of Korea under communist rule—a plan that led to the Korean War. Noncommunist United Nations countries, led by the United States, rushed to aid South Korea. China's communist leaders eventually sent troops to help North Korea. The fighting finally ended in 1953—without a peace treaty or a victory for either side. By the 1960s, two separate countries with their own ways of life had developed in the Korean Peninsula. Today the United States continues to encourage peaceful relations between the two Koreas.

JAPAN AND THE KOREAS: Land Use and Resources

MAP STUDY Although North Korea has many resources, South Korea's economy is more developed. **PLACE: What North Korean resources are shown here?**

CHINA RUSSIA

Sapporo

NORTH KOREA Chongjin

Pyongyang Hungnam

Sea of Japan

40°N

Wonsan

Niigata

Yellow Sea

Seoul SOUTH KOREA

JAPAN

Taegu Kanazawa Tokyo
Shimizu

Pusan Kobe Nagoya
Okayama Osaka

Kure

Omuta PACIFIC OCEAN 140°E

East China Sea

30°N

Agriculture
☐ Little or no farming
▨ Commercial farming
■ Manufacturing area

Resources
⛏ Coal
🐟 Fish & other seafood
⚡ Hydroelectric power
⚙ Lead
▨ Tungsten
▫ Zinc

130°E

0   150   300 mi.
0   150   300 km

Bonne projection

South Korea's modern capital city is home to almost one-fourth of its people.
PLACE: What are some of South Korea's most important exports?

Place
South Korea

South Korea lies at the southern end of the Korean Peninsula. About 38,120 square miles (98,731 sq. km) in area, South Korea is slightly larger than Indiana. The Taebaek Sanmaek Mountains cover most of central and eastern South Korea. Plains with hills and fertile river valleys spread along the southern and western coasts. Most South Koreans live in these coastal areas.

The Climate South Korea has a climate affected by monsoons. As a result, fierce winds and heavy rains are common to South Koreans. During the summer, a monsoon from the south brings hot, humid weather. In winter, a monsoon blows in from the north, bringing cold weather.

The Economy South Korea's mineral resources include iron ore, tungsten, and **anthracite**, a hard coal. During the 1980s, South Korea had a strong industrial economy. Manufacturing, high-technology, and service industries grew tremendously. Many of these privately run companies made products for overseas markets. Today South Korea is still a major exporter of ships, cars, textiles, and computers. However, mismanagement in key banks and businesses has weakened its industrial performance.

Agriculture also plays an important role in South Korea's economy. South Korean farmers own their land. Most of their farms are very small—about 2.7 acres (1.1 ha) in size. The major crops are rice, apples, barley, Chinese cabbage, onions, and potatoes. Many farmers add to their income by fishing. The map on page 643 shows you that South Korea, like Japan, is a major fishing country.

The People The people of the two Koreas belong to the same Korean ethnic group. South Korea has a population of 47 million people. About 79 percent of South Koreans live in cities and towns in the coastal plains. Since the mid-1950s, South Korea's capital of Seoul has grown into a busy, modern city of more than 11 million people.

Most people in South Korea's cities live in tall apartment buildings and modern homes. Many own cars, but they also rely on buses, subways, and trains to get from one place to another. In rural areas many people live in small, one-story houses made of bricks or concrete blocks. Some rural dwellers still follow traditional ways. A large number of South Koreans have also emigrated to the United States since the end of the Korean War.

Religion and the Arts South Koreans enjoy freedom of religion. Although most practice Buddhism or the teachings of Confucius, some are Christians. The traditional arts of Korea were influenced by Chinese religion and culture. The Koreans, however, have developed their own culture. The most widely practiced art forms are music, poetry, pottery, sculpture, and painting.

If you visit South Korea, you can see examples of traditional Korean art and architecture. In Seoul stand ancient palaces that were modeled after the Imperial Palace in Beijing, China. Ancient Buddhist temples dot the hills and valleys of the Korean countryside. Within these temples are beautifully sculpted figures of the Buddha in stone, iron, and gold. One of the great achievements of early Koreans was well-crafted pottery. Even today, Korean potters still make bowls and dishes that are admired throughout the world.

Towering Buddha

Statues of the Buddha are common sights at temples in South Korea.
MOVEMENT: What two neighboring countries have had a major influence on the history and culture of Korea?

Place
North Korea

Communist North Korea lies at the northern end of the Korean Peninsula. Slightly larger than South Korea, North Korea covers 46,490 square miles (120,409 sq. km). Rugged mountains run through the center of North Korea. A group of narrow valleys separate these ranges. Plains and lowlands run along the western and eastern coasts.

The Climate Monsoons also affect climate in North Korea. Most of North Korea has hot summers and cold, snowy winters. Because the central mountains block the full effects of the winter monsoon, the east coast generally has warmer winters than the rest of the country.

The Economy Like South Korea, North Korea has an industrial economy. With more minerals than the south, the northern part of the peninsula was the major industrial area for many years. The map on page 643 shows you that North Korea has minerals such as anthracite, tungsten, and zinc. After the 1950s, however, South Korea surpassed North Korea in industrial growth because of its dynamic, free enterprise economy.

In North Korea the communist government owns and runs factories, businesses, and farms. Under the government's direction, North Korean industrial workers produce chemicals, iron and steel, machinery, and textiles. Most farmers work on government-run farms, where they raise livestock and grow rice and vegetables. Rice is the basic food item. A popular Korean side dish is *kimchi*, a spicy blend of Chinese cabbage, onions, and other vegetables.

The People North Korea has about 22.2 million people. About 59 percent of the population live in urban areas along the coasts and river valleys. Pyongyang is North Korea's capital and largest city. Largely rebuilt since the Korean War, Pyongyang has many modern buildings and monuments to communist leaders.

JAPAN AND THE KOREAS: Population Density

MAP STUDY
About one-half of Japan's people are crowded into a 320-mile stretch of land on the island of Honshu.
PLACE: What are the most densely populated areas of the Koreas?

Persons per

sq. mi.	sq. km
2-60	1-25
60-125	25-50
125-250	50-100
Over 250	Over 100

CITIES

- City with more than 3,000,000 people
- City with 1,000,000 to 3,000,000 people
- City with 500,000 to 1,000,000 people
- City with 100,000 to 500,000 people

Bonne projection

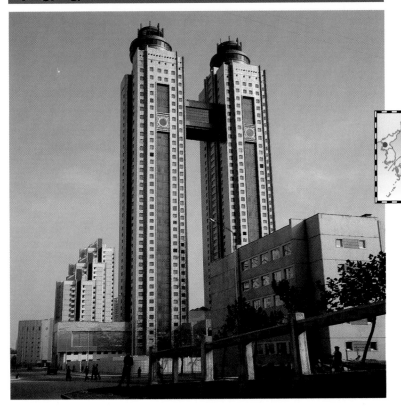

A modern hotel is surrounded by office buildings and apartments in North Korea's capital. **PLACE: Before Korea was divided, why was most industry located in North Korea?**

Under communist rule North Koreans have had to put aside much of their traditional culture in favor of communist ways. For example, the government discourages the practice of religion, although many people still hold on to their beliefs. The government also places the needs of the communist system over the needs of individuals or families. During the 1990s North Korea's government and economy became unstable. Longtime leader Kim Il Sung died in 1994. His son Kim Jong Il succeeded him after a power struggle. By the late 1990s, crop failures resulted in severe food shortages for many North Koreans.

SECTION 2 ASSESSMENT

REVIEWING TERMS AND FACTS

1. Define the following: anthracite.

2. LOCATION What body of water borders Korea on the east?

3. MOVEMENT How did Korea's location on a peninsula affect its history?

4. HUMAN/ENVIRONMENT INTERACTION What farm products are grown in South Korea?

MAP STUDY ACTIVITIES

5. Look at the land use map on page 643. What are three of South Korea's large manufacturing areas?

6. Turn to the population density map on page 646. What are the two most densely populated South Korean cities shown?

BUILDING GEOGRAPHY SKILLS

Using a Map and a Graph

A map and a graph both show you a picture. They can show geographic information but in different ways. Maps show locations, while graphs display information—usually data in numbers—about those locations. Comparing maps and graphs can help you understand more about a location. Comparing also helps show relationships between locations. In using a map and a graph, apply these steps:

- Read the map/graph title to see how the two are related.

- On the map, locate places included in the graph.

- Use information on the graph to draw conclusions about the places on the map. Use the map to help explain the information on the graph.

Glencoe's **Skillbuilder Interactive Workbook, Level 1** provides instruction and practice in key social studies skills.

ASIA'S PACIFIC RIM

Source: *World Almanac, 1998*

Geography Skills Practice

1. How are the map and the graph related?

2. Which country shown on the map and listed on the graph has the largest land area?

3. Which country has the most exports and imports?

4. How does the physical geography of this region explain the trading activity shown on the graph?

648

Important Things to Know About Japan and the Koreas

SECTION 1 JAPAN

- Japan is made up of four main islands and thousands of smaller islands.
- Japan lies on the Pacific Ring of Fire and experiences many earthquakes.
- Japan's strong economy is based on manufacturing and trade.
- Japan—a densely crowded country—holds a population almost half the size of that of the United States.
- The Japanese follow modern ways of life but keep many of their traditions.
- The religions of Shinto and Buddhism have influenced the Japanese arts.

SECTION 2 THE TWO KOREAS

- The Korean Peninsula is divided between communist North Korea and noncommunist South Korea.
- After World War II, communist troops from the Soviet Union took over the northern half of Korea. American troops occupied the southern half. Korea eventually divided along the 38th parallel.
- Both Koreas have inland mountains and coastal plains.
- Monsoon winds affect the climate of the Koreas, bringing hot weather in the summer and cold weather in winter.
- South Korea has a free enterprise economy that exports many industrial goods to other countries.
- A communist government controls North Korea's economy.
- South Korea has about 46.4 million people; North Korea, about 22.2 million.
- Most South Koreans practice Buddhism or the teachings of Confucius. Under communism, North Koreans are discouraged from practicing religion.

Tokyo, Japan ▶

REVIEWING KEY TERMS

Match the numbered terms in Set A with their lettered definitions in Set B.

A

1. megalopolis
2. anthracite
3. shogun
4. samurai
5. intensive cultivation
6. archipelago
7. tsunami

B

A. an urban area made up of several large cities
B. the warrior class of early Japan
C. huge sea wave created by an undersea earthquake
D. farming nearly every area of land
E. a group of islands
F. hard coal
G. Japanese military leader

Mental Mapping Activity

Draw a freehand map of Japan and the two Koreas. Label the following:

- Honshu
- North Korea
- Pacific Ocean
- Kyushu
- Kobe
- Tokyo

REVIEWING THE MAIN IDEAS

Section 1

1. **REGION** What is the Ring of Fire?
2. **PLACE** Why does Hokkaido have cold winters?
3. **HUMAN/ENVIRONMENT INTERACTION** Why are Japanese farmers able to produce high crop yields?
4. **HUMAN/ENVIRONMENT INTERACTION** How has Japan tried to improve its environment?
5. **PLACE** What do the religions of Shinto and Buddhism teach?

Section 2

6. **REGION** Why was Korea divided after World War II?
7. **REGION** How do monsoons affect climate in the two Koreas?
8. **PLACE** What is South Korea's capital and largest city?
9. **LOCATION** Where is most mineral wealth on the Korean Peninsula found?
10. **PLACE** How many North Koreans live in urban areas?

CRITICAL THINKING ACTIVITIES

1. **Drawing Conclusions** Do you think other countries would want to model their economies after Japan's economy? Explain.
2. **Making Comparisons** How do ways of life differ in North Korea and South Korea?

CONNECTIONS TO ECONOMICS

Cooperative Learning Activity The United States is an important trading partner of Japan and South Korea. Work in groups to find out what products from Japan and South Korea the members of your group use. Look at home and school for products made in these two countries. Make a list of the products and where they were made. As a group, prepare a list of your findings and share the list with the class.

GeoJournal Writing Activity

A haiku is a three-line poem, usually about nature and human emotions. The traditional haiku requires 17 syllables—5 in the first line, 7 in the second line, and 5 in the third line. In your journal, write your own haiku in which you poetically sketch a scene from nature, such as a snowfall or a sunrise.

TECHNOLOGY ACTIVITY

Building a Database Collect information about North Korea and South Korea. Organize your findings in a database comparing the two countries. Include information about population, major imports and exports, literacy rate, birthrate, death rate, and life expectancy. Use your database to write a paragraph that summarizes the differences and similarities between the two Koreas.

PLACE LOCATION ACTIVITY: JAPAN AND THE TWO KOREAS

Match the letters on the map with the places and physical features of Japan and the two Koreas. Write your answers on a separate sheet of paper.

1. Seoul
2. Honshu
3. Taebaek Sanmaek Mountains
4. Hokkaido
5. East China Sea
6. Inland Sea
7. Sapporo
8. Tokyo
9. Pyongyang
10. Sea of Japan

Cultural HERITAGE:
ASIA

MUSIC ▶ ▶ ▶ ▶

The music of India is played mostly on guitarlike stringed instruments and drums. Ancient melodies, called *ragas,* sound very different from Western music because they use a different scale.

ARTIFACTS ▲ ▲ ▲ ▲

This tiny stone carving was one of many discovered at Mohenjo-Daro in the Indus River valley. At least 4,000 years old, it was probably used by traders as a stamp or seal to mark their merchandise.

ARCHITECTURE ▶ ▶ ▶ ▶

Buddhist pagodas can be found throughout southern Asia. Most pagodas are eight-sided with an odd number of stories. Each story has an umbrella-shaped roof made of tiles.

652

Actors with wigs, painted faces, and elaborate costumes perform in Japan's popular Kabuki theaters. Kabuki performers act out historic events or real-life experiences in a lively, dramatic way. All Kabuki actors are men who begin their training at a very young age.

ISLAMIC ARCHITECTURE ▶ ▶ ▶ ▶

The magnificent Taj Mahal was built by an Indian ruler in the 1600s as a tomb and monument to his beloved wife. The white marble dome and minarets reflect the Islamic influence in India at the time. It took 20,000 laborers almost 20 years to complete this elaborate structure.

◄ ◄ ◄ ◄ DECORATIVE ART

These colorful, hand-painted umbrellas are an art form in Thailand. The umbrellas are made from paper and bamboo and decorated with colorful flowers, dragons, and birds.

APPRECIATING CULTURE

1. Compare and contrast the architecture of the Taj Mahal and the Buddhist pagoda.

2. The animal seal from Mohenjo-Daro was probably used as a stamp or trademark to indicate ownership of goods. Design your own personal trademark.

SOUTHEAST ASIA: Political

ASIA

100°E   110°E   120°E   130°E

Tropic of Cancer

Mandalay
MYANMAR   Hanoi
Chiang Mai   LAOS
        Vientiane   South China Sea
Yangon
THAILAND   Da Nang   20°N
Bangkok   VIETNAM   Philippine Sea
CAMBODIA   Quezon City
Phnom Penh   Manila   PACIFIC OCEAN
        Ho Chi Minh City   PHILIPPINES
            Iloilo   Cebu
Pinang   Zamboanga   Davao   10°N
Medan   BRUNEI
    Kuala Lumpur   Bandar Seri Begawan
    MALAYSIA   Celebes Sea
Singapore
Equator   SINGAPORE   0°
        Pontianak
INDIAN OCEAN   Palembang   INDONESIA
        Java Sea
    Jakarta   Surabaya

— National boundary
✪ National capital
● Other city
Mercator projection

0   250   500 mi.
0   250   500 km

MAP STUDY ACTIVITY

As you read Chapter 25, you will learn about Southeast Asia.

1. What countries in Southeast Asia border China?
2. What Southeast Asian countries are made up of islands?
3. What three countries share one island?

Mainland Southeast Asia

PREVIEW

Words to Know
- alluvial plain
- deforestation
- delta

Places to Locate
- Myanmar
- Thailand
- Laos
- Cambodia
- Vietnam
- Bangkok
- Mekong River

Read to Learn . . .
1. what countries make up mainland Southeast Asia.
2. what minerals are found in mainland Southeast Asia.
3. why the economies of Laos, Cambodia, and Vietnam are not fully developed.

Myanmar, a country in Southeast Asia. You would see that many village homes are built on poles. Homes are built this way to protect the occupants from floods and wild animals.

Imagine visiting a village deep in the forests of

South of China and east of India lies a region known as Southeast Asia. The peninsulas and thousands of islands that make up this region cover an area of about 1,750,000 square miles (4,536,000 sq. km). Including its seas, Southeast Asia spreads over an area as big as the contiguous United States. On the peninsulas of mainland Southeast Asia, you will find the countries of Myanmar, Thailand, Laos, Cambodia, Vietnam, and part of Malaysia.

Location
Myanmar

Southeast Asia's northernmost country is Myanmar. Once called Burma, Myanmar for many years was part of British India. It became an independent republic in 1948. Since independence, military leaders have turned Myanmar into a socialist country. The government runs the economy and forbids any criticism of its policies. It also limits Myanmar's contacts with the outside world.

The Land and Economy Myanmar's 253,880 square miles (657,549 sq. km) make it about the size of Texas. Rugged mountains run through the eastern

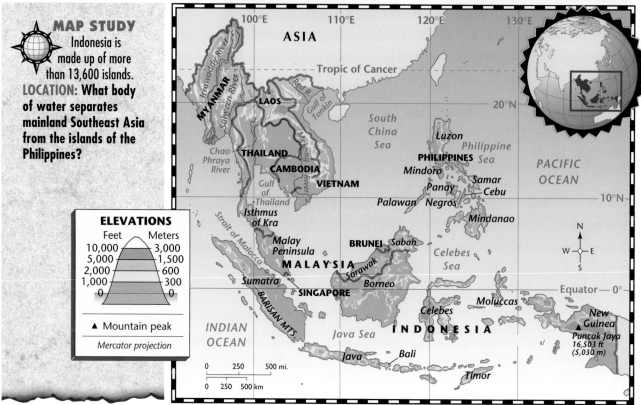

MAP STUDY
Indonesia is made up of more than 13,600 islands.
LOCATION: What body of water separates mainland Southeast Asia from the islands of the Philippines?

ELEVATIONS

Feet	Meters
10,000	3,000
5,000	1,500
2,000	600
1,000	300
0	0

▲ Mountain peak

Mercator projection

and western parts of the country. Between the mountain ranges flow two major rivers—the Irrawaddy (IHR•uh•WAH•dee) and the Salween. The land along these rivers contains Myanmar's most fertile soil.

Southern Myanmar has tropical climates. Monsoon winds from the Indian Ocean bring rain during Myanmar's summers. Dry monsoons from the north occur during winter. As is typical in high elevations, temperatures are cooler in Myanmar's northern mountains.

Myanmar's economy is based on farming. Rice is the major food crop. Some farmers work their fields with tractors, but most rely on plows drawn by water buffalo. Forests cover large areas of Myanmar and provide about 80 percent of the world's teakwood. Mines yield minerals such as tin, copper, and tungsten. Gemstones—rubies, sapphires, and jade—also come from Myanmar.

The People About 75 percent of Myanmar's 47.1 million people live in small villages. They build their homes on poles above the ground to protect themselves from floods and wild animals. The most densely populated area of the country is the fertile Irrawaddy River valley.

Many rural people in Myanmar follow traditional ways. In cities you will notice a blend of old and new. The capital and largest city, Yangon, is famous for both its modern university and its gold-covered Buddhist temples. Buddhism is the major religion of Myanmar.

Thailand

Southeast of Myanmar lies Thailand. The map on page 654 shows you that Thailand looks like a flower on a stem. The "flower" is the northern part of Thailand, located on the mainland. The "stem" is a very narrow strip of Thailand that runs southward to the Malay Peninsula.

Once called Siam, Thailand means "land of the free." It is the only Southeast Asian country that has never been a European colony. The people of Thailand have skillfully blended modern ways with traditional practices and a loyalty to Thailand's royal family.

The Land and Economy Mountains, plateaus, and river valleys spread through northern Thailand. In the central part of the country, the Chao Phraya (chow•PRY•uh) River has formed a large alluvial plain. An **alluvial plain** is a land area built up by a river's soil deposits.

Because of its fertile soil, central Thailand has most of the country's people, farms, and industries. Farther south the thin strip of Thailand along the Malay Peninsula boasts thick forests, rubber trees, and mineral wealth.

The map below shows you that Thailand has tropical and subtropical climates. Monsoon winds bring dry and wet seasons. Rainfall is heaviest in the south and southeast. Thailand is an agricultural country. Thai farmers grow rice

SOUTHEAST ASIA: Climate

MAP STUDY
Most of Southeast Asia has a hot, humid, and rainy climate.
PLACE: What countries on mainland Southeast Asia have a mid-latitude climate?

CLIMATE
Tropical
- Tropical rain forest
- Tropical savanna
Mid-Latitude
- Humid subtropical
- Highland

Mercator projection

0   250   500 mi.
0   250 500 km

Traffic on the crowded streets of Thailand's capital has created an air pollution problem. **HUMAN/ENVIRONMENT INTERACTION: What percentage of Thailand's people live in cities?**

as their major crop. Plantations in the south provide rubber for export. Teak and other wood products come from Thailand's forests. In recent years developers have cut down so many forests that many Thai people fear the complete loss of one of their country's most valuable resources. The government now tries to limit **deforestation,** or the widespread cutting of trees.

Thailand is rich in mineral resources. It is one of the world's leading exporters of tin and gemstones. Most of Thailand's manufacturing is located around Bangkok, the capital and largest city. Thai workers there produce textiles, cement, and paper products.

The People Most of Thailand's 61.1 million people belong to the Thai ethnic group and follow the Buddhist religion. Hundreds of Buddhist temples called *wats* dot cities and the countryside. Bangkok alone has more than 300 Buddhist temples! Every morning Buddhist monks, or holy men, carrying small bowls and wearing yellow-orange robes walk among the people to receive food offerings. Buddhism inspires many Thai festivals celebrated with parades and colorful flowers.

About 70 percent of Thailand's people live in rural villages. Bangkok, however, is growing rapidly as more and more people move into the city from rural areas. Today Bangkok has about 6.5 million people. Thirteen-year-old Chuan Soonsiri notices the contrasts of life in Bangkok. He points out beautiful Buddhist temples and royal palaces next to modern skyscrapers and crowded streets filled with cars and people. Although he worries about the air pollution that gets worse every year, Chuan is proud to see dancers in elaborate costumes perform traditional Thai dances. He also enjoys Thai boxing, in which the boxers use both their hands and feet to fight.

Place
Laos

Laos lies north of Thailand in the center of mainland Southeast Asia. Once a French colony, Laos became independent in 1953. A civil war soon tore Laos apart, and a communist government finally came to power in 1975. In the late 1980s the government relaxed some of its rigid policies and opened Laos to the outside world.

The Land and Economy The only landlocked country in Southeast Asia, Laos is covered by rugged mountains. Because of the cooling effect of the mountains, Laos has a humid subtropical climate. Southern Laos includes a fertile farming area along the Mekong (MAY•KAWNG) River. Southeast Asia's longest river, the Mekong provides landlocked Laos with access to the ocean. It flows about 2,600 miles (4,180 km) before emptying into the South China Sea.

Laos's communist government runs the country's economy, which is mostly agricultural. Farmers grow fruits, vegetables, and rice along the fertile banks of the Mekong River. Industry is still largely undeveloped because of isolation and years of civil war.

The People About 80 percent of Laos's 5.3 million people live in villages and towns along the Mekong River. You find Vientiane (vyehn•TYAHN), the largest city and capital, near the river. The communist government discourages religion, but most of Laos's people remain Buddhists.

Place
Cambodia

South of Thailand and Laos is Cambodia. About 1,000 years ago, Cambodia was the center of a large empire that ruled much of Southeast Asia. Today you can still see the remains of Angkor, the ancient empire's capital. In modern times Cambodia was under French rule, finally becoming independent in 1953.

Cambodians have faced almost constant warfare since the 1960s. A communist government took control of the country in the mid-1970s, and the people suffered great hardships. More than 1 million Cambodians died. Many fled overseas to the United States and other countries. Since the mid-1990s political disputes have divided the country.

The Land and Economy Low mountains, lakes, and forested plains stretch across Cambodia. The Mekong River and a number of smaller rivers crisscross the country, providing water, fertile soil, and waterways for transportation. The map on page 657 shows you that Cambodia has tropical climates.

For many years Cambodia was a rich farming country that exported rice and rubber. By the 1980s its economy was in ruins because of war and harsh communist rule. Today the government is trying to rebuild the economy. Rice and soybeans are the major crops.

The People Most of Cambodia's 10.8 million people belong to the Khmer (kuh•MEHR) ethnic group. They live in rural villages and farm the land. Only about 14 percent live in cities such as the capital, Phnom Penh (NAHM PEHN). Buddhism is the major religion of Cambodia.

Teen Scene

Happy New Year!

In Thailand the New Year is celebrated in April, one of the hottest months of the year. Vina Charas and her sister Uma look forward to the celebration. This year they will be in their village parade. After the parade, the fun begins. On New Year's Day, people drench anyone and everyone with buckets of water. The tradition started many years ago by people hoping for rain for the crops. Young people splash anyone who comes near. "No one seems to mind because it's so hot!" Vina says.

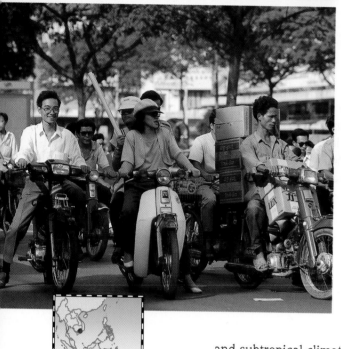

Ho Chi Minh City, Vietnam

Rush-hour traffic in Vietnam's largest city means curb-to-curb mopeds.
PLACE: What is the capital of Vietnam?

Place
Vietnam

Vietnam lies along the east coast of mainland Southeast Asia. A few decades ago, Americans talked about Vietnam every day. United States forces were fighting a war there. Today Vietnam is a communist country, but its leaders are opening Vietnam to Western ideas and practices.

The Land and Economy Vietnam has a long coastline bordering the South China Sea and the Gulf of Thailand. Rugged mountains and high plateaus cover most of Vietnam. The rest of the country is made up of coastal lowlands and river deltas. A **delta** is an area of land formed by soil deposits at the mouth of a river. Two important river deltas lie at opposite ends of Vietnam. One is the Red River delta in the north; the other is the Mekong River delta in the south. Vietnam has tropical and subtropical climates. Monsoons bring wet and dry seasons.

Vietnam's communist government runs the economy. But it has reduced controls since the late 1980s. Coal, zinc, and other mineral resources are plentiful in north and central Vietnam. Most of Vietnam's industries are located there. Years of warfare have kept Vietnam's industries from fully developing. The country is rich in fertile soil, and agriculture is the major economic activity.

The People About 85 percent of Vietnam's 78.5 million people belong to the Vietnamese ethnic group. The rest are Chinese, Cambodians, and other Asian ethnic groups. Most Vietnamese are crowded along the coasts and river deltas. The largest cities are Ho Chi Minh (HOH chee MIHN) City in the Mekong delta, and Hanoi, the capital, in the north. The most widespread religion is Buddhism.

SECTION 1 ASSESSMENT

REVIEWING TERMS AND FACTS
1. Define the following: alluvial plain, deforestation, delta.
2. LOCATION Where is Myanmar located?
3. REGION How do monsoons affect climate in mainland Southeast Asia?
4. PLACE What major food crop is grown in mainland Southeast Asia?

MAP STUDY ACTIVITIES
5. Look at the physical map on page 656. What river flows through Cambodia?
6. Study the map on page 657. What are the major climates of mainland Southeast Asia?

BUILDING GEOGRAPHY SKILLS

Reading a Contour Map

Hills and valleys have highs and lows. How do you show this on a flat map? One way is with a contour map. Contour maps use lines, called *isolines,* to outline the shape—or contour—of the landscape. Each isoline connects all points that are at the same elevation. If you walked along one isoline, you would always be at the same height above sea level.

Where isolines are far apart, the land rises gradually. Where they are close together, the land rises steeply. To read a contour map, follow these steps:

- Name the area shown on the map.
- Read the numbers on the isolines to find out how much the elevation increases with each line.
- Identify areas of steep and level terrain.

Glencoe's **Skillbuilder Interactive Workbook, Level 1** provides instruction and practice in key social studies skills.

BORNEO: Contour Map

South China Sea

Borneo

Celebes Sea

Contour intervals in meters

Mercator projection

Equator

Geography Skills Practice

1. What area of Southeast Asia is shown on the map?

2. What elevations are shown by the isolines?

Island Southeast Asia

Words to Know
- cassava
- free port
- abaca

Places to Locate
- Indonesia
- Malaysia
- Singapore
- Brunei
- Philippines
- Jakarta
- Manila
- Java

Read to Learn . . .
1. what groups of people live in island Southeast Asia.
2. why people in Malaysia, Singapore, and Brunei have high standards of living.

This volcano is part of a chain on the island of Java, one of thousands of islands that make up the country of Indonesia. The islands of Southeast Asia lie along the Pacific Ocean's Ring of Fire. People living here constantly face the threat of volcanic activity and earthquakes.

Indonesia, Malaysia, Singapore, Brunei (bru•NY), and the Philippines are the island countries of Southeast Asia. The map on page 656 shows you that these countries lie either wholly or partly on islands.

Location

Indonesia

Indonesia is Southeast Asia's largest country. Its 705,190 square miles (1,826,443 sq. km) consist of an archipelago of more than 13,600 islands. Look at the map on page 656 and find the major islands of Indonesia: Sumatra, Java, Celebes (SEH•luh•BEEZ), and the western part of the island of New Guinea.

The Land and Economy Mountains tower over much of Indonesia. Many of these mountains are active or inactive volcanoes. Volcanic ash provides farmers with fertile soil, and thick forests spread over much of the islands.

Because Indonesia lies on or near the Equator, its climate is tropical. Monsoons blow across the islands, bringing a wet season and a dry season. Indonesia's major economic activities are farming, mining, and manufacturing. Indonesian farmers grow rice, coffee, spices, and **cassava,** a plant root used in making flour. Forests supply teak and other hardwoods. Indonesia also mines tin, petroleum, nickel, and other minerals. The graph below shows that Indonesia is one of the world's leading producers of tin.

Low labor costs attract manufacturing and processing industries to Indonesia from all over the world. You find most of Indonesia's industries on the island of Java. Factories there churn out steel products, chemicals, textiles, and cement.

The People Indonesia has about 208 million people—the largest population of any country in Southeast Asia. Its rapidly growing population has made it one of the most densely populated countries in the world. About 60 percent of Indonesia's people live on the island of Java. There you will find Jakarta (juh•KAHR•tuh), Indonesia's capital and largest city. Jakarta has modern buildings and streets crowded with cars and bicycles.

Most Indonesians belong to the Malay ethnic group. They are divided into about 250 to 300 smaller groups with their own languages and dialects. The official language, Bahasa Indonesia, is taught in schools. Some urban Indonesians also understand the Dutch language. Why? The Dutch ruled Indonesia from the 1600s to the mid-1900s. In 1945 Indonesia declared itself an independent republic.

Islam—brought to the islands some 500 years ago by Arab traders—is the major religion of the country. Some Indonesians are Hindus or Christians, or they practice traditional religions. In past centuries, cultural influences from China and India affected Indonesian ways of life. Today European and American influences are also widespread.

WHAT IN THE WORLD?

Waxing Cloth?

Indonesia and Malaysia are known for a striking art form called *batik*—a Javanese word meaning "drop." To create a *batik* pattern, wax is first dripped onto fabric. When the fabric is dyed, the dye reaches only the fabric not covered with wax. After the dye has dried, the fabric is boiled to remove the wax. A beautiful pattern is revealed.

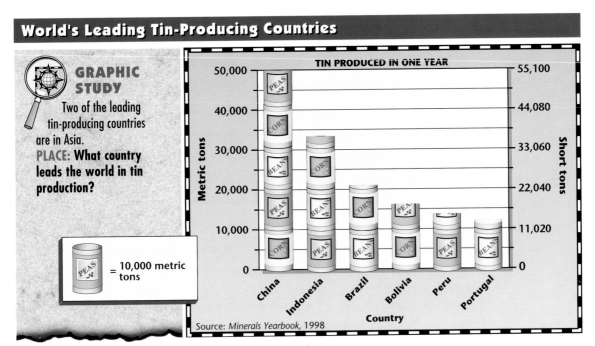

World's Leading Tin-Producing Countries

GRAPHIC STUDY

Two of the leading tin-producing countries are in Asia.

PLACE: What country leads the world in tin production?

= 10,000 metric tons

TIN PRODUCED IN ONE YEAR

Metric tons: 50,000 / 40,000 / 30,000 / 20,000 / 10,000 / 0

Short tons: 55,100 / 44,080 / 33,060 / 22,040 / 11,020 / 0

Country: China, Indonesia, Brazil, Bolivia, Peru, Portugal

Source: *Minerals Yearbook*, 1998

Young boys join in a dance at a Bali religious festival *(left)*. A Malaysian rubber worker taps a rubber tree *(right)*.
PLACE: What is the most important economic activity in Malaysia?

Place

Malaysia

North of Indonesia is Malaysia, a Southeast Asian country with an abundance of natural resources. Malaysia has two separate areas. One is the mainland part, called Malaya, on the Malay Peninsula. The other is made up of two territories—Sarawak (suh•RAH•wahk) and Sabah (SAH•buh)—on the northern edge of the island of Borneo.

The Land and Economy Mountains cover the center of Malaya. Low-lying plains are found east and west of these mountains. In Sarawak and Sabah, coastal swamps, rain forests, and rugged mountains make up most of the landscape. The map on page 657 shows you that both parts of Malaysia have a tropical rain forest climate. They have high temperatures and plenty of rain.

Agriculture is a major economic activity in Malaysia. Most farmers own small plots of land and raise rice, fruits, and vegetables. Plantation owners grow rubber, oil palms, and coconuts for export. Malaysia leads the world in the production of natural rubber and palm oil.

Malaysia is rich in tin, bauxite, petroleum, and iron ore. It is rapidly developing its oil industry. The government uses money from tin and oil exports to develop new industries that produce consumer goods. Malaysians perform manufacturing tasks for industries across the globe. For example, many computer parts are produced in Malaysia and then shipped to the United States.

The People About 22.2 million people live in Malaysia. Most belong to the Malay ethnic group, but a large Chinese population lives in the cities. People from India, Pakistan, Bangladesh, and Sri Lanka also make their homes in Malaysia. In the marketplaces you can hear Malay, Chinese, Tamil, and English spoken. Most Malaysians are Muslims, but there are large numbers of Hindus, Buddhists, Christians, and followers of traditional Chinese religions.

About 57 percent of Malaysia's people live in urban centers; the rest live in rural areas. In rural villages many people live in thatched-roof homes built on posts a few feet off the ground. Most people in the cities live in high-rise apartments. Kuala Lumpur (KWAH•luh LUM•PUR), located on the Malay Peninsula, is the capital and largest city.

Movement

Singapore

Singapore is made up of 58 islands off the southern shore of the Malay Peninsula. With only 236 square miles (611 sq. km), Singapore is the smallest country in Southeast Asia. The city of Singapore takes up much of the largest island. In the early 1800s, Singapore was covered with rain forests and swamps. Today it is one of the world's leading commercial and trading centers.

The Land and Economy The central part of Singapore is hilly; coastal areas are flat. Urban centers with modern buildings, streets, and highways have replaced much of the rain forest. Like Malaysia, Singapore has a hot, humid climate.

Singapore's economy relies on trade and manufacturing. The city of Singapore has one of the world's busiest harbors. It is a **free port,** a place where goods can be loaded, stored, and shipped again without payment of import taxes. Singapore's workers add to the country's wealth by making industrial goods for export.

SOUTHEAST ASIA: Land Use and Resources

MAP STUDY Malaysia produces more natural rubber than any other country in the world.
LOCATION: What city in Malaysia is a center of manufacturing?

Agriculture
- Plantation farming
- Subsistence farming
- Manufacturing area

Resources
- Coal
- Copper
- Chromite
- Fish & other seafood
- Forest
- Gems
- Lead
- Manganese
- Natural gas
- Nickel
- Petroleum
- Tin
- Tungsten
- Zinc

Mercator projection

Singapore, the largest port in Southeast Asia, has been described as one of the cleanest and safest cities in the world.
MOVEMENT: Why is Singapore called a *free port?*

The People Most of Singapore's nearly 4 million people are Chinese, but Malays, Indians, and Europeans also live there. Singapore's people enjoy a high standard of living. More than 90 percent of them live in the capital city of Singapore.

Place

Brunei

On the northern coast of Borneo lies another small nation—Brunei. Brunei's 2,035 square miles (5,271 sq. km) make it about the size of Delaware. The map on page 654 shows you that Brunei borders the South China Sea. Malaysia divides Brunei into two parts. The western part has low plains and coastal swamps. The eastern part has forested hills and mountains. All of Brunei experiences a hot and humid tropical climate.

The Economy and People Oil and natural gas are Brunei's main exports and sources of income. With money from these resources, the government of Brunei is building new industries. Farming and fishing are other important economic activities. Brunei's farmers grow rice, pepper, coconuts, and fruit.

Most of Brunei's 300,000 people are either Malays or Chinese. Malay, Chinese, and English are the most commonly spoken languages. Islam is the leading religion. About 67 percent of the people of Brunei live in cities. The capital and largest city is Bandar Seri Begawan (BUHN•duhr sehr•EE buh•GAH•wuhn). Because of their rich oil and natural gas resources, the people of Brunei have a high standard of living.

Place

The Philippines

East of Vietnam in the South China Sea lies the Philippines. The Philippines is an archipelago with more than 7,000 islands. Only about 900 of the islands are inhabited. Only 11 islands hold 95 percent of the Filipino people. The map on page 656 shows you that the largest of the Philippine islands are Luzon (loo•ZAHN) and Mindanao (MIHN•duh•NAH•oh).

The Philippines was a Spanish colony for more than 300 years. In the late 1800s, it came under the rule of the United States. In 1946 the Philippines became an independent democracy. Twenty-five years later, Filipino President Ferdinand Marcos set up a dictatorship. A national uprising in 1986 overthrew Marcos and restored democracy.

The Land Volcanic mountains and forests spread over the landscape of the Philippines. Because of steep mountain slopes, only one-third of the land is suitable for farming. The climate of the Philippines is tropical, with wet and dry seasons. Typhoons often cause flooding and much loss of life and property.

MAP STUDY Indonesia ranks fourth in world population after China, India, and the United States. **PLACE:** What Indonesian island has the highest population density?

Persons per

sq. mi.	sq. km
Under 2	Under 1
2-60	1-25
60-125	25-50
125-250	50-100
Over 250	Over 100

Mercator projection

CITIES
- ■ City with more than 1,000,000 people
- ● City with 500,000 to 1,000,000 people
- ○ City with 100,000 to 500,000 people

The Economy and People Agriculture, mining, and industry are the major economic activities in the Philippines. Filipino farmers harvest rice, sugarcane, pineapples, and **abaca,** a plant fiber used to make rope. Filipino workers produce textiles, chemicals, electronic products, and other manufactured goods.

About 75.3 million people live in the Philippines. Most Filipinos live on the island of Luzon. Manila, the capital and largest city, is located on Luzon and is one of the great commercial centers of Asia.

The Filipinos are Malay in ethnic background. Their culture, however, blends Malay, Spanish, and American influences. About 90 percent of Filipinos practice the Roman Catholic faith, brought to the islands by Spanish missionaries. American influences show up in the products sold along busy city streets.

SECTION 2 ASSESSMENT

REVIEWING TERMS AND FACTS

1. Define the following: cassava, free port, abaca.

2. PLACE What are the four major islands of Indonesia?

3. REGION What are Singapore's two important economic activities?

MAP STUDY ACTIVITIES

4. Look at the population density map above. What two cities in the Philippines have more than 1 million people?

MAKING CONNECTIONS

| MATH | SCIENCE | HISTORY | LITERATURE | TECHNOLOGY |

Buried deep in the soils of Southeast Asia are minerals that take the form of rare and sparkling gemstones. Most of the world's rubies, sapphires, and jade are mined in Myanmar and Thailand.

RUBIES AND SAPPHIRES Rubies and sapphires come from the same mineral— corundum. Only one other pure mineral—the diamond—has a hardness greater than corundum. Impurities in corundum determine whether a gem is a ruby or a sapphire.

Corundum that has a trace of chromium oxide produces rubies—the rarest of gemstones. A ruby's color may be pink or deep bluish-red. Myanmar produces the finest rubies. A perfect Myanmar ruby is large and red and worth twice as much as a diamond of the same size. Thailand's rubies are yellow-red.

Corundum containing iron and titanium produces blue sapphires. Star sapphires—the most precious of all the blues—reflect light as white, glowing, starlike rays. Sapphires come in a rainbow of colors, but blue sapphires are the most prized.

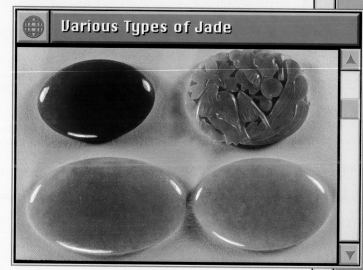

Various Types of Jade

JADE Jade is a hard, tough gemstone with a soft, shiny finish. Its unusual inner structure of interlocking needles makes jade strong and therefore good for delicate detailing. It is used in jewelry and carvings. The finest jade, found mainly in Myanmar but also in California and Mexico, comes from the rare mineral jadeite. The most beautiful colors of this gemstone include rich shades of light and dark greens, as well as softer shades of lilac and pink. The rarest and best-quality jadeite appears as a clear, bright green.

Making the Connection

1. What precious gemstones come from Southeast Asia?
2. Which Southeast Asian countries produce the gems?

Important Things to Know About Southeast Asia

SECTION 1 MAINLAND SOUTHEAST ASIA

- Mainland Southeast Asia includes the countries of Myanmar, Thailand, Laos, Cambodia, and Vietnam.
- Plentiful water supplies and fertile soil enable farmers to grow rice as a major food crop.
- Most of this area of Southeast Asia has tropical and subtropical climates.
- Most mainland Southeast Asians live in rural villages, but cities are growing in population.
- Most people in mainland Southeast Asia practice Buddhism.

SECTION 2 ISLAND SOUTHEAST ASIA

- The islands of Southeast Asia lie along the Pacific Ocean's Ring of Fire. Their people face the threat of volcanic activity and earthquakes.
- Indonesia is the largest country in Southeast Asia in area and population.
- The city of Singapore is one of the world's busiest trading and commercial centers.
- The people of Malaysia come from many different ethnic backgrounds.
- The culture of the Philippines shows Malay, Spanish, and American influences.

Floating market in Bangkok, Thailand ▶

REVIEWING KEY TERMS

Match the numbered terms in Set A with their lettered definitions in Set B.

A

1. cassava
2. deforestation
3. abaca
4. delta
5. alluvial plain
6. free port

B

A. land area formed by a river's soil deposits

B. plant fiber used in making rope

C. place where goods are unloaded, stored, and reshipped without import taxes

D. land formed by soil deposits at a river's mouth

E. widespread cutting of trees

F. plant root used in making flour

Mental Mapping Activity

Draw a freehand map of Southeast Asia. Label the following:

- Java
- Kuala Lumpur
- South China Sea
- Thailand
- Bangkok
- Vietnam

REVIEWING THE MAIN IDEAS

Section 1

1. **PLACE** Which Southeast Asian country was never a colony?
2. **HUMAN/ENVIRONMENT INTERACTION** What two major agricultural products are grown in Thailand?
3. **HUMAN/ENVIRONMENT INTERACTION** Where do most people live in Myanmar and Thailand?
4. **MOVEMENT** Why did many people flee Cambodia during the 1970s?

Section 2

5. **PLACE** What is the major religion of Indonesia and Malaysia?
6. **HUMAN/ENVIRONMENT INTERACTION** Why is only one-third of the Philippines suitable for farming?
7. **MOVEMENT** Why is Singapore important to the economies of Southeast Asia?
8. **REGION** How are Indonesia and the Philippines alike geographically?

CRITICAL THINKING ACTIVITIES

1. **Drawing Conclusions** Why is the Mekong River important to the people of Southeast Asia?
2. **Predicting Outcomes** Experts believe that Brunei has enough oil reserves to last until 2018. What might happen to the country's economy and standard of living at that time?

CONNECTIONS TO WORLD CULTURES

Cooperative Learning Activity Work in a group of three to learn about one of the countries of Southeast Asia. Each group should select one country. Then each member should choose one of the following topics to research: (a) the art; (b) holidays and festivals; or (c) the music and literature. Share your information with your group and then as a group, prepare a written report with illustrations or photos that illustrate the group's findings.

GeoJournal Writing Activity

Imagine you are a news reporter on assignment in Southeast Asia to report on an active volcano. Write about the volcanic activity as if you were an eyewitness.

TECHNOLOGY ACTIVITY

Using E-Mail Use your local library or access the Internet to locate an E-mail address for the United States Embassy in Manila, the Philippines. Compose a letter requesting information about the eruption of Mount Pinatubo in 1991. Using this information, create a bulletin board showing the chronology of the volcanic eruption. Provide photographs and captions with your display.

PLACE LOCATION ACTIVITY: SOUTHEAST ASIA

Match the letters on the map with the places and physical features of Southeast Asia. Write your answers on a separate sheet of paper.

1. Myanmar
2. Mekong River
3. Singapore
4. Jakarta
5. Sumatra
6. Java Sea
7. Vietnam
8. Brunei
9. Manila
10. Indian Ocean

Asia

HABITAT LOSS

PROBLEM

Over the last 100 years, Asia has suffered greater destruction of habitats than any other continent. Asian countries have drained wetlands, felled forests, and plowed under grasslands to feed growing populations and boost their economies. As the demand for resources increases, species disappear at an alarming rate. Scientists estimate that every few hours one plant or animal species in Asia becomes extinct.

SOLUTIONS

● India has created more than 370 national parks and preserves since 1960 to protect endangered wildlife such as the tiger. Since 1970 the population of Indian tigers in the wild has doubled.

● Countries in Asia have passed tough laws protecting wildlife. In China, poachers are executed.

● China has established 12 reserves for its giant pandas over the past few decades and plans to create 14 additional protected areas.

● In Indonesia, villagers now learn how to use the forests without destroying them. Some locals are hired as park rangers and tourist guides; others make money raising and selling butterflies or growing forest crops of nuts and palm leaves.

This tiger in India's Ranthambhore National Park is part of the success story of Project Tiger. Since the effort to protect tigers was launched in 1973, the number of tigers living in the park's forest has grown from around 14 to more than 40.

HABITAT LOSS FACT BANK

🌿 In 1900, 40,000 tigers lived in the wild in India alone; today about 6,000 survive, mostly in Asia.

🌿 In 1900, 40 percent of India was forested; today, only 15 percent is forested—and the number of endangered species has increased tenfold.

🌿 Indonesia has 210 endangered plant and animal species—more than any other nation in the world.

🌿 Javan and Sumatran rhinos are among the world's most endangered species. Fewer than 800 animals survive.

🌿 An estimated 1,200 giant pandas survive in bamboo forests in China. Poachers kill 40 or more pandas a year.

Oil palms advance on the wilderness. Hundreds of thousands of acres of Malaysia's rain forests have been lost to commercial projects such as this one on a Malaysian plantation.

TEEN TRIBUTE

Maria Martinez, a student at Boston English High School in Boston, Massachusetts, wanted to do something to save endangered Asian wildlife. So she got a job. Maria works two to three hours a day at the World Society for the Protection of Animals. She sends out petitions that call for the end of inhumane treatment of endangered Asiatic black bears in China. Maria also answers letters from other young people who want to help.

These men in Foshan, China, carry bamboo poles for sale in local markets. Pandas and villagers often compete for bamboo.

environmental activities

TAKE A CLOSER LOOK

1 What has happened to Asia's habitats in the last 100 years?

2 What growing demand has caused the most destruction of Asia's plants and animals?

WHAT CAN YOU DO?

🍃 Talk to your parents. Ask them to vote to keep our national parks and nature preserves.

🍃 Save a tree—carry your own shopping bag. The average American uses up seven trees a year.

🍃 Stuff envelopes or help a group raise money to protect an endangered animal.

🍃 Make a bird feeder. Spread a pinecone with peanut butter and hang it from a tree.

Save the
Ancient Forests

Unit 9

Australia, Oceania, and Antarctica

What Makes Australia, Oceania, and Antarctica a Region?

Most people share . . .

• a location mostly south of the Equator.

• a location near or in the Pacific Ocean.

• unique animals and vegetation.

• specialized economies.

To find out more about Australia, Oceania, and Antarctica, see the Unit Atlas on pages 676–687.

The Ross Sea, Antarctica

EXPLORING THE INTERNET

To learn more about Australia, Oceana, and Antarctica, visit the Glencoe Social Studies Web site at **www.glencoe.com** for information, activities, and links to other sites.

GeoJournal Activity

Many unique and interesting animals live in Australia, Oceania, and Antarctica. As you read this unit, choose one of the animals mentioned and write a story about it that would appeal to younger students. Illustrate your story with colorful drawings and a sketch map of where this animal lives.

UNIT 9 ATLAS

NATIONAL
GEOGRAPHIC
SOCIETY

IMAGES
of the
WORLD

1. **Kangaroo and joey, Australia**
2. **Three cowboys, Australia**
3. **Chinstrap penguins, Antarctica**
4. **Stone faces, Easter Island**
5. **Sutherland Falls, New Zealand**
6. **Boab tree, Western Australia**
7. **Traditional fishing, Vanuatu**

All photos viewed against the soaring roofline of Sydney's Opera House, Australia.

Regional Focus

The region of Australia, Oceania, and Antarctica lies in the Pacific Ocean southeast of Asia. It includes two continents—Australia and Antarctica. Australia is the only place on the earth that is both a continent *and* a country. Antarctica is the world's coldest and iciest continent. This region also takes in Oceania—an area of thousands of islands in the Pacific Ocean.

Region
The Land

The region of Australia, Oceania, and Antarctica lies mostly south of the Equator. It spreads out across millions of square miles of the Pacific Ocean. Long distances and rugged landscapes have kept many parts of the region isolated from each other and the rest of the world.

Kangaroo Crossing?

NEXT 8 km

In some parts of Australia, kangaroo populations are so large that signs are posted to warn motorists. **HUMAN/ENVIRONMENT INTERACTION: In what ways do you think humans could be a threat to the kangaroo?**

Australia A vast spread of dry, flat land makes up most of Australia. Through the central part of the country, however, runs a thick ribbon of pastureland. Underground pools of water allow farming and ranching to take place in this area. Hills and mountains stretch along Australia's east coast. A thin coastal strip faces the Pacific Ocean.

Oceania Oceania is made up of different kinds of Pacific islands. Some of the islands are mountainous. They are known for volcanic and earthquake activity. Others are massive formations of rock that rise from the ocean floor. Still other islands are low-lying, ring-shaped coral islands.

Antarctica Antarctica spreads over the southern end of the globe. It lies under an enormous sheet of ice. Mountains run through Antarctica and divide it into two parts. To the east is a high, flat plateau. A landmass largely below sea level lies to the west.

Place
Climate and Vegetation

Location and wind and ocean currents account for the extremes of temperature in Australia, Oceania, and Antarctica. Because of centuries of isolation, the region has animals and vegetation found nowhere else in the world.

Australia's eastern coast receives Pacific Ocean rains and enjoys mild climates year-round. Mountains block this moisture from reaching inland areas, which have dry or partly dry climates.

Oceania has mostly tropical climates, with wet and dry seasons. Warm days follow each other in an almost unbroken chain. Tropical plants, such as coconut palms, cover many of the islands.

Antarctica is one of the coldest places on earth. It is also one of the windiest, highest, and driest of the continents. The icy winds that sweep down from the plateau are unable to carry much moisture. As a result, only an average of 2 inches (50 mm) of precipitation, in the form of snow, falls each year.

Emperor Penguins

Penguins thrive in the Southern Hemisphere where icy Antarctic currents flow.
REGION: What do you think makes up the main portion of a penguin's diet?

Human/Environment Interaction
The Economy

Agriculture is the major economic activity of Oceania. Because of great distances and high development costs, manufacturing is limited to Australia and the island country of New Zealand. The mining of minerals, such as uranium, bauxite, iron ore, copper, nickel, and gold, is important to Australia. Modern means of transportation have increased trade between the region of Australia, Oceania, and Antarctica and the rest of the world.

Australia Only a small area of Australia is good for farming. Australian farmers make good use of their country's limited land and water resources. Australia has many cattle and sheep ranches. It is a major exporter of beef, lamb, and wool. Australians also mine uranium, bauxite, iron ore, copper, nickel, and gold. Factories produce cars, machinery, food products, and textiles.

Oceania The soil in much of Oceania limits the growth of crops for export. Most people raise only enough food to feed themselves. Some larger islands, however, have rich volcanic soil and abundant rain that allows for cash crops, such as tropical fruits, sugar, coffee, and coconut products. New Zealand, located between Australia and Oceania, relies on both agriculture and manufacturing. It exports mainly meat, wool, and dairy products. Fishing is an important industry throughout Oceania.

Antarctica Because there are no permanent settlements and because of its harsh climate, Antarctica produces no farm crops. Its icy coastal waters, however, are a rich source of seafood. The continent is believed to be rich in minerals. To preserve Antarctica as the world's last wilderness, many nations have agreed—for now—not to mine this mineral wealth.

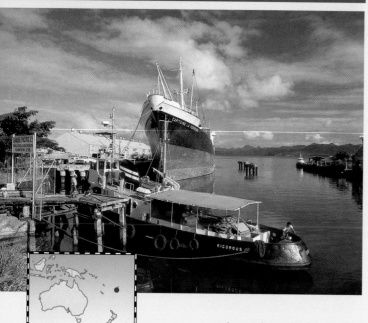

Docking at Suva, Fiji

Fiji's capital and largest city is a busy seaport.
PLACE: What physical features do you think are necessary for a city to be a seaport?

Movement
People

Australia and Oceania are a blend of European, traditional Pacific, and Asian cultures. In Australia, the original settlers were the Aborigines; in New Zealand, they were the Maori. In the late 1700s and early 1800s, the British settled and ruled Australia and New Zealand. These lands became independent in the early 1900s. Other South Pacific areas won their freedom after World War II. Today most countries in the region have democratic forms of government.

Population In spite of its vast size the region today has only about 30 million people. Nearly 18.7 million are in Australia, and most of them live in coastal cities, such as Sydney and Melbourne. Another 3.8 million live in New Zealand, which also has large urban populations. The rest of the South Pacific islands are less urbanized. Many Pacific islanders, especially young people, leave their villages and head to the region's major cities to find work. Although Antarctica has no permanent population, multinational groups of scientists live there for brief periods to carry out research.

The Arts Traditional Pacific cultures created many art forms still practiced today. For example, Aborigines paint and Maori carve beautiful wooden masks and figures. European settlers brought traditions from their homelands. In recent years traditional Pacific and European ways have blended to form a new culture unique to the region.

Multimedia Unit 9 Activities

NATIONAL GEOGRAPHIC SOCIETY

Picture Atlas of the World

Comparing and Contrasting Places

Using the CD-ROM The lands of Oceania, Australia, and Antarctica are unique. Oceania is an area of thousands of islands. Australia is the only place on earth that is both a continent and a country. Antarctica is the world's coldest and iciest continent. Explore these places using the *Picture Atlas of the World* CD-ROM. Imagine you are an anthropologist and create a file that uses photographs, statistics, or essays to compare and contrast these places with the United States. Then use the file as the basis of a class presentation. Explain the differences and similarities you've discovered, and why you think these differences and similarities exist.

Surfing the "Net"

The Antarctic Ozone Hole

The ozone layer is a thin layer of atmosphere that protects us from the sun. The ozone blocks the sun's most dangerous ultraviolet, or UV, rays from reaching the earth. However, scientists recently have recorded a steady loss of ozone in the earth's upper atmosphere. After discovery of an "ozone hole," scientific teams raced to research the problem and environmental agencies have pushed national governments to do something about it. To find out more about the ozone hole, search the Internet.

Getting There

Follow these steps to gather information on the ozone hole.

1. Use a search engine. Type in the words *ozone layer.*

2. Enter words like the following to focus your search: *South Pole, ozone depletion, ozone hole, CFC, Antarctica.*

3. The search engine will provide you with a number of links to follow.

What To Do When You Are There

Click on the links to navigate through the pages of information and gather your findings. Use your findings to create a pamphlet on ozone depletion. Include facts and figures to help explain why ozone depletion affects our lives and how we can do our part to reverse the problem. Be sure to explain the problem and resolution using terms and illustrations that a general audience could easily understand. Share your pamphlet with the class.

Physical Geography

AUSTRALIA, OCEANIA, AND ANTARCTICA: Physical

ELEVATIONS

Feet	Meters
10,000	3,000
5,000	1,500
2,000	600
1,000	300
0	0

▲ Mountain peak
☐ Ice cap
☐ Ice shelf

Mercator projection

PACIFIC OCEAN

Equator

MICRONESIA

POLYNESIA

MELANESIA

INDIAN OCEAN

Coral Sea

AUSTRALIA

Great Sandy Desert
Macdonnell Ranges
Gibson Desert
Great Victoria Desert
Great Artesian Basin
Great Barrier Reef
Lake Eyre
Darling R.
Great Dividing Range
Murray R.
Great Australian Bight

Tropic of Capricorn

▲ Mt. Kosciusko 7,310 ft. (2,228 m)

PACIFIC OCEAN

Tasmania

Tasman Sea

North Island

Mt. Cook 12,349 ft. (3,764 m)

NEW ZEALAND

South Island
Southern Alps

0   250   500 mi.
0   250   500 km

South Pole

▲ Vinson Massif 16,066 ft. (4,897 m)

Antarctic Circle

0   250 mi.
0   250 km

Map Study

1. **LOCATION** What reef lies off the northeastern coast of Australia?
2. **PLACE** About how much of Antarctica is covered by ice cap?

ELEVATION PROFILE: Australia

10,000 ft.   3,048 m

Macdonnell Ranges

Hamersley Range

5,000 ft.   1,524 m

Great Sandy Desert

Great Dividing Range

Indian Ocean

Pacific Ocean

2,000 ft.   610 m

1,000 ft.   305 m

Sea level   Sea level

⟵ West to East at 23.5°S latitude ⟶

Source: *Goode's World Atlas*, 19th edition

GeoFacts

Highest point: Vinson Massif (Antarctica) 16,066 ft. (4,897 m) high

Lowest point: Lake Eyre (Australia) 52 ft. (16 m) below sea level

Longest river: Murray-Darling (Australia) 2,310 mi. (3,717 km) long

Largest lake: Lake Eyre (Australia) 3,600 sq. mi. (9,324 sq. km)

Largest waterfall: Sutherland Falls (New Zealand) 1,904 ft. (580 m)

Largest desert: Gibson Desert (Australia) 120,000 sq. mi. (310,800 sq. km)

AUSTRALIA/OCEANIA/ANTARCTICA AND THE UNITED STATES: Land Comparison

Graphic Study

1. **PLACE** What is the highest point in the Australia/Oceania/Antarctica region?
2. **PLACE** How would you describe the size of the United States compared with the combined sizes of Australia, Oceania, and Antarctica?

UNIT 9 ATLAS

Cultural Geography

AUSTRALIA AND OCEANIA: Political

120°E   135°E   150°E   165°E   180°   165°W   150°W

Tropic of Cancer

15°N

Wake Island (U.S.)

Hawaii (U.S.)

Guam (U.S.)

NORTHERN MARIANA IS. (U.S.)

MARSHALL ISLANDS

PACIFIC OCEAN

Koror ★

Majuro ★

N
W ◇ E
S

PALAU

Palikir ★

FEDERATED STATES OF MICRONESIA

WALLIS & FUTUNA (Fr.)

0°

Tarawa ★

Equator

PAPUA NEW GUINEA

★ Yaren
NAURU

KIRIBATI

Port Moresby ★

SOLOMON IS.
Honiara ★

Funafuti ★
TUVALU

TOKELAU (N.Z.)

SAMOA

15°S

VANUATU

Apia ★

AMERICAN SAMOA (U.S.)

FRENCH POLYNESIA (Fr.)

Port-Vila ★

Suva ★
FIJI

Nuku'alofa ★

Tropic of Capricorn

AUSTRALIA

NEW CALEDONIA (Fr.)

TONGA

NIUE (N.Z.)

COOK ISLANDS (N.Z.)

PITCAIRN (Br.)

30°S

Canberra ★

NEW ZEALAND

International Date Line

— National boundary
★ National capital

0   125   250 mi.
0 125 250 km

Mercator projection

Wellington ★

Map Study

1. **PLACE** What city is Australia's national capital?
2. **LOCATION** Which Pacific island capital lies closest to both the Equator and the International Date Line?

COMPARING POPULATION:
Australia/Oceania and the United States

Australia/
Oceania

 = 25,000,000

United
States

Source: *Population Reference Bureau, 1998*

GeoFacts

Biggest country (land area):
Australia 2,951,521 sq. mi.
(7,644,439 sq. km)

Smallest country (land area): Tuvalu
9 sq. mi. (23 sq. km)

Largest city (population): Sydney
(1997) 3,800,000; (2015 projected) 3,900,000

Highest population density:
Nauru 1,267 people per sq. mi.
(489 people per sq. km)

Lowest population density: Australia
6 people per sq. mi. (2 people
per sq. km)

AUSTRALIA: Population Growth

Population (millions)

Year

Sources: *Population Reference Bureau, Inc., 1998*
Encyclopedia Britannica Book of the Year, 1998

*projected

Graphic Study

1. **REGION** What is the combined population of Australia and Oceania?
2. **PLACE** How much did Australia's population grow between 1960 and 1990?

Countries at a Glance

Australia

CAPITAL:
Canberra
MAJOR LANGUAGE(S):
English, Aboriginal languages
POPULATION:
18,700,000

LANDMASS:
2,951,521 sq. mi./
7,644,439 sq. km
MONEY:
Australian Dollar
MAJOR EXPORT:
Crude Oil
MAJOR IMPORT:
Machinery

FEDERATED STATES OF
Micronesia

 Palikir

CAPITAL:
Palikir
MAJOR LANGUAGE(S):
English
POPULATION:
100,000

LANDMASS:
270 sq. mi./
699 sq. km
MONEY:
U.S. Dollar
MAJOR EXPORT:
Copra
MAJOR IMPORT:
Food and Beverages

Fiji

 Suva

CAPITAL:
Suva
MAJOR LANGUAGE(S):
English, Fijian, Hindi
POPULATION:
800,000

LANDMASS:
7,054 sq. mi./
18,270 sq. km
MONEY:
Fiji Dollar
MAJOR EXPORT:
Sugar
MAJOR IMPORT:
Machinery

Kiribati

 Tarawa

CAPITAL:
Tarawa
MAJOR LANGUAGE(S):
English, Gilbertese
POPULATION:
82,449

LANDMASS:
313 sq. mi./
811 sq. km
MONEY:
Australian Dollar
MAJOR EXPORT:
Copra
MAJOR IMPORT:
Machinery

Marshall Islands

 Majuro

CAPITAL:
Majuro
MAJOR LANGUAGE(S):
English, Marshallese, Japanese
POPULATION:
100,000

LANDMASS:
70 sq. mi./
181 sq. km
MONEY:
U.S. Dollar
MAJOR EXPORT:
Crude Coconut Oil
MAJOR IMPORT:
Food and Live Animals

Nauru

 Yaren

CAPITAL:
Yaren
MAJOR LANGUAGE(S):
Nauruan, English
POPULATION:
10,390

LANDMASS:
21 sq. mi./
54 sq. km
MONEY:
Australian Dollar
MAJOR EXPORT:
Phosphates
MAJOR IMPORT:
Food

New Zealand

 Wellington

CAPITAL:
Wellington
MAJOR LANGUAGE(S):
English, Maori
POPULATION:
3,800,000

LANDMASS:
103,470 sq. mi./
267,987 sq. km
MONEY:
New Zealand Dollar
MAJOR EXPORT:
Food and Live Animals
MAJOR IMPORT:
Machinery

Palau

 Koror

CAPITAL:
Koror
MAJOR LANGUAGE(S):
English, Palauan
POPULATION:
20,000

LANDMASS:
190 sq. mi./
492 sq. km
MONEY:
U.S. Dollar
MAJOR EXPORT:
Tuna
MAJOR IMPORT:
Food

Papua New Guinea

Port Moresby

CAPITAL:
Port Moresby
MAJOR LANGUAGE(S):
English, Melanesian, Papuan languages
POPULATION:
4,300,000

LANDMASS:
174,850 sq. mi./
452,862 sq. km
MONEY:
Kina
MAJOR EXPORT:
Gold
MAJOR IMPORT:
Machinery

Samoa

 Apia

CAPITAL:
Apia
MAJOR LANGUAGE(S):
Samoan, English
POPULATION:
200,000

LANDMASS:
1,090 sq. mi./
2,823 sq. km
MONEY:
Tala
MAJOR EXPORT:
Coconut Oil
MAJOR IMPORT:
Food

Countries not drawn to scale.

Solomon Islands

Honiara

CAPITAL:
Honiara
MAJOR LANGUAGE(S):
English, Papuan, Melanesian, Polynesian languages
POPULATION:
400,000

LANDMASS:
10,810 sq. mi./
27,998 sq. km
MONEY:
Solomon Islands Dollar
MAJOR EXPORT:
Fish Products
MAJOR IMPORT:
Machinery

Tonga

Nuku'alofa

CAPITAL:
Nuku'alofa
MAJOR LANGUAGE(S):
Tongan, English
POPULATION:
107,335

LANDMASS:
290 sq. mi./
751 sq. km
MONEY:
Pa'anga
MAJOR EXPORT:
Squash
MAJOR IMPORT:
Food and Live Animals

Tuvalu

Funafuti

CAPITAL:
Funafuti
MAJOR LANGUAGE(S):
Tuvaluan, English
POPULATION:
10,297

LANDMASS:
9 sq. mi./
23 sq. km
MONEY:
Australian Dollar
MAJOR EXPORT:
Copra
MAJOR IMPORT:
Food

Vanuatu

Port-Vila

CAPITAL:
Port-Vila
MAJOR LANGUAGE(S):
Bislama, French, English
POPULATION:
200,000

LANDMASS:
4,710 sq. mi./
12,199 sq. km
MONEY:
Vatu
MAJOR EXPORT:
Copra
MAJOR IMPORT:
Machinery, Food

Delivering Supplies to Antarctica

A Coast Guard icebreaker cuts through the ice to deliver passengers and supplies to a science station in Antarctica.

Overlooking Sydney, Australia

A bridge over Sydney Harbor carries traffic from the main business district to the suburbs.

Australia and New Zealand

MAP STUDY ACTIVITY

In this chapter you will read about Australia and New Zealand, which are completely surrounded by water.

1. What is the national capital of Australia?
2. What sea separates Australia and New Zealand?

SECTION 1 Australia

Words to Know
- coral
- outback
- station
- marsupial
- bush

Places to Locate
- Australia
- Great Barrier Reef
- Great Dividing Range
- Western Plateau
- Canberra
- Sydney
- Melbourne

Read to Learn . . .
1. why most Australians live in coastal areas.
2. why Australia has a strong economy.
3. what groups have influenced Australia's culture.

" I started the morning routine—boil the tea, pack the gear, saddle the camels—and head south once more. . . . At Areyonga I filled my drinking-water bag with rainwater and set off for Ayers Rock. . . ." Explorer Robyn Davidson describes her recent trek across the desert of Australia. Ayers Rock—a huge red island of stone rising 1,000 feet (305 m)—is a landmark to all who travel through central Australia.

Australia lies far south on the globe between the Indian Ocean and the Pacific Ocean. People often call Australia the Land Down Under because it is located entirely within the Southern Hemisphere.

Location
The Land

Surrounded by water, Australia is a country that is a continent all by itself! Why isn't it called an island? It is too large. Instead geographers describe it as a continent—the smallest one in the world. The world's largest island, Greenland, has only about one-third of Australia's land area. With a land area of 2,951,521 square miles (7,644,439 sq. km), Australia is the world's sixth-largest country—about the size of the continental United States.

Not only is Australia the smallest continent—it is also the oldest. Australia does not have a wide variety of physical features. It is made up of mostly deserts and dry grasslands, with a few low mountains and coastal plains. Winds and time have worn the land into the flattest and lowest continent in the world.

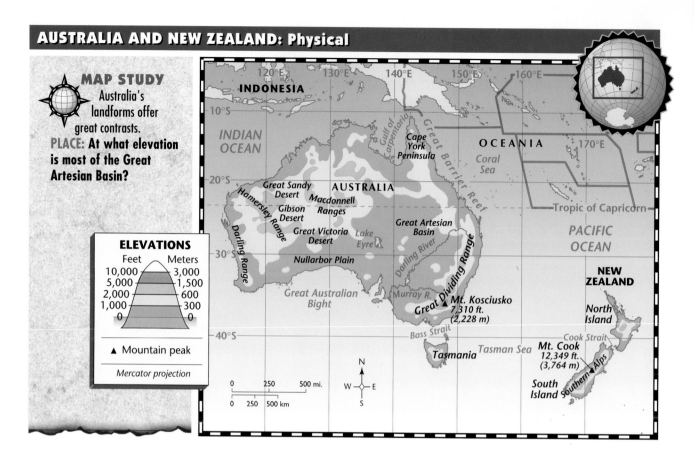

MAP STUDY
Australia's landforms offer great contrasts.
PLACE: At what elevation is most of the Great Artesian Basin?

ELEVATIONS

Feet	Meters
10,000	3,000
5,000	1,500
2,000	600
1,000	300
0	0

▲ Mountain peak

Mercator projection

Off Australia's northeastern coast lies one of the world's great natural wonders—the Great Barrier Reef. It is a 1,250-mile (2,011 km) chain of colorful **coral** formations and islands rising out of blue-green Pacific waters. Coral is a hard, rocklike material made of the skeletons of small sea animals. To Australia's southeast lies the small island of Tasmania.

The Great Dividing Range The Great Dividing Range stretches along Australia's Pacific coast. It divides the flow of Australia's rivers—eastward toward the Pacific Ocean or westward to inland areas. Two of Australia's major rivers—the Murray and the Darling—begin in the Great Dividing Range and flow westward into central Australia.

In Australia's southeastern corner, you find a narrow coastal plain. This fertile flatland boasts Australia's best farmland. You can see on the map on page 700 that it also includes some of Australia's most densely populated areas. The southern end of the Great Dividing Range hugs this narrow plain. In this area rise the peaks of the Australian Alps, Australia's highest mountains. At 7,310 feet (2,228 m), Mount Kosciusko (KAH•zee•UHS•koh) is Australia's highest peak.

The Central Lowlands As you move inland, the Great Dividing Range levels off into pastureland known as the Central Lowlands. This and other inland parts of Australia are called the **outback**. Partly dry grasslands cover much of the Central Lowlands. Here in the outback, mining towns and huge **stations**—Australian sheep and livestock ranches—are scattered over a vast area.

A resource prized above all others, water is scarce or lacking across 75 percent of the country. An unusual feature of the Central Lowlands is the Great Artesian Basin, where water is found deep underground. The basin is like a huge pail that catches water from eastern mountain rivers. Ranchers drill wells to make the underground water available for irrigating grazing land.

The Western Plateau Picture a carpet of sand twice as large as Alaska, Texas, California, and New Mexico combined. That's about the size of Australia's Western Plateau. Travel across the plateau, which covers about 75 percent of Australia, is mostly by airplane.

The map on page 690 shows you the huge deserts that spread across much of the Western Plateau. This part of the outback, however, is not a wasteland—it is rich in mineral wealth. To the south, a narrow coastal plain is home to almost all of the Western Plateau's farms and people.

The Climate Look at Australia's climate regions on the map on page 692. You can see that most of the country is dry with desert or partly desert grassland. But there are several other climate regions. Northern Australia—the part of the country closest to the Equator—has a tropical climate with rainy and dry seasons and year-round hot or warm temperatures. Coastal areas in the south and southeast have warm summers and mild winters. Only the Australian Alps and the southern island of Tasmania have winter temperatures that fall below freezing for more than a day.

A Busy Station in the Outback

Sprawling cattle and sheep ranches, called stations, dot the landscape of Australia's outback.
LOCATION: Where in Australia do you find the outback?

Animals and Plants Unless you visit a zoo, you probably don't see kangaroos or koalas near your home. Kangaroos and koalas are native only to Australia. These animals and about 120 similar kinds are called **marsupials**, or mammals that carry their young in a pouch. Why do they live only in Australia?

For millions of years, Australia was isolated from other continents. This separation led to a very special wildlife population. Dingoes, wombats, kookaburras, emus, bandicoots, and dugongs are just some of the animals found in Australia. One particularly unusual Australian animal—the platypus—lays eggs but has a furry body, a large bill, and webbed feet. Rare plants such as the eucalyptus are also native to Australia. The long, leathery leaves of the eucalyptus are the only food a koala will eat.

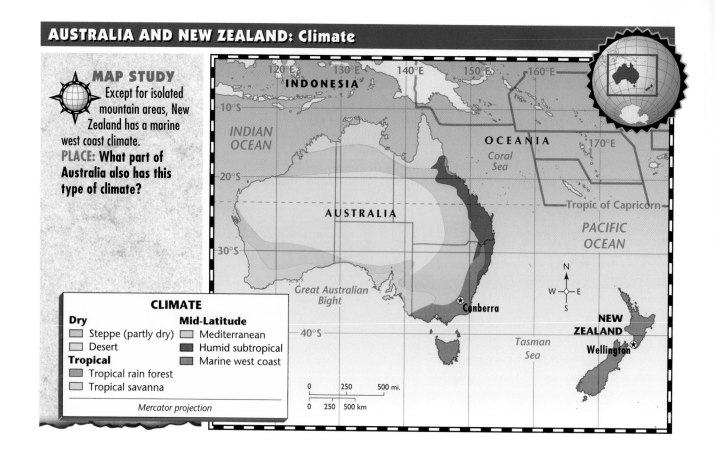

MAP STUDY
Except for isolated mountain areas, New Zealand has a marine west coast climate.
PLACE: What part of Australia also has this type of climate?

CLIMATE

Dry
- Steppe (partly dry)
- Desert

Tropical
- Tropical rain forest
- Tropical savanna

Mid-Latitude
- Mediterranean
- Humid subtropical
- Marine west coast

Mercator projection

Movement

The Economy

A treasure chest overflowing with mineral resources—that's Australia. The continent's strong economy relies on exporting these resources. In the past the United Kingdom ranked as Australia's most important trading partner. Today Australia trades more with Japan and the United States.

Many of the products that are manufactured in the country meet local needs. Australian factories produce cars, trains, computers, and consumer goods. Tourism is also an important industry. Many tourists flock to Australia each year, and the country's service industries thrive on the tourist trade.

Agriculture Australia's dry climate limits farming. Only about 10 percent of Australia's land is good for growing crops. Farmers rely on machines and irrigation to improve crop yields. Wheat is the main crop. Other grains, sugarcane, fruits, and vegetables are also grown. Most of Australia's land is set aside for grazing. Ranchers raise cattle for beef and sheep for meat and wool. The graph on page 693 shows that Australia is the world's leading wool-producing country.

Mining When gold was discovered in Australia in the mid-1800s, thousands flocked to the outback. But gold is only one of the country's many mineral resources. Australia is the world's leading producer of bauxite and lead. The map on page 698 shows you the location of Australia's coal, iron ore, uranium, silver, opal, and zinc mines.

692

Place
The People

For its huge area, Australia has very few people—only 18.7 million. Most Australians live in scattered urban areas along the coasts. Australia has long needed more skilled workers to develop its open land and boost its economy. To meet this goal, the Australian government has encouraged people from other countries to settle in Australia.

Past and Present A small part of the continent's current population were the first Australians—the Aborigines (A•buh•RIHJ•neez). The Aborigines came to Australia from Asia about 30,000 to 40,000 years ago. They moved throughout the continent hunting animals and gathering plants. The Aborigines developed a unique culture. Ancient cave paintings show the work of their artists.

The voyages of Captain James Cook provided the British with a claim to Australia in the late 1700s. At first the United Kingdom used Australia as a colony for prisoners. Then other British emigrants settled in Australia. These settlers took land from the Aborigines and forced them far into the outback. Many Aborigines died of European diseases.

In 1901 the British colonies became states and united to form the independent Commonwealth of Australia. Australia is divided into seven states as shown on the map on page 688. Australians created a British-style parliamentary

WHAT IN THE WORLD?

On Target

Hunters around the world could take a lesson from Australia's Aborigines. They invented a hunting tool called the boomerang. Shaped like a bent wing, the wooden boomerang—thrown by a hunter—sails out toward its target. If the boomerang misses, it returns to land near the person who threw it!

Leading Wool-Producing Countries

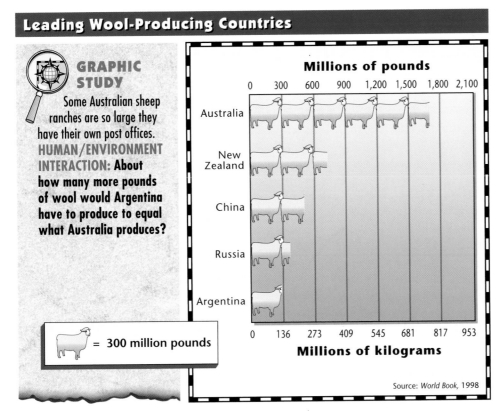

GRAPHIC STUDY

Some Australian sheep ranches are so large they have their own post offices. **HUMAN/ENVIRONMENT INTERACTION: About how many more pounds of wool would Argentina have to produce to equal what Australia produces?**

🐑 = 300 million pounds

Millions of pounds

	0	300	600	900	1,200	1,500	1,800	2,100
Australia								
New Zealand								
China								
Russia								
Argentina								

| 0 | 136 | 273 | 409 | 545 | 681 | 817 | 953 |

Millions of kilograms

Source: *World Book*, 1998

democracy and preserved much of their British heritage. Australia has developed its own national character, however. The "new" Australia comes from the diversity of its people. Many present-day Australians have Italian, Greek, Slavic, Aboriginal, or Chinese backgrounds.

City Life About 85 percent of Australia's population live in cities. Sydney and Melbourne—on the southeastern coast—are the largest cities. With populations of more than 3 million, both are lively cultural and commercial centers. Australia's next largest cities—Adelaide, Brisbane, and Perth—also are located on the coast. Canberra, the national capital, lies a relatively short distance inland from Sydney and Melbourne. With about 300,000 people, Canberra was developed through a government plan designed to draw people away from the coasts and into the outback.

Rural Life Only about 15 percent of Australians live in rural areas known as the **bush**. Many rural people live on stations that raise sheep or cattle. Thirteen-year-old Alice Adams lives on a sheep station in the Central Lowlands. She and her family live in a large, comfortable farmhouse. Working on the station is a family effort. Alice and other rural Australians sometimes find life in the bush very lonely. The Adamses' station covers more than 300 square miles (700 sq. km). The nearest settlement is about 50 miles (81 km) away. A trip to the market or shopping center is not quick. Alice and her family travel two hours on unpaved roads to reach a distant rural town.

Teen Scene

Winter in June

It's June in Australia—time to get out the skis! Because the seasons in Australia are opposite of those in the Northern Hemisphere, Paul Noone and his friends plan their winter activities from June to September. Paul and his family go to Snowy Mountains to ski. This area lies just south of Canberra in one of Australia's many national parks. From the chairlift, Paul can see Australia's highest peak, Mount Kosciusko.

SECTION 1 ASSESSMENT

REVIEWING TERMS AND FACTS

1. **Define the following:** coral, outback, station, marsupial, bush.

2. **PLACE** What is the landscape of the central three-fourths of the country like?

3. **PLACE** What important agricultural products does Australia produce?

4. **MOVEMENT** Who were the first people to settle Australia?

MAP STUDY ACTIVITIES

5. Compare the maps on pages 688 and 690. What large Australian city lies closest to the Great Barrier Reef?

6. Turn to the climate map on page 692. What area of Australia enjoys a Mediterranean climate?

Using Technology

Analyzing a LANDSAT Image

Look carefully at the photograph below. What does it show? A LANDSAT satellite carrying cameras took this picture of southern Florida from space. The cameras record millions of energy waves invisible to the human eye. LANDSAT satellites relay these signals to receiving stations here on the earth. Computers then change this information into pictures of the earth's surface.

LANDSAT carries scanning instruments that pick up sunlight reflected off of water, rocks, plants, and other objects. Geographers use the different colors of reflected light to analyze the area. In LANDSAT images, the colors red or pink mean healthy vegetation. Deep blue shows areas of clear water, while light blue shows unclear water. These images help to pinpoint polluted areas.

To interpret a LANDSAT image, apply these steps:

- Name the area shown in the image.
- Point out the natural and human-made features.
- Look for areas of healthy vegetation and clean water, and areas showing signs of pollution.
- Look for connections between the areas of pollution and the human-made features.

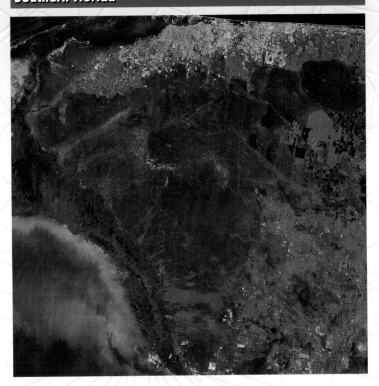

Southern Florida

Technology Skills Practice

1. What geographic area is shown in this image?

2. Where do you see the healthiest vegetation?

3. Where in the picture do you see water that might be polluted or muddy?

SECTION 2

New Zealand

PREVIEW

Words to Know
- *manuka*
- fjord
- geothermal power

Places to Locate
- New Zealand
- North Island
- South Island
- Wellington
- Auckland
- Southern Alps
- Canterbury Plains

Read to Learn . . .
1. what two large islands make up most of New Zealand.
2. what products New Zealand exports to other countries.
3. how New Zealanders spend their leisure time.

What country has more than 15 times as many sheep as people? New Zealand is the answer. Rolling green hills provide excellent grazing land for some 55 million sheep. New Zealand is one of the world's leading producers of lamb and wool.

New Zealand is an island country in the southwest Pacific Ocean. It lies about 1,200 miles (1,930 km) southeast of its nearest neighbor, Australia. For centuries, distance and isolation separated New Zealand from other parts of the world. Today it is a modern Pacific nation with one of the highest standards of living in the world.

Human/Environment Interaction
The Land

If you were shown two photographs—one of a desert and one of a lush green landscape—you could probably guess which one was Australia and which New Zealand. Although New Zealand lies relatively close to Australia, its landscape is very different from that of its larger neighbor. With 103,470 square miles (267,987 sq. km), New Zealand is about the size of the state of Colorado. The map on page 690 shows you that New Zealand is a long, narrow country. Anywhere you stand in New Zealand, you are not more than 80 miles (129 km) from the sea. New Zealand includes two main islands—North Island and South Island—as well as many smaller islands.

North Island A large volcanic plateau forms the center of North Island. Three active volcanoes and the perfectly shaped cone of inactive Mount Egmont rise above the island's fertile plains. Small shrubs called *manuka* grow well in the plateau's volcanic soil.

Farther north on the plateau you see geysers spewing hot water as high as 100 feet (30 m) in the air. Nearby flow icy cold streams. Engineers use natural steam from the geysers and other volcanic activity to produce electricity for New Zealand's industries, farms, and urban areas.

Fertile lowlands, forested hills, and sandy beaches surround the North Island's volcanic plateau. On the plateau's slopes, sheep and cattle graze. Fruits and vegetables are grown on the coastal lowlands. Seaside resorts offer tourists deep-sea fishing for marlin, shark, and tuna.

South Island A massive mountain chain called the Southern Alps runs along South Island's west coast. Snowcapped Mount Cook, the highest peak in New Zealand, soars 12,349 feet (3,764 m) in the Southern Alps.

This mountainous region reveals some of New Zealand's most beautiful scenery. Glaciers lie on mountain slopes high above thick, green forests and sparkling lakes. Along the southwestern coast, long narrow fingers of the sea called **fjords** cut into the land. New Zealand's fjords are similar to those in Norway.

From the Southern Alps to the east coast stretch the Canterbury Plains. They form New Zealand's largest area of flat or nearly flat land. Farmers grow grains and ranchers raise sheep here. The map on page 698 shows you the kinds of products New Zealand produces.

Animals and Plants As in Australia, animals and plants in New Zealand are found nowhere else. New Zealanders take pride in this fact. They chose the unusual kiwi (KEE•wee)—a long-beaked bird that cannot fly—as their national symbol. You may have eaten a fruit called a kiwi. This fruit—really a Chinese gooseberry—originated in New Zealand and was named for the kiwi bird.

Giant Australian kauri trees once covered all of North Island. European settlers cut down much of the kauri forest to build homes and ships. Today the kauri trees are protected. One of them is more than 2,000 years old!

The Climate New Zealand has a mild, wet climate. Compare the map on page 692 to the map on page 94. You see that New Zealand lies in a marine west coast region similar to the Pacific Northwest coast of the United States.

"Big Splash" is one of the many spectacular geysers created by volcanic activity in northern New Zealand.
HUMAN/ENVIRONMENT INTERACTION: How are New Zealand's engineers using geysers as a source of energy?

Ocean breezes from the west warm the land in winter and cool it in summer. As in the Pacific Northwest, rain falls throughout the year in New Zealand.

Because New Zealand lies south of the Equator, its seasons are the opposite of those in the Northern Hemisphere. July is New Zealand's coolest month, while January and February are the warmest months. Temperatures get cooler as you move from the north to the south.

Movement

The Economy

About 55 percent of New Zealand's land—its greatest resource—is cropland or pastureland. With its mild climate and fertile soil, New Zealand supports a thriving farm economy and exports many farm products. In recent years, manufacturing and tourism also have become important sources of income for New Zealand.

Farming A return to the use of natural fibers in clothing has boosted New Zealand's economy. A large percentage of the world's wool comes from New Zealand ranches. Its farmers and ranchers also produce dairy products and meat. The major agricultural exports of New Zealand are wool, lamb, butter, and cheese. Wheat, barley, oats, apples, and kiwifruit are also grown there.

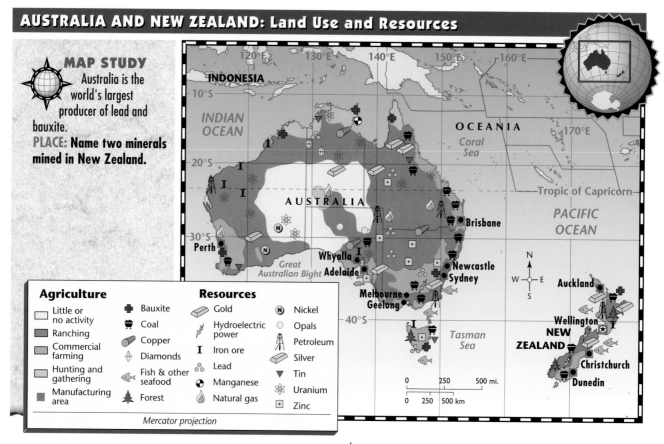

AUSTRALIA AND NEW ZEALAND: Land Use and Resources

MAP STUDY
Australia is the world's largest producer of lead and bauxite.
PLACE: Name two minerals mined in New Zealand.

Agriculture
- Little or no activity
- Ranching
- Commercial farming
- Hunting and gathering
- Manufacturing area

Resources
- Bauxite
- Coal
- Copper
- Diamonds
- Fish & other seafood
- Forest
- Gold
- Hydroelectric power
- Iron ore
- Lead
- Manganese
- Natural gas
- Nickel
- Opals
- Petroleum
- Silver
- Tin
- Uranium
- Zinc

Mercator projection

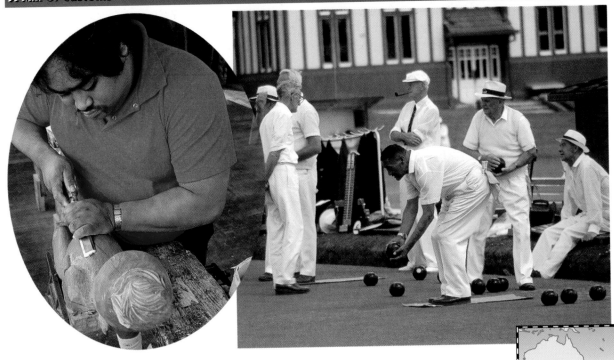

A Maori wood-carver practices his skill *(left)*. The British sport of lawn bowling is popular with New Zealanders of European descent *(right)*.
PLACE: What percentage of New Zealand's population is Maori?

Mining and Manufacturing New Zealand has only a few minerals but is rich in **geothermal power**, or electric power produced from natural steam. The major source of power, however, is hydroelectricity.

In recent years, New Zealand has developed its industrial economy. Its factories now produce cars, furniture and other wood products, clothing, and electronic equipment. Most manufacturing, however, involves making food products such as butter, milk, and cheese.

Place
The People

Picture this scene: The year is about A.D. 1300. Small canoes paddled by a Polynesian people called the Maori reach the New Zealand shore. The lush, green landscape is a welcome sight. A quick hunt produces a large mao bird and a lizard for dinner. The Maori decide to stay.

The arrival of the first people in New Zealand could have happened just this way. Today about 9 percent of the population are Maori (MOWR•ee). Most of the rest of New Zealand's 3.8 million people trace their ancestry to British settlers who came to the islands in the 1800s. Immigrants still come to New Zealand from the United Kingdom and other countries.

Influences of the Past The Maori are believed to have arrived in New Zealand about 700 years ago from Pacific islands far to the northeast. They developed skills in farming, weaving, fishing, and bird hunting and became well-known for their artistic wood carvings.

A few European explorers first came to New Zealand in the mid-1600s. Almost 200 years passed before European settlers—most of them British—arrived in large numbers. Then the British government decided to add New Zealand to its empire. In 1840 British officials signed a treaty with Maori leaders. The Maori agreed to accept British rule in return for the right to keep their lands. British settlers, however, eventually moved into Maori territory. Although the Maori fought to keep their lands, the British eventually defeated them.

New Zealand is a country of "firsts." In 1893 it became the first country in the world to give women the right to vote. New Zealand was also among the first countries to provide government help to the elderly, the sick, and those without jobs.

In 1907 New Zealand became independent of the United Kingdom. A parliamentary democracy, the New Zealand government works to improve housing, job opportunities, and education for all of its citizens, including Maori. Many Maori also want the government to return lands taken from them under British rule. In 1994 the New Zealand government paid one Maori group millions of dollars for land taken by the British.

Way of Life About 85 percent of New Zealanders live in urban areas. You can see where these cities are located on the map on page 698. The largest cities are Auckland (AW•kluhnd), a major port, and Wellington, the national capital. Both lie on North Island where three-fourths of New Zealanders live. Two smaller cities—Christchurch and Dunedin—are manufacturing centers on South Island.

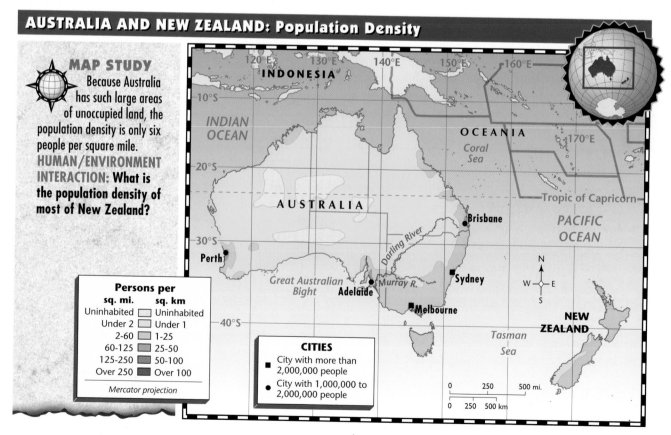

AUSTRALIA AND NEW ZEALAND: Population Density

MAP STUDY
Because Australia has such large areas of unoccupied land, the population density is only six people per square mile.
HUMAN/ENVIRONMENT INTERACTION: What is the population density of most of New Zealand?

Persons per

sq. mi.	sq. km
Uninhabited	Uninhabited
Under 2	Under 1
2-60	1-25
60-125	25-50
125-250	50-100
Over 250	Over 100

Mercator projection

CITIES
■ City with more than 2,000,000 people
● City with 1,000,000 to 2,000,000 people

New Zealanders love outdoor activities. In New Zealand's mild climate, they enjoy camping, hiking, hunting, boating, and mountain climbing in any season. The people of New Zealand also enjoy sports such as cricket, a British game played with a bat and ball, and rugby, a British form of football.

Many New Zealanders still observe British customs. Yet immigrants from Asia, the Pacific, and various European nations have brought cultural diversity to New Zealand. Today, the growing Maori population also receive more recognition than they did in the past.

New Zealand is rapidly becoming a modern Pacific nation that blends European and Maori ways. This mix is evident in the life of 15-year-old Ruth Erutoe, a Maori teenager who lives in a suburb of Auckland. Ruth and her family listen to Italian opera and admire Kiri Te Kanawa (KEE•ree teh KAN• ah•wah), the world-famous opera star from New Zealand. The Erutoes also remain close to their Maori heritage. For weddings and other special occasions, they go to a *marae*, or a Maori meetinghouse. Some meetinghouses are simple buildings. Others are decorated with elaborate wood carvings. Turn to page 708 to see an example of a Maori wood carving.

Bustling Auckland, New Zealand

Auckland is New Zealand's largest city, chief seaport, and industrial center.
PLACE: What is the capital of New Zealand?

SECTION 2 ASSESSMENT

REVIEWING TERMS AND FACTS

1. **Define the following:** *manuka*, fjord, geothermal power.

2. **REGION** What physical feature lies in the center of North Island?

3. **MOVEMENT** From where did the Maori come?

4. **LOCATION** Where is the city of Wellington in relation to Auckland?

MAP STUDY ACTIVITIES

5. Look at the land use map on page 698. What mineral resources does New Zealand have?

6. Turn to the population density map on page 700. Where do the fewest people of New Zealand live?

MAKING CONNECTIONS

MATH	SCIENCE	HISTORY	LITERATURE	TECHNOLOGY

Australia is home to more than 120 kinds of marsupials—mammals whose young grow and mature inside a pouch on the mother's belly. Wallabies, wombats, and other marsupials are unfamiliar to people outside Australia. Kangaroos and koala bears, however, are known throughout the world.

KANGAROOS No matter what their size or where they live, all kangaroos have one thing in common: big hind feet. Either red or gray, kangaroos bound along at about 20 miles (32 km) per hour. Some may race up to 40 miles (65 km) per hour. In a single jump a kangaroo can hop 10 feet (3 m) high and cover a distance of 45 feet (14 m)!

Kangaroos also have big ears. Sensitive instruments, a kangaroo's ears are never still. One ear points forward, the other backward. Female kangaroos have front pouches that open at the top to hold their joeys, or infants. These big pockets provide nourishment and protection for several months.

KOALAS Despite their name, koalas are not bears. Like their kangaroo cousins, female koalas protect and nourish their young in pouches on their bellies. A female koala's pouch, however, opens at the bottom. Strong muscles keep the pouch shut and the young koalas safe inside.

Koala Mom and Joey

Koalas make their homes in the eucalyptus trees of southeastern Australia. Quiet, calm, and sleepy, the cuddly-looking animals spend at least 20 hours a day dozing high in a favorite tree. Koalas are fussy eaters. They eat nothing but eucalyptus leaves—about 2.5 pounds (1.2 kg) a day. The leaves also provide the animals with all the moisture they need.

Making the Connection

1. About how many kinds of marsupials live in Australia?
2. How are kangaroos and koalas alike? How are they different?

Chapter 26 Highlights

Important Things to Know About Australia and New Zealand

SECTION 1 AUSTRALIA

- Australia is both a country and the world's smallest continent.
- Deserts and grasslands cover most of the country west of the Great Dividing Range.
- Australia's economy relies mostly on farming and mining.
- Australia is the world's leading wool-producing country. It also leads in the production of bauxite and lead.
- The first Australians were the Aborigines. Others are of European and Asian descent.
- Most Australians live in cities. Sydney, Melbourne, Adelaide, Brisbane, and Perth are the largest.

SECTION 2 NEW ZEALAND

- New Zealand includes two major islands—North Island and South Island—and many smaller islands.
- New Zealand has a mild, wet climate.
- New Zealand's agricultural exports—especially wool—are the mainstays of its economy.
- New Zealand gets most of its electricity from geothermal energy.
- The Maori, a Polynesian ethnic group from the South Pacific, were the first people to settle New Zealand.
- New Zealand's culture at one time was mainly influenced by British traditions. Now it is a mix of many cultures, including those of the Maori and other immigrants.

Sydney, Australia ▶

REVIEWING KEY TERMS

Match the numbered terms in Set A with their lettered definitions in Set B.

A

1. *manuka*
2. bush
3. geothermal power
4. outback
5. marsupial
6. fjord
7. coral
8. station

B

A. inlet of the sea that cuts into the land
B. hard material made of the skeletons of small sea animals
C. electricity produced from natural steam
D. Australian sheep or cattle ranch
E. vast inland areas of Australia
F. small shrubs that grow on New Zealand's volcanic soil
G. Australian word for rural areas
H. mammal that carries its young in a pouch

REVIEWING THE MAIN IDEAS

Mental Mapping Activity

Draw a freehand map of Australia and New Zealand. Label the following:
- Sydney
- Melbourne
- Auckland
- North Island
- South Island
- Wellington

Section 1

1. LOCATION Why is Australia called the Land Down Under?
2. MOVEMENT What two countries are Australia's major trading partners?
3. PLACE Why was the city of Canberra built?

Section 2

4. PLACE What large mountain range runs down the western coast of South Island?
5. MOVEMENT What are New Zealand's major agricultural exports?
6. HUMAN/ENVIRONMENT INTERACTION What leisure activities do New Zealanders enjoy that are made possible by the country's climate?

CRITICAL THINKING ACTIVITIES

1. **Making Comparisons** How does the climate of Australia compare with that of New Zealand?
2. **Making Inferences** Why do you think most Australians live in coastal cities?

CONNECTIONS TO WORLD CULTURES

Cooperative Learning Activity Work in a group of three to learn more about the people and cultures of Australia and New Zealand. Each group will choose a country. Then each member will select *one* of the following topics to research: (a) leisure activities; (b) arts and crafts; or (c) music and dance. Share your information with the rest of your group. Prepare a written report, a poster, or a travel brochure that presents your group's findings.

GeoJournal Writing Activity

Imagine that you are visiting Australia. Using the map on page 688, prepare a list of places to see—one place for each state of the country. Write an itinerary describing the places you want to visit, what you hope to see there, and how many miles (km) you will travel from place to place.

TECHNOLOGY ACTIVITY

Using a Computerized Card Catalog

Use a computerized card catalog in your school or local library to locate sources about Australia's Great Barrier Reef. Write a report describing the formation of the reef, its animal life, and environmental threats to it. Be sure to include a map showing the location of the reef. Share your report with the rest of the class.

PLACE LOCATION ACTIVITY: AUSTRALIA AND NEW ZEALAND

Match the letters on the map with the places and physical features of Australia and New Zealand. Write your answers on a separate sheet of paper.

1. Brisbane
2. Great Barrier Reef
3. Wellington
4. Darling River
5. Canberra
6. Great Dividing Range
7. Auckland
8. Southern Alps
9. Perth
10. Tasmania

GeoLab ACTIVITY

From the classroom of Rebecca Revis, Sylvan Hills Junior High School, Sherwood, Arkansas

GLACIERS: Earth's Scouring Pads

Background

Antarctica, the world's coldest and iciest region, has mountains, valleys, and lowlands underneath its ice cap. Like the Arctic Circle, the Antarctic Circle also has many glaciers. Glaciers and rivers erode the land and change it a great deal. In this activity, you'll observe how glaciers and rivers change the earth's surface.

Glacier-created valley, New Zealand

Believe it or NOT!

Glaciers cover about one-tenth of the earth's land and hold about 85 percent of all freshwater. The power of glaciers is enormous. Consider that the Great Lakes were formed by a glacier scouring out a river valley.

Materials

- water
- sand, gravel, and clay
- stream table with sand
- lamp with reflector
- ruler

(NOTE: You will be using electrical equipment near water in this GeoLab. Please keep these items away from one another.)

What To Do

A. Set up the stream table and lamp as shown.

B. Make an ice block by mixing water with sand, gravel, and clay in a container that measures about 2 inches (5 cm) by 8 inches (20 cm) by 1 inch (2 cm). Then freeze this container.

C. Make a V-shaped river channel. Measure and record its width and depth. Draw a sketch that includes these measurements.

D. Place the ice block, to act as a moving glacier, at the upper end of the stream table.

E. Gently push the glacier along the river channel until it is under the light, halfway between the top and bottom of the stream table.

F. Turn on the light and allow the ice to melt. Observe and record what happens.

G. Measure and record the width and depth of the glacial channel. Draw a sketch of the channel and include these measurements in your journal.

Lab Activity Report

1. How can you figure out the direction from which a glacier traveled?

2. How can you tell how far down the valley the glacier traveled?

3. How do glaciers affect the surface over which they move?

4. **Drawing Conclusions** How can you identify land that was once covered by a glacier?

Go A Step Further

+2   +2

Before your "glacier" melts completely, take one small part of it and rub it over a piece of wood. What happens in the wood's surface? How do glaciers make similar patterns in rocks?

Cultural HERITAGE:
AUSTRALIA AND OCEANIA

ARCHITECTURE ▶ ▶ ▶ ▶

The opera house in Sydney's harbor is a landmark recognized throughout the world. The overlapping white shells of its roofline were designed to imitate the shapes of boat sails in the harbor.

◀ ◀ ◀ ◀ WOOD CARVING

The Maori of New Zealand are expert wood-carvers. Many of their intricately textured carvings portray ancestors. The carvings decorate homes and community meetinghouses.

PAINTING ▶ ▶ ▶ ▶

Nature plays an important role in the lives of the Australian Aborigines, and it is reflected in their art. This painting, done on bark, shows many animal, plants, and landscape features.

708

◄ ◄ ◄ ◄ MASKS

This mask, with its large eyes and bright colors, represents the face of an owl. The people of Papua, New Guinea, make animal masks to use in traditional dances.

THATCHED BUILDINGS ▶ ▶ ▶ ▶

New Guinea builders use the trunks of palm trees to build the frames for their beautiful spirit houses. The walls and roof are woven from palm leaves. Only men are allowed in these buildings, which hold each village's religious relics.

BOOMERANGS ▲ ▲ ▲ ▲

Australian boomerangs come in many shapes and sizes. The Aborigines use boomerangs mostly for hunting. Some are carved or painted for use in religious ceremonies. The small boomerangs are toys for children.

APPRECIATING CULTURE

1. What natural materials do the Aborigines, Maori, and people of New Guinea need to create their artwork and buildings?

2. How would you describe the Sydney Opera House to someone who has not seen it?

Chapter 27

Oceania and Antarctica

MAP STUDY ACTIVITY

You are ending your geographic "tour" of the world by learning about Oceania and Antarctica.

1. What is the capital of Papua New Guinea?

2. How many research stations does the United States have in Antarctica?

Oceania

PREVIEW

Words to Know
- continental island
- copra
- high island
- low island
- atoll
- phosphate
- trust territory

Places to Locate
- Melanesia
- Micronesia
- Polynesia

Read to Learn . . .
1. what geographic areas make up Oceania.
2. how land and climate affect the way people in Oceania earn their livings.
3. what groups have settled in Oceania.

What do you picture when you hear the word "paradise"? You might see one of the more than 30,000 tropical islands that dot the blue waters of the Pacific Ocean. Some of the islands, like New Guinea shown here, are mountainous.

The Pacific island region is called Oceania. Great distances separate this region from other parts of the world. The islands of Oceania—about 25,000 of them—are spread out across 70 million square miles (181.3 million sq. km). Because of Oceania's vast distances, geographers group the islands into three main regions: Melanesia, Micronesia, and Polynesia.

Location
Melanesia

North and east of Australia lie the islands of Melanesia (MEH•luh•NEE•zhuh). Because of their dense vegetation, Melanesia's islands are often called the "black islands." Melanesia's land and ocean area combined almost match the land area of the continental United States. The largest country in size and population is Papua New Guinea (PA•pyuh•wuh noo GIH•nee). It lies on the eastern half of the island of New Guinea.

Southeast of Papua New Guinea are three other independent island countries: the Solomon Islands, Fiji, and Vanuatu (VAN•WAH•TOO). Near these countries is New Caledonia, a group of islands ruled by France.

The Climate and Economy Melanesia consists mostly of continental islands. A **continental island** is formed by chunks of land split off from a larger continent or through the erosion of a link of land that once connected the island to the mainland. Rugged mountains and thick rain forests cover the continental islands of Melanesia. Strips of fertile plains hug island coastlines.

Thermometers record little change in temperatures in Melanesia year-round. The map on page 720 shows you that most of Melanesia has a tropical climate. The temperature along island coasts seldom falls below 70°F (21°C) or rises above 80°F (27°C).

Most Melanesians are subsistence farmers, growing only enough to feed their families. Papua New Guinea and Fiji, however, cultivate agricultural products for export. Farmers in Papua New Guinea grow cacao, tea, and coffee. Those in Fiji raise sugarcane. A major money-making product of Melanesia—and the rest of Oceania—is **copra**, or dried coconut meat. Countries around the world use coconut oil from copra to make margarine, soap, and other products.

Some Melanesian islands, such as Papua New Guinea and New Caledonia, hold rich mineral resources. Rugged mountains and vast shipping distances, however, make it costly to develop mining and other industries.

The Past and Present Melanesians share many different cultures and languages. More than 700 languages are spoken in Papua New Guinea alone! To ease communication, English is the language of business and government throughout most of Melanesia. From the 1800s to the mid-1900s, Western countries ruled most of Melanesia. Many island countries today are a blend of Western and Melanesian cultures.

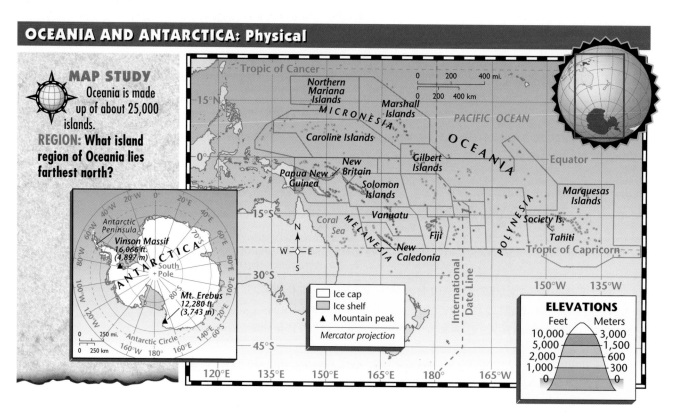

OCEANIA AND ANTARCTICA: Physical

MAP STUDY
Oceania is made up of about 25,000 islands.
REGION: What island region of Oceania lies farthest north?

712

UNIT 9

Many Melanesians still live in small villages in houses made of grass and other natural materials. They keep strong ties to their local group and hold on to traditional customs. Only a few Melanesians live in cities. Port Moresby in Papua New Guinea and Suva in Fiji are among the largest urban areas. Many people in these cities live in modern houses and have jobs in business and government.

More Melanesians live in small villages like this one in the Solomon Islands *(left)* than in modern cities such as Fiji's capital of Suva *(right)*. **PLACE: How are the lifestyles of rural Melanesians different from those who live in the city?**

Region
Micronesia

North of Melanesia lies another island region—Micronesia. The name refers to the "tiny islands" in this region. Look at the map on page 712 to see the contrasts between the two regions. The map shows you that the islands of Micronesia are scattered across a vast ocean area. The independent countries of Micronesia are the Federated States of Micronesia, the Marshall Islands, Palau (puh•LOW), Nauru (nah•OO•roo), and Kiribati (KIHR•uh•BAS). The Northern Mariana Islands and the island of Guam are territories linked to the United States.

High and Low Islands Rich soil, ribbonlike waterfalls, and thick green vegetation blanket Micronesia's **high islands**. Volcanic activity formed most of these rugged islands many centuries ago. The rest of Micronesia includes **low islands** usually made of coral, and have little vegetation. Skeletons of millions of tiny sea animals formed the low islands over thousands of years. Most of the low islands are **atolls**, or ring-shaped coral reefs that surround small lagoons. You often will find atolls built up on the rims of underwater volcanoes that no longer erupt. The chart on page 714 shows you how a typical atoll is formed.

The Climate and Economy Micronesia has a tropical climate. Daily temperatures average about 80°F (27°C) year-round, and rain is plentiful across the region. Tropical breezes flowing over these islands are not always gentle, however. From July to October, fierce storms called typhoons sometimes strike the islands, causing loss of life and much destruction.

Subsistence farming is the major economic activity on Micronesia's high islands. Farmers there grow food crops in the fertile soil and raise cattle, sheep, and goats. On some high islands, copra is a major export. People on the low coral islands rely on the sea for food.

Most Micronesian island countries depend on aid from the United States, Australia, and Europe. With this aid they are building roads, ports, and airfields so that industry can develop in the future. The only exception is the tiny island republic of Nauru. For years the 10,400 people of Nauru have prospered from the mining of **phosphate,** a mineral used in making fertilizers. With Nauru's phosphate deposits running out, however, the people are looking for other sources of income.

The Past and Present Southeast Asians first settled Micronesia about 4,000 years ago. European explorers, traders, and missionaries settled on the Micronesian islands during the 1700s and early 1800s. By the early 1900s, many European countries, the United States, and Japan owned colonies in this region.

During World War II, the United States and Japan fought a number of bloody battles on Micronesian islands. Why? Look at the map on page A30 to see the islands' location in relation to Japan and the United States. Following World War II, most of Micronesia was turned over to the United States as **trust territories**. These territories were under temporary United States control. Since the 1970s, many of the Micronesian islands have become independent.

Formation of an Atoll/Coral Reef

GRAPHIC STUDY
An atoll begins as a ring of coral around a volcanic island.
PLACE: Why do you think a lagoon is not very deep?

Today Micronesia's 400,000 people speak 11 languages and several dialects. Most of them live in villages headed by local chiefs. In recent years many young people have left the villages to find jobs in towns.

Place
Polynesia

East of Melanesia and Micronesia lie the tropical islands often pictured on travel brochures—the islands that make up Polynesia. The name refers to the "many islands" in the region. The map on page 712 shows you that Polynesia is the largest of the three Pacific island regions. Three independent countries—Samoa, Tonga, and Tuvalu—are found in Polynesia. Other island groups are under French rule and are known as French Polynesia. Tahiti, Polynesia's largest island, is part of this French territory.

The Climate and Economy Most Polynesian islands are high volcanic islands, some with tall, rugged mountains. Thick rain forests cover mountain valleys and coastal plains. Other Polynesian islands are of the low coral type. With little soil, the only vegetation is scattered coconut palms. Because most of Polynesia lies in the tropics, the climate is hot and humid.

Most people in Polynesia raise crops or fish for their food. Some farmers raise coconuts and tropical fruits for export. Tourism is the fastest-growing industry of Polynesia. Each year thousands of visitors come by air or sea to its emerald-green mountains and white, palm-lined beaches. New roads, hotels, shops, and restaurants serve these tourists.

The Past and Present Settlers came later to Polynesia than to the other two Pacific regions. The first Polynesians were probably Melanesians or Micronesians who sailed to the islands in canoes.

During the late 1800s, the stronger European powers divided up Polynesia among themselves. Military bases were built on these well-located islands in the 1900s. They were perfect refueling stops for airplanes crossing the Pacific. Beginning in the 1960s, some Polynesian territories chose independence while others decided to remain under Western rule.

Today about 580,000 people live in Polynesia. Modern influences have affected the islands, yet some Polynesians live traditionally in villages. Women in Samoa and Tonga still make tapa cloth. They first strip the inner bark from paper

Teen Scene

Island Life

Kaulana Pau lives on a tiny atoll surrounded by ocean. The atoll is in the Caroline Islands in Micronesia. Kaulana has visited some of the cities on the larger islands and plans to go the University of Guam someday. But when asked if she would like to move to a city, she politely answers, "No, thank you." The ocean is a part of Kaulana's life. "It gives us food, it's our highway to other islands, and it's how my family earns a living," she says. Kaulana's family takes the fish they catch to a processing plant on one of the larger islands. There it is either dried or canned for export.

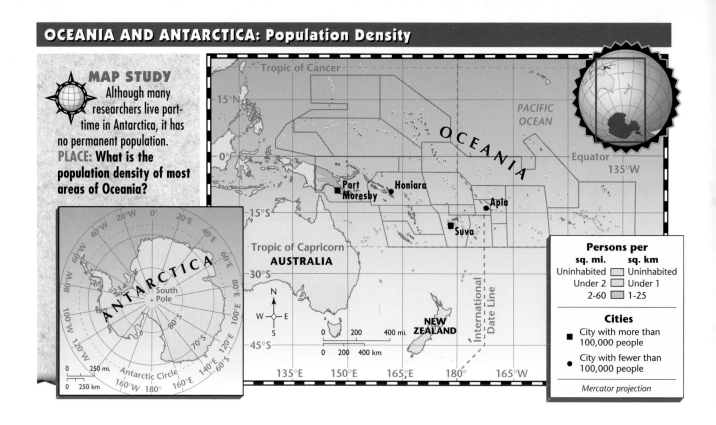

MAP STUDY
Although many researchers live part-time in Antarctica, it has no permanent population.
PLACE: What is the population density of most areas of Oceania?

Persons per

sq. mi.	sq. km
Uninhabited	Uninhabited
Under 2	Under 1
2-60	1-25

Cities
■ City with more than 100,000 people
● City with fewer than 100,000 people

Mercator projection

mulberry trees. Then they soak the bark and beat it with wooden clubs to form the cloth which is used to make clothing.

An increasing number of Polynesians live in cities or towns. Thirteen-year-old Henri Moeino lives in Papeete (PAH•pee•AY•tee), the largest city and port on the island of Tahiti. Henri points out that Papeete and its surrounding area are home to more than 100,000 people. He and other Tahitians belong to an interesting mix of peoples. Henri has Polynesian and French ancestry. Like most urban Polynesians, Henri follows both European and American ways.

SECTION 1 ASSESSMENT

REVIEWING TERMS AND FACTS

1. Define: continental island, copra, high island, low island, atoll, phosphate, trust territory.

2. REGION What are the three island regions of Oceania?

3. PLACE How do the high and low islands in Micronesia differ in appearance?

4. HUMAN/ENVIRONMENT INTERACTION How do most people in Oceania make a living?

MAP STUDY ACTIVITIES

5. Turn to the political map on page 710. What is the capital of Fiji?

6. Look at the physical map on page 712. What is the largest island in Oceania?

BUILDING GEOGRAPHY SKILLS

Analyzing a Photograph

You can learn much about the geography and culture of a place from a photograph. The key is to examine clues in the photo. Because photographs show only a small "slice" of reality, however, they can be misleading. For example, a picture of the wealthiest part of a city does not accurately show the living standards of all of the city's people. To accurately interpret a photograph, follow these steps:

- Read the caption.
- Name the landforms, climate, vegetation, cultural features, and human activities in the photograph.
- Think about what may be excluded from this view.

Glencoe's **Skillbuilder Interactive Workbook, Level 1** provides instruction and practice in key social studies skills.

Drying Copra on the Solomon Islands

A woman collects dried coconuts, called copra, which will be pressed to produce coconut oil. About 30 coconuts are needed to make 1 gallon of oil. The oil is then used to make soaps, margarine, detergents, cosmetics, and many other products.

Geography Skills Practice

1. What is the main topic of this photograph?

2. What natural features are included in the photograph?

3. What information about culture is shown?

4. What information do you think is left out of the photograph?

SECTION 2 Antarctica

PREVIEW

Words to Know
- rookery
- ice shelf
- crevasse
- krill
- ozone

Places to Locate
- Antarctica
- Transantarctic Mountains
- South Pole

Read to Learn . . .
1. where Antarctica is located.
2. why Antarctica is called a polar desert.
3. how Antarctica is like a scientific laboratory.

Who doesn't love penguins? Their shiny "tuxedos" and waddling walk have fascinated people for years. Scientists study the habits of penguins, the largest group of marine animals in Antarctica. For example, studying where they build their nests—or **rookeries**—gives scientists more clues to understanding the vast continent of Antarctica.

Antarctica—surrounded by icy ocean water—sits on the southern end of the earth. It covers about 5,400,000 square miles (14,000,000 sq. km). It is larger in size than either Europe or Australia. Mysterious Antarctica is the least explored of all the continents.

Location

Landforms

Picture Antarctica—a rich, green land covered by forests and lush plants. Does this description match your mental picture of the continent? Fossils discovered there tell scientists that millions of years ago Antarctica's landscape was inhabited by dinosaurs and small mammals.

Today a huge ice cap buries nearly 98 percent of Antarctica's land area. In many places, the ice cap is 1.5 to 2 miles (2.4 to 3.2 km) thick—about the height of 10 tall skyscrapers. This sea of ice holds about 70 percent of the world's freshwater. Where the ice cap spreads beyond the land and over the ocean, it forms an **ice shelf.**

Icy Coasts The ice cap is heavy. In some areas, it forms **crevasses**, or cracks, more than 100 feet (30 m) deep. As glaciers meet the sea, large chunks of ice break off to form icebergs. Antarctica borders the Atlantic, Pacific, and Indian oceans. As these oceans reach Antarctica, they become cooler and less salty, which allows them to freeze. Some of the fish in these waters have a special antifreeze—a protein in their blood that keeps it from freezing.

Landforms Beneath the packed layers of the ice cap lie highlands, valleys, and lowlands—the same features you would find on other continents. A long mountain range called the Transantarctic Mountains crosses Antarctica and splits it in two. The highest peak on the continent—Vinson Massif—rises here to 16,066 feet (4,897 m). The Transantarctic Mountains sweep out into the Antarctic Peninsula, which reaches within 600 miles (965 km) of South America's Cape Horn.

A high, flat plateau covers the area east of the Transantarctic Mountains. The earth's southernmost point, the South Pole, lies on the plateau at the center of Antarctica. West of the mountains is a group of low islands buried under layers and layers of ice. On Ross Island rises the peak of Mount Erebus. At 12,220 feet (3,743 m), it is Antarctica's most active volcano.

Place

Climate

Now that you have a mental picture of Antarctica's ice cap, think about this: Antarctica receives so little precipitation that it is the world's largest, coldest desert! Inland Antarctica receives no rain and hardly any new snow each year.

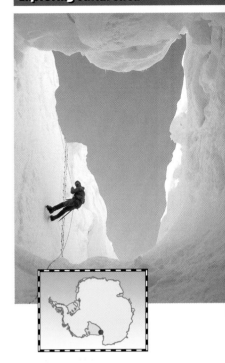

A scientist lowers into a crevasse near his research station. **HUMAN/ENVIRONMENT INTERACTION: What may happen to Antarctica's environment if too many people work there?**

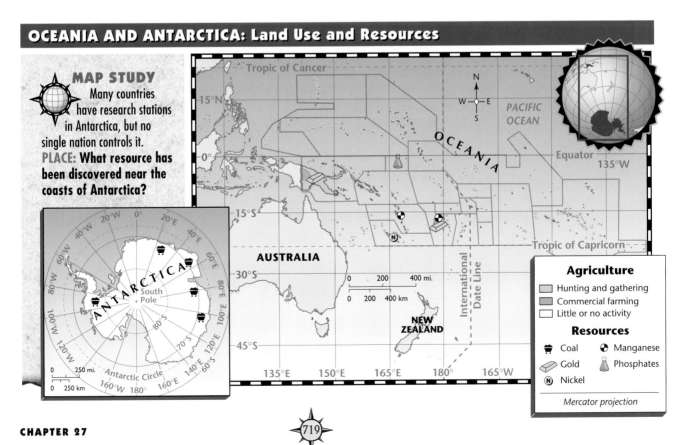

OCEANIA AND ANTARCTICA: Land Use and Resources

MAP STUDY
Many countries have research stations in Antarctica, but no single nation controls it.
PLACE: What resource has been discovered near the coasts of Antarctica?

Tropic of Cancer

15°N

PACIFIC OCEAN

OCEANIA

Equator
135°W

0°

15°S

Tropic of Capricorn

AUSTRALIA

30°S

International Date Line

NEW ZEALAND

45°S

ANTARCTICA
South Pole
Antarctic Circle

135°E   150°E   165°E   180°   165°W

Agriculture
▢ Hunting and gathering
▢ Commercial farming
▢ Little or no activity

Resources
⛏ Coal   ◉ Manganese
▱ Gold   ⚗ Phosphates
Ⓝ Nickel

Mercator projection

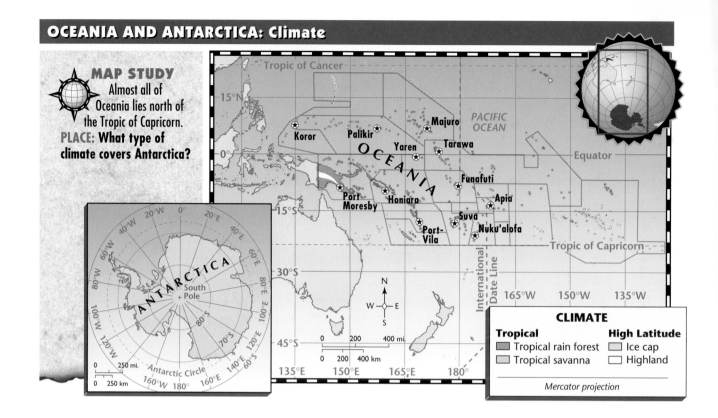

MAP STUDY

Almost all of Oceania lies north of the Tropic of Capricorn.

PLACE: What type of climate covers Antarctica?

The map above shows you that Antarctica has a polar ice cap climate. Imagine summer in a place where temperatures may fall as low as −30°F (−34.5°C) and climb only to 32°F (0°C)! Antarctic summers last from December through February. Winter temperatures along the coasts fall to −40°F (−40°C), and in inland areas to a low of −100°F (−73°C).

Region
Resources

Scientists believe that the Antarctic ice hides a treasure chest of minerals. The mining of resources on this continent is a source of international disagreement, however.

Mineral Resources Antarctica has major deposits of coal, and lesser amounts of copper, gold, iron ore, manganese, and zinc hidden underneath its ice cap. Petroleum may lie offshore. None of Antarctica's mineral resources have been developed. Many people believe that mining these resources would harm Antarctica's fragile environment.

Plants and Animals What is the largest permanent land animal in Antarctica? Most people would say the penguin. They would be incorrect, however. Penguins are marine animals, not land animals. Today the life-form considered to be the largest permanent land animal is *Beligica antarctica,* a wingless insect about one-tenth of an inch long.

Only a few small plants and insects can survive in Antarctica's cold, dry, inland areas. Most plants on the continent are algae and mosses that grow along the coast on rocky surfaces. The waters and coasts around Antarctica, however, are home to penguins, fish, whales, and many kinds of flying birds. A small shrimplike animal called **krill** is a key source of food for other animals in Antarctica.

Human/Environment Interaction
Exploration and Research

Because of its harsh climate, Antarctica is the only continent that has no permanent human settlement. Its largely unspoiled environment has made it a favorable place for scientific research.

WHAT IN THE WORLD?

Operation Highjump
In 1946 the United States carried out the largest exploration of Antarctica up to that time. Captain Richard E. Byrd led 4,700 people in Operation Highjump. With 13 ships and 23 airplanes, Byrd and his group found more than 25 new islands and photographed 1,400 miles (2,300 km) of uncharted coastline.

Explorers and Scientists Europeans first sighted Antarctica during the early 1800s. In 1911 explorers competed with one another to reach the South Pole. You can read about this exciting race on page 722. The discovery of the South Pole opened the rest of Antarctica for exploration.

By the 1960s scientists from 12 countries had set up research centers on Antarctica. The map on page 710 shows you the major research centers. To preserve Antarctica as a peaceful scientific research lab, 12 countries signed the Antarctic Treaty in 1959. In the early 1990s, a number of countries agreed to keep Antarctica free of mining for 50 years.

Much research in Antarctica deals with **ozone,** a form of oxygen in the atmosphere. You learned in Chapter 3 that ozone protects all living things on the earth from certain harmful rays of the sun. In the 1980s scientists discovered a weakening or "hole" in the ozone layer above Antarctica. Studying this layer will help scientists learn more about possible changes in the world's climates.

SECTION 2 ASSESSMENT

REVIEWING TERMS AND FACTS
1. Define the following: rookery, ice shelf, crevasse, ozone.
2. LOCATION What oceans surround Antarctica?
3. PLACE What kind of climate does Antarctica have?
4. HUMAN/ENVIRONMENT INTERACTION Why was the 1959 Antarctic Treaty important?

MAP STUDY ACTIVITIES
5. Look at the map on page 719. What major mineral resource lies in Antarctica?
6. Turn to the climate map on page 720. How do the climates of Oceania and Antarctica differ?

MAKING CONNECTIONS

MATH | **SCIENCE** | **HISTORY** | **LITERATURE** | **TECHNOLOGY**

The big news in the fall of 1911 was the race between Norway's Roald Amundsen and Britain's Robert Scott. The two seasoned explorers took on the challenge of finding the exact location of the South Pole.

READY, SET . . . Arriving at Ross Island, Scott and his crew set up headquarters at Cape Evans. Their equipment included 21 ponies and 3 tractor-like, motorized sleds.

Amundsen and his team pitched camp at the extreme western edge of the Ross Ice Shelf. To make the journey easier, Amundsen brought trained sled dogs and special skis.

. . . GO!! Amundsen's crew and dogsleds pulled out on October 19. Their expedition cut a new route over the Great Ice Barrier and through Antarctica's great central plateau. During the 1,400-mile (2,253-km) trip, the men left supplies in seven well-marked places. They reached the South Pole on December 14. There they put up a small tent on the Pole's exact location and left a letter inside for Scott. The team arrived back at their original campsite on January 25, 1912, in good health and high spirits.

On November 1, Scott and his 15-member team headed for the central plateau on a well-known route across Beardmore Glacier. The trip was a disaster. Their motorized sleds bogged down in soft snow, and supplies ran low. Eleven men and all the ponies died. Only Scott and 4 others made it to the South Pole on January 17, 1912. On the return trip to Cape Evans, however, the men were unable to find their poorly marked supply sites in the vast windy Antarctic wastes. All died from hunger and cold.

Scott's Expedition

Making the Connection

1. What transportation equipment did each team bring?
2. How did Antarctica's geography and climate defeat Scott?

Important Things to Know About Oceania and Antarctica

SECTION 1 OCEANIA

- Oceania is made up of three regions—Melanesia, Micronesia, and Polynesia.
- Oceania has three kinds of islands: continental islands separated from continents, high islands formed by volcanoes, and low islands made from coral reefs.
- Most islands of Polynesia were trust territories at one time. Today many are independent.
- The cultures of these island groups are a mixture of local traditions, the cultures of European settlers, and modern influences.
- Farming, fishing, and tourism are the major economic activities of Oceania.
- The largest island region in Oceania by size is Polynesia.

SECTION 2 ANTARCTICA

- A huge ice cap covers most of Antarctica.
- The earth's southernmost point, the South Pole, lies near the center of Antarctica.
- Potential uses of Antarctica's resources include mining of minerals and transforming ice into freshwater that could be used by the rest of the world.
- Animals such as penguins, fish, whales, birds, and krill make their homes in the icy waters and on the coasts of Antarctica.
- Antarctica is the only continent with no permanent human settlement.
- Antarctica is a major center of international scientific research.

Port Ucla, Vanuatu ▶

REVIEWING KEY TERMS

Match the numbered terms in Set A with their lettered definitions in Set B.

A
1. krill
2. atoll
3. crevasse
4. high island
5. copra
6. low island
7. continental island
8. phosphate

B
A. large island thrust up from the ocean
B. large break in the Antarctic ice
C. mineral used to make fertilizer
D. shrimplike animal found in Antarctic waters
E. island formed from coral reefs
F. coral reef surrounding a bay
G. island made from volcanoes
H. dried coconut meat

Mental Mapping Activity

Draw a freehand map of Antarctica. Label the following:
- Atlantic Ocean
- Pacific Ocean
- Antarctic Peninsula
- South Pole
- Antarctic Circle

REVIEWING THE MAIN IDEAS

Section 1
1. LOCATION Where is Oceania located?
2. REGION What is the major climate found in Melanesia, Micronesia, and Polynesia?
3. PLACE What mineral is mined in the island republic of Nauru?
4. MOVEMENT Why do people in Polynesia leave their islands?

Section 2
5. LOCATION What lies under the ice cap of Antarctica?
6. PLACE What is summer like in Antarctica?
7. PLACE What kinds of plants grow in Antarctica?
8. REGION Why is Antarctica considered a good place for scientific research?

CRITICAL THINKING ACTIVITIES

1. **Drawing Conclusions** Why is tourism a growing industry in Oceania?
2. **Predicting Consequences** What might have happened to Antarctica if the Antarctic treaties had not been signed?

CONNECTIONS TO WORLD CULTURES

Cooperative Learning Activity Work in groups to learn more about one of the island countries of Oceania. Each group will choose one country from Melanesia, Micronesia, or Polynesia. Then each group member will select one topic to research for a group essay entitled: "One Day of My Life in _____." The essay should describe what a person's daily activities in that location might be like. Put your group's information together to write an essay. Add illustrations if possible. Share your essays with the rest of the class.

GeoJournal Writing Activity

Imagine that you are a scientist working in Antarctica. Write a letter home describing your work and the work of other scientists at your research station.

TECHNOLOGY ACTIVITY

Using a Database Research the wildlife of Australia, Oceania, and Antarctica. Create a database of your information with separate fields for the following: animal, natural habitat, diet, natural predators, introduced predators, and population status. Use the database to create a map showing the locations of each animal group in the region.

PLACE LOCATION ACTIVITY: OCEANIA AND ANTARCTICA

Match the letters on the map with the places and features of Oceania and Antarctica. Write your answers on a separate sheet of paper.

1. Port Moresby
2. Solomon Islands
3. French Polynesia
4. South Pole
5. Fiji
6. Federated States of Micronesia
7. Antarctic Peninsula
8. Pacific Ocean

EYE ON THE ENVIRONMENT

Great Barrier Reef
TROUBLE DOWN UNDER

PROBLEM

Australia's Great Barrier Reef, the world's largest coral reef, is threatened by human activity. Pollution and commercial fishing endanger the reef. The possibility of a major oil spill—hundreds of oil tankers pass near the reef each year—looms as a constant worry. But tourism poses the most serious threat to the reef's health. And every year more than *2 million* people visit the reef!

SOLUTIONS

● To protect the reef and its treasures, the government of Australia works with environmental organizations around the world.

● New laws restrict where and how people may fish, dive, sail, snorkel, or build near the reef.

● Oil tankers, other large ships, and ships carrying hazardous cargo must carry a specially trained pilot to help navigate the reef.

● Specific areas of the reef are set aside for certain tourist activities. Other areas are off-limits except to scientists.

A leopard moray eel pokes its head out of coral. The Great Barrier Reef supports fish, whales, turtles, and countless other sea creatures.

CORAL REEF FACT BANK

🍃 Coral reefs, formed by the accumulated skeletons of coral, are "fish factories" crucial to the world's food chain.

🍃 The Great Barrier Reef covers about 135,000 square miles (350,000 sq. km). It is 1,250 miles (2,011 km) long and contains 2,600 separate reefs and about 300 islands.

🍃 It is home to more than 1,500 species of fish, 400 types of coral, 4,000 species of mollusks, and 22 types of whales.

🍃 The Great Barrier Reef—the largest structure built by living creatures anywhere in the world—is clearly visible from space.

An island—among more than 300 in the Great Barrier Reef—rises from the crystal-clear Coral Sea. Agricultural runoff and other pollution endanger the sea's delicate chemistry and the reef's colonies of coral.

NEW ZEALAND

TEEN TRIBUTE

Five students from Pioneer State High School, in Mackay, Australia, set up a self-guided snorkeling tour of the Great Barrier Reef that keeps tourists off the coral. The students studied an area and then laid out an underwater trail. By carefully choosing the path and placing information markers on the trail, the students help protect the reef—and educate sightseers.

environmental activities

WHAT CAN YOU DO?

TAKE A CLOSER LOOK

1 Where is the Great Barrier Reef located?

2 What human activities have threatened the reef?

🍃 Write to oil companies, encouraging them to be watchful when shipping oil.

🍃 Leave nature the way you find it whenever hiking or camping in state and national parks.

🍃 Find out about a natural area in your community or state that people are trying to protect. Join in!

🍃 Support the International Green Cross—an environmental protection group organized at the recent Earth Summit.

Equal Rights for All Species

A diver explores the reef, eyeing table coral and other wonders in this enchanted undersea garden that stretches for more than a thousand miles.

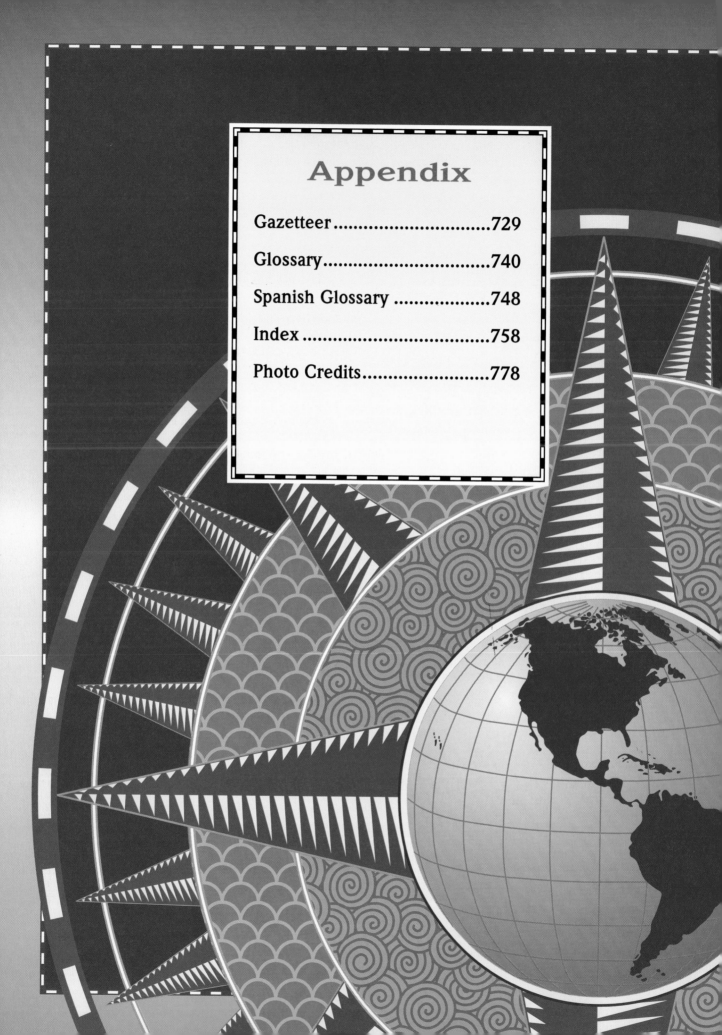

Appendix

Gazetteer

A Gazetteer (GAZ•uh•TIR) is a geographic index or dictionary. It shows latitude and longitude for cities and certain other places. Latitude and longitude are shown in this way: 48°N 2°E, or 48 degrees north latitude and two degrees east longitude. This Gazetteer lists most of the world's largest independent countries, their capitals, and several important geographic features. The page numbers tell where each entry can be found on a map in this book. As an aid to pronunciation, most entries are spelled phonetically.

A

Abidjan [A•bih•JAHN] Capital and port of Côte d'Ivoire, Africa. 5°N 4°W (p. 476)

Abu Dhabi [AH•boo DAH•bee] Capital of the United Arab Emirates, on the Persian Gulf. 24°N 54°E (p. 414)

Abuja [ah•BOO•jah] Capital of Nigeria. 8°N 9°E (p. 476)

Accra [uh•KRAH] Port city and capital of Ghana. 6°N 0° longitude (p. 476)

Addis Ababa [A•duhs A•buh•buh] Capital of Ethiopia. 9°N 39°E (p. 476)

Adriatic [AY•dree•A•tihk] **Sea** Arm of the Mediterranean Sea between the Balkan Peninsula and Italy. 44°N 14°E (p. 246)

Afghanistan [af•GA•nuh•STAN] Country in central Asia, west of Pakistan. 33°N 63°E (p. 414)

Albania [al•BAY•nee•uh] Country on the east coast of the Adriatic Sea, south of Serbia and Montenegro. 42°N 20°E (p. 248)

Algeria [al•JIHR•ee•uh] Country in North Africa. 29°N 1°E (p. 414)

Algiers [al•JIHRZ] Capital of Algeria. 37°N 3°E (p. 414)

Alps [ALPS] Mountain system extending east to west through central Europe. 46°N 9°E (p. 246)

Amazon [A•muh•ZAHN] **River** Largest river in the world by volume and second-largest in length. 2°S 53°W (p. 144)

Amman [ah•MAHN] Capital of Jordan. 32°N 36°E (p. 414)

Amsterdam [AMP•stuhr•DAM] Capital of the Netherlands. 52°N 5°E (p. 248)

Andes [AN•DEEZ] Mountain system extending north to south along the western side of South America. 13°S 75°W (p. 144)

Andorra [an•DAWR•uh] Small country in southern Europe, between France and Spain. 43°N 2°E (p. 248)

Angola [ang•GOH•luh] Country in Africa, west of Zambia. 14°S 16°E (p. 476)

Ankara [ANG•kuh•ruh] Capital of Turkey. 40°N 33°E (p. 414)

Antananarivo [AN•tuh•NA•nuh•REE•VOH] Capital of Madagascar. 19°S 48°E (p. 476)

Arabian [uh•RAY•bee•uhn] **Peninsula** Large peninsula of southwest Asia, extending north to south into the Arabian Sea. 28°N 40°E (p. 412)

Argentina [AHR•juhn•TEE•nuh] Country in the southern part of South America, east of Chile on the Atlantic Ocean. 36°S 67°W (p. 146)

Armenia [ahr•MEE•nee•uh] Southeastern European country between the Black Sea and the Caspian Sea. 40°N 45°E (p. 354)

Ashkhabad [ASH•kuh•BAD] Capital of Turkmenistan. 38°N 58°E (p. 354)

Asmara [az•MAHR•uh] Capital of Eritrea. 16°N 39°E (p. 476)

Astana [ah•STAH•nah] Capital of Kazakhstan. 52°N 72°E (p. 354)

Asunción [uh•SOONT•see•OHN] Capital of Paraguay. 25°S 58°W (p. 146)

Athens [A•thuhnz] Capital and largest city in Greece. 38°N 24°E (p. 248)

Australia [aw•STRAYL•yuh] Country and continent southeast of Asia. 23°S 135°E (p. 682)

Austria [AWS•tree•uh] Country in central Europe, east of Switzerland and south of Germany and the Czech Republic. 47°N 12°E (p. 248)

Azerbaijan [A•zuhr•BY•JAHN] European-Asian country on the Caspian Sea. 40°N 47°E (p. 354)

B

Baghdad [BAG•DAD] Capital of Iraq. 33°N 44°E (p. 414)

Bahama [buh•HAH•muh] **Islands** Country made up of many islands, between Cuba and the United States. 23°N 74°W (p. 145)

Baku [bah•KOO] Port city and capital of Azerbaijan. 40°N 50°E (p. 354)

Balkan [BAWL•kuhn] **Peninsula** Peninsula in southeastern Europe, mostly covered by the country of Greece. 42°N 20°E (p. 246)

Baltic [BAWL•tihk] **Sea** Sea in northern Europe that is an arm of the Atlantic Ocean connected to the North Sea. 55°N 17°E (p. 246)

Bamako [BAH•muh•KOH] Capital of Mali. 13°N 8°W (p. 476)

Bangkok [BANG•KAHK] Capital of Thailand. 14°N 100°E (p. 580)

Bangladesh [BAHNG•gluh•DEHSH] Country in South Asia, bordered by India and Myanmar. 24°N 90°E (p. 580)

Bangui [BAHNG•GEE] Capital of the Central African Republic. 4°N 19°E (p. 476)

Banjul [BAHN•JOOL] Port city and capital of Gambia. 13°N 17°W (p. 476)

Barbados [bahr•BAY•DOHS] Island country between the Atlantic Ocean and the Caribbean Sea. 14°N 59°W (p. 146)

Beijing [BAY•JIHNG] Cultural and industrial center and capital of China. 40°N 116°E (p. 580)

Beirut [bay•ROOT] Capital of Lebanon. 34°N 36°E (p. 414)

Belarus [BEE•luh•ROOS] Eastern European country west of Russia and east of Poland. 54°N 28°E (p. 354)

Belgium [BEHL•juhm] Country in northwestern Europe, south of the Netherlands. 51°N 3°E (p. 248)

Belgrade [BEHL•GRAYD] Capital of Yugoslavia (Serbia). 45°N 21°E (p. 248)

Belize [buh•LEEZ] Country in Central America, east of Guatemala. 18°N 89°W (p. 146)

Belmopan [BEHL•moh•PAN] Capital of Belize. 17°N 89°W (p. 146)

Benin [buh•NIHN] Country in western Africa. 8°N 2°E (p. 476)

Berlin [BUHR•LIHN] Capital of Germany. 53°N 13°E (p. 248)

Bern [BUHRN] Capital of Switzerland. 47°N 7°E (p. 248)

Bhutan [boo•TAHN] Country in the eastern Himalayas, northeast of India. 27°N 91°E (p. 580)

Bishkek [bihsh•KEHK] Largest city and capital of Kyrgyzstan. 43°N 75°E (p. 354)

Bissau [bih•SOW] Capital of Guinea-Bissau. 12°N 16°W (p. 476)

Black Sea Large sea between Europe and Asia. 43°N 32°E (p. 352)

Bogotá [BOH•guh•TAH] Capital of Colombia. 5°N 74°W (p. 146)

Bolivia [buh•LIH•vee•uh] Country in the central part of South America, north of Argentina. 17°S 64°W (p. 146)

Bosnia-Herzegovina [BAHZ•nee•uh HEHRT•suh•goh•VEE•nuh] Southeastern European country between Yugoslavia and Croatia. 44°N 18°E (p. 248)

Botswana [baht•SWAH•nuh] Country in Africa, north of the Republic of South Africa. 22°S 23°E (p. 476)

Brasília [bruh•ZIHL•yuh] Capital of Brazil. 16°S 48°W (p. 146)

Bratislava [BRA•tuh•SLAH•vuh] Capital and largest city of Slovakia. 48°N 17°E (p. 248)

Brazil [bruh•ZIHL] Largest country in South America. 9°S 53°W (p. 146)

Brazzaville [BRA•zuh•VIHL] Port city and capital of the Congo Republic in west central Africa. 4°S 15°E (p. 476)

Brunei [bru•NY] Country in Southwest Asia, on northern coast of the island of Borneo. 5°N 114°E (p. 578)

Brussels [BRUH•suhlz] Capital of Belgium. 51°N 4°E (p. 248)

Bucharest [BOO•kuh•REHST] Capital of Romania. 44°N 26°E (p. 248)

Budapest [BOO•duh•PEHST] Capital of Hungary. 48°N 19°E (p. 248)

Buenos Aires [BWAY•nuhs AR•eez] Capital of Argentina, on the Río de la Plata. 34°S 58°W (p. 146)

Bujumbura [BOO•juhm•BUR•uh] Capital of Burundi in eastern Africa near Lake Tanganyika. 3°S 29°E (p. 476)

Bulgaria [BUHL•GAR•ee•uh] Country in southeastern Europe, south of Romania. 42°N 24°E (p. 248)

Burkina Faso [bur•KEE•nuh FAH•soh] Country in western Africa, south of Mali. 12°N 3°E (p. 476)

Burundi [bu•ROON•dee] Country in central Africa at the northern end of Lake Tanganyika. 3°S 30°E (p. 476)

C

Cairo [KY•ROH] Capital of Egypt, on the Nile River. 31°N 32°E (p. 414)

Cambodia [kam•BOH•dee•uh] Country in Southeast Asia, south of Thailand. 12°N 104°E (p. 580)

Cameroon [KA•muh•ROON] Country in west Africa, on the northeast shore of the Gulf of Guinea. 6°N 11°E (p. 476)

Canada [KA•nuh•duh] Northernmost country in North America. 50°N 100°W (p. 84)

Canberra [KAN•buh•ruh] Capital of Australia. 35°S 149°E (p. 684)

Cape Town Port city and legislative capital of the Republic of South Africa. 34°S 18°E (p. 544)

Caracas [kuh•RAH•kuhs] Capital of Venezuela. 11°N 67°W (p. 146)

Caribbean [KAR•uh•BEE•uhn] **Sea** Part of the Atlantic Ocean, bordered by the West Indies, South America, and Central America. 15°N 76°W (p. 144)

Caspian [KAS•pee•uhn] **Sea** Salt lake between Europe and Asia that is the world's largest inland body of water. 40°N 52°E (p. 352)

Caucasus [KAW•kuh•suhs] **Mountains** Mountain range in the southern part of the former Soviet Union. 43°N 42°E (p. 352)

Central African Republic Country in central Africa, south of Chad. 8°N 21°E (p. 476)

Chad [CHAD] Country in central Africa, west of Sudan. 18°N 19°E (p. 476)

Chang [CHANG] **River** Principal river of China that rises in Tibet and flows into the East China Sea near Shanghai. 31°N 117°E (p. 578)

Chile [CHIH•lee] South American country, west of Argentina. 35°S 72°W (p. 146)

China [CHY•nuh] Country in eastern and central Asia, known officially as the People's Republic of China. 37°N 93°E (p. 580)

Chisinau [KEE•shih•NOW] Largest city and capital of Moldova. 47°N 29°E (p. 354)

Colombia [kuh•LUHM•bee•uh] Country in South America, west of Venezuela. 4°N 73°W (p. 146)

Colombo [kuh•LUHM•BOH] Capital of Sri Lanka. 7°N 80°E (p. 580)

Comoros [KAH•muhr•ROHS] **Islands** Small island country in Indian Ocean between the island of

Madagascar and the southeast African mainland. 13°S 43°E (p. 476)

Conakry [KAH•nuh•kree] Capital of Guinea. 10°N 14°W (p. 476)

Congo [KAHNG•GOH] **Republic** Country in equatorial Africa, south of the Central African Republic. 3°S 14°E (p. 476)

Congo [KAHNG•GOH] **Democratic Republic of the** African country on the Equator, north of Zambia and Angola. 1°S 22°E (p. 476)

Copenhagen [KOH•puhn•HAY•guhn] Capital of Denmark. 56°N 12°E (p. 248)

Costa Rica [KAHS•tuh REE•kuh] Central American country, south of Nicaragua. 11°N 85°W (p. 146)

Côte d'Ivoire [KOHT dee•VWAHR] West African country, south of Mali. 8°N 7°W (p. 476)

Croatia [kroh•AY•shuh] Southeastern European country on the Adriatic Sea. 46°N 16°E (p. 248)

Cuba [KYOO•buh] Island in the West Indies. 22°N 79°W (p. 146)

Cyprus [SY•pruhs] Island country in the Mediterranean Sea, south of Turkey. 35°N 31°E (p. 248)

Czech [CHEHK] **Republic** European country south of Germany and Poland. 50°N 15°E (p. 248)

D

Dakar [DA•KAHR] Port city and capital of Senegal. 15°N 17°W (p. 476)

Damascus [duh•MAS•kuhs] Capital of Syria. 34°N 36°E (p. 414)

Dar es Salaam [DAHR•ehs suh•LAHM] Capital of Tanzania. 7°S 39°E (p. 520)

Denmark [DEHN•MAHRK] Country in northwestern Europe, between the Baltic and North Seas. 56°N 9°E (p. 248)

Dhaka [DA•kuh] Capital of Bangladesh. 24°N 90°E (p. 580)

Djibouti [juh•BOO•tee] Country in east Africa, on the Gulf of Aden. 12°N 43°E (p. 476)

Dodoma [DOH•doh•mah] Future capital of Tanzania. 7°S 36°E (p. 476)

Doha [DOH•HAH] Capital of Qatar. 25°N 51°E (p. 414)

Dominican [duh•MIH•nih•kuhn] **Republic** Country in the West Indies on the eastern part of Hispaniola Island. 19°N 71°W (p. 174)

Dublin [DUH•bluhn] Port city and capital of Ireland. 53°N 6°W (p. 248)

Dushanbe [doo•SHAM•buh] Largest city and capital of Tajikistan north of Pakistan. 39°N 69°E (p. 354)

E

Ecuador [EH•kwuh•DAWR] Country in South America, south of Colombia. 0° latitude 79°W (p. 146)

Egypt [EE•juhpt] Country in northern Africa on the Mediterranean Sea. 27°N 27°E (p. 414)

El Salvador [el SAL•vuh•DAWR] Country in Central America, southwest of Honduras. 14°N 89°W (p. 146)

Equatorial Guinea [EE•kwuh•TOHR•ee•uhl GIH•nee] Country in western Africa, south of Cameroon. 2°N 8°E (p. 476)

Eritrea [EHR•uh•TREE•uh] Country in eastern Africa on the Red Sea, north of Ethiopia. 17°N 39°E (p. 476)

Estonia [eh•STOH•nee•uh] Northern European country on the Baltic Sea, north of Latvia. 59°N 25°E (p. 248)

Ethiopia [EE•thee•OH•pee•uh] Country in eastern Africa, north of Somalia and Kenya. 8°N 38°E (p. 476)

Euphrates [yu•FRAY•TEEZ] **River** River in southwestern Asia that flows through Syria and Iraq and joins the Tigris River. 36°N 40°E (p. 412)

F

Fiji [FEE•JEE] Country comprised of an island group in the southwest Pacific Ocean. 19°S 175°E (p. 684)

Finland [FIHN•luhnd] Country in northern Europe, east of Sweden. 63°N 26°E (p. 248)

France [FRANTS] Country in western Europe, south of the English Channel. 47°N 1°E (p. 248)

Freetown [FREE•TOWN] Port city and capital of Sierra Leone, in western Africa. 9°N 13°W (p. 476)

French Guiana [gee•AH•nah] French-owned territory in northern South America. 5°N 53°W (p. 146)

G

Gabon [ga•BOHN] Country in western Africa on the Atlantic Ocean, west of Congo. 0° latitude 12°E (p. 476)

Gaborone [GAH•buh•ROH•NAY] Capital of Botswana, in southern Africa. 24°S 26°E (p. 476)

Gambia [GAM•bee•uh] Country in western Africa, along the Gambia River. 13°N 16°W (p. 476)

Georgetown [JAWRJ•TOWN] Capital of Guyana. 8°N 58°W (p. 146)

Georgia [JAWR•juh] Asian-European country bordering the Black Sea, south of Russia. 42°N 43°E (p. 354)

Germany [JUHR•muh•nee] Country in north central Europe, officially called the Federal Republic of Germany. 52°N 10°E (p. 248)

Ghana [GAH•nuh] Country in western Africa on the Gulf of Guinea, east of Côte d'Ivoire. 8°N 2°W (p. 476)

Great Plains The continental slope extending through the United States and Canada. 45°N 104°W (p. 82)

Greece [GREES] Country in southern Europe, mostly on the Balkan Peninsula. 39°N 22°E (p. 246)

Greenland [GREEN•luhnd] Island in northwestern Atlantic Ocean and the largest island in the world. 74°N 40°W (p. 84)

Guatemala [GWAH•tuh•MAH•luh] Country in Central America, south of Mexico. 16°N 92°W (p. 146)

Guatemala City Capital of Guatemala and the largest city in Central America. 15°N 91°W (p. 146)

Guinea [GIH•nee] West African country on the Atlantic coast north of Sierra Leone. 11°N 12°W (p. 476)

Guinea-Bissau [GIH•nee bih•SOW] West African country on the Atlantic coast. 12°N 20°W (p. 476)

Gulf of Mexico Gulf on the southeast coast of North America. 25°N 94°W (p. 82)

Guyana [gy•A•nuh] South American country on the Atlantic coast, between Venezuela and Suriname. 8°N 59°W (p. 146)

H

Haiti [HAY•tee] Country on Hispaniola Island in the West Indies. 19°N 72°W (p. 174)

Hanoi [ha•NOY] Capital of Vietnam. 21°N 106°E (p. 580)

Harare [huh•RAH•RAY] Capital of Zimbabwe. 18°S 31°E (p. 476)

Havana [huh•VA•nuh] Seaport, capital city of Cuba, and largest city of the West Indies. 23°N 82°W (p. 146)

Helsinki [HEHL•SIHNG•kee] Capital of Finland. 60°N 24°E (p. 248)

Himalayas [HI•muh•LAY•uhs] Mountain range in South Asia, bordering the Indian subcontinent on the north. 30°N 85°E (p. 578)

Honduras [hahn•DUR•uhs] Central American country, on the Caribbean Sea. 15°N 88°W (p. 146)

Hong Kong [HAHNG KAHNG] Administrative district and port in southern China. 22°N 115°E (p. 580)

Huang He [HWAHNG•HE] River in north central and eastern China, also known as the Yellow River. 35°N 114°E (p. 578)

Hungary [HUHNG•guh•ree] Central European country, south of Slovakia. 47°N 18°E (p. 248)

I

Iberian [y•BIHR•ee•uhn] **Peninsula** Peninsula in southwest Europe, occupied by Spain and Portugal. 41°N 1°W (p. 246)

Iceland [YS•luhnd] Island country between the North Atlantic and the Arctic oceans. 65°N 20°W (p. 248)

India [IHN•dee•uh] South Asian country, south of China and Nepal. 23°N 78°E (p. 580)

Indonesia [IHN•duh•NEE•zhuh] Group of islands that forms the Southeast Asian country known as the Republic of Indonesia. 5°S 119°E (p. 580)

Indus [IHN•duhs] **River** River in Asia that rises in Tibet and flows through Pakistan to the Arabian Sea. 27°N 68°E (p. 578)

Iran [ih•RAHN] Southwest Asian country that was formerly named Persia, east of Iraq. 31°N 54°E (p. 414)

Iraq [ih•RAHK] Southwest Asian country, south of Turkey. 32°N 43°E (p. 414)

Ireland [YR•luhnd] Island west of England, occupied by the Republic of Ireland and by Northern Ireland. 54°N 8°W (p. 248)

Islamabad [ihs•LAH•muh•BAHD] Capital of Pakistan. 34°N 73°E (p. 580)

Israel [IHZ•ree•uhl] Country in southwest Asia, south of Lebanon. 33°N 34°E (p. 414)

Italy [IH•tuhl•ee] Southern European country, south of Switzerland and east of France. 44°N 11°E (p. 248)

J

Jakarta [juh•KAHR•tuh] Capital of Indonesia. 6°S 107°E (p. 580)

Jamaica [juh•MAY•kuh] Island country in the West Indies. 18°N 78°W (p. 146)

Japan [juh•PAN] Country in east Asia, consisting of the four large islands of Hokkaido, Honshu, Shikoku, and Kyushu, plus thousands of small islands. 37°N 134°E (p. 580)

Jerusalem [juh•ROO•suh•luhm] Capital of Israel and a holy city for Christians, Jews, and Muslims. 32°N 35°E (p. 414)

Jordan [JAWR•duhn] Country in southwest Asia, south of Syria. 30°N 38°E (p. 414)

K

Kabul [KAH•buhl] Capital of Afghanistan. 35°N 69°E (p. 414)

Kampala [kahm•PAH•luh] Capital of Uganda. 0° latitude 32°E (p. 476)

Kathmandu [KAT•MAN•DOO] Capital of Nepal. 28°N 85°E (p. 580)

Kazakhstan [KA•zak•STAN] Large Asian country south of Russia, bordering the Caspian Sea. 48°N 59°E (p. 354)

Kenya [KEH•nyuh] Country in eastern Africa, south of Ethiopia. 1°N 37°E (p. 476)

Khartoum [kahr•TOOM] Capital of Sudan. 16°N 33°E (p. 476)

Kiev [KEE•ehf] Capital of Ukraine. 50°N 31°E (p. 354)

Kigali [kih•GAH•lee] Capital of Rwanda, in central Africa. 2°S 30°E (p. 476)

Kingston [KIHNG•stuhn] Capital of Jamaica. 18°N 77°W (p. 146)

Kinshasa [kihn•SHAH•suh] Capital of the Democratic Republic of the Congo. 4°S 15°E (p. 476)

Kuala Lumpur [KWAH•luh LUM•PUR] Capital of Malaysia. 3°N 102°E (p. 580)

Kuwait [ku•WAYT] Country between Saudi Arabia and Iraq, on the Persian Gulf. 29°N 48°E (p. 414)

Kyrgyzstan [KIHR•gih•STAN] Small central Asian country on China's western border. 41°N 75°E (p. 354)

L

Lagos [LAY•GAHS] Port city of Nigeria. 6°N 3°E (p. 495)

Laos [LOWS] Southeast Asian country, south of China and west of Vietnam. 20°N 102°E (p. 580)

La Paz [luh PAHZ] The administrative capital of Bolivia, and the highest capital in the world. 17°S 68°W (p. 146)

Latvia [LAT•vee•uh] Northeastern European country on the Baltic Sea, west of Russia. 57°N 25°E (p. 248)

Lebanon [LEH•buh•nuhn] Country on the Mediterranean Sea, south of Syria. 34°N 34°E (p. 414)

Lesotho [luh•SOH•TOH] Country in south Africa, within the borders of the Republic of South Africa. 30°S 28°E (p. 476)

Liberia [ly•BIHR•ee•uh] West African country, south of Guinea. 7°N 10°W (p. 476)

Libreville [LEE•bruh•VIHL] Port city and capital of Gabon. 1°N 9°E (p. 476)

Libya [LIH•bee•uh] North African country on the Mediterranean Sea, west of Egypt. 28°N 15°E (p. 414)

Liechtenstein [LIHK•tuhn•SHTYN] Small country in central Europe, between Switzerland and Austria. 47°N 10°E (p. 248)

Lilongwe [lih•LAWNG•WAY] Capital of Malawi, in southeastern Africa. 14°S 34°E (p. 476)

Lima [LEE•muh] Capital of Peru. 12°S 77°W (p. 146)

Lisbon [LIHZ•buhn] Port city and capital of Portugal. 39°N 9°W (p. 248)

Lithuania [LIH•thuh•WAY•nee•uh] Northeastern European country on the Baltic Sea, west of Belarus. 56°N 24°E (p. 248)

Ljubljana [lee•OO•blee•AH•nuh] Largest city and capital of Slovenia. 46°N 14°E (p. 248)

Lomé [loh•MAY] Port city and capital of Togo in Africa. 6°N 1°E (p. 476)

London [LUHN•duhn] Capital of the United Kingdom, on the Thames River. 52°N 0° longitude (p. 248)

Luanda [lu•AN•duh] Port city and capital of Angola. 9°S 13°E (p. 476)

Lusaka [loo•SAH•kuh] Capital of Zambia. 15°S 28°E (p. 476)

Luxembourg [LUHK•suhm•BUHRG] Small European country between France, Belgium, and Germany. 50°N 7°E (p. 248)

M

Macao [muh•KOW] Administrative district and port in southern China. 22°N 113°E (p. 580)

Macedonia [MA•suh•DOH•nee•uh] **Former Yugoslav Republic of** Southeastern European country north of Greece. 42°N 22°E (p. 248). Macedonia also refers to a geographic region in the Balkan Peninsula.

Madagascar [MA•duh•GAS•kuhr] Island in the Indian Ocean off the southeast coast of Africa. 18°S 43°E (p. 476)

Madrid [muh•DRIHD] Capital of Spain. 40°N 4°W (p. 248)

Malabo [mah•LAH•BOH] Capital of Equatorial Guinea. 4°N 9°E (p. 476)

Malawi [muh•LAH•wee] Southeastern African country, south of Tanzania and east of Zambia. 11°S 34°E (p. 476)

Malaysia [muh•LAY•zhuh] Federation of states in Southeast Asia on the Malay Peninsula and the island of Borneo. 4°N 101°E (p. 578)

Maldive [MAWL•DEEV] **Islands** Island country in the Indian Ocean near South Asia. 5°N 42°E (p. 580)

Mali [MAH•lee] Country in western Africa, east of Mauritania and south of Algeria. 16°N 0° longitude (p. 476)

Managua [muh•NAH•gwuh] Capital of Nicaragua. 12°N 86°W (p. 146)

Manila [muh•NIH•luh] Port city and capital of the Republic of the Philippines. 15°N 121°E (p. 580)

Maseru [MA•suh•ROO] Capital of Lesotho, in southern Africa. 29°S 27°E (p. 476)

Mauritania [MAWR•uh•TAY•nee•uh] Western African country, north of Senegal. 20°N 14°W (p. 476)

Mauritius [maw•RIH•shuhs] Small island country in the Indian Ocean east of Madagascar. 21°S 58°E (p. 476)

Mbabane [EHM•bah•BAH•nay] Capital of Swaziland, in southeastern Africa. 26°S 31°E (p. 476)

Mediterranean [MEH•duh•tuh•RAY•nee•uhn] **Sea** Large inland sea surrounded by Europe, Asia, and Africa. 36°N 13°E (p. 246)

Mekong [MAY•KAWNG] **River** River in Southeast Asia that rises in Tibet and empties into the South China Sea. 18°N 104°E (p. 578)

Mexico [MEHK•sih•KOH] Country in North America, south of the United States. 24°N 104°W (p. 146)

Mexico City Capital and most populous city of Mexico. 19°N 99°W (p. 146)

Minsk [MIHNTSK] Capital of Belarus. 54°N 28°E (p. 354)

Mississippi [MIH•suh•SIH•pee] **River** Large river system in the central United States that flows southward into the Gulf of Mexico. 32°N 92°W (p. 82)

Mogadishu [MAH•guh•DIH•SHOO] Major seaport and capital of Somalia, in eastern Africa. 2°N 45°E (p. 476)

Moldova [mahl•DOH•vuh] Small European country between Ukraine and Romania. 48°N 28°E (p. 354)

Monaco [MAH•nuh•KOH] Small country in southern Europe, on the French Mediterranean coast. 44°N 8°E (p. 248)

Mongolia [mahn•GOH•lee•uh] Country in Asia between Russia and China 46°N 100°E (p. 580)

Monrovia [MUHN•ROH•vee•uh] Major seaport and capital of Liberia, in western Africa. 6°N 11°W (p. 476)

Montevideo [MAHN•tuh•vuh•DAY•OH] Seaport and capital of Uruguay in South America. 35°S 56°W (p. 146)

Morocco (muh•RAH•KOH) Country in northwestern Africa on the Mediterranean Sea and the Atlantic Ocean. 32°N 7°W (p. 414)

Moscow (MAHS•KOH) Capital and largest city of Russia. 56°N 38°E (p. 354)

Mount Everest (EHV•ruhst) Highest mountain in the world, in the Himalayas between Nepal and Tibet. 28°N 87°E (p. 578)

Mozambique (MOH•zuhm•BEEK) Country in southeastern Africa, south of Tanzania. 20°S 34°E (p. 476)

Muscat (MUHS•KAT) Seaport and capital of Oman. 23°N 59°E (p. 414)

Myanmar (MYAHN•MAHR) Country in Southeast Asia, south of China and India, formerly called Burma. 21°N 95°E (p. 580)

N

Nairobi [ny•ROH•bee] Capital of Kenya. 1°S 37°E (p. 476)

Namibia [nuh•MIH•bee•uh] Country in southwestern Africa, south of Angola on the Atlantic Ocean. 20°S 16°E (p. 476)

Nassau [NA•SAW] Capital of the Bahamas. 25°N 77°W (p. 146)

N'Djamena [EN•juh•MAY•nuh] Capital of Chad. 12°N 15°E (p. 476)

Nepal [nuh•PAWL] Mountain country between India and China. 29°N 83°E (p. 580)

Netherlands [NEH•thuhr•lundz] Western European country on the North Sea, north of Belgium. 53°N 4°E (p. 248)

New Delhi [NOO DEH•lee] Capital of India. 29°N 77°E (p. 580)

New Zealand [NOO ZEE•luhnd] Major island country in the South Pacific, southeast of Australia. 42°S 175°E (p. 684)

Niamey [nee•AH•may] Capital and commercial center of Niger, in western Africa. 14°N 2°E (p. 476)

Nicaragua [NI•kuh•RAH•gwuh] Country in Central America, south of Honduras. 13°N 86°W (p. 146)

Nicosia [NIH•kuh•SEE•uh] Capital of Cyprus. 35°N 33°E (p. 248)

Niger [NY•juhr] Landlocked country in western Africa, north of Nigeria. 18°N 9°E (p. 476)

Nigeria [ny•JIHR•ee•uh] Country in western Africa, south of Niger. 9°N 7°E (p. 476)

Nile [NYL] **River** Longest river in the world, flowing north and east through eastern Africa. 19°N 33°E (p. 412)

North Korea [kuh•REE•uh] Asian country in the northernmost part of the Korean Peninsula. 40°N 127°E (p. 580)

Norway [NAWR•WAY] Country on the Scandinavian Peninsula. 64°N 11°E (p. 248)

Nouakchott [noo•AHK•SHAHT] Capital of Mauritania. 18°N 16°W (p. 476)

O

Oman [oh•MAHN] Country on the Arabian Sea and the Gulf of Oman, east of Saudi Arabia. 20°N 58°E (p. 414)

Oslo [AHZ•loh] Capital and largest city of Norway. 60°N 11°E (p. 248)

Ottawa [AH•tuh•wuh] Capital of Canada. 45°N 76°W (p. 84)

Ouagadougou [WAH•guh•DOO•goo] Capital of Burkina Faso, in western Africa. 12°N 2°W (p. 476)

P

Pakistan [PA•kih•STAN] South Asian country on the Arabian Sea, northwest of India. 28°N 68°E (p. 580)

Palau [pah•LOW] Island country in the Pacific Ocean. 7°N 135°E (p. 684)

Panama [PA•nuh•MAH] Country in Central America, on the Isthmus of Panama. 9°N 81°W (p. 146)

Panamá Capital city of Panama. 9°N 79°W (p. 146)

Papua New Guinea [PA•pyuh•wuh NOO GIH•nee] Independent island country in the Pacific Ocean north of Australia. 7°S 142°E (p. 684)

Paraguay [PAR•uh•GWY] Country in South America, north of Argentina. 24°S 57°W (p. 146)

Paramaribo [PAIR•uh•MAIR•uh•BOH] Port city and capital of Suriname. 6°N 55°W (p. 146)

Paris [PAIR•uhs] River port and capital of France. 49°N 2°E (p. 248)

Persian [PUHR•zhuhn] **Gulf** Arm of the Arabian Sea between Iran and Saudi Arabia. 28°N 51°E (p. 412)

Peru [puh•ROO] Country in South America, south of Ecuador and Colombia. 10°S 75°W (p. 146)

Philippines [FIH•luh•PEENZ] Country in the Pacific Ocean, southeast of Asia. 14°N 125°E (p. 580)

Phnom Penh [NAWM•PEN] Capital of Cambodia. 12°N 106°E (p. 580)

Poland [POH•luhnd] Country on the Baltic Sea in eastern Europe. 52°N 18°E (p. 248)

Port-au-Prince [POHRT•oh•PRINTS] Port city and capital of Haiti. 19°N 72°W (p. 146)

Port Moresby [MOHRZ•bee] Port city and capital of Papua New Guinea. 10°S 147°E (p. 684)

Port of Spain [SPAYN] Capital of Trinidad and Tobago in the West Indies. 11°N 62°W (p. 146)

Porto-Novo [POHR•tuh•NOH•voh] Port city and capital of Benin, in western Africa. 7°N 3°E (p. 476)

Portugal [POHR•chih•guhl] Country on the Iberian Peninsula, south and west of Spain. 39°N 8°W (p. 246)

Prague [PRAHG] Capital of the Czech Republic. 51°N 15°E (p. 248)

Pretoria [prih•TOHR•ee•uh] Capital of South Africa. 26°S 28°E (p. 476)

Puerto Rico [PWEHR•tuh•REE•koh] Island in the Caribbean Sea; U.S. Commonwealth. 19°N 67°W (p. 146)

Pyongyang [pee•AWNG•YAHNG] Capital of North Korea. 39°N 126°E (p. 580)

Q

Qatar [KAH•tuhr] Country on the southwestern shore of the Persian Gulf. 25°N 53°E (p. 414)

Quito [KEE•toh] Capital of Ecuador. 0° latitude 79°W (p. 146)

R

Rabat [ruh•BAHT] Capital of Morocco. 34°N 7°W (p. 414)

GEOGRAPHY: The World and Its People

Reykjavík [RAY•kyuh•VIK] Capital of Iceland.
64°N 22°W (p. 248)

Rhine [RYN[**River** River in western Europe that
flows into the North Sea. 51°N 7°E (p. 246)

Riga [REE•guh] Capital and largest city of Latvia.
57°N 24°E (p. 248)

Rio Grande [REE•OH•GRAND] River that forms the
boundary between the United States and
Mexico. 30°N 103°W (p. 82)

Riyadh [ree•YAHD] Capital of Saudi Arabia. 25°N
47°E (p. 414)

Rocky Mountains Mountain system in western
North America. 50°N 114°W (p. 82)

Romania [roo•MAY•nee•uh] Country in eastern
Europe, east of Hungary. 46°N 23°E (p. 248)

Rome [ROHM] Capital of Italy. 42°N 13°E (p. 248)

Russia [RUH•shuh] Largest country in the world,
covering parts of Europe and Asia. 60°N 90°E
(p. 354)

Rwanda [roo•AHN•duh] Country in Africa, south
of Uganda. 2°S 30°E (p. 476)

S

Sahara [suh•HAIR•uh] Desert region in northern
Africa that is the largest desert in the world.
24°N 2°W (p. 412)

Saint Lawrence [LAWR•uhns] **River** River that
flows from Lake Ontario to the Atlantic Ocean
and forms part of the boundary between the
United States and Canada. 48°N 70°W (p. 82)

San'a [sa•NAH] Capital of Yemen. 15°N 44°E
(p. 414)

San José [SAN•uh•ZAY] Capital of Costa Rica. 10°N
84°W (p. 146)

San Marino [SAN•mah•REE•noh] Small European
country, located in the Italian Peninsula. 44°N
13°E (p. 248)

San Salvador [san•SAL•vuh•DAWR] Capital and
industrial center of El Salvador. 14°N 89°W
(p. 146)

Santiago [SAN•tee•AH•goh] Capital and major
industrial center of Chile. 33°S 71°W (p. 146)

Santo Domingo [SAN•tuh•duh•MIN•goh] Capital
of the Dominican Republic. 19°N 70°W (p. 146)

São Tomé and Príncipe [SOWN•tuh•MAY PRIN•
suh•puh] Small island country in Gulf of Guinea
off the coast of Central Africa. 1°N 7°E (p. 474)

Sarajevo [SAR•uh•YAY•voh] Capital of Bosnia-
Herzegovina. 43°N 18°E (p. 248)

Saudi Arabia [SOW•dee uh•RAY•bee•uh]
Country on the Arabian Peninsula. 23°N 46°E
(p. 412)

Senegal [SEH•nih•GAWL] Country on the coast of
western Africa, on the Atlantic Ocean. 15°N
14°W (p. 476)

Seoul [SOHL] Capital of South Korea. 38°N 127°E
(p. 580)

Serbia [SUHR•bee•uh] European country south of
Hungary. 44°N 21°E (p. 248)

Seychelles [say•SHELZ] Small island country in
the Indian Ocean near East Africa. 6°S 56°E
(p. 476)

Sierra Leone [see•EHR•uh•lee•OHN] Country in
western Africa, south of Guinea. 8°N 12°W
(p. 476)

Singapore [SIHNG•uh•POHR] Multi-island country
in Southeast Asia near tip of Malay Peninsula.
2°N 104°E (p. 578)

Skopje [SKAW•PYAY] Capital of the Former
Yugoslav Republic of Macedonia, in southeastern
Europe. 42°N 21°E (p. 248)

Slovakia [sloh•VAH•kee•uh] Central European
country south of Poland. 49°N 19°E (p. 248)

Slovenia [sloh•VEE•nee•uh] Small central
European country on the Adriatic Sea, south of
Austria. 46°N 15°E (p. 248)

Sofia [SOH•fee•uh] Capital of Bulgaria. 43°N 23°E
(p. 248)

Solomon [SAW•lah•mahn] **Islands** Island country
in the Pacific Ocean, northeast of Australia. 7°S
160°E (p. 684)

Somalia [soh•MAH•lee•uh] Country in Africa, on
the Gulf of Aden and the Indian Ocean. 3°N
45°E (p. 476)

South Africa [A•frih•kuh] Country at the southern
tip of Africa. 28°S 25°E (p. 476)

South Korea [kuh•REE•uh] Country in Asia on
the Korean Peninsula between the Yellow Sea
and the Sea of Japan. 36°N 128°E (p. 580)

Spain [SPAYN] Country on the Iberian Peninsula.
40°N 4°W (p. 246)

Sri Lanka [sree•LAHNG•kuh] Country in the
Indian Ocean south of India, formerly called
Ceylon. 9°N 83°E (p. 580)

Stockholm [STAHK•HOHLM] Capital of Sweden.
59°N 18°E (p. 248)

Sucre [SOO•kray] Constitutional capital of Bolivia. 19°S 65°W (p. 146)

Sudan [soo•DAN] Northeast African country on the Red Sea. 14°N 28°E (p. 476)

Suriname [SUHR•uh•NAH•muh] South American country on the Atlantic Ocean between Guyana and French Guiana. 4°N 56°W (p. 146)

Suva [SOO•vuh] Port city and capital of Fiji. 18°S 177°E (p. 684)

Swaziland [SWAH•zee•LAND] South African country west of Mozambique, almost entirely within the Republic of South Africa. 27°S 32°E (p. 476)

Sweden [SWEE•duhn] Northern European country on the eastern side of the Scandinavian Peninsula. 60°N 14°E (p. 246)

Switzerland [SWIT•suhr•luhnd] European country in the Alps, south of Germany. 47°N 8°E (p. 246)

Syria [SIHR•ee•uh] Country in Asia on the east side of the Mediterranean Sea. 35°N 37°E (p. 414)

T

Taipei [TY•PAY] Capital of Taiwan. 25°N 122°E (p. 580)

Taiwan [TY•WAHN] Island country off the southeast coast of China, and the seat of the Chinese Nationalist government. 24°N 122°E (p. 580)

Tajikistan [tah•JIH•kih•STAN] Central Asian country east of Turkmenistan. 39°N 70°E (p. 354)

Tallinn [TA•luhn] Largest city and capital of Estonia. 59°N 25°E (p. 248)

Tanzania [TAN•zuh•NEE•uh] East African country on the coast of the Indian Ocean, south of Uganda and Kenya. 7°S 34°E (p. 476)

Tashkent [tash•KENT] Capital of Uzbekistan and a major industrial center. 41°N 69°E (p. 354)

Tbilisi [tuh•BEE•luh•see] Capital of the Republic of Georgia. 42°N 45°E (p. 354)

Tegucigalpa [tuh•GOO•suh•GAL•puh] Capital of Honduras. 14°N 87°W (p. 146)

Tehran [TAY•RAN] Capital of Iran. 36°N 52°E (p. 414)

Thailand [TY•LAND] Southeast Asian country south of Myanmar. 17°N 101°E (p. 580)

Thimphu [THIHM•boo] Capital of Bhutan. 28°N 90°E (p. 580)

Tigris [TY•gruhs] **River** River in southeast Turkey and Iraq that merges with the Euphrates River. 35°N 44°E (p. 412)

Tiranë [tih•RAH•nuh] Capital of Albania. 42°N 20°E (p. 248)

Togo [TOH•goh] West African country between Benin and Ghana, on the Gulf of Guinea. 8°N 1°E (p. 474)

Tokyo [TOH•kee•OH] Capital of Japan. 36°N 140°E (p. 580)

Trinidad and Tobago [TRIH•nih•DAD tuh•BAY•goh] Island country between the Atlantic Ocean and the Caribbean Sea, near Venezuela. 11°N 61°W (p. 146)

Tripoli [TRIH•puh•lee] Capital of Libya. 33°N 13°E (p. 414)

Tunis [TOO•nuhs] Port city and capital of Tunisia. 37°N 10°E (p. 414)

Tunisia [too•NEE•zhuh] North African country on the Mediterranean Sea between Libya and Algeria. 35°N 10°E (p. 414)

Turkey [TUHR•kee] Country in southeastern Europe and western Asia. 39°N 32°E (p. 414)

Turkmenistan [TUHRK•MEH•nuh•STAN] Central Asian country on the Caspian Sea. 41°N 56°E (p. 354)

U

Uganda [oo•GAN•duh] East African country south of Sudan. 2°N 32°E (p. 476)

Ukraine [yoo•KRAYN] Large eastern European country west of Russia, on the Black Sea. 49°N 30°E (p. 354)

Ulan Bator [OO•LAHN•BAH•TAWR] Capital of Mongolia. 48°N 107°E (p. 580)

United Arab Emirates [ih•MIR•uhts] Country made up of seven states on the eastern side of the Arabian Peninsula. 24°N 54°E (p. 414)

United Kingdom Country in western Europe made up of England, Scotland, Wales, and Northern Ireland. 57°N 2°W (p. 248)

United States of America Country in North America made up of 50 states, mostly between Canada and Mexico. 38°N 110°W (p. 84)

Uruguay [UR•uh•GWY] South American country, south of Brazil on the Atlantic Ocean. 33°S 56°W (p. 146)

Uzbekistan [OOZ•BEH•kih•STAN] Central Asian country south of Kazakhstan, on the Caspian Sea. 42°N 60°E (p. 354)

V

Vanuatu [VAN•WAH•TOO] Country made up of islands in the Pacific Ocean, east of Australia. 17°S 170°W (p. 684)

Vatican [VA•tih•kuhn] **City** Headquarters of the Roman Catholic Church, located in the city of Rome in Italy. 42°N 13°E (p. 253)

Venezuela [VEH•nuh•ZWAY•luh] South American country on the Caribbean Sea, between Colombia and Guyana. 8°N 65°W (p. 146)

Vienna [vee•EH•nuh] Capital of Austria. 48°N 16°E (p. 248)

Vientiane [VYEHN•TYAHN] Capital of Laos. 18°N 103°E (p. 580)

Vietnam [vee•EHT•NAHM] Southeast Asian country, east of Laos and Cambodia. 18°N 107°E (p. 580)

Virgin Islands Island territory of the United States, east of Puerto Rico in the Caribbean Sea. 18°N 65°W (p. 146)

W

Warsaw [WAWR•SAW] Capital of Poland. 52°N 21°E (p. 248)

Washington, D.C. Capital of the United States, in the District of Columbia. 39°N 77°W (p. 84)

Wellington [WEH•lihng•tuhn] Capital of New Zealand. 41°S 175°E (p. 684)

West Indies [IHN•deez] Islands in the Caribbean Sea, between North America and South America. 19°N 79°W (p. 144)

Windhoek [VIHNT•HOOK] Capital of Namibia, in southwestern Africa. 22°S 17°E (p. 476)

Y

Yamoussoukro [YAH•muh•SOO•kroh] Second capital of Côte d'Ivoire, in western Africa. 7°N 6°W (p. 496)

Yangon [YAHN•GOHN] Capital of Myanmar. 17°N 96°E (p. 580)

Yaoundé [yown•DAY] Capital of Cameroon, in western Africa. 4°N 12°E (p. 476)

Yemen [YEH•muhn] Country on the Arabian Peninsula, south of Saudi Arabia on the Gulf of Aden and the Red Sea. 15°N 46°E (p. 414)

Yerevan [YEHR•uh•VAHN] Largest city and capital of Armenia. 40°N 44°E (p. 354)

Z

Zagreb [ZAH•GREHB] Largest city and capital of Croatia. 46°N 16°E (p. 248)

Zambia [ZAM•bee•uh] Country in south central Africa, south of the Democratic Republic of the Congo and Tanzania. 14°S 24°E (p. 476)

Zimbabwe [zim•BAH•bwee] Country in south central Africa. 18°S 30°E (p. 476)

Glossary

A

abaca [a•buh•KAH] plant fiber used to make rope (p. 671)

absolute location the exact position of a place on the earth's surface (pp. 5, 21)

acid rain precipitation in which water carries large amounts of chemicals, especially sulfuric acid (pp. 68, 100, 283)

adobe [uh•DOH•bee] sun-dried clay brick (p. 166)

alluvial [uh•LOO•vee•uhl] **plain** plain built up from soil deposited by a river (pp. 435, 657)

altiplano [AL•tih•PLAH•NOH] high plateau region of the Andes (p. 222)

altitude [AL•tuh•TOOD] height above sea level (pp. 156, 202)

anthracite [AN•thruh•SYT] hard coal (p. 644)

apartheid [uh•PAHR•TAYT] South African legal restrictions and practices separating racial and ethnic groups, word means "apartness" (p. 549)

aquifer [AH•kwuh•fuhr] underground rock layer that stores large amounts of water (p. 39)

archipelago [AHR•kuh•PEH•luh•GOH] large group or chain of islands (pp. 183, 633)

atmosphere thick cushion of gases surrounding the earth, made up mainly of the gases nitrogen and oxygen (p. 32)

atoll [A•TAWL] ring-shaped coral reef or island surrounding a small bay (pp. 604, 713)

autobahn [AW•toh•BAHN] a superhighway in Germany (p. 284)

autonomy [aw•TAH•nuh•mee] self-government (p. 532)

axis (plural, **axes**) the horizontal (bottom) or vertical (side) line of measurement on a graph (p. 13)

B

bar graph graph in which vertical or horizontal bars represent quantities (p. 13)

basin broad flat lowland area surrounded by higher land (pp. 155, 195, 511)

bauxite [BAWK•SYT] mineral ore from which aluminum is taken (pp. 178, 497)

bazaar a marketplace (p. 451)

Bedouin [BEH•duh•wuhn] member of the nomadic desert peoples of North Africa and Southwest Asia (p. 429)

bilingual having or speaking two languages (p. 129)

birthrate number of children born each year for every 1,000 people (p. 62)

bog low-lying marshy land (pp. 261, 323)

buffer state small country located between larger, often hostile, states (p. 208)

bush Australian term for remote rural areas (p. 694)

C

cacao [kuh•KOW] tropical tree whose seeds are used to make cocoa and chocolate (p. 487)

calligraphy [kuh•LIH•gruh•fee] the art of beautiful handwriting (p. 622)

campesino [KAM•puh•SEE•noh] farmer in Latin America (p. 220)

canopy topmost layer of a rain forest, which shades the forest floor (p. 505)

cardinal directions the basic directions on the earth: north, south, east, west (p. 7)

casbah [KAZ•BAH] old area of cities with narrow streets and small shops in North Africa (p. 458)

cash crop crop grown to be sold, often for export (p. 220)

cassava [kuh•SAH•vuh] plant whose roots are ground into flour and eaten; in tapioca pudding, for example (pp. 210, 495, 663)

caudillo [kaw•DEE•yoh] in Latin American history, a military dictator (p. 203)

chart graphic way of presenting information clearly (p. 17)

chicle juice of the sapodilla tree, used in making chewing gum (p. 177)

circle graph round or pie-shaped graph showing how a whole is divided (p. 14)

city-state in history, an independent city and the lands around it (p. 306)

civil war conflict involving different groups within one country (pp. 430, 534)

civilization highly developed culture, usually with organized religion and laws (p. 56)

clan group of people or families related to one another (pp. 538, 637)

climate usual pattern of weather events in an area over a long period of time (pp. 15, 41)

climate region a broad area of earth with the same climate (p. 12)

climograph combination bar and line graph giving information about temperature and precipitation (p. 15)

cloves spice made from flower buds of clove trees (p. 529)

cold war era from late 1940s to early 1990s in which the United States and Soviet Union competed for world influence (p. 371)

colony overseas settlement made by a parent country (pp. 103, 187)

command economy economic system in which the government owns land, resources, and means of production and makes all economic decisions (p. 364)

commonwealth term for a republic or state governed by the people; the official title of Puerto Rico (p. 189)

communism authoritarian political system in which the central government controls the economy and society (pp. 187, 282, 319, 364)

compass rose device drawn on maps to show the directions (p. 7)

compound in rural Africa, a group of houses surrounded by a wall (p. 488)

condensation process in which water vapor changes into a liquid form (p. 38)

constitutional monarchy form of government headed by a monarch but with most power given to an elected legislature (pp. 259, 430)

consumer goods products for personal use, such as clothing and household goods (pp. 336, 366, 449, 615)

contiguous referring to areas that touch or share a boundary (p. 89)

continent one of the major land areas of the earth (p. 30)

continental island land originally part of a continent, separated by rising water or by geological activity (p. 712)

contour line on a contour map, line connecting all points at the same elevation (p. 9)

cooperative in Cuba, a farm owned and operated by the government (p. 188)

copper belt in Zambia, region of rich copper mines (p. 557)

copra dried inner meat of coconuts (p. 712)

coral rocklike material formed of the skeletons of small sea animals (pp. 521, 690)

coral reef low-lying ocean ridge made of coral (p. 93)

cordillera [KAW•duhl•YEHR•uh] group of mountain chains that run side by side (pp. 118, 217)

core central layer of the earth, probably composed of hot iron and nickel, solid in the inner core and molten in the outer (p. 29)

cottage industry home- or village-based industry in which family members supply their own equipment to make such goods as cloth and metalware (p. 590)

crevasse [krih•VAS] deep crack in an ice cap or glacier (p. 718)

crust outer layer of the earth (p. 29)

cultural diffusion process by which knowledge and skills spread from one area to another (p. 56)

culture way of life of a group of people who share similar beliefs and customs, including language and religion (p. 55)

currents moving streams of water, warm or cold, in the oceans; also streams of air (p. 42)

cyclone intense storm system with heavy rain and high winds blowing in a circular pattern (p. 596)

czar [ZAHR] title of the former emperors of Russia (p. 370)

D

death rate number of deaths each year for every 1,000 people (p. 62)

deforestation loss of forests due to widespread cutting of trees (p. 658)

delta triangle-shaped area at a river's mouth, formed of mud and sand deposited by water (pp. 448, 596, 660)

demographer scientist who studies population (p. 62)

desertification process in which grasslands become drier and desert areas expand (p. 491)

developed country country that is industrialized rather than agricultural (p. 62)

developing country country in the process of becoming industrialized (p. 62)

diagram drawing that shows steps in a process or parts of an object (p. 16)

dialect local form of a language (pp. 188, 284, 300)

GLOSSARY

dictatorship government under the control of a single all-powerful leader (p. 455)

dike high bank of soil or concrete built to hold back the water of a river or ocean (p. 611)

drought [DROWT] extended period of extreme dryness and water shortages (pp. 490, 537)

dry farming method of wheat farming in dry areas that conserves moisture by deep plowing (p. 98)

dynasty a family of rulers (p. 619)

dzong Buddhist center for prayer and study (p. 601)

E

earthquake violent jolting or shaking of the earth caused by movement of rocks along a fault (p. 30)

elevation height above sea level (pp. 9, 48, 310)

elevation profile cutaway diagram showing changes in elevation of land (p. 9)

emigrate to move from one's native country to another country (pp. 60, 312)

empire group of lands or states under the rule of one nation or ruler (pp. 223, 623)

enclave small nation or distinct region located inside a larger country (p. 545)

environment natural surroundings (p. 23)

equinox day in March and September when the sun's rays are directly overhead at the Equator, making day and night of equal length (p. 27)

erg desert region of shifting sand dunes (p. 458)

erosion wearing away of the earth's surface, mainly by water, wind, or ice (p. 31)

escarpment steep cliff separating two fairly flat land surfaces, one higher than the other (pp. 196, 522, 546)

estancia [ehs•TAHN•syah] a large ranch in Argentina (p. 230)

ethnic group people who share a common cultural background, including ancestry and language (pp. 104, 371, 438, 487)

evaporation process in which water from oceans, lakes, and streams is turned into a gas or vapor by the sun's heat (p. 38)

exclave small part of a nation separated from the main part of the country (p. 552)

F

famine lack of food, affecting a large number of people (p. 63)

farm belt region of the midwestern United States with flat land and fertile soil (p. 98)

fault crack in the rocks of the earth's crust along which movement occurs (pp. 30, 391, 522)

favela [fuh•VEH•luh] in Brazil, term used for urban slum areas (p. 199)

fellahin [fehl•uh•HEEN] Egyptian farmers and farm workers (p. 450)

fjord [FYOHRD] long, narrow, steep-sided inlet from the sea (pp. 266, 697)

flow chart type of diagram that shows direction or movement (p. 16)

food processing industry in which foods are prepared and packaged for sale (p. 393)

fossil fuels group of nonrenewable mineral resources—coal, oil, natural gas—formed in the earth's crust from plant and animal remains (pp. 66, 124)

free enterprise basis of a market economy in which people start and run businesses to make a profit with little government intervention (p. 58)

free enterprise system economic system based on free enterprise (see above) (pp. 96, 365)

free port area where goods can be loaded, stored, and reshipped without payment of import-export taxes (p. 666)

G

galaxy huge system in the universe including millions of stars (p. 25)

gaucho in southern South America, a cowhand on horseback (pp. 208, 230)

geography the study of the earth and its land, water, and plant and animal life (p. 21)

geothermal power electric power produced by natural underground sources of steam (p. 699)

geyser hot spring that spouts steam and hot water through a crack in the earth (p. 269)

glasnost [GLAZ•nohst] Russian term for "openness," used for President Gorbachev's policy in late 1980s (p. 371)

great circle route ship or airplane route following a great circle, the shortest distance between two points on the earth (p. 6)

grid system network of imaginary lines on the earth's surface, formed by the crisscrossing patterns of the lines of latitude and longitude (pp. 5, 22)

groundwater water stored in rock layers beneath the earth's surface (p. 39)

H

hajj religious journey made by Muslims to Makkah (p. 432)

harmattan [HAHR•muh•TAN] dry wind that blows southward from the Sahara in winter (p. 486)

heavy industry production of industrial goods such as machinery and military equipment (p. 365)

hemisphere one-half of the globe; the Equator divides the earth into Northern and Southern hemispheres; the Prime Meridian divides it into Eastern and Western hemispheres (pp. 4, 22)

hieroglyphs ancient form of Egyptian writing using pictographs (p. 451)

high island in Micronesia, a mountainous volcanic island (p. 713)

high-technology industry factory that produces computers or other electronic equipment (p. 624)

high veld flat, grassy plateau region of southern Africa (p. 546)

Holocaust [HOH•luh•KAWST] term for the mass imprisonment and slaughter of European Jews and others by German Nazis during World War II (pp. 284, 426)

humid continental climate climate in continental interiors, with cold winters and short, hot summers (p. 47)

humid subtropical climate warm, mild, rainy mid-latitude climate (p. 47)

hurricane fierce tropical storm system with high-speed winds, formed over warm oceans (pp. 43, 177)

hydroelectricity/hydroelectric power electric power generated by falling water (pp. 68, 202, 449, 507)

I

ice shelf part of an ice cap that extends from the land over the ocean (p. 718)

immigrant person who moves from one place to make a permanent home in another (p. 102)

industrialized describing a country in which industry has replaced farming as the main economic activity (p. 161)

intensive cultivation farming method using all available land, producing several crops a year (p. 635)

interdependent referring to countries or people that rely on one another (p. 100)

intermediate direction any direction between the cardinal directions, such as southeast or northwest (p. 7)

invest to put money into a company in return for a share of its profits (pp. 329, 615)

isthmus [IHS•muhs] narrow piece of land connecting two larger pieces of land (pp. 32, 181)

J-K

jute [JOOT] plant fiber used in making rope and burlap bags (p. 589)

key on a map, an explanation of the symbols used (p. 7)

krill small shrimplike shellfish, source of food for many sea animals (p. 721)

L

ladino in Guatemala, a person who speaks Spanish and follows a Spanish-American, not Native American, lifestyle (p. 180)

lagoon pool of water surrounded by reefs or sandbars (p. 604)

land bridge narrow strip of land that joins two larger landmasses (p. 153)

landlocked describing a country that has no land on a sea or ocean (p. 207)

language family group of languages that comes from a common ancestor (p. 57)

latitude location north or south of the Equator, measured by imaginary lines (parallels) numbered in degrees north or south (pp. 5, 22, 155)

GLOSSARY

leap year year with 366 days to account for the extra one-fourth day in Earth's revolution around the sun (p. 26)

light industry production of consumer goods, such as food products and household goods (pp. 188, 365)

line graph graph in which one or more lines connect dots representing changing quantities (p. 14)

literacy rate percentage of adults in a society who can read and write (pp. 58, 181)

llanos [LAH•nohs] large, grassy plains regions of Latin America (pp. 202, 218)

loch [LAHK] long, narrow bay with mountains on either side; also, a lake (p. 256)

loess [LEHS] fine-grained fertile soil deposited by the wind (pp. 283, 611)

longitude location east or west of the Prime Meridian, measured by imaginary lines (meridians) numbered in degrees east or west (pp. 5, 22)

low island in Micronesia, a low-lying island formed of coral (p. 713)

M

magma [MAG•muh] melted rock within the earth's mantle (p. 30)

mainland the main landmass of a country, as contrasted with nearby islands (p. 309)

mangrove tropical tree that grows in swampy land, it has roots both above and below the water (p. 485)

mantle middle layer of the earth, composed of thick hot rock (p. 29)

manuka shrub typical of volcanic soil in New Zealand (p. 697)

maquiladoras [mah•KEE•luh•DOH•rahz] factories that assemble parts shipped in from other countries, producing automobiles, stereos, etc. (p. 161)

marine west coast climate coastal climate with mild winters and cool summers (p. 47)

marsupial type of mammal that carries its young in a pouch as the infants mature (p. 691)

Mediterranean climate mild mid-latitude coastal climate with rainy winters and hot, dry summers (p. 47)

megalopolis [MEH•guh•LAH•puh•luhs] area in which neighboring urban areas blend into one "super city" (pp. 91, 638)

mestizo [meh•STEE•zoh] person of mixed Native American and European ancestry (p. 165)

migrate to move to another place (p. 421)

mobile moving from place to place (p. 105)

monotheism belief in one God (p. 425)

monsoon seasonal winds that bring rain to parts of Asia (pp. 43, 589)

moor in the United Kingdom, a treeless, windy highland area (p. 256)

mosque [MAHSK] place of worship for followers of Islam (pp. 338, 421)

movement one of the geographic themes, describing how people from different places interact (p. 23)

multicultural referring to something that includes many different cultures (p. 104)

multinational firm a company that has offices in several countries and does business in several countries (p. 289)

N

national park public lands set aside for recreation and wilderness protection (p. 106)

natural resource anything from the natural environment that people use to meet their needs (p. 65)

nature preserve land that is set aside by a government to protect plants and wildlife (pp. 332, 387)

navigable [NA•vih•guh•buhl] describing a body of water wide and deep enough for ships to pass (pp. 222, 278)

neutrality policy of refusing to take sides in international disputes and wars (p. 290)

newsprint type of paper used for printing newspapers (p. 124)

nomads people who move from place to place, often with herds of sheep or other animals (p. 396)

nonrenewable resources metals and other minerals that cannot be replaced once they are used up (p. 66)

nutrients minerals in soil that supply growing plants with food (p. 177)

O

oasis (plural, **oases**) place with water and green vegetation surrounded by desert (pp. 398, 432)

oil shale layered rock that contains oil (p. 320)

orbit elliptical path that a planet follows in revolving around the sun (p. 25)

outback remote inland regions of Australia (p. 690)

ozone form of oxygen (O_3) in the atmosphere (pp. 72, 721)

P

pagoda many-storied tower built as a temple or shrine (p. 622)

parliamentary democracy form of government in which voters elect representatives to a law-making body (parliament), which then chooses a leader, the prime minister (pp. 128, 259)

peat partly decayed plant matter, found in bogs, used for fuel and fertilizer (p. 261)

peninsula piece of land surrounded by water on three sides (pp. 32, 153)

permafrost permanently frozen lower layers of soil in Arctic regions (pp. 47, 362)

pesticide chemicals used to kill insects and other pests (p. 67)

phosphate mineral salt containing phosphorus, used in fertilizers (pp. 424, 714)

pictograph graph in which small symbols represent quantities (p. 15)

place one of the geographic themes, describing the typical characteristics that distinguish one place from another (p. 22)

plantation large farm on which a single cash crop is raised (pp. 161, 177)

plateau flat landform whose surface is raised above the surrounding land, with a steep cliff on one side (pp. 32, 297)

plate tectonics theory in geology that the earth's crust is made up of huge, moving plates of rock (p. 30)

poacher person who hunts and kills animals illegally (p. 523)

polder [POHL•duhr] in the Netherlands, an area of land reclaimed from the sea (p. 289)

pollution putting impure or poisonous substances into land, water, or air (p. 67)

pope title of the head of the Roman Catholic Church (p. 326)

population density average number of people living in a square mile or square kilometer (pp. 12, 61)

potash [PAHT•ASH] mineral salt, often used in fertilizers (p. 424)

prairie rolling, inland grassland area with fertile soil (p. 118)

precipitation water that falls to the earth as rain, snow, or sleet (p. 38)

Prime Meridian Line of 0° longitude from which east and west locations are measured, runs through Greenwich, United Kingdom (p. 22)

prime minister government leader chosen in a parliamentary democracy by members of parliament (p. 128)

projection in mapmaking, a way of drawing the round Earth on a flat surface (p. 2)

Q

quinoa [KEEN•WAH] cereal grain grown in Bolivia (p. 226)

R

rain forest dense forest in tropical regions with heavy, year-round rainfall (p. 45)

rain shadow area on the inland side of mountain ranges, where little rain falls (p. 43)

reef narrow ridge of coral, rock, or sand near the surface of water (p. 522)

refugee person who has had to flee to another country for safety from disaster or danger (pp. 60, 534)

region one of the geographic themes, defining parts of the earth that share common characteristics (p. 23)

relative location the position of a place on the earth's surface in relation to another place (p. 22)

relief differences in height in a landscape; how flat or rugged the surface is (p. 9)

renewable resource resource that is replaced naturally or can be grown quickly (p. 66)

GLOSSARY

republic government without a monarch, in which people elect important officials (pp. 103, 280)

revolution for a planet, one complete trip around the sun (p. 26); in politics, a sudden radical change in government (p. 103)

rookery nesting place for large numbers of birds or marine animals (p. 718)

rural relating to the countryside, not the city (p. 91)

S

samurai class of warrior-nobles in feudal Japan (p. 637)

savanna tropical grassland with scattered trees, usually with wet and dry seasons (pp. 46, 485)

scale the relationship between distance on a map and actual distance on the earth (p. 8)

scale bar on a map, a divided line showing the map scale, usually in feet, miles, or kilometers (p. 8)

selva thick tropical forests of the Amazon basin in Brazil (p. 195)

serfs farm laborers bound to the land they worked (p. 370)

service industry business that provides services to people rather than producing goods (pp. 67, 97, 159, 310, 333)

shah title held by kings of Iran, formerly Persia (p. 437)

shogun military ruler or dictator of feudal Japan (p. 637)

silt particles of soil carried and deposited by running water (p. 448)

sirocco [shuh•RAH•koh] hot, dry wind that blows across southern Europe from North Africa (p. 304)

sisal [SY•suhl] plant fiber used to make rope (pp. 197, 529)

slash-and-burn farming farming techniques in which areas of forest are cleared for farmland by burning (p. 562)

smog fog mixed with smoke and chemicals (p. 162)

socialism economic system in which government sets economic goals and may own some businesses (p. 58)

sodium nitrate mineral used in making fertilizer and explosives (p. 227)

solar energy power produced by the heat of the sun (p. 68)

solar system group of planets and other bodies that revolve around the sun (p. 25)

solstice day in June and December when the sun is directly overhead at the Tropic of Cancer (23 1/2° N) or Tropic of Capricorn (23 1/2° S), marking the beginning of summer or winter (p. 26)

sorghum tall grass used as grain and to make syrup (p. 557)

standard of living measure of quality of life based on income and material possessions (p. 58)

station Australian term for a sheep or cattle ranch (p. 690)

steppe dry treeless grasslands, often found at the edges of deserts (pp. 48, 384)

strait narrow body of water lying between two pieces of land (pp. 32, 419)

subcontinent large landmass that is part of another continent but distinct from it, such as South Asia (p. 587)

subsistence farm/farming farm that produces only enough to support a family's needs (pp. 67, 161)

suburbs smaller communities surrounding a central city (p. 311)

T

table graphic way of organizing and presenting statistics or facts (p. 17)

taiga [TY•guh] huge, subarctic evergreen forests in northern Europe, Asia, and North America (p. 361)

tannin substance from tree bark used in turning hides into leather (p. 229)

teak tropical wood used in furniture and shipbuilding (p. 597)

terraced field hillside field cut in steplike strips to hold water (p. 617)

textile fabrics and clothing (p. 299)

timberline elevation above which trees cannot grow (p. 48)

township in South Africa, term for some settlements outside cities (p. 550)

GEOGRAPHY: The World and Its People

tributary small stream or river that flows into a larger river (p. 595)

tropics region of the world located between the Tropics of Cancer and Capricorn (about 30° North and 30° South), with a generally hot climate (p. 41)

trust territory region placed under control of a another country by international agreement (p. 714)

tsetse fly insect whose bite causes sleeping sickness (p. 512)

tsunami [tsoo•NAH•mee] huge sea wave caused by an earthquake on the ocean floor (pp. 30, 634)

tundra broad, dry, treeless plain in the high latitudes (pp. 47, 361)

tungsten hard, grayish metallic element used in electrical equipment (p. 616)

typhoon a hurricane, or tropical storm system, that forms in the Pacific Ocean (pp. 43, 612)

U-V

urban related to a city or densely populated area (p. 91)

urbanization tendency of a country's people to move from rural areas to cities (p. 62)

vegetation plant life in a region (p. 37)

W-X-Y-Z

water cycle process by which the earth's water moves from the oceans to the air to the land and back to the oceans (p. 37)

water vapor water in the form of a gas (p. 37)

watershed a region that drains into a common waterway or body of water (pp. 290, 533)

weather changes in temperature and precipitation over a short period of time (p. 41)

weathering process by which surface rocks are broken down into smaller pieces by water, chemicals, or frost (p. 31)

welfare state country in which government money is used to provide needy people with health care, unemployment benefits, and so on (pp. 208, 268)

yurt large, round tents of animal skin, used by nomads in Mongolia (p. 624)

Spanish Glossary

A

abaca [a•buh•KAH]**/abacá** fibra de una planta la cual es usada para hacer soga (p. 671)

absolute location/localización absoluta la posición exacta de un lugar en la superficie de la Tierra (pp. 5, 21)

acid rain/lluvia ácida precipitación la cual posee grandes cantidades de químicos, especialmente ácido sulfúrico (pp. 68, 100, 283)

adobe [uh•DOH•bee]**/adobe** ladrillo secado al Sol (p. 166)

alluvial [uh•LOO•vee•uhl] **plain/plano aluvial** plano que fue creado por la tierra acumulada de un río (pp. 435, 657)

altiplano [AL•tih•PLAH•NOH]**/altiplano** región altiplana de los Andes (p. 222)

altitude [AL•tuh•TOOD]**/altitud** altura sobre el nivel del mar (pp. 156, 202)

anthracite [AN•thruh•SYT]**/antracita** carbón duro (p. 644)

apartheid [uh•PAHR•TAYT]**/apartheid** restricciones y prácticas legales sudafricanas que segregan a los grupos raciales y étnicos, la palabra significa "aparte" (p. 549)

aquifer [AH•kwuh•fuhr]**/acuífer** capa de tierra subterránea que contiene grandes cantidades de agua (p. 39)

archipelago [AHR•kuh•PEH•luh•GOH]**/archipiélago** grupo grande o cadenas de islas (pp. 183, 633)

atmosphere/atmósfera cojín espeso de gases que rodean a la Tierra, formados principalmente de los gases nitrógeno y oxígeno (p. 32)

atoll [A•TAWL]**/atolón** arrecife o isla coralina de forma anular que rodea a una laguna pequeña (pp. 604, 713)

autobahn [AW•toh•BAHN]*/autobahn* una autopista en Alemania (p. 284)

autonomy [aw•TAH•nuh•mee]**/autonomía** auto gobierno (p. 532)

axis (plural, **axes**)**/axis** la línea o eje horizontal o vertical de medida usado en una gráfica (p. 13)

B

bar graph/gráfica de franjas gráfica en la cual las franjas verticales u horizontales representan cantidades (p. 13)

basin/cuenca extensa área de tierra baja plana, la cual está rodeada por tierra más alta (pp. 155, 195, 511)

bauxite [BAWK•SYT]**/bauxita** mineral metálico del cual se saca el aluminio (pp. 178, 497)

bazaar/bazar un mercado público (p. 451)

Bedouin [BEH•duh•wuhn]**/beduino** miembro de los nómadas del desierto del África del norte y del sudoeste de Asia (p. 429)

bilingual/bilingüe persona que habla dos idiomas (p. 129)

birthrate/índice de natalidad el número de niños que nace cada año por cada 1,000 personas (p. 62)

bog/pantano área de tierra baja y pantanosa (pp. 261, 323)

buffer state/estado intermedio pequeño país que sirve de valla entre dos naciones rivales (p. 208)

bush/área remota término australiano que designa a las áreas rurales remotas (p. 694)

C

cacao [kuh•KOW]**/cacao** árbol tropical cuyas semillas se emplean para hacer cacao y chocolate (p. 487)

calligraphy [kuh•LIH•gruh•fee]**/caligrafía** el arte de escribir con letra bonita (p. 622)

campesino [KAM•puh•SEE•noh]**/campesino** granjero de Latinoamérica (p. 220)

canopy/bóveda capa superior de un bosque tropical, la cual resguarda el suelo del bosque (p. 505)

cardinal directions/puntos cardinales las direcciones básicas: el norte, sur, este y oeste (p. 7)

casbah [KAZ•BAH]**/casbah** la parte vieja de las ciudades en África del norte donde hay calles estrechas y mercados pequeños (p. 458)

cash crop/cosecha al contado cosecha que se cultiva para la venta, a menudo con fines de exportación (p. 220)

cassava [kuh•SAH•vuh]**/yuca** planta cuyas raíces se transforman en harina y se comen, tal como en el pudín de tapioca, por ejemplo (pp. 210, 495, 663)

caudillo [kaw•DEE•yoh]**/caudillo** un dictador militar en la historia de Latinoamérica (p. 203)

SPANISH GLOSSARY

chart/diagrama forma gráfica de representar datos claramente (p. 17)

chicle/chicle jugo del árbol de zapotillo, el cual se usa en la producción de la goma de mascar (p. 177)

circle graph/gráfica circular gráfica redonda, la cual muestra cómo se divide un conjunto (p. 14)

city-state/ciudad estado en la historia, consiste de una ciudad independiente y las tierras a su alrededor (p. 306)

civil war/guerra civil conflicto que incluye a diferentes grupos de ciudadanos en un mismo país (pp. 430, 534)

civilization/civilización cultura altamente desarrollada, usualmente posee la religión organizada y leyes (p. 56)

clan/clan grupo de personas o familias relacionadas unas a las otras (pp. 538, 637)

cloves/clavos de especia especia que se produce de los capullos de las flores del clavero (p. 529)

climate/clima los patrones normales del clima de un área a través de un largo período de tiempo (pp. 15, 41)

climate region/región climática un área extensa del mundo con el mismo clima (p. 12)

climograph/climograma una combinación de gráfica lineal y de franjas, la cual provee información sobre la temperatura y precipitación (p. 15)

cold war/la guerra fría época desde los finales del 1940 al comienzo de los 1990 en la cual los EE. UU. y la Unión Soviética compitieron por la influencia mundial (p. 371)

colony/colonia colonización extranjera hecha por un país matriarcal (pp. 103, 187)

command economy/economía autoritaria sistema económico en el cual el gobierno toma posesión de las propiedades, los recursos y medios de producción, y hace todas las decisiones económicas (p. 364)

commonwealth/estado libre asociado término usado para designar a una república o un estado gobernado por la gente; el título oficial de Puerto Rico (p. 189)

communism/comunismo sistema político autoritario en el cual el gobierno central controla a la economía y a la sociedad (pp. 187, 282, 319, 364)

compass rose/rosa de los vientos emblema que aparece dibujado en los mapas para señalar direcciones (p. 7)

compound/campamento grupo de viviendas rodeadas por una muralla en el África rural (p. 488)

condensation/condensación paso del vapor de agua al estado líquido (p. 38)

constitutional monarchy/monarquía constitucional forma de gobierno encabezado por un monarca pero donde el mayor control es otorgado a la legislatura electa (pp. 259, 430)

consumer goods/bienes del consumidor productos para el consumo personal, tales como la ropa y los productos caseros (pp. 336, 366, 449, 615)

contiguous/contiguo se refiere a las áreas adyacentes o que comparten una frontera (p. 89)

continent/continente una de las áreas de población más grandes de la Tierra (p. 30)

continental island/isla continental tierra que fue originalmente parte de un continente, separada por agua creciente o por alguna actividad geológica (p. 712)

contour line/curva de nivel en un mapa topográfico, la línea que une a todos los puntos en la misma elevación (p. 9)

cooperative/cooperativa en Cuba, es una finca controlada y operada por el gobierno (p. 188)

copper belt/región cobreña en Zambia, región de valiosas minas de cobre (p. 557)

copra/copra médula del coco seco (p. 712)

coral/coral material rocoso formado de los esqueletos de animales marinos pequeños (pp. 521, 690)

coral reef/arrecife de coral arrecife que yace en un nivel bajo del océano y está hecho de coral (p. 93)

cordillera [KAW•duhl•YEHR•uh]**/cordillera** grupo de montañas enlazadas entre si (pp. 118, 217)

core/núcleo capa central de la Tierra, probablemente compuesta de hierro caliente y níquel, es sólida en su núcleo interno y fundida en su exterior (p. 29)

cottage industry/industria autosuficiente industria casera o iniciada en un pueblo donde los miembros de la familia suplen su propio equipo de trabajo para producir bienes tal como las telas y efectos de metal (p. 590)

crevasse [krih•VAS]**/grieta** rajadura profunda en una capa de hielo o glaciar (p. 718)

crust/corteza la capa externa de la Tierra (p. 29)

cultural diffusion/difusión cultural el proceso por el cual los conocimientos y las destrezas se diseminan de un área a la otra (p. 56)

culture/cultura forma de vida de un grupo de gente que comparten costumbres y creencias similares, tanto como un mismo idioma y religión (p. 55)

currents/corrientes corrientes de agua, caliente o fría, en los océanos (p. 42)

cyclone/ciclón tormenta intensa que produce fuertes lluvias y vientos veloces que giran en forma circular (p. 596)

czar [ZAHR]**/zar** título de los emperadores antiguos de Rusia (p. 370)

D

death rate/índice de mortalidad número de muertes que ocurren cada año por cada 1,000 personas (p. 62)

deforestation/deforestación la pérdida de los bosques debido a la extensa práctica de cortar los árboles (p. 658)

delta/delta área triangular en la boca de un río, la cual se forma debido al lodo y la arena depositadas por el agua (pp. 448, 596, 660)

demographer/demógrafo científico que estudia la población (p. 62)

desertification/desiertificación proceso por el cual los prados se secan y las áreas desiertas aumentan (p. 491)

developed country/país desarrollado país que es industrial en vez de ser agricultural (p. 62)

developing country/país en vías de desarrollo país en proceso de industrialización (p. 62)

diagram/diagrama dibujo que muestra los pasos de un proceso o las partes de un objeto (p. 16)

dialect/dialecto variante regional de un idioma (pp. 188, 284, 300)

dictatorship/dictadura un gobierno que está bajo el control de un sólo líder que posee todo el poder (p. 455)

dike/dique banco alto hecho de tierra o concreto, el cual es construido para contener el agua de un río u océano (p. 611)

drought [DROWT]**/sequía** un largo período de extrema sequía y escasez de agua (pp. 490, 537)

dry farming/cultivo seco método de cultivar el trigo en áreas secas, el cual conserva humedad por medio del arado profundo (p. 98)

dynasty/dinastía una familia de gobernantes (p. 619)

dzong/dzong centro budista para el rezo y el estudio (p. 601)

E

earthquake/terremoto estremecimiento violento o temblor de la tierra causado por el movimiento de rocas en una falla (p. 30)

elevation/elevación la altura sobre el nivel del mar (pp. 9, 48, 310)

elevation profile/perfil de elevación diagrama transversal que muestra los cambios en la elevación de la Tierra (p. 9)

emigrate/emigrar trasladarse de su país nativo a otro país (pp. 60, 312)

empire/imperio grupo de países o estados bajo el mando de una nación o un gobernante (pp. 223, 623)

enclave/enclave pequeña nación o región específica establecida dentro de un país más grande (p. 545)

environment/medio ambiente el ambiente natural (p. 23)

equinox/equinoccio día en los meses de marzo y septiembre en que los rayos del Sol caen directamente sobre el ecuador, causando que el día y la noche tengan la misma duración (p. 27)

erg/ergio región desértica con dunas de arena movedizas (p. 458)

erosion/erosión desgaste de la superficie de la Tierra, principalmente por el agua, el viento o el hielo (p. 31)

escarpment/escarpadura acantilado alto que separa a dos superficies de terreno plano, una más alta que la otra (pp. 196, 522, 546)

estancia [ehs•TAHN•syah]**/estancia** rancho grande en Argentina (p. 230)

ethnic group/grupo étnico personas que comparten una historia cultural común, tanto como la misma raza e idioma (pp. 104, 371, 438, 487)

evaporation/evaporación el proceso por el cual

el agua de los océanos, lagos y arroyos se transforma en un gas o vapor por el calor del Sol (p. 38)

exclave la parte pequeña de una nación que está separada del área principal del país (p. 552)

F

famine/hambre escasez de alimentos que afecta a un gran número de personas (p. 63)

farm belt/zona de cultivo la región del centro occidental de los EE. UU. donde el terreno es plano y la tierra es fértil (p. 98)

fault/falla fractura de las rocas en la corteza de la Tierra, a lo largo de la cual ocurren desplazamientos (pp. 30, 391, 522)

favela [fuh•VEH•luh]**/*favela*** en el Brasil, término que se refiere a los barrios urbanos pobres (p. 199)

fellahin [fehl•uh•HEEN]**/*fellahin*** granjeros egipcios y trabajadores de la granja (p. 450)

fjord (FYOHRD)**/fiordo** entradas que provienen del mar, las cuales son largas, estrechas y de lados profundos (pp. 266, 697)

flow chart/diagrama de progreso tipo de diagrama que muestra dirección o movimiento (p. 16)

food processing/proceso de comidas la industria en la que las comidas son preparadas y empaquetadas para la venta (p. 393)

fossil fuels/combustibles fósiles grupo de recursos minerales no renovables — el carbón, el petróleo, el gas natural — formados en la corteza de la Tierra de los restos de plantas y animales (pp. 66, 124)

free enterprise/empresa libre la base de una economía de mercados en la cual las personas comienzan y manejan sus propios negocios para lograr una ganancia con poca intervención del gobierno (p. 58)

free enterprise system/sistema libre de empresa sistema económico basado en la libre empresa (ver definición anterior) (pp. 96, 365)

free port/puerto libre el área donde los artículos pueden ser cargados, almacenados y reembarcados sin pagar impuestos de importación-exportación (p. 666)

G

galaxy/galaxia sistema enorme en el universo, el cual incluye a millones de estrellas (p. 25)

***gaucho*/gaucho** en la parte sur de América Latina, es un ganadero a caballo (pp. 208, 230)

geography/geografía el estudio de la Tierra y sus regiones, su agua y su vida vegetal y animal (p. 21)

geothermal power/energía geotérmica energía eléctrica producida por fuentes de vapor naturales subterráneas (p. 699)

geyser/géiser manantial caliente que arroja vapor y agua caliente a través de una rajadura en la Tierra (p. 269)

glasnost [GLAZ•nohst]**/*glasnost*** término ruso que significa "política abierta"; lema usado por Gorbachev en su política a finales de los 1980 (p. 371)

great circle route/ruta del gran círculo ruta tomada por un barco o avión en la cual éste hace un círculo grande, la distancia más corta entre dos puntos de la Tierra (p. 6)

grid system/sistema de cuadrícula red de líneas imaginarias sobre la superficie de la Tierra, formadas cuando las líneas de latitud y longitud se cruzan, creando patrones (pp. 5, 22)

groundwater/agua subterránea el agua que está almacenada en las capas de roca bajo la superficie de la Tierra (p. 39)

H

***hajj*/hajj** viaje religioso que los musulmanes hacen al Makkah (p. 432)

harmattan [HAHR•muh•TAN]**/harmatán** viento seco que sopla hacia el sur desde el Sahara en el invierno (p. 486)

heavy industry/industria pesada producción de bienes industriales tales como las maquinarias y equipo militar (p. 365)

hemisphere/hemisferio una mitad del globo terráqueo; el ecuador divide a la Tierra en los hemisferios norte y sur; el primer meridiano lo divide en los hemisferios oriental y occidental (pp. 4, 22)

hieroglyphs/jeroglífico estilo antiguo de escritura egipcia, el cual usa pictografías (p. 451)

high island/isla montañosa es una isla volcánica montañosa en Micronesia (p. 713)

high-technology industry/industria de tecnología avanzada fábrica que produce computadoras u otros equipos electrónicos (p. 624)

high veld/estepa región altiplana y herbosa de Sudáfrica (p. 546)

Holocaust [HOH•luh•KAWST]**/Holocausto** término usado para describir el encarcelamiento y matanza de judíos europeos por los nazi alemanes durante la Segunda Guerra Mundial (pp. 284, 426)

humid continental climate/clima húmedo continental el clima en el interior del continente, con inviernos fríos y veranos cortos y calientes (p. 47)

humid subtropical climate/clima húmedo subtropical el clima cálido, templado y lluvioso de la altitud media (p. 47)

hurricane/huracán tormenta tropical devastadora, con fuertes vientos, la cual se forma en las aguas cálidas del océano (pp. 43, 177)

hydroelectric power (hydroelectricity)/ energía hidroeléctrica (hidroelectricidad) energía eléctrica generada por el agua que cae (pp. 68, 202, 449, 507)

I

ice shelf/capa de hielo parte de una capa espesa de hielo que se extiende desde la tierra hasta el océano (p. 718)

immigrant/inmigrante persona que se muda de un lugar y forma un hogar permanente en otro lugar (p. 102)

industrialized/industrializado término que describe a un país en el que la industria ha reemplazado al cultivo como actividad económica principal (p. 161)

intensive cultivation/cultivo intenso método de cultivo que utiliza toda la tierra disponible para producir varias cosechas al año (p. 635)

interdependent/interdependiente se refiere a los países o a personas que dependen unos de otros (p. 100)

intermediate direction/dirección intermedia cualquier dirección que está entre los puntos cardinales, tal como el sudeste o el noreste (p. 7)

invest/invertir poner dinero en una compañía a cambio de recibir un porcentaje de sus ganancias (pp. 329, 615)

isthmus [IHS•muhs]**/istmo** lengua de tierra que une a dos partes más grandes (pp. 32, 181)

J-K

jute [JOOT]**/yute** fibra de una planta, se usa para hacer cordeles y telas de saco (p. 589)

key/clave la explicación de los símbolos usados en un mapa (p. 7)

krill/crustáceo marisco pequeño parecido al camarón, el cual es fuente de alimento para muchos animales marinos (p. 721)

L

ladino/**ladino** en Guatemala, se refiere a una persona que habla español y que sigue el estilo de vida español-americano, no el nativo americano (p. 180)

lagoon/laguna cuerpo de agua rodeado de arrecifes o bancos de arena (p. 604)

land bridge/puente terrestre pedazo estrecho de tierra que une a dos áreas mayores (p. 153)

landlocked/rodeado de tierra término que describe a un país cuya tierra no tiene salida al mar o al océano (p. 207)

language family/familia de idiomas grupo de idiomas que proviene de la misma lengua predecesora (p. 57)

latitude/latitud distancia al norte o sur del ecuador, la cual se mide con líneas imaginarias (paralelos) contadas en grados al norte o sur (pp. 5, 22, 155)

leap year/año bisiesto año que tiene 366 días, establecido para compensar por la fracción adicional de un cuarto de día que se produce cuando la Tierra gira alrededor del Sol (p. 26)

light industry/industria liviana producción de bienes al consumidor, tales como productos comestibles y del hogar (pp. 188, 365)

GEOGRAPHY: The World and Its People

line graph/gráfica lineal gráfica en la cual una o más líneas conectan los puntos que representan cantidades variantes (p. 14)

literacy rate/índice de alfabetización porcentaje de adultos en una sociedad que pueden leer y escribir (pp. 58, 181)

llanos [LAH•nohs]/**llanos** las amplias regiones llanas y verdosas de Latinoamérica (pp. 202, 218)

loch [LAHK]/**ensenada** bahía larga y estrecha con montañas a cada lado; también, un lago (p. 256)

loess [LEHS]/**loes** tierra fértil de grano fino, depositada por el viento (pp. 283, 611)

longitude/longitud distancia al este u oeste del primer meridiano, la cual se mide con líneas imaginarias (meridianas) contadas en grados al este u oeste (pp. 5, 22)

low island/isla baja es una isla en Micronesia situada a nivel bajo y formada de coral (p. 713)

M

magma [MAG•muh]/**magma** roca derretida situada dentro de la capa intermedia de la Tierra (p. 30)

mainland/territorio continental el área principal y de más volumen de tierra que tiene un país, en contraste con las islas adyacentes (p. 309)

mangrove/mangle árbol tropical que crece en tierra pantanosa, tiene raíces tanto sobre como bajo la superficie del agua (p. 485)

mantle/capa capa intermedia de la Tierra, compuesta de roca espesa y caliente (p. 29)

manuka/*manuka* arbusto típico de la tierra volcánica de Nueva Zelandia (p. 697)

maquiladoras [mah•KEE•luh•DOH•rahz]/**maquiladoras** factorías que ensamblan las partes recibidas de otros países para producir automóviles, sistemas de sonido estereofónicos, etc. (p. 161)

marine west coast climate/clima marino de la costa occidental clima costeño, el cual tiene inviernos templados y veranos frescos (p. 47)

marsupial/marsupial tipo de mamífero que lleva a sus crías en una bolsa abdominal donde terminan su desarrollo (p. 691)

Mediterranean climate/clima mediterráneo clima templado costeño a mitad de latitud, el cual tiene inviernos lluviosos y veranos calientes y secos (p. 47)

megalopolis/la megalópolis región en la que las áreas urbanas adyacentes están integradas, formando así una "gran ciudad" (pp. 91, 638)

mestizo [meh•STEE•zoh] persona nacida de padres procedentes de las razas americana nativa y europea (p. 165)

migrate/migrar mudarse a otro lugar (p. 421)

mobile/móvil mudarse de lugar a lugar (p. 105)

monotheism/monoteísmo la creencia en un sólo Dios (p. 425)

monsoon/monzón vientos estacionales que traen la lluvia a ciertas partes de Asia (pp. 43, 589)

moor/páramo un terreno alto y sin árboles pero ventoso en el Reino Unido (p. 256)

mosque [MAHSK]/**mezquita** lugar de devoción de los que siguen la religión del Islam (pp. 338, 421)

movement/movimiento uno de los temas geográficos que describen cómo las personas de diferentes lugares se comunican (p. 23)

multicultural/multicultural se refiere a un asunto que incluye a muchas culturas diferentes (p. 104)

multinational firm/empresa multinacional una compañía que tiene oficinas y comercia en varios países (p. 289)

N

national park/parque nacional terrenos públicos que se reservan para el recreo de los visitantes al área y para la protección de su estado virgen (p. 106)

natural resource/recurso natural cualquier cosa que proviene del medio ambiente natural y que las personas usan para satisfacer sus necesidades (p. 65)

nature preserve/santuario terreno reservado por el gobierno para proteger a las plantas y a la fauna silvestre (pp. 332, 387)

navigable/navegable término que describe a un cuerpo de agua lo suficientemente ancho y profundo para permitir el paso a los barcos (pp. 222, 278)

neutrality/neutralidad la política que rechaza la preferencia de una u otra posición en lo relativo a desacuerdos y guerras internacionales (p. 290)

newsprint/papel de periódico tipo de papel usado para imprimir los periódicos (p. 124)

nomads/nómadas personas que se mudan de un lugar a otro, a menudo se llevan consigo a sus rebaños de ovejas u otros animales (p. 396)

nonrenewable resources/recursos no renovables metales y otros minerales que no pueden ser reemplazados después de ser utilizados (p. 66)

nutrients/nutrientes los minerales de la tierra que suplen alimento a las plantas en crecimiento (p. 177)

O

oasis (plural, **oases**)/**oasis** lugar donde el agua y la vegetación verdosa está rodeada por un desierto (pp. 398, 432)

oil shale/esquisto roca arcillosa en capas, la cual contiene aceite (p. 320)

orbit/órbita trayectoria elíptica que sigue un planeta cuando da vueltas alrededor del Sol (p. 25)

outback/llanura desértica regiones distantes del interior de Australia (p. 690)

ozone/ozono forma de oxígeno (O_3) en la atmósfera (pp. 72, 721)

P

pagoda/pagoda una torre de muchos pisos, la cual fue construida para servir de templo o lugar de adoración (p. 622)

parliamentary democracy/democracia parlamentaria estilo de gobierno en el cual los votantes eligen a representantes para formar parte de un cuerpo creador de leyes (parlamento), el cual después escoge a un líder, el primer ministro (pp. 128, 259)

peat/turba materia de las plantas en un estado parcialmente descompuesto, se encuentra en pantanos y es usada como combustible y fertilizante (p. 261)

peninsula/península pedazo de tierra rodeado por agua en tres de sus lados (pp. 32, 153)

permafrost/permagel capas inferiores de la tierra en las regiones árticas, las cuales están permanentemente congeladas (pp. 47, 362)

pesticide/insecticida químicos usados para matar a los insectos y a otros animales dañinos (p. 67)

phosphate/fosfato sal mineral que contiene fósforo, usado en fertilizantes (pp. 424, 714)

pictograph/pictografía gráfica en la que los símbolos pequeños representan cantidades (p. 15)

place/lugar uno de los temas geográficos, el cual describe las características típicas que distinguen a un lugar de otro (p. 22)

plantation/hacienda granja de gran tamaño donde se cultiva sólo una cosecha al contado (pp. 161, 177)

plateau/meseta forma terrestre plana cuya superficie está por encima de la tierra que le rodea, con una colina muy alta en uno de sus lados (pp. 32, 297)

plate tectonics/tectónicas de lámina teoría en el campo de geología la cual dice que la corteza de la Tierra está compuesta de enormes láminas movedizas de roca (p. 30)

poacher/cazador furtivo persona que caza y mata a los animales ilegalmente (p. 523)

polder [POHL•duhr]/**pólder** área de tierra en los Países Bajos, la cual fue recuperada del mar (p. 289)

pollution/contaminación el arrojar substancias impuras o venenosas en la tierra, agua o aire (p. 67)

pope/papa título del cabecilla de la Iglesia Católica Romana (p. 326)

population density/densidad de la población número promedio de personas que viven en una milla cuadrada o kilómetro cuadrado (pp. 12, 61)

potash [PAHT•ASH]/**potasio** sal mineral; usada a menudo en fertilizantes (p. 424)

prairie/pradera terreno ondulado de pastoreo, se encuentra en áreas interiores con tierra fértil (p. 118)

precipitation/precipitación agua que cae sobre la Tierra en forma de lluvia, nieve o aguanieve (p. 38)

Prime Meridian/primer meridiano la línea de longitud de 0° desde la cual se miden las distancias al este y al oeste, atraviesa a Greenwich, Reino Unido (p. 22)

prime minister/primer ministro líder gubernamental el cual es seleccionado en una democracia parlamentaria por los miembros del parlamento (p. 128)

projection/proyección en la cartografía, es una manera de dibujar la redondez de la Tierra en una superficie plana (p. 2)

Q

quinoa [KEEN•WAH]/**quinoa** grano de cereal que se crece en Bolivia (p. 226)

R

rain forest/bosque tropical bosque espeso en las regiones tropicales, donde llueve mucho todo el año (p. 45)

rain shadow/sombra de lluvia región en la parte interior de las cordilleras de montañas, donde cae muy poca lluvia (p. 43)

reef/arrecife hilera estrecha de coral, roca o arena cerca de la superficie del agua (p. 522)

refugee/refugiado persona que ha tenido que escapar a otro país para protegerse de un desastre o de peligro (pp. 60, 534)

region/región uno de los temas geográficos, el cual define a las partes de la Tierra que comparten características comunes (p. 23)

relative location/ubicación relativa la ubicación de un lugar en la superficie de la Tierra con relación a otro lugar (p. 22)

relief/relieve diferencias en la altura de un terreno; cuán plano o desigual es su superficie (p. 9)

renewable resource/recurso renovable recurso que puede ser reemplazado naturalmente o que se puede desarrollar con rapidez (p. 66)

republic/república un gobierno sin monarca, en el cual las personas eligen a los oficiales importantes (pp. 103, 280)

revolution/revolución al referirse a un planeta, es un recorrido completo alrededor del Sol (p. 26); en la política, es un cambio radical y repentino de gobierno (p. 103)

rookery/criadero nido para un gran número de pájaros o animales marinos (p. 718)

rural/rural relativo al campo, no a la ciudad (p. 91)

S

samurai/samurai clase de guerreros aristocráticos en el Japón feudal (p. 637)

savanna/sabana terreno de pastoreo tropical con árboles dispersos, generalmente tiene épocas lluviosas y secas (pp. 46, 485)

scale/escala la relación entre la representación de una distancia en un mapa y la distancia verdadera en la Tierra (p. 8)

scale bar/barra de escala la línea dividida en un mapa, la cual muestra la escala del mapa, generalmente en pies, millas o kilómetros (p. 8)

selva/**selva** bosque tropical espeso en la cuenca del Amazonas de Brasil (p. 195)

serfs/siervos labradores vinculados a la tierra en la que han trabajado (p. 370)

service industry/industria de servicio comercio que provee un servicio a las personas en vez de producir bienes para el consumidor (pp. 67, 97, 159, 310, 333)

shah/sha título de los reyes de Irán, país anteriormente llamado Persia (p. 437)

shogun/shogún mandatario militar o dictador del Japón feudal (p. 637)

silt/sedimento partículas de tierra que son arrastradas y depositadas por el agua (p. 448)

sirocco [shuh•RAH•koh]/**siroco** viento caliente y seco que sopla a través de Europa desde el África del Norte (p. 304)

sisal [SY•suhl]/**sisal** fibra de una planta, la cual se usa para hacer cordeles (pp. 197, 529)

slash-and-burn farming/agricultura de tala y quemado técnicas agrícolas en las cuales ciertas áreas forestales son despejadas para el cultivo por medio de incendios (p. 562)

smog/smog humo mezclado con niebla y productos químicos (p. 162)

socialism/socialismo sistema económico en el que el gobierno establece las metas económicas y puede poseer algunos comercios (p. 58)

sodium nitrate/nitrato de sodio mineral que se usa al preparar los abonos y en explosivos (p. 227)

solar energy/energía solar la energía producida por el calor del Sol (p. 68)

solar system/sistema solar grupo de planetas y otros cuerpos celestes que dan vuelta alrededor del Sol (p. 25)

solstice/solsticio día en junio y diciembre cuando el Sol está directamente sobre el Trópico de Cáncer (23 1/2° N) o el Trópico de Capricornio (23 1/2° S), lo que marca el comienzo del verano o el invierno (p. 26)

sorghum/melaza hierba alta que se usa como un grano y también para hacer almíbar (p. 557)

standard of living/nivel de vida término que mide la calidad de vida de una persona con base en su ingreso y posesiones materiales (p. 58)

station/estación término australiano que se refiere a un rancho de ovejas o ganado (p. 690)

steppe/estepa tierras secas y sin árboles utilizadas para el pastoreo, a menudo se encuentran a los bordes de los desiertos (pp. 48, 384)

strait/desfiladero estrecho cuerpo de agua que yace entre dos pedazos de tierra (pp. 32, 419)

subcontinent/subcontinente gran área de tierra que forma parte de otro continente, pero es distinto a éste, tal como el Asia del Sur (p. 587)

subsistence farm (farming)/granja de subsistencia/cultivo granja que sólo produce lo suficiente para satisfacer las necesidades de una familia (pp. 67, 161)

suburbs/suburbios comunidades más pequeñas que rodean a una ciudad central (p. 311)

T

table/tabla forma gráfica de organizar y representar datos o estadísticas (p. 17)

taiga [TY•guh]**/taiga** enormes selvas subárticas de árboles siempre verdes en el norte de Europa, en Asia y América del Norte (p. 361)

tannin/tanino substancia que proviene de la corteza de los árboles y que se usa para convertir las pieles de animales en cuero (p. 229)

teak/teca madera tropical que se usa en la construcción de muebles y barcos (p. 597)

terraced field/campo abancalado campo donde la ladera ha sido cortada en franjas parecidas a escaleras para contener el agua (p. 617)

textile/textil telas y ropa (p. 299)

timberline/altura límite límite de elevación sobre el cual los árboles no pueden crecer (p. 48)

township/municipio término usado para describir a varios pueblos a las afueras de las ciudades en el África del Sur (p. 550)

tributary/tributario arroyo pequeño o río que desemboca en un río más grande (p. 595)

tropics/tropical región del mundo ubicada entre los Trópicos de Cáncer y Capricornio (alrededor de 30° al norte y 30° al sur), generalmente es de clima caliente (p. 41)

trust territory/territorio bajo administración fiduciaria región que está bajo el control de otro país debido a un pacto internacional (p. 714)

tsetse fly/mosca tse-tsé insecto cuya picada causa la enfermedad del sueño (p. 512)

tsunami [tsoo•NAH•mee]**/tsunami** ola gigantesca de mar causada por un terremoto en el suelo del océano (pp. 30, 634)

tundra una llanura extensa, seca y sin árboles en las latitudes altas (pp. 47, 361)

tungsten/tungsteno elemento metálico duro y de color gris, usado en los equipos eléctricos (p. 616)

typhoon/tifón un huracán o tormenta tropical, el cual se forma en el Océano Pacífico (pp. 43, 612)

U-V

urban/urbano relacionado a una ciudad o área densamente poblada (p. 91)

urbanization/urbanización la tendencia de la gente de un país a mudarse de áreas rurales a las ciudades (p. 62)

vegetation/vegetación la vida vegetal de una región (p. 37)

W-X-Y-Z

water cycle/ciclo de agua proceso por el cual el agua de la Tierra se mueve de los océanos al aire, a la tierra y vuelve otra vez a los océanos (p. 37)

water vapor/vapor de agua agua en forma de gas (p. 37)

watershed/cuenca arrecife alto del cual los ríos de un área fluyen en direcciones diferentes (pp. 290, 533)

weather/clima cambios de temperatura y de precipitación que ocurren en un período corto de tiempo (p. 41)

weathering/acción corrosiva proceso donde las rocas en la superficie se desmoronan en trozos más pequeños debido a la acción corrosiva del agua, los elementos químicos o la congelación (p. 31)

welfare state/estado benefactor país donde se usa el dinero del gobierno para proveer cuidado de la salud, beneficios de desempleo y otros servicios a las personas necesitadas (pp. 208, 268)

yurt/yurta tiendas de campaña grandes y redondas, las cuales están hechas de piel de animales y son usadas por los nómadas en Mongolia (p. 624)

SPANISH GLOSSARY

Index

B

D

INDEX

T

INDEX

Photo Credits

Cover, F. Mels/Westlight; **vi,** Rich Buzzelli/Tom Stack & Associates; **vii,** James P. Blair/National Geographic Society; **viii,** Jodi Cobb/National Geographic Society; **ix,** Sheila Nardulli/Liaison International; **x,** (t) Paul A. Zahl/National Geographic Society, (b) Sam Abell/National Geographic Society; **xii,** Martin Harvey/The Wildlife Collection; **18-19,** Bob Sacha/used with permission, Christian Science Mapparium, Boston, Massachusetts; **20,** ©Telegraph Colour Library/FPG International; **21,** ©Superstock, Inc.; **22,** (l) ©Ann & Myron Sutton/Superstock, Inc., (r) ©Galen Rowell/Mountain Light; **23,** ©Guy Marche/FPG International; **25,** NASA/National Geographic Society; **28,** James P. Blair/National Geographic Society; **29,** Otis Imboden/National Geographic Society; **30,** (l) Walter Meayers Edwards/National Geographic Society, (r) ©Douglas Faulkner/Photo Researchers, Inc.; **33,** ©Telegraph Colour Library/FPG International; **36,** ©F. Stuart Westmorland/Photo Researchers, Inc.; **37,** Steve Raymer/National Geographic Society; **39,** Robert W. Madden/National Geographic Society; **41,** James P. Blair/National Geographic Society; **43,** (l) ©Michael P. Gadomski/Photo Researchers, Inc., (r) David S. Boyer/National Geographic Society; **45,** Susan Snyder; **48,** Walter Meayers Edwards/National Geographic Society; **49,** ©F. Stuart Westmorland/Photo Researchers, Inc.; **52,** (l) ©Stephen J. Krasemann/Photo Researchers, Inc., (r) Dwight Kuhn; **53,** Matt Meadows; **54,** Dick Durrance II/National Geographic Society; **55,** Ed Kim/National Geographic Society; **58,** (l) James L. Amos/National Geographic Society, (r) ©Superstock, Inc.; **60,** David Alan Harvey/National Geographic Society; **63,** James P. Blair/National Geographic Society; **64,** David R. Frazier Photolibrary; **65,** ©C. Shambroom/Photo Researchers, Inc.; **68,** (l) ©Simon Fraser/Science Photo Library/Photo Researchers, Inc., (r) Bryan Hodgson/National Geographic Society; **69,** Dick Durrance II/National Geographic Society; **72,** Robert W. Madden/National Geographic Society; **72-73,** (background) Aaron Haupt; **73,** (t) NASA/GSFC/National Geographic Society, (br) Bruce Dale/National Geographic Society; **74-75,** Phil Schemeister/National Geographic Society; **76,** (l) George F. Mobley/National Geographic Society, (b) James P. Blair/National Geographic Society; **76-77,** (t,b) James P. Blair/National Geographic Society, (c) James L. Amos/National Geographic Society; **77,** (t,b) James P. Blair/National Geographic Society, (r) George F. Mobley/National Geographic Society; **78,** Walter Meayers Edwards/National Geographic Society; **79,** George F. Mobley/National Geographic Society; **80,** Johnny Johnson; **88,** Mark Burnett; **89,** ©John W. Warden/Superstock, Inc.; **90,** (l) David R. Frazier Photolibrary, (r) Tim Courlas; **91,** ©James Blank/FPG International; **93,** Mark E. Gibson; **96,** Robert W. Madden/National Geographic Society; **98,** (t) Bruce Dale/National Geographic Society, (b) David M. Dennis; **99,** ©Superstock, Inc.; **101,** John Youger; **102,** James L. Amos/National Geographic Society; **103,** Larry Hamill; **104,** ©Mark Rightmire/The Orange County Register; **107,** Mark Burnett; **110,** (l) Rich Buzzelli/Tom Stack & Associates, (r) Matt Meadows; **111,** Matt Meadows; **112,** (t) Craig Lowell/Viesti Associates, Inc., (c) Tim Courlas, (b) Bridgeman Art Library/Art Resource; **113,** (t) Jodi Cobb/National Geographic Society, (bl) George F. Mobley/National Geographic Society, (br) Art Resource; **114,** Rick Stewart/Allsport; **115,** Gordon W. Gahan/National Geographic Society; **116, 119,** David R. Frazier Photolibrary; **121,** George F. Mobley/National Geographic Society; **124,** (l) George F. Mobley/National Geographic Society, (r) David R. Frazier Photolibrary; **126,** Archive Photos; **127,** George F. Mobley/National Geographic Society; **128,** (l) George F. Mobley/National Geographic Society, (r) David S. Boyer/National Geographic Society; **130,** Bruce Dale/National Geographic Society; **131,** Rick Stewart/Allsport; **134,** James L. Stanfield/National Geographic Society; **134-135,** (background) Aaron Haupt; **135,** (t,bl) Joseph H. Bailey/National Geographic Society; **136-137,** William Albert Allard/National Geographic Society; **138,** (l) Otis Imboden/National Geographic Society, (b) Walter Meayers Edwards/National Geographic Society; **138-139,** (c) Bruce Dale/National Geographic Society, (background) James P. Blair/National Geographic Society; **139,** (tl,br) James P. Blair/National Geographic Society, (tr) O. Louis Mazzatenta/National Geographic Society, (cr) Otis Imboden/National Geographic Society; **140,** ©Tom Tracy/FPG International; **141,** ©Telegraph Colour Library/FPG International; **142,** ©Superstock, Inc.; **151,** Jan Butchofsky/Dave G. Houser; **152,** Ted Streshinsky/Photo 20-20; **153,** Buddy Mays/Travel Stock; **155, 159,** Robert Frerck/Odyssey; **163,** Dallas & John Heaton/Westlight; **164,** David Ryan/Photo 20-20; **165,** Robert Frerck/Odyssey; **166,** David R. Frazier Photolibrary; **166,** Robert Frerck/Odyssey; **167,** Ted Streshinsky/Photo 20-20; **168,** Donna Carroll/Travel Stock; **169,** Ted Streshinsky/Photo 20-20; **172,** (l) Reggie David/Pacific Stock, (r) Matt Meadows; **173,** Matt Meadows; **174,** D. Donne Bryant/DDB Stock Photo; **175, 179,** ©Superstock, Inc.; **180,** James C. Simmons/Dave G. Houser; **183,** ©Messerschmidt/FPG International; **185,** (l) Suzanne Murphy-Lamrond/DDB Stock Photo, (r) Winfield Parks/National Geographic Society; **188,** ©Carol Lee/Tony Stone Images; **191,** D. Donne Bryant/DDB Stock Photo; **194,** ©Ary Diesendruck/Tony Stone Images; **195,** ©Tom McHugh/Photo Researchers, Inc.; **198,** Robert Fried/DDB Stock Photo; **201,** Robert W. Madden/National Geographic Society; **203,** ©Marco Corsetti/FPG International; **205,** Buddy Mays/Travel Stock; **206,** Robert Frerck/Odyssey; **207, 208,** ©Superstock, Inc.; **210,** (l) O. Louis Mazzatenta/National Geographic Society, (r) Peter Lang/DDB Stock Photo; **211,** ©Ary Diesendruck/Tony Stone Images; **214,** (t) Janice Sheldon/Photo 20-20, (c) Barry W. Barker/Odyssey, (b) O. Louis Mazzatenta/National Geographic Society; **215,** (t) Scalkwijk/Art Resource, (r) Photo 20-20, (b) Robert Frerck/Odyssey; **216,** David L. Perry; **217,** ©Sheryl McNee/FPG International; **221,** Bates Littlehales/National Geographic Society; **222,** Gilbert M. Grosvenor/National Geographic Society; **224,** David L. Perry; **225,** Gordon W. Gahan/National Geographic Society; **227,** (l) ©Philip & Karen Smith/Tony Stone Images, (r) George F. Mobley/National Geographic Society; **228,** James P. Blair/National Geographic Society; **230,** (l) ©John Warden/Tony Stone Images, (r) ©Neil Beer/Tony Stone Images; **233,** David L. Perry; **236,** Paul A. Zahl/National Geographic Society; **236-237,** (background) Aaron Haupt; **237,** (t & br) James P. Blair/National Geographic Society; **238-239,** James L. Stanfield/National Geographic Society; **240,** Bruce Dale/National Geographic Society; **240-241,** (c,background) Sam Abell/National Geographic Society, (b) O. Louis Mazzatenta/National Geographic Society; **241,** (tl,bl,br) James L. Stanfield/National Geographic Society, (tr) George F. Mobley/National Geographic Society; **242,** ©Bruce Stoddard/FPG International; **243,** TRIP/J. Bartos; **244,** ©Al Michaud/FPG International; **254,** ©Tony Stone Images; **255,** ©David H. Endersbee/Tony Stone Images; **256,** George F. Mobley/National Geographic Society; **257,** ©Marcus Brooke/FPG International; **260,** ©James P. Rowan/Tony Stone Images; **261,** ©Ric Ergenbright Photography; **262,** Winfield Parks/National Geographic Society; **266,** Bryan & Cherry Alexander; **267,** ©Superstock, Inc.; **268,** ©Chad Ehlers/Tony Stone Images; **271,** ©Tony Stone Images; **274,** (t) ©Superstock, Inc., (c) James L. Stanfield/National Geographic Society , (b) Smithsonian Institution; **275,** (t) Department of the Environment, London, (c,b) Scala/Art Resource; **276,** ©Thomas Craig/FPG International; **277,** ©Charlie Waite/Tony Stone Images; **279,** (l) Bruce Dale/National Geographic Society, (r) James L. Stanfield/National Geographic Society; **282,** ©Peter Turnley/Black Star; **283,** ©Josef Beck/FPG International; **285,** Patrick Piel/Liaison International; **286,** Anthony Suau/Liaison International; **287,** ©David Noble/FPG International; **290,** Thomas J. Abercrombie/National Geographic Society; **291,** James L. Stanfield/National Geographic Society; **293,** ©Thomas Craig/FPG International; **295,** Rudi von Briel; **296,** ©Robert Frerck/Tony Stone Images; **297,** ©George Hunter/Tony Stone Images; **299,** (l) ©Guy Marche/FPG International, (r) Ric Ergenbright Photography; **300,** ©Travelpix/FPG International; **303,** ©Telegraph Colour Library/FPG International; **304,** ©Superstock, Inc.; **306,** Albert Moldvay/National Geographic Society; **307,** ©J.E. Stevenson/FPG International; **308,** James P. Blair/National Geographic Society; **310,** (t) Winfield Parks/National Geographic Society, (b) Otis Imboden/National Geographic Society; **313,** Robert Frerck/Tony Stone Images; **316,** (l) ©Ian Bradshaw/Zefa-UK/The Stock Market,

(r) Matt Meadows; **317,** Matt Meadows; **318,** ©B. Bisson/Sygma; **319,** TRIP/W. Jacobs; **321,** TRIP/T. Noorits; **323,** ©Superstock, Inc.; **325, 326,** James P. Blair/National Geographic Society; **327,** The Granger Collection; **328,** ©Superstock, Inc; **329,** TRIP/M. Barlow; **331,** ©Superstock, Inc.; **332,** James L. Stanfield/National Geographic Society; **333,** ©Peter Turnley/Black Star; **335,** TRIP/I. Wellbelove; **338,** James L. Stanfield/National Geographic Society; **339,** ©B. Bisson/Sygma; **342,** James P. Blair/National Geographic Society; **342-343,** (background) Aaron Haupt; **343,** (t) James L. Stanfield/National Geographic Society, (b) Albert Moldvay/National Geographic Society; **344-345,** National Geographic Society; **346,** Dean Conger/National Geographic Society; **346-347,** (c) Bruce Dale/National Geographic Society, (background) Bruce Dale/National Geographic Society; **347,** Steve Raymer/National Geographic Society; **348, 349,** Novosti/Sovfoto/Eastfoto; **350,** Bruce Dale/National Geographic Society; **357,** (t) ©Shinichi Kanno/FPG International, (b) Steve Raymer/National Geographic Society; **358,** Dean Conger/National Geographic Society; **359,** Sovfoto/Eastfoto; **362,** Steve Raymer/National Geographic Society; **364,** ©Bill Swersey/Liaison International; **365,** ©Superstock, Inc.; **369,** ©G. Pinkhassov/Magnum Photos, Inc.; **370,** ©De Keerle/Sygma; **373,** (l) Steve Raymer/National Geographic Society, (r) ©Dave Bartruff/Artistry International; **374,** Steve Raymer/National Geographic Society; **375,** Dean Conger/National Geographic Society; **378,** (l) Wolfgang Kaehler, (r) Matt Meadows; **379,** Matt Meadows; **380,** (t) ©Superstock, Inc., (c) TRIP/S. Pozharskij, (b) Tate Gallery, London/Art Resource; **381,** (t) Dean Conger/National Geographic Society, (bl) ©Forbes Magazine Collection/Superstock, Inc., (b) George F. Mobley/National Geographic Society; **382,** Steve Raymer/National Geographic Society; **383,** Sovfoto/Eastfoto; **387,** ©Jeremy Hartley/Panos Pictures; **389,** ©TRIP/V. Kolpakov; **390,** G. Romantsova from Sovfoto/Eastfoto; **391, 392,** George F. Mobley/National Geographic Society; **394,** ©TRIP/V. Slapinia; **395,** Buddy Mays/Travel Stock; **397,** Sovfoto/Eastfoto; **398,** Tass/Sovfoto/Eastfoto; **399,** Steve Raymer/National Geographic Society; **402,** George F. Mobley/National Geographic Society; **402-403,** (background) Aaron Haupt; **403,** (t) William H. Bond/National Geographic Society, (br) Steve Raymer/National Geographic Society; **404-405,** Kenneth Garrett/National Geographic Society; **406,** (l) James L. Stanfield/National Geographic Society, (b) Steve Raymer/National Geographic Society; **406-407,** (t,background) David Alan Harvey/National Geographic Society, (c) James L. Stanfield/National Geographic Society; **407,** (t,br) Jodi Cobb/National Geographic Society, (bl) Winfield Parks/National Geographic Society; **408,** ©Nik Wheeler; **409,** Robert Harding Picture Library; **410,** Robert Harding Picture Library; **418, 419,** James L. Stanfield/National Geographic Society; **421,** file photo; **423,** ©Richard T. Nowitz; **425,** (t) Aaron Haupt, (b) Jodi Cobb/National Geographic Society; **426,** Sygma; **427,** ©Katrina Thomas/Photo Researchers, Inc.; **428, 430,** ©Superstock, Inc.; **431,** TRIP Photographic; **432,** ©J. Langevin/Sygma; **433,** ©Nabeel Turner/Tony Stone Images; **434,** ©Christina Dameyer/Photo 20-20; **436,** James P. Blair/National Geographic Society; **437,** ©Bernard Sioberstein/FPG International; **439,** James L. Stanfield/National Geographic Society; **442,** (l) ©Stephen Marks/The Image Bank, (r) Matt Meadows; **443,** Matt Meadows; **444,** (t) Victoria & Albert Museum/Art Resource, (c) D.W. Funt/Art Resource, (b) Erich Lessing/Archaeological Museum, Cairo, Egypt/Art Resource; **445,** (t) ©Superstock, Inc., (c) ©Josef Beck/FPG International, (b) ©Richard T. Nowitz; **446,** ©Murray & Associates/Tony Stone Images; **447,** Leo de Wys, Inc./©Fridmar Damm; **449,** ©F. Lazi/FPG International; **452,** Robert Harding Picture Library; **454,** ©Superstock, Inc.; **456,** Thomas J. Abercrombie/National Geographic Society; **457, 458,** ©Dave Bartruff/Artistry International; **460,** The Granger Collection; **461,** ©Murray & Associates/Tony Stone Images; **464,** James L. Stanfield/National Geographic Society; **464-465,** (background) Aaron Haupt; **465,** (t) James L. Stanfield/National Geographic Society, (b) David Alan Harvey/National Geographic Society; **466-467,** James P. Blair/National Geographic Society; **468,** (l) George F. Mobley/National Geographic Society, (br)

Steve Raymer/National Geographic Society; **468-469,** (c) James L. Stanfield/National Geographic Society, (background) Thomas J. Abercrombie/National Geographic Society; **469,** (tl) James L. Stanfield/National Geographic Society, (tr) Steve Raymer/National Geographic Society, (cr,br) George F. Mobley/National Geographic Society; **470,** Jeremy Hartly/Panos Pictures; **471,** ©Gerry Ellis Nature Photography; **472,** N. Durrell McKenna/Panos Pictures; **483,** (tl) Jeremy Hartley/Panos Pictures, (tr) Betty Press/Panos Pictures, (bl) Jason Lauré; **484,** Panos Pictures; **485,** Bruce Paton/Panos Pictures; **487,** Betty Press/Panos Pictures; **490,** Jeremy Hartley/Panos Pictures; **492,** Marcus Rose/Panos Pictures; **493,** Sara Leigh/Panos Pictures; **494, 497,** Dave G. Houser; **498,** Ron Giling/Panos Pictures; **499,** Panos Pictures; **502,** (t,c) Boltin Picture Library, (b) ©Travelpix/FPG International; **503,** (t) ©C.M. Hardt/Liaison International, (bl) Boltin Picture Library, (br) ©Superstock, Inc.; **504,** Nick Robinson/Panos Pictures; **505,** Robert Harding Picture Library; **507,** Jason Lauré; **509,** Dave G. Houser; **511,** ©Marco Corsetti/FPG International; **514,** Martin Adler/Panos Pictures; **517,** Nick Robinson/Panos Pictures; **520,** ©Gerald Cubitt/FPG International; **521,** Emory Kristof/National Geographic Society; **523,** Joseph J. Scherschel/National Geographic Society; **525,** Trygue Bolstad/Panos Pictures; **527,** Bruce Dale/National Geographic Society; **529,** Jason Lauré; **530,** Robert F. Sisson/National Geographic Society; **531,** Sarah Leen/National Geographic Society; **533,** Emory Kristof/National Geographic Society; **534,** Marc Schlossman/Panos Pictures; **535,** TRIP/Helen Rogers; **537,** (l) James P. Blair/National Geographic Society, (r) Liba Taylor/Panos Pictures; **538,** Betty Press/Panos Pictures; **539,** ©Gerald Cubitt/FPG International; **542, 543,** Matt Meadows; **544,** Johann Van Tonder/Images of Africa Photobank; **545,** James P. Blair/National Geographic Society; **547,** (l) Volkmar Wentzel/National Geographic Society, (r) Neil Cooper/Panos Pictures; **549,** (l) Liaison International, (r) Jason Lauré; **550,** David Atchinon-Jones/Robert Harding Picture Library; **552,** Rob Cousins/Panos Pictures; **554,** Bruce Paton/Panos Pictures; **555,** Walter Meayers Edwards/National Geographic Society; **556,** James L. Stanfield/National Geographic Society; **557,** Trygve Bolstad/Panos Pictures; **559,** Gary John Norman/Panos Pictures; **560,** James L. Stanfield/National Geographic Society; **561,** Mark Schlossman/Panos Pictures; **563,** Alan Carey; **564,** Steve Raymer/National Geographic Society; **565,** Johann Van Tonder/Images of Africa Photobank; **568,** James L. Stanfield/National Geographic Society; **568-569,** (background) Aaron Haupt; **569,** (t) Emory Kristof/National Geographic Society, (b) Gordon W. Gahan/National Geographic Society; **570-571,** Paul Chesley/National Geographic Society; **572,** (l) Dean Conger/National Geographic Society, (br) George F. Mobley/National Geographic Society; **572-573,** (c) Jodi Cobb/National Geographic Society, (background) George F. Mobley/National Geographic Society; **573,** (tl) Sam Abell/National Geographic Society, (tr,cl) James L. Stanfield/National Geographic Society, (br) David Alan Harvey/National Geographic Society; **574,** Dean Conger/National Geographic Society; **575,** James L. Stanfield/National Geographic Society; **576,** Dallas & John Heaton/Westlight; **584,** (t) ©Superstock, Inc., (b) James P. Blair/National Geographic Society; **585,** ©Josef Beck/FPG International; **586,** ©N. Shah/Superstock, Inc.; **587,** George F. Mobley/National Geographic Society; **589,** (l) James L. Stanfield/National Geographic Society, (r) George F. Mobley/National Geographic Society; **591,** Steve Raymer/National Geographic Society; **594,** James L. Stanfield/National Geographic Society; **596,** George F. Mobley/National Geographic Society; **597,** Dick Durrance II/National Geographic Society; **598,** Steve Raymer/National Geographic Society; **599,** ©Naomi Duguid/Asia Access; **601,** Paul von Stroheim/Westlight; **602,** ©Travelpix/FPG International, Inc.; **604,** (l) ©Superstock, Inc., (r) James L. Stanfield/National Geographic Society; **605,** ©N. Shah/Superstock, Inc.; **608, 609,** ©Superstock, Inc.; **612,** (l) Bruce Dale/National Geographic Society, (r) ©Antoinette Jong/Superstock, Inc.; **614,** ©Superstock, Inc.; **617,** (l,r) Dean Conger/National Geographic Society; **618,** The Metropolitan Museum of Art, Edward Elliott Family Collection, Purchase, The Dillon Fund Gift, 1982.; **619,** Nik Wheeler/Westlight;

620, Dean Conger/National Geographic Society; **622,** Bruce Dale/National Geographic Society; **623,** ©Superstock, Inc.; **624,** R. Ian Lloyd/Westlight; **625,** Anat Givon/AP/Wide World Photos; **626,** Jodi Cobb/National Geographic Society; **627,** ©Superstock, Inc.; **630,** (l) ©Jeffery Alford/Asia Access, (r) RMIP/Richard Haynes; **631,** RMIP/Richard Haynes; **632,** David Alan Harvey/National Geographic Society; **633,** ©Tony Stone Images; **635,** Mike Yamashita/Westlight; **637,** Charles O'Rear/Westlight; **639,** Larry Hamill; **640,** (l) David Alan Harvey/National Geographic Society, (r) George F. Mobley/National Geographic Society; **641,** Dean Conger/National Geographic Society; **642,** Brent Bear/Westlight; **644,** ©Superstock, Inc.; **645,** Westlight; **647,** ©Superstock, Inc.; **649,** David Alan Harvey/National Geographic Society; **652,** (t) R. Ian Lloyd/Westlight, (c) James P. Blair/National Geographic Society, (b) Dean Conger/National Geographic Society; **653,** (t) James L. Stanfield/National Geographic Society, (c) Bruce Dale/National Geographic Society, (b) Dallas & John Heaton/Westlight; **654,** Mike Yamashita/Westlight; **655,** Wilber E. Garrett/National Geographic Society; **658,** Mark Downey; **659,** Asia Access; **660,** ©Sheila Nardulli/Liaison International; **662,** Dean Conger/National Geographic Society; **664,** (l) Gilbert M. Grosvenor/National Geographic Society, (r) R. Ian Lloyd/Westlight; **666,** ©Joe Lynch/Liaison International; **668,** Ward's Natural Science; **669,** Mike Yamashita/Westlight; **672,** George F. Mobley/National Geographic Society; **672-673,** (background) Aaron Haupt; **673,** (t) James P. Blair/National Geographic Society, (b) Luis Marden/National Geographic Society; **674-675,** Gerald L. Kooyman/Polar Images; **676,** (cr) James L. Amos/National Geographic Society, (cl) Gordon W. Gahan/National Geographic Society, (b) Sam Abell/National Geographic Society; **676-677,** (background) Robert W. Madden/National Geographic Society; **677,** (t) Gordon W. Gahan/National Geographic Society, (cl) James P. Blair/National Geographic Society, (cr) Sam Abell/National Geographic Society, (b) George F. Mobley/National Geographic Society; **678,** (l) Bill Bachman/Pacific Stock, (r) James L. Stanfield/National Geographic Society; **679, 680,** Dave G. Houser; **687,** (t) George F. Mobley/National Geographic Society, (b) Robert W. Madden/National Geographic Society; **688,** ©Superstock, Inc.; **689,** Dean Lee/The Wildlife Collection; **691,** Joseph J. Scherschel/National Geographic Society; **694,** ©David Austin/Tony Stone Images; **695,** EROS Data Center; **696,** James L. Amos/National Geographic Society; **697,** ©Hideo Kurihara/Tony Stone Images; **699,** (l) ©Dave G. Houser, (r) Albert Moldvay/National Geographic Society; **701,** Bates Littlehales/National Geographic Society; **702,** Martin Harvey/The Wildlife Collection; **703,** ©Superstock, Inc.; **706,** G.R. Roberts; **707,** RMIP/Richard Haynes; **708,** (t) ©TravelPix/FPG International, (c) Bates Littlehales/National Geographic Society, (b) Auscape International; **709,** (t,c) Jean-Paul Ferrero/Auscape International, (b) M. Gillam/Auscape International; **710,** Jean-Paul Ferrero/Auscape International; **711,** Peter Stone/Pacific Stock; **713, 715, 717,** Wolfgang Kaehler; **718,** ©Hans Reinhard/Tony Stone Images; **719,** George F. Mobley/National Geographic Society; **722,** Herbert Ponting/Popperfoto/Archive Photo; **723,** Jean-Paul Ferrero/Auscape International; **726,** Bates Littlehales/National Geographic Society; **726-727,** (background) Aaron Haupt; **727,** (t) Gordon W. Gahan/National Geographic Society, (b) Bates Littlehales/National Geographic Society.

GEOGRAPHY: The World and Its People